Torts I

Practicing Tort Law

Fourth Edition

Nelson P. Miller

Torts I–

Practicing Tort Law

Fourth Edition

Nelson P. Miller

Publisher:
Crown Management LLC – July 2018
1527 Pineridge Drive
Grand Haven, MI 49417
USA

ISBN-13: 978-1-7322387-5-6

All Rights Reserved
© 2018 Nelson P. Miller
c/o 111 Commerce Avenue S.W.
Grand Rapids, MI 49503
(616) 560-0632

Of man's first disobedience, and the fruit
  Of that forbidden tree, whose mortal taste
Brought death into the world, and all our woe,
  With loss of Eden, till one greater Man
Restore us, and regain the blissful seat,
  Sing, Heav'nly Muse, that on the secret top
Of Oreb, or of Sinai, didst inspire
  That shepherd who first taught the chosen seed
In the beginning how the heav'ns and earth
  Rose out of Chaos... .

John Milton, *Paradise Lost* (1668)

PREFACE

This course book differs from the ordinary law school casebook. That difference is due in part to Thomas McIntyre Cooley. Justice Cooley had a polite and circumspect debate with Dean Christopher Columbus Langdell at Harvard Law School on the occasion of Harvard University's 250th anniversary, when Justice Cooley received Harvard's honorary degree. History credits (or shall we say *curses*?) Dean Langdell with inventing law school's case method and traditional casebook. Dean Langdell denigrated practical studies while championing science-like case studies. His Harvard comrade-in-arms Justice Oliver Wendell Holmes denigrated ethical studies. By contrast, Justice Cooley expressed concern that the law must not depart from the practical and ethical—hence Western Michigan University Cooley Law School's mission integrating knowledge, skills, and ethics to train law's sturdy practitioners.

Casebooks today do tend to include some introductory text and, often, author notes and questions. They also include statutes, law review articles, and other commentary. Going beyond those designs, this course book adds pedagogical (teaching), androgogical (learner-centered), and heutogogical (inclusive, learner-controlled) forms such as learner objectives, skills and ethics paths, tort-practice forms and vignettes, case studies, career advice, and explicit instruction on legal analysis. Especially when used with its companion workbook, these designs help you place tort law in its practice context while developing a professional identity as a member of a community of professional practice. Hence, its subtitle *Practicing Tort Law*.

The book's design is also to give you greater control over your learning. In its much-anticipated report *Educating Lawyers*, the Carnegie Foundation on Higher Education urged precisely these reforms—to integrate skills and ethics into a more explicit study of the knowledge or doctrinal dimension of law, to foster an apprenticeship of practice. Although professors at my law school already follow these practices (the Carnegie Foundation report vindicated the school's mission and programs), this book makes those practices clearer. It is another example of the student-centered innovation that lends Western Michigan University Cooley Law School its preeminence at practice preparation. I hope you appreciate this design. I welcome your comments, evaluation, and encouragement.

TABLE OF CONTENTS

PREFACE vii

CHAPTER
I. **THE LAW OF CARE—INTRODUCTION** 1
    A. Rationale 1
    B. Practice Context 3
II. **INTENTIONAL TORTS—PERSON** 7
    A. Battery 16
    B. Assault 25
    C. False Imprisonment 32
    D. Intentional Infliction of Emotional Distress 39
III. **INTENTIONAL TORTS—PROPERTY** 52
    A. Trespass to Land and Nuisance 52
    B. Trespass to Chattels 65
    C. Conversion 70
IV. **INTENTIONAL TORTS—DEFENSES** 77
    A. Consent 80
    B. Self-Defense and Defense of Others 89
    C. Defense and Recovery of Property 93
    D. Policy Defenses 103
V. **NEGLIGENCE** 114
    A. Duty 117
        1. Generally 117
        2. Standards of Care 126
        3. Qualified Duties 147
            a. Contracts 148
            b. Omissions 157
            c. Economic Loss 172
            d. Emotional Distress 179
            e. Prenatal Harm 195
    B. Breach 203
        1. Proof of Fault 204
        2. Res Ipsa Loquitur 213
        3. Violation of Statute 221
VI. **CAUSATION** 238
    A. Cause-in-Fact 239
    B. Proximate or Legal Cause 264
        1. Direct Sequence 268
        2. Foreseeability 274
        3. Intervening Causes 287
VII. **MALPRACTICE** 309

	A. Duty	309
	B. Standard of Care	318
	C. Causation	341
	D. Informed Consent	349
VIII.	**PREMISES LIABILITY**	355
	A. Generally	355
	B. Classifying the Plaintiff	365
	1. Invitees	366
	2. Licensees	373
	3. Trespassers	378
	4. Children	382
	C. Off the Premises	386
IX.	**NEGLIGENCE—DEFENSES**	391
	A. Contributory or Comparative Fault	391
	B. Assumption of Risk	401

CONCLUSION 412

CHAPTER I

THE LAW OF CARE— INTRODUCTION

A. Rationale

OBJECTIVE: Given a client, witness, juror, or other person involved in a tort claim, communicate the tort system's rationale, consistent with the history, philosophy, and morality reflected in this chapter.

Case Study: A prospective client is considering retaining your law firm to pursue tort claims relating to an incident in which a dog severely bit and maimed him. The dog had been roaming loose in the neighborhood when the prospective client tried to catch it to return it to its home. As the prospective client reached for the dog's collar, the dog bit and tore at his hand, severing a tendon and damaging nerves. The prospective client missed six weeks of work and remains partially disabled at using the computer keyboard at his financial management work. He had two surgeries, incurred $15,000 in medical expenses, and has scars on his hand. The family who owns the dog has homeowner's liability insurance covering dog-bite claims. ***Explain tort law's rationale for the prospective client, who is hesitant to pursue his rights.***

Rationale. The skill that the above objective and case study require—justifying the tort system—is critical for torts practice. As surprising as it might have seemed 50 or even just 25 years ago, tort practice today is controversial. Until recently, tort law was out of the public eye and governed largely by the common law. Yet for the past couple of decades, tort law has been the subject of significant political debate and legislative reform. The public scrutiny of tort law is due in part to the relaxation of rules against lawyer advertising, bringing personal-injury advertising and practices into the public eye. It is also due in part to insurance and industry lobbying and advertising, investment cycles affecting insurance premiums, media reporting of jury verdicts, changes in the global economy, and changes in the way that we understand law itself. In this volatile social environment, lawyers must help clients, witnesses, jurors, judges, and others who participate in the tort system understand its justification and rationale.

History. Tort law is inescapable. It is a part of the earliest recovered fragments of legal codes, the Laws of Ur-Nammu and Code of Lipit Ishtar from 4,000 years ago. It makes up a significant part of the ancient Mesopotamian Laws of Eshnunna from 3,700 years ago and of the earliest complete legal code yet recovered, the Code of Hammurabi from about 3,600 years ago. It is in the Torah's (Old Testament's) Covenant Code, the codes of Assyrian kings from 2,700 years ago, the Talmud, Rome's Twelve Tables of 449 B.C., right through to the Institutes of Justinian in 533 A.D. The longest of the Roman Twelve Tables devotes itself solely to tort law. Scholars find tort law in the pre-Norman Laws of King Ethelbert, Ine, King Alfred, and

Ethelred, and in the Winchester Code of King Cnut. Natural law's father Hugo Grotius detailed its features in the early 1600s, as did the first law professor Samuel Pufendorf in 1673. The social Darwinism of the 19th century and pragmatic materialism of the 20th century briefly hid its grand history from the likes of Main, Wigmore, and Holmes, but we know today that tort law's history is as long, rich, complex, and subtle as any area of law.

> **The Code of Hammurabi** (circa 1700 B.C.)
> 229: If a builder has built a house for a man, and his work is not strong, and if the house he has built falls in and kills the householder, that builder shall be slain.
> 232: If goods have been destroyed, he shall replace all that has been destroyed; and because the house that he built was not made strong, and it has fallen in, he shall restore the fallen house out of his own personal property.
> 235: If a boat-builder has built a boat for a man and his work is not firm, and in that same year that boat is disabled in use; then the boat-builder shall overhaul that boat, and strengthen it with his own material, and he shall return the strengthened boat to the boat-owner.
> 236: If a man has given his boat on hire to a boatman, and the boatman is careless, and the boat is sunk and lost; then the boatman shall replace the boat to the boat-owner.

Definition. Tort law has always existed and will always exist because it is fundamental to an ordered, civil society. Tort law is the law of care, love, the Golden Rule, and Kant's categorical imperative. The word *tort*, meaning a compensable harm or wrong, derives from similar Latin and French words suggesting an event, condition, or relationship twisted at its root. Tort law is the law of social relations between both friends and strangers. Its reasonable-person standard brings order and a community's good sense to the operation of vehicles, construction of roads, practice of professions, maintenance of property, and manufacture of products. In that respect, tort law stands next to the law of bargain, covenant, contract, or promise, and property law, at the foundation of civil society.

Policy. Tort law is purposeful, compensating for loss while deterring loss's occurrence. ***Compensation*** restores, buying medical care and equipment, hiring nursing aides, replacing lost wages, and saving businesses from bankruptcy, marriages from divorce, and homes from foreclosure. ***Deterrence*** protects, influencing the redesign of defective products, updating of outmoded medical procedures, repair of deteriorating sidewalks and bridges, and safe maintenance of vehicles and equipment. In economic terms, tort law places the burden of liability on the least-cost risk avoider—on the one most able to change an unreasonably dangerous practice or, if they choose not to, then to pay for the harm it causes. Tort law internalizes costs (damage to life, limb, property, and environment) to those who produce them. In that respect, tort law sustains responsible liberty, imposing no constraints on our choices but holding us responsible for their untoward consequences.

Place. Tort law is a proper subject for public discussion and court or legislative reform. We should, though, understand and appreciate tort law's history, ubiquity, purpose, and necessity in the process, or reform will distort. Tort-law reform tends to be a pendulum swinging back and forth in favor of the injured or the putative wrongdoer, with liability expanding or contracting in response to public and private interests, technological development, and economic cycles. Yet that tort reform behaves like a pendulum means that tort law has a central point toward which it necessarily gravitates. The best tort lawyers can articulate and communicate tort law's pivotal nature. Consider, then, how effectively or poorly tort law redresses the corruption, brutality, and carelessness of person toward person.

B. Practice Context

OBJECTIVE: Given a client who must litigate a tort claim, communicate its probable course, consistent with the practice conventions and procedures reflected in this section.

Case Study: The prospective client in the prior case study has signed a contingency-fee agreement with your law firm and now wants to know what is next. ***Summarize for the client a typical course that would lead to the tort claim's resolution.***

Local Practice. Tort practice involves primarily state law and local influences rather than federal law (although federal statutory tort causes of action exist). Each state has its own tort law and practice conventions, and each local bar, judge, and jury pool can have peculiar attitudes about tort law. Tort lawyers who have a national practice, specializing in fields like drug and product defects, airline crashes, and other complex litigation, often associate with local counsel both to comply with bar admission rules and to ensure competence in the state law and local rules, and familiarity with local practice conventions and the local jury pool. In-office conventions, conduct of the relationship with opposing counsel, and settlement procedure and dynamics can also have distinctly local character.

National Character. Parochial limitations aside, tort law does have a generally unified, national character, enough to test on the Multi-State Bar Exam comprising a significant portion of most states' bar examination. Law schools teach tort law as if a unified body with peculiar state exceptions and adaptations. Although tort law has some well-known cases, practitioners recall those cases for their memorable illustration of widely accepted principles rather than as controlling authority within the jurisdiction. Fully competent tort practitioners may recall the names and facts of few or no controlling cases. Yet they can project the intricate workings of tort principles in endless circumstances, follow circuit and probate court rules, know the impact of tort-reform statutes, and sense the trends and leanings of appellate and trial courts on liability issues. Tort practitioners must also have a clear strategic sense of the probable course of tort litigation. As you read the following example, do not be concerned if you do not understand the law and procedures. Instead, try to identify the tort-law knowledge, the practical skills, and the ethical sense the lawyers used to pursue the case.

A Representative Case. The lawyer's pastor telephoned her at her law office explaining that a young congregation member had just been seriously hurt on the job, losing a hand in a machine accident. The lawyer had no experience with workplace injuries and products liability but knew who did. She called an experienced plaintiff's lawyer who quickly did a conflict check to ensure that he and the members of his law firm had no conflicts of interest in representing the young man. The experienced lawyer, his associate, and the referring lawyer then arranged to meet the young man just days after his injury. The referring lawyer would eventually receive one-third of the one-third contingency fee the lawyers earned on the case, for making this referral while maintaining responsibility for the file.

The young man's wife had to drive him to the meeting place because his hand was swathed in bandages. There, the lawyers learned that the young man and his wife were newly married, without health insurance or savings, and now very concerned about their future. The experienced lawyer explained that the employer's worker-compensation insurer would be paying accident-related medical expenses, 80% of lost wages, and a lump-sum benefit. The lawyers gave the young couple a state-published booklet on worker's compensation rights and benefits. The lawyers then asked what had happened.

The young man explained that when things got slow at work, his supervisor had sent him over to a sister company to operate a machine. The plant manager there had given the young man no instructions other than to keep his hand out of the machine when it closed. The machine had double-hand controls requiring the operator to have both hands on the controls when the machine closed. Workers relied on the double-hand controls to ensure that the machine did not close when the workers were reaching into the machine to remove the finished parts.

Those controls had failed the moment of the young man's injury. The young man did not know how they had failed, but he was certain that he had pressed the controls once, waited while the machine closed and opened, and then reached in to remove the finished part just at the moment that the machine made a second, unexpected cycle, crushing his hand. The young man had heard since his injury that one of the reasons his supervisor sent him to the plant to operate the machine was that other workers had refused because of its propensity to double-cycle. Co-workers rushed the young man to the hospital, where his treatment had been surprisingly brief. He would continue to see a hand specialist, but the doctors had little they could do. The young man's total medical expense was about $25,000. He would not work again at the manual labor for which he was qualified.

Ethics

In *Bates v. State Bar of Arizona*, 433 U.S. 350 (1977), the United States Supreme Court held that lawyer advertising that is truthful and not misleading is a First Amendment, commercial-speech right. *Bates* and other Supreme Court cases following it permitted broader lawyer advertising than most states had previously permitted. Although *Bates* involved family law services, one of the cases that followed it, *Zauderer v Office of Disciplinary Counsel of the Supreme Court of Ohio*, 471 U.S. 626 (1985), involved a personal injury lawyer advertising in the newspaper for clients allegedly injured by a contraceptive product (the Dalkon Shield). Most consumers are familiar with personal-injury advertising, like targeted mailings for motor-vehicle accidents, television advertising for prescription drug defects, and billboards or online advertising for worker's compensation and Social Security disability claims, and construction and industrial accidents.

Rule 7.1 of the ABA Model Rules of Professional Conduct prohibits false or misleading advertising, stating "A lawyer shall not make a false or misleading communication about the lawyer's services. A communication is false or misleading if it contains a material misrepresentation of fact or law, or omits a fact necessary to make the statement considered as a whole not materially misleading." Comment 3 to Rule 7.1 indicates that an advertisement that raises false expectations or makes unsubstantiated comparisons may be misleading. Would a tort law advertisement that listed seven multi-million dollar verdicts or settlements that the lawyer had won violate these provisions? Do marketing plans have their place in a professional practice? If so, how would you market a tort law practice? Notice how the lawyers met the clients in the case under discussion.

The lawyers explained to the young couple how they would investigate and pursue negligence and products-liability claims against the responsible companies if warranted. They explained that the exclusive-remedy provision of the worker-compensation act would probably bar the young man's claims against his employer and supervisor. The lawyers had the young man sign authorizations for release of medical, employment, and other information. Within days, the lawyers had located and retained a machine expert to inspect the press. The inspection revealed that the machine's control-box mounting had failed allowing the machine to make the unactivated cycle. The lawyers determined the identity of the machine's manufacturer, the machine's original purchaser, a second company that had resold the machine, the machine's installer, and the die manufacturer and installer. The lawyers again ensured that they had no conflicts of interest. They researched products-liability and worker-compensation law. They also met with the state OSHA investigator, obtaining and reviewing his official investigation report. They then decided to recommend suing four defendants on negligence, products liability, and intentional-tort theories. The clients approved, and the lawyers filed suit three weeks after the accident.

The lawyers for all parties conducted pretrial discovery for the next two years. They drafted and served interrogatories, document requests, and admission requests, and answers and responses to those discovery requests. They took two-dozen depositions in several different states. Discovery confirmed that while the machine manufacturer had long been out of business, it had an insurance policy and maintained one employee to manage its records and litigation. The machine had no records other than for its sale. All defendants denied knowledge of the machine's propensity to fail. The lawyers discovered no record of failure, although co-workers testified that they witnessed and reported failures before the young man's injury. The court dismissed the claim against one of the defendants. The remaining claims then went to case evaluation where three independent attorneys evaluated the claims at figures ranging between $15,000 and $500,000. All parties rejected the evaluations. In subsequent negotiations, the young couple settled for modest amounts with two of the defendants, leaving just one defendant in the case for trial. Most of the modest settlements went to reimburse the lawyers for litigation expenses, with the young couple receiving the small remainder.

Three years after the young man's injury, the lawyers tried to eight jurors the young couple's products-liability claim against the machine's manufacturer. During trial, the young couple's lawyers called twenty witnesses including plant-safety experts, metallurgist expert, hand specialist, rehabilitation expert, labor economist, co-workers and supervisors, the lone employee of the machine's defunct manufacturer, and the young couple. The defendant manufacturer called one machine expert. On cross-examination, one of the young couple's lawyers had the defense expert stand in front of the jury demonstrating with the expert's own machine mockup exactly how the machine had failed. After deliberating for eight hours over two days, the jury returned a unanimous verdict of two million dollars also finding the young man thirty-percent comparatively negligent. The lawyers drafted a settlement agreement reflecting the verdict, exchanged the signed agreement and settlement check, and presented the court with a dismissal. The young couple structured their settlement payments in a tax-free annuity that guaranteed them an income stream and lump-sum payments for life. They also appealed the court's dismissal of one defendant, obtained a reversal of that dismissal, and then reached a settlement with that defendant, adding substantially to their overall monetary recovery.

> **Skills**
> Some tort lawyers advertise. Others do not, preferring to maintain referral networks and work from an existing client base. Discuss with classmates the contents of an advertisement you think would be appropriate to run. What do you want potential clients to understand about you? What might be your strengths? What should your advertisement reflect about the justice system? What do you think interests and motivates potential clients to choose and contact certain attorneys over other attorneys? What kind of clients, with what expectations, do you want your marketing to attract? Discuss the media in which and the geographic region where you would like the advertisement to run. Consider your advertising budget. Law firms budget anywhere between a few hundred to several million dollars per year for advertising.

INQUIRY

Tort-Practice Skills. Notice that the above example case included these skills common to tort-law practice: (1) forming lawyer/client relationships; (2) investigating and evaluating claims; (3) advising clients; (4) drafting and serving court pleadings; (5) conducting pretrial discovery; (6) arguing pretrial motions; (7) participating in alternative dispute resolution procedures; (8) preparing for and conducting trials; (9) managing settlements and client funds; and (10) conducting appeals. Tort lawyers must comply with professional-conduct rules, law-practice standards, and other duties at each of these stages of tort litigation. They also draw on knowledge of tort, contract, tax, corporate, and administrative law, civil procedure, evidence, and other areas of substantive and procedural law. Notice how a tort lawyer's knowledge, skill, and ethics work together with practice management to serve clients in need. Appreciate tort law and practice.

> **Career**
> Mentors can make a difference in finding employment and succeeding in tort practice. Tort practice involves substantial professional-identity issues. Attracting, serving, and representing tort clients involves not just what you know but also **who you are** and **what you become**. Your professional identity must reflect good standing and discernment, to succeed in tort practice. Seeing experienced tort lawyers in action can help you form your own professional identity, not so much by emulation but by the insight they share and confidence your interaction engenders. Begin that interaction when in law school, where formal mentor programs are available. Also, look for mentors on your own. Do not choose as your only mentor someone like yourself. Instead, find experienced lawyers who are different from you, from whom you can learn. Base the mentor relationship on relevant training, not having a good time or impressing one another. Ask your mentor what makes a good tort lawyer, and then record, reflect on, and incorporate what your mentor says.

CHAPTER II

INTENTIONAL TORTS—PERSON

OBJECTIVE: Given law practice settings involving various personal injury claims, sort those injuries caused intentionally from those not intentional, also stating the effects of that determination, consistent with the following text.

Case Study: A crazed stranger attacked and beat a hotel guest in his room, after the hotel clerk carelessly gave the stranger a programmed key card to the guest's room. ***Distinguish and explain for the guest whether his claims against the stranger and hotel are for intentional or unintentional torts, and identify the probable procedural and substantive effects of that determination.***

Differentiation. Tort practice involves examining conduct to identify, pursue, defend, and settle or try claims. Intentional torts—harms that a person in some sense desires to bring about, as opposed to harms that may result from carelessness—are the first class of claims within tort law. Tort law divides itself up into intentional torts, torts of negligence, and strict-liability torts. Because of liability insurance, negligence law rather than the law of intentional torts is the heart of modern tort-law practice. Insurers generally do not underwrite intentional wrongs. For public-policy reasons, law may not enforce agreements to insure against a person's intentional torts and crimes. Tort lawyers deal primarily with negligence, not intentional torts. Yet studying intentional torts makes good tort-law training. Malfeasance—the malicious desire to harm—is often more easy to recognize than the carelessness that identifies negligence claims. Law also more clearly defines intentional-tort claims and elements. Begin your studies, then, with intentional torts, even while recognizing that tort practice primarily involves negligence claims.

Intentional Torts. This text presents seven intentional torts: assault, battery, false imprisonment, intentional infliction of emotional distress, trespass to land, trespass to chattels, and conversion. This chapter addresses the four intentional torts, assault, battery, false imprisonment, and intentional infliction of emotional distress, that involve injury to persons—what some call the "dignitary" torts. The next chapter addresses the three remaining intentional torts, trespass to land, trespass to chattels, and conversion, that involve damage to or deprivation of property. The first three of the personal intentional torts, assault, battery, and false imprisonment, involve traditional common law. The last of one, intentional infliction of emotional distress, is a newer intentional tort not necessarily recognized, or recognized by different name or in different form, from state to state.

Knowledge

In tort practice, lawyers must be able to identify legal claims out of client interviews, witness statements, medical records, police reports, and other case materials. Tort lawyers must have a mental list of claims (including their elements) to which to resort while actively sorting that data. Tort law defines most claims by their elements. By *element*, law means a

> necessary condition to finding that the tort was committed and the liability claim exists. The facts must satisfy all elements of a tort, or the claim does not exist. The skill of spotting claims becomes difficult when the facts only approximate the elements of various tort claims. The lawyer must generalize facts, hoping to match (or if representing a defendant, hoping not to match) the elements of the various torts. For example, when a lawyer hears that one person "shoved" another, the lawyer generalizes "shoved" to alert the lawyer to the possibility that the conduct satisfies the *contact* element of battery. Likewise, a lawyer may generalize "pointed the gun" into the *imminent-apprehension* element of assault or "displayed the carcass" into the *outrageous-conduct* element of the intentional infliction of emotional distress.

Intent. Intentional torts begin with the consideration of intent. *Intent* is an element of each of the intentional torts. The Restatement (Third) of Torts: Liability for Physical and Emotional Harm §5 states, "An actor who intentionally causes physical harm is subject to liability for that harm." States, though, require more than intent, to hold a person liable for harm. The person harmed must also prove the other elements of one of the intentional torts, like the *contact* element of battery or the *restraint* element of false imprisonment. As the following cases suggest, a lawyer can satisfy the intent element of the intentional torts by showing that the defendant desired to bring about the plaintiff's harm. The Restatement (Third) of Torts: Liability for Physical and Emotional Harm §1, defines *intent* by stating, "A person acts with intent to produce a consequence if: (a) the person acts with the purpose of producing that consequence; or (b) the person acts knowing that the consequence is substantially certain to result." The defendant's motive to harm the plaintiff may have been ill will, malice, vengeance, or the like. Evidence of malicious motive can go a long way toward proving intent, although strictly speaking, motive is not an element of these torts, and the plaintiff need not prove motive. Proof (direct or circumstantial) of the defendant's desire to harm is enough to establish intent. Consider as an example the following case.

Williams v. Kearbey
Kansas Court of Appeals
13 Kan. App.2d 564, 775 P.2d 670 (1989)

DAVIS, J. ... Defendant Alan Kearbey, a minor, shot and wounded plaintiff Don Harris and plaintiff Daniel Williams, also a minor. Plaintiffs brought this action against Kearbey for battery. The jury found for plaintiffs. It also found, in answer to a special question, that Kearbey was insane at the time. The trial court entered judgment for plaintiffs and Kearbey appeals, arguing: (1) that an insane person should not be held civilly liable for his torts; and (2) that an insane person cannot commit a battery because he is incapable of forming the necessary intent.

.... On January 21, 1985, Alan Kearbey, who was then 14 years old, shot several people at Goddard Junior High School. The principal was killed and three other people were wounded. Among the wounded were plaintiff Don Harris, a teacher at the school, and plaintiff Daniel Williams, a student at the school. Both were shot in the leg.

Harris and Williams brought this action against Kearbey, his parents, and the Goddard School District (U.S.D. No. 265). The trial court held that Harris' claim against the school district was barred by the Kansas Workers' Compensation Act and, at the close of plaintiffs' case, granted the school district's motion for a directed verdict against plaintiff Williams based on governmental immunity. These rulings were not appealed. The jury was allowed, however, to apportion fault to the school district. The court denied Alan Kearbey's motion for a directed verdict on the grounds of insanity. ...

In 1927, the Kansas Supreme Court held that "[a]n insane person who shoots and kills another is civilly liable in damages to those injured by his tort." *Seals v. Snow*, 123 Kan. 88, Syl. ¶1, 254 P. 348 (1927). In 1940, the Supreme Court reaffirmed this holding in dicta, saying: "It is definitely settled in this state that the defendant, Toepffer, if in fact insane, would have been civilly liable in damages for his torts." *Toepffer v. Toepffer,* 151 Kan. 924, 929, 101 P.2d 904 (1940). The appellate courts of this state have not spoken on this subject since 1940.

The tort liability of insane persons presents a policy question. In resolving this question, American courts have unanimously chosen to impose liability on an insane person rather than leaving the loss on the innocent victim. *Seals v. Snow* is a leading case in support of this view.

In *Seals v. Snow,* Martin Snow shot and killed Arthur Seals. ...

On appeal, Snow argued that he should not be held liable for his torts since he was insane. The court responded: "It is conceded that the great weight of authority is that an insane person is civilly liable for his torts. This liability has been based on a number of grounds, one that where one of two innocent persons must suffer a loss, it should be borne by the one who occasioned it. Another, that public policy requires the enforcement of such liability in order that relatives of the insane person shall be led to restrain him and that tort-feasors shall not simulate or pretend insanity to defend their wrongful acts causing damage to others, and that if he was not liable there would be no redress for injuries, and we might have the anomaly of an insane person having abundant wealth depriving another of his rights without compensation." 123 Kan. at 90, 254 P. 348.

Kearbey argues (1) the loss should fall upon plaintiffs rather than himself since he was not capable of avoiding his conduct and, hence, was not at fault; (2) it no longer makes sense to impose liability on an insane person in order to encourage his relatives to confine him since public policy no longer favors confinement of the mentally ill unless the insane person presents a danger to other people, in which case liability should be imposed directly on the insane person's relatives for failing to confine him, rather than on the insane person himself; and (3) concern over feigned insanity is no longer warranted since psychiatrists and psychologists now have improved methods of proving or disproving insanity.

Taking up Kearbey's arguments in reverse order, it is obvious that Kearbey's confidence in modern psychiatry is not widely shared. Comments to the Restatement (Second) of Torts list several valid reasons why liability is still imposed on insane persons. These reasons include: "the unsatisfactory character of the evidence of mental deficiency in many cases, together with the ease with which it can be feigned, the difficulty of estimating its existence, nature and extent; and some fear of introducing into the law of torts the confusion that has surrounded the defense of insanity in the criminal law." Restatement (Second) of Torts § 895J comment a (1977).

Next, Kearbey argues that liability should not be imposed on an insane person in order to encourage his relatives to confine him since public policy no longer favors confinement of the mentally ill. We agree that this is not a particularly strong reason for imposing liability. It is also clear, however, that removing this rationale would not have changed the court's decision in *Seals v. Snow*.

The main rationale of *Seals v. Snow* and the one which keys our affirmance of the trial court in this case is that, as between an insane person who injures another and an innocent person, it is more just for the insane person to bear the loss he caused than to visit the loss on the injured person. As stated in *Seals v. Snow*:

> "Undoubtedly, there is some appearance of hardship, even of injustice, in compelling one to respond for that which, for want of the control of reason, he was unable to avoid; that it is imposing upon a person already visited with the inexpressible calamity of mental obscurity an obligation to observe the same care and precaution respecting the rights of others that the law demands of one in the full possession of his faculties. But the question of liability in these cases, as well as in others, is a question of policy; and it is to be disposed of as would be the question whether the incompetent person should be supported at the expense of the public, or of his neighbors, or at the expense of his own estate. If his mental disorder makes him dependent, and at the same time prompts him to commit injuries, there seems to be no greater reason for imposing upon the neighbors or the public one set of these consequences, rather than the other; no more propriety or justice in making others bear the losses resulting from his unreasoning fury, when it is spent upon them or their property, than there would be in calling upon them to pay the expense of his confinement in an asylum, when his own estate is ample for the purpose." 123 Kan. at 90-91, 254 P. 348 (quoting 1 Cooley on Torts 172 [3d ed.1906]).

Although the above language is somewhat dated, the reasoning is still well grounded in sound public policy. Someone must bear the loss and, as between the tortfeasor, the injured party, and the general public, sound public policy favors placing the loss on the person who caused it, whether sane or not.

With one exception, it appears that every American court dealing with the question has reached this same result. A leading case is *McGuire v. Almy,* 297 Mass. 323, 8 N.E.2d 760 (1937), in which the court affirmed a verdict against an insane person for tortious assault and battery. ....

Kearbey argues that he did not commit the tort of battery because his insanity prevented him from forming the intent necessary for that tort. The prevailing American view as set forth above is that a finding of insanity does not preclude a finding that a defendant acted intentionally. A jury may find that an insane person acted intentionally if he intended to do what he did, even though his reasons and motives were entirely irrational. Restatement (Second of Torts § 895J comment c (1977); Prosser & Keeton on Torts § 135, p. 1074 (5th ed.1984).

The requirements of the prevailing American view for imposing liability for an intentional tort are satisfied in this case. In finding for the plaintiffs, the jury necessarily found that Alan Kearbey touched or struck the plaintiffs "with the intent of bringing about either a contact or an apprehension of contact, that is harmful or offensive." The fact that Kearbey did not "understand the nature of his acts" or did not "understand that what he was doing was prohibited by law" does not preclude the jury from finding that Kearbey acted intentionally in discharging a weapon in Goddard Junior High School.

Affirmed.

Practice

The two lawyers finally found the tumbledown house on the nameless streets—thieves having stolen the street signs long ago. They knocked loudly when it appeared no one inside could hear. Finally, they heard a resident unbolt the door's several locks. A shy and

> smiling young woman invited them in. The lawyers sat at a kitchen table with the woman and a muscled, older man she described as her boyfriend, reviewing a contingency-fee agreement for her tort claim. Other loud knocks came from the door. Each time, the boyfriend would make his way to the door, peer through its peephole, undo its several locks, and talk in hushed tones with the person on the outside. He would then lock the door again, make his way to a room at the back of the house, emerge with a hand in his pocket, make his way back to the door, undo its several locks, talk in hushed tones with the person on the outside, and lock the door again before returning to the kitchen table. Four of these mysterious transactions occurred during the lawyers' half-hour-long consultation, leaving the lawyers wondering about the challenges of representing a drug dealer's girlfriend.

INQUIRY

Voluntariness. Other jurisdictions follow the rule of *Williams v. Kearbey*. The critical consideration is the voluntariness of the defendant's actions, not the rationality of or motive for those actions. Consider the tort claims upheld in Delahanty v. Hinckley, 799 F. Supp. 184 (D. D.C. 1992), by persons who were struck by bullets aimed at President Reagan, even though the assailant John Hinckley's insanity resulted in his acquittal on the criminal charges. Consider also Colman v. Notre Dame Convalescent Home, 968 F. Supp. 809 (D. Conn. 1997), in which a demented nursing home patient was subject to intentional-tort liability for hitting an entertainer at the nursing home with the entertainer's own guitar. Still, the difference between intent to contact and intent to harm can be important for insurance-coverage purposes. Liability-insurance policies typically exclude coverage for intended harms. On the other hand, the intentional-acts exclusions of insurance policies leave open the possibility that insurance will cover harm resulting from intentional contact not meant to cause harm. *See* Baldinger v. Consolidated Mut. Ins. Co., 222 N.Y.S.2d 736 (N.Y. App. Div. 1961), *affd.*, 183 N.E.2d 908 (N.Y. 1962) (coverage for injury to girl intentionally pushed by five-year-old boy who did not mean to hurt the girl). As to insurance coverage, the insurance-policy language will control. Even though the tort rule is different, insurance cases have held that the defendant must have intended not only the contact but also intended harm or offense. *See* White v. Muniz, 999 P.2d 814 (Colo. 2000) (plaintiff maintaining claim against defendant Alzheimer's sufferer must prove that defendant intended not only the contact but that the plaintiff be harmed or offended).

Substantial Certainty. Law extends intent's definition to deal with other circumstances. Persons sometimes act knowing the substantial certainty of another's harm, without necessarily desiring the harm. A despairing motorist intentionally crosses the centerline into oncoming traffic in a botched suicide attempt that unintentionally kills an innocent motorist. A frustrated worker sprays gunfire into a company cafeteria, unintentionally wounding co-worker friends. A protestor ignites a suitcase of explosives at a national event, unintentionally killing innocent spectators. The actors may not have intended to bring about the harm of others, but when they do, law has good reason to hold them liable for an intentional tort. When the actor knows to a substantial certainty that the harm will result, tort law considers the intent element satisfied. The best-known case is Garratt v. Dailey, 279 P.2d 1091 (Wash. 1955), *after remand*, 304 P.2d 681 (1956), in which a five-year-old boy pulled a chair out from under his aunt, not intending to hurt her but knowing that she was just about to sit. But consider the following more-recent case involving a well-known defendant.

Doe v. Johnson
United States District Court
817 F.Supp. 1382 (W.D. Mich. 1993)

ENSLEN, D.J. This case is before the Court on defendant's motion to dismiss under Federal Rule of Civil Procedure 12(b)(6), or in the alternative, for a more definite statement under Rule 12(e). ...

Facts

This case raises unique legal and *policy* issues, but has fairly straight forward facts. Plaintiff, Jane Doe, alleges that defendant, Earvin Johnson, Jr., wrongfully transmitted the human immunodeficiency virus ("HIV virus") to her through consensual sexual contact. Ms. Doe alleges that the wrongful transmission of the HIV virus occurred on or about the evening of June 22, 1990, or the morning of June 23, 1990, or both, at her home in Ingham County, Michigan. Plaintiffs' Complaint at 3-4. Ms. Doe and Mr. Johnson had "sexual contact" which allegedly led to the transmission of the HIV virus. Ms. Doe alleges that immediately prior to the encounter, she asked Mr. Johnson to use a condom. Mr. Johnson allegedly refused to do so. Nonetheless, Ms. Doe engaged in consensual sexual contact with Mr. Johnson. *Id.* at 4.

Prior to the evening of June 22, 1990 or morning of June 23, 1990, Ms. Doe claims that Mr. Johnson "was sexually active, having sexual contact and engaging in sexual intercourse with multiple partners." *Id.* at 3. Thus, Ms. Doe claims that Mr. Johnson "knew or should have known" that he had a high risk of becoming infected with the HIV virus because of his "sexually active, promiscuous lifestyle." *Id.* Accordingly, Ms. Doe argues that Mr. Johnson should have (1) warned her about his past lifestyle; (2) informed her that he "may have HIV"; (3) informed her that he did in fact "have HIV"; (4) not engaged in sexual contact with her; or (5) used a condom or other method to protect her from the HIV virus.

As a result of this wrongful transmission, Ms. Doe states that she suffers, and will continue to suffer, many consequences including physical illness, severe emotional distress, loss of enjoyment of life, extreme embarrassment, humiliation, shame, medical expenses, and lost wages and benefits. *Id.* at 5. Moreover, Ms. Doe notes that she will eventually develop acquired immunodeficiency syndrome ("AIDS") and "suffer a slow, certain, and painful death." *Id.* ....

Battery (Count III)

Defendant argues that count III of plaintiffs' Complaint should be dismissed because plaintiffs have failed to state a claim for battery. Specifically, defendant argues that plaintiffs did not allege that he "intended to transmit the virus" to Ms. Doe, or believed that such transmission was "substantially certain" to occur. Defendant's Brief at 16. Defendant also raises a statute of limitations argument.

Battery is the willful and harmful or offensive touching of another person against their will. *Tinkler v. Richter,* 295 Mich. 396, 401, 295 N.W. 201 (1940); *see also* Restatement (Second) of Torts §§ 13, 18 (1985) (battery is defined as the "intentional, harmful, or offensive, and unprivileged contact with the person of another.") (hereinafter "Restatement" or "Restatement of Torts"). The Restatement of Torts states that where

"[X] consents to sexual intercourse with [Y], who knows that [X] is ignorant of the fact that [Y] has a venereal disease, [Y] is subject to liability for battery." Restatement of Torts § 892B, illustration 5; *see also Kathleen K. v. Robert B.*, 150 Cal.App.3d 992, 198 Cal.Rptr. 273 (1984).

Sexual activity between two individuals satisfies the contact requirement for battery. *See, e.g.,* Douglas W. Baruch, *AIDS in the Courts: Tort Liability for the Sexual Transmission of Acquired Immune Deficiency Syndrome*, 22 Tort & Ins.L.J. 165, 176 (1987). The intent required for a showing of battery does not require a desire to harm someone. Instead, it only requires the intent to make contact and encompasses not only "those consequences which are desired, but also ... those which the actor believes are substantially certain to follow from what the actor does." W. Prosser & W. Keeton, Prosser and Keeton on the Law of Torts §§ 8, 11 (5th ed. 1984); *see also Schroeder v. Auto Driveaway Co.*, 11 Cal.3d 908, 114 Cal.Rptr. 622, 631, 523 P.2d 662, 671 (1975); *State v. Lankford*, 29 Del. 594, 102 A. 63 (1917).

Defendant argues that plaintiffs have failed to state a claim because they did not state that defendants "intended to transmit," or knew with "substantial certainty" that he could transmit, the HIV virus to Ms. Doe. I disagree. Under Rule 12(b)(6) I must accept all allegations in the Complaint as true and construe these allegations "in the light most favorable to plaintiff[s]." *Scheuer v. Rhodes*, 416 U.S. 232, 236, 94 S.Ct. 1683, 1686, 40 L.Ed.2d 90 (1974). In so doing, I find that plaintiffs have alleged a cause of action for the wrongful transmission of an infectious disease under a battery theory. Specifically, under the liberal Rule 12(b)(6) standard, I find that plaintiffs have alleged that defendant knew with "substantial certainty" that he could transmit the HIV virus to Ms. Doe.

INQUIRY

Variations. Law may permit a lesser *recklessness* form of intent to satisfy the intent element of the intentional-infliction-of-emotional-distress (IIED) tort. While the other intentional torts require the desire to harm or knowledge of substantial certainty of harm, IIED's *recklessness* definition of intent holds the element satisfied on knowledge of high probability of harm. Recklessness is acting with knowledge of high probability of harm. The Restatement (Third) of Torts: Liability for Physical and Emotional Harm §2 has a more elaborate and sensitive definition, stating, "A person acts recklessly in engaging in conduct if: (a) the person knows of harm created by the conduct or knows facts that make the risk obvious to another in the person's situation, and (b) the precaution that would eliminate or reduce the risk involves burdens that are so slight relative to the magnitude of the risk as to render the person's failure to adopt the precaution a demonstration of the person's indifference to the risk." Good policy reasons exist for modifying the intent element for the IIED tort, as you will see later from your study of that tort.

> **Figure**
> Trial lawyer Kathleen Flynn Peterson, a president and executive-committee member of the American Association of Justice (formerly the Association of Trial Lawyers of America), has been representing injured individuals for over 25 years. She was a registered nurse before beginning her tort-law career and has put her medical education and

experience to good use litigating medical-malpractice and personal-injury cases from her Minneapolis law firm, Robins, Kaplan, Miller & Ciresi, for which she has also been the personal-injury section chair. She is a director of her law firm's foundation promoting public health, social justice, and education, and a tireless speaker on those topics before hundreds of organizations. Ms. Peterson has been recognized as an influential lawyer and woman by a host of local, regional, and national organizations.

Transferred Intent. Intent transfers among the five traditional intentional torts assault, battery, false imprisonment, trespass to chattels, and trespass to land. By *transfer* of intent from tort to tort, law means that a person intending one of these five traditional intentional torts satisfies the intent element of any of the other four of those five torts—even when the person did not intend that other tort. *See* Alteiri v. Colasso, 362 A.2d 798 (Conn. 1975) (intent to assault satisfies intent to commit battery). Intent transfers not only among these five torts but also from intended to unintended victims of these torts. A person intending harm to one victim satisfies the intent element of harm toward an unintended victim. *See* Holloway v. Wachovia Bank and Trust Co., 428 S.E.2d 453 (N.C. Ct. App. 1993) (intent to frighten vehicle driver transfers to satisfy intent element as to frightened vehicle passenger), *revd. in part on other grounds*, 425 S.E.2d 233 (N.C. 1994). Identify in the following case the torts and victims from which and to which intent transferred.

Talmage v. Smith
Michigan Supreme Court
101 Mich. 370, 59 N.W. 656 (1894).

MONTGOMERY, J. The plaintiff recovered in an action of trespass. The case made by plaintiff's proofs was substantially as follows: On the evening of September 11, 1891, some limekilns were burning a short distance from defendant's premises, in Portland, Ionia county. Defendant had on his premises certain sheds. He came up to the vicinity of the sheds, and saw six or eight boys on the roof of one of them. He claims that he ordered the boys to get down, and they at once did so. He then passed around to where he had a view of the roof of another shed, and saw two boys on the roof. The defendant claims that he did not see the plaintiff, and the proof is not very clear that he did, although there was some testimony from which it might have been found that he was within his view. Defendant ordered the boys in sight to get down, and there was testimony tending to show that the two boys in defendant's view started to get down at once. Before they succeeded in doing so, however, defendant took a stick, which is described as being two inches in width, and of about the same thickness, and about 16 inches long, and threw it in the direction of the boys; and there was testimony tending to show that it was thrown at one of the boys in view of the defendant. The stick missed him, and hit the plaintiff just above the eye with such force as to inflict an injury which resulted in the total loss of the sight of the eye. Counsel for the defendant contends that the undisputed testimony shows that defendant threw the stick without intending to hit anybody, and that under the circumstances, if it in fact hit the plaintiff,—defendant not knowing that he was on the shed,—he was not liable. ...

The circuit judge charged the jury as follows: "If you conclude that Smith did not know the Talmage boy was on the shed, and that he did not intend to hit Smith, or the young man that was with him, but simply, by throwing the stick, intended to frighten

Smith, or the other young man that was there, and the club hit Talmage, and injured him, as claimed, then the plaintiff could not recover. If you conclude that Smith threw the stick or club at Smith, or the young man that was with Smith,—intended to hit one or the other of them,—and you also conclude that the throwing of the stick or club was, under the circumstances, reasonable, and not excessive, force to use towards Smith and the other young man, then there would be no recovery by this plaintiff. But if you conclude from the evidence in this case that he threw the stick, intending to hit Smith, or the young man with him,—to hit one of them,—and that that force was unreasonable force, under all the circumstances, then Smith, you see (the defendant), would be doing an unlawful act, if the force was unreasonable, because he has no right to use it. Then he would be doing an unlawful act. He would be liable then for the injury done to this boy with the stick, if he threw it intending to hit the young man Smith, or the young man that was with Smith on the roof; and the force that he was using, by the throwing of the club, was excessive and unreasonable, under all the circumstances of the case, if it was, and then the stick went on and hit the boy, as it seems to have hit him, if it was unreasonable and excessive, then he would be liable for the consequences of it, because he was doing an unlawful act in the outset; that is, he was using unreasonable and unnecessary force—excessive force—against Smith and the young man, to get them off the shed." We think the charge a very fair statement of the law of the case. ... The right of the plaintiff to recover was made to depend upon an intention on the part of the defendant to hit somebody, and to inflict an unwarranted injury upon some one. Under these circumstances, the fact that the injury resulted to another than was intended does not relieve the defendant from responsibility. The cases cited in defendant's brief, we think, support this rule. ...

... The judgment will be affirmed, with costs.

Practice

The older man, fastidiously dressed and groomed, greeted the lawyer formally through the translator, who had herself assumed a more formal posture than usual. The man client began to speak with a pained expression of an old grievance with a former business partner nearly a decade ago. He then moved on to stories of bureaucratic bungling, family problems, and employment issues. The lawyer tried a few times to interject some legal counsel, but it only slowed the client before he moved on to the next grievance. The lawyer silently listed on a legal pad ten different marginally legal issues including three tort claims that the client's long story evoked—the client rebuffing the lawyer's every effort to speak. When the client finally ended, the lawyer said simply, "You are obviously a man of great faith and distinction. You have persevered with courage through so difficult a life. I thank you for honoring me with your account." For the first time smiling and looking like a great weight had been lifted from his shoulders, the client rose, bowed formally, extended his hand, and left in complete satisfaction.

INQUIRY

Minority. How young can a child be and still be capable of committing an intentional tort? *Compare* Bailey v. C.S., 12 S.W.3d 159 (Tex. App. 2000) (four-year-old child subject to liability for crushing babysitter's larynx with blow to throat); Ortega v. Montoya, 97 N.M. 159, 637 P.2d 841 (1981) (eight-year-old subject to liability for shooting another with BB gun); Weisbart v Flohr, 260 Cal. App. 2d 281, 67 Cal. Rpotr. 114 (1968) (seven-year-old boy subject to liability for shooting five-year-old girl with arrow from bow), *with* Fromenthal v. Clark, 442 So.2d 608 (La. App. 1983), *cert. denied*, 444 So.2d 1242 (1984) (two-year-old too young to form intent); Carey v. Reeve, 56 Wash. App. 18, 781 P.2d 904 (1989) (children under age seven presumed incapable of forming intent); Queen Ins. Co. v. Hammond, 374 Mich. 655, 132 N.W.2d 792 (1965) (same). Is a parent liable? Cases generally do not hold parents liable for their children's intentional torts unless they had specific reason to know of the need to restrain the child from committing an imminent harm. *See* Dinsmore-Poff v. Alvord, 972 P.2d 978 (Alaska 1999). On the other hand, statutes in many states create parental liability for the intentionally tortious acts of children known to have a miscreant nature. *See* Or. Rev. Stat. §30.765 (parental responsibility statute). Parental responsibility statutes often cap parental liability at just a few thousand dollars. *See id.* ($7,500 cap); *see also* Ala. Code §65-380 ($1,000 plus court costs); Cal. Civ. Code §§1714.1, 1714.3 ($30,000 per person, $60,000 per occurrence); Conn. Gen. Stats. §52-572 ($5,000); Wyo. Stat. Ann. §14-2-203 ($2,000).

Mistake. What if the intentional tort results from an actor's mistake as to the circumstances—reasonable or unreasonable? Mistakes are generally held not to excuse the defendant from intentional tort liability. The well-known historical case is Ranson v. Kitner, 31 Ill.App. 241 (1889), in which the defendant was held liable to pay $50 for shooting another's dog, reasonably thinking the dog was a wolf. Surgeons who mistakenly operate on the wrong person or limb, *see* Gill v. Selling, 125 Or. 587, 267 P. 812 (1928), or those who cut timber on another's land thinking it is their own land, *see* Perry v. Jefferies, 61 S.C. 292, 39 S.E. 515 (1901), are generally liable for an intentional tort (battery or trespass in those two examples) without respect to the reasonableness of their actions.

Transfer of Intent. Is the doctrine of transferred intent an anomaly, or is it significant to tort actions today? *See* Davis v. White, 18 B.R. 246 (Bankr. E.D. Va. 1982) (non-dischargeable intentional tort obligation arising under doctrine of transferred intent, when defendant's stray bullet struck plaintiff); Hall v. McBryde, 919 P.2d 910 (Colo. App. 1996) (youth attempting to scare motorist with gunfire held subject to intentional tort liability for accidental injury to neighbor); Holloway v Wachovia Bank and Trust Co., 109 N.C. App. 403, 428 S.E.2d 453 (1993) (defendant purposefully pointing gun at car driver in attempt to repossess car liable to passenger plaintiff, under doctrine of transferred intent).

Significance. What difference does it make whether a tort is intentional or merely negligent? Intentional torts more likely expose wrongdoers to punitive damage awards, less likely provide defenses of contributory or comparative negligence, less likely give rise to employer vicarious liability, likely have shorter limitation periods, and likely do not have insurance coverage. Although workplace injuries are ordinarily compensable only through statutory worker's compensation schemes, intentional torts are an exception to those schemes' exclusive-remedy provisions. Causation may also extend to a greater reach in the case of an intentional tort. Claimants need not prove damages in the case of the personal (dignitary) intentional torts. If a claimant shows no injury, then presumed or nominal damages may still be due for an intentional tort. Torts of negligence require proof of damages.

A. Battery

OBJECTIVE: Given facts suggesting an intentional-tort claim, recall and apply the battery elements, analyzing whether the facts satisfy those elements, consistent with the following text.

Case Study: A tenant rents an apartment. The property owner employs a maintenance person, giving him a master key to all apartments. The maintenance person supplements his income by stealing from tenants, using the master key. The maintenance person believed that the tenant was away one evening. He entered her apartment using the master key, with the intent to steal. Leaving the lights off, he edged his way into the apartment's bedroom, stumbling against the tenant's bed and mistakenly putting his hand on the sleeping tenant's leg. The tenant awoke and screamed, causing the maintenance person to flee. Authorities arrested the maintenance person and convicted him of attempted theft. ***Analyze whether the tenant has a battery claim against the maintenance person.***

Battery. Now consider the remaining elements, after intent, of the first of the four personal or dignitary intentional torts: battery. Battery occurs when a person intentionally brings about a harmful or offensive contact with another person, without that other person's consent. Restatement (Second) of Torts §13 (1965), states, "An actor is subject to liability to another for battery if (a) he acts intending to cause a harmful or offensive contact with the person of the other or a third person, or an imminent apprehension of such a contact, and (b) a harmful contact with the person of the other directly or indirectly results." Restatement (Second) of Torts §18 adds that the defendant is also liable for a battery if an *offensive* rather than *harmful* contact results.

Battery-Dignitary Offenses. When thinking of battery, shootings and other intentional blows may first come to mind, but the harm need not be physical. Some of the more common cases involve not physical harm but dignitary offenses like grabbing the breast of a man's coat in confrontation, spitting in another's face, Alcorn v Mitchell, 63 Ill. 553 (1872), knocking off another's hat, Seigel v. Long, 169 Ala. 79, 53 So. 753 (1910), or sexual touches, Gates v. State, 110 Ga.App. 303, 138 S.E.2d 473 (1964) (buttocks); Skousen v. Nidy, 90 Ariz. 215, 367 P.2d 248 (1961) (pubic area). The old English case of Cole v. Turner, 90 Eng. Rep. 958 (Nisi Prius 1704), established for us that "the least touching of another in anger is battery," although interpret "anger" in the modern sense to mean expected offense. Consider the following well-known case involving an unusual claim of harm and then another case even more unusual.

Leichtman v. WLW Jacor Communications, Inc.
Ohio Court of Appeals
92 Ohio App.3d 232, 634 N.E.2d 697 (1994)

PER CURIAM. The plaintiff-appellant, Ahron Leichtman, appeals from the trial court's order dismissing his complaint against the defendants-appellees, WLW Jacor Communications ("WLW"), William Cunningham and Andy Furman, for battery, invasion of privacy, and a violation of Cincinnati Bd. of Health Reg. No. 00083. ...

In his complaint, Leichtman claims to be "a nationally known" antismoking advocate. Leichtman alleges that, on the date of the Great American Smokeout, he was invited to appear on the WLW Bill Cunningham radio talk show to discuss the harmful effects of smoking and breathing secondary smoke. He also alleges that, while he was in the studio, Furman, another WLW talk-show host, lit a cigar and repeatedly blew smoke in Leichtman's face "for the purpose of causing physical discomfort, humiliation and distress."

Leichtman contends that Furman's intentional act constituted a battery. The Restatement of the Law 2d, Torts (1965), states:

"An actor is subject to liability to another for battery if

"(a) he acts intending to cause a harmful or offensive contact with the person of the other * * *, and

"(b) a harmful contact with the person of the other directly or indirectly results[; or][fn omitted]

"[c] an offensive contact with the person of the other directly or indirectly results."[fn omitted]

In determining if a person is liable for a battery, the Supreme Court has adopted the rule that "[c]ontact which is offensive to a reasonable sense of personal dignity is offensive contact." *Love v. Port Clinton* (1988), 37 Ohio St.3d 98, 99, 524 N.E.2d 166, 167. It has defined "offensive" to mean "disagreeable or nauseating or painful because of outrage to taste and sensibilities or affronting insultingness." *State v. Phipps* (1979), 58 Ohio St.2d 271, 274, 12 O.O.3d 273, 275, 389 N.E.2d 1128, 1131. Furthermore, tobacco smoke, as "particulate matter," has the physical properties capable of making contact. R.C. 3704.01(B) and 5709.20(A); Ohio Adm.Code 3745-17.

As alleged in Leichtman's complaint, when Furman intentionally blew cigar smoke in Leichtman's face, under Ohio common law, he committed a battery. No matter how trivial the incident, a battery is actionable, even if damages are only one dollar. *Lacey v. Laird* (1956), 166 Ohio St. 12, 1 O.O.2d 158, 139 N.E.2d 25, paragraph two of the syllabus. The rationale is explained by Roscoe Pound in his essay "Liability": "[I]n civilized society men must be able to assume that others will do them no intentional injury—that others will commit no intentioned aggressions upon them." Pound, An Introduction to the Philosophy of Law (1922) 169.

Other jurisdictions also have concluded that a person can commit a battery by intentionally directing tobacco smoke at another. *Richardson v. Hennly* (1993), 209 Ga.App. 868, 871, 434 S.E.2d 772, 774-775. We do not, however, adopt or lend credence to the theory of a "smoker's battery," which imposes liability if there is substantial certainty that exhaled smoke will predictably contact a nonsmoker. Ezra, Smoker Battery: An Antidote to Second-Hand Smoke (1990), 63 S.Cal.L.Rev. 1061, 1090. Also, whether the "substantial certainty" prong of intent from the Restatement of Torts translates to liability for secondary smoke via the intentional tort doctrine in employment cases as defined by the Supreme Court in *Fyffe v. Jeno's, Inc.* (1991), 59 Ohio St.3d 115, 570 N.E.2d 1108, paragraph one of the syllabus, need not be decided here because Leichtman's claim for battery is based exclusively on Furman's commission of a deliberate act. Finally, because Leichtman alleges that Furman deliberately blew smoke into his face, we find it unnecessary to address offensive contact from passive or secondary smoke under the "glass cage" defense of *McCracken v. Sloan* (1979), 40 N.C.App. 214, 217, 252 S.E.2d 250, 252, relied on by the defendants. ...

Arguably, trivial cases are responsible for an avalanche of lawsuits in the courts. They delay cases that are important to individuals and corporations and that involve important social issues. The result is justice denied to litigants and their counsel who must wait for their day in court. However, absent circumstances that warrant sanctions for frivolous appeals under App.R. 23, we refuse to limit one's right to sue. Section 16,

Article I, Ohio Constitution states, "All courts shall be open, and every person, for an injury done him in his land, goods, person, or reputation, shall have remedy by due course of law, and shall have justice administered without denial or delay."

This case emphasizes the need for some form of alternative dispute resolution operating totally outside the court system as a means to provide an attentive ear to the parties and a resolution of disputes in a nominal case. Some need a forum in which they can express corrosive contempt for another without dragging their antagonist through the expense inherent in a lawsuit. Until such an alternative forum is created, Leichtman's battery claim, previously knocked out by the trial judge in the first round, now survives round two to advance again through the courts into round three. ...

Judgment accordingly.

> **Knowledge**
>
> Legal analysis has high structure. Analysis begins by identifying the disputing parties. Analysis is within an adversarial field. Lawyers must know the parties and their opposing interests. Tort law typically involves an injured plaintiff seeking compensation from an insured defendant who resists paying it, although many tort cases have more than one plaintiff or one defendant. Analysis must identify victims suffering loss and wrongdoers bringing loss about, pairing victims with wrongdoers to determine for each pair whether a tort claim exists. Lawyers cannot always immediately identify parties by name and may even have to sue before identification is possible—perhaps a hit-and-run driver, vehicle owner, or employer, joint venturer, or principal of an agent. Lawyers who do not diligently identifying opposing parties run a malpractice risk.

Borhmann v. Maine Yankee Atomic Power Co.
United States District Court
926 F. Supp. 211 (D. Maine 1996)

CARTER, C.J. Plaintiffs, several University of Southern Maine students, have filed the present action against Maine Yankee Atomic Power Company ("Maine Yankee") for injuries they allegedly sustained after being exposed to radiation when touring Defendant's nuclear power plant in Wiscasset, Maine. Plaintiffs seek recovery pursuant to theories of common law negligence, negligent infliction of emotional distress, intentional infliction of emotional distress, strict liability, fraud, battery, failure to meet State safety reporting requirements pursuant to 35-A M.R.S.A. § 4334(1)(A), and federal public liability pursuant to the Atomic Energy Act. ...

The facts alleged in the Complaint are as follows. Plaintiffs are five University of Southern Maine students who were among a group of chemistry students invited to tour Defendant's facility. Complaint and Demand for Jury Trial (Docket No. 1) ¶¶ 12, 13. Plaintiffs allege that approximately two weeks before their tour, there was a radioactive gas leak in Defendant's primary auxiliary building (PAB) as a result of design flaws and faulty engineering when Defendant "sluiced the demineralizers in its Chemical and Volume Control System." Id. ¶ 11. The students toured Maine Yankee on the morning of October 11, 1994, at which time, Defendant allegedly was in the process of repairing the leakage problem. Id. ¶¶ 1, 11, 13, 14, 15. Plaintiffs claim that "Maine Yankee officials had decided to flush out resin 'hot spots' in the demineralizer" and scheduled the procedure to occur during Plaintiffs' tour. Id. ¶ 15. Plaintiffs further allege that the officials were aware that the flushing procedure would release radioactive gases. Id. Plaintiffs claim that they were never apprised of the problems at Defendant's facility. Id. ¶¶ 16, 19.

Plaintiffs allege that each student was given a pocket-sized Self-Reading Dosimeter, which measures only gamma radiation. Id. ¶ 17. The students were not provided with Thermo-Luminescent Dosimeters, which also measure beta radiation and which are worn by the employees of Defendant. Id. ¶ 17.

Plaintiffs claim that despite his being warned that radioactive gases would be released in the PAB, the lead tour guide led the students into the "hot" side of the plant. Id. ¶¶ 18, 20. Plaintiffs allege that the tour guides knowingly took the students through a plume of unfiltered radioactive gases. Id. ¶¶ 35, 46. While the students were walking through the radioactive gases, the continuous air monitor in the PAB was sounding an alarm. Id. ¶ 35. After spending thirty to forty minutes on the "hot" side of the plant, the students returned to the "hot" side's entry point and stepped into portal monitors. Id. ¶ 23. Plaintiffs and the tour guides allegedly "alarmed out," indicating that they had all been exposed to excessive radioactive contamination from the tour. Id. ¶¶ 23, 24. In fact, Plaintiffs Bohrmann and Ortman continued to "alarm out" up to twenty minutes after they left the PAB. Id. ¶ 25.

Plaintiffs allege that Maine Yankee employees never suggested that the students remove their contaminated clothing or that the students take a shower and wash themselves. Id. ¶ 25. Two hours after the exposure to radioactive gases, Defendant told a few students that they needed to go for a "whole body count" to assess their radiation exposure. Id. ¶ 27. Plaintiff Gagnon allegedly was told that he had nothing to worry about and was not told to undergo a whole body count. Id. ¶ 27. Plaintiffs claim that Maine Yankee employees falsely told them that they had not been subjected to gamma radiation and that only gamma radiation was "bad." Id. ¶ 28. Defendant's employees allegedly told Plaintiffs that they had not been exposed to anything that would pose a health risk. Id. ¶ 29. …

Plaintiffs assert that Defendant deliberately failed to report the contamination of Plaintiffs and the tour guides to the Nuclear Regulatory Commission or the State Nuclear Safety Inspector until after the contamination was reported in the media several days later. Id. ¶ 30. Plaintiffs allegedly did not become aware of the extent of their exposure until they read a newspaper report of the incident later that week. Id. ¶ 29. Defendant allegedly destroyed the charts showing the level of radioactive gases in the PAB soon after October 11, 1994. Id. ¶ 40. Plaintiffs assert that such destruction makes it impossible to quantify the release of radiation to which they had been exposed and allegedly constitutes a violation of federal regulations mandating the retention of the records. Id. ¶¶ 40, 44.

Plaintiff Bohrmann claims to have suffered a significant decrease in his white blood cell count. Id. ¶ 49. In addition, Plaintiffs allege that they live with "the significant distress and uncertainty caused by exposure to unreasonably high levels of nuclear radiation." Id. ¶ 50. Plaintiffs now seek compensatory and punitive damages. …

As concerns Plaintiffs' claims for damages pursuant to theories of intentional infliction of emotional distress and battery, the Court concludes that such intentional tort claims are not inconsistent with the federal safety standards. To recover on either theory, Plaintiffs must demonstrate that Defendant intentionally exposed Plaintiffs to radiation without their consent, and that such intentional conduct on the part of Defendant caused them damages. See, e.g., Latremore v. Latremore, 584 A.2d 626, 631 (Me.1990) (setting forth elements of intentional infliction of emotional distress); Pattershall v. Jenness, 485 A.2d 980, 984 (Me.1984) (an element of battery is an intentional act).[fn]

There is no reason apparent to this Court to believe that Congress intended that a defendant be insulated from liability for its intentional acts solely by complying with the federal safety standards. Instead, *compliance* with the federal regulations merely demonstrates the absence of negligence. See Coley, 768 F.Supp. at 629. The federal safety standards have no bearing on a defendant's liability for its intentional acts. While a plaintiff may recover on an intentional tort theory without proving exposure to radiation exceeding the federal safety standards, a plaintiff may not recover without first proving that he sustained damages, and such proof may be difficult to establish in the absence of proving a violation of the federal safety standards. See, e.g., Laswell v. Brown, 683 F.2d 261, 269 (8th Cir.1982) (concluding that "lawsuit for personal injuries cannot be based only upon the mere possibility of some future harm"), cert. denied, 459 U.S. 1210, 103 S.Ct. 1205, 75 L.Ed.2d 446 (1983); Johnston v. United States, 597 F.Supp. 374, 425-26 (D.Kan.1984); Bubash v. Philadelphia Elec. Co., 717 F.Supp. 297, 300 (M.D.Pa.1989) (concluding that mere exposure to radiation is not an actionable physical injury). Nevertheless, the absence of a violation of the federal standards does not necessarily establish the absence of an actual injury. ...

Fisher v. Carrousel Motor Hotel, Inc.
Texas Supreme Court
424 S.W.2d 627 (Tex. 1967)

GREENHILL, J. This is a suit for actual and exemplary damages growing out of an alleged assault and battery. The plaintiff Fisher was a mathematician with the Data Processing Division of the Manned Spacecraft Center, an agency of the National Aeronautics and Space Agency, commonly called NASA, near Houston. The defendants were the Carrousel Motor Hotel, Inc., located in Houston, the Brass Ring Club, which is located in the Carrousel, and Robert W. Flynn, who as an employee of the Carrousel was the manager of the Brass Ring Club. ... The questions before this Court are whether there was evidence that an actionable battery was committed, and, if so, whether the two corporate defendants must respond in exemplary as well as actual damages for the malicious conduct of Flynn.

The plaintiff Fisher had been invited by Ampex Corporation and Defense Electronics to a one day's meeting regarding telemetry equipment at the Carrousel. The invitation included a luncheon. The guests were asked to reply by telephone whether they could attend the luncheon, and Fisher called in his acceptance. After the morning session, the group of 25 or 30 guests adjourned to the Brass Ring Club for lunch. The luncheon was buffet style, and Fisher stood in line with others and just ahead of a graduate student of Rice University who testified at the trial. As Fisher was about to be served, he was approached by Flynn, who snatched the plate from Fisher's hand and shouted that he, a Negro, could not be served in the club. Fisher testified that he was not actually touched, and did not testify that he suffered fear or apprehension of physical injury; but he did testify that he was highly embarrassed and hurt by Flynn's conduct in the presence of his associates.

The jury found that Flynn 'forceably dispossessed plaintiff of his dinner plate' and 'shouted in a loud and offensive manner' that Fisher could not be served there, thus subjecting Fisher to humiliation and indignity. It was stipulated that Flynn was an employee of the Carrousel Hotel and, as such, managed the Brass Ring Club. The jury also found that Flynn acted maliciously and awarded Fisher $400 actual damages for his humiliation and indignity and $500 exemplary damages for Flynn's malicious conduct.

The Court of Civil Appeals held that there was no assault because there was no physical contact and no evidence of fear or apprehension of physical contact. However, it has long been settled that there can be a battery without an assault, and that actual physical contact is not necessary to constitute a battery, so long as there is contact with clothing or an object closely identified with the body. 1 Harper & James, The Law of Torts 216 (1956); Restatement of Torts 2d, ss 18 and 19. ...

Under the facts of this case, we have no difficulty in holding that the intentional grabbing of plaintiff's plate constituted a battery. The intentional snatching of an object from one's hand is as clearly an offensive invasion of his person as would be an actual contact with the body. "To constitute an assault and battery, it is not necessary to touch the plaintiff's body or even his clothing; knocking or snatching anything from plaintiff's hand or touching anything connected with his person, when, done is an offensive manner, is sufficient." Morgan v. Loyacomo, 190 Miss. 656, 1 So.2d 510 (1941).

Such holding is not unique to the jurisprudence of this State. In S. H. Kress & Co. v. Brashier, 50 S.W.2d 922 (Tex.Civ.App.1932, no writ), the defendant was held to have committed "an assault or trespass upon the person" by snatching a book from the plaintiff's hand. The jury findings in that case were that the defendant "dispossessed plaintiff of the book' and caused her to suffer 'humiliation and indignity."

The rationale for holding an offensive contact with such an object to be a battery is explained in 1 Restatement of Torts 2d s 18 (Comment p. 31) as follows: "Since the essence of the plaintiff's grievance consists in the offense to the dignity involved in the unpermitted and intentional invasion of the inviolability of his person and not in any physical harm done to his body, it is not necessary that the plaintiff's actual body be disturbed. Unpermitted and intentional contacts with anything so connected with the body as to be customarily regarded as part of the other's person and therefore as partaking of its inviolability is actionable as an offensive contact with his person. There are some things such as clothing or a cane or, indeed, anything directly grasped by the hand which are so intimately connected with one's body as to be universally regarded as part of the person."

We hold, therefore, that the forceful dispossession of plaintiff Fisher's plate in an offensive manner was sufficient to constitute a battery, and the trial court erred in granting judgment notwithstanding the verdict on the issue of actual damages. ...

The judgments of the courts below are reversed, and judgment is here rendered for the plaintiff for $900 with interest from the date of the trial court's judgment, and for costs of this suit.

> **Knowledge**
> Lawyers must evaluate whether facts satisfy a claim's elements. Facts must satisfy each element for the claimant to have a claim. The claimant must produce evidence supporting each element, so that a reasonable juror could conclude that the claimant has proven the claim. Defining an element differs from determining whether facts satisfy an

> element. Lawyers evaluate by approximation whether facts meet the element's requirements. Approximating the relationship between the elements and facts involves comparing and contrasting similar law-fact terms. For example, given that the defendant shoved the plaintiff, a lawyer would conclude that the contact element of battery was met. "Shove" (the fact) equates with "contact" (the element). For a more difficult approximation, when the defendant struck the hood of a car occupied by the plaintiff, a lawyer would ask whether "struck the hood of a car" equates with "contact." The lawyer might need to explore the functional nature of the contact element. Did striking the car hood transmit any offensive physical sensation to the plaintiff? Or did it offensively invade the plaintiff's personal space?

INQUIRY

Permitted Contact. Where does one draw the line between permissible and impermissible contact—between what is harmful or offensive, and what is not? *See* Lambertson v. United States, 528 F2d 441 (2d Cir. 1976) (meat inspector jumping on back of worker and screaming "boo" while covering worker's eyes subject to battery liability for undesired injury when worker struck face on meathook); White v. University of Idaho, 115 Idaho 564, 768 P.2d 827 (Idaho Ct. App. 1989) (music professor making unexpected piano-striking contact to musician's back demonstrating playing, subject to battery liability for resulting undesired injury); Caudle v. Betts, 512 So.2d 389 (La. 1987) (company executive liable in battery for injury to employee from electrical shock intended as a joke). Would a polite tap from behind on the shoulder to communicate with another ever constitute a battery? *See* Wallace v. Rosen, 765 N.E.2d 192 (Ind. Ct. App. 2002) (teacher's touching parent on the back to get her attention to clear the way during a fire drill held not to constitute a battery) (quoting Holmes, "even a dog knows the difference between being tripped over and being kicked").

Motive. Should the actor's motive, including for example the actor's good intention to help someone who does not want that help, make a difference whether the touching constitutes a battery? *See* Clayton v. New Dreamland Roller Skating Rink, Inc., 14 N.J. Super. 390, 82 A.2d 458 (1951), *cert. denied*, 13 N.J. 527, 100 A.2d 567 (1953) (skating rink employee with first aid experience subject to battery liability for attempting to set patron's broken arm over patron's and patron's husband's protests); *see also* Cohen v. Smith, 269 Ill. App.3d 1087, 207 Ill. Dec. 873, 648 N.E.2d 329 (1995) (male nurse subject to battery liability for touching female patient during regular course of Cesarean section, after patient had been reassured that her religious beliefs against such touching would be respected); Roberson v. Provident House, 576 So.2d 992 (La. 1991) (battery claim over medical treatment rendered against plaintiff's expressed wishes). The context in which the touching occurs—even if the plaintiff would not have permitted it if knowing the full circumstances—can still be important. *See* Brzoska v. Olson, 668 A.2d 1355 (Del. 1995) (no battery claim over defendant HIV-infected dentist performing plaintiff patient's dental work without disclosing HIV status).

Employment. Should supervisors have greater or lesser liberty to touch subordinates in the course of employment? *See* Snyder v. Turk, 90 Ohio App.3d 18, 627 N.E.2d 1053 (1993) (surgeon subject to battery liability for grabbing scrub nurse's shoulder to pull her face down toward the patient's surgical opening while admonishing nurse over inefficient supplying of surgical instruments); *see also* Koffman v. Garnett, 265 Va. 12, 574 S.E.2d 258 (2003) (260-pound football coach subject to battery liability for, without warning, demonstrating tackling technique on 144-pound 13-year-old player, breaking player's humerus).

Eggshell-Skull Rule. Should a person who commits a battery in which one would reasonably expect only a mild harm pay for the full extent of unpredictable damage? The answer—yes—is one that torts practitioners call the *eggshell-skull rule* after the case of McCahill v. New York Transp. Co., 201 N.Y. 221, 94 N.E. 616 (1911). The scope of harm for which the defendant must pay arises again when you consider the proximate-cause element of negligence claims in a later chapter. Consider the following famous case illustrative of the eggshell-skull rule in the intentional-tort context.

Vosburg v. Putney
Wisconsin Supreme Court
80 Wis. 523, 50 N.W. 403 (1891)

.... The other facts fully appear in the following statement by LYON, J.:

The action was brought to recover damages for an assault and battery, alleged to have been committed by the defendant upon the plaintiff on February 20, 1889. The answer is a general denial. At the date of the alleged assault the plaintiff was a little more than 14 years of age, and the defendant a little less than 12 years of age. The injury complained of was caused by a kick inflicted by defendant upon the leg of the plaintiff, a little below the knee. The transaction occurred in a school-room in Waukesha, during school hours, both parties being pupils in the school. ... The facts of the case, as they appeared on both trials, are sufficiently stated in the opinion by Mr. Justice ORTON on the former appeal, and require no repetition. On the last trial the jury found a special verdict, as follows: "(1) Had the plaintiff during the month of January, 1889, received an injury just above the knee, which became inflamed, and produced pus? Answer. Yes. (2) Had such injury on the 20th day of February, 1889, nearly healed at the point of the injury? A. Yes. (3) Was the plaintiff, before said 20th of February, lame, as the result of such injury? A. No. (4) Had the *tibia* in the plaintiff's right leg become inflamed or diseased to some extent before he received the blow or kick from the defendant? A. No. (5) What was the exciting cause of the injury to the plaintiff's leg? A. Kick. (6) Did the defendant, in touching the plaintiff with his foot, intend to do him any harm? A. No. (7) At what sum do you assess the damages of the plaintiff? A. Twenty-five hundred dollars." ... Thereupon judgment for plaintiff, for $2,500 damages and costs of suit, was duly entered. The defendant appeals from the judgment. ...

LYON, J., (*after stating the facts.*) Several errors are assigned, only three of which will be considered.

I. The jury having found that the defendant, in touching the plaintiff with his foot, did not intend to do him any harm, counsel for defendant maintain that the plaintiff has no cause of action, and that defendant's motion for judgment on the special verdict should have been granted. ... Had the parties been upon the play-grounds of the school, engaged in the usual boyish sports, the defendant being free from malice, wantonness, or negligence, and intending no harm to plaintiff in what he did, we should hesitate to hold the act of the defendant unlawful, or that he could be held liable in this action. Some consideration is due to the implied license of the play-grounds. But it appears that the injury was inflicted in the school, after it had been called to order by the teacher, and after the regular exercises of the school had commenced. Under these circumstances, no implied license to do the act complained of existed, and such act was a violation of the order and decorum of the school, and necessarily unlawful. Hence we are of the opinion that, under the evidence and verdict, the action may be sustained.

II. The plaintiff testified, as a witness in his own behalf, as to the circumstances of the alleged injury inflicted upon him by the defendant, and also in regard to the wound he received in January, near the same knee, mentioned in the special verdict. The defendant claimed that such wound was the proximate cause of the injury to plaintiff's leg, in that it produced a diseased condition of the bone, which disease was in active progress when he received the kick, and that such kick did nothing more than to change the location, and perhaps somewhat hasten the progress, of the disease. The testimony of Dr. Bacon, a witness for plaintiff, (who was plaintiff's attending physician,) elicited on cross-examination, tends to some extent to establish such claim. Dr. Bacon first saw the injured leg on February 25th, and Dr. Philler, also one of plaintiff's witnesses, first saw it March 8th. Dr. Philler was called as a witness after the examination of the plaintiff and Dr. Bacon. On his direct examination he testified as follows: "I heard the testimony of Andrew Vosburg in regard to how he received the kick, February 20th, from his playmate. I heard read the testimony of Miss More, and heard where he said he received this kick on that day." (Miss More had already testified that she was the teacher of the school, and saw defendant standing in the aisle by his seat, and kicking across the aisle, hitting the plaintiff.) The following question was then propounded to Dr. Philler: "After hearing that testimony, and what you know of the case of the boy, seeing it on the 8th day of March, what, in your opinion, was the exciting cause that produced the inflammation that you saw in that boy's leg on that day?" An objection to this question was overruled, and the witness answered: "The exciting cause was the injury received at that day by the kick on the shin-bone." ....

III. Certain questions were proposed on behalf of defendant to be submitted to the jury, founded upon the theory that only such damages could be recovered as the defendant might reasonably be supposed to have contemplated as likely to result from his kicking the plaintiff. The court refused to submit such questions to the jury. The ruling was correct. The rule of damages in actions for torts was held in Brown v. Railway Co., 54 Wis. 342, 11 N. W. Rep. 356, 911, to be that the wrongdoer is liable for all injuries resulting directly from the wrongful act, whether they could or could not have been foreseen by him. The chief justice and the writer of this opinion dissented from the judgment in that case, chiefly because we were of the opinion that the complaint stated a cause of action *ex contractu,* and not *ex delicto,* and hence that a different rule of damages—the rule here contended for—was applicable. We did not question that the rule in actions for tort was correctly stated. That case rules this on the question of damages. The remaining errors assigned are upon the rulings of the court on objections to testimony. These rulings are not very likely to be repeated on another trial, and are not of sufficient importance to require a review of them on this appeal. The judgment of the circuit court must be reversed, and the cause will be remanded for a new trial.

Knowledge

A simple way to express how to evaluate an element is by using a "was-when-because" formulation. For example: "The duty element WAS satisfied WHEN defendant undertook the repairs, BECAUSE defendant should then have foreseen the likelihood of injury." Or: "The intent element WAS not met WHEN defendant fell onto the plaintiff,

BECAUSE the fall was clearly accidental." Or: "The malice element WAS very likely satisfied WHEN defendant called the plaintiff a racial slur, BECAUSE it expressed defendant's ill will toward the plaintiff." You need not restrict your evaluation to a single sentence but can extend it into several sentences or paragraphs. But analysis can also be concise in this fashion. Begin by identifying the element. Then state whether the facts satisfy the element. Then identify the facts that support your evaluation. Finally, show your reasoning. The "was-when-because" rubric provides the cues.

B. Assault

OBJECTIVE: Given facts suggesting an intentional tort claim for assault, recall and apply the assault elements analyzing whether the facts satisfy the claim, consistent with the following text.

Case Study: A man wanted a woman never to forget that he was the toughest man in town. Dressed in hunting gear, he walked up to the counter in the store where she was working, pulled his knife from his boot, raised it shoulder high, and swung it down hard toward her, stabbing its tip in the counter right in front of her. She jumped back and passed out. *Analyze whether these facts satisfy the elements of assault.*

Assault. Assault is an intentional tort closely related to battery. Although one often hears *assault and battery* in that singular form, the torts of (1) assault and (2) battery are two separate torts. While assault often occurs with battery and vice versa, either tort can occur without the other. An assault is the reasonable apprehension of an imminent battery, when the perpetrator has the apparent present ability to carry it out. The Restatement (Second) of Torts §21 (1965) holds that, "An actor is subject to liability to another for assault if (a) he acts intending to cause a harmful or offensive contact with the person of the other or a third person, or an imminent apprehension of such a contact, and (b) the other is thereby put in such imminent apprehension." The sense of the tort of assault is that the one who is about to suffer a battery sees it coming and thus suffers that additional harm anticipating the contact. If a battery does not actually occur (perhaps the perpetrator misses), then one has only an assault. If the perpetrator commits a battery from behind where the victim cannot see the approach, or with the victim unconscious, then only battery occurs and not assault. Consider the following illustrative cases.

Beach v. Hancock
New Hampshire Supreme Court
27 N.H. 223 (1853)

Trespass, for an assault.
Upon the general issue it appeared that the plaintiff and defendant, being engaged in an angry altercation, the defendant stepped into his office, which was at hand, and brought out a gun, which he aimed at the plaintiff in an excited and threatening manner, the plaintiff being three or four rods distant. The evidence tended to show that the defendant snapped the gun twice at the plaintiff, and that the plaintiff did not know whether the gun was loaded or not, and that, in fact, the gun was not loaded.
The court ruled that the pointing of a gun, in an angry and threatening manner, at a person three or four rods distant, who was ignorant whether the gun was loaded or not,

was an assault, though it should appear that the gun was not loaded, and that it made no difference whether the gun was snapped or not.

The court, among other things, instructed the jury that, in assessing the damages, it was their right and duty to consider the effect which the finding of light or trivial damages in actions for breaches of the peace, would have to encourage a disregard of the laws and disturbances of the public peace.

The defendant excepted to these rulings and instructions.

The jury, having found a verdict for the plaintiff, the defendant moved for a new trial by reason of said exceptions. ...

GILCHRIST, C.J. ... One of the most important objects to be attained by the enactment of laws and the institutions of civilized society is, each of us shall feel secure against unlawful assaults. Without such security society loses most of its value. Peace and order and domestic happiness, inexpressibly more precious than mere forms of government, cannot be enjoyed without the sense of perfect security. We have a right to live in society without being put in fear of personal harm. But it must be a reasonable fear of which we complain. And it surely is not unreasonable for a person to entertain a fear of personal injury, when a pistol is pointed at him in a threatening manner, when, for aught he knows, it may be loaded, and may occasion his immediate death. The business of the world could not be carried on with comfort, if such things could be done with impunity.

We think the defendant guilty of an assault, and we perceive no reason for taking any exception to the remarks of the court. Finding trivial damages for breaches of the peace, damages incommensurate with the injury sustained, would certainly lead the ill-disposed to consider an assault as a thing that might be committed with impunity. But, at all events, it was proper for the jury to consider whether such a result would or would not be produced. [C]

Judgment on the verdict.

Figure

Dennis Archer was the first African-American president of the American Bar Association, the world's largest professional organization. He has also been the mayor of Detroit, president of the National League of Cities, and a Michigan Supreme Court justice. Yet first and last, he was a trial lawyer in torts cases. Mr. Archer started his law career representing individuals with tort claims and those in need of a trial lawyer for criminal defense. As his trial practice grew, so did the size and influence of the law firms he joined and causes he undertook—medical malpractice, products liability, personal injury, and other civil claims in addition to criminal defense. Mr. Archer also got involved in politics, first managing a successful judicial campaign for his law partner before embarking on campaigns of his own. His eight years as mayor of Detroit saw a decline in violent crime and increase in economic development. Mr. Archer returned to private law practice after his stint on Michigan's high court to chair the 240-lawyer firm Dickinson Wright, conducting substantial medical-malpractice, consumer class-action, defamation, business-tort, and other litigation practice.

Cullison v. Medley
Indiana Supreme Court
570 N.E.2d 27 (Ind. 1991)

KRAHULIK, J. Dan R. Cullison (Appellant-Plaintiff below) petitions this Court to accept transfer of this cause in order to reverse the trial court's entry of summary judgment against him and in favor of the Appellees-Defendants below (collectively "the Medleys"). The Court of Appeals affirmed the entry of summary judgment. *Cullison v. Medley* (1990), Ind.App., 559 N.E.2d 619. For the reasons set forth below, we grant transfer, vacate the opinion of the Court of Appeals, reverse the entry of summary judgment and remand to the trial court.

... We conclude that the evidence presented to the trial court construed in favor of the non-moving party, Cullison, establishes questions of fact which require jury resolution on three of the four counts alleged in Cullison's complaint.

According to Cullison's deposition testimony, on February 2, 1986, he encountered Sandy, the 16-year-old daughter of Ernest, in a Linton, Indiana, grocery store parking lot. They exchanged pleasantries and Cullison invited her to have a Coke with him and to come to his home to talk further. A few hours later, someone knocked on the door of his mobile home. Cullison got out of bed and answered the door. He testified that he saw a person standing in the darkness who said that she wanted to talk to him. Cullison answered that he would have to get dressed because he had been in bed. Cullison went back to his bedroom, dressed, and returned to the darkened living room of his trailer. When he entered the living room and turned the lights on, he was confronted by Sandy Medley, as well as by father Ernest, brother Ron, mother Doris, and brother-in-law Terry Simmons. Ernest was on crutches due to knee surgery and had a revolver in a holster strapped to his thigh. Cullison testified that Sandy called him a "pervert" and told him he was "sick," mother Doris berated him while keeping her hand in her pocket, convincing Cullison that she also was carrying a pistol. Ron and Terry said nothing to Cullison, but their presence in his trailer home further intimidated him. Primarily, however, Cullison's attention was riveted to the gun carried by Ernest. Cullison testified that, while Ernest never withdrew the gun from his holster, he "grabbed for the gun a few times and shook the gun" at plaintiff while threatening to "jump astraddle" of Cullison if he did not leave Sandy alone. Cullison testified that Ernest "kept grabbing at it with his hand, like he was going to take it out," and "took it to mean he was going to shoot me" when Ernest threatened to "jump astraddle" of Cullison. Although no one actually touched Cullison, his testimony was that he feared he was about to be shot throughout the episode because Ernest kept moving his hand toward the gun as if to draw the revolver from the holster while threatening Cullison to leave Sandy alone.

As the Medleys were leaving, Cullison suffered chest pains and feared that he was having a heart attack. Approximately two months later, Cullison testified that Ernest glared at him in a menacing manner while again armed with a handgun at a restaurant in Linton. On one of these occasions, Ernest stood next to the booth where Cullison was seated while wearing a pistol and a holster approximately one foot from Cullison's face. Shortly after the incident at his home, Cullison learned that Ernest had previously shot a man. This added greatly to his fear and apprehension of Ernest on the later occasions when Ernest glared at him and stood next to the booth at which he was seated while armed with a handgun in a holster.

Cullison testified that as a result of the incident, he sought psychological counseling and therapy and continued to see a therapist for approximately 18 months. Additionally, Cullison sought psychiatric help and received prescription medication which prevented him from operating power tools or driving an automobile, thus injuring Cullison in his sole proprietorship construction business. Additionally, Cullison testified that he suffered from nervousness, depression, sleeplessness, inability to concentrate and impotency following his run-in with the Medleys. ....

II. *Assault*

In count two of his complaint, Cullison alleged an assault. The Court of Appeals decided that, because Ernest never removed his gun from the holster, his threat that he was going to "jump astraddle" of Cullison constituted conditional language which did not express any present intent to harm Cullison and, therefore, was not an assault. Further, the Court of Appeals decided that even if it were to find an assault, summary judgment was still appropriate because Cullison alleged only emotional distress and made no showing that the Medleys' actions were malicious, callous, or willful or that the alleged injuries he suffered were a foreseeable result of the Medleys' conduct. We disagree.

It is axiomatic that assault, unlike battery, is effectuated when one acts intending to cause a harmful or offensive contact with the person of the other or an imminent apprehension of such contact. Restatement (Second) of Torts § 21 (1965). It is the right to be free from the apprehension of a battery which is protected by the tort action which we call an assault. As this Court held approximately 90 years ago in *Kline v. Kline* (1901), 158 Ind. 602, 64 N.E. 9, an assault constitutes "a touching of the mind, if not of the body." Because it is a touching of the mind, as opposed to the body, the damages which are recoverable for an assault are damages for mental trauma and distress. "Any act of such a nature as to excite an apprehension of a battery may constitute an assault. It is an assault to shake a fist under another's nose, to aim or strike at him with a weapon, or to hold it in a threatening position, to rise or advance to strike another, to surround him with a display of force...." W. Prosser & J. Keaton, Prosser and Keaton on Torts § 10 (5th ed. 1984). Additionally, the apprehension must be one which would normally be aroused in the mind of a reasonable person. *Id.* Finally, the tort is complete with the invasion of the plaintiff's mental peace.

The facts alleged and testified to by Cullison could, if believed, entitle him to recover for an assault against the Medleys. A jury could reasonably conclude that the Medleys intended to frighten Cullison by surrounding him in his trailer and threatening him with bodily harm while one of them was armed with a revolver, even if that revolver was not removed from its holster. Cullison testified that Ernest kept grabbing at the pistol as if he were going to take it out, and that Cullison thought Ernest was going to shoot him. It is for the jury to determine whether Cullison's apprehension of being shot or otherwise injured was one which would normally be aroused in the mind of a reasonable person. It was error for the trial court to enter summary judgment on the count two allegation of assault. ...

[Reversed in part and remanded.]

Knowledge

Tort lawyers must recall elements of torts claims. While experienced lawyers probably do not use any particular memory device, instead knowing the elements from years of usage, you may find some memory device helpful. A mnemonic (acrostic) constructs a memorable sound or word from the first letter of each element. For example, if battery is *intentional harmful or offensive contact*, then IHOC is an appropriate mnemonic. If assault occurs upon the apprehension of an imminent battery with the perpetrator's apparent present ability to carry it out, then AI IHOC APA is an appropriate (though unwieldy)

> mnemonic. A less abstract, more functional memory aid is to categorize elements by what the actor thinks, does, and causes. For battery, the actor *thinks* with intention, *does* an act causing contact, and *causes* something harmful or offensive. For assault, the actor *thinks* with intention, *does* an act creating apprehension of imminent battery, and *causes* reasonable fear. To know elements, you must first recall them.

Present Ability. Now consider an additional element of the tort of assault, one that the above cases imply, that the putative victim must reasonably believe that the alleged perpetrator has the present ability to carry out an imminent battery.

Western Union Telegraph Co. v. Hill
Alabama Court of Appeals
25 Ala. App. 540, 150 So. 709 (1933)

SAMFORD, J. The action in this case is based upon an alleged assault on the person of plaintiff's wife by one Sapp, an agent of defendant in charge of its office in Huntsville, Ala. The assault complained of consisted of an attempt on the part of Sapp to put his hand on the person of plaintiff's wife coupled with a request that she come behind the counter in defendant's office, and that, if she would come and allow Sapp to love and pet her, he "would fix her clock."

The first question that addresses itself to us is, Was there such an assault as will justify an action for damages?

Blackstone's definition of an assault is: "An attempt or offer to beat another, without touching him; as if one lifts up his cane or his fist in a threatening manner; or strikes at him but misses him." …

In this state an assault and battery is: "Any touching by one person of the person of another in rudeness or in anger." Seigel v. Long, 169 Ala. 79, 53 So. 753, 754, 33 L. R. A. (N. S.) 1070; Jacobi v. State, 133 Ala. 17, 32 So. 158.

While every battery includes an assault, an assault does not necessarily require a battery to complete it. What it does take to constitute an assault is an unlawful attempt to commit a battery, incomplete by reason of some intervening cause; or, to state it differently, to constitute an actionable assault there must be an intentional, unlawful, offer to touch the person of another in a rude or angry manner under such circumstances as to create in the mind of the party alleging the assault a well-founded fear of an imminent battery, coupled with the apparent present ability to effectuate the attempt, if not prevented. …

Solicitation by a man to a woman for intercourse unaccompanied by an assault is not actionable. … Insulting words used when not accompanied by an assault are not the subject of an action for damages. …

What are the facts here? Sapp was the agent of defendant and the manager of its telegraph office in Huntsville. Defendant was under contract with plaintiff to keep in repair and regulated an electric clock in plaintiff's place of business. When the clock needed attention, that fact was to be reported to Sapp, and he in turn would report to a special man, whose duty it was to do the fixing. At 8:13 o'clock p.m. plaintiff's wife reported to Sapp over the phone that the clock needed attention, and, no one coming to attend to the clock, plaintiff's wife went to the office of defendant about 8:30 p. m. There she found Sapp in charge and behind a desk or counter, separating the public from the part of the room in which defendant's operator worked. The counter is four feet and two inches high, and so wide that, Sapp standing on the floor, leaning against the counter and stretching his arm and hand to the full length, the end of his fingers reaches just to the outer edge of the counter. The photographs in evidence show that the counter was as high as Sapp's armpits. Sapp had had two or three drinks and was "still slightly feeling the effects of whisky; I felt all right; I felt good and amiable." When plaintiff's wife came into the office, Sapp came from towards the rear of the room and asked what he could do for her. She replied: "I asked him if he understood over the phone that my clock was out of order and when he was going to fix it. He stood there and looked at me a few minutes and said: 'If you will come back here and let me love and pet you, I will fix your clock.' This he repeated and reached for me with his hand, he extended his hand toward me, he did not put it on me; I jumped back. I was in his reach as I stood there. He reached for me right along here (indicating her left shoulder and arm)." The foregoing is the evidence offered by plaintiff tending to prove an assault. Per contra, aside from the positive denial by Sapp of any effort to touch Mrs. Hill, the physical surroundings as evidenced by the photographs of the locus tend to rebut any evidence going to prove that Sapp could have touched plaintiff's wife across that counter even if he had reached his hand in her direction unless she was leaning against the counter or Sapp should have stood upon something so as to elevate him and allow him to reach beyond the counter. However, there is testimony tending to prove that, notwithstanding the width of the counter and the height of Sapp, Sapp could have reached from six to eighteen inches beyond the desk in an effort to place his hand on Mrs. Hill. The evidence as a whole presents a question for the jury. This was the view taken by the trial judge, and in the several rulings bearing on this question there is no error. ...

[Reversed as to the liability of Sapp's employer for the actions of Sapp, insofar as Sapp had not acted within the scope of his employment.]

INQUIRY

Criminal Assault. A criminal assault typically requires that the defendant have the *actual* ability to harm, not merely the *apparent* ability—the latter enough to constitute a tort, as the above *Western Union* case indicates. Why the difference?

Overt Acts. In the *Cullison* case above, one of the defendants repeatedly grabbed for and shook his gun while others made veiled threats. Is holding (but not aiming or brandishing) a gun or other weapon, or simply wearing a holstered gun, enough to constitute an assault, when combined with threatening words? *See* Cucinotti v. Ortmann, 399 Pa. 26, 159 A.2d 216 (1960) (allegations that defendants carried blackjacks while threatening to use them not enough without accompanying overt acts creating imminent apprehension); Penny v. State, 114 Ga. 77, 39 S.E. 871 (1901) (gun brought along for an interview not enough to constitute an assault unless so extraordinary as to constitute an overt act). What overt acts are sufficient? Some states create statutory tort actions for stalking—conduct that may not involve threats of imminent harm but that foreseeably alarm or harass the victim. Cal. Civ. Code §1708.7.

Imminent Apprehension. What if the plaintiff who claims an assault only learned about the imminent battery after it had occurred—as when the plaintiff did not notice the defendant aiming a gun at the plaintiff but learned about it later? *See* Tom v. Lenox Hill Hosp., 165 Misc.2d 313, 627 N.Y.S.2d 874 (N.Y. 1995) (surgeon not liable for assault on unconscious patient alleging surgery for which no consent was given); State v. Barry, 45 Mont. 598, 124 P. 775 (1912) (no assault where plaintiff did not learn of the threat until it had passed). Law is clear that the plaintiff who does not see it coming (does not anticipate the harm) will not have a claim. Koffman v. Garnett, 265 Va. 12, 574 S.E.2d 258 (2003) (football coach subject to battery liability for tackling 13-year-old student player without warning but not liable for assault).

Imminence. How imminent must the threatened battery be for the threat to constitute an assault? *See* Brower v. Ackerley, 88 Wash. App. 87, 943 P.2d 1141, 1145 (1997) (threats to "find out where you live and kick your ass" and to "cut you in your sleep" not sufficiently imminent to constitute an assault); Brooker v. Silverthorne, 99 S.E. 350 (S.C. 1919) (telephone threats not sufficient to constitute an assault). A comment to Restatement (Second) of Torts §29(1) states that "[i]mminent does not mean immediate, in the sense of instantaneous contact" but "means rather that there will be no significant delay." Is this statement helpful?

Contact. Assaults may occur when the anticipated imminent harm is a blow from a fist, shot from a gun, stab from a knife, and other common forms of intentional harm. Anything else? *See* Vetter v. Morgan, 913 P.2d 1200 (Kan. App. 1995) (perpetrator's road-rage style threats at a traffic light to use van to run victim's car off road, followed by veering actions of the van toward victim's car, can constitute assault). Keep in mind with respect to assault, that a wide range of forces can satisfy the contact element of battery. It need not be the perpetrator's own body that applies the direct force or that the perpetrator apply force directly to the victim, if the force transmits from perpetrator to victim and the other elements are present.

Skills

Rank the following matters (each drawn from the authors' experience) in the order in which you would prefer to undertake the client's representation, with "1" being the client you would most like to represent and "10" being the client you would least like to represent. As you do so, consider what criteria you use, and why. Your answers to these questions would influence not only the economics of your law practice but also your professional identity, job or career satisfaction, and reputation as a lawyer.

A A 42-year-old postal delivery person with scars on the face and neck, in a strict liability claim against the owner of the pit bull that bit the delivery person, where the owner was a 22-year-old unemployed tenant renting a bedroom in an old house for $250 per month.

B The estate of a 40-year-old married shop manager with two teenage children, in a wrongful death action against his girlfriend and the owner of the vehicle in which he was killed as a passenger, when the girlfriend (who was drunk) ran off the road at 2 a.m. crashing into a tree.

C A 58-year-old married man whose neck, jaw, nose, and eye orbit were fractured, and who suffered a severe closed-head injury, in a negligence action against the owner and operator of a boat that ran over him from behind, when he was piloting his own boat at a slow speed.

D The estate of a 42-year-old married environmental engineer with a teenage child, in a wrongful death action against the pilot and owner of a helicopter in which the engineer was killed, when the engine malfunctioned and the pilot (who was drunk) failed to auto-rotate the helicopter safely to the ground.

E The estate of a 45-year-old married laborer with no children, in a wrongful death action against the owner and builder of a moto-cross track, after the laborer was killed when his go-cart (for which the track was not designed) flipped over and landed on him at the bottom of a large ramp/jump he attempted to take.

> **F** A 38-year-old married woman who claimed disabling jaw pain and dysfunction, in a dental malpractice claim against the oral surgeon who performed temporomandibular (jaw) joint surgery on her in an unsuccessful attempt to relieve her dysfunction and pain.
> **G** A 52-year-old unmarried man who claimed three *months* of work disability from back pain, in a negligence (third-party no-fault) claim against the negligent driver who injured him, where the driver's insurance agent has shown you that the man altered his doctor's off-work slip saying three *days*.
> **H** A 47-year-old married woman with lumbar disk and non-displaced hip fractures, in a negligence (third-party no-fault) claim against the negligent driver and vehicle owner, when the driver (who was drunk) ran into the woman's vehicle from behind on the driver's way to purchase drugs.
> **I** A 45-year-old married woman with neck strain limiting her ability to work long cleaning shifts and to bowl in leagues as previously, in a negligence (third-party no-fault) claim against the negligent driver of a vehicle who struck her vehicle in the side running a red light.
> **J** A seven-year-old girl with severe scars on her face, in a strict liability claim against the owner of the Rottweiler dog that knocked the girl down, stood over her, and bit in the face, where the owner owned the home two-doors away from the girl's residence.

C. False Imprisonment

OBJECTIVE: Given an intentional tort claim for false imprisonment, recall and apply the elements analyzing whether the facts satisfy those elements, consistent with the following text.

Case Study: At a sorority-house party, a man drugged a young woman who fell unconscious under the drug's influence on a sitting room couch. The young man then locked and barricaded the unconscious woman in the sitting room as a prank. Early the next morning, another young woman noticed the barricaded door, removed the barricade and unlocked it, and found the young woman still unconscious inside. ***Analyze whether these facts satisfy the elements of a false imprisonment claim against the young man.***

False Imprisonment. After assault and battery, false imprisonment is the third personal or dignitary intentional tort. The definition or elements of a false imprisonment claim are that the perpetrator intentionally restrained the victim against the victim's will, while not authorized by law—intentional unauthorized restraint against will. Although they are independent torts, assault, battery, and false imprisonment can occur sequentially. Restraint may (though need not) involve the kind of offensive contact that would satisfy a battery claim—false imprisonment and battery occurring together. The victim may also anticipate the contact and restraint in a way that would satisfy an assault claim—false imprisonment, battery, and assault occurring together. As you read the following cases, see if you can articulate scenarios where these three torts occur sequentially and separately.

Federal Claims. Both private individuals and government officers can commit the false-imprisonment tort. In the case of government officers, law sometimes refers to the claim as *false arrest*. In those cases, claimants may have the benefit of suing not only under the common law of false imprisonment but also under a federal statute 42 U.S.C. §1983. Section 1983 authorizes damages actions when individuals lose, under color of law, constitutional and other federal rights—such as Fourth Amendment (and, incorporating the same rights as to state officers, Fourteenth Amendment) rights not to be subject to unreasonable seizure. Section 1983 actions have the added benefit of affording statutory attorney's fees to prevailing plaintiffs. An officer or private citizen who claims but lacks legal authority to detain may at the same time be liable for common-law false imprisonment. Whitman v. Atchison, T. & S.F. R. Co., 85 Kan. 150, 116 P. 234 (1911) (train conductor subject to liability when falsely telling injured passenger that the law required passenger to remain to make out a report). If, on the other hand, law provides for arrest or confinement, then ordinarily no false imprisonment claim arises—unless the actor fails to follow mandated confinement procedures. *See* Foshee v. Health Mgt. Assocs., 675 So.2d 957 (Fla. App. 1996).

Big Town Nursing Home, Inc. v. Newman
Texas Court of Civil Appeals
461 S.W.2d 195 (Tex. Civ. App. 1970)

This is an appeal by defendant nursing home from a judgment for plaintiff Newman for actual and exemplary damages in a false imprisonment case.

Plaintiff Newman sued defendant nursing home for actual and exemplary damages for falsely and wrongfully imprisoning him against his will from September 22, 1968 to November 11, 1968. ... The trial court entered judgment on the verdict for plaintiff for $25,000. ...

Plaintiff is a retired printer 67 years of age, and lives on his social security and a retirement pension from his brother's printing company. He has not worked since 1959, is single, has Parkinson's disease, arthritis, heart trouble, a voice impediment, and a hiatal hernia. He has served in the army attaining the rank of Sergeant. He has never been in a mental hospital or treated by a psychiatrist. Plaintiff was taken to defendant nursing home on September 19, 1968 by his nephew who signed the admission papers and paid one month's care in advance. Plaintiff had been arrested for drunkenness and drunk driving in times past (the last time in 1966) and had been treated twice for alcoholism. Plaintiff testified he was not intoxicated and had nothing to drink during the week prior to admission to the nursing home. The admission papers provided that patient "will not be forced to remain in the nursing home against his will for any length of time." Plaintiff was not advised he would be kept at the nursing home against his will. On September 22, 1968 plaintiff decided he wanted to leave and tried to telephone for a taxi. Defendant's employees advised plaintiff he could not use the phone, or have any visitors unless the manager knew them, and locked plaintiff's grip and clothes up. Plaintiff walked out of the home, but was caught by employees of defendant and brought back forceably, and thereafter placed in Wing 3 and locked up. Defendant's Administrator testified Wing 3 contained senile patients, drug addicts, alcoholics, mentally disturbed, incorrigibles and uncontrollables, and that "they were all in the same kettle of fish." Plaintiff tried to escape from the nursing home five or six times but was caught and brought back each time against his will. He was carried back to Wing 3 and locked and taped in a "restraint chair," for more than five hours. He was put back in the chair on subsequent occasions. He was not seen by the home doctor for some 10 days after he was admitted, and for 7 days after being placed in Wing 3. The doctor wrote the social security office to change payment of plaintiff's social security checks without plaintiff's authorization. Plaintiff made every effort to leave and repeatedly asked the manager and assistant manager to be permitted to leave. The home doctor is actually a resident studying pathology and has no patients other than those in two nursing homes. Finally on November 11, 1968 plaintiff escaped and caught a ride into Dallas, where he called a taxi and was taken to the home of a friend. During plaintiff's ordeal he lost 30 pounds. There was never any court proceeding to confine plaintiff. Defendant's assistant manager testified that plaintiff attempted to leave the home five or six times, and on each occasion was brought back against his will.

False imprisonment is the direct restraint of one person of the physical liberty of another without adequate legal justification. ...

Defendant placed plaintiff in Wing 3 with insane persons, alcoholics and drug addicts knowing he was not in such category; punished plaintiff by locking and taping him in the restraint chair; prevented him from using the telephone for 51 days; locked up his clothes; told him he could not be released from Wing 3 until he began to obey the rules of the home; and detained him for 51 days during which period he was demanding to be released and attempting to escape. ...

Defendant acted in the utter disregard of plaintiff's legal rights, knowing there was no court order for commitment, and that the admission agreement provided he was not to be kept against his will. ...

However, from this record, we are of the opinion that the verdict and judgment of the trial court is excessive in the sum of $12,000., and that this cause should be reversed for that reason only. ...

Reversed and Remanded. [Plaintiff accepted the remittitur and received judgment for $13,000.]

McCann v. Wal-Mart Stores, Inc.
United States Court of Appeals, First Circuit
210 F.3d 51 (1st Cir. 2000)

BOUDIN, C.J. This case involves a claim for false imprisonment. On December 11, 1996, Debra McCann and two of her children—Jillian, then 16, and Jonathan, then 12—were shopping at the Wal-Mart store in Bangor, Maine. After they returned a Christmas tree and exchanged a CD player, Jonathan went to the toy section and Jillian and Debra McCann went to shop in other areas of the store. After approximately an hour and a half, the McCanns went to a register and paid for their purchases. One of their receipts was time stamped at 10:10 p.m.

As the McCanns were leaving the store, two Wal-Mart employees, Jean Taylor and Karla Hughes, stepped out in front of the McCanns' shopping cart, blocking their path to the exit. Taylor may have actually put her hand on the cart. The employees told Debra McCann that the children were not allowed in the store because they had been caught stealing on a prior occasion. In fact, the employees were mistaken; the son of a *different* family had been caught shoplifting in the store about two weeks before, and Taylor and Hughes confused the two families.

Despite Debra McCann's protestations, Taylor said that they had the records, that the police were being called, and that the McCanns "had to go with her." Debra

McCann testified that she did not resist Taylor's direction because she believed that she had to go with Taylor and that the police were coming. Taylor and Hughes then brought the McCanns past the registers in the store to an area near the store exit. Taylor stood near the McCanns while Hughes purportedly went to call the police. During this time, Debra McCann tried to show Taylor her identification, but Taylor refused to look at it.

After a few minutes, Hughes returned and switched places with Taylor. Debra McCann told Hughes that she had proof of her identity and that there must be some proof about the identity of the children who had been caught stealing. Hughes then went up to Jonathan, pointed her finger at him, and said that he had been caught stealing two weeks earlier. Jonathan began to cry and denied the accusation. At some point around this time Jonathan said that he needed to use the bathroom and Hughes told him he could not go. At no time during this initial hour or so did the Wal-Mart employees tell the McCanns that they could leave.

Although Wal-Mart's employees had said they were calling the police, they actually called a store security officer who would be able to identify the earlier shoplifter. Eventually, the security officer, Rhonda Bickmore, arrived at the store and informed Hughes that the McCanns were not the family whose son had been caught shoplifting. Hughes then acknowledged her mistake to the McCanns, and the McCanns left the store at approximately 11:15 p.m. In due course, the McCanns brought suit against Wal-Mart for false imprisonment (a defamation claim was also made but was rejected by the jury).

The jury awarded the McCanns $20,000 in compensatory damages on their claim that they were falsely imprisoned in the Wal-Mart store by Wal-Mart employees. Wal-Mart has now appealed the district court's denial of its post-judgment motions for judgment as a matter of law and for a new trial. ...

Both of Wal-Mart's claims of error depend on the proper elements of the tort of false imprisonment. Although nuances vary from state to state, the gist of the common law tort is conduct by the actor which is intended to, and does in fact, "confine" another "within boundaries fixed by the actor" where, in addition, the victim is either "conscious of the confinement or is harmed by it." *Restatement (Second), Torts* § 35 (1965). ...

While "confinement" can be imposed by physical barriers or physical force, much less will do—although how much less becomes cloudy at the margins. It is generally settled that mere threats of physical force can suffice, *Restatement, supra,* § 40; and it is also settled ... that the threats may be implicit as well as explicit, *see id.* cmt. a; 32 Am.Jur.2d *False Imprisonment* § 18 (1995) (collecting cases), and that confinement can also be based on a false assertion of legal authority to confine. *Restatement, supra,* § 41. Indeed, the *Restatement* provides that confinement may occur by other unspecified means of "duress." *Id.* § 40A.

Against this background, we examine Wal-Mart's claim that the evidence was insufficient, taking the facts in the light most favorable to the McCanns, drawing reasonable inferences in their favor, and assuming that the jury resolved credibility issues consistent with the verdict. *See Gibson v. City of Cranston,* 37 F.3d 731, 735 (1st Cir.1994); *Sanchez v. Puerto Rico Oil Co.,* 37 F.3d 712, 716 (1st Cir.1994). Using this standard, we think that a reasonable jury could conclude that Wal-Mart's employees intended to "confine" the McCanns "within boundaries fixed by" Wal-Mart, that the employees' acts did result in such a confinement, and that the McCanns were conscious of the confinement.

The evidence, taken favorably to the McCanns, showed that Wal-Mart employees stopped the McCanns as they were seeking to exit the store, said that the children were not allowed in the store, told the McCanns that they had to come with the Wal-Mart employees and that Wal-Mart was calling the police, and then stood guard over the McCanns while waiting for a security guard to arrive. The direction to the McCanns, the reference to the police, and the continued presence of the Wal-Mart employees (who at one point told Jonathan McCann that he could not leave to go to the bathroom) were enough to induce reasonable people to believe either that they would be restrained physically if they sought to leave, or that the store was claiming lawful authority to confine them until the police arrived, or both. ... Affirmed.

Dupler v. Seubert
Wisconsin Supreme Court
69 Wis.2d 373, 230 N.W.2d 626 (1975)

WILKIE, C.J. This is a false imprisonment action. On April 23, 1971, plaintiff-appellant Ethel M. Dupler was fired from her job with the defendant-respondent Wisconsin Telephone Company. She was informed of her discharge during an hour-and-a-half session with her two superiors, defendants-respondents Keith Peterson and Helen Seubert, who Dupler claims, falsely imprisoned her during a portion of this time period. A jury found that Peterson and Seubert did falsely imprison Dupler and fixed damages at $7,500. ...

Dupler had worked for the Telephone Company as a customer service representative since 1960. At approximately 4:30 on April 23rd, Seubert asked Dupler to come to Peterson's office. When all three were inside, sitting down, with the door closed, Seubert told Dupler the Telephone Company would no longer employ her and that she could choose either to resign or be fired. Dupler testified that she refused to resign and that in the conversation that followed, Peterson discussed several alternatives short of dismissal, all of which had been considered but rejected.

At approximately 5 o'clock, Dupler testified, she began to feel sick to her stomach and said "You have already fired me. Why don't you just let me go." She made a motion to get up but Peterson told her to sit down in "a very loud harsh voice." Then, Dupler testified, she began to feel violently ill and stated "I got to go. I can't take this any more. I'm sick to my stomach. I know I'm going to throw up." She got up and started for the door but Seubert also arose and stood in front of the door. After Dupler repeated that she was sick, Seubert allowed her to exit, but followed her to the men's washroom, where Dupler did throw up. Following this, at approximately 5:25, Seubert asked Dupler to return to Peterson's office where she had left her purse to discuss the situation further. Dupler testified that she went back to the office and reached for her purse; Seubert again closed the door and Peterson said '(i)n a loud voice 'Sit down. I'm still your boss. I'm not through with you." At approximately 5:40 Dupler told Peterson her husband was waiting for her outside in a car and Peterson told her to go outside and ask her husband to come inside. Dupler then went outside and explained the situation to her husband who said "You get back in there and get you coat and if

you aren't right out I'll call the police." Dupler returned to Peterson's office and was again told in a loud tone of voice to sit down. She said Seubert and Peterson were trying to convince her to resign rather than be fired and again reviewed the alternatives that had been considered. Dupler then said: "What's the sense of all this. Why keep torturing me. Let me go. Let me go." She stated that Peterson replied "No, we still aren't finished. We have a lot of things to discuss, your retirement pay, your vacation, other things." Finally, at approximately 6:00 Peterson told Dupler they could talk further on the phone or at her house, and Dupler left. When asked why she had stayed in Peterson's office for such a long time, Dupler replied: Well, for one thing, Helen, Mrs. Seubert, had blocked the door, and tempers had been raised with all the shouting and screaming, I was just plain scared to make an effort. There were two against one."
...

The essence of false imprisonment is the intentional, unlawful, and unconsented restraint by one person of the physical liberty of another.[fn omitted] ... In Maniaci v. Marquette University,[50 Wis.2d 287, 184 N.W.2d 168 (1971)] the court adopted the definition of false imprisonment contained in sec. 35 of the Restatement of Torts 2d, which provides in part:

False Imprisonment

(1) An actor is subject to liability to another for false imprisonment if (a) he acts intending to confine the other or a third person within boundaries fixed by the actor, and (b) his act directly or indirectly results in such a confinement of the other, and the other is conscious of the confinement or is harmed by it.[fn omitted]

Secs. 39[] and 40[] provide that the confinement may be caused by physical force or the threat of physical force, and the comment to sec. 40 indicates the threat may either be express, or inferred from the person's conduct. ...

... [W]e conclude that the record contains sufficient evidence from which the jury could have concluded that Mrs. Dupler was intentionally confined, against her will, by an implied threat of actual physical restraint. She testified that defendant Peterson ordered her in a loud voice to remain seated several times, after she expressed the desire to leave. She reported being "berated, screamed and hollered at," and said the reason she did not just walk out of the room was that "Mrs. Seubert had blocked the door, and tempers had been raised with all the shouting and screaming, I was just plain scared to make an effort. There were two against one." The jury obviously believed Mrs. Dupler's rather than the defendants' account of what transpired, as it had the right to do, and we conclude her testimony was sufficient to support the jury's verdict. ...

We conclude that ... the jury could properly find that defendants falsely imprisoned Dupler by compelling her to remain in Peterson's office against her will after 5 p.m. We conclude the imprisonment ceased when Dupler left the building to visit her husband, but resumed when she reentered Peterson's office to get her coat in order to leave, but was commanded to stay. ...

[The appellate court affirmed but modified Mrs. Dupler's award. It found that the jury had not had the opportunity to distinguish between Mrs. Dupler's compensable harm for false imprisonment and the non-compensable distress she suffered over her firing—her firing having been otherwise lawful but for the attendant false imprisonment.]

INQUIRY

Means of Restraint. What other means of confinement satisfies the restraint element of the false-imprisonment tort? *Compare* Bureerong v. Uvawas, 959 F. Supp. 1231 (C.D. Cal. 1997) (defendants' threats to use physical force against plaintiff immigrant garment workers and their families could constitute restraint to laborer complex); Banks v. Fritsch, 39 S.W.3d 474 (Ky. App. 2001) (false-imprisonment liability for teacher chaining frequently absent student to tree); Fischer v. Famous-Barr Co., 646 S.W. 2d 819 (Mo. App. 1982) (store employee's seizing plaintiff's handbag could constitute restraint to store premises); Noguchi v. Nakamura, 2 Haw. App. 655, 638 P.2d 1383 (1982) (false imprisonment in moving car); Whittaker v. Sandford, 110 Me. 77, 85 A. 399 (Maine 1912) (defendant's refusal to take plaintiff to shore could constitute restraint on defendant's yacht); *with* Trahan v. Bellsouth Telecommunications, Inc., 881 F. Supp. 1080 (W.D. La. 1995) (employer's threat to fire employee if employee leaves premises not a restraint); Lopez v. Winchell's Donut House, 466 N.E.2d 1309 (Ill. App. Ct. 1994) (employee who remained in order to protect reputation against false accusation that she gave goods to customer was not restrained); Hardy v. La Belle's Distrib. Co., 661 P.2d 35 (Mont. 1983) (employee who accompanied employer representatives to office and remained to defend herself against false accusation of theft was not restrained); Marcano v. Northwestern Chrysler-Plymouth Sales, Inc., 550 F. Supp. 595 (N.D. Ill. 1982) (no false imprisonment where dealer intentionally locked plaintiff's keys in car, and plaintiff voluntarily stayed at the dealership for five hours); Snyder v. Evangelical Orthodox Church, 216 Cal. App.3d 297, 264 Cal. Rptr. 640 (1989) (bishop not restrained by church's order to meditate in isolation or have his adulterous relationship revealed).

Form of Restraint. What form of confinement may the restraint take? *See* Shen v. Leo A. Daly Co., 222 F.2d 472 (8th Cir. 2000) (island of Taiwan too large an area to be considered false imprisonment); Smith v. Comair Inc., 134 F.3d 254 (4th Cir. 1998) (airline's refusal to permit passenger to board flight after layover does not constitute restraint within the terminal area, where passenger was at all times free to leave the airport); Cullen v. Dickenson, 33 S.D. 27, 144 N.W. 656 (1913) (refusal to readmit plaintiff to defendant's dance hall not false imprisonment); Marrone v. Washington Jockey Club, 35 App. D.C. 82 (1910) (refusal to readmit plaintiff to defendant's race track not false imprisonment); *but see* Albright v. Oliver, 975 F.3d 343 (7th Cir. 1992) (suggesting in dicta that confinement may be to an area as large as a state). Although they would not have false imprisonment claims, persons who are excluded from premises based on protected characteristics such as disability or membership in a protected class such as by race or ethnicity may have federal or state civil rights actions. *See* 42 U.S.C. §2000a. Even in the absence of a federal civil right, a member of the public may have a common-law right of access to a public utility or common carrier. *See* Restatement (Second) of Torts §191 (1965).

Escape. What if the putative victim knows of a means of escape? Furlong v. German-American Press Assn., 189 S.W. 385 (Mo. 1916) (no false imprisonment if known means of escape presents no unreasonable peril); Restatement (Second) of Torts §36, comment a (escape is unreasonable if involving personal danger or exposure, or harm to clothing); *cf.* Talcott v. National Exhibition Co., 144 App.Div.

337, 128 N.Y.S. 1059 (1911) (plaintiff must know of available means of escape, or it must be apparent).

Knowledge. Must the putative victim know of the confinement? *See* Parvi v. City of Kingston, 41 N.Y.2d 553, 362 N.E.2d 960 (1977) (drunken person conscious of unlawful arrest and confinement at the time but without subsequent recollection can maintain false-imprisonment claim); Restatement (Second) of Torts §42 (1965) (false-imprisonment claimant must know of the confinement). Although the claimant must ordinarily be conscious of the confinement in order to state a false imprisonment claim, should some circumstances constitute false imprisonment even without consciousness? *See* Katjazi v. Katjazi, 488 F. Supp. 15 (E.D. N.Y. 1978) (mother permitted to maintain infant child's false imprisonment against father, when father abducted child to Yugoslavia, without showing of the child's capacity to comprehend the restraint); Restatement (Second) of Torts §35 (false-imprisonment liability without consciousness if wrongdoer harms victim).

D. Intentional Infliction of Emotional Distress

OBJECTIVE: **Given various fact scenarios involving a person's humiliation or embarrassment by another, recall and apply the elements of the tort of intentional infliction of emotional distress analyzing whether the facts satisfy those elements, consistent with the following text.**

Case Study: Two young men were rivals at work, fishing, hunting, and sports. One young man went to the other's home when the other and his parents were away, and spray painted profanities on the garage door that (translated politely) meant that the other was in an incestuous relationship. The offended young man grew depressed as a result of the incident, the public attention it drew to him, and the embarrassment and hectoring it caused him. A counselor who recorded his sleep disruption, moderate anxiety disorder, and moderate weight gain from the stress surrounding the matter. ***Analyze whether these facts satisfy the elements of an intentional infliction of emotional distress claim.***

Intentional Infliction of Emotional Distress. From the standpoint of the English and early American common law, intentional infliction of emotional distress is not one of the five traditional intentional torts assault, battery, false imprisonment, trespass to land, and trespass to chattels. Not all states recognize the newer IIED tort, and not all states recognizing it give it the same name and elements. Some courts call it *outrage* while others call it intentional infliction of *mental* (rather than *emotional*) distress. Lawyers often plead intentional infliction with the tort of negligent infliction of emotional distress, treated in the chapter on negligence claims. The intentional-infliction tort fills gaps in the law of intentional torts, where the traditional claims like assault and battery do not cover misconduct so reprehensible that it must give rise to a tort claim. An example would be outrageous threats of serious future harm that, because they are not of imminent harm, the law could not redress through a claim for assault. The law fills some of those gaps in other ways. For example, states tend to recognize tort liability for the mishandling of corpses. *See* Alderman v. Ford, 146 Kan. 698, 72 P.2d 981 (1937); Gostkowski v. Roman Catholic Church, 262 N.Y. 320, 186 N.E. 798 (1933); Gadbury v. Bleitz, 133 Wash. 134, 233 P.299 (1925). Courts also tend to hold certain parties, such as common carriers and innkeepers, to higher duties with respect to emotional insults, *see* Emmke v. De Silva, 293 F. 17 (8th Cir. 1923) (innkeeper); Lipman v. Atlantic Coast Line R.R. Co., 108 S.C. 151, 93 S.E. 714 (1917) (rail carrier).

Severe Distress. One of the most-infamous early cases supporting the outrage tort is Nickerson v. Hodges, 84 So. 37 (La. 1920), in which three conspirators (one of them the plaintiff's own daughter) played an elaborate hoax on the plaintiff, who for some time had been deluded by a fortune teller's tip that about a pot of buried gold on her land. The elaborate hoax, including much digging, discovery of a chest, and a parade with the chest, played on the plaintiff's known susceptibility, ended in her humiliation at a public ceremony, and resulted in her complete mental demise. This example suggests an important aspect of the IIED tort—that not every intentional distress states a claim. (Imagine the huge number of claims if the law so generously defined it.) Instead, law requires that the intentional conduct inflicting distress be *outrageous*, meaning beyond all bounds of decency in civil society, and that the resulting distress be severe—sometimes with the additional requirement that the victim physically manifest the distress for another person to observe and confirm it.

Direct and Bystander Claims. Intentional-infliction claims arise in two contexts. The first deals with extreme and outrageous conduct directed at the plaintiff. The second has to do with conduct directed at or involving someone else but done either with knowledge of substantial certainty that the conduct would cause severe emotional distress to the plaintiff (meaning done intentionally) or with deliberate indifference to that result (meaning done recklessly). The first category raises what the law calls *direct* claims, while the second category raises what the law calls *bystander* claims. Obviously, intent is an element of the intentional-infliction tort—one typically proven by the defendant's desire to harm or knowledge of the plaintiff's substantial certainty of harm. As noted above in the section on intent, *recklessness*, defined as knowledge of a high probability of harm, also satisfies the intent element of intentional infliction of emotional distress. The same distinction between direct and bystander claims exists in claims alleging negligent infliction of emotional distress, discussed in the chapter on negligence below.

Purpose and Plaintiff's Presence. Many states require the plaintiff to show that the defendant directed the outrageous conduct at the plaintiff. *See* Taylor v. Vallelunga, 171 Cal. App.2d 107, 339 P.2d 910 (1959) (no IIED claim where perpetrator did not intend beating of plaintiff's father in her presence to cause her suffering). In those states, a defendant's injuring or murdering the plaintiff's spouse, sibling, or other family member would not be enough unless the defendant's actions were for inflicting the plaintiff with distress. Other states do not require an element of purpose but do require the plaintiff's presence—and the defendant's knowledge of the plaintiff's presence. *See* Bevan v. Fix, 42 P.3d 1013 (Wyo. 2002) (IIED claim allowed for children who heard their mother's beating by defendant); *but see* Schurk v. Christensen, 80 Wash.2d 652, 497 P.2d 937 (1972) (child's mother permitted IIED claim for child's molestation notwithstanding that she was not present); Knierim v. Izzo, 22 Ill.2d 73, 174 N.E.2d 157 (1961) (presence not required). In those cases of a bystander's distress from a defendant's intentional actions, some courts require the bystander to prove bodily harm as manifesting the distress's severity. *See* Hill v. Kimball, 76 Tex. 210, 13 S.W. 59 (1890) (defendant liable for plaintiff's severe distress and miscarriage when defendant beat two other persons in her presence). Consider the following cases.

State Rubbish Collectors Assn. v. Siliznoff
California Supreme Court
240 P.2d 282 (Cal. 1952)

TRAYNOR, J. On February 1, 1948, Peter Kobzeff signed a contract with the Acme Brewing Company to collect rubbish from the latter's brewery. Kobzeff had been in the rubbish business for several years and was able to secure the contract because Acme was dissatisfied with the service then being provided by another collector, one Abramoff. Although Kobzeff signed the contract, it was understood that the work should be done by John Siliznoff, Kobzeff's son-in-law, whom Kobzeff wished to assist in establishing a rubbish collection business.

Both Kobzeff and Abramoff were members of the plaintiff State Rubbish Collectors Association, but Siliznoff was not. The by-laws of the association provided that one member should not take an account from another member without paying for it. Usual prices ranged from five to ten times the monthly rate paid by the customer, and disputes were referred to the board of directors for settlement. After Abramoff lost the Acme account he complained to the association, and Kobzeff was called upon to settle the matter. Kobzeff and Siliznoff took the position that the Acme account belonged to Siliznoff, and that he was under no obligation to pay for it. After attending several meetings of plaintiff's board of directors Siliznoff finally agreed, however, to pay Abramoff $1,850 for the Acme account and join the association. The agreement provided that he should pay $500 in thirty days and $75 per month thereafter until the whole sum agreed upon was paid. Payments were to be made through the association, and Siliznoff executed a series or promissory notes totaling $1,850. None of these notes was paid, and in 1949 plaintiff association brought this action to collect the notes then payable. Defendant cross-complained and asked that the notes be cancelled because of duress and want of consideration. In addition he sought general and exemplary damages because of assaults made by plaintiff and its agents to compel him to join the association and pay Abramoff for the Acme account. The jury returned a verdict against plaintiff and for defendant on the complaint and for defendant on his cross-complaint. It awarded him $1,250 general and special damages and $7,500 exemplary damages. The trial court denied a motion for a new trial on the condition that defendant consent to a reduction of the exemplary damages to $4,000. Defendant filed the required consent, and plaintiff has appealed from the judgment.

Plaintiff's primary contention is that the evidence is insufficient to support the judgment. Defendant testified that shortly after he secured the Acme account, the president of the association and its inspector, John Andikian, called on him and Kobzeff. They suggested that either a settlement be made with Abramoff or that the job be dropped, and requested Kobzeff and defendant to attend a meeting of the association. At this meeting defendant was told that the association "ran all the rubbish from that office, all the rubbish hauling," and that if he did not pay for the job they would take it away from him. "We would take it away, even if we had to haul for nothing.' * * * (O)ne of them mentioned that I had better pay up, or else." Thereafter, on the day when defendant finally agreed to pay for the account, Andikian visited defendant at the Rainier Brewing Company, where he was collecting rubbish. Andikian told defendant that "We will give you up till tonight to get down to the board meeting and make some kind of arrangements or agreements about the Acme Brewery, or otherwise we are going to beat you up.' * * * He says he either would hire somebody or do it himself. And I says, 'Well, what would they do to me?' He says, well, they would physically beat me up first, cut up the truck tires or burn the truck, or otherwise put me out of business completely. He said if I didn't appear at the meeting and make some kind of an agreement that they would do that, but he says up to then they would let me alone, but if I walked out of that meeting that night they would beat me up for sure." Defendant attended the meeting and protested that he owed nothing for the Acme account and in any event could not pay the amount demanded. He was again told by the president of the association that "that table right there (the board of directors) ran all the rubbish collecting in Los Angeles and if there was any routes to be gotten that they would get them and distribute them among their members * * *." After two hours of further discussion defendant agreed to join the association and pay for the Acme account. He promised to return the next day and sign the necessary papers. He testified that the only reason "they let me go home, is that I promised that I would sign the notes the very next morning." The president "made me promise on my honor and everything else, and I was scared, and I knew I had to come back, so I believed he knew I was scared and that I would come back. That's the only reason they let me go home." Defendant also testified that because of the fright he suffered during his dispute with the association he became ill and vomited several times and had to remain away from work for a period of several days.

Plaintiff contends that the evidence does not establish an assault against defendant because the threats made all related to action that might take place in the future; that neither Andikian nor members of the board of directors threatened immediate physical harm to defendant. ... We have concluded, however, that a cause of action is established when it is shown that one, in the absence of any privilege, intentionally subjects another to the mental suffering incident to serious threats to his physical well-being, whether or not the threats are made under such circumstances as to constitute a technical assault. ...

The view has been forcefully advocated that the law should protect emotional and mental tranquillity as such against serious and intentional invasions... , and there is a growing body of case law supporting this position. ... In recognition of this development the American Law Institute amended section 46 of the Restatement of Torts in 1947 to provide: "One who, without a privilege to do so, intentionally causes severe emotional distress to another is liable (a) for such emotional distress, and (b) for bodily harm resulting from it." ...

There are persuasive arguments and analogies that support the recognition of a right to be free from serious, intentional, and unprivileged invasions of mental and emotional tranquility. If a cause of action is otherwise established, it is settled that damages may be given for mental suffering naturally ensuing from the acts complained of, ... and in the case of many torts, such as assault, battery, false imprisonment, and defamation, mental suffering will frequently constitute the principal element of damages. ... In cases where mental suffering constitutes a major element of damages it is anomalous to deny recovery because the defendant's intentional misconduct fell short of producing some physical injury.

It may be contended that to allow recovery in the absence of physical injury will open the door to unfounded claims and a flood of litigation, and that the requirement that there be physical injury is necessary to insure that serious mental suffering actually occurred. The jury is ordinarily in a better position, however, to determine whether outrageous conduct results in mental distress than whether that distress in turn results in physical injury. From their own experience jurors are aware of the extent and character of the disagreeable emotions that may result from the defendant's conduct, but a difficult medical question is presented when it must be determined if emotional distress resulted in physical injury. ... Greater proof that mental suffering occurred is found in the defendant's conduct designed to bring it about than in physical injury that may or may not have resulted therefrom. ...

In the present case plaintiff caused defendant to suffer extreme fright. By intentionally producing such fright it endeavored to compel him either to give up the Acme account or pay for it, and it had no right or privilege to adopt such coercive methods in competing for business. In these circumstances liability is clear. ....

The judgment is affirmed.

Skills

Lawyers decline matters with some frequency. Indeed, lawyers must decline some cases because of the lawyer's workload or health. *See* ABA Model Rules of Professional Conduct, Rule 1.16. The timeliness and manner in which lawyers decline matters can be important. When a lawyer waits too long to let a potential client know that the lawyer will not pursue the claim, and a limitations period then bars the claim, an unhappy and aggrieved client may pursue a malpractice claim against the lawyer. *See Togstad v. Vesely, Otto, Miller & Keefe*, 291 N.W.2d 686 (Minn. 1980). If a lawyer tells a potential client that the client has no claim when, to the contrary, a claim exists, then the lawyer may again have committed malpractice. What other purposes does the following decline letter serve? Should the letter have evaluated the potential client's claim? Why or why not?

[law firm letterhead]

[date]

[Client's name and address]

Dear **[Client]**:

Thank you for meeting with me last week concerning **[describe the subject matter]**. After giving your matter considered reflection, I must respectfully decline to represent you. I am returning your materials with this correspondence and taking no further action on your behalf. The reasons for my declining your matter may have to do as much with my present workload as with the merits of your claim. I am not saying that you have no legal claim. To the contrary, I encourage you to seek other counsel if you feel that you have a claim and still wish to pursue it. There are, however, limitations periods within which your claims must be filed. These limitations periods may be as short as **[state the shortest applicable period]** or as long as **[state the longest applicable period]** from the date your claim arose. Limitations periods may also be tolled under certain circumstances. But, if you wish to proceed, you should not delay in having your claim reviewed by another attorney. If you are unable to locate another attorney on your own, **[the _____ Bar Association has a lawyer-referral service you may use by telephoning _____]**. You may also call or contact me again if you have other matters for review. I appreciate your confidence and am sorry that I am unable to help you with your present matter.

Sincerely,
[name of law firm]
/s/ _____
[Attorney name]

Enclosures **[Client's materials]**

Severe Outrage. On occasion, a claim falls within the ambit of the traditional tort claims, but the outrage may be so severe that an intentional-infliction claim seems a more-appropriate vehicle for redress than traditional claims like assault and battery—or the plaintiff may have other reasons to pursue the newer claim. Consider the following case attempting to distinguish the newer IIED tort from the traditional torts.

Dickens v. Puryear
North Carolina Supreme Court
276 S.E.2d 325 (N.C. 1981)

EXUM, J. Plaintiff's complaint is cast as a claim for intentional infliction of mental distress. It was filed more than one year but less than three years after the incidents complained of occurred. Defendants moved for summary judgment before answer was due or filed. Much of the factual showing at the hearing on summary judgment related to assaults and batteries committed against plaintiff by defendants. Defendants' motions for summary judgment were allowed on the ground that plaintiff's claim was for assault and battery; therefore it was barred by the one-year statute of limitations applicable to assault and battery. G.S. 1-54(3).

[Plaintiff appealed on the basis in part that the claim should not have been barred by the one-year limitation period for assault and battery.]

The facts brought out at the hearing on summary judgment may be briefly summarized: For a time preceding the incidents in question plaintiff Dickens, a thirty-one year old man, shared sex, alcohol and marijuana with defendants' daughter, a seventeen year old high school student. On 2 April 1975 defendants, husband and wife, lured plaintiff into rural Johnston County, North Carolina. Upon plaintiff's arrival defendant Earl Puryear, after identifying himself, called out to defendant Ann Puryear who emerged from beside a nearby building and, crying, stated that she "didn't want to see that SOB." Ann Puryear then left the scene. Thereafter Earl Puryear pointed a pistol between plaintiff's eyes and shouted "Ya'll come on out." Four men wearing ski masks and armed with nightsticks then approached from behind plaintiff and beat him into semi-consciousness. They handcuffed plaintiff to a piece of farm machinery and resumed striking him with nightsticks. Defendant Earl Puryear, while brandishing a knife and cutting plaintiff's hair, threatened plaintiff with castration. During four or five interruptions of the beatings defendant Earl Puryear and the others, within plaintiff's hearing, discussed and took votes on whether plaintiff should be killed or castrated. Finally, after some two hours and the conclusion of a final conference, the beatings ceased. Defendant Earl Puryear told plaintiff to go home, pull his telephone off the wall, pack his clothes, and leave the state of North Carolina; otherwise he would be killed. Plaintiff was then set free.[fn omitted]

Plaintiff filed his complaint on 31 March 1978. It alleges that defendants on the occasion just described intentionally inflicted mental distress upon him. He further alleges that as a result of defendants' acts plaintiff has suffered "severe and permanent mental and emotional distress, and physical injury to his nerves and nervous system." He alleges that he is unable to sleep, afraid to go out in the dark, afraid to meet strangers, afraid he may be killed, suffering from chronic diarrhea and a gum disorder, unable effectively to perform his job, and that he has lost $1000 per month income. ...

.... Defendants contend, and the Court of Appeals agreed, that this is an action grounded in assault and battery. Although plaintiff pleads the tort of intentional infliction of mental distress, the Court of Appeals concluded that the complaint's factual allegations and the factual showing at the hearing on summary judgment support only a claim for assault and battery. The claim was, therefore, barred by the one-year period of limitations applicable to assault and battery. Plaintiff, on the other hand, argues that the factual showing on the motion supports a claim for intentional infliction of mental distress a claim which is governed by the three-year period of limitations.[fn omitted] At least, plaintiff argues, his factual showing is such that it cannot be said as a matter of law that he will be unable to prove such a claim at trial. We agree with plaintiff's position. ...

North Carolina follows common law principles governing assault and battery. ... The interest protected by the action for battery is freedom from intentional and unpermitted contact with one's person; the interest protected by the action for assault is freedom from apprehension of a harmful or offensive contact with one's person. ...

The tort of intentional infliction of mental distress is recognized in North Carolina. Stanback v. Stanback, 297 N.C. 181, 254 S.E.2d 611 (1979). "(L)iability arises under this tort when a defendant's 'conduct exceeds all bounds usually tolerated by decent society' and the conduct 'causes mental distress of a very serious kind.'" Id. at 196, 254 S.E.2d at 622, quoting Prosser, s 12, p. 56. ...

... [T]he question is whether the evidentiary showing demonstrates as a matter of law that plaintiff's only claim, if any, is for assault and battery. If plaintiff, as a matter of law, has no claim for intentional infliction of mental distress but has a claim, if at all, only for assault and battery, then plaintiff cannot surmount the affirmative defense of the one-year statute of limitations and defendants are entitled to summary judgment on the ground of the statute.

Although plaintiff labels his claim one for intentional infliction of mental distress, we agree with the Court of Appeals that "(t)he nature of the action is not determined by what either party calls it... ." Hayes v. Ricard, 244 N.C. 313, 320, 93 S.E.2d 540, 545-46 (1956). The nature of the action is determined "by the issues arising on the pleading and by the relief sought," id., and by the facts which, at trial, are proved or which, on motion for summary judgment, are forecast by the evidentiary showing.

Here much of the factual showing at the hearing related to assaults and batteries committed by defendants against plaintiff. The physical beatings and the cutting of plaintiff's hair constituted batteries. The threats of castration and death, being threats which created apprehension of immediate harmful or offensive contact, were assaults. Plaintiff's recovery for injuries, mental or physical, caused by these actions would be barred by the one-year statute of limitations.

The evidentiary showing on the summary judgment motion does, however, indicate that defendant Earl Puryear threatened plaintiff with death in the future unless plaintiff went home, pulled his telephone off the wall, packed his clothes, and left the state. The Court of Appeals characterized this threat as being "an immediate threat of harmful and offensive contact. It was a present threat of harm to plaintiff ...." 45 N.C.App. at 700, 263 S.E.2d at 859. The Court of Appeals thus concluded that this threat was also an assault barred by the one-year statute of limitations.

We disagree with the Court of Appeals' characterization of this threat. The threat was not one of imminent, or immediate, harm. It was a threat for the future apparently intended to and which allegedly did inflict serious mental distress; therefore it is actionable, if at all, as an intentional infliction of mental distress. ...

The threat, of course, cannot be considered separately from the entire episode of which it was only a part. The assaults and batteries, construing the record in the light most favorable to the plaintiff, were apparently designed to give added impetus to the ultimate conditional threat of future harm. Although plaintiff's recovery for injury, mental or physical, directly caused by the assaults and batteries is barred by the statute of limitations, these assaults and batteries may be considered in determining the outrageous character of the ultimate threat and the extent of plaintiff's mental or emotional distress caused by it.[fn omitted]

Having concluded, therefore, that the factual showing on the motions for summary judgment was sufficient to indicate that plaintiff may be able to prove at trial a claim for intentional infliction of mental distress, we hold that summary judgment for defendants based upon the one-year statute of limitations was error and we remand the matter for further proceedings against defendant Earl Puryear not inconsistent with this opinion. ...

Knowledge

Lawyers advocate tort law from codes, cases, core meanings, and concrete considerations. Codes—whether state or federal constitution or legislation, administrative regulations, or local ordinances—involve democratic, representative judgments, deciding by group mandate. Codes have a European social-contract basis and represent deductive reasoning. Cases, or the common law—that accumulation of individual cases any one or group of which may be controlling or at least advisory—represent tradition, deciding disputes as a community historically and usually decides them. The common law has an English tradition and represents inductive reasoning. Core meanings—like fairness, equity, proportion, justice, responsibility, and liberty—represent truths of the human condition, as the wisdom and experience of the ages condensed into attributes and values. They have an Aristotelian, Roman, and Thomist history and represent moral reasoning. Finally, tort lawyers consider the concrete or instrumental effects of law—the pragmatic consequences of adopting various legal rules. These instrumental arguments have their basis in social science. All these reasoning forms are legitimate.

INQUIRY

Limitations Periods. Considering *Puryear*, what is the effect of a statute of limitation—to bar IIED claims for all of what law would have redressed as a traditional tort (were it not for the statute of limitations), or not to bar any part of an IIED claim even if a time-barred traditional tort would have redressed it? *Compare* Restatement (Second) §47 and K.G. v. R.T.R., 918 S.W.2d 795 (Mo. 1996) (IIED merely supplements traditional torts, relief for which claimant must pursue within the applicable limitations period), *with* Jones v. Clinton, 974 F. Supp. 712 (E.D. Ark. 1997) (IIED claim permitted notwithstanding that battery and false imprisonment claims arguably encompassing all of the complained-of conduct were time-barred). If the traditional torts are not time-barred, and IIED does not cover conduct that would fall outside of those claims, may the victim still maintain an IIED claim? *See* Miller v. National Broadcasting Co., 187 Ca. App. 3d 1463 (Ct. App. 1986) (IIED claim permitted notwithstanding that it relied on the same misconduct for which trespass and invasion of privacy were pled); Burgess v. Taylor, 44 S.W.3d 806 (Ky. Ct. App. 2001) (IIED claim permitted notwithstanding that it relied on the same misconduct for which conversion could have been alleged). The misconduct in *Miller* involved a television crew entering the decedent's home with emergency medical technicians and taping his death due to heart attack, for broadcast. The misconduct in *Burgess* involved the intentional slaughter of two loaned horses by a defendant who had misrepresented himself to be a horse lover. Is IIED the better way to redress the outrage associated with those torts?

Outrageousness. What does it mean for conduct to be extreme and outrageous? *See* Restatement of Torts §46, Comment d (extreme and outrageous mean "to go beyond all possible bounds of decency, and to be regarded as atrocious, and utterly intolerable in a civilized community"); *see also* Field v. Philadelphia Elec. Co., 388 Pa. Super, 400, 565 A.2d 1170 (Pa. Sup. Ct. 1988) (knowing exposure to high levels of radioactivity, and the concealing of that exposure). Is the solicitation of a sexual relationship enough? *See* Reed v. Maley, 115 Ky. 816, 74 S.W. 1079 (1903) (no); *see also* Jones v. Clinton, 990 F. Supp. 657, 677 (E.D. Ark. 1998) ("a mere sexual proposition or encounter, albeit an odious one, [does not] give rise to a claim of outrage"). Is a gross insult enough? *See* Slocum v. Food Fair Stores of Florida, Inc., 100 So.2d 396 (1958) (no) (plaintiff suffered mental distress and heart attack after store employee refused to tell her a product's price, adding "you stink to me"). Can abusive and harassing use of email and social-media accounts constitute outrageous conduct? Dennis v Napoli, 49 N.Y.S.3d 652, 148 A.D.3d 446 (N.Y. Sup. Ct. App. Div. 2017) (yes).

Special Relationships. Some courts take a categorical approach, recognizing intentional-infliction claims more readily in certain relationships. So, for instance, what if the defendant is a common carrier or utility—would a gross insult be enough then? *See* Restatement (Second) of Torts §48 (yes); *see, e.g.*, Lipman v. Atlantic Coast Line R. Co., 93 S.E. 714 (S.C. 1917) (conductor telling passenger that he belonged in a lunatic asylum with two black eyes is sufficiently outrageous in common-carrier relationship); *but see* Bethel v. N.Y.C. Transit Authority, 703 N.E.2d 1214 (N.Y. 1998) (no higher duty for common carriers). What is the justification for holding common carriers and utilities, and perhaps also innkeepers, liable for lesser insults? They may be monopolies or be in special relationship to their customers. One commentator suggests instead that class bias exists against employees of these entities. John L. Diamond, Cases and Materials on Torts 45 (West 2001). What about the special relationship of marriage—should law more-readily recognize intentional-infliction claims between spouses, less-readily recognize them, or not recognize them at all? *See* McCulloh v. Drake, 24 P.3d 1162 (Wyo. 2001) (joining trend toward recognizing IIED claims within marriages but setting higher standard); Henriksen v. Cameron, 622 A.2d 1135 (Me. 1993) (same). Interspousal immunity, now recognized in less than one-half of the states and treated in a subsequent chapter on negligence defenses, becomes an issue.

Repetition. What if the defendant frequently repeats less-than-outrageous insults or draws them together in a way that seems particularly pernicious? *See* Rulon-Miller v. International Business Machines Corp., 162 Cal. App.3d 241, 208 Cal. Rptr. 524 (1984) (IIED liability for the "combination of statements and conduct" that would not otherwise have been enough); Samms v. Eccles, 11 Utah 2d 289, 358 P.2d 344 (1961) (hounding late-night telephone calls from May to December are enough); *but see* Harris v. Jones, 281 Md. 560, 380 A.2d 611 (1977) (repeatedly mimicking stutterer over five month period may or may not be enough, depending on whether it produced severe distress). What if the conduct is basically lawful but done in an extraordinarily distressing manner? *See* Johnson v. Wayne County, 213 Mich. App. 143, 540 N.W.2d 66 (1995) (claim stated for lawfully holding juror in contempt for failing to serve at murder trial but incarcerating juror in a cell with the alleged murderer). What if the distressing conduct pursues legal rights? *See* Davis v. Currier, 704 A.2d 1207 (Maine 1997) (no IIED counter-claim for civil suit alleging assault liability notwithstanding defendant's criminal acquittal on related charges).

Employment. Should the fact that the defendant employs the person claiming intentional infliction of emotional distress work for or against the claimant? *See* Texas Farm Bureau Mut. Ins. Cos. V. Sears, 84 S.W.3d 604, 611 (Tex. 2002) (employer has discretion to supervise and criticize, and "only very unusual employment disputes" will give rise to IIED claims); Anderson v. Oklahoma Temp. Svcs., Inc., 925 P.2d 574 (Okla. App. 1996) (supervisor's profanity, smoking, and vulgar behavior toward employee not sufficiently extreme and outrageous); *but see* Ford v. Revlon, Inc., 153 Ariz. 38, 734 P.2d 580 (1987) (employer liable for intentional infliction of emotional distress for assaults and vulgarity toward employee). What if the person alleged to have committed the intentional infliction has done so in the course of the person's employment—for instance, to collect on a bill the plaintiff owed? *Contrast* Hamilton v. Ford Motor Credit Co., 502 A.2d 1057 (Md. Ct. Spec. App. 1986) (threats and persistent telephone calls not extreme and outrageous enough), *with* Bowden v. Spiegel, Inc., 96 Cal App.2d 793, 216 P.2d 571 (1950) (bill collector subject to IIED claim for implying that his telephone call was an emergency and that the message was "going to be a shock").

Knowledge

Law is fraught with ambiguity. Legal analysis itself is inherently uncertain—but useful in that uncertainty. We think law to be solely rule-based, but law's reasoning is not essentially formal. It is dialectical—a back-and-forth proposition. Law is necessarily indeterminate. Legal language is intentionally ambiguous while also being precise. Ambiguity creates room for reflection and opportunity for compromise—for incorporating the views of others and expanding options and possibilities. Ambiguity allows lawyers to deal more sensitively with the humanity of parties, allowing that humanity to flourish. Ambiguity can accommodate an infinite variety of circumstances

> and interests. Lawyers satisfy law's formal needs by using expressions like *probable, quite certain, unlikely, possible,* and *doubtful,* to reflect and quantify uncertainty.

Susceptibility. The outrageousness element of intentional infliction of emotional distress depends on an objective or community standard, not the plaintiff's subjective evaluation of the conduct. *See* Slocum v. Food Fair Stores of Florida, Inc., *supra*. But what if the perpetrator knows that the victim is particularly sensitive? *See* Drezja v. Vaccaro, 650 A.2d 1308 (D.C. App. 1994) (propriety of interview of rape victim judged by victim's condition and circumstance); Korbin v. Berlin, 177 So.2d 551 (Fla. App. 1965) (IIED claim stated on behalf of six-year-old child for defendant's having told her that God would punish her mother for stealing another woman's husband); Delta Fin. Co. v. Ganakas, 93 Ga. App. 297, 91 S.W.2d 383 (1956) (IIED claim stated on behalf of 11-year-old child whom defendant told that her mother would be jailed if the child did not open the door to allow defendant to repossess a television).

> **Skills**
>
> Lawyers begin a lawsuit by preparing **pleadings**—complaints, answers, counter-claims, cross-claims, and third-party complaints naming the parties and claims they assert and defend. (Discovery requests and their responses, motions and their responses, briefs, and the other papers lawyers file are court papers, not pleadings.) Below is a typical complaint for a tort case, beginning with allegations of jurisdiction and venue, then alleging facts, and then stating separate counts each titled with the name of the tort and alleging all elements, finally ending with a prayer for relief. Has the attorney pled facts supporting each element of the claims?

STATE OF MICHIGAN
IN THE LAKE COUNTY CIRCUIT COURT

TED PRICE and **BETTY PRICE**, Case No. 10-_____-NP
    Plaintiffs,
    v Hon. _____
DIRK MONK,
    Defendant.

[Name, address, and telephone]
Attorneys for Plaintiffs

PLAINTIFFS' COMPLAINT

Plaintiffs Ted Price and Betty Price complain against defendant Dirk Monk as follows:
JURISDICTION AND VENUE
1. Ted and Betty Price are husband and wife residing in Monroe County.
2. Dirk Monk resides in Lake County.
3. This civil case is for damages above $25,000 within the Court's venue and jurisdiction.
FACT ALLEGATIONS
4. Mr. and Mrs. Price were camping at the Pine River Campground on May 1, 2011.
5. Mr. Monk was living out of his pickup truck at an adjacent campsite.

6. Mr. Monk made crude and profane remarks directed toward Mrs. Price.
7. Mrs. Price objected to Mr. Monk's remarks, alerting Mr. Price.
8. Mr. Price requested that Mr. Monk desist and leave Mrs. Price alone.
9. Mr. Monk approached Mr. Price in a threatening and profane manner.
10. Mr. Monk was under the influence of alcohol and is over six feet tall.
11. Mr. and Mrs. Price are both elderly and under five-and-a-half feet tall.
12. Mr. Price requested that Mr. Monk leave Mr. Price alone, as well.
13. Mr. Monk aggressively shoved Mr. Price while laughing at Mrs. Price.
14. From Mr. Monk's shove, Mr. Price fell back, fracturing his elbow.
15. Police were called to restore order, and ambulance removed Mr. Price.
16. As a further result, Mr. Price suffered fear, fright, shock, pain, embarrassment, humiliation, mortification, mental and emotional distress, disability, and loss of enjoyment of life, and incurred medical expense.
17. As a further result, Mrs. Price suffered fear, fright, shock, embarrassment, humiliation, and severe mental and emotional distress, manifested in depression, sleeplessness, and weight and hair loss.
18. These losses, expenses, and damages will continue into the future.

This reference incorporates the above paragraphs into the following counts.

COUNT I: BATTERY

19. Mr. Monk committed a battery on Mr. Price, in that Mr. Monk intentionally harmed and offended Mr. Price through Mr. Monk's physical contact with Mr. Price, causing Mr. Price the above loss and damage.

COUNT II: ASSAULT

20. Mr. Monk committed an assault on Mr. Price, in that Mr. Monk intentionally placed Mr. Price in reasonable fear of an imminent harmful and offensive contact, while Mr. Monk's ability to carry out that harmful and offensive contact was apparent to Mr. Price, causing Mr. Price the above loss and damage.

COUNT III: INTENTIONAL INFLICTION OF EMOTIONAL DISTRESS

21. Mr. Monk intentionally inflicted emotional distress on Mrs. Price, in that Mr. Monk intended, by his outrageously crude and profane remarks and the threat to and injury of her husband beyond all bounds of decency in civil society, to cause her severe distress that she did in fact suffer in physical manifestation.

ON THESE GROUNDS, plaintiffs Ted Price and Betty Price pray that the Court grant judgment in their favor and against defendant Dirk Monk for all damages to which they are found entitled, together with an award of interest, costs, and attorney's fees.

[signature block for plaintiff's counsel]

Career

Networking can make a difference in finding employment and succeeding in tort practice. Tort practice takes place within a community of professionals, most of whom maintain good relationships with one another. Your introduction to one tort practitioner gives you access to a network of tort practitioners who tend to know who is providing what legal service to whom, through what marketing and relationships. Tort practitioners tend to know who is busy, meaning who may be hiring. They share resources and tips with another, such as the names of qualified (and unqualified) expert witnesses, medical examiners, investigator, animators, and illustrators. Get to know tort practitioners in the geographic area where you plan to practice. Learn their relative skills, specialty areas, and referral policies. It may help you find or keep a job, and will make you more knowledgeable and skilled at serving your torts clients.

CHAPTER III

INTENTIONAL TORTS—PROPERTY

A. Trespass to Land and Nuisance

OBJECTIVE: Given descriptions of situations in which there are various entries of persons or things onto another person's land, recall and apply the elements of the tort of trespass to land, analyzing whether the facts satisfy those elements, consistent with this section of the text.

Case Study: A car hit a patch of black ice and spun into a yard in the middle of the night. The inebriated driver decided to sleep it off in a barn in the yard. Early the next morning, he called a friend asking that the friend use his four-wheel-drive truck to drag the car out of the yard. The friend did so, leaving deep ruts in the yard. ***Recall and apply the elements of trespass to determine whether and for what actions the property owner has trespass claims against the inebriated driver and friend.***

Trespass to Land. Trespass to land is an intentional, unauthorized entry onto the land of another, interfering with its exclusive possession. Entry will alone not do—it must be intentional. Negligent entries onto land, such as the motor vehicle driver who speeds around an icy corner unintentionally causing the vehicle to slide from the road and into someone's yard, may be actionable in negligence claims but are not trespasses. *See also* Hammontree v. Jenner, 97 Cal. Rptr. 739 (Ct. App. 1971) (no property-damage liability without fault for driver losing control of car from unexpected seizure). Although we typically think of trespass as a person going onto another's land, the entry need not be of a person but must be tangible. A person may intentionally direct something else onto another's land, constituting a trespass—perhaps by throwing a rock or shooting a bullet onto the land, constructing a deck or driveway, or rerouting runoff water. Intentional, industrial activities that send smoke, gas, and odor onto another's land are not ordinarily not tangible-enough invasions to constitute trespass but may instead give rise to causes of action in nuisance (a related property tort). Although we commonly think of trespass as a person sneaking onto another's land—that is, entering the land without the landowner's knowledge—in fact, trespass can be open and notorious, such as where neighbors dispute who owns the land and the non-owner wrongfully enters and acts as if owning it.

Mistake and Intent. This latter scenario suggests another important feature of trespass law that one is liable for trespass even when acting in good faith, under reasonable mistake as to ownership and authority for entry. Here, as elsewhere in the law of intentional torts, mistake does not negate intent. Peters v. Archambault, 278 N.E.2d 729 (Mass. 1991), is an example, where the plaintiff obtained an injunction requiring the defendant to raze the substantial portion of the house defendant had mistakenly built on the plaintiff's neighboring land. Note that damage is not an element of trespass. Trespass claims can involve huge financial losses. Yet without proof of loss, law presumes damages. Courts may award nominal damages for so little as a leisurely stroll across another's grass. A landowner must have an enforceable legal right to exclude another even without financial loss, to forestall a trespasser's claim for a prescriptive easement or right. In that sense, the element that the entry must *interfere with exclusive possession* refers not to the damage or annoyance a trespass might cause but to violating the owner's right to exclude others. Only in the case of intangible entries, such as microscopic particles, will the courts either require proof of trespass damages or, if the condition interferes with use and enjoyment but does not appear to be an entry (as with noise and smells), shunt the claim to the grab-bag tort of nuisance. Consider the following illustrative trespass-to-land cases.

Hannabalson v. Sessions
Iowa Supreme Court
116 Iowa 457, 90 N.W. 93 (1902)

WEAVER, J. Plaintiff and defendant live upon adjoining lots. There is frequent war between the families. ... Upon the boundary line between the lots is a tight board fence, a part of which was built by plaintiff's husband; but, unfortunately, this barrier, while all sufficient to prevent the passage of the dove of peace, is neither high enough nor tight enough to prevent the interchange of brick bats or the bandying of opprobrious epithets. On May 30, 1898, the defendant, while at work in his garden, claimed to have narrowly escaped a brick hurled in his direction by one of plaintiff's children, and in his indignation at the unprovoked bombardment threatened the lad with arrest. Plaintiff and her husband, being at work near by, heard the threat, and took up the quarrel. About this time plaintiff's husband discovered that a ladder belonging to defendant was hanging upon a peg or block attached to the partition fence, and, conceiving this to be a cloud upon his title, he forthwith attempted to remove it, while defendant, seeing the peril in which his property was placed, rushed to its defense. Whether plaintiff herself laid violent hands on the ladder is a matter of grave dispute. She denies it, and says that the height and depth of her offending consisted in her leaning up against the fence with one arm quietly hanging over the top thereof, and in stimulating her husband's zeal by audible remarks about the "crazy fool" who was bearing down upon them from the other side. She further avers that while occupying this position of strict neutrality the defendant assaulted her vi et armis, and with his clenched fist struck the arm which protruded over the fence top into his domain. Defendant denies the striking, and says that plaintiff, instead of being a peaceable and impartial observer of the skirmish, was herself a principal actor, and that in aid of her husband she climbed upon some convenient pedestal, and, hanging herself across the fence, reached down, and with malice aforethought seized the ladder and wrenched it from its resting place. Thereupon, actuated by a natural and lawful desire to protect his property from such ravishments, and being goaded on by statements from the other side of the fence reflecting upon his mother and casting doubt upon his proper rank in the animal kingdom, he gently, and without unreasonable force, laid his open hand upon plaintiff's arm, and mildly but firmly suggested the propriety of her "keeping on her own side of the fence." ...

3. It is also said that the court erred in instructing the jury that, if plaintiff leaned over the partition fence and attempted to interfere with the ladder, defendant had the right to use such force upon her as was reasonably necessary to cause her to desist, and to expel her from his premises. ... The general doctrine announced in the instruction is, in our judgment, correct. The mere fact that plaintiff did not step across the boundary line does

not make her any less a trespasser if she reached her arm across the line, as she admits she did. It is one of the oldest rules of property known to the law that the title of the owner of the soil extends, not only downward to the center of the earth, but upward usque ad cœlum, although it is, perhaps, doubtful whether owners as quarrelsome as the parties in this case will ever enjoy the usufruct of their property in the latter direction. The maxim, "Ubi pars est ibi est totum,"—that where the greater part is there is the whole,—does not apply to the person of a trespasser, and the court and jury could therefore not be expected to enter into any inquiry as to the side of the boundary line upon which plaintiff preponderated, as she reached over the fence top. It was enough that she thrust her hand or arm across the boundary to technically authorize the defendant to demand that she cease the intrusion… .

We are not prepared to hold with counsel that the mere fact that this particular part of the fence was built by plaintiff's husband makes defendant a wrongdoer in hanging his ladder upon it. The entire fence, by whomsoever built, being placed upon the boundary, is in a just sense common property, and it would be an intolerable conclusion to say that neither party could touch the portion not built by himself without danger of a lawsuit. The law as it is affords sufficient opportunity for spiteful and contentious persons to harass their neighbors by strict insistence upon technical rights, and it would be little less than a calamity to establish the precedent for which appellant contends. This case is one with which the courts ought not to be burdened, and we can justify giving it the serious attention we have only in the hope that an exhibition of its petty and ridiculous features may tend to check such litigation.

The judgment of the district court is affirmed.

Knowledge

Generating rules is a critical skill for a lawyer. Lawyers must select and state rules from various textual sources for varying contexts. Experienced lawyers can take a complex statute or court rule, administrative regulation, or judicial opinion, and from those sources generate any number of specific rules and sub-rules. Judicial opinions often state rules and holdings but sometimes do not, leaving the reader to infer the rules and holdings from the context of the facts, discussion, and outcome. What an authority presents in a case or statute as a single rule may include several sub-rules. Try stating tort-law rules in terms of who, what, when, and where—the *who* often being a party, the *what* being a claim or element, the *when* stating the conduct involved, and the *where* naming the context or circumstance. Be able to generate tort-law rules from varied sources.

Herrin v. Sutherland
Montana Supreme Court
74 Mont. 587, 241 P.328 (1925)

Action by H. J. Herrin against William Sutherland. Judgment for plaintiff, and defendant appeals. Affirmed.

The complaint contains eight causes of action, in the first of which the plaintiff alleges himself to be the owner in fee and in the actual possession of a large tract of land in Lewis and Clark County, abutting for several miles on both sides of the Missouri river, a nontidal but navigable stream. It is then alleged that about the 18th of September, 1924, the defendant, being engaged on a fishing and hunting expedition, rowed a boat down the channel of the stream between plaintiff's lands "abutting on each side thereof, and intermittently cast for and caught fish in said channel, shot at and killed wild ducks floating thereon or in flight thereover, in violation of plaintiff's right of possession and control of the channel of said stream, to plaintiff's damage in the sum of $10;" that on that day and while on said fishing and hunting expedition the defendant rowed the boat to the west bank of the stream, and there moored the same above the ordinary low water mark of the stream, and thereafter, while fishing in the river, "walked and tramped along said bank on the land of plaintiff, above the ordinary low water mark and in and above the ordinary high water mark, and between said water marks, tramped upon and destroyed native and planted grasses upon said land," in violation of plaintiff's rights and to his damage.

In the second cause of action plaintiff alleges his ownership and actual possession of what he terms his "home ranch," which ranch is devoted to the raising of hay and grain and the breeding and raising of sheep and cattle. There flows through this ranch a small unnavigable stream known as Fall Creek, about 15 feet in width and about 2 feet deep, which stream is inhabited by game fish. That on or about the 3d of August, 1924, the defendant entered the stream at its mouth, where it empties into the Missouri river, "and waded up and down the same fishing with a line and rod, in violation of plaintiff's right to the undisturbed, peaceful, and exclusive enjoyment of said stream for fishing and other purposes, to plaintiff's damage in the sum of $10;" and when not wading in the channel of the stream the defendant walked up and down the banks thereof, tramping on and destroying hay growing on said banks, and breaking and cutting willows growing along the banks, to plaintiff's damage.

The third cause of action also relates to the home ranch, it being alleged that on the 18th of September, 1924, the defendant, while engaged in hunting ducks and other water fowl and other migratory game birds, and while standing on the lands of another, repeatedly discharged a Winchester shotgun at water fowl in flight over plaintiff's said premises, dwelling house and over his cattle, "thereby preventing plaintiff from the quiet, undisturbed, peaceful enjoyment of his dwelling house, ranch, and property, to plaintiff's damage in the sum of $10." …

After defendant's general demurrer to the several causes of action was overruled he declined to answer, and his default was entered. Upon the suggestion of counsel for plaintiff that only nominal damages would be demanded, the court rendered judgment in favor of the plaintiff for damages in the sum of $1 upon the eight causes of action collectively, with costs of the action. From this judgment the defendant has appealed.

CALLAWAY, C. J. (after stating the facts as above). 1. First cause of action. At the outset it is conceded that the Missouri river is a navigable stream; also that the plaintiff does not own any land beyond low water mark. Nevertheless he claims that, as he exercises complete dominion to the low water mark on both sides of the stream, as an incident to that right he may control the use of the channel of the stream for all purposes except navigation. …

At an early date in England title to the land beneath the sea and tidal rivers was conceived to be in the king, whereas title to the land under inland waters where the tide did not ebb and flow was in the private riparian proprietors. Originally the right to fish in the sea and tidal rivers was held to be the exclusive prerogative of the king as lord of the soil (Royal Fishery of the Banne, Davies Rep. 149; Hale, De Juris Maris, 18), but by a process of legal evolution this right came to be regarded as held in trust for the public; and the general rule now is that in tidal waters all have an equal right to fish. ...

While plaintiff's position that he may control the use of the channel for any purposes is untenable, still he may maintain his first cause of action, for the defendant went upon the land of plaintiff "above the ordinary low water mark and in and above the ordinary high water mark and between said water marks," and tramped upon and destroyed native and planted grasses upon said land. In going upon plaintiff's land in the fashion described, the defendant was a trespasser. [Cc] ...

2. The defendant trespassed also when he waded up and down Fall creek fishing. The channel of the creek belonged to the plaintiff [c], and while the plaintiff did not own the fish, feræ naturæ, he had the exclusive right to fish for them while they were in the waters of Fall Creek within his land. [C] It would seem clear that a man has no right to fish where he has no right to be. So it is held uniformly that the public have no right to fish in a nonnavigable body of water, the bed of which is owned privately. [Cc] ...

Likewise the plaintiff trespassed when he tramped upon and destroyed the hay and broke and cut the willows growing upon the banks of the stream.

3. It must be held that when the defendant, although standing upon the land of another, fired a shotgun over plaintiff's premises, dwelling and cattle, he interfered with "the quiet, undisturbed, peaceful enjoyment" of the plaintiff, and thus committed a technical trespass at least. The plaintiff was the owner of the land. "Land," says Blackstone, "in its legal signification has an indefinite extent, upwards as well as downwards; whoever owns the land possesses all the space upwards to an indefinite extent; such is the maxim of the law." Cooley's Blackstone, Book II, 18; vol. 1, 445; Kent's Com. 401. ...

Sir Frederick Pollock, in the tenth edition of his valuable work on Torts, page 363, observes that it has been doubted whether it is a trespass to pass over land without touching the soil, as one may in a balloon, or to cause a material object, as a shot fired from a gun, to pass over it. ... Continuing he observes: "As regards shooting it would be strange if we could object to shots being fired point blank across our land only in the event of actual injury being caused, and the passage of the foreign object in the air above our soil being thus a mere incident and a distinct trespass to person or property."

But he concludes that, when taking into account the extreme flight of projectiles fired from modern artillery which may pass thousands of feet above the land, the subject is not without difficulty. That shortly it will become one of considerable importance is indicated by the rapid approach of the airplane as an instrumentality of commerce [c]. However, it seems to be the consensus of the holdings of the courts in this country that the air space, at least near the ground, is almost as inviolable as the soil itself. [Cc] It is a matter of common knowledge that the shotgun is a firearm of short range. To be subjected to the danger incident to and reasonably to be anticipated from the firing of this weapon at water fowl in flight over one's dwelling house and cattle would seem to be far from inconsequential, and, while plaintiff's allegations are very general in character, it cannot be said that a cause of action is not stated for nominal damages at least. ...

The judgment is affirmed.

> **Skills**
> Tort lawyers often depend on paralegals, secretaries, or other staff, or on other lawyers, to record the basic information on which they will evaluate a potential client's matter. The intake process can be critical to the office's efficient, ethical operation—and to the potential client's claim. What do you think is the critical information that the intake person must record when a potential client calls or visits a law office? Start with the client's name and contact information because the lawyer must have a way to reach the potential client, whether the lawyer decides to represent the client or not. A lawyer's letting a potential client know that the lawyer has declined a matter can be critical to the potential client's ability to timely retain another lawyer. Also critical is recording enough information to identify the nature of the claims and when they arose, so that the lawyer can calculate the limitations period and either make a timely filing or, if turning down the matter, do so timely alerting the potential client to pursue the claim promptly if the client intends to seek another lawyer. Consider the following intake form.

NEW CLIENT INTAKE FORM

PERSONAL:
NAME:_____
HOME TELEPHONE:_____ WORK TELEPHONE:_____
FACSIMILE:_____ E-MAIL:_____
HOME ADDRESS:_____
DATE OF BIRTH:_____ SOCIAL SECURITY NUMBER:_____

FAMILY:
MARRIED?_____ SPOUSE'S NAME_____
                      SPOUSE'S EMPLOYER:_____
DIVORCED?_____ FORMER SPOUSE'S NAME:_____
CHILDREN?_____ NAME/AGE:_____

EMPLOYMENT: NAME/AGE:_____
JOB TITLE/DESCRIPTION:_____
WAGES (HOURLY):_____ WAGES (ANNUAL):_____
EMPLOYER'S ADDRESS:_____

LEGAL SERVICE: CLAIM or DEFENSE
SUBJECT MATTER:_____
DATE CLAIM AROSE:_____ /LIMITATIONS PERIOD:_____ /EXPIRES ON:_____
OPPOSING PARTY:_____
OPPOSING PARTY'S ADDRESS:_____
OPPOSING PARTY'S LAWYER:_____
OPPOSING PARTY'S EMPLOYMENT/BUSINESS:_____
DESCRIPTION:_____
_____

WITNESS:_____ /TELEPHONE/ADDRESS:_____
WITNESS:_____ /TELEPHONE/ADDRESS:_____
PHYSICIAN:_____ /ADDRESS:_____

BILLING: CONTINGENCY or HOURLY
REFERRING ATTORNEY:_____ REFERRAL FEE:_____
MARKETING: GOT OUR NAME FROM:_____
DISPOSITION: INSTRUCTIONS GIVEN TO CLIENT:_____
DECLINED:_____ / AT FIRST CONTACT or BY FOLLOW-UP TELEPHONE or BY CORRESPONDENCE
INVESTIGATION UNDERTAKEN:_____
FILE OPENED?_____ FEE AGREEMENT?_____ CASE FILED?_____

Kopka v. Bell Telephone Co.
Pennsylvania Supreme Court
91 A.2d 232 (Pa. 1952)

STERN, J. This litigation involves the question of the right of a possessor of land to recover damages for personal injuries sustained by him in consequence of a trespasser's invasion of his property.

At the request of residents of a township in Indiana County for telephone service the Bell Telephone Company of Pennsylvania, defendant in this suit, had its engineers stake out a line along a road bordering the farm of the plaintiff, Walter V. Kopka.[fn] It then proceeded to obtain rights-of-way from property owners along the road upon which the line was to be constructed, but no such right was obtained from the plaintiff.

Under an arrangement between the Company and one Jud Sedwick, additional defendant, the latter proceeded to erect the necessary poles to carry the wires and for that purpose drilled holes, one of which was dug inside the road on plaintiff's property; in this hole there was to be placed an anchor rod supporting a guy wire for bracing one of the poles. The Company had indicated to Sedwick where the holes were to be dug and the poles and anchor rods erected. This particular hole, 6 1/2 feet deep and 17 inches wide, was dug on December 19, 1947. Two days later, on the 21st, plaintiff was informed by a neighbor about it and went out to investigate, it having been dug without his permission or knowledge. It was in the latter half of the afternoon of a cloudy day and starting to get dark. While walking around to find the hole plaintiff's left leg slipped into it with the result that he allegedly sustained certain injuries. He testified, although there was strong evidence to the contrary, that there was no mound or ring of dirt thrown up around the hole and that the ground seemed level at that point. The hay field through which he passed he described as being "rough and rolling, grass growed up, kind of spongy and spots of snow around in the fields." Around where the hole was "it was all weeds and briars and whatever it was." Other testimony on behalf of the plaintiff was to the effect that that corner of the field "was left in weeds, briar and morning-glory vines."

Suit was instituted against the Telephone Company in the Court of Common Pleas of Allegheny County. The complaint alleged the defendant had, without plaintiff's permission, trespassed upon his farm and dug a hole there, and that property damage as well as personal injuries to plaintiff resulted from the negligence of defendant in thus trespassing and causing others to trespass on his farm, digging the hole there and leaving it unprotected and without barriers, thereby creating a dangerous trap. Defendant filed an answer denying that the acts complained of were done by its agents or employes, but that, on the contrary, the installation of the poles and anchor rods was made by Jud Sedwick, an independent contractor. Defendant brought Sedwick on the record as additional defendant, alleging that any damage done to plaintiff's property or injuries suffered by him were the result of additional defendant's negligence and not that of defendant. ...

The trial resulted in a verdict in favor of plaintiff and against defendant in the sum of $11,000, and a verdict in favor of the additional defendant. The court ... ordered that judgment be entered on the verdict, from which judgment defendant now appeals. ...

Before considering the question of the liability of a trespasser for personal injuries suffered by the possessor of land as an indirect result of the trespass, there are two relevant legal principles to be borne in mind. The first is that the fact that a trespass results from an innocent mistake and, in that sense, is not deliberate or wilful, does not relieve the trespasser of liability therefor or for any of the results thereof. [C] Thus, in Restatement, Torts, § 163, comment (b), it is said: "If the actor intends to be upon the particular piece of land in question, it is not necessary that he intend to invade the actor's interest in the exclusive possession of his land. The intention which is required to make the actor liable * * * is an intention to enter upon the particular piece of land in question irrespective of whether the actor knows or should know that he is not entitled to enter thereon. It is, therefore, immaterial whether or not he honestly and reasonably believes that the land is his own, or that he has the consent of the possessor or of a third person having power to give consent on his behalf, or that he has a mistaken belief that he has some other privilege to enter." ...

The second important principle to be noted is that one who authorizes or directs another to commit an act which constitutes a trespass to another's land is himself liable as a trespasser to the same extent as if the trespass were committed directly by himself, and this is true even though the authority or direction be given to one who is an independent contractor. [Cc] ...

The liability of defendant Company for the trespass involved in the digging of the hole on plaintiff's land without his knowledge or consent being thus established, does such liability extend to the personal injuries sustained by him as the result of his falling into the hole? The authorities are clear to the effect that where the complaint is for trespass to land the trespasser becomes liable not only for personal injuries resulting directly and proximately from the trespass but also for those which are indirect and consequential.[fn] ...

[The appellate court found the verdict excessive.] On the whole, a verdict in the amount of $7,000 would seem generous compensation for the injuries he sustained, and the verdict should accordingly be reduced to that amount.

As far as the verdict in favor of the additional defendant is concerned, it is clear, from what has previously been stated, that Sedwick, however innocent his act of trespass, incurred thereby the same liability to plaintiff as did the original defendant. However, there has been no appeal by plaintiff from the verdict in Sedwick's favor, nor has defendant ever made any claim on its own behalf against the additional defendant. Therefore the propriety of the verdict in the latter's favor is not here in question.

As modified the judgment is affirmed.

Knowledge

Lawyers read and cite cases for the rules of law on which the outcome of those cases depended—what lawyers call the case's *holding*. Case opinions often state holdings but sometimes do not. Occasionally, an opinion will begin, "We hold...," and then state something that is *not* the case's holding. A case's holding is not merely a rule of law the case opinion announces. Opinions will occasionally announce or repeat rules having nothing directly to do with the case facts, issue, and outcome. Lawyers call those asides *dicta*. A holding is a rule of law that the case facts place in issue, on which the case's outcome depends. Arriving at a case's holding is thus a more-complex analytic skill than it might first seem. It requires constructing an acontextual rule that you express with precision, out of a context-laden source.

INQUIRY

Intangible Entries. In some cases, the interference with the landowner's exclusive possession is less clear than the above examples, leaving questions whether the one ostensibly interfering has even entered the land. Think of the impact on neighboring lands of any noisy, dusty, smoky, or odorous activity—whether industrial, agricultural, or recreational—that a landowner may wish to conduct on the landowner's own land. In such cases, the *entry* and *interference with exclusive possession* elements of trespass work less well or not at all as a conceptual framework for determining the parties' rights, causing the courts and parties to turn to an alternative *nuisance* claim. Law defines nuisance as intentional interference with another's use or enjoyment of their land. Law recognizes both public and private nuisances. Public nuisance deals with conditions that interfere with public health, safety, or convenience—perhaps to passersby on a highway or users of a park, or to a large number of neighboring landowners. *See* Restatement (Second) of Torts §821B (1965); Armory Park Neighborhood Assn. v. Episcopal Commun. Services, 712 P.2d 914 (Ariz. 1985) (enjoining church from offering meals to the indigent, as a public nuisance). Private nuisance deals with an interference with the private use and enjoyment of privately owned land. *See* Restatement (Second) of Torts §822 (1965). Some authority also exists for negligent nuisance claims holding the defendant to a duty not to unreasonably (but unintentionally) allow conditions to develop or exist on the defendant's land that interfere with the use and enjoyment of other lands. Consider the following case.

Bradley v. American Smelting and Refining Co.
Washington Supreme Court
104 Wash.2d 677, 709 P.2d 782 (1985)

CALLOW, J. This comes before us on a certification from the United States District Court for the Western District of Washington. Plaintiffs, landowners on Vashon Island, had sued for damages in trespass and nuisance from the deposit on their property of microscopic, airborne particles of heavy metals which came from the American Smelting and Refining Company (ASARCO) copper smelter at Ruston, Washington. ...

Plaintiffs' property is located some 4 miles north of defendant's smelter. Defendant's primary copper smelter (also referred to as the Tacoma smelter), has operated in its present location since 1890. ... As a part of the industrial process of smelting copper at the Tacoma smelter, various gases such as sulfur dioxide and particulate matter, including arsenic, cadmium and other metals, are emitted. Particulate matter is composed of distinct particles of matter other than water, which cannot be detected by the human senses. ...

The parties stipulated that as a part of the smelting process, particulate matter including arsenic and cadmium was emitted, that some of the emissions had been deposited on the plaintiffs' land and that the defendant has been aware since 1905 that the wind, on occasion, caused these emissions to be blown over the plaintiffs' land. The defendant cannot and does not deny that whenever the smelter was in operation the whim of the winds could bring these deleterious substances to the plaintiffs' premises.

The insistence that a trespass involve an invasion by a "thing" or "object" was repudiated in the well known (but not particularly influential) case of *Martin v. Reynolds*

Metals Co., [221 Or. 86, 342 P.2d 790 (1959)], which held that gaseous and particulate fluorides from an aluminum smelter constituted a trespass for purposes of the statute of limitations: "[L]iability on the theory of trespass has been recognized where the harm was produced by the vibration of the soil or by the concussion of the air which, of course, is nothing more than the movement of molecules one against the other." * * * The view recognizing a trespassory invasion where there is no "thing" which can be seen with the naked eye undoubtedly runs counter to the definition of trespass expressed in some quarters. [Citing the Restatement (First), Torts and Prosser]. It is quite possible that in an earlier day when science had not yet peered into the molecular and atomic world of small particles, the courts could not fit an invasion through unseen physical instrumentalities into the requirement that a trespass can result only from a *direct* invasion. But in this atomic age even the uneducated know the great and awful force contained in the atom and what it can do to a man's property if it is released. In fact, the now famous equation $E=MC^2$ has taught us that mass and energy are equivalents and that our concept of "things" must be reframed. If these observations on science in relation to the law of trespass should appear theoretical and unreal in the abstract, they become very practical and real to the possessor of land when the unseen force cracks the foundation of his house. The force is just as real if it is chemical in nature and must be awakened by the intervention of another agency before it does harm. ....

Martin v. Reynolds Metals Co., 221 Or. 86, 90-91, 101, 342 P.2d 790 (1959), was an action in trespass brought against the defendant corporation for causing gases and fluoride particulates to settle on the plaintiffs' land making it unfit for livestock. ... In addition, the court stated: "Trespass and private nuisance are separate fields of tort liability relating to actionable interference with the possession of land. They may be distinguished by comparing the interest invaded; an actionable invasion of a possessor's interest in the exclusive possession of land is a trespass; an actionable invasion of a possessor's interest in the use and enjoyment of his land is a nuisance. [C]" ...

We hold that the defendant's conduct in causing chemical substances to be deposited upon the plaintiffs' land fulfilled all of the requirements under the law of trespass. ...

Having held that there was an intentional trespass, we adopt, in part, the rationale of *Borland v. Sanders Lead Co.,* 369 So.2d 523, 529 (Ala.1979), which stated in part: "Although we view this decision as an application, and not an extension, of our present law of trespass, we feel that a brief restatement and summary of the principles involved in this area would be appropriate. Whether an invasion of a property interest is a trespass or a nuisance does not depend upon whether the intruding agent is "tangible" or "intangible." Instead, an analysis must be made to determine the interest interfered with. If the intrusion interferes with the right to exclusive possession of property, the law of trespass applies. If the intrusion is to the interest in use and enjoyment of property, the law of nuisance applies. As previously observed, however, the remedies of trespass and nuisance are not necessarily mutually exclusive." ...

We accept and approve the elements of trespass by airborne pollutants as set forth by the *Borland* case. [Cc] ...

When airborne particles are transitory or quickly dissipate, they do not interfere with a property owner's possessory rights and, therefore, are properly denominated as nuisances. [Cc] When, however, the particles or substance accumulates on the land and does not pass away, then a trespass has occurred. *Borland v. Sanders Lead Co., supra; Martin v. Reynolds Metals Co., supra.* While at common law any trespass entitled a landowner to recover nominal or punitive damages for the invasion of his property, such a rule is not appropriate under the circumstances before us. No useful purpose would be served by sanctioning actions in trespass by every landowner within a hundred miles of a manufacturing plant. Manufacturers would be harassed and the litigious few would cause the escalation of costs to the detriment of the many. The elements that we have adopted for an action in trespass from *Borland* require that a plaintiff has suffered actual and substantial damages. Since this is an element of the action, the plaintiff who cannot show that actual and substantial damages have been suffered should be subject to dismissal of his cause upon a motion for summary judgment. ...

In conclusion, we answer the certified questions as follows: ...

2. An intentional deposit of microscopic particulates, undetectable by the human senses, gives rise to a cause of action for trespass as well as a claim of nuisance.

3. A cause of action under such circumstances requires proof of actual and substantial damages. ...

The United States District Court for the Western District of Washington shall be notified for such further action as it deems appropriate.

INQUIRY

Damages. What is the plaintiff landowner to do when the landowner suffers only nominal damages, but the defendant, willing to pay the usual $1, refuses to leave the land? Courts recognize actions for *ejectment*, the sheriff forcibly removing the defendant according to the court's judgment. The plaintiff landowner may also file a quiet-title action (a property-law form), pleading trespass only for damage recovery or to end ongoing interference with exclusive possession. Are punitive damages available against a trespasser when the trespass causes only nominal damages? *See* Jacque v. Steenberg Homes, Inc., 209 Wis.2d 605, 563 N.W.2d 154 (1997) (yes) (defendant bulldozed snow-path across plaintiff's land to deliver mobile home, even though plaintiff repeatedly refused permission to do so).

> **Figure**
> Trial lawyer Michael Sillyman is a past president of the Hispanic National Bar Association, Public Lawyers Section of the Arizona State Bar Association, Ninth Circuit Judicial Conference, and several other professional and civic organizations and associations. He has also served as a judge pro tem of the Arizona Court of Appeals, an arbitrator for the National Association of Securities Dealers and New York Stock Exchange, and a speaker for the ABA Business Litigation Section, the NASD, the Commodity Futures Trading Commission, and several other organizations. But the mainstay of his law practice is representing government agencies, private corporations, and their directors, officers, and employees in constitutional and civil-rights claims, defamation and invasion-of-privacy actions, and other business-tort actions. He is a partner at the law firm Kutak Rock LLP in Scottsdale, Arizona.

Personal Injury. The above cases show that a trespassing defendant may be liable not only for property damage but also for related personal injury. Trespass actions can provide a recovery where a negligence action would not. *See* Beavers v. West Penn Power Co., 436 F.2d 869 (3d Cir. 1971) (trespass claim against power company for death of ten-year-old child who was electrocuted when contacting power lines trespassing over home in which child resided) (approving jury instruction that would hold defendant liable without regard to fault). If trespass claims can redress injury or death, then what about recovery for emotional distress? *See* Johnson v. Marcel, 251 Va. 58, 465 S.W.2d 815 (1996) (emotional distress damages allowed for trespass with aggravated circumstances).

Benefit and Causation. What if the defendant's trespass benefits the plaintiff? *See* Longenecker v. Zimmerman, 175 Kan. 719, 267 P.2d 543 (1954) (defendant liable in trespass for topping plaintiff's trees, even though action was reasonable precaution beneficial to both parties). What if the defendant merely leaves something on the land beyond the period for which the defendant had permission to leave it, and it causes an injury? *See* Rogers v. Board of Road Comrs., 319 Mich. 661, 30 N.W.2d 358 (1947) (trespass liability for snow-fence anchor post left on land into summer months, causing injury). Courts may extend causation to a greater degree for the intentional tort of trespass than for ordinary negligence. *See* Baker v. Shymkiv, 6 Ohio St.3d 151 (1983) (trespassers held liable for heart-attack death of landowner upset at the trespass); Keesecker v. G.M. McKelvey Co., 141 Ohio St. 162, 47 N.E.2d 211 (1943) (trespasser held liable for injury to child who fell through open door trespasser had left open in the course of the trespass); Wyant v. Crouse, 127 Mich. 158, 86 N.W. 527 (1901) (trespasser held liable for destruction of blacksmith shop by fire trespasser had built in the forge).

Exceeding Consent. What if one who has permission to enter the land for one purpose engages in another purpose that the landowner would not have authorized? *See* Copeland v. Hubbard Broadcasting, Inc., 526 N.W.2d 402 (Minn. App. 1995) (trespass liability for television reporter's surreptitious video-recording of veterinary treatment of animal in plaintiff's residence, where reporter gained entry by posing as veterinary student). A landowner may wish to bar a particular person's entry when to do so would implicate civil rights. What is the effect on a landowner's trespass claim, of state and federal statutes that bar discrimination in the provision of public service? *See* Dilworth v. Riner, 343 F.2d 226 (5th Cir. 1965) (members of groups protected by civil rights statutes may enter businesses open to the public for service, without trespass liability in the event that owner unlawfully demands their exit). What is the effect on a landowner's trespass claim against one who has a public statement to make, if the landowner controls an area that First Amendment law construes to be a public forum? *See* PruneYard Shopping Center v. Robins, 447 U.S. 74 (1980) (upholding state constitution's provision protecting public expression at privately owned shopping centers); Hudgens v. N.L.R.B. 424 U.S. 507 (1976) (First Amendment will deem public for expression's purpose, private property that supplants municipal government); Marsh v. Alabama, 326 U.S. 501 (1946) (private company town may be public for First Amendment-expression purposes).

Interference. The above cases raise the question of what constitutes a sufficient interference with exclusive possession of land. Distinguishing what is tangible from what is intangible is one way in which the courts have treated this issue, although as shown above, some authority regards gases and particulates as sufficiently tangible to constitute an entry. *See* Martin v. Reynolds Metals Co., 221 Or. 86, 342 P.2d 790 (Or. 1959). What about nauseating odors and bacteria from a nearby sewage-treatment plant? *See* Brown v. County Commissioners of Scioto County, 87 Ohio App.3d 704, 622 N.E.2d 1153 (1993) (not a trespass claim, although fact issue as to whether it constitutes a nuisance); Spur Indus., Inc., v. Del E. Webb Development Co., 108 Ariz. 178, 494 P.2d 700 (1972) (homeowners entitled to injunction against neighboring cattle feedlot, provided that developer who sold to homeowners offered to pay costs of relocating feedlot). What if the defendant merely shines light on the plaintiff's land? *See* Amphitheaters, Inc. v. Portland Meadows, 184 Or. 336, 198 P.2d 847 (1948) (race-track lights not a trespass).

Nuisance. In these cases of intangible entries, courts clearly prefer nuisance, which asks whether the condition interferes with use and enjoyment of land, over trespass for analyzing the claim. *See* Boomer v. Atlantic Cement Co., 26 N.Y.2d 219, 309 N.Y.S.2d, 257 N.E.2d 870 (1970) (nuisance action requiring defendant cement-plant owner to compensate nearby landowners for plant's dirt, smoke, and vibration); *see also* Armory Park Neighborhood Assn. v. Episcopal Community Services in Arizona, 148 Ariz. 1, 712 P.2d 914 (Ariz. 1985) (upholding preliminary injunction against defendants who drew large numbers of indigent persons to public park for free meals, resulting in litter, trespassing, and other problems for nearby landowners). As the *Bradley* opinion above intimates, the interference must be substantial. Minor annoyances that come with urban living do not establish a nuisance. *See* Karpiak v. Russo, 676 A.2d 270 (Pa. Super. 1996) (noise, smell, and dust of landscaping business); Langan v. Bellinger, 611 N.Y.S.2d 59 (App. Div. 1994) (church bells); Beckman v. Marshall, 85 So.2d 552 (Fla. 1956) (nursery-school noise). Does it matter who is there first? *See* Spur Indus., Inc. v. Del E. Webb Dev. Co., *supra* (enjoining feed-lot operation but requiring complainant new development to pay for feedlot loss); *see also* City of Burbank v. Lockheed Air Terminal Inc., 411 U.S. 624 (1973) (provisions of Noise Control Act of 1972, 42 U.S.C. §§4901-4918, supersede local control). Does nuisance depend on a subjective or objective test of the sensibilities of enjoyment? *See* Layton v. Yankee Caithness Joint Venture, 774 F. Supp. 576 (D. Nev. 1991) (exceptionally sensitive neighbor to geothermal power plant not entitled to nuisance recovery for noise); Impellizerri v. Jamesville Federated Church, 104 Misc.2d 620, 428 N.Y.S.2d 550 (1979) (nuisance claim over music from church carillon denied because not an interference with the ordinary person's enjoyment) ("plaintiffs have a special problem"); *see also* Adkins v. Thomas Solvent Co., 440 Mich 293, 487 N.W.2d 715 (1992) (ungrounded fear of groundwater contamination below plaintiff's land cannot constitute a nuisance); *see also* Restatement (Second) of Torts §821F (1965) (nuisance liability "only to those whom it causes significant harm, of a kind that would be suffered by a normal person").

Airspaces. The above cases suggest that objects entering the "immediate reaches" of the airspace over the land can constitute an entry for trespass purposes. What about air traffic? *See* Restatement (Second) of Torts §159 (air travel is a trespass if it "enters into immediate reaches of the air space next to the land and ... interferes substantially with the others' use and enjoyment of the land"); Hinman v. Pacific Air Transport, 84 F.2d 755 (9th Cir. 1936) (same); *but see* Nestle v. Santa Monica, 6 Cal.3d 920, 496 P.2d 480, 101 Cal. Rptr. 568 (1972) (over-flights are not trespasses) (actions lie in negligence or nuisance); Atkinson v. Bernard, Inc., 223 Or. 624, 355 P.2d 229 (1960) (same). Is there another way to address over-flights that destroy the value of land? *See* Brown v. United States, 73 F.3d 1100 (Fed. Cir. 1996) (Fifth Amendment takings claim for repeated Air Force touch-and-go over-flights); *see also* Loretto v. Teleprompter Manhattan CATV Corp., 458 U.S. 419 (1982) (landowners entitled to Fifth Amendment takings claim for regulations that required landowners to permit cable-television lines to be attached to landowners' buildings); Boomer v. Atlantic Cement Co., 26 N.Y.2d 219, 257 N.E.2d 870, 309 N.Y.S.2d 312 (1970) (inverse condemnation claim for noise and vibration). The advent of inexpensive video-camera-equipped drones substantially increases this question's relevance. Trespass law can help an aggrieved landowner address drone entries, although administrative regulation of drone use will also clarify landowner and drone owner rights.

Beneath the Land. How does trespass law treat subsurface entries under lands? *See* Chance v. BP Chemicals, 77 Ohio St.3d 17, 670 N.E.2d 985 (1996) (injected waste chemicals migrating far below plaintiff's land do not interfere with plaintiff's property rights); Boehringer v. Montalto, 142 Misc. 560, 254 N.Y.S. 276 (1931) (sewer line 150 feet below surface of plaintiff's land not a trespass); *but see* JBG/Twinbrook Metro Ltd. Partnership v. Wheeler, 697 A.2d 898 (Md. 1997) (trespass claim for subsurface gas leakage); Edwards v. Sims, 232 Ky. 791, 24 S.W.2d 619 (1929) (use of cave below plaintiff's land, as tourist attraction, subject to plaintiff's trespass claim); *see generally* Restatement (Second) of Torts §159 (1965) ("a trespass may be committed on, beneath, or above the surface of the earth"). Where a landowner or predecessor has not already sold subsurface mining rights, cases tend to hold that mining below another's land is a trespass, except in some western states where mining interests may follow the vein.

Knowledge

When lawyers encounter a rule in one setting, they must often generalize the rule into a broader statement applicable in other settings. One may state a rule at different levels of specificity. Skillful lawyers recognize a narrow rule's broader relevance, broader rules emanating from specific rules. For example, when a waiter grabs a plate from the hand of a diner whom the waiter refused to serve based on the diner's race, a case opinion may hold satisfied the contact element of the battery tort. A lawyer interested in using the opinion to support another case may have to generalize the rule into something like "an offensive touching of anything closely connected with the plaintiff's body satisfies the contact element of battery." To generalize a rule, substitute appropriate broader terms for the narrow terms the opinion offers—a lexicographic skill.

B. Trespass to Chattels

OBJECTIVE: Given descriptions of situations in which one person uses, misuses, or interferes with another person's personal property, recall and apply the elements of the trespass to chattels tort analyzing whether the facts satisfy those elements, consistent with this section of the text.

Case Study: In the previous case study, the inebriated driver also found a pair of shears in the barn when he woke early the next morning and for a prank cut the long tails off two draft horses stalled in the barn. ***Recall and apply the elements of the trespass to chattels tort to determine whether the horses' owner has a claim against the inebriated driver.***

Trespass to Chattels. Trespass to chattels is the intentional impairment or deprivation of personal property, causing some damage or loss less than the personal property's full or substantial value. Trespass to chattels' elements are similar to those of trespass to land except that trespass to chattels applies to personal property—livestock, vehicles, equipment, and the like—rather than land. Note also that trespass to chattels requires proof of some compensable damage or loss, unlike trespass-to-land actions, which landowners may maintain without proof of damage to the land. *See* Hecht v.

Components Intern., Inc., 22 Misc.3d 360, 370, 867 N.YS.2d 889 (N.Y. Sup.Ct. 2008) (fired chief executive's deleting emails was "harmless intermeddling," not trespass to chattels). Consider the following cases illustrating these points.

Jamgotchian v. Slender
California Court of Appeals
89 Cal.Rptr.3d 122 (2009)

KRIEGLER, J.

Plaintiff and appellant Jerry Jamgotchian..., the owner of a horse named John's Kinda Girl (JKG), contends a triable issue of fact exists as to whether [defendant and appellant George] Slender, a racing steward, is liable for trespass to chattels based on his actions preventing Jamgotchian from retrieving JKG from the Del Mar Race Track grounds and requiring that the horse be raced against Jamgotchian's wishes. We reverse, holding that triable issues of fact exist....

... Jamgotchian filed a complaint against Slender and Mark Glatt, JKG's trainer, for trespass to chattels and injunctive relief based on allegations that they raced JKG against his express instructions. ...

The undisputed evidence submitted in connection with the summary judgment pleadings showed the following facts. Slender has been a racing steward appointed by the California Horse Racing Board (CHRB) for more than 33 years. Jamgotchian is licensed by the CHRB and owns more than 100 thoroughbred race horses, including JKG.

In August 2005, Jamgotchian and Glatt discussed potential races for JKG. They preferred a race scheduled to be held at Del Mar on August 17, 2005. Their second choice was a stakes race in Seattle, Washington on August 21, 2005, for which JKG had been nominated. Their third choice was a stakes race at Del Mar on September 1, 2005. Their fourth choice was a race scheduled to be held at Del Mar on August 14, 2005.

... The deadline to request to withdraw a horse from a race is called the "scratch time." The scratch time for the August 14 race was 9:30 a.m. on August 13, 2005. In general, after the scratch time has passed, a horse may not be entered in another race unless the horse is excused from the first race by the stewards. However, a horse may be scratched from a race and entered into a stakes race without obtaining the permission of the stewards. Glatt would not know whether the August 17 race was going forward before the scratch time for the August 14 race.

In order to get race cards filled and generate additional revenue for the racetrack and the horsemen, it is a long-standing practice of the racing secretary's office to solicit and accept "provisional" entries that allow the licensee to scratch a horse from the race. ... [W]hen the racing secretary's office has accepted a provisional entry, the stewards routinely permit the licensee to scratch the horse. ...

On August 14, 2005, Slender was one of three stewards on the board of stewards which supervised the horse racing meeting at the track. He was the duty steward, which meant he reported early and was responsible for handling entries and scratches before the other stewards arrived.

At 9:30 a.m., Jamgotchian told Glatt that he wanted JKG withdrawn from the August 14 race in order to enter JKG in the stakes race in Seattle. Glatt called and spoke to Slender to request a scratch of JKG from the race. Glatt said JKG had no physical infirmities and was sound and fit to race.

Slender stated: "We are not going to allow any horse owner to control our multi-million-dollar business. You're obligated to run. If you do not race the horse, you are ... being threatened with a 60–day suspension of your license." Glatt responded with disbelief and tried to explain the situation Slender was putting him in, but Slender was steadfast in his decision. ...

Based on information from Glatt, Jamgotchian told Slender that JKG had an injured heel that would be better with a few more days of rest. ...

Slender told Glatt that if he did not saddle and race JKG that day, he would be immediately fined and immediately have his trainer's license suspended for a period of 30 to 60 days. ...

At about 11:00 a.m., Slender called CHRB investigator Douglas Aschenbrenner and asked him to prevent Jamgotchian from taking JKG off the Del Mar grounds. Slender told Aschenbrenner that Jamgotchian wanted to scratch JKG and run the horse somewhere else, but he did not want that. Slender said to go to the barn to make sure the horse did not leave the grounds. ...

At 4:00 p.m., Jamgotchian faxed a letter to the stewards stating that he had learned from Glatt that JKG would not be allowed to leave Del Mar. He asked to make arrangements to have the horse removed within the hour. At 4:15 p.m., Jamgotchian faxed a letter to the stewards again requesting permission to scratch JKG from the race and to remove her from Del Mar. He received no response to the faxes or to telephone messages. ...

Miller arranged for a commercial van company to pick up the horse. Jamgotchian called Glatt at 4:30 p.m. and said he had arranged for a shipping company to pick up the horse. At 4:33 p.m., he sent a fax to the stewards stating that he had a shipping company waiting to pick up JKG and remove her from the Del Mar grounds, but no one had contacted him and authorized her to leave. He pleaded for someone to contact him so that he could get his horse immediately.

At 4:40 p.m., Glatt saddled JKG in the paddock. At 5:00 p.m., JKG raced. Miller saw JKG run the race. Afterward, Miller saw JKG get on the van, which took the horse to Miller's barn at San Luis Rey Downs. Running in the race injured JKG's front foot and caused her to be lame. ...

Jamgotchian contends that a triable issue of fact exists as to whether Slender committed trespass to chattel. We agree.

"Dubbed by Prosser the 'little brother of conversion,' the tort of trespass to chattels allows recovery for interferences with possession of personal property 'not sufficiently important to be classed as conversion, and so to compel the defendant to pay the full value of the thing with which he has interfered.' (Prosser & Keeton, Torts (5th ed.1984) § 14, pp. 85–86.)

"Though not amounting to conversion, the defendant's interference must, to be actionable, have caused some injury to the chattel or to the plaintiff's rights in it. Under California law, trespass to chattels 'lies where an intentional interference with the possession of personal property *has proximately* caused injury.' [Citation omitted.] In cases of interference with possession of personal property not amounting to conversion, 'the owner has a cause of action for trespass or case, *and may recover only the actual damages suffered by reason of the impairment of the property or the loss of its use.*' (Citations omitted.) In modern American law generally, '[t]respass [to chattels] remains as an occasional remedy for minor interferences, *resulting in some damage,* but not sufficiently serious or sufficiently important to amount to the greater tort' of conversion." (Prosser & Keeton, Torts, *supra,* § 15, p. 90, italics added.)

"The Restatement, too, makes clear that some actual injury must have occurred in order for a trespass to chattels to be actionable. Under section 218 of the Restatement Second of Torts, dispossession alone, without further damages, is actionable (see *id.,* par. (a) & com. d, pp. 420–421), but other forms of interference require some additional harm to the personal property or the possessor's interests in it. (*Id.,* pars. (b)-(d).) 'The interest of a possessor of a chattel in its inviolability, unlike the similar interest of a possessor of land, is not given legal protection by an action for nominal damages for harmless intermeddlings with the chattel. In order that an actor who interferes with another's chattel may be liable, his conduct must affect some other and more important interest of the possessor. *Therefore, one who intentionally intermeddles with another's chattel is subject to liability only if his intermeddling is harmful to the possessor's materially valuable interest in the physical condition, quality, or value of the chattel, or if the possessor is deprived of the use of the chattel for a substantial time, or some other legally protected interest of the possessor is affected as stated in Clause (c)....* (Citation omitted.)" (*Intel Corp. v. Hamidi* (2003) 30 Cal.4th 1342, 1350–1351, 1 Cal.Rptr.3d 32, 71 P.3d 296.)

The Restatement 2nd Torts, section 217, provides, "A trespass to a chattel may be committed by intentionally [¶] (a) dispossessing another of the chattel, or [¶] (b) using or intermeddling with a chattel in the possession of another." The Restatement 2nd Torts, section 221, provides that "A dispossession may be committed by intentionally ... barring the possessor's access to a chattel[.]"

A triable issue of fact exists as to whether Slender's conduct in ordering CHRB investigators and race security staff to prevent Jamgotchian from retrieving his horse was a substantial factor in causing Jamgotchian's harm. Had Jamgotchian been permitted to retrieve JKG, the horse would not have been raced and injured. In addition, Slender's threat to suspend Glatt for failing to race the horse would have been easier to challenge had the horse had been retrieved by Jamgotchian prior to the race. It is for the trier of fact to determine whether Slender intentionally interfered with Jamgotchian's right to possession of the JKG in light of Jamgotchian's: arrangements for a van and an alternate trainer to pick up the horse; knowledge that Slender had ordered the security officers at the race track gate to prevent any attempt to remove JKG; and increasingly frantic attempts to secure approval from race officials to remove the horse from the grounds. A reasonable trier of fact could conclude that Jamgotchian was not required to provoke a confrontation to be dispossessed of the horse under the circumstances of the case. ...

The judgment [of dismissal] is reversed. Appellant Jerry Jamgotchian is awarded his costs on appeal.

Intel Corp. v. Hamidi
California Supreme Court
30 Cal.4th 1342, 71 P.3d 296 (2003)

WERDEGAR, J. Intel Corporation (Intel) maintains an electronic mail system, connected to the Internet, through which messages between employees and those outside the company can be sent and received, and permits its employees to make reasonable nonbusiness use of this system. On six occasions over almost two years, Kourosh

Kenneth Hamidi, a former Intel employee, sent e-mails criticizing Intel's employment practices to numerous current employees on Intel's electronic mail system. Hamidi breached no computer security barriers in order to communicate with Intel employees. He offered to, and did, remove from his mailing list any recipient who so wished. Hamidi's communications to individual Intel employees caused neither physical damage nor functional disruption to the company's computers, nor did they at any time deprive Intel of the use of its computers. The contents of the messages, however, caused discussion among employees and managers.

On these facts, Intel brought suit, claiming that by communicating with its employees over the company's e-mail system Hamidi committed the tort of trespass to chattels. The trial court granted Intel's motion for summary judgment and enjoined Hamidi from any further mailings. A divided Court of Appeal affirmed.

After reviewing the decisions analyzing unauthorized electronic contact with computer systems as potential trespasses to chattels, we conclude that under California law the tort does not encompass, and should not be extended to encompass, an electronic communication that neither damages the recipient computer system nor impairs its functioning. Such an electronic communication does not constitute an actionable trespass to personal property, i.e., the computer system, because it does not interfere with the possessor's use or possession of, or any other legally protected interest in, the personal property itself. [Cc] The consequential economic damage Intel claims to have suffered, i.e., loss of productivity caused by employees reading and reacting to Hamidi's messages and company efforts to block the messages, is not an injury to the company's interest in its computers—which worked as intended and were unharmed by the communications—any more than the personal distress caused by reading an unpleasant letter would be an injury to the recipient's mailbox, or the loss of privacy caused by an intrusive telephone call would be an injury to the recipient's telephone equipment. ...

... Intel's claim fails not because e-mail transmitted through the Internet enjoys unique immunity, but because the trespass to chattels tort—unlike the causes of action just mentioned—may not, in California, be proved without evidence of an injury to the plaintiff's personal property or legal interest therein. ...

Hamidi, a former Intel engineer, together with others, formed an organization named Former and Current Employees of Intel (FACE-Intel) to disseminate information and views critical of Intel's employment and personnel policies and practices. FACE-Intel maintained a Web site (which identified Hamidi as Webmaster and as the organization's spokesperson) containing such material. In addition, over a 21-month period Hamidi, on behalf of FACE-Intel, sent six mass e-mails to employee addresses on Intel's electronic mail system. The messages criticized Intel's employment practices, warned employees of the dangers those practices posed to their careers, suggested employees consider moving to other companies, solicited employees' participation in FACE-Intel, and urged employees to inform themselves further by visiting FACE-Intel's Web site. The messages stated that recipients could, by notifying the sender of their wishes, be removed from FACE-Intel's mailing list; Hamidi did not subsequently send messages to anyone who requested removal.

Each message was sent to thousands of addresses (as many as 35,000 according to FACE-Intel's Web site), though some messages were blocked by Intel before reaching employees. Intel's attempt to block internal transmission of the messages succeeded only in part; Hamidi later admitted he evaded blocking efforts by using different sending computers. When Intel, in March 1998, demanded in writing that Hamidi and FACE-Intel stop sending e-mails to Intel's computer system, Hamidi asserted the organization had a right to communicate with willing Intel employees; he sent a new mass mailing in September 1998.

The summary judgment record contains no evidence Hamidi breached Intel's computer security in order to obtain the recipient addresses for his messages; indeed, internal Intel memoranda show the company's management concluded no security breach had occurred.[fn] Hamidi stated he created the recipient address list using an Intel directory on a floppy disk anonymously sent to him. Nor is there any evidence that the receipt or internal distribution of Hamidi's electronic messages damaged Intel's computer system or slowed or impaired its functioning. Intel did present uncontradicted evidence, however, that many employee recipients asked a company official to stop the messages and that staff time was consumed in attempts to block further messages from FACE-Intel. According to the FACE-Intel Web site, moreover, the messages had prompted discussions between "[e]xcited and nervous managers" and the company's human resources department. ...

Though not amounting to conversion, the defendant's interference must, to be actionable, have caused some injury to the chattel or to the plaintiff's rights in it. Under California law, trespass to chattels "lies where an intentional interference with the possession of personal property has proximately caused injury." (Thrifty-Tel, Inc. v. Bezenek (1996) 46 Cal.App.4th 1559, 1566, 54 Cal.Rptr.2d 468, italics added.) In cases of interference with possession of personal property not amounting to conversion, "the owner has a cause of action for trespass or case, and may recover only the actual damages suffered by reason of the impairment of the property or the loss of its use." (Zaslow v. Kroenert, supra, 29 Cal.2d at p. 551, 176 P.2d 1, italics added; [c].) ...

The dispositive issue in this case, therefore, is whether the undisputed facts demonstrate Hamidi's actions caused or threatened to cause damage to Intel's computer system, or injury to its rights in that personal property, such as to entitle Intel to judgment as a matter of law. To review, the undisputed evidence revealed no actual or threatened damage to Intel's computer hardware or software and no interference with its ordinary and intended operation. Intel was not dispossessed of its computers, nor did Hamidi's messages prevent Intel from using its computers for any measurable length of time. Intel presented no evidence its system was slowed or otherwise impaired by the burden of delivering Hamidi's electronic messages. Nor was there any evidence transmission of the messages imposed any marginal cost on the operation of Intel's computers. In sum, no evidence suggested that in sending messages through Intel's Internet connections and internal computer system Hamidi used the system in any manner in which it was not intended to function or impaired the system in any way. ...

Intel connected its e-mail system to the Internet and permitted its employees to make use of this connection both for business and, to a reasonable extent, for their own purposes. In doing so, the company necessarily contemplated the employees' receipt of unsolicited as well as solicited communications from other companies and individuals. That some communications would, because of their contents, be unwelcome to Intel management was virtually inevitable. Hamidi did nothing but use the e-mail system for its intended purpose-to communicate with employees. The system worked as designed, delivering the messages without any physical or functional harm or disruption. These occasional transmissions cannot reasonably be viewed as impairing the quality or value of

Intel's computer system. We conclude, therefore, that Intel has not presented undisputed facts demonstrating an injury to its personal property, or to its legal interest in that property, that support, under California tort law, an action for trespass to chattels.

> *Knowledge*
> If generalizing rules is a lawyer's skill, so too is specifying them. Applying a general rule requires making it specific to the disputed matter. The skill requires a lawyer to substitute narrow terms for broad ones, moving down from a high-level rule to a low-level, specific rule. Take again, for example, the broad statement of the tort-law rule that contact with anything closely connected with the person satisfies battery's contact element. A lawyer with a case in which someone slammed their fist on the hood of a car occupied by the client would re-state the tort-law rule as "striking the hood of an occupied car satisfies the contact element of a battery claim as to the car's occupant." A court may not accept this specification (narrowing) of the tort-law rule, but the lawyer should consider it, to test the rule's fit, considering factors or the rule's goal. Lawyers argue factors and goals within the framework of the specified rule.

C. Conversion

OBJECTIVE: Given descriptions of situations in which one person uses, misuses, or interferes with another person's personal property, recall and apply the elements of the conversion tort analyzing whether the facts satisfy those elements, consistent with this section of the text.

Case Study: A woman lent her pearl necklace to a friend for the friend's job interview. The friend did not return the necklace but instead gave the necklace to her boyfriend to get money to buy crack cocaine. The boyfriend took the necklace to a barber who gave the boyfriend money and marked the necklace for sale in his barbershop. The necklace's owner learned these facts when authorities arrested the boyfriend on drug charges. ***Recall and apply the elements of conversion to determine whether the necklace's owner has that claim against her friend, the boyfriend, and the barber.***

Conversion. As *Intel Corp. v. Hamidi* intimates, conversion relates to trespass to chattels. Conversion is the intentional deprivation of personal property of another. The primary distinction between conversion and trespass to chattels is the degree to which the tortfeasor deprives the personal property's owner of the personal property's use. In trespass to chattels, the tortfeasor deprives the owner of some but not all use of the personal property. The tortfeasor may have taken the personal property for a time before returning it or may have damaged it requiring repair but leaving remaining value. For conversion, the owner must prove that the owner lost all use of the personal property— whether because of its theft, conveyance to another from whom the owner cannot reasonably recover it, or its destruction. Plaintiffs occasionally plead the two torts together, although for tactical reasons the plaintiff may plead only one or the other of the two torts—depending on whether the plaintiff wants the personal property returned or thinks that the personal property has a salvageable value. Businesses will often use conversion claims to resolve disputed claims over equipment that one party has leased, loaned, or conveyed to another, but with damage, depreciation, or no remaining use or value. In such cases, the equipment's owner claims conversion, while the equipment's possessor attempts to convey the equipment back to its owner. The Restatement (Second) of Torts §222A, titled "What Constitutes Conversion," recognizes this rather more functional nature of the conversion tort. The Restatement defines conversion as "an intentional exercise of dominion or control over a chattel which so seriously interferes with the right of another to control it that the actor may justly be required to pay the other the full value of the chattel," and then lists factors determining the conversion claim's justice. Those factors include the extent and duration of the defendant's control over the personal property, the defendant's intent and good faith in controlling it, any damage done to it, and the expense and inconvenience caused to the owner. Consider the following case.

Pearson v. Dodd
United States Court of Appeals, District of Columbia Circuit
410 F.2d 701 (D.C. Cir.), cert. denied, 395 U.S. 947 (1969)

SKELLY WRIGHT, C.J. This case arises out of the exposure of the alleged misdeeds of Senator Thomas Dodd of Connecticut by newspaper columnists Drew Pearson and Jack Anderson. The District Court has granted partial summary judgment to Senator Dodd, appellee here, finding liability on a theory of conversion. … We … reverse its grant of summary judgment for conversion.

The undisputed facts in the case were stated by the District Court as follows: "* * * On several occasions in June and July, 1965, two former employees of the plaintiff, at times with the assistance of two members of the plaintiff's staff, entered the plaintiff's office without authority and unbeknownst to him, removed numerous documents from his files, made copies of them, replaced the originals, and turned over the copies to the defendant Anderson, who was aware of the manner in which the copies had been obtained. The defendants Pearson and Anderson thereafter published articles containing information gleaned from these documents."[fn] …

The District Court ruled that appellants' receipt and subsequent use of photocopies of documents which appellants knew had been removed from appellee's files without authorization established appellants' liability for conversion. We conclude that appellants are not guilty of conversion on the facts shown. …

Conversion is the substantive tort theory which underlay the ancient common law form of action for trover. A plaintiff in trover alleged that he had lost a chattel which he rightfully possessed,[fn] and that the defendant had found it and converted it to his own use. With time, the allegations of losing and finding became fictional, leaving the question of whether the defendant had "converted" the property the only operative one.[fn]

The most distinctive feature of conversion is its measure of damages, which is the value of the goods converted.[fn] The theory is that the "converting" defendant has in some way treated the goods as if they were his own, so that the plaintiff can properly ask the court to decree a forced sale of the property from the rightful possessor to the converter.[fn]

Because of this stringent measure of damages, it has long been recognized that not every wrongful interference with the personal property of another is a conversion.[fn] Where the intermeddling falls short of the complete or very substantial deprivation of possessory rights in the property, the tort committed is not conversion, but the lesser wrong of trespass to chattels.[fn]

The Second Restatement of Torts [§222A(1) (1965)] has marked the distinction by defining conversion as: "* * * An intentional exercise of dominion or control over a chattel which so seriously interferes with the right of another to control it that the actor may justly be required to pay the other the full value of the chattel."[fn] Less serious interferences fall under the Restatement's definition of trespass.

The difference is more than a semantic one. The measure of damages in trespass is not the whole value of the property interfered with, but rather the actual diminution in its value caused by the interference.[fn] More important for this case, a judgment for conversion can be obtained with only nominal damages, whereas liability for trespass to chattels exists only on a showing of actual damage to the property interfered with.[fn] Here the District Court granted partial summary judgment on the issue of liability alone, while conceding that possibly no more than nominal damages might be awarded on subsequent trial. Partial summary judgment for liability could not have been granted on a theory of trespass to chattels without an undisputed showing of actual damages to the property in question.

It is clear that on the agreed facts appellants committed no conversion of the physical documents taken from appellee's files. Those documents were removed from the files at night, photocopied, and returned to the files undamaged before office operations resumed in the morning. Insofar as the documents' value to appellee resided in their usefulness as records of the business of his office, appellee was clearly not substantially deprived of his use of them.

This of course is not an end of the matter. It has long been recognized that documents often have value above and beyond that springing from their physical possession.[fn] They may embody information or ideas whose economic value depends in part or in whole upon being kept secret. The question then arises whether the information taken by means of copying appellee's office files is of the type which the law of conversion protects. The general rule has been that ideas or information are not subject to legal protection,[fn] but the law has developed exceptions to this rule. Where information is gathered and arranged at some cost and sold as a commodity on the market, it is properly protected as property.[fn] Where ideas are formulated with labor and inventive genius, as in the case of literary works[fn] or scientific researches,[fn] they are protected. Where they constitute instruments of fair and effective commercial competition, those who develop them may gather their fruits under the protection of the law.[fn] ...

The question here is not whether appellee had a right to keep his files from prying eyes, but whether the information taken from those files falls under the protection of the law of property, enforceable by a suit for conversion. In our view, it does not. The information included the contents of letters to appellee from supplicants, and office records of other kinds, the nature of which is not fully revealed by the record. Insofar as we can tell, none of it amounts to literary property, to scientific invention, or to secret plans formulated by appellee for the conduct of commerce. Nor does it appear to be information held in any way for sale by appellee, analogous to the fresh news copy produced by a wire service.[fn]

Appellee complains, not of the misappropriation of property bought or created by him, but of the exposure of information either (1) injurious to his reputation or (2) revelatory of matters which he believes he has a right to keep to himself. Injuries of this type are redressed at law by suit for libel and invasion of privacy respectively, where defendants' liability for those torts can be established under the limitations created by common law and by the Constitution.[fn]

Because no conversion of the physical contents of appellee's files took place, and because the information copied from the documents in those files has not been shown to be property subject to protection by suit for conversion, the District Court's ruling that appellants are guilty of conversion must be reversed.

Knowledge

In some instances, proving a claim or satisfying one of its elements requires evaluating and weighing factors. Factors are various non-exclusive considerations that, by their accumulation or weight, tend to make the proof of a claim or element more or less likely. The experienced lawyer knows that one factor, satisfied by the strongest of evidence, may alone satisfy the element or claim that several factors address. The experienced lawyer knows just as well that an accumulation of factors, satisfied by only weak evidence, may yet prove the element or claim. Weighing factors requires (1) recalling or developing a list of factors, followed by (2) aligning case facts with the factors to which they relate. In effect, the lawyer makes successive approximations matching facts to law.

INQUIRY

Identifying the Converter. In claiming conversion, must the plaintiff show that the defendant took possession of the personal property? *See* Kelley v. LaForce, 288 F.3d 1 (1st Cir. 2002) (defendant police officers subject to claim for depriving bar owner of personal property inside the bar when the police officers locked the bar owner out). What if the defendant took the property but conveyed it to another—against whom does the owner have a conversion claim? The traditional rule is that the owner of converted property may pursue conversion claims against either or both of the original converter and subsequent holders of the property, even if the subsequent holders purchased the property in good faith. The rule may first seem counterintuitive and unfair to the property's purchaser. Yet the rule in many cases places the burden where it belongs—on the purchaser to be sure to buy only from reputable sellers. One who purchases an expensive watch at a fraction of its value from a street-corner seller (a fence for thieves) should not have a claim superior to the watch's rightful owner. A convenient way to remember the rule is that thieves do not obtain and cannot convey good title. What, though, if the purchaser buys from an ordinary merchant in that kind of good, to whom the owner entrusted the good (perhaps for safekeeping or repair)? The Uniform Commercial Code would grant the purchaser good title in such cases—presumably because the owner had the better opportunity to judge the converter's reliability and would more likely have a collectable claim against the identifiable converter. The same would be true in cases in which a person obtains personal property by misrepresentation. In those cases, title transfers. One who purchases property from a defrauder has good title and is not liable in conversion. The defrauded party's claim is against the defrauder, for misrepresentation, not conversion.

Good Faith. Considering the issue from another perspective, is the alleged converter's good faith relevant? *See* Baer v. Slater, 261 Mass. 153, 158 (N.E. 328 (1927) (bailee liable in conversion to bailor for delivering goods to credible impostor); Potomac

Ins. Co. v. Nickson, 64 Utah 395, 231 P. 445 (1924) (conversion liability of garage for mis-delivering vehicle to person presenting stolen ticket). Law ordinarily requires bailees to deliver to the right person, failing which they may be liable in conversion. Recall that the converter's fault is not an element of a conversion claim. See the case cited above in the section on intent, Ranson v. Kitner, 31 Ill. App. 241 (1889), in which the defendant shot a dog reasonably believing that it was a wolf and yet was liable in conversion.

Interference. What is a sufficient interference with a chattel to make the claim one for conversion rather than trespass to chattels? *See* Zaslow v. Kroenert, 29 Cal.2d 541, 176 P.2d 1 (1946) (defendant who unlawfully removed personal property but timely informed plaintiff of its location not liable in conversion); Borg & Powers Furniture Co. v. Reiling, 213 Minn. 539, 7 N.W.2d 310 (1942) (conversion where defendant moves plaintiff's furniture to warehouse but fails to notify plaintiff); Hicks Rubber Co., Distributors v. Stacy, 133 S.W.2d 249 (Tex. Civ. App. 1939) (conversion where defendant stores plaintiff's furniture in defendant's name, intending to keep it); McCurdy v. Wallblom Furniture & Carpet Co., 94 Minn. 326, 102 N.W. 873 (1905) (conversion where defendant stores plaintiff's furniture which fire destroys before plaintiff can recover it). Conversion claims can readily arise in the landlord-tenant context or in other instances where landowners have an interest in removing another's personal property from the premises. Does a conversion occur when a person whom the owner initially authorized to use the personal property keeps it over-long or uses it for an unauthorized purpose? *See* Swish Mfg. Southeast v. Manhattan Fire & Marine Ins., 675 F.2d 1218 (11th Cir. 1982) (conversion for using aircraft to transport contraband rather than, as authorized, passengers); Doolittle v. Shaw, 92 Iowa 348, 60 N.W. 621 (1894) (driving horse miles beyond the authorized destination not a conversion where horse was not injured); *but see* Baxter v. Woodward, 191 Mich. 379, 158 N.W. 137 (1916) (conversion where horse injured in taking it beyond the authorized distance).

Personal Property. Do medical patients have a conversion claim when treating or examining care providers use patient tissue for their own research and commercial purposes? *See* Moore v. Regents of the Univ. of California, 51 Cal.3d 120, 271 Cal. Rptr. 146, 793 P.2d 479 (1990) (no conversion claim, but medical care providers have duties to disclose other purposes of the treatment and examination that may affect the patient's decision to permit them). Do family members have a conversion claim for the unauthorized harvesting of body parts from a deceased loved one? *See* Wint v. Alabama Eye & Tissue Bank, 675 So.2d 383 (Ala. 1996) (affirming dismissal of woman's conversion suit for unauthorized removal of her deceased husband's eyes, where insufficient evidence existed as to who took the eyes, and the claim was time-barred); Whaley v. County of Tuscola, 58 F.3d 1111 (6th Cir. 1995) (unconstitutional deprivation of property interest to remove corneas and eyes during autopsy, without authorization). The question of what property one can convert extends beyond the unusual issue of body parts. Can one convert intangible property like electronic records? *See* Thyroff v. Nationwide Mut. Ins. Co., 8 N.Y.3d 283, 292-293, 864 N.E.2d 1272 (N.Y. Ct. App. 2007) (yes, where indistinguishable from printed documents). A domain name? *See* Kremen v. Cohen, 337 F.3d 1024 (9th Cir. 2003) (plaintiff states conversion claim for deprivation of "sex.com" address). Securities? *See* Herrick v. Humphrey Hardware Co., 73 Neb. 809, 103 N.W. 685 (1905) (stockholder has conversion claim for officer's refusal to record stock transfer on company books). Law-firm files? *See* Parker v. Kowalski & Hirschhorn, 124 Md. App. 447, 722 A.2d 441 (1999) (attorney subject to conversion claim for taking files when changing firms, but firm deprived of files is not entitled to fees the second firm earned on those files).

> *Skills*
>
> Personal injury attorneys typically handle torts cases on a contingency-fee basis under agreements like the one that follows. Choose a student with whom to work on this exercise. One student assume the role of an attorney who is competent in the type of tort claim under consideration and the other the role of the potential client. Discuss the contingency-fee agreement with one another. Explore with one another whether you will enter into the agreement with the other. As you engage one another and negotiate over the agreement, consider your criteria—both attorney and client—for whether to proceed with the representation. Clients may take interest in the one-third fee provision, cost-reimbursement terms and how much the costs will be, how sure the attorney is of the claim, and what happens if the client loses the claim. Clients are making judgments about the attorney's personal character, competence, and diligence. Attorneys take interest in the client's credibility, expectations for the amount of the recovery, and willingness to take the attorney's advice. The ethics of attorney's fees are a subject in another chapter.

FEE AGREEMENT

Client retains Attorneys to represent Client as legal counsel to maintain a civil action for damages in connection with a motor vehicle accident on or about July 28, 2007. Unless otherwise agreed in writing, the representation does include pursuing the personal injury claim arising out of that incident through trial but does not include appeals from orders or judgments in the matter or claims for property-damage collision-coverage insurance benefits. THE TERMS OF THE REPRESENTATION ARE AS FOLLOWS:

This document is the entire agreement and is not modified by oral promises or statements. Attorneys have made no promises or guarantees regarding the outcome of Client's matter. Attorneys will devote their professional skills to Client's matter. Client will cooperate with Attorneys. Client will maintain a current address, failing which Attorneys may terminate this agreement. Client binds Client's personal representatives, conservators, and assigns to this agreement. Attorneys will communicate settlement offers to Client for Client's decision. Attorneys will advance costs (e.g., transcripts, court fees, expert witness fees, process server fees, copying, mail and courier, and travel). Client will reimburse Attorneys for costs. At attorneys' option, costs may be reimbursed from recovery. Client will pay Attorneys one third of the recovery after reimbursing costs. ***If no recovery is made, Client will pay no fee.*** Attorneys have offered Client hourly or per-day fee arrangements that Client has declined. Client approves that Attorneys will share their fee with the referring attorney John Doe. Attorneys may withdraw without cause, in which event Client will owe no fee to Attorneys. If Attorneys withdraw due to Client misconduct or are discharged, then Client will reimburse costs and pay Attorneys at the higher of $175 per hour or one third of the amount last offered by opposing parties. If costs and attorney's fees are recovered, then Attorneys have the option of the costs and attorney's fees or adding the costs and attorneys' fees to the other money recovered and receiving one third. If the recovery includes future payments, the present value of the future payments will be used for purposes of calculating the one-third fee. Attorneys have a lien on Client's file and recovery before reducing owed costs and fees to judgment. Client authorizes Attorneys to pay insurance or other liens or assignments out of the recovery. Attorneys own Client's file except for specifically identified Client property such as stock certificates, personal photographs, original wills, contracts, and unrecorded deeds. Client files will be destroyed without notice to the client five years from the last date of service, except that Client property such as stock certificates, personal photographs, original wills, contracts, and unrecorded deeds will be retained indefinitely for safekeeping or returned to Client if Client has kept Attorneys advised of a current address. Client agrees to pay a reasonable search and copying charge.

ATTORNEYS CLIENT

_____/_____   _____/_____
           dated   dated

Career

Torts I—Practicing Tort Law

> Membership can make a difference in finding employment and succeeding in tort practice. National, state, and local bars have torts-practice sections. Even as a student, you can join those sections to receive their journals, notices, and job postings, and to have access to their practice network and resources. Membership introduces you to a network of professionals. It also gives you standing within that network. Attend torts-practice section meetings and events. Introduce yourself and give your business card to torts practitioners at those meetings and events. Ask them how their tort practice is going, for trends. Torts lawyers attending professional gatherings will often speak much more openly and reflectively about the challenges and successes of their law practice than in proceedings in which they represent a client. List your torts-related memberships on your resume indicating your interest in the field and your recognition that professional fellowship improves your skill.

Chapter IV

INTENTIONAL TORTS—DEFENSES

OBJECTIVE: Given various intentional tort claims for personal injury, identify those claims in which the facts support one or more defenses such as consent, self-defense, or defense of others, consistent with your study of intentional tort defenses in the text.

Case Study: A patron stepped toward a bartender saying threatening words about what he was going to do to the bartender for having offended his girlfriend sitting next to him at the bar. The bartender picked up a beer bottle, gripping it by its neck and raising it to shoulder level in an offensive posture. The patron took another step toward the bartender. The bartender started to take a swing at the patron with the bottle. The girlfriend screamed. The patron managed to knock the bartender's arm aside and slug the bartender in the stomach. ***Identify those claims in which these facts support the defenses of consent, self-defense, or defense of others.***

Legal analysis is not over once the lawyers have evaluated the elements of a tort claim, finding a provable case. The lawyers turn next to defenses. The plaintiff has the burden of proof on the elements of a tort claim—usually by a preponderance of the evidence but occasionally by a higher proof burden like clear-and-convincing evidence. The defendant has the burden of proof on defenses—again, usually by a preponderance of the evidence. That the defendant has the burden of proof on defenses may be why in answers lawyers often title them as *affirmative* defenses. Significantly, the defendant must ordinarily plead defenses in an answer to put the plaintiff on fair notice of that additional dimension to the case. The defendant who fails to plead a defense may lose the right to maintain it. At trial, the defendant would ordinarily be the first party to present proofs on a defense because the defendant, who has the proof burden on defenses, will also have the burden of production—of producing sufficient evidence for the defense to reach the jury. The plaintiff would then have an opportunity to present opposing evidence. In practice, though, claims and defenses can overlap and depend on the same evidence. For example, battery's *harmful or offensive* element and a *consent* defense may both depend on the plaintiff's desire for, expectation of, and response to the defendant's contact. Yet for analysis, keep claims and their elements distinct from defenses.

Defenses to intentional tort claims justify the alleged misconduct. For that reason, law may call intentional-tort defenses *privileges,* implying that the alleged misconduct was instead responsible. For example, the defendant who asserts a consent defense to a battery claim is not arguing that the conduct was wrong but excusable. Rather, the defendant is arguing that the plaintiff desired and expected that the conduct occur. In that respect, intentional-tort defenses tend to be categorical—either/or propositions on which the case resolves for one side or the other in its entirety. By contrast, defenses to unintentional torts (torts of negligence or strict liability) tend to rely on excuses. The contributory or comparative negligence defense is an example, where the defendant is not (by the assertion of the defense) claiming that law justifies the defendant's own conduct but instead blames the plaintiff for contributing to the event that the defendant is in effect (by the assertion of the defense) acknowledging was harmful. Note, then, that contributory or comparative negligence is not traditionally a defense to an intentional tort. That the plaintiff may recover for an intentional tort even if the plaintiff has been careless represents a judgment that the volitional character of an intentional tort makes it more reprehensible than mere carelessness, which is not volitional in character. Some jurisdictions nonetheless recognize a contrary rule permitting comparative negligence as a defense to an intentional tort. Even in those jurisdictions that do not, the plaintiff's carelessness may indirectly support the defendant's other intentional-tort defenses.

This chapter addresses intentional-tort defenses based on the plaintiff's conduct—consent, self defense, defense of others, defense and recovery of property, necessity, discipline, authority of law, and justification. The text treats other defenses in a chapter following the chapters on negligence. All of the defenses in that chapter apply to negligence claims, and several of the defenses in that chapter apply *only* to negligence claims. One of those other defenses, though, also applies to intentional torts—the statute of limitations. Statutes of limitations typically provide for separate limitations periods for intentional torts, often a year or two shorter than the two- to three-year limitations period typical for negligence claims—but in rare cases longer, such as a five-year limitations period in one state for spousal-battery claims. Mich. Comp. L. §600.5806. The immunity defense treated in the chapter following the negligence chapters may apply to intentional-tort claims or may not apply, depending on the state's statutes or common law. Keep in mind when studying the intentional-tort defenses below that other defenses may apply.

> **Skills**
>
> One conventional way for a defendant to plead defenses is in the defendant's formal answer to the complaint, under a title "Affirmative Defenses" immediately following the defendant's paragraph-by-paragraph answers to the complaint's paragraphs. An example follows. Note the counter-claim.
>
> *[caption]*
>
> ### DEFENDANT'S ANSWER, DEFENSES, AND COUNTER-CLAIM
>
> #### Answer
>
> Defendant Dirk Monk answers the complaint of plaintiffs Ted Price and Betty Price as follows:
>
> JURISDICTION AND VENUE
> 1. No contest.
> 2. Admitted.
> 3. Denied as untrue that Mr. and Mrs. Price have stated a claim and are entitled to damages in any amount, but no contest as to the court's jurisdiction and venue.
>
> FACT ALLEGATIONS
> 4. Admitted.
> 5. Admitted.
> 6. Denied as untrue.
> 7. Denied as untrue in the manner and form alleged.
> 8. Denied as untrue in the manner and form alleged.
> 9. Denied as untrue.

10. The allegation regarding alcohol is denied as untrue. Admitted that Mr. Monk is over six feet tall, but denied as untrue that Mr. Monk presented any threat to Mr. or Mrs. Price.

11. No contest as to age or height of Mr. and Mrs. Price, leaving them to their proofs.

11. Denied as untrue in the manner and form alleged.

12. Denied as untrue in the manner and form alleged. Mr. Monk defensively raised his hands as Mr. Price approached, and Mr. Price pushed against Mr. Monk's hands.

13. Denied as untrue in the manner and form alleged.

14. Admitted that police came to the scene and that ambulance removed Mr. Price, but denied as untrue that there was any need to "restore order" and that Mr. Monk was in any way responsible for Mr. Price's need for medical treatment that was instead the sole result of actions by Mr. Price.

15. Denied as untrue in the manner and form alleged.

16. Denied as untrue in the manner and form alleged.

17. Denied as untrue in the manner and form alleged.

This reference incorporates the above paragraphs into the following counts.

COUNT I: BATTERY

18. Denied as untrue.

COUNT II: ASSAULT

19. Denied as untrue.

COUNT III: INTENTIONAL INFLICTION OF EMOTIONAL DISTRESS

20. Denied as untrue.

ON THESE GROUNDS, defendant Dirk Monk prays that the Court dismiss plaintiffs Ted and Betty Price's complaint with prejudice and with an award of costs.

Affirmative Defenses

For his separate affirmative defenses, defendant Dirk Monk states:

A. Plaintiffs did not file their complaint within the applicable period of limitations.
B. Plaintiff Ted Price consented to the conduct about which he now complains.
C. Mr. Monk's acts were in self-defense.
D. Mr. Monk's acts were in recovery of his property.
E. Mr. Monk reserves additional affirmative defenses pending discovery.

ON THESE DEFENSES, defendant Dirk Monk prays that the Court dismiss plaintiffs Ted and Betty Price's complaint with prejudice and an award of costs.

Counter-Claim

For his counter-claim, defendant Dirk Monk complains against plaintiff Ted Price saying:

COUNT I: BATTERY

1. Mr. Price aggressively ran against Mr. Monk while shouting profanities, with no cause or excuse, and out of confusion and misunderstanding.

2. Mr. Price's actions were intentional and caused contact between them that was offensive to Mr. Monk.

ON THESE GROUNDS, defendant Dirk Monk prays that the court grant judgment in his favor and against plaintiff Ted Price for all damages to which Mr. Monk is found entitled, together with an award of interest, costs, and attorney's fees.

[signature block for defense counsel]

A. Consent

Consent involves a plaintiff's conduct indicating plaintiff's agreement that the defendant's alleged misconduct occur or plaintiff's willingness to accept it without legal recourse. That tort law recognizes consent as a defense indicates the value we place on personal liberty and autonomy—that people should, to a point, do as they wish, when they are hurting only themselves and, possibly, others who wish hurt with them. Yet more to the point, the defense of consent reflects a matter of personal responsibility—that one who consents to conduct should not later complain of its foreseeable consequences. Consent can be either express or implied—expressed through what the plaintiff purposefully communicates or reasonably implied from the plaintiff's actions within the circumstances. Law evaluates consent from the objective standpoint of the reasonable observer under the circumstances, not from the subjective standpoint of the plaintiff or the defendant. When the plaintiff behaves in a way that the reasonable person would construe to be consent, law holds the plaintiff has consented. Similarly, law will not accept that it appeared to the defendant as if the plaintiff had consented, if the plaintiff's conduct would have indicated to the reasonable person that the plaintiff was objecting. As suggested above, law may treat consent as a defense or in the plaintiff's prima-facie case as a question of the conduct's harmfulness or offensiveness (with respect to battery) or whether it was authorized (with respect to false imprisonment and trespass claims). In that respect, the defendant who fails to assert consent as a defense may be able to present the same evidence and make similar arguments within the plaintiff's case. Consider the following cases.

O'Brien v. Cunard S.S. Co.
Massachusetts Supreme Court
154 Mass. 272, 28 N.E. 266 (1891)

KNOWLTON, J. This case present[s the question of] whether there was any evidence to warrant the jury in finding that the defendant, by any of its servants or agents, committed an assault on the plaintiff.... . [T]he plaintiff relied on the fact that the surgeon who was employed by the defendant vaccinated her on ship-board, while she was on her passage from Queenstown to Boston. On this branch of the case the question is whether there was any evidence that the surgeon used force upon the plaintiff against her will. In determining whether the act was lawful or unlawful, the surgeon's conduct must be considered in connection with the surrounding circumstances. If the plaintiff's behavior was such as to indicate consent on her part, he was justified in his act, whatever her unexpressed feelings may have been. In determining whether she consented, he could be guided only by her overt acts and the manifestations of her feelings. [Cc] It is undisputed that at Boston there are strict quarantine regulations in regard to the examination of emigrants, to see that they are protected from small-pox by vaccination, and that only those persons who hold a certificate from the medical officer of the steam-ship, stating that they are so protected, are permitted to land without detention in quarantine, or vaccination by the port physician. It appears that the defendant is accustomed to have its surgeons vaccinate all emigrants who desire it, and who are not protected by previous vaccination, and give them a certificate which is accepted at quarantine as evidence of their protection. Notices of the regulations at quarantine, and of the willingness of the ship's medical officer to vaccinate such as needed vaccination, were posted about the ship in various languages, and on the day when the operation was performed the surgeon had a right to presume that she and the other women who were vaccinated understood the importance and purpose of vaccination for those who bore no marks to show that they were protected. By the plaintiff's testimony, which, in this particular, is undisputed, it appears that about 200 women passengers were assembled below, and she understood from conversation with them that they were to be vaccinated; that she stood about 15 feet from the surgeon, and saw them form in a line, and pass in turn before him; that he "examined their arms, and, passing some of them by, proceeded to vaccinate those that had no mark;" that she did not hear him say anything to any of them; that upon being passed by they each received a card, and went on deck; that when her turn came she showed him her arm; he looked at it, and said there was no mark, and that she should be vaccinated; that she told him she had been vaccinated before, and it left no mark; "that he then said nothing; that he should vaccinate her again;" that she held up her arm to be vaccinated; that no one touched her; that she did not tell him she did not want to be vaccinated; and that she took the ticket which he gave her, certifying that he had vaccinated her, and used it at quarantine. She was one of a large number of women who were vaccinated on that occasion, without, so far as appears, a word of objection from any of them. They all indicated by their conduct that they desired to avail themselves of the provisions made for their benefit. There was nothing in the conduct of the plaintiff to indicate to the surgeon that she did not wish to obtain a card which would save her from detention at quarantine, and to be vaccinated, if necessary, for that purpose. Viewing his conduct in the light of the surrounding circumstances, it was lawful; and there was no evidence tending to show that it was not. The ruling of the court on this part of the case was correct. …

Exceptions overruled.

Koffman v. Garnett
Virginia Supreme Court
574 S.E.2d 258 (Va. 2003)

LACY, J. In this case we consider whether the trial court properly dismissed the plaintiffs' second amended motion for judgment for failure to state causes of action for gross negligence, assault, and battery. …

In the fall of 2000, Andrew W. Koffman, a 13-year old middle school student at a public school in Botetourt County, began participating on the school's football team. It was Andy's first season playing organized football, and he was positioned as a third-string defensive player. James Garnett was employed by the Botetourt County School Board as an assistant coach for the football team and was responsible for the supervision, training, and instruction of the team's defensive players.

The team lost its first game of the season. Garnett was upset by the defensive players' inadequate tackling in that game and became further displeased by what he perceived as inadequate tackling during the first practice following the loss.

Garnett ordered Andy to hold a football and "stand upright and motionless" so that Garnett could explain the proper tackling technique to the defensive players. Then Garnett, without further warning, thrust his arms around Andy's body, lifted him "off his feet by two feet or more," and "slamm[ed]" him to the ground. Andy weighed 144 pounds, while Garnett weighed approximately 260 pounds. The force of the tackle broke the humerus bone in Andy's left arm. During prior practices, no coach had used physical force to instruct players on rules or techniques of playing football.

… [Andy's father, as Andy's next friend,] alleged that Andy was injured as a result of Garnett's simple and gross negligence and intentional acts of assault and battery. Garnett filed a demurrer …, asserting that the second amended motion for judgment did not allege sufficient facts to support a lack of consent to the tackling demonstration and, therefore, did not plead causes of action for either gross negligence, assault, or battery. The trial court dismissed the action, finding that … the facts alleged were insufficient to state causes of action for gross negligence, assault, or battery because the instruction and playing of football are "inherently dangerous and always potentially violent." …

The disparity in size between Garnett and Andy was obvious to Garnett. Because of his authority as a coach, Garnett must have anticipated that Andy would comply with his instructions to stand in a non-defensive, upright, and motionless position. Under these circumstances, Garnett proceeded to aggressively tackle the much smaller, inexperienced student football player, by lifting him more than two feet from the ground and slamming him into the turf. According to the Koffmans' allegations, no coach had tackled any player previously so there was no reason for Andy to expect to be tackled by Garnett, nor was Andy warned of the impending tackle or of the force Garnett would use.

As the trial court observed, receiving an injury while participating in a tackling demonstration may be part of the sport. The facts alleged in this case, however, go beyond the circumstances of simply being tackled in the course of participating in organized football. Here Garnett's knowledge of his greater size and experience, his instruction implying that Andy was not to take any action to defend himself from the force of a tackle, the force he used during the tackle, and Garnett's previous practice of not personally using force to demonstrate or teach football technique could lead a reasonable person to conclude that, in this instance, Garnett's actions were imprudent and were taken in utter disregard for the safety of the player involved. …

The Koffmans' second amended motion for judgment does not include an allegation that Andy had any apprehension of an immediate battery. This allegation cannot be supplied by inference because any inference of Andy's apprehension is discredited by the affirmative allegations that Andy had no warning of an imminent forceful tackle by Garnett. The Koffmans argue that a reasonable inference of apprehension can be found "in the very short period of time that it took the coach to lift Andy into the air and throw him violently to the ground." At this point, however, the battery alleged by the Koffmans was in progress. Accordingly, we find that the pleadings were insufficient as a matter of law to establish a cause of action for civil assault.

The second amended motion for judgment is sufficient, however, to establish a cause of action for the tort of battery. The Koffmans pled that Andy consented to physical contact with players "of like age and experience" and that neither Andy nor his parents expected or consented to his "participation in aggressive contact tackling by the adult coaches." Further, the Koffmans pled that, in the past, coaches had not tackled players as a method of instruction. Garnett asserts that, by consenting to play football, Andy consented to be tackled, by either other football players or by the coaches.

Whether Andy consented to be tackled by Garnett in the manner alleged was a matter of fact. Based on the allegations in the Koffmans' second amended motion for judgment, reasonable persons could disagree on whether Andy gave such consent. Thus, we find that the trial court erred in holding that the Koffmans' second amended motion for judgment was insufficient as a matter of law to establish a claim for battery.

For the above reasons, we will reverse the trial court's judgment that the Koffmans' second amended motion for judgment was insufficient as a matter of law to establish the causes of actions for gross negligence and battery and remand the case for further proceedings consistent with this opinion.[fn]   [The court permitted the Koffmans to pursue a claim for punitive damages.]

Reversed and remanded.

Duncan v. Scottsdale Medical Imaging, Ltd.
Arizona Supreme Court
205 Ariz. 306, 70 P.3d 435 (2003)

JONES, C.J. ... We granted review of two questions raised by petitioner, Martha Duncan, to determine whether the trial court and court of appeals erred in dismissing Duncan's battery claim against respondent, Scottsdale Medical Imaging ("SMI")... .

SMI performed a magnetic resonance imaging ("MRI") examination on Duncan on June 19, 1998. The procedure was performed at Scottsdale Memorial Hospital North. Duncan required sedation due to a back condition that would not allow her to lie still for the duration of the MRI procedure. On the day of the procedure, Duncan spoke by telephone to an SMI nurse. Duncan told the nurse she would only accept demerol or morphine for sedation and no other drug. The nurse assured Duncan that only demerol or morphine would be administered.

On the day of the procedure, Duncan asked Nurse Gary Fink, allegedly an employee of SMI, what drug she would be given. Nurse Fink said it was fentanyl, a synthetic drug similar to demerol and morphine. Duncan expressly rejected fentanyl, again stating that she did not want to receive anything but demerol or morphine. She repeated this request three separate times and asked Nurse Fink to call her doctor to discuss the medication or reschedule the MRI. Duncan finally agreed to proceed when Nurse Fink told her the medication had been changed to morphine. Duncan later learned that Nurse Fink, contrary to express understanding, had actually given her fentanyl. The administration of fentanyl led to serious complications, including severe headache, projectile vomiting, breathing difficulties, post-traumatic stress disorder, and vocal cord dysfunction.

Duncan sued SMI and Hospital Radiologists, Ltd. ("defendants"), alleging she informed defendants and/or their agents that she suffered allergic reactions to certain medications and that she specifically instructed that she was not to be given any synthetic drugs. Duncan alleged that defendants and/or their agents administered fentanyl, through injection, despite assuring her that the proper medication was being used. ...

Duncan then moved for summary judgment on the issue of battery, asking the trial court to allow her claim to proceed outside the MMA [(the state's medical malpractice act)] without the need to present expert testimony on the standard of care. SMI contended the MMA barred the battery claim and cross-moved for summary judgment, seeking dismissal of the so-called malpractice claim because Duncan failed to name an expert witness to testify that SMI's treatment fell below standard and that such failure was the cause of injury. The trial court denied Duncan's motion and granted SMI's motion, holding that evidence of the applicable standard of care and causation was essential to the claim. ...

We must first determine whether the administration of a drug against a patient's express wishes constitutes a battery under Arizona law. An actor is subject to liability to another for battery if the actor intentionally engages in an act that results in harmful or offensive contact with the person of another. See Restatement (Second) of Torts §§ 13, 18

(1965) (hereafter "Restatement"). The law is well established that a health care provider commits a common law battery on a patient if a medical procedure is performed without the patient's consent. [C] A battery claim is defeated, however, when consent is given. See Restatement §§ 13 cmt. d, 18 cmt. f, 892-892D. Thus, the central question in a case of medical battery is whether the patient has effectively given his or her consent to the procedure. ...

Courts generally recognize two theories of liability for unauthorized medical treatment or therapy rendered by physicians to their patients: a traditional intentional tort claim for battery and a negligence claim for lack of informed consent. [C] ... As explained by the California Supreme Court in Cobbs v. Grant, battery and informed consent theories apply in different situations: "The battery theory should be reserved for those circumstances when a doctor performs an operation to which the patient has not consented. When the patient gives permission to perform one type of treatment and the doctor performs another, the requisite element of deliberate intent to deviate from the consent given is present. However, when the patient consents to certain treatment and the doctor performs that treatment but an undisclosed inherent complication with a low probability occurs, no intentional deviation from the consent given appears; rather, the doctor in obtaining consent may have failed to meet his due care duty to disclose pertinent information. In that situation the action should be pleaded in negligence." 8 Cal.3d 229, 104 Cal.Rptr. 505, 502 P.2d 1, 8 (1972). ...

The court of appeals found that Duncan's battery claim should fail because she consented to receive the injection. We disagree. Her general authorization of an injection does not defeat her battery claim because her consent was limited to certain drugs. Duncan explicitly conditioned her consent on the use of morphine or demerol and rejected the use of any other drug. Conduct involving the use of a sedative other than morphine or demerol, contrary to explicit instruction and understanding, cannot be viewed as consensual.

The Restatement requires that consent, to be effective, must be "to the particular conduct, or substantially the same conduct." Restatement § 892A (2)(b). The terms and reasonable implications of the consent given determine the scope of the particular conduct covered. Restatement § 892A cmt. d. ...

The relevant inquiry here is not whether the patient consented to an injection; the issue is whether the patient consented to receive the specific drug that was administered. Duncan could have given broad consent to the administration of any painkiller, but she gave specific instructions that she would accept only morphine or demerol and nothing else. We hold that when a patient gives limited or conditional consent, a health care provider has committed a battery if the evidence shows the provider acted with willful disregard of the consent given. [C] ...

Even assuming arguendo that there was consent to this procedure, there would remain the question of whether that consent was obtained by misrepresentation and thus invalid. ...

According to Restatement § 892B(2), consent is ineffective if obtained by another's misrepresentation: "If the person consenting to the conduct of another is induced to consent by a substantial mistake concerning the nature of the invasion of his interests or the extent of the harm to be expected from it and the mistake is known to the other or is induced by the other's misrepresentation, the consent is not effective for the unexpected invasion or harm." ... Accordingly, we hold that if a patient's consent is obtained by a health care provider's fraud or misrepresentation, a cause of action for battery is appropriate. [C] ...

Duncan's evidence supports the claim for battery because she alleges SMI and/or its agents administered fentanyl without consent. ...

We vacate the court of appeals' memorandum decision, reverse the judgment of the trial court, and remand the case to the trial court for further proceedings consistent with this opinion.

Practice

The lawyer, who had practiced personal injury law for ten years, was making his first hospital visit to a potential client. As he got off the elevator, he smiled to himself, thinking again of scenes from *The Rainmaker* and wondering, "Has it come to this?" But the potential client's husband, who had located the lawyer's name in the telephone book, had already been to the lawyer's office. His wife had a fractured hip and life-threatening bleeding from a severe auto accident, and was not going anywhere for weeks. She just wanted to meet her lawyer and sign the contingency fee agreement so that the lawyer could get started on her case. She had been on her way to work early one morning when her car was read-ended by a drunken young woman who was heading off to buy drugs, in a car the young woman had no permission to use, while driving on a license already suspended for drunken driving. The lawyer knew from the potential client's husband that his wife was having a hard time dealing with a life shattered by such irresponsibility—that in this hospital visit his wife would have hard questions not only about tort law but about a criminal justice system that seemed not yet to have worked.

INQUIRY

Medical Treatment. As the foregoing case suggests, consent can be a significant issue with respect to providing medical care, when the care results in injury from a risk associated with the procedure but not disclosed to the patient. This text treats those lack-of-informed-consent cases in the chapter on medical malpractice. The issue of consent as a defense is clearest in those cases when the medical treatment meets the standard of care, no malpractice claim exists, and the plaintiff's only recourse is through a battery claim. Does it make any difference to the claim if the plaintiff benefited by the unauthorized medical treatment? *See* Pugsley v. Privette, 220 Va. 892, 263 S.E.2d 69 (1980) (no consent where plaintiff permitted operation only if her own physician attended, but he did not attend); Mohr v. Williams, 95 Minn. 261, 104 N.W. 12 (1905) (ear specialist liable for extending treatment to other ear without patient's consent, while patient was under general anesthetic) (remanded for retrial of excessive jury verdict). The *Mohr* case may indicate the difference that the beneficence of the treatment makes. The first trial resulted in a $14,322.50 jury verdict that the court held excessive. The retrial resulted in a $39 verdict that no party appealed. What are the damages in battery when medical-care providers violate a patient's DNR (do not resuscitate) order? *See* Campbell v. Delbridge, 670 N.W.2d 108 (Iowa 2003) (emotional distress damages); Anderson v. St. Francis-St. George Hosp., Inc., 77 Ohio St.3d 82, 671 N.E.2d 225 (1996) (nominal damages only).

Capacity. To give valid consent, a person must have sufficient mental capacity to understand the nature of the conduct to which the person is consenting—and its attendant consequences and risks. A mentally disabled or incapacitated person may not be able to give consent. *See* Restatement (Second) of Torts §59, Comment *a* (1965) (intoxication may prevent consent); *see also* Reavis v. Slominski, 551 N.W.2d 528 (Neb. 1996) (approving plaintiff's request for a jury instruction that plaintiff's consent to intercourse could be ineffectual because of childhood sexual abuse). Could a person be incapable of *withholding* consent? An example is Miller v. Rhode Island Hosp., 625 A.2d 778 (R.I. 1993), where the case held that the defendant physicians properly ignored the drunken plaintiff's objections to an emergency surgery because the plaintiff lacked the capacity to withhold consent. The plaintiff's intoxicated condition may nullify either the giving or the withholding of consent to conduct not directly related to the activities surrounding the intoxication—meaning, on the other hand, that the plaintiff's voluntary intoxication is probably consent to its obvious and necessary consequences. What might those be?

Substituted Consent. Who must consent to protect medical care providers from battery claims, when a child needs medical treatment? *See* Kozup v. Georgetown Univ. Hosp., 851 F.2d 437 (D.C. Cir. 1988) (physician must show that there was no time to seek parents' consent to life-saving transfusion for infant); Bonner v. Moran, 126 F.2d 121 (D.C. Cir. 1941) (parent, not minor, must consent); Zoski v. Gaines, 271 Mich. 1, 260 N.W. 99 (1935) (same); Lacey v. Laird, 166 Ohio St. 12, 139 N.E.2d 25 (1956) (same) (minor seeking nose job). What if the parent refuses life-saving treatment for a child? *See* Miller v. HCA, Inc., 118 S.W.3d 758 (Tex. 2003) (parents sue physician for battery for resuscitating premature infant without their consent); In re Sampson, 29 N.Y.2d 900, 328 N.Y.S.2d 686, 278 N.E.2d 918 (1972) (court may overrule parent for life-saving treatment of minor); *but see* In re Green, 448 Pa. 338, 292 A.2d 387 (1972) (court may not overrule parent). What if the parent insists that one child be a transplant donor for another? *See* Hart v. Brown, 29 Conn. Supp. 368, 289 A.2d 386 (1972) (parent can consent, but court review wise); Strunk v. Strunk, 445 S.W.2d 145 (Ky. 1969) (guardian may consent to donation of incompetent ward's organ if doing so would benefit incompetent). May a parent grant consent for a child to be part of medical research that will not help the child and risks the child's injury? *See* Grimes v. Kennedy Krieger Institute, Inc., 366 Md. 29, 782 A.2d 807 (2001) (no).

Emergencies. How does the law treat consent to emergency medical care? Will the law hold a medical-care provider liable in tort for treating a patient whose injury or youth prevents the physician from obtaining the patient's consent? *See* Luka v. Lowrie, 171 Mich. 122, 136 N.W.1106 (1912) (physician not liable for amputating unconscious patient's crushed foot, where procedure was life-saving). The medical care provider may act without consent if the patient cannot give consent, death or serious injury will result without treatment, a reasonable person would consent, and the provider has no reason to believe that the patient would withhold consent. What if the patient refuses necessary treatment that the reasonable person would accept? *See* Schloendorff v. Society of New York Hosp., 211 N.Y. 125, 105 N.E. 92 (1914) (physician liable for unauthorized removal of tumor that patient had specifically forbid, during exploratory surgery the patient had authorized); *see also* Stamford Hosp. v. Vega, 236 Conn. 646, 674 A.2d 821 (1996) (competent patient may refuse life-saving transfusion); In re Osborne, 294 A.2d 372 (D.C. App. 1972) (bedside hearing confirms patient's refusal to accept life-saving transfusion under any circumstances); Thor v. Superior Court, 5 Cal.4th 725, 855 P.2d 375, 21 Cal. Rptr.2d 357 (1993) (adult serving life prison sentence entitled to refuse life-saving medical care); *but see* Application of the President and Directors of Georgetown

College, 331 F.2d 1000 (D.C. Cir. 1964) (plaintiff accepts judge's order for transfusion for plaintiff who refused to authorize it).

Limitations on Consent. What if the patient consents to treatment only by certain care providers and forbids treatment by others? *See* Cohen v. Smith, 269 Ill. App.3d 1087, 648 N.E.2d 329 (1995) (male nurse subject to battery liability for seeing and touching plaintiff who had expressed religious belief that she should not be seen unclothed or touched by males). What if the patient limits consent to a surgery to the surgeon's using family members' blood for any transfusion? *See* Ashcraft v. King, 278 Cal. Rptr. 900 (Cal. Ct. App. 1991) (recognizing claim when use of non-family member blood resulted in plaintiff's contracting HIV). What can a medical care provider do to minimize hindsight disputes over consent? *See* Rothe v. Hull, 352 Mo. 926, 180 S.W.2d 7 (1944) (patient's execution of standard consent form sufficient for physician to do what the physician believes is necessary). Whose job is it to get the consent—the physician or hospital? *See* Ward v. Lutheran Hosps. & Homes Soc. Of Amer., Inc., 963 P.2d 1031 (Alaska 1998) (hospitals do not owe duty to independent physician's patients to obtain consent for that physician's treatment). When should a care provider obtain consent? *See* Perry v. Shaw, 106 Cal. Rptr.2d 70 (Cal. Ct. App. 2001) (consent ineffective when patient was heavily medicated for surgical procedure when consent was obtained and had refused procedure twice before).

Deceit in Obtaining Consent. As the above cases suggest, that the defendant engaged in deceit is a plaintiff's common response when the defendant argues the plaintiff's consent. Imagination seems to be the only limit to man's capability for deception. *See* Sanchez-Scott v. Alza Pharmaceuticals, 86 Cal. App. 4th 365, 103 Cal. Rptr.2d 410 (2001) (no consent to drug salesman's witnessing plaintiff's breast exam, where doctor introduced salesman not as salesman but as someone following the doctor's work); Hogan v. Tavzel, 660 So.2d 350 (Fla. App. 1995) (battery liability for not revealing genital warts before sex); Neal v. Neal, 125 Idaho 617, 873 P.2d 871 (1994) (jury question whether wife has battery claim against husband for consensual intimate relations between them while husband was having an affair); Barbara A. v. John G., 145 Cal. App.3d 369, 193 Cal. Rptr. 422 (1983) (man who falsely tells woman he cannot get her pregnant, knowing statement is false, and in order to induce sexual relationship, subject to liability for woman's ectopic pregnancy); Commonwealth v. Gregory, 132 Pa. Super. 507, 1 A.2d 501 (1938) (no consent where man induces woman to disrobe for examination by calling on her while representing himself to be a doctor, when man was only a doctor of theology). What if the deception involves unhealthy ingredients of a consumable product? *See* Naegele v. R.J. Reynolds Tobacco Co., 50 P.3d 769 (Cal. 2002) (summary dismissal of smoker's fraud claim reversed); Commonwealth v. Stratton, 114 Mass. 303, 19 Am. Rep. 350 (1873) (no consent where defendant gave plaintiff chocolate candy laced with poison). Does it make any difference if the deceiver provides a useful service in the course of the deception? *See* Taylor v. Johnston, 985 P.2d 460 (Alaska 1999) (person falsely claiming to be licensed physician subject to battery liability even if providing medical treatment). Does it make any difference if the deceiver acts unintentionally and does not know that the statements are deception? *See* McPherson v. McPherson, 712 A.2d 1043 (Me. 1998) (husband not liable for infecting wife with venereal disease where husband did not know, nor should he have known, that he was a carrier).

Scope of Consent. How does one determine the scope or limits of consent? *See* Peters v. Rome City School Dist., 298 A.D.2d 864, 747 N.Y.S.2d 867 (App. Div. 2002) (school held liable for placing child with behavioral problems in a small, padded cell that smelled of urine, even though parents had consented to plan for a time-out room); Ames v. Oceanside Welding & Towing Co., 767 A.2d 677 (R.I. 2001) (implied consent for apartment complex to tow plaintiff's vehicle under policy not to park in street after snowstorm); Wartman v. Swindell, 25 A. 356 (N.J. 1892) (series of practical jokes between plaintiff and defendant may establish implied consent). When, for instance, will tort liability arise for violent conduct within the confines of a violent sport to which the party claiming the tort was a willing participant? *See* Hackbart v. Cincinnati Bengals, 601 F.2d 516, *cert. denied*, 444 U.S. 931 (1979) (angered offensive player strikes blow to the back of a kneeling defensive player's head after conclusion of play) (battery claim remanded for trial, where there was evidence that the conduct violated both the safety rules and general customs of the game); *see also* Greer v. Davis, 921 W.W.2d 325 (Tex. App. 1996) (jury question whether base runner intentionally violated safety rules of game by colliding with catcher guarding base); Knight v. Jewett, 834 P.2d 696 (Cal. 1992) (over-exuberant participant in backyard touch-football game is not liable for violent contact which is not "totally outside the range" of the sport's activity); Gauvin v. Clark, 404 Mass. 450, 537 N.W.2d 94 (1989) (college hockey player not liable for striking another player, where act was not willful in nature); Tavernier v. Maes, 242 Cal. App.2d 532, 51 Cal. Rptr. 575 (1966) (jury issue as to implied consent of plaintiff to defendant's sliding into second base in family softball game, breaking plaintiff's ankle).

Illegal Acts. Can a person consent to an illegal act? *See* Janelsins v. Button, 102 Md. App. 30, 648 A.2d 1039 (1994) (jurisdictions split on whether consent to illegal prizefight is valid, or whether battery claim may be maintained for fighter's injury or death); Hart v. Geysel, 159 Wash. 632, 294 P. 570 (1930) (same); Gaither v. Meacham, 214 Ala. 343, 108 So. 2 (1926) (15-year-old cannot consent to sex in violation of statutory-rape law). The cases generally allow a tort claim by the person giving the invalid consent, if the person was a member of the class whom the legislature intended the statute to protect. *See* Elkington v. Foust, 618 P.2d 37 (Utah 1980) (minor plaintiff may maintain sexual battery claim against stepfather without facing jury instruction on consent).

Consent and Trespass. Is consent a defense to trespass to land? *See* Marsh v. Colby, 39 Mich. 626 (1878) (consent to cross plaintiff's land to fish in ponds established by testimony as to local custom). Do the same limitations apply with respect to consent obtained by deceit? *See* Food Lion, Inc. v. Captial Cities/ABC, Inc., 194 F.3d 505 (4th Cir. 1999) (trespass for broadcaster to send employees to plaintiff's stores, posing as job applicants, in order to video-record meat-handling practices for expose); Copeland v. Hubbard Broadcasting, Inc., 526 N.W.2d 402 (Minn. App. 1995) (trespass liability for reporter posing as veterinarian's assistant, gaining entry to plaintiff's home); *but see* Desnick v. American Broadcasting Co., 44 F.3d 1345 (7th Cir. 1995) (no trespass claim against broadcaster that secretly sent seven test patients to clinics with hidden cameras, where there was no interference with the owner's use of the land).

Duress. When should consent be considered invalid because it is not voluntary (is not really consent)? *See* Vaughn v. Ruoff, 253 F.3d 1124 (8th Cir. 2001) (consent to sterilization may not have been valid where it was obtained by suggestion that it would lead to mildly mentally disabled mother's getting her two children back from foster care); Wende C. v. United Methodist Church, 6 A.D.3d 1047, 776 N.Y.S.2d 390 (App. Div.

2004) (plaintiff engaging in adulterous relationship with her minister held to have consented notwithstanding counseling relationship); Banks v. Fritsch, 39 S.W.3d 474 (Ky. App. 2001) (defendant teacher chains plaintiff student to tree as a joke to prevent student from skipping class); Reavis v. Slominski, 250 Neb. 711, 551 N.W.2d 528 (1996) (jury should be instructed that consent is invalid if plaintiff is substantially impaired from weighing the proposed conduct to which consent is given) (supervisor presses employee to resume sexual relationship); *see also* Miller v. Rhode Island Hosp., 625 A.2d 778 (R.I. 1993) (hospital personnel perform involuntary, life-saving surgery on drunken motor vehicle accident victim, who then sues for battery) (competence to refuse consent depends on ability to appreciate the benefit and risk of the proposed conduct).

> ### *Knowledge*
> Classifying parties and persons—categorizing them or giving them a particular status—is a common method of legal analysis. Status is, in essence, a problem-solving device. The statuses common to parties in a case can be both procedural and substantive in nature. Parties first take on an alignment as plaintiff (the party bringing the suit), defendant (the party responding to the suit), or even third-party defendant (a party brought in by the defendant to answer for what the plaintiff alleges) or cross- or counter-claim defendant. Lawyers and law students must remain constantly aware of which party is on which side of whatever claim or issue is under consideration. But a second kind of classification can be equally important, involving what status the substantive law assigns a party, for instance as a trespasser, public official, private actor, and so on. Keeping in mind each party's procedural alignment (the sides on any given issue) and substantive status (how the law regards them) is a skill critical to law practice.

B. Self-Defense and Defense of Others

While the consent defense reflects a judgment about personal autonomy and responsibility, self-defense reflects a judgment about personal integrity—that individuals must be free to preserve their own life and health against unlawful, intentional efforts to harm or destroy them. *See* Restatement (Second) of Torts §63 (self-defense by force less than that threatening death or serious harm; Restatement (Second) of Torts §65 (self defense by force threatening death or serious harm). Defense of others has the same purpose of preserving personal integrity but adds to it another policy connotation—that individuals should be free, to a point, to intercede and act on behalf of other persons who lack the capacity or will to preserve their own personal integrity. In those respects, self-defense and defense of others are perfect fits for tort law, in that they promote life and health against conduct that threatens it. Yet both self-defense and defense of others are in another respect ill at ease with tort law because they are defenses that authorize and protect harm-causing conduct. This tension defines the conceptual contours and limits of both defenses, while having its influence on tort practice. Tort practitioners often loathe pursuing battery claims in which self-defense will be an issue—and not just because liability for battery claims is typically uninsured. The outcome of *fight* cases in which the one who got the worse of it sues the other (occasionally for serious injuries) is notoriously difficult to predict. They often depend not only on the credibility of witnesses on each side, who vehemently contradict one another, but on the tenuous ordering and re-ordering of what may well have been coincident facts as to who hit whom first. They also readily generate counter-claims. Juror reaction to fight cases may be "a pox on both your houses," reflecting good-sense social policy to settle disputes in court rather than by vigilante violence. For these reasons, self-defense is a significantly greater issue in criminal practice, where its treatment is in much greater depth than would be appropriate here. Consider the following one representative case.

Haeussler v. De Loretto
California Court of Appeals
240 P.2d 654 (Cal. App. 1952)

VALLÉE, J. Appeal by plaintiff from a judgment for defendant in an action for damages for assault and battery. The cause was tried by the court without a jury.

The evidence, stated in the light most favorable to the prevailing litigant, discloses that on May 21, 1950, about 10:30 p.m., plaintiff went to the home of defendant, a neighbor, to inquire about his dog which was missing and which frequently had gone to defendant's home. The dog had been the subject of disagreement between the wives of the parties on several previous occasions. When defendant, in response to plaintiff's knock, opened the door, the dog ran out from inside the house. Defendant testified that plaintiff immediately started talking in a loud tone of voice, told him he did not want defendant or his wife to feed the dog or keep it at their house; that plaintiff kept "waving his hands, and while he talked, his face was pretty flushed and he was pretty excited, like he had been drinking, and he kept arguing with me and one word led to another, and I don't know the man, but I do know of him. I know he had trouble with the Teamster's Union and Frowiss and him beat up a couple of friends of mine, and I got a little afraid, and towards the end, after I had asked him to go three times, and he kept waving his hands, I thought he was going to strike me, and I struck him or pushed him, and I went in and closed the door." Plaintiff called the police but no arrest was made nor was any criminal action had.

The court found that plaintiff precipitated the argument; defendant ordered plaintiff to leave his premises; plaintiff advanced threateningly toward defendant; defendant struck him once; two of plaintiff's teeth were loosened, necessitating dental care; defendant used reasonable force in defense of himself and in removing plaintiff from his premises; plaintiff failed to prove by a preponderance of evidence that defendant used or attempted to use wilful and unlawful force upon the person of plaintiff.

The issue of self defense was pleaded by defendant and litigated. The determination of which of the two parties precipitated the fight, and whether defendant acted in self defense, and whether in so doing he used more force than was reasonably necessary under the circumstances, were questions for the trier of fact. [C] One who is involved in an altercation with another has the right to use such force as is necessary to protect himself from bodily injury, and the question of the amount of force justifiable under the circumstances of a particular case is also one for the trier of fact. [Cc] As the court found that defendant used reasonable force in defense of himself, it necessarily follows the force used was not wilful or unlawful and that plaintiff failed to sustain the burden of proof. Since the conflicts in the evidence were resolved in defendant's favor, and the foregoing narration of the evidence supports the findings, this court may not disturb the judgment.

Affirmed.

INQUIRY

Proof Burdens. In a battery case in which the defendant's harmful actions respond to some perceived threat by the plaintiff (in the nature of self defense), what must plaintiff prove, and who has the burden of proof? *See* Edson v. City of Anaheim, 63 Cal. App.4th 1269, 74 Cal. Rptr.2d 614 (1998) (collecting cases showing that plaintiff's battery claim depends on showing defendant's unreasonable use of force but that defendant has burden of proof on self defense, unless defendant was a police officer, in which case plaintiff has burden of proof). Who decides whether self-defense is an issue? *See* Coleman v. Strohman, 821 P.2d 88 (Wyo. 1999) (upholding trial judge's decision to give self-defense instruction requiring reasonableness of defendant's actions); Goldfuss v. Davidson, 79 Ohio St.3d 116, 679 N.E.2d 1099 (1997) (upholding trial judge's refusal to give self-defense jury instruction, where defendant shot from his locked house at trespassers fleeing from his barn 100 feet away). How much force can be used in self-defense? *See* Price v. Gray's Guard Serv., Inc., 298 So.2d 461 (Fla. Ct. App. 1974) (guard beaten with his own club entitled to shoot assailants); McDonald v. Terrebonne Parish School Bd., 252 So.2d 558 (La. App. 1971) (smaller boy justified to throw broom at larger boy presenting weaponless threat); Greenberg v. Mobil Oil Corp., 318 F. Supp. 1025 (N.D. Tex. 1970) (threat must be of death or serious injury to justify self defense using deadly force); Silas v. Bowen, 277 F. Supp. 314 (D. S.C. 1967) (small man justified in shooting at large man's feet in self-defense of larger man's weaponless threat). What if the defender misses the one making the threat but hits another—does the defender still have the defense? *See* McDonald, *supra* (yes); Silas, *supra* (same); Shaw v. Lord, 41 Okl. 347, 137 P. 885 (1914) (same). Just as intent will transfer to hold a defendant liable, so, too, will intent transfer to protect a defendant who intends self-defense.

Retaliation. When does self-defense turn into actionable retaliation for which the original defender is liable? *See* Edgar v. Emily, 637 S.W.2d 412 (Mo. App. 1982) (self-defense for defendant with stick to threaten plaintiff's husband with stick but then defend himself from plaintiff who had a hatchet or hammer and struck defendant in the face, because defendant had retreated and was no longer a threat); Germolus v. Sausser, 83 Minn. 141, 85 N.W. 946 (1901) (defendant liable for striking plaintiff with whip defendant had taken from plaintiff because plaintiff's threat had terminated). Does tort law recognize provocation as a defense—that the plaintiff so angered or otherwise provoked the defendant that the defendant was entitled to commit a battery? *See* Landry v. Bellinger, 851 So.2d 943 (La. 2003) (provoking a fight does not bar a battery claim for injuries arising out of it); Manning v. Michael, 188 Conn. 607, 452 A.2d 1157 (1982) (provocation does not justify battery but may be used to oppose punitive damages); Crotteau v. Karlgaard, 48 Wis.2d 245, 179 N.W.2d 797 (1970) (plaintiff's demand that defendant "[g]et out of the way, you dumb son of a bitch" not sufficient to justify defendant's retaliation); Prell Hotel Corp. v. Antonacci, 86 Nev. 390, 469 P.2d 399 (1970) (calling defendant a degrading name not sufficient provocation to justify retaliation); *but cf.* Gortarez v. Smitty's Super Valu, Inc., 680 P.2d 807 (Ariz. 1984) (security guard who induced fight with patron cannot claim self-defense in injury of patron); Silas v. Bowen, 277 F. Supp. 314 (D. S.C. 1967) (words combined with physical threat can justify self-defense).

Retreat. Must a person retreat before using force in self-defense, if retreat is possible and reasonable? A person need not retreat if using force less than that likely to cause death or serious injury. A majority of jurisdictions appear to allow the use of deadly force in response to a deadly threat without requiring retreat. Certainly, retreat would not ordinarily be an issue when the person making the threat has a gun and is capable of causing immediate death or serious injury. Yet some jurisdictions and the Restatement (Second) of Torts §65 require retreat before using force likely to cause death or serious injury, if that retreat is possible and reasonable. How far must a defendant retreat before using force in self-defense, in the minority of jurisdictions requiring retreat? The traditional vernacular is "retreat to the wall." Law is reasonably clear that no retreat is required if the person is in the person's own home.

Law Enforcement. How does the law treat consent when the person using or threatening force is a police officer? An arrestee has no right to defend a police officer's lawful use of force to make arrest and perform other duties in a lawful and reasonable manner. One would expect courts and juries to appreciate and respect the need for the use of force in law enforcement. Yet cases generally find a limited right of self-defense to excessive force from a police officer. *See* State v. Panella, 43 Conn. App. 76, 682 A.2d 532 (1996) (self-defense instruction appropriate where without provocation or notice of arrest, police officer attacked defendant with flashlight causing defendant to fear for his life, and defendant held reasonable belief that officers committed beatings); Robinson v. United States, 649 A.2d 584 (D.C. App. 1994) (limited right of self-defense after showing that officer exceeded permissible force). Courts split on whether one has a right to resist an unlawful arrest in which the force necessary to make the arrest is not in itself excessive. *Contrast* Commonwealth v. Hill, 264 Va. 541, 570 S.E.2d 805 (2001) (no right to resist unlawful detention and pat down); State v. Hobson, 577 N.W.2d 825 (Wis. 1998) (abrogating common-law privilege to resist unlawful arrest), *with* White v. Morris, 345 So.2d 461 (La. 1977) (right to resist unlawful arrest); *see also* Ala. Code §13A-3-28 (1994) (abrogating right to resist unlawful arrest).

Mistake. What does the law do if the defendant claiming self-defense was wrong because there was no real threat? *See* Smith v. Delery, 238 La. 180, 114 So.2d 857 (1959) (defendant claims self-defense to shoot boy who was merely retrieving his dog from behind defendant's house); Bunten v. Davis, 82 N.H. 304, 133 A. 16 (1926) (defendant claims self-defense to shoot at plaintiff who was merely setting off fireworks). The cases turn on whether the defendant's belief that defendant was about to suffer harm was reasonable. *See* Crabtree v. Dawson, 119 Ky. 148, 83 S.W. 557 (1904) (question of reasonableness where defendant heard that person he had just ejected for intoxication was outside getting bricks, and plaintiff ran toward defendant when defendant stepped outside); Keep v. Quallman, 68 Wis. 451, 32 N.W. 233 (1887) (defendant entitled to jury instruction on reasonable grounds to fear an immediate threat from plaintiff, after defendant hit plaintiff with a cane in an argument when plaintiff, who was known to shoot people, suddenly reached into pocket).

Defense of Others. The defense of others is co-extensive with self-defense. The actor must perceive an imminent threat to defend. *See* State v. Wright, 163 Ariz. 184, 786 P.2d 1035 (Ariz. App. 1989) (error to deny defense-of-others instruction where defendant was attempting to save friend from fight); McCullough v. McAnelly, 248 So.2d 7 (La. Ct. App. 1971) (privilege to use deadly force to defend one's son); Beavers v. Calloway, 271 A.D. 820 (N.Y. App. Div. 1946) (privilege of bar patron to intervene in altercation between others); *cf.* State v. Pounders, 913 S.W.2d 904 (Mo. App. 1996) (no defense of others, where third person had left scene before defendant used deadly force against victim); Brumley v. State, 804 S.W.2d 659 (Texas 1991) (defendant not entitled to defense-of-others defense with respect to unborn child, against trespass for blocking office where abortion was believed to be imminent). The force used to defend others must be reasonable. *See* Lopez v. Surchia, 112 Cal. App.2d 314, 246 P.2d 111 (1952) (excessive force for defendant to shoot boy who was fighting with defendant's son). Law encounters defense of others often in battery cases involving family members. *See* McCullough v. McAnelly, 238 So.2d 7 (La. App. 1971) (defendant shot teenage boy who attacked defendant's son); Boyer v. Waples, 206 Cal. App.2d 725, 24 Cal. Rptr. 192 (1962) (defendant shot plaintiff after plaintiff threatened defendant's family, and plaintiff was outside family home at night); Lopez, *supra*; Frew v. Teagarden, 111 Kan. 107, 205 P. 1023 (1922).

Mistake. What does the law provide when the plaintiff against whom the defendant used force *and* the person whom the defendant was acting to protect knew no genuine threat existed, and defendant was mistaken? Jurisdictions split on the effect of mistake in the defense of others. The Restatement (Second) of Torts §76 would allow the defense for reasonable mistake. *See also* Bell v. Smith, 488 S.E.2d 91 (Ga. Ct. App. 1997) (following reasonableness analysis); Sloan v. Pierce, 85 P.812 (Kan. 1906) (same). Other jurisdictions hold that the defendant has the defense of others only where the person the defendant acted to protect would have had the right to self-defense—holding the defendant liable if, especially, the defendant has mistakenly helped the aggressor rather than the person threatened. *See* State v. Wegner, 390 N.E.2d 801 (Ohio 1979) (intervention is at one's peril regarding mistake, even if action is reasonable); Morgan v. State, 545 S.W.2d 811 (Texas Ct. App. 1977) (no defense of others where defendant's sister was in fact out of danger); Robinson v. Decatur, 32 Ala. App. 654, 29 So.2d 429 (1947) (person defended was aggressor).

Practice

"Hey, lawyer-man," the smiling client greeted the pro-bono lawyer. "Hey, Jimmy," the lawyer answered, "You're looking well. Where's the crutch." "Got rid of that thing—doing lots better," the client responded as he settled into the plastic chair next to the steel desk at which the lawyer sat in the soup kitchen where he offered free legal advice. The lawyer and client then went over the status of Jimmy's motor-vehicle no-fault insurance claim with which the lawyer had helped. Jimmy had been crossing the street one evening when a vehicle making a right-hand turn struck him. In this no-fault state, Jimmy would be entitled to medical and work-loss benefits whether or not the driver or Jimmy was at fault. The trouble was that Jimmy had no vehicle of his own and did not reside with a relative who had an insured vehicle. So the driver's or vehicle owner's insurer should have paid his no-fault benefits. Jimmy had lost both of his jobs and his hotel room because of his injury. The lawyer had met him when Jimmy hobbled into the soup kitchen's day room on crutches, showing the lawyer his badly swollen and slightly scarred ankle where the vehicle had struck him. The lawyer easily got Jimmy the benefits he needed, simply by knowing the legal and insurance-policy requirements, forming a plan of action, making a telephone call, and writing a couple of letters. These tasks were just the sort for which the tradesman Jimmy had no experience. He had not been able to read and understand the insurer's letters. As Jimmy gathered his papers to leave, elated at his paid medical bills and that he was headed back to work, off the street, and back in the hotel with his modest work-loss benefits, the lawyer gently encouraged him about some emergency planning. The lawyer

> asked, "How about that daughter of yours? Could she help you with some financial planning?" Jimmy seemed encouraged. "Yeah, she's a good one, that girl of mine," he replied, "I didn't want to trouble her—her old man being hurt and all that. But maybe now that I'm alright."

C. Defense and Recovery of Property

OBJECTIVE: Given a description of a personal injury caused by a homeowner, shopkeeper, or other person attempting to defend or recover property, determine whether privilege to take those actions defeats an intentional tort claim, consistent with your study of intentional tort defenses in the text.

Case Study: A private merchandise-security officer watched security-camera monitors for evidence of shoplifting by a lone customer wandering aimlessly about the store. Although the video images were not clear, the officer believed that she witnessed the customer attempt to pocket and conceal store items. The officer stepped in front of the customer at the front door as he prepared to leave without having gone through customer checkout. The officer reached into the customer's jacket pocket and pulled out its contents, which were nothing more than the customer's wallet. The shocked customer protested, reaching toward the officer to take back his wallet. The officer stepped back from the customer, accusing the customer of shoplifting and starting to thumb through the customer's wallet as other customers stared. The customer pulled out his cell phone, pretended to dial 911, and said loudly into the phone that someone was trying to steal his wallet, causing the officer to return the wallet. **Discuss and evaluate whether privilege protects the officer's actions.**

Tort law regards a person's right to defend property as similar to the rights of self-defense and defense of others, in that the force used must be reasonable and in response to a reasonably perceived and imminent threat. Yet the defense of property is distinct from self-defense and defense of others in other ways. A person may ordinarily not, in the defense of property, use force likely to cause death or serious injury—presumably because of the much greater value we place on life than property. This distinction is, however, often less significant than one might think because defense of property can so easily turn into self-defense. When a person uses or prepares to use force to defend property, that person may also be in a position to use force to defend self and others. *See* Tipsword v. Potter, 31 Idaho 509, 174 P.133 (1918) (homeowner permitted to use deadly force when intruder attempts to enter occupied homestead at night). If the putative perpetrator is willing to confront force to accomplish the property's destruction or theft, then that same perpetrator is reasonably likely to be willing to direct force back at the one who is making the property's defense or at others whom the defender may then defend with all reasonable force—including, if necessary, deadly force. Also, a person is not entitled to defend property, where the person made a mistake in defending the property—even if the mistake was a reasonable mistake. The defender of property must ensure a real, not imagined, risk of the property's destruction or theft. Consider the following case as an introduction to the variety of cases found in the defense and recovery of property.

Katko v. Briney
Iowa Supreme Court
183 N.W. 2d 657 (Iowa 1971)

MOORE, C.J. The primary issue presented here is whether an owner may protect personal property in an unoccupied boarded-up farm house against trespassers and thieves by a spring gun capable of inflicting death or serious injury.

We are not here concerned with a man's right to protect his home and members of his family. Defendants' home was several miles from the scene of the incident to which we refer infra.

Plaintiff's action is for damages resulting from serious injury caused by a shot from a 20-gauge spring shotgun set by defendants in a bedroom of an old farm house which had been uninhabited for several years. Plaintiff and his companion, Marvin McDonough, had broken and entered the house to find and steal old bottles and dated fruit jars which they considered antiques.

At defendants' request plaintiff's action was tried to a jury consisting of residents of the community where defendants' property was located. The jury returned a verdict for plaintiff and against defendants for $20,000 actual and $10,000 punitive damages.

After careful consideration of defendants' motions for judgment notwithstanding the verdict and for new trial, the experienced and capable trial judge overruled them and entered judgment on the verdict. Thus we have this appeal by defendants. ...

... In 1957 defendant Bertha L. Briney inherited her parents' farm land in Mahaska and Monroe Counties. Included was an 80-acre tract in southwest Mahaska County where her grandparents and parents had lived. No one occupied the house thereafter. Her husband, Edward, attempted to care for the land. He kept no farm machinery thereon. The outbuildings became dilapidated.

For about 10 years, 1957 to 1967, there occurred a series of trespassing and housebreaking events with loss of some household items, the breaking of windows and "messing up of the property in general." The latest occurred June 8, 1967, prior to the event on July 16, 1967 herein involved.

Defendants through the years boarded up the windows and doors in an attempt to stop the intrusions. They had posted "no trespass" signs on the land several years before 1967. The nearest one was 35 feet from the house. On June 11, 1967 defendants set "a shotgun trap" in the north bedroom. After Mr. Briney cleaned and oiled his 20-gauge shotgun, the power of which he was well aware, defendants took it to the old house where they secured it to an iron bed with the barrel pointed at the bedroom door. It was rigged with wire from the doorknob to the gun's trigger so it would fire when the door was opened. Briney first pointed the gun so an intruder would be hit in the stomach but at Mrs. Briney's suggestion it was lowered to hit the legs. He admitted he did so "because I was mad and tired of being tormented" but "he did not intend to injure anyone." He gave to explanation of why he used a loaded shell and set it to hit a person already in the house. Tin was nailed over the bedroom window. The spring gun could not be seen from the outside. No warning of its presence was posted.

Plaintiff lived with his wife and worked regularly as a gasoline station attendant in Eddyville, seven miles from the old house. He had observed it for several years while hunting in the area and considered it as being abandoned. He knew it had long been uninhabited. In 1967 the area around the house was covered with high weeds. Prior to July 16, 1967, plaintiff and McDonough had been to the premises and found several old bottles and fruit jars which they took and added to their collection of antiques. On the latter date about 9:30 p.m. they made a second trip to the Briney property. They entered the old house by removing a board from a porch window which was without glass. While McDonough was looking around the kitchen area plaintiff went to another part of the house. As he started to open the north bedroom door the shotgun went off striking him in the right leg above the ankle bone. Much of his leg, including part of the tibia, was blown away. Only by McDonough's assistance was plaintiff able to get out of the house and after crawling some distance was put in his vehicle and rushed to a doctor and then to a hospital. He remained in the hospital 40 days.

Plaintiff's doctor testified he seriously considered amputation but eventually the healing process was successful. Some weeks after his release from the hospital plaintiff returned to work on crutches. He was required to keep the injured leg in a cast for approximately a year and wear a special brace for another year. He continued to suffer pain during this period.

There was undenied medical testimony plaintiff had a permanent deformity, a loss of tissue, and a shortening of the leg. ...

The main thrust of defendants' defense in the trial court and on this appeal is that "the law permits use of a spring gun in a dwelling or warehouse for the purpose of preventing the unlawful entry of a burglar or thief." ...

Instruction 6 stated: "An owner of premises is prohibited from willfully or intentionally injuring a trespasser by means of force that either takes life or inflicts great bodily injury; and therefore a person owning a premise is prohibited from setting out "spring guns" and like dangerous devices which will likely take life or inflict great bodily injury, for the purpose of harming trespassers. The fact that the trespasser may be acting in violation of the law does not change the rule. The only time when such conduct of setting a "spring gun" or a like dangerous device is justified would be when the trespasser was committing a felony of violence or a felony punishable by death, or where the trespasser was endangering human life by his act."

The overwhelming weight of authority, both textbook and case law, supports the trial court's statement of the applicable principles of law.

Restatement of Torts, section 85, page 180, states: "The value of human life and limb, not only to the individual concerned but also to society, so outweighs the interest of a possessor of land in excluding from it those whom he is not willing to admit thereto that a possessor of land has, as is stated in §79, no privilege to use force intended or likely to cause death or serious harm against another whom the possessor sees about to enter his premises or meddle with his chattel, unless the intrusion threatens death or serious bodily harm to the occupiers or users of the premises. ... A possessor of land cannot do indirectly and by a mechanical device that which, were he present, he could not do immediately and in person. Therefore, he cannot gain a privilege to install, for the purpose of protecting his land from intrusions harmless to the lives and limbs of the occupiers or users of it, a mechanical device whose only purpose is to inflict death or serious harm upon such as may intrude, by giving notice of his intention to inflict, by mechanical means and indirectly, harm which he could not, even after request, inflict directly were he present."
...

In addition to civil liability many jurisdictions hold a land owner criminally liable for serious injuries or homicide caused by spring guns or other set devices. [Cc] ...

Study and careful consideration of defendants' contentions on appeal reveal no reversible error.

Affirmed.

Subsequent History. The *Katko v. Briney* case received substantial post-trial publicity in part because the wire service mistakenly reported that Katko's attempted theft was from the Briney's occupied home. State legislators crafted "Briney Bills" proposing to give homeowners the right to defend property by any means. After neighboring Nebraska enacted one bill, the state supreme court held it to be an unconstitutional delegation of sentencing. State v. Goodseal, 186 Neb. 359, 183 N.W.2d 258 (1971), *cert. denied*, 404 U.S. 845 (1971). Before the trial of the above civil case, Marvin Katko had pled guilty to petty larceny and paid a $50 fine. His short sentence was suspended. He had no prior convictions except for some traffic offenses. The post-trial details of the *Katko v. Briney* case itself are interesting. Mr. and Mrs. Briney sold a substantial portion of the farm to three neighbors by judgment sale in order to attempt to pay a portion of Katko's judgment. Sometime after the land rose in value, the Brineys and Katko *together* sued the land's remaining owner (a son of one of the three who bought the land from the Brineys), claiming that it had been held in trust for the Brineys who would thus have been entitled to its increase in value. The owner settled the claim for enough to pay the remaining portion of the judgment that the Brineys owed Katko. Palmer, *Katko v. Briney*: A Study in American Gothic, 56 Iowa L.Rev. 1219 (1971). Interestingly, the modern American storm over *Katko v. Briney* had its opposite long ago in England. In Illott v. Wilkes, 3 B. & Ald. 304, 106 Eng. Rep. 674 (1820), the court had refused to impose liability on a landowner who shot a poacher with a spring gun, producing such protest that Parliament made setting a spring gun a crime. Bird v. Holbrook, 4 Bing. 628, 130 Eng. Rep. 911 (1828), quickly overruled *Illott*. Consider now some more-conventional and less-well-known cases involving the defense and recovery of property.

Brown v. Martinez
New Mexico Supreme Court
68 N.M. 271, 361 P.2d 152 (1961)

MOISE, J. Appellants, being father and son, appeal from a judgment dismissing their claim for damages against appellee growing out of injuries suffered by the son when he was shot in the left leg while engaged with several other boys in a watermelon stealing escapade on appellee's property. ...

[O]n the night of September 18, 1954, appellant, a 15-year old boy, and two other boys visited appellee's garden patch adjacent to the road for the purpose of stealing melons. About 8:30 or 9:00 p. m., the next night, being September 19, 1954, appellant with several other boys again went to the farm of appellee for the purpose of stealing watermelons. While two of the boys entered the melon patch, appellant went to the southeast corner of the property and was in the highway right of way close to the fence when appellee hearing the boys in the patch came out of his house with a rifle in his hand, called to the boys to get out, and seeing the two boys running toward the southwest corner of the property fired the gun toward the southeast to scare them, the bullet striking appellant in the back of the left leg, half way between the ankle and the knee, breaking the bones and coming out of the front of the leg. ...

Our examination of the authorities convinces us that the question of the reasonableness of resort to firearms to prevent a trespass or to prevent commission of an unlawful act not amounting to a felony is one of law for the court, and that such conduct is not excusable. ...

There is no suggestion in the proof here that appellee in any way felt his safety was threatened. Accordingly, under the facts as proven and found, the appellee acted improperly and is liable for injuries caused in using a gun in the manner he did, and with such unfortunate consequences, in order to drive away trespassers on his property, or to protect his watermelons, or to scare the intruders. [Cc] ...

It follows from what has been said that the cause must be reversed and remanded with instructions that the court set aside its order of dismissal; determine appellants' damages; and otherwise proceed in a manner not inconsistent herewith.

It is so ordered.

INQUIRY

Recovery of Property. The defense of property can also quickly turn to its recovery. Under the common law, or by statute in many states, the right to use less-than-deadly force to defend property extends to the right to use force in its recovery, with the attendant limitation that the force be non-deadly and reasonable. *See* N.Y. Gen. Bus. Law §218; Wis. Stats. Ann. §943.50; Guijosa v. Wal-Mart Stores, Inc., 32 P.3d 250 (Wash. 2001) (right to detain shopper for up to 30 minutes while awaiting arrival of police, on reasonable suspicion of shoplifting); Gortarez v. Smitty's Super Value, Inc., 140 Ariz. 97, 680 P.2d 807 (1984) (shop-owner's parking-lot choke hold on boy suspected of shoplifting was unreasonable); Restatement (Second) of Torts §106 (1965). But significant additional limitations exist on the right to use force to recover property. The person seeking to recover the property must make a demand before using force, unless a demand is useless or unsafe. Restatement (Second) of Torts §104 (1965). Also, a person may use force in the recovery of property only so long as the recovery is made or attempted while the person is in fresh pursuit of the property, on or about the premises from which the wrongdoer took it. Restatement (Second) of Torts §103 (1965). A person who faces safety threat in the course of recovering property may defend with reasonable force—including up to deadly force if the threat is one of death or serious injury. *See* Hamilton v. Barker, 116 Mich. 684, 75 N.W. 133 (1898). If the thief gets away with a person's property, and its recovery requires the use of force, then the person must seek the help of the police or courts. *See* Roberts v. Speck, 169 Wash. 613, 14 P.2d 33 (1932). The overriding concern here is with keeping the peace and not authorizing vigilante justice resolving property disputes. *See, e.g.,* Auto Owners Ins. Co. v. Grier, 163 N.C. App. 560, 593 S.W.2d 804 (2004) (owner robbed of money by plaintiff, not entitled to recovery of property defense, for pursuing plaintiff from business, pulling gun on plaintiff, holding plaintiff at gunpoint, and then shooting plaintiff when plaintiff struggled).

Repossession. The fresh-pursuit limitation does not prevent the property's owner from simply taking the property back from a person who has left it available for the taking (without force) or from making demands that the person relinquish the property. The finance agreement will provide for the right to retake property sold on time payments, consistent with the Uniform Commercial Code §9-503. Section 9-503 provides that "unless otherwise agreed a secured party has on default the right to retake possession of the collateral" if "this can be done without breach of the peace." Repossession personnel must be familiar with the line between those permissible and impermissible means. Tort practitioners keep them so, pursuing many cases over injury occurring around the repossession of personal property. Other limitations on the recovery of property have to do with conduct toward the person suspected of having taken, or who did take, the property—investigating whether property is missing must be reasonable. Store merchandise-security personnel must know the line between those permissible and impermissible means because, again, tort practitioners will keep them so. Parties have filed many cases for false imprisonment, battery, invasion of privacy, and defamation, involving suspected shoplifting.

Hodgeden v. Hubbard
Vermont Supreme Court
18 Vt. 504, 46 Am. Dec. 167 (1846)

TRESPASS for assault and battery, and for taking and carrying away a stove, the property of the plaintiff. ...

On trial the plaintiff gave evidence, tending to prove, that, on the nineteenth day of September, 1842, he purchased at the Tyson ware house, in Montpelier, a stove, and gave his promissory note therefor, payable in six months; that the agent, who had charge of the warehouse, was absent at the times, and the sale was made by the defendant Hubbard, who was clerk for the agent, as was also the defendant Ayres; that on the same day, and soon after the sale, the defendants learned, that the plaintiff was irresponsible as to property, and started in pursuit of him, and overtook him about two miles from Montpelier and took the stove from him by force; but it did not appear, how much force was used, or its character; but it did appear, that, in the attempt to dispossess the plaintiff of the stove, he drew his knife, and that he was then forcibly held by one of the defendants, while the other took possession of the stove; and the testimony tended to prove, that the resistance of the plaintiff was such, that the defendants used violence and applied force to his person with great rudeness and outrage. ...

[T]he court charged the jury, that, although the plaintiff was guilty of misrepresentation and fraud, in obtaining the stove, in the manner attempted to be proved by the defendants, yet this would not justify the defendants in forcibly taking the property from him; that the property in the stove would not be changed by the purchase, and the defendants might take it peaceably, wherever they could find it; but that the defendants, having delivered the stove to the plaintiff, could not justify taking it from him by blows inflicted upon his person, or by holding him, but should resort to redress by legal process; and that, if they should find, that the property in the stove was not changed, for the reason stated, and that the defendants took it by violence, in the manner attempted to be shown by the plaintiff, although they used no more force than was necessary to accomplish that object under the resistance of the plaintiff, they would still be liable in this action; but the court, in that case, recommended to the jury to give small damages.

Verdict for plaintiff for one dollar damages. Exceptions by defendants.

The opinion of the court was delivered by WILLIAMS, Ch. J. ...

In the present case the defendants had clearly a right to retake the property, thus fraudulently obtained from them, if it could be done without unnecessary violence to the person, or without breach of the peace. ...

In the case before us it is stated, that it did not appear "how much force was used, or its character," before the defendants were assaulted by the plaintiff. To obtain possession of the property in question no violence to the person of the plaintiff was necessary, or required, unless from his resistance. It was not like property carried about the person, as a watch, or money, nor did it require a number of people to affect the object. The plaintiff had no lawful possession, nor any right to resist the attempt of the defendants to regain the property, of which he had unlawfully and fraudulently obtained the possession. By drawing his knife he became the aggressor, inasmuch as he had no right thus to protect his fraudulent attempt to acquire the stove, and the possession of the same, and it was the right of the defendants to hold him by force, and, if they made use of no unnecessary violence, they were justified; if they were guilty of more, they were liable.

The judgment of the county court is reversed.

Bonkowski v. Arlan's Dept. Store
Michigan Court of Appeals
12 Mich. App. 88, 162 N.W.2d 347 (1968)

FITZGERALD, J. This appeal from a jury verdict for false arrest and slander, rendered against the defendant store whose agent stopped and questioned the plaintiff whom he suspected of larceny, surprisingly presents questions that are novel to the appellate courts of this jurisdiction.

The plaintiff, Mrs. Marion Bonkowski, accompanied by her husband, had left the defendant's Saginaw, Michigan store about 10:00 p.m. on the night of December 18, 1962 after making several purchases, when Earl Reinhardt, a private policeman on duty that night in the defendant's store, called to her to stop as she was walking to her car about 30 feet away in the adjacent parking lot. Reinhardt motioned to the plaintiff to return toward the store, and when she had done so, Reinhardt said that someone in the store had told him the plaintiff had put three pieces of costume jewelry into her purse without having paid for them. Mrs. Bonkowski denied she had taken anything unlawfully, but Reinhardt told her he wanted to see the contents of her purse. On a cement step in front of the store, plaintiff emptied the contents of her purse into her husband's hands. The plaintiff produced sales slips for the items she had purchased, and Reinhardt, satisfied that she had not committed larceny, returned to the store.

Plaintiff brought this action against Earl Reinhardt and Arlan's Department Store, seeking damages on several counts. She complains that as a result of defendant's tortious acts she has suffered numerous psychosomatic symptoms, including headaches, nervousness, and depression. … On the counts of false arrest and slander the case went to the jury, who returned a verdict of $43,750. …

We conclude the plaintiff established a case entitling her to go to the jury on a charge of false arrest.[fn] …

To the common-law tort of false arrest, privilege is a common-law defense, and we recognize as applicable here a privilege similar to that recognized by the American Law Institute in the Restatement of Torts, 2d. In section 120A, the Institute recognizes a privilege in favor of a merchant to detain for reasonable investigation a person whom he reasonably believes to have taken a chattel unlawfully. We adopt the concept embodied in section 120A, and we state the rule for this action as follows: if defendant Arlan's agent,

Earl Reinhardt, reasonably believed the plaintiff had unlawfully taken goods held for sale in the defendant's store, then he enjoyed a privilege to detain her for a reasonable investigation of the facts.

The Commissioners' comment states the strong reason behind recognizing such a privilege: "The privilege stated in this section is necessary for the protection of a shopkeeper against the dilemma in which he would otherwise find himself when he reasonably believes that a shoplifter has taken goods from his counter. If there were no such privilege, he must either permit the suspected person to walk out of the premises and disappear, or must arrest him, at the risk of liability for false arrest if the theft could not be proved." 1 Restatement of Torts, 2d, page 202.

That the problem of shoplifting, faced by merchants, has reached serious dimensions is common knowledge, and we find compelling reason to recognize such a privilege, similar to that recognized in other jurisdictions. [C]

The privilege we recognize here goes beyond that set forth in the Restatement, for the Commissioners there stated a caveat that "the Institute expresses no opinion as to whether there may be circumstances under which this privilege may extend to the detention of one who has left the premises but is in their immediate vicinity." 1 Restatement of Torts, 2d, page 202.

... We think the privilege should be so extended here because we think it entirely reasonable to apply it to the circumstances of the case at bar, for the reason that a merchant may not be able to form the reasonable belief justifying a detention for a reasonable investigation before a suspected person has left the premises. ...

On remand on the cause for false arrest, therefore, it will be the duty of the jury to determine in accordance with the rule we have set down, whether or not the defendant's agent, Earl Reinhardt, reasonably believed the plaintiff had unlawfully taken any goods held for sale at the defendant's store. If the jury finds the defendant's agent did so reasonably believe, then it must further determine whether the investigation that followed was reasonable under all the circumstances. If the jury finds the defendant does not come within this privilege, then from the facts as discussed above, it could find a false arrest. ...

Reversed and remanded for new trial in accordance with this opinion. The award of costs to await final determination of the cause.

INQUIRY

Mistake and Confusion. A person has no right to defend property using force against a person entitled to take the property. *See* Magnuson v. Billmayer, 189 Mont. 458, 616 P.2d 368 (1980) (no force permitted to stop telephone company workers from entering land on easement and removing telephone poles belonging to company). Law permits no mistakes in using force to defend property. But what if authorized intruders in some way misled the person into using force? *See* State v. Shite, 642 So.2d 842 (Fla. App. 1994) (thinking that they were robbers, homeowner mistakenly fired at plain-clothes police who entered the home on a gambling raid after cutting off power).

Warning. Must the person who is preparing to use force to defend property warn before doing so? *See* Emmons v. Quade, 176 Mo. 22, 75 S.W. 103 (1903) (worker subject to liability for clubbing boy who was scooping up grain left over in a rail car); *but see* Higgins v. Minaghan, 78 Wis. 602, 47 N.W. 941 (1891) (no need to warn mob where warning would be useless, cause unwise delay, or itself incite violence). Will the law privilege a person who warns that they will use deadly force to protect property? In some states, it appears so. *See* Sappington v. Sutton, 501 P.2d 814 (Okl. 1972) (vicious dog); Hood v. Waldrum, 58 Tenn. App. 512, 434 S.W.2d 94 (1968) (same); *cf.* Loomis v. Terry, 17 Wend. 496, 31 Am. Dec. 306 (N.Y. 1837) (liability where no warning given). May a property owner use a dangerous form of defense that of itself gives notice, like barbed wire? *See* Quigley v. Clough, 173 Mass. 429, 53 N.E. 884 (1899) (yes). Most states do not grant a privilege to use deadly force with a warning but only permit that amount of force the owner would be entitled to use if the owner were present. *See* State v. Childers, 133 Ohio St. 508, 14 N.E.2d 767 (1938).

Contractual Consent. The text above states that property owners may use force to recover property only in fresh pursuit. *See* Watkins v. Sears Roebuck & Co., 735 N.Y.S.2d 75 (App. Div. 2001) (reasonable for guard to tackle suspected shoplifter who was fleeing store, even though tackle broke suspect's leg). What if the possessor of leased property or property purchased under a finance agreement has consented in the agreement to the seller's use of force in retaking the property? *See* Girard v. Anderson, 219 Iowa 142, 257 N.W. 400 (1934) (reflecting current view that agreement is void to the extent that it purports to permit force not authorized in the absence of agreement). Although Uniform Commercial Code §9-503 permits a secured seller of personal property to retake it without resort to the courts "if this can be done without breach of the peace," the law on retaking real property without the occupier's permission can be quite different. Most states do not permit the use of force to retake real property, instead providing streamlined court procedures for prompt recovery of real property by forcible entry and detainer. Attempts to retake real property by force are likely to violate statute, may lead to trespass and other intentional tort claims, *see* Daluiso v. Boone, 71 Cal.2d 484, 455 P.2d 811, 78 Cal. Rptr. 707 (1969) (IIED claim for intruding owner's outrageous conduct), and may result in statutory claims (even trebled) for damage to or loss of the tenant's personal property.

Shoplifting. Cases and statutes show considerable variety in what they permit shopkeepers to do to investigate suspected shoplifting by one still on or about the premises. Some hold that a shopkeeper's investigatory stop of a suspected shoplifter is at the shopkeeper's peril—that the shopkeeper had better have been right or will be subject to liability. *See* Claggett v. State, 670 A.2d 1002 (Md. App. 1996). But in general, what must a shopkeeper do before using reasonable, non-deadly force in the investigation of shoplifting? *See* Restatement (Second) of Torts §120A (make a request that the suspected shoplifter stay and submit to investigation). What is reasonable cause to make the request? *See* Grant v. Stop-N-Go Market of Texas, Inc., 994 S.W.2d 867 (Tex. Ct. App. 1999) (fact that store surveillance videotape was missing and according to police had not shown evidence of shoplifting supported that there was no cause for the plaintiff's detention). Can a shopkeeper make a second request and investigation of a suspected shoplifter, after a first request and investigation has already cleared the shopper? *See* Turner v. Hudson Salvage, Inc., 709 So.2d 425 (Miss. 1998) (unreasonable to make second request). How long can a suspected shoplifter be detained during the course of an investigation? *See* Va. Code §18.2-105 (2005) (up to one hour). What if the shopkeeper's investigations are racially discriminatory? *See* Hampton v. Dillard Dept. Stores, Inc., 247 F.3d 1091 (10th Cir. 2001) (civil rights claim under 42 U.S.C. §1981), *cert. denied*, 534 U.S. 1131 (2002). May a shopkeeper threaten to hold a suspected shoplifter until the suspect signs a confession? *See* Moffatt v. Buffums' Inc., 21 Cal. App2d 371, 69 P.2d

424 (1937) (no); W.T. Grant Co. v. Owens, 149 Va. 906, 141 S.E. 860 (1928) (no). May a service supplier detain a customer who has not paid? One would think not, ordinarily. *But see* Standish v. Narragansett S.S. Co., 111 Mass. 512, 15 Am. Rep. 66 (1873) (failure to pay for boat ride).

Knowledge

Lawyers use the skill of making successive approximations of hypothetical scenarios to the facts at hand, as a way of demonstrating why the facts should or should not state a claim. The lawyer holds in mind the actual scenario while selectively contrasting the generated scenarios one-by-one. The contrast is selective and intentional in that the lawyer determines and asserts that the hypothetical scenario is closer to or farther away from the legal standard at issue. The contrast has a purpose, showing the facts to be within or outside of a certain legal definition or standard. The lawyer must have in mind the facts and hypothesized scenario and the legal definition or standard, and be able to articulate where the facts and scenarios fall in relation to that definition or standard.

D. Policy Defenses

OBJECTIVE: Given various intentional tort claims, identify those claims in which the facts support one or more other defenses such as necessity, authority of law, discipline, or justification, consistent with your study of intentional tort defenses in the text.

Case Study: A police department authorizes off-duty officers to take actions consistent with their training and law enforcement duties when they personally witness what they reasonably believe to be a violation of the law. While walking home from a movie late one night, an off-duty officer witnessed a man using a tool to try to unlock a car door. Assuming that the man was attempting to steal the vehicle (a felony), the officer asked what the man was doing. The man merely glared back at the officer while continuing to work with the tool. So the officer pulled the man's shoulder around toward him, intending to disclose his identity as a police officer and to question the man. When the man instead pulled away, the officer shoved the man over on the hood of the car. The man then truthfully told the officer that the man was simply trying to open his own car out of which he had mistakenly locked himself. *Analyze whether the officer has defenses of necessity, authority of law, discipline, or justification.*

The defenses of consent, self-defense, defense of others, and defense and recovery of property each depend on the plaintiff's conduct. Tort law recognizes several other defenses that depend less or not at all on the plaintiff's conduct and more on public interests and policies. Among them are necessity (public and private), authority of law (arrest and search), discipline, and justification. Just as the defenses covered above reflect tort law's sensitivity to the infinite variety of individual interests and circumstance, the defenses below reflect tort law's equal ability to incorporate public policy and accommodate public interests.

Public Necessity. The first policy defense, public necessity, is a defense to the property-damage torts of trespass to land and chattels. Public necessity depends on the defendant's showing that the defendant had a public interest to preserve by the entry onto the plaintiff's land or by the destruction of plaintiff's real or personal property. Law privileges the defendant to make the entry or destroy the property. The defendant will not pay damages to the plaintiff. The public-necessity defense finds its illustrative history in Mouse's Case, 12 Co. Rep. 63, 77 Eng. Rep. 1341 (1609), in which the defendant claimed a privilege to throw a casket from a capsizing boat. The plaintiff's recourse, if any, must be through something other than tort law—perhaps property-damage insurance, public-relief programs, specific private-relief legislation, or an inverse-condemnation action if public officials are involved. Consider the following case.

Surocco v. Geary
California Supreme Court
3 Cal. 69, 58 Am. Dec. 385 (1853)

MURRAY, C.J.... . This was an action ... to recover damages for blowing up and destroying the plaintiffs' house and property, during the fire of the 24th of December, 1849.

Geary, at that time Alcalde of San Francisco, justified, on the ground that he had the authority, by virtue of his office, to destroy said building, and also that it had been blown up by him to stop the progress of the conflagration then raging.

It was in proof, that the fire passed over and burned beyond the building of the plaintiffs', and that at the time said building was destroyed, they were engaged in removing their property, and could, had they not been prevented, have succeeded in removing more, if not all of their goods.

The cause was tried by the court sitting as a jury, and a verdict rendered for the plaintiffs... .

The only question for our consideration is, whether the person who tears down or destroys the house of another, in good faith, and under apparent necessity, during the time of a conflagration, for the purpose of saving the buildings adjacent, and stopping its progress, can be held personally liable in an action by the owner of the property destroyed.
...

The right to destroy property, to prevent the spread of a conflagration, has been traced to the highest law of necessity, and the natural rights of man, independent of society or civil government. "It is referred by moralists and jurists to the same great principle which justifies the exclusive appropriation of a plank in a shipwreck, though the life of another be sacrificed; with the throwing overboard goods in a tempest, for the safety of a vessel; with the trespassing upon the lands of another, to escape death by an enemy. It rests upon the maxim, *Necessitas inducit privilegium quod jura privata.*"

The common law adopts the principles of the natural law, and places the justification of an act otherwise tortious precisely on the same ground of necessity. [C]

This principle has been familiarly recognized by the books from the time of the saltpetre case, and the instances of tearing down houses to prevent a conflagration, or to raise bulwarks for the defence of a city, are made use of as illustrations, rather than as abstract cases, in which its exercise is permitted. At such times, the individual rights of property give way to the higher laws of impending necessity.

A house on fire, or those in its immediate vicinity, which serve to communicate the flames, becomes a nuisance, which it is lawful to abate, and the private rights of the individual yield to the considerations of general convenience, and the interests of society. Were it otherwise, one stubborn person might involve a whole city in ruin, by refusing to allow the destruction of a building which would cut off the flames and check the progress of the fire, and that, too, when it was perfectly evident that his building must be consumed. …

The legislature of the State possess the power to regulate this subject by providing the manner in which buildings may be destroyed, and the mode in which compensation shall be made; and it is to be hoped that something will be done to obviate the difficulty, and prevent the happening of such events as those supposed by the respondent's counsel.

In the absence of any legislation on the subject, we are compelled to fall back upon the rules of the common law.

The evidence in this case clearly establishes the fact, that the blowing up of the house was necessary, as it would have been consumed had it been left standing. The plaintiffs cannot recover for the value of the goods which they might have saved; they were as much subject to the necessities of the occasion as the house in which they were situate; and if in such cases a party was held liable, it would too frequently happen, that the delay caused by the removal of the goods would render the destruction of the house useless.

The court below clearly erred as to the law applicable to the facts of this case. The testimony will not warrant a verdict against the defendant.

Judgment reversed.

INQUIRY

Takings. The federal and state constitutions require just compensation when government takes private property for public use. If destroying a private residence is a public necessity for the public's benefit, then should just compensation follow? *See* Wegner v. Milwaukee Mut. Ins. Co., 479 N.W.2d 38 (Minn. 1991) (state constitutional right to damages for SWAT teams having damaged private residence in which suspect took refuge); Steele v. City of Houston, 603 S.W.2d 786 (Tex. 1980) (public necessity not a bar to homeowner's damages claim for police destruction of home in attempt to capture escaped convicts); *but see* Customer Company v. City of Sacramento, 10 Cal.4th 368, 895 P.2d 900, 41 Cal. Rptr.2d 658 (1995) (no state constitutional right to damages for police apprehending suspect who took refuge in private residence); *see also* Eggleston v. Pierce County, 148 Wash.2d 760, 64 P.2d 618 (2003) (no private right of damages for destruction of property as an exercise of police power); Kelley v. Story County Sheriff, 611 N.W.2d 475 (Iowa 2000) (same). Should a private right of recovery exist for injury from a government-mandated vaccination administered to everyone as the only way to conquer the disease? *See* Lapierre v. Attorney-General of Quebec, 16 D.L.R.4th 554 (Can. 1985) (no). What if firefighters damage a landowner's timber with fire-retardant chemicals while fighting a forest fire? *See* Stocking v. Johson Flying Service, 143 Mont. 61, 387 P.2d 312 (1963) (no compensation because a public necessity). What if government must destroy a landowner's elk herd to prevent the spread of disease? *See* South Dakota Dept. of Health v Heim, 357 N.W.2d 522 (S.D. 1984) (public necessity). What if the army destroys a petroleum facility to keep the enemy from taking it? *See* United States v. Caltex, Inc., 344 U.S. 149 (1952) (not a compensable taking).

Private Necessity. Law distinguishes private necessity from public necessity both on the grounds for and effect of it. The grounds for private necessity are not to preserve a public interest, as in the case of public necessity, but rather a private interest. The actor invades another property owner's interests to preserve the actor's own private interest. The defense's effect is not to bar any claim, as with public necessity, but rather to grant the actor the privilege to use the owner's property but require the actor to pay the owner for its loss or damage. *See* Restatement (Second) of Torts §§197, 263. These private-necessity rules require the actor to make an economic determination of which will cause the greater damage: (a) to suffer the actor's own harm or loss by taking no action to preserve the actor's own interests; or (b) for the actor to make use of the other property owner's interests to preserve the actor's interests but to pay the other property owner's loss. Private necessity is in that sense an incomplete or conditional defense. One might ask then, what good is a private necessity that leaves the one asserting the defense having to pay anyway for the other property owner's damage? The answer has to do with the legal effect of the property owner's *denying* the actor's right to use the owner's property out of private necessity. In that case, the law would hold the property owner to pay the damages resulting from the refusal to accommodate a private necessity. The following case illustrates both propositions by citation to earlier cases.

Vincent v. Lake Erie Transport Co.
Minnesota Supreme Court
124 N.W. 221 (Minn. 1910)

O'BRIEN, J. The steamship Reynolds, owned by the defendant, was for the purpose of discharging her cargo on November 27, 1905, moored to plaintiff's dock in Duluth. While the unloading of the boat was taking place a storm from the northeast developed, which at about 10 o'clock p. m., when the unloading was completed, had so grown in violence that the wind was then moving at 50 miles per hour and continued to increase during the night. There is some evidence that one, and perhaps two, boats were able to enter the harbor that night, but it is plain that navigation was practically suspended from the hour mentioned until the morning of the 29th, when the storm abated, and during that time no master would have been justified in attempting to navigate his vessel, if he could avoid doing so. After the discharge of the cargo the Reynolds signaled for a tug to tow her from the dock, but none could be obtained because of the severity of the storm. If the lines holding the ship to the dock had been cast off, she would doubtless have drifted away; but, instead, the lines were kept fast, and as soon as one parted or chafed it was replaced, sometimes with a larger one. The vessel lay upon the outside of the dock, her bow to the east, the wind and waves striking her starboard quarter with such force that she was constantly being lifted and thrown against the dock, resulting in its damage, as found by the jury, to the amount of $500.

We are satisfied that the character of the storm was such that it would have been highly imprudent for the master of the Reynolds to have attempted to leave the dock or to have permitted his vessel to drift away from it. ... Nothing more was demanded of them than ordinary prudence and care, and the record in this case fully sustains the contention of the appellant that, in holding the vessel fast to the dock, those in charge of her exercised good judgment and prudent seamanship. ...

The situation was one in which the ordinary rules regulating property rights were suspended by forces beyond human control, and if, without the direct intervention of some act by the one sought to be held liable, the property of another was injured, such injury must be attributed to the act of God, and not to the wrongful act of the person sought to be charged. If during the storm the Reynolds had entered the harbor, and while there had become disabled and been thrown against the plaintiffs' dock, the plaintiffs could not have recovered. Again, if while attempting to hold fast to the dock the lines had parted, without any negligence, and the vessel carried against some other boat or dock in the harbor, there would be no liability upon her owner. But here those in charge of the vessel deliberately and by their direct efforts held her in such a position that the damage to the dock resulted, and, having thus preserved the ship at the expense of the dock, it seems to us that her owners are responsible to the dock owners to the extent of the injury inflicted.

In Depue v. Flatau, 100 Minn. 299, 111 N. W. 1, 8 L. R. A. (N. S.) 485, this court held that where the plaintiff, while lawfully in the defendants' house, became so ill that he was incapable of traveling with safety, the defendants were responsible to him in damages for compelling him to leave the premises. If, however, the owner of the premises had furnished the traveler with proper accommodations and medical attendance, would he have been able to defeat an action brought against him for their reasonable worth?

In Ploof v. Putnam, 71 Atl. 188, 20 L. R. A. (N. S.) 152, the Supreme Court of Vermont held that where, under stress of weather, a vessel was without permission moored to a private dock at an island in Lake Champlain owned by the defendant, the plaintiff was not guilty of trespass, and that the defendant was responsible in damages because his representative upon the island unmoored the vessel, permitting it to drift upon the shore, with resultant injuries to it. If, in that case, the vessel had been permitted to remain, and the dock had suffered an injury, we believe the shipowner would have been held liable for the injury done.

Theologians hold that a starving man may, without moral guilt, take what is necessary to sustain life; but it could hardly be said that the obligation would not be upon such person to pay the value of the property so taken when he became able to do so. And so public necessity, in times of war or peace, may require the taking of private property for public purposes; but under our system of jurisprudence compensation must be made.

Let us imagine in this case that for the better mooring of the vessel those in charge of her had appropriated a valuable cable lying upon the dock. No matter how justifiable such appropriation might have been, it would not be claimed that, because of the overwhelming necessity of the situation, the owner of the cable could not recover its value.

This is not a case where life or property was menaced by any object or thing belonging to the plaintiff, the destruction of which became necessary to prevent the threatened disaster. Nor is it a case where, because of the act of God, or unavoidable accident, the infliction of the injury was beyond the control of the defendant, but is one where the defendant prudently and advisedly availed itself of the plaintiffs' property for the purpose of preserving its own more valuable property, and the plaintiffs are entitled to compensation for the injury done.

Order affirmed.

Knowledge

As you can see in the above *Vincent v. Lake Erie Transport* opinion, lawyers and judges use the skill of stating hypothetical scenarios similar to the facts. Law arises by organizing facts. Lawyers constantly deal with facts and hypothetical scenarios when evaluating past events or predicting events likely to occur in the future. Lawyers make informed judgments by comparing and contrasting similar situations to the case at hand. Lawyers reason inductively, employing constructed picture-stories as metaphors for the case at hand,

> reasoning by analogy. The lawyer's ability to hypothesize and conjecture as to possible or probable facts can also help investigate and develop case theories.

INQUIRY

Effect of Negligence. What if the ship captain or harbormaster claiming private necessity to keep ships at a dock during a storm should, in the exercise of reasonable care, have moved the ships earlier to avoid the storm? *See* Pacific Alaska Fuel Services v. M/V Miyoshima Maru, 1994 WL 739434 (D. Alaska) (no private-necessity defense). What role does the actor's reasonableness play in the defense of private necessity? *See* Benamon v. Soo Line R. Co., 294 Ill. App.3d 85, 228 Ill. Dec. 494, 689 N.W.2d 366 (1997) (youth's unreasonable entry onto dangerous land does not hold landowner to higher duty to youth, where youth had other, reasonable options); Trisuzzi v. Tabatchnik, 285 N.J. Super. 15, 666 A.2d 543 (1995) (jury must be allowed to decide whether dog-bite victim acted with reasonable care in entering dog owner's land to protect himself and his family). Must the person act intentionally with respect to the use of or entry onto the other's property, to claim a private necessity? *See* Kavanaugh v. Midwest Club, Inc., 164 Ill. App.3d 213, 115 Ill. Dec. 245, 517 N.E.2d 656 (1987) (motorist suffering epileptic seizure has no private-necessity claim to a landowner's protection from a pond adjacent to roadway, where motorist did not act intentionally).

Travelers. Should a traveler have a private-necessity privilege to cross private land adjacent to a blocked road? *See* Irwin v. Yeager, 74 Iowa 174, 37 N.W. 136 (1888) (yes); Morey v. Fitzgerald, 56 Vt. 487, 48 Am. Rep. 811 (1884) (yes). Are there any private necessities that justify the taking of another person's life? *See* United States v. Holmes, 1 Wall Jr. 1, 26 Fed. Cas. 360 (E.D. Pa. 1842) (seaman criminally responsible for providing that six passengers of lifeboat were thrown overboard to save remaining twenty-six passengers and nine crew on lifeboat); Arp v. State, 97 Ala. 5, 12 So. 301 (1893) (defendant criminally responsible for taking another's life notwithstanding that armed men threatened to shoot defendant if he did not take the other's life); Regina v. Dudley, 15 Cox C.C. 624, 14 Q.B.D. 273 (1884) (three shipwreck survivors afloat in lifeboat held criminally responsible for killing and eating fourth survivor). Should necessity defend acts of civil disobedience? *See* United States v. Schoon, 955 F.2d 1238 (9th Cir. 1991) (no necessity defense for defendants to throw simulated blood on Tucson IRS office wall in protest of American presence in war-torn El Salvador).

Authority of Law. Authority of law is another policy defense to intentional torts. Authority of law protects more officials than just police officers. It may also protect corrections officers (jail guards), military personnel, medical examiners, mental health personnel, immigration officials, and even regulatory inspectors. What is or is not a permissible arrest, investigation, or detention is a constitutional matter covered in other law-school courses and is also the subject of penal codes. To state some general principles, a proper arrest made of the person named in a valid warrant is obviously privileged. *See* Restatement (Second) of Torts §113 (1965); *see also* Kelly v. Story County Sheriff, 611 N.W.2d 475 (Iowa 2000) (no property-damage recovery for damage to front door done by officers executing arrest warrant). *Proper arrest* means the arresting person has not used excessive force, for which battery and civil-rights liability would exist. *Contrast* Thurman v. City of Milwaukee, 197 F. Supp.2d 1141 (E.D. Wis. 2002) (off-duty officer subject to liability for shooting and killing man who stole lawnmower from officer's garage), *with* Richardson v. McGriff, 762 A.2d 48 (Md. 2000) (use of deadly force was reasonable when officer found the plaintiff hiding in a closet and reasonably mistook vacuum for gun). The officer making the arrest must arrest the right person. The law does not allow mistake in identity, even if reasonable. If the warrant is valid on its face, then law privileges the officer to make the arrest. Law does not privilege an officer if the warrant is obviously invalid such as when it is from a court without jurisdiction.

Arrest. Law permits arrests without warrant under common-law rules providing generally as follows. Officers and citizens may arrest to stop a felony, or to keep the peace, in the arresting person's presence—with reasonable mistakes allowed. Officers may arrest suspects for felonies outside the officers' presence, and may make reasonable mistakes in doing so, if probable cause exists for their actions. Citizens may also do so, except that the citizen has no authority-of-law defense if no felony in fact occurred. Misdemeanor arrests require a warrant, except in a few jurisdictions that now allow misdemeanor arrests by an officer if the misdemeanor occurs in the officer's presence. The authority-of-law defense's protections do not extend to news-media coverage of arrests and the execution of search and arrest warrants. *See* Wilson v. Lane, 526 U.S. 603 (1999).

Discipline. Discipline is another policy defense, this one based on the relationship of the parties, granting one party the privilege to act toward the other in ways that might otherwise constitute an assault, battery, or false imprisonment. The relationships in which discipline may apply as a defense include parent and child, teacher and student, military superior and subordinate, and ship captain and crew or passengers. According to the Restatement (Second) of Torts §150, parent-child discipline should depend on a range of factors that may include the child's age, sex, and sensitivity; the reprehensibility of the act for which the parent disciplined; the effect of the act and discipline on other children in the family; the discipline's probability of increasing the child's obedience; and the discipline's degrading, injurious, or otherwise harmful nature. A person who temporarily acts for the parents may have some, though probably reduced, benefit of the privilege. Teacher-student physical discipline (corporal punishment), where allowed, must be reasonable. *Contrast* Neil v. Fulton County Bd., 229 F.3d 1069 (11th Cir. 2000) (striking student with metal lock may be unreasonable discipline), and Baikie v. Luther High School, 366 N.E.2d 542 (Ill. Ct App. 1977) (shoving student into locker may be unreasonable discipline), *with* Roy v. Continental Ins. Co., 313 So.2d 349 (La. Ct. App. 1975) (five paddle hits on buttocks is reasonable discipline). The scope of teacher-student discipline may depend on maintaining safety and order in the educational environment, ruling out reforming the student through physical discipline. *See* LaFrentz v. Gallagher, 105 Ariz. 255, 462 P.2d 804 (1969). Indeed, corporal-punishment statute may permit teacher-student contact only to protect safety and preserve order rather than for punishment. *See, e.g.,* Mich. Comp. L. §380.1312 (teachers may use reasonable force to maintain order and control); Rinehart v. Board of Educ., 87 Ohio App.2d 214, 621 N.E.2d 1365 (1993); *but see* Okla. Stat. Tit. 21, §844 (teachers may use ordinary force as discipline). Teachers may be liable for excessive force in the course of discipline, *see* Johnson v. Horace Mann Mut. Ins. Co., 241 So.2d 588 (La. App. 1970), and are especially at risk of suit when acting out of anger or motive other than to ensure safety and maintain order, *see* Story v. Martin, 217 So.2d 758 (La. App. 1969).

Justification. Justification is the final policy defense for consideration—obviously, from its name, a catchall category for compelling circumstances not covered by other, more-specific defenses. As an intentional-tort defense, justification has no particular contour. Apparently, too many circumstances exist where good excuse exists to intentionally damage or injure, to define this final defense with any greater precision than its title. See if you can discern its contours from the following two cases.

Drabek v. Sabley
Wisconsin Supreme Court
31 Wis.2d 184, 142 N.W.2d 798 (1966)

The jury found no false imprisonment and no assault and battery. ... Plaintiff has appealed.

Plaintiff Thomas Drabek, 10 years old, lived with his parents on highway 67, just north of the village of Williams Bay. On February 23, 1964, shortly before 6:00 p.m., Tom and four other boys were across the highway from the Drabek home, throwing snowballs at passing cars. Defendant, Dr. Nanito Sabley, drove by, and his car was hit by a snowball, apparently thrown by one of the other boys. Dr. Sabley stopped his car and the boys ran. Dr. Sabley pursued Tom for about 100 yards, caught him, and, holding him by the arm, took him to the car and directed him to enter it. Dr. Sabley asked and was told Tom's name, but did not ask where he lived. Dr. Sabley, who had been driving north, turned his car around and drove into the village. He located a police officer, and turned Tom over to him. Tom told the officer the names of the other boys involved, and the officer took Tom to his home. Tom was with the defendant some 15 to 20 minutes. ...

FAIRCHILD, J. Interpreting the evidence, where in conflict, most favorably to the verdict, defendant effectively restrained Tom's physical liberty, and took him into the village for the purpose of having him tell the police officer the names of the other boys. Defendant held Tom by the arm both on the way to the car before driving into the village, and, at times, while they were in the village. ...

Defendant claims justification in that he witnessed acts that were dangerous to defendant and others and took reasonable steps to prevent further dangerous activities.

It is recognized that one may be privileged to interfere with the liberty of another, within limits, for the purpose of defending one's self, defending a third person, or preventing the commission of a crime.[fn] Dr. Sabley did not act in self defense, since he was no longer in danger. It is true that the boys momentarily terminated their offensive activity when he stopped his car, but it was reasonable to expect them to renew it. We perceive that throwing snowballs at moving cars creates danger, as much because of the likelihood of startling the driver as of damage to the cars. Although it is a close question whether the threat to the safety of others was sufficiently immediate, after the boys had run away, it seems to us that Dr. Sabley, though not an officer, was privileged to take reasonable steps to prevent the resumption of the activity.

We conclude that Dr. Sabley's actions presented a jury question of reasonableness up to the time he put the boy in his car and drove away. Up to that time he had obtained the boy's name, and admonished him, according to the defendant's testimony, against carrying on the activity. The jury was entitled to believe that in holding the boy he used only such force as was reasonable for the purpose. Dr. Sabley may well have been justified in marching Tom across the road to his home and notifying his parents. We conclude, however, that it was unreasonable, as a matter of law, for Dr. Sabley to put 10-year-old Tom in his car a few yards from his home and drive him into the village for the purposes he did and under the circumstances of this case.

Accordingly we conclude that the jury finding, in effect, that Dr. Sabley's conduct was reasonable exonerates him up to the time he put Tom in the car, but not afterward. The restraint of Tom's liberty continued, and after that point there was false imprisonment. Dr. Sabley admitted holding Tom while they looked for the officer, and this was a battery, though nominal. ...

Judgment reversed, cause remanded for further proceedings.

Sindle v. New York City Transit Authority
Court of Appeals of New York
33 N.Y.2d 293, 307 N.E.2d 245, 352 N.Y.S.2d 183 (1973)

JASEN, J. At about noon on June 20, 1967, the plaintiff, then 14 years of age, boarded a school bus owned by the defendant, New York City Transit Authority, and driven by its employee, the defendant Mooney. It was the last day of the term at the Elias Bernstein Junior High School in Staten Island and the 65 to 70 students on board the bus were in a boisterous and exuberant mood. Some of this spirit expressed itself in vandalism, a number of students breaking dome lights, windows, ceiling panels and advertising poster frames. There is no evidence that the plaintiff partook in this destruction.

The bus made several stops at appointed stations. On at least one occasion, the driver admonished the students about excessive noise and damage to the bus. When he reached the Annadale station, the driver discharged several more passengers, went to the rear of the bus, inspected the damage and advised the students that he was taking them to the St. George police station.

The driver closed the doors of the bus and proceeded, bypassing several normal stops. As the bus slowed to turn onto Woodrow Road, several students jumped without apparent injury from a side window at the rear of the bus. Several more followed, again without apparent harm, when the bus turned onto Arden Avenue.

At the corner of Arden Avenue and Arthur Kill Road, departing from its normal route, the bus turned right in the general direction of the St. George police station. The plaintiff, intending to jump from the bus, had positioned himself in a window on the right-rear side. Grasping the bottom of the window sill with his hands, the plaintiff extended his legs (to mid-thigh), head and shoulders out of the window. As the bus turned right, the right rear wheels hit the curb and the plaintiff either jumped or fell to the street. The right rear wheels then rolled over the midsection of his body, causing serious personal injuries.

The plaintiff, joined with his father, then commenced an action to recover damages for negligence and false imprisonment. At the outset of the trial, the negligence cause was waived and plaintiffs proceeded on the theory of false imprisonment. ... The court also excluded all evidence bearing on the justification issue.

We believe that it was an abuse of discretion for the trial court ... to exclude the evidence of justification. It was the defendants' burden to prove justification—a defense that a plaintiff in an action for false imprisonment should be prepared to meet.... . The trial court's rulings precluded the defendants from introducing any evidence in this regard and were manifestly unfair. Accordingly, the order of the Appellate Division must be reversed and a new trial granted.

In view of our determination, it would be well to outline some of the considerations relevant to the issue of justification. In this regard, we note that, generally, restraint or detention, reasonable under the circumstances and in time and manner, imposed for the purpose of preventing another from inflicting personal injuries or interfering with or damaging real or personal property in one's lawful possession or custody is not unlawful. [C] Also, a parent, guardian or teacher entrusted with the care or supervision of a child may use physical force reasonably necessary to maintain discipline or promote the welfare of the child. [C]

Similarly, a school bus driver, entrusted with the care of his student-passengers and the custody of public property, has the duty to take reasonable measures for the safety and protection of both—the passengers and the property. In this regard, the reasonableness of his actions—as bearing on the defense of justification—is to be determined from a consideration of all the circumstances. At a minimum, this would seem to import, a consideration of the need to protect the persons and property in his charge, the duty to aid the investigation and apprehension of those inflicting damage, the manner and place of the occurrence, and the feasibility and practicality of other alternative courses of action. ...

For the reasons stated, the order of the Appellate Division should be reversed and the case remitted for a new trial.

MEDICAL RECORDS

Tort lawyers work extensively with medical records. Those records may include admission records, consent forms, physicians' notes, orders, and consults, laboratory and imaging reports, nurses' notes, therapy and progress reports, discharge summaries, and other documentation. Lawyers must know how to choose, obtain, summarize, and analyze medical records, organize them for retrieval, and use them in pretrial matters and at trial. Here are a few practical tips. On *choosing records,* in many cases, the attorneys involved in the case will need to obtain all medical records. In cases involving unusually voluminous records, the lawyers may begin by seeking admission records, physician and consult reports, imaging interpretations, and discharge summaries. To *obtain records,* the attorneys will often write cover letters to the medical-care providers, enclosing the patient's signed authorization for release of medical information. Other attorneys prefer to use medical-record services that charge fees for obtaining records. To *organize records,* when the records arrive, attorneys keep them in the form produced (important for later identification), often number-stamping each page for ready identification. Copies will then be put in chronological or other meaningful order in a single master file and tabbed so that they are available for prompt retrieval. A good first step in *analyzing records* is for attorneys to be sure that the records are complete. One then reads the complete records with care taken to decode abbreviations and code numbers, and (using a medical dictionary) to define unknown terms. Attorneys may look for inconsistent diagnoses, unnatural progression of conditions, and interruptions in care including missed appointments and treatment refused. Attorneys may also *summarize records* both chronologically and by provider.

> **Career**
> Technology can make a difference in finding employment and succeeding in tort practice. By using the Internet, one can learn a lot about potential employers and their needs and interests. You can also use e-portfolios, slide shows, websites, and electronic writing samples to demonstrate your knowledge and skill. Torts practitioners level the professional playing field with technology. They depend on technology for research, discovery, trial preparation and presentation, timekeeping, billing, practice and case management, and client communication. When you demonstrate your technology skills, you increase your value to prospective clients and employers, while also conveying to opposing counsel and the court your professional competence. Firms maintaining torts practices hire new lawyers for the technology skills they bring to the firm. Develop and demonstrate your technology skills.

CHAPTER V

NEGLIGENCE—GENERALLY

OBJECTIVE: Given descriptions of personal injury and property damage in a variety of circumstances, recall the elements of negligence and identify the facts that if present would satisfy each element in each circumstance, consistent with this section of the text.

As the introduction suggests, negligence as a legal concept has been around since the earliest known laws—the most-ancient Code of Hammurabi providing for liability for loss from a house not made strong, a boat not made firm, and a boatman acting carelessly. Among other early tort laws like those found in the Covenant Code, the Torah, and the Mesopotamian region, the later Roman codes were the most-developed in negligence law. Early Roman laws tended to combine negligence and criminal provisions. An example is the tenth statement of the Twelve Tables (449 B.C.). It provides, "If a man willfully set fire to a house, or to a stack of corn set up near a house, he shall be bound, scourged, and burned alive; if the fire rose through accident, that is, through negligence, he shall make compensation, and, if too poor, he shall undergo a moderate punishment." But by the Institutes of Justinian (533 A.D.), Roman law treated negligence separately and divided it into five gradations—gross negligence, ordinary negligence, and slight neglect in one hierarchy, and lack of diligence within a trade or the neglect of the ordinary care of a lay person in another hierarchy. Law then traces the negligence tort, reflecting an imperative of care, into and through the Continental code and English common-law traditions, down to today.

Negligence owes its rise to modern prominence, though, to two other phenomena. One is the increased danger in the workplace that accompanied industrialization in the mid-to-late 1800s. The other is the development of liability insurance for maritime trade during the same period. Industrialization caused so many careless injuries in the workplace that by the early 1900s, worker's compensation acts were in place that provided a hope (realized or not) for reasonable compensation for the injured worker. As to liability insurance, negligence claims are today the heart and soul of tort law (and the practitioner's bread and butter) because of the liability insurance available to fund judgments and settlements for negligence claimants. Even in the few remaining motor-vehicle no-fault states, laws mandate negligence-liability insurance for motor vehicles operated on public highways. Many of those laws refuse vehicle registration without proof of insurance. One cannot obtain a home mortgage without proof of homeowner's insurance that typically includes negligence-liability coverage. Professionals may not be able to obtain or renew their professional licenses without proof of malpractice-liability insurance coverage or may have to disclose whether they have insurance. Government and others routinely require companies to carry liability insurance as a condition of doing business, to ensure compensation to negligence victims and avoid indirect-liability suits aimed at deeper pockets. One can hardly overstate the centrality of negligence claims to the tort system.

One other consideration important to maintaining negligence claims bears mention. The pursuit of a negligence claim can require dozens or even hundreds of hours of attorney time, depending on the size and complexity of the case. It can also require tens of thousands of dollars in advanced costs for expert witnesses, accident reconstruction, deposition transcripts, and mediation and court costs—costs that are recovered (if at all) at the conclusion of a case that may take years to resolve. Injured plaintiffs tend not to have the finances available with which to retain lawyers and advance litigation costs. Plaintiff's lawyers routinely handle negligence claims under contingency-fee agreements like the example earlier in this text. The insurance companies that indemnify and defend parties liable for injury and loss tend not to have these resource constraints. Their concerns are instead over quality service to their customers, and profit and loss. Although some insurance companies use in-house counsel, they tend to retain defense lawyers case-by-case from approved counsel lists and pay them by the hour, under increasingly strict budgets and cost controls. Without these financing mechanisms, the tort system would not look like what it does today. Without contingency fees, injured persons would have little access to the courts.

> **Ethics**
> Statute, court rules, and ethics rules all govern contingency-fee agreements. Rule 1.5 of the ABA Model Rules of Professional Conduct prohibits a lawyer from charging an unreasonable fee. The reasonableness of a fee depends on factors including the time and labor required, novelty and difficulty of the case, skill level required, fee customarily charged, amount involved, results obtained, and the lawyer's reputation. Rule 1.5 expressly permits contingency-fee agreements (except for certain non-tort cases) but requires that they be in writing and signed by the client, explain how the fee is calculated, and state the expenses and manner of their calculation. Rule 1.5 also prohibits lawyers in different firms from dividing a fee unless the client agrees and the lawyers share responsibility for the matter or divide the fee in proportion to their services—in effect, limiting referral fees. Rule 1.8(e) prohibits a lawyer from providing financial assistance to a client (loans, for example) in connection with litigation except to advance litigation costs. Some lawyers reproduce this last rule—no loans to litigation clients—on their contingency-fee agreements. Can you see why?

Negligence is both the name of the modern cause of action—like *assault*, *battery*, and *false imprisonment*—and one of the elements of the tort by the same name. The negligence cause of action has four elements: duty, breach, causation, and damages. Lawyers often use the word *negligence* to refer only to the *breach* element of negligence claims. When a lawyer says that the defendant "was negligent," they mean that the defendant's conduct breached the applicable standard of care (that evidence satisfies the breach element of a negligence claim), not necessarily that all other elements of a negligence claim (duty, causation, and damages) are present. Likewise, the Restatement (Third) of Torts: Liability for Physical and Emotional Harm §3 (2005) defines *negligence* not as the cause of action including all four of its elements (duty, breach, causation, and damages) but as the breach element of the negligence cause:

> A person acts negligently if the person does not exercise reasonable care under all the circumstances. Primary factors to consider in ascertaining whether the

person's conduct lacks reasonable care are the foreseeable likelihood that the person's conduct will result in harm, the foreseeable severity of any harm that may ensue, and the burden of precautions to eliminate or reduce the risk of harm.

The four elements of a negligence claim influence one another and are sometimes difficult to analyze separately. Different lawyers might characterize a single negligence issue as a question of duty, or of breach, or of causation, or of damages. For instance, when a court considers whether to hold a slingshot manufacturer liable in negligence for one boy's putting out the eye of another using the slingshot as it was designed (even if not for its intended purpose), the question could be whether the manufacturer owed a duty to the victim. The question could also be whether the manufacturer breached any duty, the breach was a cause of the unfortunate incident, or the foreseeable injury was serious enough to justify liability. See Moning v. Alfono, 400 Mich 425, 254 N.W.2d 759 (1977) (manufacturer subject to liability under duty analysis).

Those cautions aside, the duty element of a negligence claim requires determining whether the law required the defendant to conform the defendant's conduct to a certain standard—whether, for instance, of reasonable care of an adult or of a child of the same age, or of a minimally competent professional, or of a specialist in the field, and so on. Determining duty requires law knowledge and application of law to the parties' circumstance. The breach element of a negligence claim requires determining whether the defendant's conduct conformed to the standard of care. Breach involves primarily a factual determination. The causation element of a negligence claim requires determining whether a sufficient connection existed between the defendant's breach and plaintiff's injury. Causation is initially a factual question but, as the connection grows more remote, can also involve policy judgments. The damages element of a negligence claim requires proof of the plaintiff's injury or loss. If the plaintiff has no damages, then the plaintiff has no negligence claim. Where a defendant's conduct creates an unreasonable risk that has not yet hurt anyone, the action, if any, would be one for nuisance, not negligence. Negligence is in that sense a law of responsible liberty. It imposes no bar to careless conduct—only a deterrent and remedy. It is neither bar nor deterrent to reasonably careful conduct, for harm in connection with which it provides no remedy.

This text treats the four negligence elements in their logical and traditional order—first duty, then breach, then causation, and finally damages. Yet torts practitioners, judges, juries, and liability-insurance representatives do not necessarily approach torts claims so logically. The damage element may be the primary matter about which all participants are most concerned. Plaintiff's lawyers often begin an opening statement and closing argument with what happened to the plaintiff, addressing damages. The story is often much more about how severely the event affected the plaintiff's life (damages) than what the defendant owed the plaintiff (duty) or precisely what caused the loss (causation)—although like damages, the defendant's culpability (breach) can also be a large part of the story. By contrast, defendants and their counsel tend instead to focus on the duty and causation (especially proximate cause) elements, those which counsel find easier to defend. In any tort case, all but one of the elements may be largely undisputed, and the whole case may turn on the remaining element, which may be any one of the four elements. Tort practice thus requires broad knowledge and a variety of skills, from legal research on duty, to administrative investigation of industry standards, accident reconstruction, questions of scientific cause, and medical and social issues relating to injury. Consider next the subtlety of negligence rules, responding to the wonderful and awful variety in human relationship and circumstance.

Skills

Attorneys do well to anticipate and know their client's interests, preferences, and needs. When a potential client meets with an attorney over whether to enter into a contingency-fee agreement, the potential client may be considering: (a) whether the attorney will take less than the proposed percentage fee; (b) what the cost reimbursement provision means, and how much the costs will be; (c) how sure the attorney is that the client will win the case, and for how much; (d) what experience the attorney has in the field and how well-thought-of the attorney is by judges and bar; (e) whether the attorney will return the client's telephone calls and keep the client well-informed; (f) what happens if the client wants to fire the attorney part way through the claim; and (g) whether the client will have to pay the attorney anything if the case is lost. The attorney should have answers to these questions. Choose another student with whom to work, choose attorney and potential client roles, and see if you can come to an agreement over whether to sign the contingency-fee agreement reproduced above or negotiate another one like it.

A. Duty

OBJECTIVE: Given negligence claims involving a variety of defendants or potential defendants, determine whether each defendant owed the plaintiff a duty, and if so, identify the standard of care as to each, consistent with this section of the text.

Case Study: A contractor drove his pickup truck into the intersection colliding with a vehicle driven by a mother. The mother had her three-year-old daughter riding in her car without a child seat. The collision injured both mother and daughter. A subcontractor's compressor was stored loose in the back of the contractor's pickup truck. The collision damaged the compressor beyond repair. On her way to the scene, an emergency vehicle driver raced through an intersection causing a motorist to drive his vehicle hard up against a curb. ***Identify the facts that if present would satisfy the elements of a negligence claim as to each instance of personal injury or property damage.***

1. Generally

Duty. Law is much about duty. Deontological (duty-based) theories pervade all of law including tort law because of the volitional and discrete nature of our existence. We are both volitionally independent and consciously purposeful beings. And so of necessity (at least if we are to be rational about it), we must regard others as also volitionally independent and consciously purposeful—that self-evident truth about which Jefferson wrote in the Declaration of Independence that God created all equal. Thus, the easiest category in which tort duties arise is where a person acts creating a foreseeable risk of harm. In choosing to move, walk, sit, run, shoot, fly, design, construct, sell, operate, or do any of the other myriad of activities of which we are capable, we must also consider the effect of our choices on others, unless we wish to relinquish our own opportunity to choose and act with conscious purpose (our liberty, that is). Tort law describes this fundamental other-consideration as *care*. We could more prosaically call it *love* (the Greek agape form, not eros). Thus, we describe tort-law duties at their fundamental level using terms like *reasonable care*, *ordinary care*, and the *reasonably prudent person*, referring to an objective standard outside of the individual whose conduct is at issue.

The Restatement (Third) of Torts: Liability for Physical and Emotional Harm §7 defines the scope of a person's duty as follows:

> (a) An actor ordinarily has a duty to exercise reasonable care when the actor's conduct creates a risk of physical harm.
>
> (b) In exceptional cases, when an articulated countervailing principle or policy warrants denying or limiting liability in a particular class of cases, a court may decide that the defendant has no duty or that the ordinary duty of reasonable care requires modification.

Under the Restatement's approach, each of us generally has a duty to conduct ourselves with reasonable care whenever our acts create a foreseeable risk of physical harm to others. Because we create risks with much of what we do, the law rarely disputes duty when our actions are the factual cause of another's harm. Contrary to the analysis of many cases, *see, e.g.*, Wiener v. Southcoast Children Centers, Inc., 88 P.3d 517 (Cal. 2004); Remsburg v. Docusearch, Inc., 816 A.2d 1001 (N.H. 2003), the existence of a duty to behave with reasonable care should not depend on the foreseeability of risk. Foreseeability is relevant to whether a person or entity has breached a duty and whether the breach was the proximate cause of injury (both topics discussed later). As discussed later in this chapter, the law may eliminate or modify the general duty of reasonable care in circumstances where public policy demands it.

Behavior Standards. Tort law has always employed objective standards for behavior. The reasonably prudent-person standard had its modern genesis in Vaughan v. Menlove, 3 Bing. (N.C.) 468, 132 Eng. Rep. 490 (1837). The *Vaughan* defendant built a hayrick near the plaintiff's cottages. After the rick caught fire, destroying the plaintiff's cottages, the trial judge instructed the jury deciding the plaintiff's negligence claim that the defendant "was bound to proceed with such reasonable caution as a prudent man would have exercised under such circumstances." The defendant maintained on appeal that the question should have been "whether he had acted bona fide to the best of his judgment." The opinions held instead that the trial judge had been correct, that negligence liability should not rise and fall "co-extensive with the judgment of each individual," and that the standard was "the conduct of a man of ordinary prudence…." The reasonably prudent-person standard suffers some academic criticism. But the standard demands only an obtainable and sustainable merit—in its quaint, English conception, the conduct expected of "'the man in the street' or 'the man in the Clapham omnibus,' or … 'the man who takes the magazines at home, and in the evening pushes the lawn mower in his shirt sleeves.'" Hall v. Brooklands Club, 1 K.B. 205, 224 (1933). Consider the following case.

Delair v. McAdoo

Pennsylvania Supreme Court
324 Pa. 392, 188 A. 181 (1936)

KEPHART, C.J. Plaintiff brought an action in trespass to recover for damages to his person and property sustained as a result of a collision between his automobile and that owned by the defendant. The accident occurred when defendant, proceeding in the same direction as plaintiff, sought to pass him. As defendant drew alongside of plaintiff, the left rear tire of his car blew out, causing it to swerve and come into contact with the plaintiff's car. The latter's theory at trial was that defendant was negligent in driving with defective tires. The jury found for plaintiff in the sum of $7,500. The court ... refused [defendant's] motion for a judgment n. o. v. Its ruling on the ... motion is here for review. ...

It is common experience that the blow-out of an automobile tire is a hazardous occurrence. A blow-out has a known tendency to cause the vehicle to swerve and become unmanageable, rendering possible injury to others due to the lack of control. [C] ...

While blow-outs may result from untoward accidents for which no responsibility exists such as from spikes and other causes [cc], where they result from defects in the tire arising from age or wear, there seems little doubt that responsibility should attend the dereliction of the vehicle owner in using such equipment, if the faults would be disclosed on reasonable inspection. ...

It has been held in other states that the question whether a particular person is negligent in failing to know that his tires are in too poor a condition for ordinary operation on the highways is a question of fact for the jury. [Cc] In the instant case the testimony relative to the defect was as follows: A witness for the plaintiff stated that the tire "was worn pretty well through. You could see the tread in the tire—the inside lining." The witness later described this inside lining as the "fabric." The fact that the tire was worn through to and into the fabric over its entire area was corroborated by another witness. The repairman who replaced the tire which had blown out stated that he could see "the breaker strip" which is just under the fabric of a tire. ...

The question was raised at bar whether plaintiff should not have had expert testimony to show that a tire in the condition testified to was dangerous. It would seem, however, that this is a matter as to which the ordinary man's experience is sufficient to enable him to make a sound judgment. ...

A jury is just as well qualified to pass judgment as to the risk of danger in the condition of an article in universal use under a given state of facts as experts. We have in this state more than a million automobiles and trucks, approximately two for every three families. Their daily use over the highways is common, and requires a certain amount of knowledge of the movable parts, particularly the tires; it is imperative that a duty or standard of care be set up that will be productive of safety for other users of the highways. Any ordinary individual, whether a car owner or not, knows that when a tire is worn through to the fabric, its further use is dangerous and it should be removed. When worn through several plies, it is very dangerous for further use. All drivers must be held to a knowledge of these facts. An owner or operator cannot escape simply because he says he does not know. He must know. The hazard is too great to permit cars in this condition to be on the highway. It does not require opinion evidence to demonstrate that a trigger pulled on a loaded gun makes the gun a dangerous instrument when pointed at an individual, nor could one escape liability by saying he did not know it was dangerous. The use of a tire worn through to the fabric presents a similar situation. The rule must be rigid if millions are to drive these instrumentalities which in a fraction of a second may become instruments of destruction to life and property. There is no series of accidents more destructive or more terrifying in the use of automobiles than those which come from "blow-outs." The law requires drivers and owners of motor vehicles to know the condition of those parts which are likely to become dangerous where the flaws or faults would be disclosed by a reasonable inspection. It will assume they do know of the dangers ascertainable by such examination.

Order affirmed.

INQUIRY

Degrees of Duty. Is there a higher standard of care than ordinary or reasonable care? *See* Stewart v. Motts, 539 Pa. 596, A.2d 535 (1995) ("there is but one standard of care to be applied to negligence actions," although reasonableness may require greater care regarding dangerous instrumentalities); Butler v. Acme Markets, Inc., 177 N.J. Super. 279, 426 A.2d 521 (1981) (the standard remains the same, although greater danger may require greater care), affd., 89 N.J. 270, 445 A.2d 1141 (1982); Purtle v. Shelton, 251 Ark. 519, 474 S.W.2d 123 (1971) (affirming refusal of trial judge to give requested instruction that defendant should have used "high degree of care commensurate with the dangers" of hunting, in favor of "ordinary care under the circumstances" instruction); *but see* Wood v. Groh, 269 Kan. 420, 7 P.3d 1163 (2000) (requiring "extraordinary care" when the danger from conduct is high). Traditionally, common carriers have been held to a higher degree of care variously described as the "highest duty of care," *see* Jones v. Port Auth. of Allegheny County, 583 A.2d 512 (Pa. Comm. 1990) (ordering new trial for failure to instruct jury that defendant bus authority owed patron rider the highest duty of care), or even the "utmost care," although there may be a modern trend to employ the reasonable care standard, *see* Bethel v. New York City Transit Auth., 703 N.E.2d 1214 (N.Y. 1998) (heightened standard unnecessary). Given higher standards of care, should *lower* standards of care than reasonable care also exist? Some courts require certain plaintiffs, like trespassers, to prove defendant's recklessness—meaning that the defendant knew or (in negligence actions) should have known of a high probability of harm. *See* Beausoleil v. National R.R. Passenger Corp., 145 F. Supp.2d 119, 125-126 (D. Mass. 2001). The no-recklessness standard is, in effect, a lower standard than reasonable care.

Duty to Protect. One of the more difficult duty questions involves the duty of a person or entity—particularly a business—to protect others against crimes by third persons. A shopping mall and its security company are well aware that of frequent crimes, including escalating crimes of violence against women, inside the mall and in its parking area but fail to take reasonable action to alert and protect mall customers. A perpetrator rapes a woman shopper in the mall. Can the woman hold the mall and security company liable in tort based on a duty to take reasonable measures to protect against crime? *See* L.A.C. v. Ward Parkway Shopping Ctr., 75 S.W.3d 247 (Mo. 2002) (yes). The duty question may not be as simple as it sounds in this context.

Society reserves most police functions to the government. Business owners may not have the resources or expertise to engage in the kind of aggressive policing that some communities require to combat entrenched crime. Police agencies and communities may not want private businesses—even sophisticated security companies—engaging in police functions. Yet some circumstances nonetheless seem to compel a duty. *See* Stewart v. Federated Dept. Stores, Inc., 234 Conn. 597, 662 A.2d 753 (1995) (store liable for murder of customer in unguarded parking garage that invited violence). Previous crimes make foreseeability of the liability incident more likely. *See* Erichsen v. No-Frills Supermarkets of Omaha, Inc., 246 Neb. 238, 518 N.W.2d 116 (1994). Yet courts can disagree about what constitutes a sufficiently similar crime. *Contrast* Liszewski v. Target Corp., 374 F.3d 597 (8th Cir. 2004) (other crimes dissimilar), *with* Sturbridge Partners, Ltd. v. Walker, 267 Ga. 785, 482 S.E.2d 339 (1997) (prior burglaries may be similar enough to create duty to prevent rape). Prior threats can also make a difference. *See* Metropolitan School Dist. v. Jackson, 9 N.E.3d 230 (Ind. Ct. App. 2014) (duty to protect against school shooter expelled for fifty discipline referrals and threat to blow up school). Do you think that the balancing test applied in the following case is an appropriate means by which to account for the various factors on whether a duty should exist to prevent crime?

Posecai v. Wal-Mart Stores, Inc.
Louisiana Supreme Court
752 So.2d 762 (La. 1999)

MARCUS, J. Shirley Posecai brought suit against Sam's Wholesale Club ("Sam's") in Kenner after she was robbed at gunpoint in the store's parking lot. On July 20, 1995, Mrs. Posecai went to Sam's to make an exchange and to do some shopping. She exited the store and returned to her parked car at approximately 7:20 p.m. It was not dark at the time. As Mrs. Posecai was placing her purchases in the trunk, a man who was hiding under her car grabbed her ankle and pointed a gun at her. The unknown assailant instructed her to hand over her jewelry and her wallet. ... She lost [jewelry] ... valued at close to $19,000. ...

At the time of this armed robbery, a security guard was stationed inside the store to protect the cash office from 5:00 p.m. until the store closed at 8:00 p.m. He could not see outside and Sam's did not have security guards patrolling the parking lot. ...

An expert on crime risk assessment and premises security, David Kent, was qualified and testified on behalf of the plaintiff. It was his opinion that the robbery of Mrs. Posecai could have been prevented by an exterior security presence. He presented crime data from the Kenner Police Department indicating that between 1989 and June of 1995 there were three robberies or "predatory offenses"[fn] on Sam's premises, and provided details from the police reports on each of these crimes.[fn] ...

... Mr. Kent ... found a total of eighty-three predatory offenses in the six and a half years before Mrs. Posecai was robbed [in the area of the Wal-Mart store]. Mr. Kent concluded that the area around Sam's was "heavily crime impacted".... .

A threshold issue in any negligence action is whether the defendant owed the plaintiff a duty. [C] Whether a duty is owed is a question of law. [Cc] In deciding whether to impose a duty in a particular case, the court must make a policy decision in light of the unique facts and circumstances presented. [C] The court may consider various moral, social, and economic factors, including the fairness of imposing liability; the economic impact on the defendant and on similarly situated parties; the need for an incentive to prevent future harm; the nature of defendant's activity; the potential for an unmanageable flow of litigation; the historical development of precedent; and the direction in which society and its institutions are evolving. [Cc]

This court has never squarely decided whether business owners owe a duty to protect their patrons from crimes perpetrated by third parties.[fn] ... Most state supreme courts that have considered the issue agree that business owners do have a duty to take reasonable precautions to protect invitees from foreseeable criminal attacks.[fn]

We now join other states in adopting the rule that although business owners are not the insurers of their patrons' safety, they do have a duty to implement reasonable measures to protect their patrons from criminal acts when those acts are foreseeable. We emphasize, however, that there is generally no duty to protect others from the criminal activities of third persons. [C] This duty only arises under limited circumstances, when the criminal act in question was reasonably foreseeable to the owner of the business. Determining when a crime is foreseeable is therefore a critical inquiry. ...

We agree that a balancing test is the best method for determining when business owners owe a duty to provide security for their patrons. The economic and social impact of requiring businesses to provide security on their premises is an important factor. Security is a significant monetary expense for any business and further increases the cost of doing business in high crime areas that are already economically depressed. Moreover, businesses are generally not responsible for the endemic crime that plagues our communities, a societal problem that even our law enforcement and other government agencies have been unable to solve. At the same time, business owners are in the best position to appreciate the crime risks that are posed on their premises and to take reasonable precautions to counteract those risks.

With the foregoing considerations in mind, we adopt the following balancing test to be used in deciding whether a business owes a duty of care to protect its customers from the criminal acts of third parties. The foreseeability of the crime risk on the defendant's property and the gravity of the risk determine the existence and the extent of the defendant's duty. The greater the foreseeability and gravity of the harm, the greater the duty of care that will be imposed on the business. A very high degree of foreseeability is required to give rise to a duty to post security guards, but a lower degree of foreseeability may support a duty to implement lesser security measures such as using surveillance cameras, installing improved lighting or fencing, or trimming shrubbery. The plaintiff has the burden of establishing the duty the defendant owed under the circumstances.

The foreseeability and gravity of the harm are to be determined by the facts and circumstances of the case. The most important factor to be considered is the existence, frequency and similarity of prior incidents of crime on the premises, but the location, nature and condition of the property should also be taken into account. It is highly unlikely that a crime risk will be sufficiently foreseeable for the imposition of a duty to provide security guards if there have not been previous instances of crime on the business' premises. ...

We conclude that Sam's did not possess the requisite degree of foreseeability for the imposition of a duty to provide security patrols in its parking lot. ... Accordingly,

Sam's owed no duty to protect Mrs. Posecai from the criminal acts of third parties under the facts and circumstances of this case. ...

For the reasons assigned, the judgment of the court of appeal is reversed. It is ordered that judgment be rendered in favor of Wal-Mart Stores, Inc. ...

INQUIRY

Duty as a Question of Law. As you can see from the *Posecai* case, not every claim goes to the jury. When the *Posecai* appellate court stated that whether a defendant owes a duty is a question of law, the court meant that the trial judge should decide, not the jury. Trial judges usually make those duty decisions on the defendant's motion well before trial. Juries decide disputed *fact* issues, while judges determine questions of *law*. You will study this law-fact distinction, including its constitutional and historical source, in civil-procedure courses. For now, know that trial judges define the limits of tort-law duties, while juries decide disputed facts. For another example of a duty question for the trial judge, do high-school officials owe a duty to maintain a closed campus so that students do not drive recklessly from the campus and hurt one another? *See* Rogers v. Retrum, 825 P.2d 20 (Ariz. App. 1991) (although schools owe duties of reasonable care to their students with respect to school policies, the duty does not extend to preventing off-campus motor-vehicle accidents). Does a city owe a duty to construct highway medians so that drivers do not lose control of their vehicles when they drive onto and across them? *See* Washington v. City of Chicago, 720 N.W.2d 1030 (Ill. 1999) (no duty to construct planter boxes on median so that emergency vehicle can negotiate median without lost control). Consider the following case on the limits of duty as a matter of law, before studying other, more-specific limits in following sections on qualified duties.

Galanti v. United States
United States Court of Appeals for the Eleventh Circuit
709 F.2d 706 (1983)

MORGAN, J. Vivian W. Galanti, plaintiff-appellant, brought this action against the government in the District Court for the Northern District of Georgia under the Federal Tort Claims Act (FTCA), 28 U.S.C. §1346(b), claiming that her husband, Isaac N. Galanti, died as a result of negligence committed by an agent of the Federal Bureau of Investigation (FBI). The district court concluded that no actionable negligence exists under the pertinent facts and granted the government's motion to dismiss for failure to state a claim. We affirm the district court's order for the following reasons.

The facts giving rise to appellant's claim are undisputed.[fn] In October of 1978, Isaac N. Galanti and Roger Dean Underhill were shot to death on a secluded tract of undeveloped property in Fulton County, Georgia. Galanti was interested in purchasing the property from Underhill, and the two men were inspecting it at the time of their deaths. Unknown to Galanti, Underhill was a key witness in the government's investigation into the criminal activity of Michael G. Thevis. Thevis, a convicted felon, had escaped from federal custody six months earlier and was still a fugitive at the time of the murders. He was apprehended a month later and eventually convicted in federal court of violating Underhill's civil rights by having him murdered, along with the innocent bystander Galanti, in order to prevent Underhill's testimony in the government's case.

For several months before his death, Underhill traveled a great deal and kept a low profile, although he frequently contacted F.B.I. Agent Paul V. King, Jr. King was in charge of the Thevis investigation and knew that Thevis had made earlier attempts to kill Underhill. King considered Underhill to be in extreme danger at all times. For this reason, the government arranged for Underhill to enter a witness protection program in which Underhill would be given a permanent, new identity with government assistance, but Underhill refused to enter the program until he sold the undeveloped property in Fulton County. He ignored advice to retain a real estate agent and insisted on personally handling the sale of his property. In the week preceding his death, Underhill repeatedly visited the property even though King advised him of the needless danger involved. On the night before the murders, Underhill called and informed King that he would be showing the property the next day to Galanti who had answered a newspaper advertisement. King made no attempt to contact and warn Galanti of the potential danger, nor did he arrange for surveillance of the property. This is the conduct which formed the basis of appellant's suit in the district court. She claimed that King's failure to warn or protect Nicholas Galanti against a specific, foreseeable danger was a negligent act and the proximate cause of her husband's death.[fn]

This action was necessarily filed in federal court under the provisions of the FTCA since appellant seeks to hold the government liable for the negligence of its employee, but both parties agree that Georgia law controls the negligence issue. [C] In Georgia there are four essential elements of a negligence action:

> (1) A legal duty to conform to a standard of conduct raised by the law for the protection of others against unreasonable risks of harm;
> (2) A breach of this standard;
> (3) A legally attributable causal connection between the conduct and the resulting injury; and,
> (4) Some loss or damage flowing to the plaintiff's legally protected interest as a result of the alleged breach of the legal duty.

Bradley Center v. Wessner, 250 Ga. 199, 200, 296 S.E.2d 693 (1982). It is the first element with which we are concerned in this appeal. The court below concluded that under no circumstances could appellant establish a legal duty owed by King to Nicholas Galanti, and accordingly granted the government's motion to dismiss for failure to state a claim. Appellant vigorously challenges this conclusion and relies on a large number of state and federal cases, some very recent, in order to support her argument. After a careful review of the various claims and the relevant law, we find that the district court's order must be affirmed.[fn]

The general rule in Georgia is that one has no duty to warn or protect another person from a foreseeable risk of harm simply because of one's knowledge of the danger. [Cc] In other words, the mere foreseeability of injury to another person does not of itself create a duty to act.[FN4. The Second Restatement of Torts provides the best codification of this common law rule: "The fact that the actor realizes or should realize that action on his part is necessary for another's aid or protection does not of itself impose upon him a duty to take such action." Restatement (Second) of Torts § 314 (1965).] This rule is not applicable in three distinct factual situations, however, and appellant contends that each of the three exceptions is present here. First, the duty to protect or warn against danger will arise if the defendant has in any way taken an affirmative step to create the danger. In the recent case of United States v. Aretz, 248 Ga. 19, 26, 280 S.E.2d 345, 350 (1981), the Georgia Supreme Court held that "where one by his own act, although without negligence on his part, creates a dangerous situation, he is under a duty to remove the hazard or give warning of the danger so as to prevent others from being injured where it is reasonably foreseeable that this will occur." In that case, the United States Army provided one of its contractors with mistaken information concerning the appropriate storage classification of explosive materials. The Army later realized the mistake, but failed to communicate it to the contractor, and the materials exploded causing injury and death to several of the contractor's employees. The Georgia court, upon certification from the Fifth Circuit Court of Appeals, held that the Army's failure to inform the contractor of the change in classification was a breach of duty which arose when the Army mistakenly classified the materials in the first place. The *Aretz* decision relied heavily on an earlier Georgia case, Hardy v. Brooks, 103 Ga.App. 124, 118 S.E.2d 492 (1961), where the defendant hit and killed a cow without negligence while driving his car on a public road. The Georgia Court of Appeals held that the defendant's act of killing the cow created the duty to act in the face of foreseeable danger to other drivers on the road. Therefore, *Aretz* and *Hardy* stand for the proposition that a duty to warn or protect a third person from danger will arise if the defendant affirmatively contributes to the creation of the danger. [C] In the present case, FBI Agent King did nothing to create the foreseeable danger. He was merely aware of the risk to Galanti and for whatever reason chose not to act. Georgia law does not hold him legally responsible for knowledge alone.

A second exception to the general rule concerns the defendant's failure to properly exercise his ability to control the foreseeably dangerous instrument. The most recent Georgia decision involving this principle is Bradley Center, Inc. v. Wessner, 250 Ga. 199, 296 S.E.2d 693 (1982). In that case, a private mental hospital released one of its patients despite its ability to keep the patient confined, and despite its knowledge that the patient might cause harm to a specific third party. Under these facts the Georgia court held that the hospital owed a legal duty to the third party even in the absence of the usual doctor-patient privity. Appellant argues that *Bradley* stands for the proposition that one must always warn or protect a third person from a foreseeable criminal act, but this argument is incorrect. *Bradley,* and other cases like it, hold that the legal duty arises only if the defendant failed to exercise his ability to control the potential criminal. [C] This is not the situation we are faced with here. Appellant has not alleged, and the relevant facts do not support the theory, that FBI Agent King or his associates had the ability and failed to control Michael Thevis.[fn] Thevis was a wanted fugitive beyond King's control during the relevant time period, and thus King had no duty to warn or protect Galanti merely because of the danger posed by Thevis' known criminal intent.

Finally, law enforcement officials may have the legal duty to warn or protect against danger if they have voluntarily assumed or incurred that duty to a specific individual. [Cc] However, this duty, if at all applicable here, would extend only to Roger Dean Underhill, and he repeatedly ignored warnings and refused protection.

Appellant cannot cite to any Georgia statute or case which charges law enforcement officials with the duty to warn or protect members of the general public simply upon learning of a possible danger.

We recognize that the result in this case may appear harsh because Galanti's death very likely would have been avoided if King had chosen to act rather than to remain silent. Nonetheless, Georgia law did not impose any legal duty on King to act on behalf of Galanti, and therefore appellant's complaint did not establish a viable claim. For this reason, the order of the district court is

AFFIRMED.

2. Standards of Care

As the above cases suggest, standards of care involve more than vague generalities like reasonable care and the reasonably prudent person. Tort lawyers plead, argue, and prove standards of care with greater specificity. For example, reasonable care in a case in which an auto mechanic made a shoddy vehicle repair leading to an accident may involve duties to reasonably inspect, report, advise, repair, and test—and, possibly, to comply with vehicle-repair laws and regulations, mechanic-licensing requirements, shop training, and repair-industry standards. Reasonable care in a case in which a vehicle driver has collided with and injured a pedestrian may include duties to keep a lookout for and yield to pedestrians. It may require maintaining control of the vehicle and keeping the vehicle on the traveled portion of the highway. It may require maintaining a safe speed, adjusting speed to weather and lighting conditions, and taking evasive action to avoid obstacles including pedestrians. It may also require observing traffic signs and signals, not to mention complying with traffic laws and regulations, driving rules (common rules of the road), and license restrictions. It may also require repairing and maintaining the vehicle for safe operation. Depending on the circumstances of each case, standards of care may depend on local or industry customs, the presence of an emergency, the defendant's age or physical characteristics, and many other considerations. While reading the following cases, try to articulate the more-specific standard of care the appellate court applied to reach its conclusion.

Lubitz v. Wells
Connecticut Superior Court
19 Conn. Sup. 322, 113 A.2d 147 (1955)

TROLAND, J. The complaint alleges that James Wells was the owner of a golf club and that he left it for some time lying on the ground in the backyard of his home. That thereafter his son, the defendant James Wells, Jr., aged eleven years, while playing in the yard with the plaintiff, Judith Lubitz, aged nine years, picked up the golf club and proceeded to swing at a stone lying on the ground. In swinging the golf club, James Wells, Jr., caused the club to strike the plaintiff about the jaw and chin.

Negligence alleged against the young Wells boy is that he failed to warn his little playmate of his intention to swing the club and that he did swing the club when he knew she was in a position of danger.

In an attempt to hold the boy's father, James Wells, liable for his son's action, it is alleged that James Wells was negligent because although he knew the golf club was on the ground in his backyard and that his children would play with it, and that although he knew or "should have known" that the negligent use of the golf club by children would cause injury to a child, he neglected to remove the golf club from the backyard or to caution James Wells, Jr., against the use of the same.

The demurrer challenges the sufficiency of the allegations of the complaint to state a cause of action or to support a judgment against the father, James Wells.

It would hardly be good sense to hold that this golf club is so obviously and intrinsically dangerous that it is negligence to leave it lying on the ground in the yard. The father cannot be held liable on the allegations of this complaint. [Cc]

The demurrer is sustained.

Knowledge

Lawyers construct conceptual continuums. Improve your contrast of hypothetical scenarios by scaling them. *Scaling* means to arrange scenarios along a continuum that has exaggerated contrasting points at either end. Scenarios on one end will have one outcome under a legal rule, while scenarios at the other end will have the opposite outcome. The lawyer advocates where the facts of the case at issue lie on the constructed continuum. For example, in a case in which the plaintiff alleges that leaving a golf club in a yard was negligent, a continuum would place "reasonable care" or "not negligent" at one end to "negligent" or even "grossly negligent" at the other end. Toy stuffed animals, rubber balls, and other items for play would be at the "not negligent" end of the continuum, while poisonous chemicals, toxic pesticides, and power tools would be toward the other end. The continuum makes more evident how to consider a golf club—as a recreational item one might reasonably leave in a yard.

Chicago, B. & Q.R. Co. v. Krayenbuhl
Nebraska Supreme Court
65 Neb. 889, 91 N.W. 880 (1902)

ALBERT, J. This action was brought on behalf of Leo Krayenbuhl, whom we shall hereafter call the plaintiff, by his next friend, against the Chicago, Burlington & Quincy Railroad Company to recover for personal injuries received by the plaintiff while playing on a turntable belonging to the defendant.

... [D]efendant operated a line of railroad, which extended through the village of Palmer, at which point it maintained a passenger depot, roundhouse, coalhouse, water tank, and turntable. ... The turntable was situated between ... two branches, at a point about 1,600 feet from the depot, and about 100 feet from each branch, and a track extended to it from the point of divergence of the two branches. A path or footway, beginning some distance northwest of the turntable, extended in a southeasterly direction, passed within about 70 feet of it, and crossed the track at the south. This path was in common use, not only by the members of the family to which the plaintiff belonged, but by the public generally, and there was no fence between it and the turntable. The turntable was provided with a movable bolt, which by means of a lever could be thrown into a socket in the surrounding framework, thus holding the turntable in position. Provision was also made for locking it with a padlock. The rules of the defendant in force at the time required the foreman of the roundhouse, or in his absence the station agent, to keep the turntable locked when not in use; but there is considerable evidence to the effect that this rule was frequently disregarded, and that, owing to the looseness of one of the staples used in connection with the lock, even when thus fastened, it could be unfastened by young children without much difficulty. The plaintiff's father was in the employ of the defendant as section foreman, and, with his family, occupied a small house on the right of way near the station, within about 30 feet of the track, and about 1,600 feet from the turntable. Another family resided on the right of way, a few rods from the turntable. The two families visited back and forth, using the right of way for a path. The plaintiff's father kept a cow, which was pastured on the right of way, sometimes near the turntable, and it appears from the evidence that his children drove it back and forth on the right of way as occasion required. There is evidence tending to show that it was the common practice for the children of the family and other children in the neighborhood to resort to the coalhouse, roundhouse, and turntable, and to amuse themselves by revolving the turntable, and riding on it while it was in motion, and that this practice was known to the defendant, who permitted it without protest.

On the 20th day of October, 1895, in the absence of his parents, the plaintiff,—he was then four years of age,—in company with some other members of the family, the oldest of whom was eleven years old, and some other children, the oldest of whom was fourteen, were playing with a push car, moving it up and down on the railroad track. The agent in charge of the station joined them, and rode a short distance on the car. He then left them.... The children continued to push the car, and finally reached the turntable. There is evidence sufficient to sustain a finding that they found the turntable unlocked and unguarded, but the evidence is conflicting on that point. The plaintiff and some of the other children got on the turntable, while two of the others set it in motion. While it was in motion the plaintiff's foot was caught between the rails, and severed at the ankle joint. The injury thus sustained is that for which damages is sought in this action. A trial was had to a jury, which resulted in a verdict and judgment for the plaintiff. The defendant brings error. ...

... [W]here the owner of dangerous premises knows, or has good reason to believe, that children so young as to be ignorant of the danger will resort to such premises he is bound to take such precautions to keep them from such premises, or to protect them from injuries likely to result from the dangerous condition of the premises while there, as a man of ordinary care and prudence, under like circumstances, would take. At first sight, it would seem that the principle, thus stated, is too broad, and that its application would impose unreasonable burdens on owners, and intolerable restrictions on the use and enjoyment of property. But it must be kept in mind that it requires nothing of the owner that a man of ordinary care and prudence would not do of his own volition, under like circumstances. Such a man would not willingly take up unreasonable burdens, nor vex himself with intolerable restrictions.

It is true, as said in Loomis v. Terry, 17 Wend. 497, 31 Am. Dec. 306, "the business of life must go forward"; the means by which it is carried forward cannot be rendered absolutely safe. Ordinarily, it can be best carried forward by the unrestricted use of private property by the owner; therefore the law favors such use to the fullest extent consistent with the main purpose for which, from a social standpoint, such business is carried forward, namely, the public good. Hence, in order to determine the extent to which such use may be enjoyed, its bearing on such main purpose must be taken into account, and a balance struck between its advantages and disadvantages. ... [A] turntable is a dangerous contrivance, which facilitates railroading; the general benefits resulting from its use outweigh the occasional injuries inflicted by it; hence the public good demands its use. ... But the danger incident to its use may be lessened by the use of a lock which would prevent children, attracted to it, from moving it; the interference with the proper use of the turntable occasioned by the use of such lock is so slight that it is outweighed by the danger to be anticipated from an omission to use it; therefore the public good, we think, demands the use of the lock. ...

Hence, in all cases of this kind in the determination of the question of negligence, regard must be had to the character and location of the premises, the purpose for which they are used, the probability of injury therefrom, the precautions necessary to prevent such injury, and the relations such precautions bear to the beneficial use of the premises. The nature of the precautions would depend on the particular fact in each case. In some cases a warning to the children or the parents might be sufficient; in others, more active measures might be required. But in every case they should be such as a man of ordinary care and prudence would observe under like circumstances. If, under all the circumstances, the owner omits such precautions as a man of ordinary care and prudence, under like circumstances, would observe, he is guilty of negligence.

[The court reversed the verdict for plaintiff because of other error in the jury instruction.]

INQUIRY

Particularity. Does a landowner owe a duty to remove a tree stump from a yard to prevent someone from tripping over it? *See* Johnson v. Krueger, 36 Colo. App. 242, 539 P.2d 1296 (1975) (no negligence to leave stump in yard). To look under one's car before driving off, in case an infant has crawled under it? *See* Williams v. Jordan, 208 Tenn. 456, 346 S.W.2d 583 (1961) (no duty to check under car for infant). To construct and maintain a wooden guardrail for pedestrian and horse travel, to anticipate that a motor vehicle might run against it someday? *See* Davison v. Snohomish, 149 Wash. 109, 270 P. 422 (1928) (no duty); *but cf.* Barlett v. Northern Pacific R. Co. 74 Wash.2d 881, 447 P.2d 735 (1968) (jury question) ("We do not consider the ideas of the court, expressed 40 years ago, as necessarily authoritative on the engineering and financial phases of the same problem today."). To manufacture a snowmobile to prevent injury to a young boy who accidentally toboggans under it? *See* Whiteford v. Yamaha Motor Corp., 582 N.W.2d 916 (Minn. 1998) (no duty because danger remote). To not manufacture a slingshot to sell to an 11-year-old, in order that he not shoot out the eye of a 12-year-old? *See* Moning v. Alfono, 400 Mich. 425, 254 N.W.2d 759 (1977) (question of fact for jury). To make power lines visible to helicopter pilots? *See* Arizona Public Service Co. v. Brittain, 107 Ariz. 278, 486 P.2d 176 (1971) (fact question for the jury). One occasionally sees bright-orange balls strung along power lines that hang across highways or canyons. When one person or entity develops and uses a safety device, does it create a duty on the part of others to use it?

Weather. What duties does a person owe with respect to predicting the weather? To bury pipes deep enough to prevent their breaking twenty-five years later in an extremely severe freeze, and flooding a house? *See* Blyth v. Birmingham Waterworks Co., 11 Exch. 781, 156 Eng. Rep. 1047 (1856) (no duty to bury pipes to meet extremely unusual freeze). To protect an oil storage tank against lightning strikes? *See* Tex-Jersey Oil Corp. v. Beck, 292 S.W.2d 803 (Tex. Civ. App. 1956) (yes, a duty). To protect golfers on a golf course against lightning strikes? *See* Hames v. State of Tennessee, 808 S.W.2d 41 (Tenn. 1991) (no duty); *but cf.* Maussner v. Atlantic City Country Club, Inc., 299 N.J. Super. 535, 691 A.2d 826 (1997) (a duty only if assumed). Does duty depend on the *possibility* of an injury or on some significant *likelihood* of it? *See* Bigbee v. Pacific Tel. & Tel. Co., 34 Cal.3d 49, 665 P.2d 947, 192 Cal. Rptr. 857 (1983) (duty depends on foreseeability that "includes whatever is likely enough in the setting of modern life that a reasonably thoughtful [person] would take account of it in guiding practical conduct); Gulf Refining Co. v. Williams, 183 Miss. 723, 185 So. 234 (1938) (some real likelihood). If possible injury was enough for a duty to prevent it, then in every case where injury occurred (thereby demonstrating its possibility, even if extremely remote), duty would be present.

Obviousness. With respect to a standard of care, must everyone know certain things? *See* Seaboard Air Line R. Co. v. Hackney, 217 Ala. 382, 115 So. 869 (1928) (plaintiff required to know that poorly stacked railroad ties will topple by gravity). Not everyone has the same knowledge of risks. We are all novices in one field or another. Should we indulge novice motor-vehicle drivers with a lower standard of care? *See* Michigan City v. Rudolph, 104 Ind. App. 643, 12 N.E.2d 970 (1938) (driver held to knowledge that vehicles lose control in sand). Does one have a duty to become knowledgeable about the risks of a new field in which the actor is a novice? *See* Gobrecht v. Beckwith, 82 N.H. 415, 135 A. 20 (1926) (landlord installing gas heater had duty to learn of its hazards, but tenant occupying premises did not have that duty). On the other hand, does the standard of care require one who has special knowledge within a field to use it? *See* Hill v. Sparks, 546 S.W.2d 473 (Mo. App. 1976) (excavator required to use special knowledge of earth-moving equipment to avoid accidental death of sister); Gulf Refining Co., *supra* (seller of gasoline drum has duty to ensure that threads of bung cap are in reasonably good repair, so as to prevent gas-igniting spark when cap is unscrewed); Restatement (Second) of Torts §289(b); *id.* at Comment *m*; *but see* Fredericks v. Castora, 241 Pa. Super. 211, 360 A.2d 696 (1976) (truck driver's 20 years of experience does not raise standard). These questions anticipate the next section on the role of industry knowledge and custom in determining a standard of care.

Trimarco v. Klein
New York Court of Appeals
56 N.Y.2d 98, 436 N.E.2d 502, 451 N.Y.S.2d 52 (1982)

FUCHSBERG, J. After trial by jury in a negligence suit for personal injuries, the plaintiff, Vincent N. Trimarco, recovered a judgment of $240,000. A sharply divided Appellate Division, 82 A.D.2d 20, 441 N.Y.S.2d 62, having reversed on the law and dismissed the complaint, our primary concern on this appeal is with the role of the proof plaintiff produced on custom and usage. The ultimate issue is whether he made out a case.

The controversy has its genesis in the shattering of a bathtub's glass enclosure door in a multiple dwelling in July, 1976. ... [A]t the time of the incident plaintiff, the tenant of the apartment in which it happened, was in the process of sliding the door open so that he could exit the tub. It is undisputed that the occurrence was sudden and unexpected and the injuries he received from the lacerating glass most severe.

The door, which turned out to have been made of ordinary glass variously estimated as one sixteenth to one quarter of an inch in thickness, concededly would have presented no different appearance to the plaintiff and his wife than did tempered safety glass, which their uncontradicted testimony shows they assumed it to be. Nor was there any suggestion that defendants ever brought its true nature to their attention. …

As part of his case, plaintiff, with the aid of expert testimony, developed that, since at least the early 1950's, a practice of using shatterproof glazing materials for bathroom enclosures had come into common use, so that by 1976 the glass door here no longer conformed to accepted safety standards. This proof was reinforced by a showing that over this period bulletins of nationally recognized safety and consumer organizations along with official Federal publications had joined in warning of the dangers that lurked when plain glass was utilized in "hazardous locations", including "bathtub enclosures." … [O]n examination of the defendants' managing agent, who long had enjoyed extensive familiarity with the management of multiple dwelling units in the New York City area, plaintiff's counsel elicited agreement that, since at least 1965, it was customary for landlords who had occasion to install glass for shower enclosures, whether to replace broken glass or to comply with the request of a tenant or otherwise, to do so with "some material such as plastic or safety glass." …

Our analysis may well begin by rejecting defendants' contention that the shower door was not within the compass of section 78 of the Multiple Dwelling Law. From early on, it was understood that this statute was enacted in recognition of the reality that occupants of tenements in apartment houses, notwithstanding their control of the rented premises, as a practical matter looked to their landlords for the safe maintenance of the tenanted quarters as well. The result was that, if responsibility for keeping "every part thereof * * * in good repair" was not placed on the landlords, defects would remain unremedied ([cc]). …

Which brings us to the well-recognized and pragmatic proposition that when "certain dangers have been removed by a customary way of doing things safely, this custom may be proved to show that [the one charged with the dereliction] has fallen below the required standard" (*Garthe v. Ruppert*, 264 N.Y. 290, 296, 190 N.E. 643). Such proof, of course, is not admitted in the abstract. It must bear on what is reasonable conduct under all the circumstances, the quintessential test of negligence.

It follows that, when proof of an accepted practice is accompanied by evidence that the defendant conformed to it, this may establish due care ([c], and, contrariwise, when proof of a customary practice is coupled with a showing that it was ignored and that this departure was a proximate cause of the accident, it may serve to establish liability ([c]). Put more conceptually, proof of a common practice aids in "formulat[ing] the general expectation of society as to how individuals will act in the course of their undertakings, and thus to guide the common sense or expert intuition of a jury or commission when called on to judge of particular conduct under particular circumstances" (Pound, Administrative Application of Legal Standards, 44 ABA Rep, 445, 456-457).

The source of the probative power of proof of custom and usage is described differently by various authorities, but all agree on its potency. Chief among the rationales offered is, of course, the fact that it reflects the judgment and experience and conduct of many ([cc]). Support for its relevancy and reliability comes too from the direct bearing it has on feasibility, for its focusing is on the practicality of a precaution in actual operation and the readiness with which it can be employed ([c]). Following in the train of both of these boons is the custom's exemplification of the opportunities it provides to others to learn of the safe way, if that the customary one be. ([c])

From all this it is not to be assumed customary practice and usage need be universal. It suffices that it be fairly well defined and in the same calling or business so that "the actor may be charged with knowledge of it or negligent ignorance" ([cc]).

However, once its existence is credited, a common practice or usage is still not necessarily a conclusive or even a compelling test of negligence ([c]). Before it can be, the jury must be satisfied with its reasonableness, just as the jury must be satisfied with the reasonableness of the behavior which adhered to the custom or the unreasonableness of that which did not ([c]). After all, customs and usages run the gamut of merit like everything else. That is why the question in each instance is whether it meets the test of reasonableness. As Holmes' now classic statement on this subject expresses it, "[w]hat usually is done may be evidence of what ought to be done, but what ought to be done is fixed by a standard of reasonable prudence, whether it usually is complied with or not" (*Texas & Pacific Ry. Co. v. Behymer*, 189 U.S. 468, 470, 23 S.Ct. 622, 622-23, 47 L.Ed. 905).

So measured, the case the plaintiff presented... was enough to send it to the jury and to sustain the verdict reached. The expert testimony, the admissions of the defendant's manager, the data on which the professional and governmental bulletins were based, the evidence of how replacements were handled by at least the local building industry for the better part of two decades, these in the aggregate easily filled that bill. Moreover, it was also for the jury to decide whether, at the point in time when the accident occurred, the modest cost and ready availability of safety glass and the dynamics of the growing custom to use it for shower enclosures had transformed what once may have been considered a reasonably safe part of the apartment into one which, in the light of later developments, no longer could be so regarded.

Furthermore, the charge on this subject was correct. The Trial Judge placed the evidence of custom and usage "by others engaged in the same business" in proper perspective, when, among other things, he told the jury that the issue on which it was received was "the reasonableness of the defendant's conduct under all the circumstances." He also emphasized that the testimony on this score was not conclusive, not only by saying so but by explaining that "the mere fact that another person or landlord may have used a better or safer practice does not establish a standard" and that it was for the jurors "to determine whether or not the evidence in this case does establish a general custom or practice."

Nevertheless, we reverse and order a new trial because the General Business Law sections should have been excluded. ...

Accordingly, the case should be remitted to Supreme Court, Bronx County, for further proceedings in accordance with this opinion.

INQUIRY

Unreasonable Customs. What if the custom within the industry carelessly creates substantial risk of serious injury or death? The case of The T.J. Hooper, 60 F.2d 737 (1932) (2nd Cir. 1932), involved the custom of tug boats pulling coal barges up the Eastern seaboard, to not have radios for warnings of approaching bad weather in time to pull into safe harbor. When plaintiff sued after a gale destroyed plaintiff's barges, and the defendant relied on the custom, Judge Learned Hand wrote for the appellate court that "a whole calling may have unduly lagged in the adoption of new and available devices. It may never set its own tests, however persuasive be its usages. Courts must in the end say what is required [because] there are precautions so imperative that their universal disregard will not excuse their omission." Indeed, for all the evidentiary value custom usually carries, a custom may be so unsafe that it would not even be admissible as relevant evidence. See Mayhew v. Sullivan Mining Co., 76 Me. 100 (1884) (proof of universal custom of cutting unlighted and unguarded ladder holes in miners' platforms "would have no tendency to show that the act was consistent with ordinary prudence"). The Restatement (Third) of Torts: Liability for Physical and Emotional Harm §13 recognizes the possibility of unreasonable customs, summarizing:

> (a) An actor's compliance with the custom of the community, or of others in like circumstances, is evidence that the actor's conduct is not negligent but does not preclude a finding of negligence.
>
> (b) An actor's departure from the custom of the community, or of others in like circumstances, in a way that increases risk is evidence of the actor's negligence but does not require a finding of negligence.

Skills

Tort lawyers must plead standards of care in a wide variety of cases. Choose one of the following cases, articulate the standard of care, and write it in the manner you would if you were drafting a complaint for the plaintiff. To help you get started, reproduced below your choices is a sample complaint reciting the standard of care in a motor-vehicle accident case in which the defendant pulled out from a stop sign and collided with a vehicle passing through the intersection on a through street.

A. For a landlord whose water heater corroded, resulting in severe leakage that destroyed valuable personal effects of a tenant.

B. For a snow-removal company that had the contract to clear a grocery-store parking lot, where a customer slipped and fell on glare ice, and was seriously injured.

C. For a motor-vehicle driver who struck and killed a disabled pedestrian who was attempting to cross at a crosswalk in a heavy downpour during a morning commute.

D. For a security company whose guard used a master key that a customer had provided, to enter an office and sexually assault the customer's employee.

E. For a cleaning service whose employees used a scouring product that marred custom furniture and cabinetry throughout a customer's premises.

F. For a service that transports the disabled, after its van driver stopped abruptly, causing a rider to slip forward off a wheelchair and severely injure herself on the floor.

[Sample Complaint—Standard of Care]

> ...
> 14. Defendant owed plaintiff a duty of reasonable care including the duties to:
>   a) obey traffic signs so as to come to a full stop until traffic was clear;
>   b) not proceed into the intersection until the way was clear;
>   c) yield to vehicles having the right-of-way;
>   d) keep a sharp lookout all ways so as to timely observe approaching vehicles;
>   e) maintain reasonable and prudent control of the vehicle so as to avoid collision;
>   f) take reasonable evasive action once a driving hazard appeared;
>   g) use headlights, horn, and signals so as to alert others during emergency action;
>   h) plan and time transportation so as not to require hurry and rush;
>   i) comply with all traffic laws, rules, and regulations including:
>   i) obey traffic control devices, MCL §257.611;
>   ii) stop and remain at the scene of an accident, MCL §257.617;
>   iii) report the accident, MCL §257.617a;
>   iv) stop and yield at a through intersection, MCL §257.668;
>   v) stop and yield at a stop sign, MCL §257.671;
>   vi) yield when turning at an intersection, MCL §257.649; and
>   vii) stop and yield when entering a highway, MCL §257.652. ...

Emergencies. How should emergencies affect the standard of care? The duty cases above define the standard of care as conduct reasonable under all circumstances then existing. It would seem that if an emergency was one of the circumstances relevant to judging a person's conduct, then the standard of care as enunciated already provides for it. In cases tried to a jury rather than to the bench (where the judge is assumed to know the law), the question can arise whether the jury should receive a special instruction on the effect of emergencies. A majority of cases have held that law requires such an instruction when requested and relevant. *See* Desrosiers v. Flight Intern. of Florida, Inc., 156 F.3d 952 (9th Cir. 1998) (California law); Whittaker v. Coca-Cola, 812 So.2d 1252 (Ala. Civ. App. 2001); Lockhart v. List, 542 Pa. 141, 665 A.2d 1176 (1995); Rivera v. New York City Transit Auth., 77 N.Y.2d 322, 567 N.Y.S.2d 629, 569 N.E.2d 432 (N.Y. 1991) (reversing plaintiff's verdict, after trial court failed to give an emergency instruction in defense of subway motorman's failure to stop train from hitting person on track); *cf.* Wilson v. Sibert, 535 P.2d 1034 (Alaska 1975) (emergency instruction not required, but it was not error to give it when requested); *but cf.* Lyons v. Midnight Sun Trans. Servs. Inc., 928 P.2d 1202 (Alaska 1996) ("the sudden emergency instruction is a generally useless appendage"). The Restatement (Third) of Torts: Liability for Physical and Emotional Harm §9 confirms, "If an actor is confronted with an unexpected emergency requiring rapid response, this is a circumstance to be taken into account in determining whether the actor's resulting conduct is that of the reasonably careful person." The Restatement (Second) of Torts §296 (1965) cautions that although "a sudden emergency ... is a factor" in determining the reasonableness of conduct, an actor remains liable for "tortious conduct which has produced the emergency." *See* Frisby v. Aggerton Logging, Inc., 323 Ark. 508, 915 S.W.2d 718 (1996). Situations may also exist in which persons should anticipate, prepare for, and protect against emergencies—perhaps when driving by a school at recess, when small children might dart onto the street. *See* Conery v. Tackmaier, 34 Wis.2d 511, 149 N.W.2d 575 (1967). Should a defendant whose negligence created the emergency be given the benefit of an emergency instruction? *See* Mitchell v.

Johnson, 641 So.2d 238 (Ala. 1994) (no). Now consider the following trial-court opinion involving a different kind of emergency.

Cordas v. Peerless Transp. Co.
City Court of New York
27 N.Y.S.2d 198 (City Ct. N.Y. 1941)

CARLIN, J. This case presents the ordinary man—that problem child of the law—in a most bizarre setting. As a lowly chauffeur in defendant's employ he became in a trice the protagonist in a breach-bating drama with a denouement almost tragic. It appears that a man, whose identity it would be indelicate to divulge was feloniously relieved of his portable goods by two nondescript highwaymen in an alley near 26th Street and Third Avenue, Manhattan; they induced him to relinquish his possessions by a strong argument ad hominem couched in the convincing cant of the criminal and pressed at the point of a most persuasive pistol. Laden with their loot, but not thereby impeded, they ... boarded defendant's taxicab, which quickly veered south toward 25th Street on 2d Avenue where he saw the chauffeur jump out while the cab, still in motion, continued toward 24th Street; after the chauffeur relieved himself of the cumbersome burden of his fare the latter also is said to have similarly departed from the cab before it reached 24th Street. The chauffeur's story is substantially the same except that he states that his uninvited guest boarded the cab at 25th Street while it was at a standstill waiting for a less colorful fare; that his "passenger" immediately advised him "to stand not upon the order of his going but to go at once" and added finality to his command by an appropriate gesture with a pistol addressed to his sacro iliac. The chauffeur in reluctant acquiescence proceeded about fifteen feet, when his hair, like unto the quills of the fretful porcupine, was made to stand on end by the hue and cry of the man despoiled accompanied by a clamourous concourse of the law-abiding which paced him as he ran; the concatenation of "stop thief," to which the patter of persistent feet did maddingly beat time, rang in his ears as the pursuing posse all the while gained on the receding cab with its quarry therein contained. The hold-up man sensing his insecurity suggested to the chauffeur that in the event there was the slightest lapse in obedience to his curt command that he, the chauffeur, would suffer the loss of his brains, a prospect as horrible to an humble chauffeur as it undoubtedly would be to one of the intelligentsia. The chauffeur apprehensive of certain dissolution from either Scylla, the pursuers, or Charybdis, the pursued, quickly threw his car out of first speed in which he was proceeding, pulled on the emergency, jammed on his brakes and, although he thinks the motor was still running, swung open the door to his left and jumped out of his car. He confesses that the only act that smacked of intelligence was that by which he jammed the brakes in order to throw off balance the hold-up man who was half-standing and half-sitting with his pistol menacingly poised. ... The plaintiff-mother and her two infant children were there injured by the cab which, at the time, appeared to be also minus its passenger who, it appears, was apprehended in the cellar of a local hospital where he was pointed out to a police officer by a remnant of the posse, hereinbefore mentioned. He did not appear at the trial. The three aforesaid plaintiffs and the husband-father sue the defendant for damages predicating their respective causes of action upon the contention that the chauffeur was negligent in abandoning the cab under the aforesaid circumstances. Fortunately the injuries sustained were comparatively slight. ... In slight paraphrase of the world's first bard it may be truly observed that the expedition of the chauffeur's violent love of his own security outran the pauser, reason, when he was suddenly confronted with unusual emergency which "took his reason prisoner." The learned attorney for the plaintiffs concedes that the chauffeur acted in an emergency but claims a right to recovery upon the following proposition taken verbatim from his brief: 'It is respectfully submitted that the value of the interests of the public at large to be immune from being injured by a dangerous instrumentality such as a car unattended while in motion is very superior to the right of a driver of a motor vehicle to abandon same while it is in motion even when acting under the belief that his life is in danger and by abandoning same he will save his life." To hold thus under the facts adduced herein would be tantamount to a repeal by implication of the primal law of nature written in indelible characters upon the fleshy tablets of sentient creation by the Almighty Law-giver, "the supernal Judge who sits on high." There are those who stem the turbulent current for bubble fame, or who bridge the yawning chasm with a leap for the leap's sake or who "outstare the sternest eyes that look outbrave the heart most daring on the earth, pluck the young sucking cubs from the she-bear, yea, mock the lion when he roars for prey" to win a fair lady and these are the admiration of the generality of men; but they are made of sterner stuff than the ordinary man upon whom the law places no duty of emulation. The law would indeed be fond if it imposed upon the ordinary man the obligation to so demean himself when suddenly confronted with a danger, not of his creation, disregarding the likelihood that such a contingency may darken the intellect and palsy the will of the common legion of the earth, the fraternity of ordinary men,—whose acts or omissions under certain conditions or circumstances make the yardstick by which the law measures culpability or innocense, negligence or care. If a person is placed in a sudden peril from which death might ensue, the law does not impel another to the rescue of the person endangered nor does it condemn him for his unmoral failure to rescue when he can; this is in recognition of the immutable law written in frail flesh. Returning to our chauffeur. If the philosophic Horatio and the martial companions of his watch were 'distilled almost to jelly with the act of fear' when they beheld "in the dead vast and middle of the night' the disembodied spirit of Hamlet's father stalk majestically by 'with a countenance more in sorrow than in anger" was not the chauffeur, though unacquainted with the example of these eminent men-at-arms, more amply justified in his fearsome reactions when he was more palpably confronted by a thing of flesh and blood bearing in its hand an engine of destruction which depended for its lethal purpose upon the quiver of a hair? When Macbeth was cross-examined by Macduff as to any reason he could advance for his sudden despatch of Duncan's grooms he said in plausible answer "Who can be wise, amazed, temperate and furious, loyal and neutral, in a moment? No man." Macbeth did not by a "tricksy word" thereby stand justified as he criminally created the emergency from which he sought escape by indulgence in added felonies to divert suspicion to the innocent. However, his words may be wrested to the advantage of the defendant's chauffeur whose acts cannot be legally construed as the proximate cause of plaintiff's injuries, however regrettable, unless nature's first law is arbitrarily disregarded. ... The chauffeur—the ordinary man in this case—acted in a split second in a most harrowing experience. To call him negligent would be to brand him coward; the court does not do so in spite of what those swaggering heroes, "whose valor plucks dead lions by the beard," may bluster to the contrary. ... Judgment for defendant against plaintiffs dismissing their complaint upon the merits.

> **Ethics**
> Rule 1.3 of the ABA Model Rules of Professional Conduct requires that lawyers "act with reasonable diligence and promptness in representing a client." Rule 1.3's admonition is particularly appropriate for the plaintiff's lawyer who represents many clients in tort claims. Plaintiff's work can require constant attention to files in order to ensure that the matters move forward—ordering medical records, retaining experts, scheduling witness interviews, and, especially, timely filing complaints, witness lists, and other court papers in order that the clients' matters not be delayed or prejudiced.

INQUIRY

Physical Characteristics. We have seen that the law may define or alter the standard of care based on customs or emergency circumstances. Should the law also modify the standard of care based on the physical characteristics of the party whose conduct is under consideration? The accepted rule is that the reasonably prudent person takes on the physical characteristics of the party whose conduct is under consideration. *See* Restatement (Second) of Torts §283C (1965). For instance, it would ordinarily be meaningless to hold a blind person to the standard of care for a person with sight. *See* Roberts v. State of Louisiana, 396 So.2d 566 (La. 1981) (affirming dismissal of negligence claim against blind operator of public concession stand, for bumping into and knocking over plaintiff while attempting to walk to the bathroom); Shepherd v. Gardner Wholesale, Inc., 288 Ala. 43, 256 So.2d 877 (1972) (plaintiff with blurred vision from cataracts not held to standard of clear sight); *cf.* Poyner v. Loftus, 694 A.2d 69 (D.C. Ct. App. 1997) (reasonable care requires visually impaired pedestrian to use cane or guide dog to prevent fall). The standard of care would also likely account for physical abilities limited by epilepsy, *see* Storjohn v. Fay, 246 Neb. 454, 519 N.W.2d 521 (1994), polio paralysis, *see* Hodges v. Jewel Cos., 72 Ill. App.3d 263, 28 Ill. Dec. 571, 390 N.E.2d 930 (1979), short stature, *see* Mahan v. State of New Uork, 172 Md. 373, 191 A. 575 (1937) (view over hood of car), deafness, *see* Otterbeck v. Lamb, 85 Nev. 456, 456 P.2d 855 (1969), and the absence of a sense of smell, *see* Stephens v. Dulaney, 78 N.M. 53, 428 P.2d 27 (1967).

Accommodation. Should a defendant have to anticipate the plaintiff's blindness or other physical limitation? *See* Hill v. Glenwood, 124 Iowa 479, 100 N.W. 522 (1904) (affirming judgment for blind plaintiff injured on street); *but see* Lauff v. Wal-Mart Stores, Inc., 2002 WL 32129976 (W.D. Mich. 2002) (under Michigan law, an invitee's blindness is immaterial to whether the claim is barred by the open and obvious doctrine); Lugo v. Ameritech Corp., 464 Mich. 512, 518n.2, 629 N.W.2d 384 (2001) (whether a plaintiff has a particular susceptibility to injury is immaterial to determining whether the open-and-obvious doctrine bars a claim); Smith v. Sneller, 147 Pa. Super. 231, 24 A.2d 61, *affd.*, 345 Pa. 68, 26 A.2d 452 (1942) (reversing judgment for blind plaintiff who had fallen into ditch without using cane). The general rule is probably that if the reasonable person would have taken a person's blindness or other physical limitation into account, then so should the defendant. *See* Fletcher v. Aberdeen, 54 Wash. 2d 174, 338 P.2d 743 (1959). Also keep in mind civil-rights statutes like the Americans with Disabilities Act, 42 U.S.C. §§12101 et seq. (1990), that require reasonable accommodation of the disabled when it comes to public services and accommodations, employment, and other areas.

Incapacity. If the plaintiff's physical incapacity is due to age, then the courts are likely to require the defendant's indulgence. *See* Tobia v. Cooper Hosp. Univ. Med. Ctr., 136 N.J. 335, 643 A.2d 1 (1994) (85-year-old fell from gurney in emergency room). If, on the other hand, the plaintiff's incapacity was due to self-induced intoxication, the courts are unlikely to impose a higher standard of care on the defendant to accommodate the intoxication. The famous quip in Robinson v. Pioche, Bayerque & Co., 5 Cal. 460 (1885), is that a "drunken man is as much entitled to a safe street as a sober one, and much more in need of it." The quip refers not to raising the standard to the level of protecting the drunk but to indulging the drunk to the same extent that we should indulge the sober.

Children. A next subject is the standard of care children owe to others. The majority rule, endorsed in the Restatement (Third) of Torts: Liability for Physical and Emotional Harm §10, is that the standard of care owed by a child is that conduct which it is reasonable to expect from a child of like age, intelligence, and experience, within certain limits:

> (a) A child's conduct is negligent if it does not conform to that of a reasonably careful person of the same age, intelligence, and experience, except as provided in Subsection (b) or (c).
> (b) A child less than five years of age is incapable of negligence.
> (c) The special rule in Subsection (a) does not apply when the child is engaging in a dangerous activity that is characteristically undertaken by adults.

See Cleveland Rolling-Mill Co. v. Corrigan, 46 Ohio St. 283, 20 N.E. 466 (1889). Several states qualify that flexible standard with rules that a child is incapable of negligence if under age six, *see* Price v. Kitsap Transit, 125 Wash.2d 456, 886 P.2d 556 (1994), or age seven, *see* Appelhans v. McFall, 757 N.E.2d 987 (Ill. App. 2001) (the "tender years" doctrine), that children ages seven to 14 are presumed incapable but may be proven capable, *see* Patterson v. Central Mills, Inc., 112 F. Supp.2d 681 (N.D. Ohio 2000), and that children over age 14 are held to an adult standard, *see* Chu v. Bowers, 656 N.E.2d 436 (Ill. App. Ct. 1995); Savage Indus., Inc. v. Duke, 598 So.2d 856 (Ala. 1992)—making for a neat "Rule of Sevens." One jurisdiction has held as old as a 17-year-old to a child-of-that-age standard. *See* Charbonneau v. MacRury, 84 N.H. 501, 153 A. 457 (1931). Others simply find very young children not to be capable of negligence but without applying any hard-and-fast age rule. *See* Mastland, Inc., v. Evans Furniture, Inc., 498 N.W.2d 682 (Iowa 1993) (three-year-old child setting crib afire with lighter not capable of negligence). What, though, if the child is doing something that only adults ordinarily attempt? Consider the following trial-court opinion.

Neumann v Shlansky
County Court of New York
58 Misc. 2d 128, 294 N.Y.S.2d 628 (1968)

MARBACH, J. Defendant moves to set aside the verdict and for a new trial on the grounds that the verdict was contrary to the law of the case since the charge given by me, as trial judge, was erroneous as a matter of law.

The question presented here is, as far as can be determined, a case of first impression not only in this state but also in the nation. The issue is the standard of care which must be exercised by an eleven year old infant defendant when he is playing golf.

The facts are relatively simple and may be summarized as follows: Defendant, an 11 year old boy was playing in a foursome at the Harrison Country Club with his mother, and two other adults. The infant defendant was on the tee of a par three hole of about 170 yards. Plaintiff had just left the green on the par 3 hole and was crossing a foot bridge, which his caddy was about to cross, about 150-160 yards from the tee in plain view of the tee when he was hit in the knee by the ball driven from the tee by the infant defendant. The infant testified that he saw the plaintiff before he hit. There was testimony that indicated that infant had yelled "fore," the traditional warning given on the golf course when a golfer sees that someone may be hit by a golf ball. Plaintiff testified he did not hear the warning. There was further testimony which indicated that the infant was a boy who had been playing golf two to three times a week during the season for the past two years. It was apparent on the trial from the shot hit by the infant that he had at least some proficiency in hitting the golf ball.

The Court charged the jury that the infant in this case was to be held to the standard of care of an adult and not to the usual standard of care of a child. The jury returned with a verdict for the plaintiff.

At the outset it should be established that a golfer owes a duty to use reasonable care to avoid injuring other players on the golf course. [Cc] Furthermore, a golf ball is a dangerous missile which can cause serious injury if it hits someone while in flight. [Cc] ... It is for this Court to determine based upon all the factors involved whether this infant defendant while he was on the golf course is to be held to the standard of care of the reasonably prudent infant or the reasonably prudent man.

This Court holds that this infant should be held to the standard of care of the reasonable man. ...

There is an exception to the general rules for infants who engage in adult activities. ...

As applied to the instant case one of the critical elements in the opinion of the Court is the risk involved when a dangerous missile is hit by a golfer. Just as a motor vehicle or other power-driven vehicle is dangerous, so is a golf ball hit with a club. Driving a car, an airplane or powerboat has been referred to as adult activity even though actively engaged in by infants. [C] Likewise, golf can easily be determined to be an adult activity engaged in by infants. Both involve dangerous instruments. [C] No matter what the age of a driver of a car or a driver of a golf ball, if he fails to exercise due care serious injury may result. Driving a car, it is true, is not a game as golf may be. However, golf is not a game in the same way that football, baseball, basketball or tennis is a game. It is a game played by an individual which in order to be played well demands an abundance of skill and personal discipline, not to mention constant practice and dedication. Custom, rules and etiquette play an important role in this game. Foremost among these is the fact, as is indicated on many scorecards, that one does not hit a ball when it is likely that the ball could or will hit someone else for the obvious reason that someone could get hurt. ...

... In the case at bar we have an 11 year old boy playing in the company of three adults. He has taken lessons and plays regularly at his club. On a par three hole of about 170 yards he sees the plaintiff within the realm of foreseeable danger and he hits a golf ball, a dangerous missile, 150-160 yeards where it hits the plaintiff. Had it hit the plaintiff in the head it may have seriously injured or even killed him. The boy knew or should have known that a golf ball can inflict serious injury. He could have waited for a few seconds until plaintiff was clear yet he chose to hit in breach of his duty and injury resulted. This particular infant defendant was for all purposes on the golf course as an adult golfer. He was playing in a foursome with adults; he had played this course in the company of adults before and he hit the ball, as well as, if not better than many adults. If this Court were to say that the standard of care which defendant must bring to a golf course is only that of an infant it would be ignoring the realities of the game as well as the situation applicable to this case.

It might be argued that the applicable standard should be that of an 11 year old boy who possesses the experience or intelligence of one who has played a great deal of golf. This subjective standard does not adequately consider the objective nature of the game, the inherent risks involved and the undisputed fact that a golf ball is a dangerous missile capable of inflicting grievous harm no matter who hits it. [C] ...

In conclusion, this Court holds that golf involves special factors which when considered together in the abstract and in conjunction with the fact situation in this particular case require this infant be held to the standard of the reasonable man on the golf course. Motion denied.

INQUIRY

Adult Activities. What qualifies as an *adult activity* to require a child performing that activity to conform to an adult standard? Some activities, like driving a motor vehicle, are obviously adult activities. *See* Stevens v. Veenstra, 226 Mich. App. 441, 578 N.W.2d 341 (1998); Nielsen v. Brown, 232 Or. 426, 374 P.2d 896 (1962). Is climbing from a truck window while it is moving—and breaking one's neck—an adult activity when done by a drunken 16-year-old? *See* Strait v. Cary, 173 Wis.2d 377, 496 N.W.2d 634 (Wis. App. 1992) (no—child standard applied to contributory-negligence question). Is shooting a firearm? *See* Purtle v. Shelton, 251 Ark. 519, 474 S.W.2d 123 (Ark. 1971) (no—17-year-old person held to child standard); *but see* Huebner v. Koelfgren, 519 N.W.2d 488 (Minn. Ct. App. 1994) (child using firearm is held to adult standard). Is pulling an inner tube on a snowmobile an adult activity? *See* Robinson v. Lindsay, 92 Wash.2d 410, 598 P.2d 392 (1979) (13-year-old held to adult standard when driving snowmobile in manner that cut off 11-year-old plaintiff's thumb). Is operating a motorboat? *See* Dellwo v. Pearson, 259 Minn. 452, 107 N.W.2d 859 (1961) (yes). A motorcycle? *See* Harrelson v. Whitehead, 236 Ark. 325, 365 S.W.2d 868 (1961) (yes). A motor scooter? *See* Medina v. McAllister, 202 So.2d 755 (Fla. 1967) (yes); Adams v. Lopez, 75 N.M. 503, 407 P.2d 50 (1965) (yes). What about riding a bicycle? *See* Appelhans v. McFall, 757 N.E.2d 987 (Ill. App. 2001) (no); Williams v. Gilbert, 239 Ark. 935, 395 S.W.2d 333 (1965) (no). Downhill skiing? *See*

Goss v. Allen, 70 N.J. 442, 360 A.2d 388 (1976). Building a campfire? Farm Bureau Ins. Group v. Phillips, 116 Mich. App. 544, 323 N.W.2d 477 (1982) (no). Can you place these cases in categories or generalize rules from them? The temptation may be to classify as an adult activity the operation of equipment that has a motor—especially transportation equipment. *But see* Hudson-Connor v. Putney, 192 Or. App. 488, 86 P.3d 106 (2004) (refusing to hold 11-year-old operating golf cart to an adult standard).

Collectability. What practical use is it to sue a child who, after all, is unlikely to have any financial resources? While suits against children are less common in part because children tend not to have assets or earnings out of which to pay a settlement or judgment, liability-insurance coverage maintained by their parents will often cover them under resident-relative or similar coverage language. Where a child has no assets or insurance coverage, one might ask what liability parents have for the negligent acts of their children? Law generally does not impose vicarious liability on parents for the negligent acts of their children. Instead, a plaintiff wishing to pursue a claim against a parent for harm caused by the act of a child must do so, if at all, under a direct (rather than indirect) theory such as negligent parental supervision. However, the policy judgment that parents should have wide latitude in deciding how to raise and supervise children narrows the negligent-supervision theory. Where the law recognizes the negligent-parental-supervision theory, states tend to require proof that the child acted maliciously and that the parent knew or should have known of the child's propensity, and tend to cap parental liability at low figures like $10,000. *See* Tenn. Code Ann. §37-10-101-103. A second direct-liability theory is the parent's negligent entrustment to the child of an unsuitable instrumentality like a weapon or vehicle. *See* Rios v. Smith, 744 N.E.2d 1156 (N.Y. 2001) (parent subject to negligence liability for entrusting all-terrain vehicle to teenage son).

Practice

Everyone, it seems, has heard of the "McDonald's coffee" case—the one in which a jury awarded $2.9 million to a woman who spilled McDonald's coffee on herself, because the coffee was too hot. Although it is the poster-child for frivolous cases, plaintiff's lawyers in jury voir dire paint a truer picture of it to defuse juror bias against the tort system. First, the compensatory award of $200,000 was because the woman suffered third-degree burns to her groin area requiring a weeklong hospitalization and skin grafting. The $2.7 million in punitive damages represented just two days' profits from McDonald's coffee sales. Testimony that McDonald's served its coffee 20 to 30 degrees hotter than its competitors, at a temperature that takes from just 3 to 12 seconds to cause third-degree burns, and that it had received over 700 complaints and paid over $500,000 in settlements for coffee burns, supported the punitive award. Finally, the trial judge reduced the award to about $500,000, after which McDonald's settled. See the documentary *Hot Coffee* about the case.

Mental Characteristics. We have seen how the standard of care adapts to the defendant's physical limitations and takes account of the defendant's young age. What if the defendant has a mental disability? The general rule is that the standard of care remains the same and is not lower to account for a defendant's diminished mental capacities. *See* Jolley v. Powell, 299 So.2d 647 (Fla. Ct. App. 1991) (mentally ill person is liable under usual reasonable-person standard); Kuhn v. Zabotsky, 9 Ohio St.2d 129, 224 N.E.2d 137 (1967) (reasonable-person standard despite sudden insanity); Johnson v. Lambotte, 147 Colo. 203, 363 P.2d 165 (1961) (reasonable-person standard despite mental illness); Restatement (Second) of Torts §283B (reasonable-person standard despite lack of intelligence). The Restatement (Third) of Torts: Liability for Physical and Emotional Harm §11 summarizes the physical and mental disability rules as follows:

(a) The conduct of an actor with a physical disability is negligent only if the conduct does not conform to that of a reasonably careful person with the same disability.
(b) The conduct of an actor during a period of sudden incapacitation or loss of consciousness resulting from physical illness is negligent only if the sudden incapacitation or loss of consciousness was reasonably foreseeable to the actor.
(c) An actor's mental or emotional disability is not considered in determining whether conduct is negligent, unless the actor is a child.

Is Alzheimer's Disease a mental or physical condition for purposes of the different rules for physical and mental limitations? *See* White v. Muniz, 999 P.2d 814 (Col. 2000) (Alzheimer's sufferer subject to negligence liability even if unable to form intent necessary to be held liable for battery); Gould v. American Family Ins. Co., 198 Wis.2d 450, 543 N.W.2d 282 (1996) (mental condition—reasonable person standard); *but cf.* Lynch v. Rosenthal, 396 S.W.2d 272 (Mo. App. 1965) (very low IQ considered with regard to plaintiff's standard). The general rule holding the mentally disabled to the reasonable-person standard may apply not only to diminished capacity but to specific predilections. *See* C.T.W. v. B.C.G., 809 S.W.2d 788 (Tex. App. 1991) (pedophile held to standard of care to avoid children and get help). Some authority exists (perhaps a trend) for modifying the rule for a mentally disabled plaintiff whose contributory negligence is in question. *See* Stacy v. Jedco Const. Co., 119 N.C. App. 115, 457 S.E.2d 875, 879 (1995) (capable of contributory negligence but not held to reasonable-person standard); Cowan v. Doering, 111 N.J. 451, 545 A.2d 159 (N.J. 1988) (contributory negligence of mentally disturbed plaintiff measured "in light of his or her mental capacity" as part of "the modern trend"). Authority also exists for lowering or eliminating the care required of an institutionalized mentally disabled person, as to tort claims brought by injured caretakers. *See* Colman v. Notre Dame Convalescent Home, 968 F. Supp. 809 (D. Conn. 1997); Berberian v. Lynn, 179 N.J. 290, 845 A.2d 122 (2004); Hofflander v. St. Catherine's Hosp., Inc., 262 Wis.2d 539, 664 N.W.2d 545 (2003); Creasy v. Rusk, 730 N.E.2d 659 (Ind. 2000). Consider a case representative of the general rule.

Breunig v. American Family Ins. Co.
Wisconsin Supreme Court
45 Wis.2d 536, 173 N.W.2d 619 (1970)

This is an action by Phillip A. Breunig to recover damages for personal injuries which he received when his truck was struck by an automobile driven by Erma Veith and insured by the defendant American Family Insurance Company (Insurance Company). …

The Insurance Company alleged Erma Veith was not negligent because just prior to the collision she suddenly and without warning was seized with a mental aberration or delusion which rendered her unable to operate the automobile with her conscious mind.

The jury returned a verdict finding her causally negligent on the theory she had knowledge or forewarning of her mental delusions or disability. ... The defendant insurance company appeals.

HALLOWS, C.J. There is no question that Erma Veith was subject at the time of the accident to an insane delusion which directly affected her ability to operate her car in an ordinarily prudent manner and caused the accident. ...

At the trial Erma Veith testified she could not remember all the circumstances of the accident and this was confirmed by her psychiatrist who testified this loss of memory was due to his treatment of Erma Veith for her mental illness. This expert also testified to what Erma Veith had told him but could no longer recall. The evidence established that Mrs. Veith, while returning home after taking her husband to work, saw a white light on the back of a car ahead of her. She followed this light for three or four blocks. Mrs. Veith did not remember anything else except landing in a field, lying on the side of the road and people talking. She recalled awaking in the hospital.

The psychiatrist testified Mrs. Veith told him she was driving on a road when she believed that God was taking ahold of the steering wheel and was directing her car. She saw the truck coming and stepped on the gas in order to become air-borne because she knew she could fly because Batman does it. To her surprise she was not air-borne before striking the truck but after the impact she was flying.

Actually, Mrs. Veith's car continued west on highway 19 for about a mile. The road was straight for this distance and then made a gradual turn to the right. At this turn her car left the road in a straight line, negotiated a deep ditch and came to rest in a cornfield. When a traffic officer came to the car to investigate the accident, he found Mrs. Veith sitting behind the wheel looking off into space. He could not get a statement of any kind from her. She was taken to the Methodist Hospital and later transferred to the psychiatric ward of the Madison General Hospital.

The psychiatrist testified Erma Veith was suffering from "schizophrenic reaction, paranoid type, acute."[fn] He stated that from the time Mrs. Veith commenced following the car with the white light and ending with the stopping of her vehicle in the cornfield, she was not able to operate the vehicle with her conscious mind and that she had no knowledge or forewarning that such illness or disability would likely occur.

... Not all types of insanity vitiate responsibility for a negligent tort. The question of liability in every case must depend upon the kind and nature of the insanity. The effect of the mental illness or mental hallucinations or disorder must be such as to affect the person's ability to understand and appreciate the duty which rests upon him to drive his car with ordinary care, or if the insanity does not affect such understanding and appreciation, it must affect his ability to control his car in an ordinarily prudent manner. And in addition, there must be an absence of notice of forewarning to the person that he may be suddenly subject to such a type of insanity or mental illness. ...

The policy basis of holding a permanently insane person liable for his tort is: (1) Where one of two innocent persons must suffer a loss it should be borne by the one who occasioned it; (2) to induce those interested in the estate of the insane person (if he has one) to restrain and control him; and (3) the fear an insanity defense would lead to false claims of insanity to avoid liability. ...

We think the statement that insanity is no defense is too broad when it is applied to a negligence case where the driver is suddenly overcome without forewarning by a mental disability or disorder which incapacitates him from conforming his conduct to the standards of a reasonable man under like circumstances. These are rare cases indeed, but their rarity is no reason for overlooking their existence and the justification which is the basis of the whole doctrine of liability for negligence, i.e., that it is unjust to hold a man responsible for his conduct which he is incapable of avoiding and which incapability was unknown to him prior to the accident.

... All we hold is that a sudden mental incapacity equivalent in its effect to such physical causes as a sudden heart attack, epileptic seizure, stroke, or fainting should be treated alike and not under the general rule of insanity. ...

... While there was testimony of friends indicating she was normal for some months prior to the accident, the psychiatrist testifies the origin of her mental illness appeared in August, 1965, prior to the accident. ...

... Since these mental aberrations were not constant, the jury could infer she had knowledge of her condition and the likelihood of a hallucination just as one who has knowledge of a heart condition knows the possibility of an attack. ...

Judgment affirmed.

INQUIRY

Utility. What do these cases on duty teach us about the care that undergirds negligence law? Trained in the lexicon of social-science, lawyers and judges tend to write about duty based on economic and instrumental effects, using concepts like the risk or probability of harm, predictability or foreseeability of harm, cost and feasibility of measures to avoid harm, and availability and cost of means of defraying loss through insurance. *See, e.g.,* Rowland v. Christian, 69 Cal.2d 108, 70 Cal. Rptr. 97, 443 P.2d 561 (1968); Restatement (Second) of Torts §291 (1965) ("the risk is unreasonable and the act is negligent if the risk is of such magnitude as to outweigh ... the utility of the act"); *id.* at §292 (measure utility by social value of the interest advanced, the chance the interest will advance, and whether less-dangerous means exist to advance it); *id.* at §293 (measure risk by the social value of the imperiled interest, the chance the actor will imperil it, the extent of the harm, and the number at peril); *but see* Kingsport Util. v. Brown, 201 Tenn. 393, 299 S.W.2d 656 (1955) ("When the likelihood of danger to human life is to be balanced against the costs of insulation [for electric wires], we do not think the latter is a good argument.").

Foundations. On the other hand, tort lawyers know that juries do not have that same training. They know that jurors understand human conditions and behaviors in non-law terms. Care, as a manifestation of the deeper condition of love, has certain attributes. Care is accountable, responsible, thoughtful, reflective, considerate, and persevering, even while it is customary and ordinary. Care is never perverse or silly. Nor is it rude, cruel, or unkind. Care does not permit inconsiderate self-seeking, greed, or thoughtlessness. It is not vengeful and does not allow us to hold things against others or discriminate unfairly. Above all, care protects rather than exposes, requires regard for one another's well-being and sensitivity in all endeavors, and encourages hope and trust among strangers, family, enemies, and friends. While we study the technical nature of tort law, we should also remember that jurors decide tort claims as much on these accessible understandings as on calculation and analysis.

Negligence Formulas. Courts have at times tried to replace jury or policy decisions concerning whether a party owes a duty (and, if so, what is the applicable standard of care) with judge-made rules of law or negligence formulas. Two examples retain some weight today. The first example is when when motorists over-drive their headlights, colliding with an obstruction in the road. *See* Marshall v. Southern Ry. Co., 233 N.C. 38, 62 S.E.2d 489 (1950) (affirming non-suit of plaintiff's case where plaintiff drove into railroad trestle supports at night); *but see* Chaffin v. Brame, 233 N.C. 377, 64 S.E.2d 276 (1951) (plaintiff's over-driving headlights and crashing into truck stopped on highway not contributory negligence as a matter of law). The second example is when motorists follow another vehicle so closely that they are unable to avoid a rear-end collision. In another attempt at fashioning a rule of law rather than a standard of care for determining negligence, the Supreme Court in B. & O.R. Co. v. Goodman, 275 U.S. 66 (1927), held with respect to railroad crossings "that if a driver cannot be sure otherwise whether a train is dangerously near he must stop and get out of his vehicle, although obviously he will not often be required to do more than to stop and look." In that opinion, Justice Holmes wrote that while it is true "that the question of due care very generally is left to the jury," "when the standard is clear it should be laid down once and for all by the courts." "Once and for all" lasted just seven years. In Pokora v. Wabash Ry. Co., 292 U.S. 98 (1934), the Supreme Court abandoned the *Goodman* rule, admitting "[s]tandards of prudent conduct are declared at times by courts, but they are taken over from the facts of life. To get out of a vehicle and reconnoiter is an uncommon precaution." *See also* Trevino v. Union Pacific R.R. Co., 916 F.2d 1230 (7th Cir. 1990) (rejecting rule of law requiring driver to notice railroad car at crossing as a rule that "buck[s] the twentieth century trend toward leaving questions of care to the jury"); *contra* Hurst v. Union Pacific R.R. Co., 958 F.2d 1002 (10th Cir. 1992).

Learned Hand's Formula. In another instance, Judged Learned Hand in Conway v. O'Brien, 111 F.2d 611, 612 (2nd Cir. 1940), attempted to articulate an economic formula for the standard of care: "The degree of care demanded of a person by an occasion is the resultant of three factors: the likelihood that his conduct will injure others, taken with the seriousness of the injury if it happens, and balanced against the interest which he must sacrifice to avoid the risk." Yet continuing on in the same passage, Judge Hand admitted, "All these are practically not susceptible of any quantitative estimate, and the second two are generally not so, even theoretically. For this reason, a solution always involves some preference, or choice between incommensurables, and it is consigned to a jury because their decision is thought most likely to accord with commonly accepted standards, real or fancied." Nevertheless, seven years later Judge Hand wrote one of the best-known tort opinions, articulating the same negligence formula with greater clarity—an opinion that continues to resonate with the social-science academy if not (as Judge Hand himself admitted in *Conway v. O'Brien*) necessarily with juries. As you read that case, consider whether Judge Hand applied his own formula—and whether there was any possibility that he could have done so.

United States v. Carroll Towing Co.
United States Court of Appeals, Second Circuit
159 F.2d 169 (2d. Cir. 1947)

HAND, J. These appeals concern the sinking of the barge, "Anna C," on January 4, 1944, off Pier 51, North River. The Conners Marine Co., Inc., was the owner of the barge, which the Pennsylvania Railroad Company had chartered; the Grace Line, Inc., was the charterer of the tug, "Carroll," of which the Carroll Towing Co., Inc., was the owner. The decree in the limitation proceeding held the Carroll Company liable to the United States for the loss of the barge's cargo of flour, and to the Pennsylvania Railroad Company, for expenses in salving the cargo and barge; and it held the Carroll Company also liable to the Conners Company for one half the damage to the barge; these liabilities being all subject to limitation. ... The Carroll Company and the Pennsylvania Railroad Company have filed assignments of error.

The facts, as the judge found them, were as follows. On June 20, 1943, the Conners Company chartered the barge, "Anna C." to the Pennsylvania Railroad Company.... On January 2, 1944, the barge, which had lifted the cargo of flour, was made fast off the end of Pier 58 on the Manhattan side of the North River, whence she was later shifted to Pier 52. At some time not disclosed, five other barges were moored outside her, extending into the river; her lines to the pier were not then strengthened. ... The Grace Line, which had chartered the tug, "Carroll," sent her down to the locus in quo to "drill" out one of the barges which lay at the end of the Public Pier.... The "harbormaster" and the deckhand went aboard the barges and readjusted all the fasts to their satisfaction, including those from the "Anna C." to the pier.

After doing so, they threw off the line between the two tiers and again boarded the "Carroll," which backed away from the outside barge, preparatory to "drilling" out the barge she was after in the tier off the Public Pier. She had only got about seventy-five feet away when the tier off Pier 52 broke adrift because the fasts from the "Anna C," either rendered, or carried away. The tide and wind carried down the six barges, still holding together, until the "Anna C" fetched up against a tanker, lying on the north side of the pier below—Pier 51—whose propeller broke a hole in her at or near her bottom. Shortly thereafter: i.e., at about 2:15 P.M., she careened, dumped her cargo of flour and sank. The tug, "Grace," owned by the Grace Line, and the "Carroll," came to the help of the flotilla after it broke loose; and, as both had syphon pumps on board, they could have kept the "Anna C" afloat, had they learned of her condition; but the bargee had left her on the evening before, and nobody was on board to observe that she was leaking. ...

... [I]f the bargee had been on board, and had done his duty to his employer, he would have gone below at once, examined the injury, and called for help from the 'Carroll' and the Grace Line tug. Moreover, it is clear that these tugs could have kept the barge afloat, until they had safely beached her, and saved her cargo. This would have avoided what we shall call the "sinking damages." Thus, if it was a failure in the Conner Company's proper care of its own barge, for the bargee to be absent, the company can recover only one third of the "sinking" damages from the Carroll Company and one third from the Grace Line. For this reason the question arises whether a barge owner is slack in the care of his barge if the bargee is absent. ...

It appears from the foregoing review [of case law] that there is no general rule to determine when the absence of a bargee or other attendant will make the owner of the barge liable for injuries to other vessels if she breaks away from her moorings. However, in any cases where he would be so liable for injuries to others obviously he must reduce his damages proportionately, if the injury is to his own barge. It becomes apparent why there can be no such general rule, when we consider the grounds for such a liability. Since there are occasions when every vessel will break from her moorings, and since, if she does, she becomes a menace to those about her; the owner's duty, as in other similar situations, to provide against resulting injuries is a function of three variables: (1) The probability that she will break away; (2) the gravity of the resulting injury, if she does; (3) the burden of adequate precautions. Possibly it serves to bring this notion into relief to state it in algebraic terms: if the probability be called P; the injury, L; and the burden, B; liability depends upon whether B is less than L multiplied by P: i.e., whether B less than PL. Applied to the situation at bar, the likelihood that a barge will break from her fasts and the damage she will do, vary with the place and time; for example, if a storm threatens, the danger is greater; so it is, if she is in a crowded harbor where moored barges are constantly being shifted about. On the other hand, the barge must not be the bargee's prison, even though he lives aboard; he must go ashore at times. We need not say whether, even in such crowded waters as New York Harbor a bargee must be aboard at night at all; it may be that the custom is otherwise, as Ward, J., supposed in "The Kathryn B. Guinan," supra; and that, if so, the situation is one where custom should control. We leave that question open; but we hold that it is not in all cases a sufficient answer to a bargee's absence without excuse, during working hours, that he has properly made fast his barge to a pier, when he leaves her. In the case at bar the bargee left at five o'clock in the afternoon of January 3rd, and the flotilla broke away at about two o'clock in the afternoon of the following day, twenty-one hours afterwards. The bargee had been away all the time, and we hold that his fabricated story was affirmative evidence that he had no excuse for his absence. At the locus in quo—especially during the short January days and in the full tide of war activity—barges were being constantly "drilled" in and out. Certainly it was not beyond reasonable expectation that, with the inevitable haste and bustle, the work might not be done with adequate care. In such circumstances we hold—and it is all that we do hold—that it was a fair requirement that the Conners Company should have a bargee aboard (unless he had some excuse for his absence), during the working hours of daylight. ...

Decrees reversed and cause remanded for further proceedings in accordance with the foregoing.

---

3. Qualified Duties

Other areas exist where tort-law duties take on a peculiar character requiring other rules. These areas lie at the borders of tort-based duties, surrounding tort law's central concern over the care that we take in our affirmative actions. Four of these border areas are where: (1) the tort-law duty depends on a contract (a hybrid, in a sense, of tort and contract law), (2) the duty involves an omission to act rather than an affirmative action, (3) the duty concerns the interests of a bystander to the primary harm, and (4) the loss does not involve any direct physical harm but does affect the tort claimant's economic interests. Consider each of these areas in turn.

a. Contracts

OBJECTIVE: Given injuries due to the negligence of persons performing or failing to perform contracts, apply the principles in this section to determine whether each person owed a duty of care the violation of which would give rise to a negligence claim.

Case Study: A cabler had a contract to run wire for a new fire alarm system in a building. The cabler got busy with other jobs and did not complete the work according to schedule. A fire occurred resulting in damage to equipment stored in the building. The fire would not have damaged the equipment, and would have been extinguished, if the cabler had completed his cabling contract timely. ***Explain whether the equipment's owner has a negligence claim against the cabler.***

A person generally owes no duty to act for the benefit of another, except that a contract may obligate the person to do so. Does tort liability exist when someone suffers injury or loss because a promisor does not perform a contract? Can the person suffering the injury or loss sue the promisor whom the contract obligated to perform? If so, then is the claim in tort, contract, or both? Depending on the circumstances, the answer can be any of those options. This section articulates the rules determining where the law permits (1) no suit at all, (2) a claim only in tort, (3) a claim only in contract, or (4) the option of suing in tort or contract.

Both tort and contract rest on the sense of obligation. The fundamental distinction is that obligations not to commit a tort and not to breach a contract arise from different sources. Tort duties arise from outside the plaintiff/defendant relationship, based on fundamental understandings regarding the nature of human existence—that treating one another with a reciprocal degree of reasonable care fits our independent corporeal form, inherent and equal value, and mutual dependence. The law imposes contract duties from within the plaintiff/defendant relationship, based on covenant or promise. Tort- and contract-based obligations, though, can overlap because the contract promise may include reasonable care performing the contract. To put it another way, the promise may be to do that which a reasonable person would have done anyway in undertaking the act without the promise. As you read the following illustrative case, discern the outer bounds of the rule permitting a tort claim—when the claim exists and when it does not.

Genen v. Metro-North Commuter R.R.
Supreme Court of New York, Appellate Division
261 A.D.2d 211, 690 N.Y.S.2d 213 (1999)

MEMORANDUM DECISION. ...

Plaintiff Abraham Genen slipped and fell on an icy platform at defendant Metro-North's Salisbury Mills station. Metro-North had previously hired defendant Hunter to perform snow removal and sanding services at the station. On January 31, 1996, the day before the accident, two inches of snow fell and, according to Hunter, it plowed and sanded the platforms and station area pursuant to its contract. Plaintiff commenced the instant action for personal injuries against Metro-North and Hunter, and Metro-North brought a third-party action against Hunter for contribution and indemnification.

The issue to be decided on this appeal is whether the plaintiff may maintain a cause of action sounding only in negligence directly against the snow removal contractor Hunter. Clearly, Hunter assumed no independent duty of care to the plaintiff *solely by virtue of its snow removal contract with Metro-North;* that is, plaintiff is not a third-party beneficiary of the snow removal contract between Hunter and Metro-North. However, Hunter may be liable to the plaintiff for its affirmative acts of negligence if those acts created or increased a hazard and were the proximate cause of plaintiff's injuries ([cc]).

In opposition to Hunter's motion for summary judgment, plaintiff presented evidence demonstrating that Hunter had performed snow removal operations on the day before the accident, in the area where plaintiff slipped. Plaintiff offered evidence showing that at the time of the accident, the area where he slipped had not been sanded and was covered with dangerous ice patches. This evidence supported plaintiff's claim in his bill of particulars that Hunter had "created the dangerous condition by incomplete ice removal." Having undertaken to clear the snow and ice, Hunter was obligated to exercise reasonable care in doing so, or be held liable in negligence where its acts created or increased the snow-related hazard). As it may reasonably be inferred that the dangerous ice patches were the residue of Hunter's incomplete and incompetent snow removal efforts, a triable issue of fact exists as to whether Hunter's conduct created or increased a hazard that would not have existed but for Hunter's actions ([c]).

While several cases from other departments, and one from this Court, appear to hold that there is no duty to a plaintiff under similar circumstances ([cc]), they are not controlling. None of them discuss the pleadings or whether the plaintiffs asserted a cause of action in negligence against the contractor based on the theory that the contractor created or increased a dangerous hazard. Further, most of them do not disclose whether the contractor had attempted snow removal operations, or if they did, the result thereof. ...

Nor are the Court of Appeals' holdings in *Eaves Brooks Costume Co. v. Y.B.H. Realty Corp.*, 76 N.Y.2d 220, 557 N.Y.S.2d 286, 556 N.E.2d 1093, and [c] controlling. ...

Significantly, in *Eaves Brooks* (*supra*, [c]), the Court of Appeals discussed tort liability in favor of a noncontracting party in the context of a contract to inspect or maintain, and where the contractors had simply failed to perform their duties under the contract. The holding in *Eaves Brooks,* it appears, is limited only to instances where the injury arose from "inaction" ([c]). When a contractor is alleged to have negligently created or increased a dangerous condition by its own affirmative acts, such conduct unquestionably constitutes misfeasance rather than nonfeasance, and the scope of the defendant's duty should be determined under traditional negligence principles, without regard to any breach of contract theory.[fn] Thus, it does not appear that the *Eaves Brooks* rationale applies to cases involving affirmative acts of negligence, such as in this instance. ...

The negligent conduct at issue in this case is completely different. A failure to perform a contract is not at issue here. Rather, the claim against Hunter arises out of its affirmative acts in improperly plowing and sanding a railroad platform and leaving dangerous icy patches on its surface. Thus, Hunter's duty to exercise reasonable care in relation to the plaintiff in this context arose not out of a contract, but rather by its own affirmative acts that created a risk of injury to members of the public using that Metro-North station ([cc]). As an aside, it should also be remembered that the area where this accident occurred, a railroad platform, is one where a heightened duty of care exists, as the potential for grave injury resulting from improper snow removal is increased (*cf., H.R. Moch Co. v. Rensselaer Water Co.,* [247 N.Y. 160, 168 159 N.E. 896 (1928) (]a tort duty arises where "the putative wrongdoer has advanced to such a point as to have launched a force or instrument of harm"). ...

Courts have frequently recognized that an actor's conduct may give rise tort liability where none otherwise would exist. For example, while ordinarily an owner or lessee of property is under no duty to remove snow and ice that naturally accumulates on a public sidewalk adjacent to its premises, if it undertakes to do so, it can be held liable in negligence where its acts create or increase a hazardous condition ([cc]). A similar scenario is presented here. Initially, Hunter assumed no duty of care to plaintiff merely by virtue of its snow removal contract. Had Hunter done nothing, a mere breach of contract would exist and plaintiff would have no direct claim against Hunter. However, once Hunter attempted snow removal operations, it was obligated to do so in a proper manner that did not create a hazard that otherwise would not have existed ([c]). Why should Hunter be able to escape liability for its own affirmative negligent acts which allegedly injured others by skating away, using as a cover, the icy slope of a contract with another? ...

As a triable issue of fact exists, Hunter's motion for summary judgment dismissing the complaint was properly denied. Hunter's motion for dismissal of the third-party complaint was also properly denied, as its liability for contribution or indemnification must await a determination of Metro-North's liability ([c]).

INQUIRY

Misfeasance or Nonfeasance. The above case illustrates the general rule that a promisor to a contract will owe a tort-based duty to a person who is not a party to the contract only if the promisor affirmatively undertakes some act performing the contract. A simpler way of stating the rule is to say that tort liability extends only to misfeasance (wrong action), not nonfeasance (inaction), performing a contract. The well-known historical case is Winterbottom v. Wright, 10 M. & W. 109, 152 Eng. Rep. 402 (Exch. Pl. 1842), in which the defendant failed to repair a mail coach as promised with the result that the coach's driver suffered injury. The Exchequer of Pleas held that the driver had no tort claim for the promisor's nonfeasance. *See also* Southwestern Bell Tel. Co. v. DeLanney, 809 S.W.2d 493 (Tex. 1991) (failure to publish promised Yellow-Pages advertisement does not give rise to tort-based duty); Leavitt v. Twin County Rental Co., 222 N.C. 81, 21 S.E.2d 890 (1942) (lessor's unfulfilled promise to repair ceiling plaster does not create a duty to plaintiff who was injured by unrepaired falling plaster); *cf.* Lee v. Rowland, 11 N.C. App. 27, 180

S.E.2d 445 (1971) (defendant liable for injury due to improper axle repair). How clear is the line between misfeasance and nonfeasance? *Contrast* Nagy v. McEachern, 28 Mich. App. 439, 184 N.W.2d 556 (1970) (defendant liable for inadequate repair of firearm safety); Flint v. Walling Mfg. Co. v. Beckett, 167 Ind. 491, 79 N.E. 503 (1906) (defendant negligent installer of windmill liable in tort for damage caused when it fell over on barn), *with* Levine v. Sears Roebuck & Co., 200 F. Supp.2d 180 (E.D. N.Y. 2002) (defendant not liable to plaintiff injured by dishwasher door that defendant had failed to repair as promised); Hart v. Ludwig, 347 Mich. 559, 79 N.W.2d 895 (1956) (failure to perform oral promise to maintain orchard not actionable in tort where defendant worked one season and began a second before refusing to go on); Newton v. Brook, 134 Ala. 269, 32 So. 722 (1902) (failure to prepare body for shipment not actionable in tort where no part of contract was performed). The *Hart* opinion just cited offers a well-written and interesting history of the rule. It also cautions, "The cases are numerous and confusing as to the dividing line between actions of contract and of tort; and there are many cases where a man may have his election to bring either action." Does it seem to you that *Hart*, itself, begs the rule—given that the defendant in that case had begun the contract?

> **Figure**
>
> The public best knows the late trial lawyer Johnnie Cochran for his successful defense of O.J. Simpson's double-murder trial. But his first notable case was a tort claim representing the widow of a man shot and killed by several police officers—a case which he lost. He then spent five years as the first African-American assistant district attorney in Los Angeles County, working (he wrote) to improve the justice system from inside, before returning to private practice—this time with greater success. His first notable tort win was a $760,000 verdict for an African-American college football player shot by police. Cochran had many other notable tort cases, so many that he formed partnerships and opened offices in over a dozen states, earning tens of millions of dollars in fees. The Cochran Law Firm continues to represent tort claimants nationwide today, after its founder's 2005 death.

Exceptions. Every rule has its exceptions. What do you think the exceptions should be, where a plaintiff should be able to sue in tort not merely for misfeasance but also for nonfeasance in the performance of a contract? What if the promisor assures the other party to the contract that the promisor has done the necessary safety work? *See* Moody v. Martin Motor Co., 76 Ga. App. 456, 46 S.E.2d 197 (1948) (promisor is liable to injured third person). Historically, common carriers whose services are generally available to the public have been subject to tort liability when they negligently fail or intentionally refuse to provide that service. *See* Zabron v. Cunard S.S. Co., 151 Iowa 345, 131 N.W. 18 (1911); Nevin v. Pullman Palace-Car Co., 106 Ill. 222, 46 Am. Rep. 688 (1883). The rationale may be that the plaintiff should not have to suffer for having been denied a right generally available to the public. The law reflects that rationale more clearly today, in that the intentional refusal of a common carrier to serve a member of the public may also be actionable as a civil rights violation, if the common carrier bases the refusal on a protected characteristic or membership in a protected class. Also, a party who contracts without any intention at the time of contracting to perform the contract will be subject to misrepresentation liability, covered in a later chapter. What about the defendant who inspects as part of a contract but does not repair? Consider the following case.

Wroblewski v. Otis Elevator Co.
Supreme Court of New York, Appellate Division
9 A.D.2d 294, 193 N.Y.S.2d 855 (3d Dept. 1959)

FOSTER, J. This is an appeal by a plaintiff from a judgment of no cause of action in a negligence action.

Appellant was an elevator operator for the New York Telephone Company, employed in its building on State Street in the City of Albany, New York. On the 11th day of May, 1953, she discharged her last passenger from the elevator she was operating, on to the seventh floor of the building, then placed the control handle in an up position, but the elevator, instead of going up, plunged downward until it forcibly struck the buffer in the pit at the foot of the elevator shaft. As a result of this fall she claimed to have received the personal injuries which formed the basis of her claim for damages in this action.

The Otis Elevator Company, the defendant-respondent, had a service contract with the New York Telephone Company with respect to the elevator in question, as well as others, maintained in the Telephone building. This contract provided for service by way of examination of the elevator, cleaning, oiling and greasing, and making necessary minor adjustments. Emergency call-back service was also provided for between regular examinations if trouble developed with the equipment and Otis was notified. For this service Otis received $754 a month.

... Appellant testified that on the morning of the day the accident happened she noticed that the elevator did not work properly, and she so notified the elevator starter who was on duty at the time. Later a service man from Otis appeared and rode with her in the elevator to the 9th floor, made some sort of an examination there, and then told her that the elevator was working all right. The service man flatly denied the testimony of appellant in this respect and on that phase of the case a sharp issue of fact was presented.

After the accident ... it was found that one of the wires, designed and installed to carry an electric current in the traveling cable, had been severed, and this break was the source of the trouble.

A great deal of evidence was taken on the trial but the foregoing will serve to indicate the questions of law involved. On the issue of liability the trial court charged the jury in this language: "Unless, from the evidence in this case, you find that the Otis Elevator Company, the defendant, made repairs or made replacements on this elevator, and that in making such repairs or replacing such parts by some act of commission or omission it brought about the accident described in the evidence in this case, the plaintiff cannot recover."

In thus limiting the consideration of the jury we think the trial court erred. As a matter of fact there was no evidence that Otis had made any repairs to the elevator, or replaced parts, prior to the accident; hence the charge quoted amounted, for practical purposes, to a direction of a verdict for the defendant. The respondent argues here that failure to inspect properly was a breach of contract, and the remedy arising therefrom belonged solely to the Telephone Company ([cc]). The trial court apparently relied upon the principle of lack of privity enunciated in such cases, but we think they do not amount to a strait jacket on the facts, such as they might be found, in this case. ... The present juridical thought on the subject was well expressed in the case of Rosenbaum v. Branster Realty Corp., 276 App.Div. 167, at page 168, 93 N.Y.S.2d 209, at page 212: "The duty of reasonable care in the performance of a contract is not always owed solely to the person with whom the contract is made or those claiming through him. It may inure to the benefit of others." ...

In this case it seems to have been overlooked that appellant testified as to a specific complaint that the elevator was not working properly, and in response to such complaint a service man from Otis appeared, examined the elevator and assured her that it was all right. This was denied but the denial only created an issue of fact. If the jury accepted appellant's testimony, then the representative of Otis was obliged to make a reasonably careful and prudent inspection. If he failed to do so and injury resulted to the appellant by reason thereof it is no defense that he did not make any repairs to the elevator under the contract or otherwise. Such a defense would be contrary to common sense. Failure to make any inspection, or non-feasance, would of course be merely a breach of contract for which Otis would not be liable in negligence, but if inspection was undertaken, in dealing with an instrumentality potentially dangerous then Otis was obliged to perform such inspection in a reasonably careful and prudent manner, and its failure to do so would inure to the benefit of a third party using the elevator. ...

The judgment should be reversed and a new trial directed.

Judgment reversed and a new trial directed, with costs to appellant to abide the event.

Ethics

Tort lawyers often work on fascinating cases involving strange events, extraordinary actions, unusual motives, bizarre relationships, large amounts of money, and (occasionally) famous and influential individuals and powerful interests and entities. As much as tort lawyers may wish to entertain with talk about the details of their work, they may not do so. Rule 1.6 of the ABA Model Rules of Professional Conduct prohibits lawyers from revealing information relating to the representation of a client without the client's informed consent or implied authorization. The rule has other exceptions, for instance to prevent a client's crime or fraud using the lawyer's services, or to collect a fee or defend a grievance. Yet the rule does not authorize entertaining talk.

INQUIRY

Relevance. What difference does it make whether the plaintiff sues in tort or in contract? Contract law and tort law may offer different procedures, proofs, and remedies. Contract claims may require prompt notice of breach and an opportunity to remedy before suit, whereas tort claims may have longer or shorter limitations periods. Plaintiffs may have to file tort and contract claims in courts of different jurisdiction or, under venue statutes, in different counties. Tort claims may not require proof of the agreement, its consideration, and its terms but will require proof of a standard of care and its breach—including, possibly, expert testimony. Contracts may require more than that required of the reasonably prudent person. Tort remedies will typically include all compensatory damages including mental and emotional distress, whereas a contract may limit remedies to repair or replacement of defective goods and other economic loss. Practitioner do well to know these differences and properly advise clients of their implications.

Shifting a Duty. What duties exist when a contractor accept a landowner's duties but then fails to perform them? Some cases hold that when a company contracts to do that which the landowner owed a duty to do, the law will not impose misfeasance and reliance as conditions to the contractor's duty. *See* Gazo v. City of Stamford, 255 Conn. 245, 765 A.2d 505 (2001) (snow-removal contractor owed landowner's duty to clear sidewalk of ice and snow); Palka v. Servicemaster Mgt. Services Corp., 83 N.Y.2d 579, 634 N.E.2d 189, 611 N.Y.S.2d 817 (1994) (inspection service owed duty of care to hospital employee that it agreed by contract to undertake on behalf of hospital employer). Do these cases gut the misfeasance/nonfeasance rule? *See* Caldwell v. Bechtel, Inc., 632 F.2d 989 (D.C. Cir. 1980) (contractor agreeing to supervise job safety owes a tort-based duty to workers injured at the site); Wilson v. Rebsamen Ins., Inc., 330 Ark. 687, 957 S.W.2d 678 (1997) (same); Hodge v. United States Fidelity & Guar. Co., 539 So.2d 229 (Ala. 1989) (insurer making inspection of employer's premises owes duty of care to employees); *but see* Schoenwald v. Farmers Coop. Assn., 474 N.W.2d 519 (S.D. 1991) (insurer making inspection of premises owes no duty of care to others).

Utilities. Notice that the above featured case, *Genen v. Metro-North Commuter R.R. Co.*, cites the case of H.R. Moch v. Rensselaer Water Co., 247 N.Y. 160, 159 N.E. 896 (1928), in which the defendant had breached its contract to provide water service to fire hydrants, resulting in the plaintiff's loss when its building caught fire. The water pressure was too low at the hydrant—arguably an act of misfeasance rather than merely nonfeasance. Yet the appellate court nonetheless found in favor of the defendant water company. The *H.R. Moch Co.* opinion, written by Justice Cardozo, illustrates a corollary rule that tort liability does not extend to third persons who are injured by the failure to provide utilities. *See* Milliken & Co. v. Consolidated Edison Co., 84 N.Y.2d 469, 644 N.E.2d 268 (1994); Goldstein v. Consolidated Edison Co., 115 A.D.2d 34, 499 N.Y.S.2d 47 (1 Dept. 1986) (power company owes no duty to tenant falling on a stairway darkened during power outage); Strauss v. Belle Realty Co., 65 N.Y.2d 399, 492 N.Y.S.2d 555, 482 N.E.2d 34 (1985) (defendant electrical utility owes no tort-based duty to maintain power—not liable for man's fall due to grossly negligent blackout); Mentzer v. New England Tel. & Tel. Co., 276 Mass 478, 177 N.E. 549 (1931) (telephone company not liable to third person for failure to provide telephone service); *cf.* Hayes v. Torrington Water Co., 88 Conn. 609, 92 A. 406 (1914) (utility subject to liability for defective water supply carrying disease); *but see* Doyle v. South Pittsburgh Water Co., 414 Pa. 199, 199 A.2d 875 (1964) (finding duty on misfeasance theory that utility had begun performance). What rationales support the rule? Justice Cardozo asserted in his *H.R. Moch Co.* opinion, "We are satisfied that liability would be unduly and indeed indefinitely extended by this enlargement of the zone of duty." What is "undue" about extending tort liability to those who fail to perform contracts in ways that create unreasonable dangers for others? The courts with some frequency have accepted that extending tort liability to meet new circumstances will "open the floodgates" of tort litigation. Do classes of injured and oppressed potential tort claimants clamor for rights to file more cases? If so, then on what principles other than docket expediency should the courts refuse to recognize them? Tort law can have a brooding class-conflict atmosphere—the haves against the have-nots. In shaping these rules, are the courts tacitly weighing the economic interests of those who have the wherewithal to make and perform contracts against the social interests of those harmed by their negligent performance?

Gravamen and Election. Will a tort action always exist when a promisor breaches a contract by misfeasance? Who has the choice of actions when both tort and contract claims exist? These can be important questions because of the law's different treatment of tort and contract procedures, proofs, and remedies. The answers to these questions can vary from state to state without clear reason. In some cases, the courts have held that the gist or gravamen of the claim was in tort and not contract. Examples are Victorson v. Bock Laundry Mach. Co., 37 N.Y.2d 395, 335 N.E.2d 275, 373 N.Y.S.2d 39 (1975), involving defects in washing machines that caused property damage, and Webber v. Herkimer & Mohawk St. R. Co., 190 N.Y. 311, 16 N.E. 358 (1888), involving a railroad passenger's injury. The gravamen of claims against attorneys, physicians, and other professionals, by those whom they contract to serve, is ordinarily only in tort—in the form of malpractice rather than breach-of-contract actions (a subject treated in greater detail in the chapter on professional negligence). In other cases, the courts have permitted the plaintiff to elect the remedy—to choose a tort action *or* contract action. *See* Collins v. Reynard, 154 Ill.2d 48, 607 N.E.2d 1185, 180 Ill. Dec. 672 (1992) (legal-malpractice action cognizable in contract or tort). Consider the following case.

Doughty v. Maine Cent. Transp. Co.
Maine Supreme Court
141 Me. 124, 39 A.2d 758 (1944)

HUDSON, J. The defendant excepts to a ruling below sustaining the plaintiff's demurrer to its plea, wherein, by way of brief statement, a special statute of limitations was set up in defense.

This action is assumpsit, brought to recover damages for personal injuries suffered by the plaintiff on June 15, 1942, while a fare-paying passenger on a motor bus owned and operated by the defendant, when the bus left the travelled portion of the highway and collided with a tree near Bethel, Maine.

In the brief statement, the defendant alleged "That under Section 11 of Chapter 66 of the Revised Statutes of Maine, 1930, it is provided that this action shall be commenced only within one year after the cause of action occurs." It was not brought within the year.

Sec. 11, reads as follows: "Actions of tort for injuries to the person or for death and for injuries to or destruction of property caused by the ownership, operation, maintenance or use on the ways of the state of motor vehicles or trailers subject to the supervision and control of the public utilities commission, shall be commenced only within one year next after the cause of action occurs."

The question is the applicability of this statute. The plaintiff contends that in place of Sec. 11, the statute governing the time in which this action could have been brought lawfully is Chap. 95, Sec. 90, Par. IV, R.S.1930, which reads in part: "The following actions shall be commenced within six years after the cause of action accrues and not afterwards. ****** IV. Actions of account, of assumpsit or upon the case, founded on any contract or liability, express or implied."

If this statute is applicable, this action was seasonably commenced.

The gist of the defendant's argument is that this "action, in substance, is one 'of tort'" and that "if the words 'of tort' are directed to the form of the action rather than to its substance, then the action is one for personal injury for negligence" and "is controlled by the limitation in Sec. 11." ...

Then what did the Legislature intend when it said "actions of tort"? Had it in mind the form of the action or the cause of action upon which it would be based? Counsel agree upon the law enunciated in Goddard v. Grand Trunk Railway, 57 Me. 202, on pages 217 and 218, 2 Am.Rep. 39, where the Court said: "The law requires the common carrier of passengers to exercise the highest degree of care that human judgment and foresight are capable of, to make his passenger's journey safe. Whoever engages in the business impliedly promises that his passenger shall have this degree of care. *** The passenger's remedy may be either in assumpsit or tort, at his election." ...

It must be assumed that the Legislature enacted Sec. 11 with knowledge of the law as to the right of choice of remedies. With this knowledge it said "actions of tort," not "actions of tort and/or contract," not simply "action to recover damages," etc., not "action to recover damages for a personal injury resulting from negligence," [c] ... but it confined the limitation to "actions of tort." This language is plain. One of two possible remedies, assumpsit or tort, was chosen for the one-year limitation. It omitted actions ex contractu, to which another statute already applied. ...

... We cannot believe that the Legislature, when it said in this statute "actions of tort," intended to include actions of assumpsit, although the claimed breach of the implied promise were founded originally on the commission of a tort. ...

This plaintiff could have sued either in assumpsit or in tort; she had her choice. She elected to sue in assumpsit, and hence the assumpsit statute of limitations rather than the tort is applicable.

Exceptions overruled.

INQUIRY

Continuing Performance. What if the contract on which a tort-based duty existed expires? Does the tort duty continue if the contractor knows of the danger? *See* Folsom v. Burger King, 135 Wash.2d 658, 958 P.2d 301 (1998) (security company owes no duty to come to the aid of victims of robbery-murder where security company had notice of alarm but disregarded it as a closed account). What if a promisor terminates a service on which a specific class of persons has come to rely, without notice to the class, creating an unreasonable danger? *See* Florence v. Goldberg, 44 N.Y.2d 189, 404 N.Y.S.2d 583, 375 N.E.2d 763 (1978) (municipality owed duty to continue school-crossing guard on which plaintiff parent had come to rely for protection of six-year-old child who was killed by traffic after guard service terminated without notice to plaintiff parent).

b. Omissions

OBJECTIVE: Given injuries due to the negligence of potential defendants in omitting or failing to act, apply the principles developed in this section to determine whether each potential defendant owed a duty of care the violation by omission of which would give rise to a claim for negligence.

Case Study: A trucker had his vehicle skid off the road in an ice storm in a remote area. Within minutes of the accident, a hunter drove by and saw the motorist waving for help in the freezing cold by the crumpled vehicle. The hunter did not stop. It was several hours before another motorist drove by and saved the trucker, who suffered severe frostbite, hypothermia, and shock because of the delay in his rescue. ***Explain whether the hunter owed the trucker a duty of care the violation of which would give rise to a claim for negligence.***

When a person acts in an affirmative manner, the existence of a duty not to unreasonably harm in the course of those acts seems clear enough. The introduction to the duty section of this chapter notes that a duty to exercise reasonable care arises when a person's acts create a foreseeable risk of physical harm. At the opposite end of the spectrum, no duty exists to protect others from harm that others cause. Yet the law recognizes several exceptions addressed below. Duty is not always so clear when the question involves a person's inaction. Fundamentally, tort law does not impose a duty to render aid to another in the absence of a special reason or relationship. Liberty and responsibility are at the core of tort law. One who unwisely chooses a course of action that carries with it certain untoward risks should not look to hold others accountable for omitting to act to prevent that harm. We are, it seems, our brothers' keepers only to a certain extent—not to the point of promoting and enabling the unreasonable conduct of others. The refusal of tort law to recognize an affirmative duty to act, and refusal to hold others liable for omissions in acting except in special situations, can seem callous at times. Some hold necessary drawing that line in order that tort law not devolve into utopian paternalism contradicting our essential right to will and to act while accepting the consequences. See if you agree with the limitation on duty imposed in the following two cases.

Hegel v. Langsam
Ohio Court of Common Pleas
29 Ohio Misc. 147, 55 Ohio Ops.2d 476,
273 N.E.2d 351 (Ct. Com. Pls. 1971)

BETTMAN, J. This matter is before the Court on defendant's motion for judgment on the pleadings. The gravamen of plaintiff's position is that the defendants permitted the minor plaintiff, a seventeen year old female student from Chicago, Illinois, enrolled at the University, to become associated with criminals, to be seduced, to become a drug user and further allowed her to be absent from her dormitory and failed to return her to her parents' custody on demand.

On our opinion plaintiffs completely misconstrue the duties and functions of a university. A university is an institution for the advancement of knowledge and learning. It is neither a nursery school, a boarding school nor a prison. No one is required to attend. Persons who meet the required qualifications and who abide by the university's rules and regulations are permitted to attend and must be presumed to have sufficient maturity to conduct their own personal affairs.

We know of no requirement of the law and none has been cited to us placing on a university or its employees any duty to regulate the private lives of their students, to control their comings and goings and to supervise their associations.

We do not believe that O.R.C. 3345.21 requiring a university to maintain "law and order" on campus, nor O.R.C. 2151.41, making it a crime to contribute to the delinquency of a child, have any bearing on the fact situation before us.

For these reasons we hold that plaintiffs have failed to state a cause of action and defendants' motion for judgment on the pleadings should be granted.

Having so determined it is not necessary to consider the defense that the University and its employees are immune from suit.

Please present entry accordingly.

Yania v. Bigan
Pennsylvania Supreme Court
397 Pa. 316, 155 A.2d 343 (1959)

JONES, J. A bizarre and most unusual circumstance provides the background of this appeal.

On September 25, 1957 John E. Bigan was engaged in a coal strip-mining operation in Shade Township, Somerset County. On the property being stripped were large cuts or trenches created by Bigan when he removed the earthen overburden for the purpose of removing the coal underneath. One cut contained water 8 to 10 feet in depth with side walls or embankments 16 to 18 feet in height; at this cut Bigan had installed a pump to remove the water.

At approximately 4 p. m. on that date, Joseph F. Yania, the operator of another coal strip-mining operation, and one Boyd M. Ross went upon Bigan's property for the purpose of discussing a business matter with Bigan, and, while there, were asked by Bigan to aid him in starting the pump. Ross and Bigan entered the cut and stood at the point where the pump was located. Yania stood at the top of one of the cut's side walls and then jumped from the side wall—a height of 16 to 18 feet—into the water and was drowned.

Yania's widow, in her own right and on behalf of her three children, instituted wrongful death and survival actions against Bigan contending Bigan was responsible for Yania's death. ...

The complaint avers negligence in the following manner: ... "After [Yania] was in the water, a highly dangerous position, having been induced and inveigled therein by [Bigan], [Bigan] failed and neglected to take reasonable steps and action to protect or assist [Yania], or extradite [Yania] from the dangerous position in which [Bigan] had placed him." Summarized, Bigan stands charged with ... failing to go to Yania's rescue after he had jumped into the water.[fn] ...

... [I]t is urged that Bigan failed to take the necessary steps to rescue Yania from the water. The mere fact that Bigan saw Yania in a position of peril in the water imposed upon him no legal, although a moral, obligation or duty to go to his rescue unless Bigan was legally responsible, in whole or in part, for placing Yania in the perilous position. [Cc] The language of this Court in Brown v. French, 104 Pa. 604, 607, 608, is apt: "If it appeared that the deceased, by his own carelessness, contributed in any degree to the accident which caused the loss of his life, the defendants ought not to have been held to answer for the consequences resulting from that accident. * * * He voluntarily placed himself in the way of danger, and his death was the result of his own act. * * * That his undertaking was an exceedingly reckless and dangerous one, the event proves, but there was no one to blame for it but himself. He had the right to try the experiment, obviously dangerous as it was, but then also upon him rested the consequences of that experiment, and upon no one else; he may have been, and probably was, ignorant of the risk which he was taking upon himself, or knowing it, and trusting to his own skill, he may have regarded it as easily superable. But in either case, the result of his ignorance, or of his mistake, must rest with himself—and cannot be charged to the defendants." The complaint does not aver any facts which impose upon Bigan legal responsibility for placing Yania in the dangerous position in the water and, absent such legal responsibility, the law imposes on Bigan no duty of rescue.

Order affirmed.

INQUIRY

Morality. In addition to *Hegel v. Langsam*, other cases have also held that a college has no tort-based duty to protect a student against drugs, alcohol, sex, and consorting with criminals. *See* Beach v. University of Utah, 726 P.2d 413 (Utah 1986); Wilson v. Continental Ins. Cos., 87 Wis.2d 310, 274 N.W.2d 679 (1979). Cases like *Yania v. Bigan* above sometime refer to a distinction between law and morality—that tort law requires less of us than moral action would require. Or did the court simply not get it right in *Yania v. Bigan*? Morality and law both demand that each of us retain certain liberties including the important right to encounter the correcting consequences of our own foolish action. Neither law nor morality would remove consequence from choice because to do so is to make the actor unaccountable. Yet if, in *Yania v. Bigan*, the defendant inveigled the plaintiff's decedent to jump, then didn't the defendant invite the plaintiff to rely that the defendant would give reasonable assistance with respect to the consequences? In other words, wasn't it both immoral and a breach of tort-based duty for the defendant to have let the plaintiff's decedent drown after the defendant arguably misrepresented the defendant's own intentions with respect to the consequences? *Cf.* Stockberger v. United States, 332 F.3d 479 (7th Cir. 2003) (liability might reduce the altruism that makes these cases unusual); Rocha v. Faltys, 69 S.W.3d 315 (Tex. App. 2002) (fraternity brother's encouraging student who could not swim to jump into water remains nonfeasance and does not create a duty of care). The Restatement (Second) of Torts §323-324 recognizes a duty to act where the defendant engages in an undertaking that creates a risk of harm or where the defendant knows that the plaintiff is relying to the plaintiff's detriment on the defendant's assistance. If the law does not base tort law at least in part on morality—on the inferable fitness of conduct between interacting parties—what gives it sanction to impose liability in any circumstance?

Affirmative Acts. One of the exceptions to the general no-duty-to-protect-others rule states that a duty to exercise reasonable care arises when a person voluntarily undertakes to protect another from risk of harm caused by other people or things. In those circumstances, liability exists if the person fails to use reasonable care and that failure increases the risk of harm or the undertaking influences the person to forgo other forms of protection. See Restatement (Third) of Torts: Liability for Physical and Emotional Harm §§42, 43. Similarly, a duty arises if a person rescues another in peril while unable to protect him- or herself from harm. Id. §44. Instances arise when a duty exists for defendant's broader undertaking even if the particular breach looks like an omission to act. *See* Kleinknect v. Gettysburg College, 989 F.2d 1360 (3d Cir. 1993) (Pennsylvania law recognizes duty of college to maintain life-saving emergency-medical equipment for member of lacrosse team); Duarte v. State, 84 Cal. App.3d 729, 148 Cal Rptr. 804 (1978) (university owed duty of security with respect to rape and murder inside dormitory). Is the difference in these cases that the defendant was engaged in an affirmative undertaking—or that the plaintiff was innocent of any foolishness? These close calls approaching the finest line between an omission to act (for which a duty is less likely) and an unreasonable act (where duty exists) seem to find their most acute expression in the police-call cases. Revisit in the section on governmental immunity one such case well-enough known for its horrible oddity that one can see a film about it. Riss v. City of New York, 22 N.Y.2d 579, 240 N.E.2d 860, 293 N.Y.S.2d 897 (1968). As you consider another gripping case—a few of the more sordid details omitted from the excerpt below—see if you can tell the precise moment at which the defendants crossed the line between no-duty and duty.

Sinthasomphone v. Milwaukee
United States District Court
785 F. Supp. 1343 (E.D. Wis. 1992)

EVANS, C.J. "I'm on 25th and State, and there is this young man. He's buck naked. He has been beaten up ... He is really hurt ... He needs some help."

With these words, a caller asked a Milwaukee Emergency 911 operator to send help to a person in need of assistance. When the call was made, on May 27, 1991, the name Jeffrey Dahmer was largely unknown. Today, everyone knows the story of the 31-year-old chocolate factory worker, a killing machine who committed the most appalling string of homicides in this city's history. ...

The telephone call for help on May 27 was made from a phone booth just a half a block away from Dahmer's apartment. The subject of the call was Konerak Sinthasomphone, a 14-year-old Laotian boy. Later that evening, after the police had responded to the call and determined that nothing was amiss, Dahmer killed Sinthasomphone. He went on to kill others, including Matt Turner in June, Jeremiah Weinberger in early July, and Oliver Lacy and Joseph Bradehoft in mid-July. He terrorized Tracy Edwards before Edwards escaped and led the police to Dahmer, who was finally arrested on July 22, 1991. After the arrest, Dahmer confessed to 17 murders. ...

As alleged in the amended *Sinthasomphone* complaint, the facts, which at this time I must legally assume to be true, are as follows.

In May of 1991, the 31-year-old Dahmer was on probation following a 1988 conviction for sexual abuse of a male child. He brought young Sinthasomphone to his apartment. There he held the boy captive, drugged him, stripped him of his clothing, and committed acts of physical and sexual abuse. All the while, the remains of previous victims of Dahmer's madness lay decaying in another room of the apartment.

Somehow, shortly before 2 a.m. on May 27, 1991, Sinthasomphone escaped from the apartment and—although he was drugged, naked, and bleeding—made his way to the street. On the street, Nichole Childress and Sandra Smith, two young black women, saw him and called the police. Before the police arrived, Dahmer appeared and tried to reassert physical control over Sinthasomphone. Childress and Smith intervened. ...

The complaint alleges ... that the officers intentionally and deliberately refused to listen to the following specific information conveyed by Nichole Childress, Sandra Smith, and others: that Sinthasomphone was a child; that he was trying to escape from Dahmer, that Dahmer had referred to Sinthasomphone by various names; that Dahmer was attempting to physically control Sinthasomphone; and that Sinthasomphone was drugged, hurt, and had been sexually abused. The officers threatened to arrest Childress and Smith if they persisted in trying to help Sinthasomphone or to provide information.

Another allegation is that the police officers took Dahmer and Sinthasomphone into actual, physical police custody and back into Dahmer's apartment, where they ultimately delivered Sinthasomphone into Dahmer's custody, without obtaining consent from Sinthasomphone or his parents. The police concluded that Dahmer and Sinthasomphone were adult homosexual partners who, at least at that time, were staying together in Dahmer's apartment. By returning young Sinthasomphone to Dahmer, it is claimed that the police interfered with any potential rescue of Sinthasomphone by private persons. ...

... The essence of the claims is that the police ignored the complaints of citizens belonging to a racial minority and allowed Dahmer to escape from their grasp. Had Dahmer been stopped on May 27, Lacy, Bradehoft, and Edwards would not have been victimized. ...

The legal difficulties posed by these cases are immediately apparent to anyone with even a passing familiarity with federal civil rights litigation. The genius of the *Sinthasomphone* complaint in trying to avoid those difficulties is also apparent. The question is whether it has succeeded.

A major difficulty is that posed by a doctrine reaffirmed in a recent case, *DeShaney v. Winnebago County Dept. of Social Services,* 489 U.S. 189, 109 S.Ct. 998, 103 L.Ed.2d 249 (1989). Essentially, it is that the purpose of the Constitution "was to protect the people from the State, not to ensure that the State protected them from each other." [C] Joshua DeShaney, who was 5 years old, was beaten and rendered profoundly retarded by his father, with whom he lived. Social workers and other local officials had received complaints that the father was abusing the boy, but they did not remove him from his father's custody. After he was beaten for the last time, Joshua and his mother brought a case in this court, pursuant to 42 U.S.C. § 1983, alleging that Joshua's substantive due process right to liberty was abridged when the officials failed to intervene to protect him from his father. Judge John Reynolds, to whom the case was assigned, found that no constitutionally recognized claim was present. The court of appeals and the Supreme Court agreed, with the higher court noting that the state's failure to protect an individual against private violence does not constitute a violation of the due process clause. ...

However, the *DeShaney* doctrine is not without some small cracks in its surface; hairline, perhaps, but cracks nonetheless. ...

Ross v. United States, 910 F.2d 1422 (7th Cir.1990), is, in fact, a case which was decided after *DeShaney.* A 12-year-old boy slipped into the water of Lake Michigan. A friend summoned help, and within 10 minutes two lifeguards, two fire fighters, one police officer, and two civilians, who were scuba-diving nearby, responded. However, before any rescue attempt could begin, a Lake County deputy sheriff arrived in a marine patrol boat. He insisted on enforcing an agreement between the city of Waukegan, Illinois, and Lake County, Illinois, which required the county to provide all police services on Lake Michigan. Pursuant to that agreement, the sheriff had promulgated a policy that directed all members of the sheriff's department to prevent any civilian from attempting to rescue a drowning person and contemplated that only divers from the city of Waukegan Fire Department could perform rescues. The deputy ordered all rescue attempts to stop. When the civilian scuba divers offered to attempt a rescue at their own risk, the deputy threatened to arrest them. Twenty minutes later, 30 minutes after the first would-be rescuers had arrived, the officially authorized divers pulled the boy from the water. He later died. The court found that the complaint stated a claim against both Lake County and the individual deputy.

The line between *DeShaney* and *Ross* may not be entirely clear, but it is discernable. Both courts, in fact, have articulated where it is. Justice Brennan, dissenting in *DeShaney,* points out that the result in a given case may depend on the characterization of the violation: is it a failure to act or an affirmative act: "In a constitutional setting that distinguishes sharply between action and inaction, one's characterization of the misconduct alleged under § 1983 may effectively decide the case. ..." 489 U.S. at 204, 109 S.Ct. at 1008. ...

Obviously, having dissected these cases, the *Sinthasomphone* plaintiffs have not merely alleged that the police officers failed to protect Konerak Sinthasomphone from Jeffrey Dahmer. Rather, they allege, among other things, that the officers actively prevented private citizens from helping Sinthasomphone and, in fact, delivered Sinthasomphone, who was a minor, not to his parents, but into Dahmer's custody. The police left him with Dahmer despite the persistent attempts of private citizens to urge them to investigate further. One of the officers assured a concerned private citizen, who later called the police station, that everything was under control. In other words, the allegations are not just of police inaction, but of police action, action which violated Konerak Sinthasomphone's substantive due process rights. I find that a claim is stated on this basis alone.

Nevertheless, other allegations deserve mention-allegations which also may serve to distinguish this case from *DeShaney.* As I stated above, in *DeShaney* the Court rejected the argument that Joshua DeShaney was in a "special relationship" with the state officials. ...

The *Sinthasomphone* case is different, but is it different enough? Sinthasomphone had escaped from Dahmer and had found persons to help him. He also, it is claimed, showed fear of Dahmer. However, he was then taken into what could be termed, at least, as brief police custody. During the time the police were in control, they prevented others from helping him. Then the police returned him to Dahmer's apartment. They were returning a minor, the complaint alleges, not to the custody of his parents, but to an unrelated adult with no legitimate claim to custody. That person then killed him almost as soon as the police left. It is a difficult question whether this creates a "special relationship." ...

In the *Sinthasomphone* case, at the motion to dismiss stage, I cannot say that no special relationship existed between Konerak and the three police officers. ...

It cannot be said, by any stretch of the imagination, that the City of Milwaukee or its police officers had a "special relationship" with Lacy, Bradehoft, or Edwards prior to Edwards' escape from Dahmer. ...

IT IS THEREFORE ORDERED that the motions of the defendants for dismissal of the *Sinthasomphone* complaint are DENIED ... .

IT IS FURTHER ORDERED that the complaints in ... the cases of Lacy, Bradehoft, and Edwards, are DISMISSED. ...

INQUIRY

Public Callings. The law regards certain undertakings as sufficiently *public* callings that it will impose a duty of reasonable care in their undertaking. Common carriers and innkeepers are two public callings for which law imposes duties of reasonable care based on that status alone. *See* Kinsey v. Hudson & Manhattan R. Co., 130 N.J.L. 285, 32 A.2d 497 (1943) (duty of carrier extends to protect passenger against attack, theft, or negligence of other passengers); Dove v. Loweden, 47 F. Supp. 546 (W.D. Mo. 1942) (innkeeper owes guest duty to help guest escape hotel fire); Yu v. New York, N.H. & H.R. Co., 145 Conn. 451, 144 A.2d 56 (1958) (common carrier owes passenger duty); Nevin v. Pullman Palace-Car Co., 106 Ill. 222, 46 Am. Rep. 688 (1883) (defendant rail line owes duty of care to plaintiff). What makes them so? Why are carriers and innkeepers engaged in a public calling but physicians and police officers are generally not (as the law regards them)? The existence—before the plaintiff's need arises—of a special relationship of plaintiff to defendant may be the critical ingredient.

Human Rights. The European Convention on Human Rights guarantees to citizens of European Union-member countries the right not to be "subjected to torture or to inhuman or degrading treatment or punishment." A jury in England acquits a stepfather of a criminal charge of beating his unruly step-child, even though the evidence was compelling that the stepfather had beaten the child. What private right of action would you anticipate? The European Court of Human Rights required the country of England to pay the child £10,000. *See* A. v. United Kingdom, 27 E.H.R.R. 611 (1999). Does American law offer any equivalent basis to hold federal or state government liable for failing to protect the personal rights and integrity of United States citizens who harm one another? *See* Sabia v. State, 164 Vt. 293, 669 A.2d 1187 (1995) (state child-protective statutes create agency duty to protect children whose peril has been identified); Jensen v. Anderson County DSS, 304 S.C. 195, 403 S.E.2d 615 (1991) (same); *see also* District of Columbia v. Harris, 770 A.2d 82 (D.C. App.

2001) (same for district law); *but see* P.W. v. Kansas Dept. of Social and Rehab. Services, 255 Kan. 827, 877 P.2d 430 (1994) (no private right of action).

> **Ethics**
> The liability insurer for the defendant in a tort action typically chooses and retains defense counsel, and pays them on an hourly basis. Defense lawyers often have a long-term professional relationship with the insurance company and may follow insurance-company guidelines regarding case reporting, billing, and other administrative matters. The defense lawyer will also typically take instructions on settlement from the insurance-company representative. The defense lawyer's client, though, is the party whom the lawyer defends in the action. This "infernal triangle" (as lawyers sometimes humorously call it) presents potential conflicts of interest for the defense lawyer. Rule 1.7(a) of the ABA Model Rules of Professional Conduct prohibits a lawyer from representing a client if the lawyer's responsibilities to a third person (like an insurance claim representative) will materially limit the lawyer's judgment. Rule 5.4(c) also provides that a lawyer must not permit someone who pays the lawyer to represent another person, to influence the lawyer's independent judgment. The insurance policy—a contract between the insurance company and the insured defendant in the tort action—addresses some of the potential conflicts by granting the decision to settle to the insurance company rather than the insured. In practice, a defense lawyer will also take pains not to let the insurance company that is paying the lawyer's bills dictate to the lawyer actions or restrictions that would compromise the lawyer's representation of the client defendant. The triangle relationship creates other ethical issues like liability in excess of the insurance policy limits and insurer bad faith. The defense lawyer and insurance claim representative will know and follow the ethics rules.

Other Special Relations. Special relationships impose special duties. Restatement (Third) of Torts: Liability for Physical and Emotional Harm §40 provides as follows:

(a) An actor in a special relationship with another owes the other a duty of reasonable care with regard to risks that arise within the scope of the relationship.

(b) Special relationships giving rise to the duty provided in Subsection (a) include:

(1) a common carrier with its passengers,

(2) an innkeeper with its guests,

(3) a business or other possessor of land that holds its premises open to the public with those who are lawfully on the premises,

(4) an employer with its employees who are:

    (a) in imminent danger; or

    (b) injured and thereby helpless,

(5) a school with its students,

(6) a landlord with its tenants, and

(7) a custodian with those in its custody, if: a) the custodian is required by law to take custody or voluntarily takes custody of the other; and b) the custodian has a superior ability to protect the other.

Can you think of special relationships where a duty to come to the assistance of another may exist? *See* Dupont v. Aavid Thermal Techns., Inc., 147 N.H. 706, 798 A.2d 587 (2002) (employer owes employee a duty of care when the employee is in a position of imminent danger); Thomas v. Williams, 105 Ga. App. 321, 124 S.E.2d 409 (1962) (jailor owes prisoner duty of care in rescue during fire); Pirkle v. Oakdale Union Grammar Sch. Dist., 40 Cal.2d 207, 253 P.2d 1 (1953) (teacher owes student duty to seek emergency medical aid); *see also* Davis v. Monroe County Bd. of Educ., 526 U.S. 629 (1999) (school district owes limited duty to protect student from harassment only when the harassment is so severe that it bars access to educational benefit and only when not to act would be deliberate indifference). Advocates did not hail the Supreme Court's decision in *Davis* as a victory, but instead a defeat, for student civil rights. *See* Matallana v. School Bd., 838 So.2d 1191 (Fla. Dist. Ct. Cp. 2003) (school owes no duty to follow its own rules in reporting pending fight in which student was killed). One must keep in mind, though, that civil rights cases like *Davis* involving governmental liability depend not on the common law of torts but on constitutional rights and statutory causes of action where the language of the statute, not broad common-law duties, control. Immunity or the rationales that support it also limit the tort-based duty that a parent owes a child. *See* Dinsmore-Poff v. Alvord, 972 P.2d 978 (Alaska 1999) (parents owe no tort-based duty to prevent murder by 17-year-old son); Williamson v. Daniels, 748 So.2d 754 (Miss. 1999) (mother not liable for shooting by 15-year-old son); Holodook v. Spencer, 36 N.Y.2d 35, 324 N.E.2d 338, 364 N.Y.S.2d 859 (1974) (no claim for negligent parental supervision); *but see* Bieker v. Owens, 234 Ark. 97, 350 S.W.2d 522 (1961) (parent liability for injury by child who had repeatedly attacked other children). As you read the following case, though, in which the appellate court held that a spouse may owe third persons a duty with respect to the conduct of the other spouse, be sure that you can enumerate the factors that the court considered when finding that a duty existed.

J.S. v. R.T.H.
New Jersey Supreme Court
155 N.J. 330, 714 A.2d 924 (1998)

HANDLER, J. In this case, two young girls, ages 12 and 15, spent substantial periods of recreational time with their neighbor at his horse barn, riding and caring for his horses. Betraying the trust this relationship established, the neighbor, an older man, sexually abused both girls for a period of more than a year. Following the man's conviction and imprisonment for these sexual offenses, the girls, along with their parents, brought this action against the man and his wife for damages, contending that the wife's negligence rendered her, as well as her husband, liable for their injuries. The man conceded liability for both the intentional and negligent injuries that he inflicted on the girls by his sexual abuse. His wife, however, denied that, under the circumstances, she could be found negligent for the girls' injuries. ...

John, 64 years old, was charged with sexually assaulting the two sisters over a period of more than a year. He pled guilty to endangering the welfare of minors and was sentenced to eighteen months in state prison. Plaintiffs, as the natural parents and guardians ad litem of their two daughters, filed a complaint against John alleging intentional, reckless, and/or negligent acts of sexual assault against each of the two girls. In an amended complaint, plaintiffs added Mary as a defendant, alleging that she "was negligent in that she knew and/or should have known of her husband's proclivities/propensities" and that as a result of her negligence the two girls suffered physical and emotional injury.[fn] ...

The trial court entered summary judgment on behalf of Mary.[fn] On appeal, the Appellate Division reversed the order and remanded for entry of an order granting plaintiffs extended discovery. [C] ...

... Mary conceded for the purposes of argument that "at all relevant times" she "knew or should have known of her husband's proclivities/propensities." ...

In determining whether a duty is to be imposed, courts must engage in a rather complex analysis that weighs and balances several, related factors, including the nature of the underlying risk of harm, that is, its foreseeability and severity, the opportunity and ability to exercise care to prevent the harm, the comparative interests of, and the relationships between or among, the parties, and, ultimately, based on considerations of public policy and fairness, the societal interest in the proposed solution. [C]

Foreseeability of the risk of harm is the foundational element in the determination of whether a duty exists. [C] The "[a]bility to foresee injury to a potential plaintiff" is "crucial" in determining whether a duty should be imposed. [C]

Foreseeability as a component of a duty to exercise due care is based on the defendant's knowledge of the risk of injury and is susceptible to objective analysis. [C] That knowledge may be an actual awareness of risk. [C] Such knowledge may also be constructive; the defendant may be charged with knowledge if she is "in a position" to "discover the risk of harm." [C] In some cases where the nature of the risk or the extent of harm is difficult to ascertain, foreseeability may require that the defendant have a "special reason to know" that a "particular plaintiff" or "identifiable class of plaintiffs" would likely suffer a "particular type" of injury. [C] Further, when the risk of harm is that posed by third persons, a plaintiff may be required to prove that defendant was in a position to "know or have reason to know, from past experience, that there [was] a likelihood of conduct on the part of [a] third person[ ]" that was "likely to endanger the safety" of another. [C] ...

Ultimately, the determination of the existence of a duty is a question of fairness and public policy. [C] In fixing the limits of liability as a matter of public policy, courts must draw on "notions of fairness, common sense, and morality." [C] Public policy must be determined in the context of contemporary circumstances and considerations. [C] Thus, " '[d]uty' is not a rigid formalism" that remains static through time, but rather is a malleable concept that "must of necessity adjust to the changing social relations and exigencies and man's relation to his fellows." [C] ...

Here, a man criminally sexually assaulted unrelated, adolescent children whom he had befriended. The defendant is the spouse of the wrongdoer. The abuse occurred on her own property over an extended period of time. The tortious, assaultive conduct is of a type that is extremely difficult to identify, anticipate, and predict. While these considerations bear on all of the factors that are relevant in determining whether a duty of care should be recognized and imposed on the spouse, they bear materially on the primary element of foreseeability.

Although conduct involving sexual abuse is often secretive, clandestine, and furtive, a number of factors are relevant when determining whether or not it is foreseeable to a wife that her husband would sexually abuse a child. These include whether the husband had previously committed sexual offenses against children; the number, date, and nature of those prior offenses; the gender of prior victims; the age of prior victims; where the prior offenses occurred; whether the prior offense was against a stranger or a victim known to the husband; the husband's therapeutic history and regimen; the extent to which the wife encouraged or facilitated her husband's unsupervised contact with the current victim; the presence of physical evidence such as pornographic materials depicting children and the unexplained appearance of children's apparel in the marital home; and the extent to which the victims made inappropriate sexual comments or engaged in age-inappropriate behavior in the husband and wife's presence. [C]

These considerations warrant a standard of foreseeability in this case that is based on "particular knowledge" or "special reason to know" that a "[p]articular plaintiff" or "identifiable class of plaintiffs" would suffer a "particular type" of injury. [Cc] "Particularized foreseeability" in this kind of case will conform the standard of foreseeability to the empirical evidence and common experience that indicate a wife may often have actual knowledge or special reason to know that her husband is abusing or is likely to abuse an identifiable victim and will accommodate the concerns over the inherent difficulties in predicting such furtive behavior. That test of foreseeability will also ensure that the wife is not subject to a broad duty that may expose her to liability to every child whom her husband may threaten and harm. Foreseeability under that definitional standard is neither unrealistic nor unfair.

The nature of the parties' interests bears on the need to recognize a duty of care. "There can be no doubt about the strong policy of this State to protect children from sexual abuse and to require reporting of suspected child abuse." [C] That policy is so obvious and so powerful that it can draw little argument. It is an interest that is massively documented. ...

"Megan's Law," N.J.S.A. 2C:7-1 to -11, provides yet more evidence of the State's intolerance of sexual abuse of children. In affirming the constitutionality of the community notification and registration requirements of Megan's Law for convicted sex offenders, this Court recognized the enormous public interest in protecting society from the threat of potential molestation, rape, or murder of women and children. [C]

While the interest in protecting children from sexual abuse is great, this Court must also take into consideration defendants' interests in a stable marital relationship and in marital privacy. ... Both courts and scholars, however, increasingly questioned whether the doctrine of marital immunity actually succeeded in promoting the marital tranquility and privacy it was designed to serve. [C] ...

Moreover, the societal interest in enhancing marital relationships cannot outweigh the societal interest in protecting children from sexual abuse. The child-abuse reporting statute itself has mandated that balance-it applies to every citizen, including a spouse. [C] ...

Considerations of fairness and public policy also govern whether the imposition of a duty is warranted. [C] Public policy considerations based in large measure on the comparative interests of the parties support overwhelmingly the recognition of a duty of care in these circumstances. This Court has recognized that the sexual abuse of children not only traumatizes the victims, but also exacts a heavy toll on society... .

Considerations of foreseeability, the comparative interests and relationships of the parties, and public policy and fairness support the recognition of a duty of care. Based in large measure on the strong public policy of protecting children from sexual abuse, we conclude that there is a sound, indeed, compelling basis for the imposition of a duty on a wife whose husband poses the threat of sexually victimizing young children. ...

Accordingly, we hold that when a spouse has actual knowledge or special reason to know of the likelihood of his or her spouse engaging in sexually abusive behavior against a particular person or persons, a spouse has a duty of care to take reasonable steps to prevent or warn of the harm. ...

It may be found that the relationship between the next-door neighbors' in this case had been close. Mary knew that the neighbors' adolescent girls were visiting at her home nearly every day and that they spent considerable amounts of time there alone with her husband. Moreover, she never "confronted" her husband about the unsupervised time he was spending with the girls. At both the trial level and on appeal, Mary conceded for the purposes of argument that "at all relevant times" she "knew or should have known of her husband's proclivities/propensities." Thus, it may be determined that it was particularly foreseeable that John was abusing the young girls. Further, the evidence at trial could support a finding of negligence on Mary's part. It is inferable, as explained by the Appellate Division, that Mary could have discharged her duty by confronting her husband and warning him, by insisting or seeing that the girls were not invited to ride or care for the horses, by keeping a watchful eye when she knew the girls to be visiting with her husband, by asking the girls' parents to ensure that the children not visit when she was not present, or by warning the girls or their parents of the risk she perceived. [C] ...

We affirm the judgment of the Appellate Division.

INQUIRY

Control of Others. The above case involves not so much the status of the defendant as a spouse of the wrongdoer, as instead the defendant's ability to control the wrongdoer and the circumstances in which the wrong will occur. *See* Haselhorst v. State, 240 Neb. 891, 485 N.W.2d 180 (1992) (agency owed duty to foster parents to warn of foster child's propensity to sexually assault other minors, including children of foster parents). The Restatement (Third) of Torts: Liability for Physical and Emotional Harm states in section 41 that,

> (a) An actor in a special relationship with another owes a duty of reasonable care to third persons with regard to risks posed by the other that arise within the scope of the relationship.
> (b) Special relationships giving rise to the duty provided in Subsection (a) include:
> (1) a parent with dependent children,
> (2) a custodian with those in its custody,
> (3) an employer with employees when the employment facilitates the employee's causing harm to third parties, and
> (4) a mental-health professional with patients.

Other cases like the above case in which duties existed include an employer's ability to control a drunken employee rather than merely sending him (driving) home, *see* Otis

Eng. Corp. v. Clark, 668 S.W.2d 307 (Tex. 1983), a convention center's ability to control an event so that it does not endanger others, *see* Connolly v. Nicollet Hotel, 254 Minn. 373, 95 N.W.2d 657 (1959), an automobile passenger's ability to warn other passengers that the driver has been drinking heavily, *see* VanHaverbeke v. Berhard, 654 F. Supp. 255 (S.D. Ohio 1986), and a school district's ability to warn another school district of a former teacher's propensity to molest students, *see* Randi W. v. Muroc Joint Unified Sch. Dist., 14 Cal.4th 1066, 929 P.2d 582 (1997). The chapter on professional negligence addresses the duty of medical professionals to warn third persons of the dangerous propensities of patients. Does the following case rely on a special relationship—or on something else?

L.S. Ayres & Co. v. Hicks
Indiana Supreme Court
220 Ind. 86, 40 N.E.2d 334 (1942)

SHAKE, C.J. The appellee recovered a judgment against the appellant for personal injuries. ...

John Hicks, the appellee, a six year old boy, visited the appellant's department store in company with his mother, who was engaged in shopping. While descending from the third floor on an escalator, the appellee fell at the second floor landing and some fingers of both his hands were caught in the moving parts of the escalator at the place where it disappears into the floor. ...

The jury found that the escalators with which the appellant's store was equipped were purchased and installed in 1934; that no escalator was made prior to the accident that was safer than the one in use; that it was not the practice of stores installing escalators to have an attendant after a year; that the escalator on which appellee was injured was equipped with switch buttons at each floor landing by which it could be stopped in about 2 1/2 steps; that appellant had clerks working within 50 feet of the place where appellee was injured, all of whom had not been instructed how to stop the escalator; that the escalator was moving at the rate of 90 feet per minute; that appellee's fingers were caught in the mechanism practically as soon as he fell; that the escalator ran 'approximately 70 steps (of 15 inches) or more' before it was stopped; that it was from 3 to 5 minutes after appellee was first injured before his fingers were released; and that the appellee's injuries were increased by the grinding effect on his fingers which continued until the escalator was stopped. ...

It may be observed, on the outset, that there is no general duty to go to the rescue of a person who is in peril. ... The effect of this rule was aptly illustrated by Carpenter, C.J., in Buch v. Amory Mfg. Co., 1897, 69 N.H. 257, 260, 44 A. 809, 810, 76 Am.St.Rep. 163, 165, as follows: "With purely moral obligations the law does not deal. For example, the priest and Levite who passed by on the other side were not, it is supposed, liable at law for the continued suffering of the man who fell among thieves, which they might, and morally ought to have, prevented or relieved."

There may be principles of social conduct so universally recognized as to be demanded that they be observed as a legal duty, and the relationship of the parties may impose obligations that would not otherwise exist. Thus, it has been said that, under some circumstances, moral and humanitarian considerations may require one to render assistance to another who has been injured, even though the injury was not due to negligence on his part and may have been caused by the negligence of the injured person. Failure to render assistance in such a situation may constitute actionable negligence if the injury is aggravated through lack of due care. [C] The case of Depue v. Flatau, 1907, 100 Minn. 299, 111 N.W. 1, 8 L.R.A.,N.S., 485, lends support to this rule. It was there held that one who invited into his house a cattle buyer who called to inspect cattle which were for sale owed him the duty, upon discovering that he had been taken severely ill, not to expose him to danger on a cold winter night by sending him away unattended while he was in a fainting and helpless condition.

After holding that a railroad company was liable for failing to provide medical and surgical assistance to an employee who was injured without its fault but who was rendered helpless, by reason of which the employee's injuries were aggravated, it was said with the subsequent approval of this court, in Tippecanoe Loan, etc., Co. v. Cleveland, etc., R. Co., 1915, 57 Ind.App. 644, 649, 650, 104 N.E. 866, 868, 106 N.E. 739: "In some jurisdictions the doctrine has been extended much further than we are required to go in deciding this case. It has been held to apply to cases where one party has been so injured as to render him helpless by an instrumentality under the control of another, even though no relation of master and servant, or carrier and passenger, existed at the time. It has been said that the mere happening of an accident of this kind creates a relation which gives rise to a legal duty to render such aid to the injured party as may be reasonably necessary to save his life, or to prevent a serious aggravation of his injuries, and that this subsequent duty does not depend upon the negligence of the one party, or the freedom of the other party from contributory negligence, but that it exists irrespective of any legal responsibility for the original injury."

From the above cases it may be deduced that there may be a legal obligation to take positive or affirmative steps to effect the rescue of a person who is helpless and in a situation of peril, when the one proceeded against is a master or an invitor or when the injury resulted from use of an instrumentality under the control of the defendant. Such an obligation may exist although the accident or original injury was caused by the negligence of the plaintiff or through that of a third person and without any fault on the part of the defendant. Other relationships may impose a like obligation, but it is not necessary to pursue that inquiry further at this time.

In the case at bar the appellee was an invitee and he received his initial injury in using an instrumentality provided by the appellant and under its control. Under the rule stated above and on the authority of the cases cited this was a sufficient relationship to impose a duty upon the appellant. Since the duty with which we are presently concerned arose after the appellee's initial injury occurred, the appellant cannot be charged with its anticipation or prevention but only with failure to exercise reasonable care to avoid aggravation. …

… Since the appellee was only entitled to recover for an aggravation of his injuries, the jury should have been limited and restricted in assessing the damages to the injuries that were the proximate result of the appellant's actionable negligence. …

The judgment is reversed with directions to sustain the appellant's motion for a new trial.

INQUIRY

Landowners. The duties landowners owe as to conditions on their lands are the subject of a separate chapter on premises liability. Some claims, though, involve not dangerous conditions of the land but help that a landowner might, and perhaps ought, to give against some danger not connected with the land. For instance, does the owner of a commercial establishment have a duty to allow someone to use a telephone on the premises to call for help relating to a danger off the premises? *See* Soldano v. O'Daniels, 141 Cal. App.3d 443, 190 Cal. Rptr. 310 (1983) (owner has duty to let a rescuer use a public telephone on the premises to call for aid for one who faces a danger off the premises). Or does one who conducts an outdoor event have a duty to warn of impending risk of lightning strike? *See* Dykema v. Gus Macker Enterps., Inc., 196 Mich App. 6, 492 N.W.2d 472 (1992) (no duty of outdoor basketball tournament to warn of approaching thunderstorm); Hames v. State, 808 S.W.2d 41 (Tenn. 1991) (no duty of golf course to warn of approaching thunderstorm); *but see* Seelbinder v. County of Volusia, 821 So.2d 1095 (Fla. Dist. Ct. App. 2002) (duty to warn of lightning exists where means of warning was available and advertised).

Instrumentalities. The above *L.S. Ayres & Co.* case has to do with duties control of an instrumentality create. A duty generally arises when one controls an instrumentality and is aware that it will injure a person or that it has injured a person whose injury will worsen if the controller takes no action. *See* South v. National R. Passenger Corp., 290 N.W.2d 819 (N.D. 1980) (rail line owes duty to assist person struck by train without rail line's negligence); Pridgen v. Boston Hous. Auth., 364 Mass. 696, 308 N.E.2d 467 (1974) (housing authority owes duty to aid trespassing minor in peril of being crushed by elevator); Restatement (Second) of Torts §322 (duty to act on behalf of one imperiled by instrumentality under one's control). A few older cases hold otherwise. *See* Griswold v. Boston & Maine R. Co., 183 Mass. 434, 67 N.E. 354 (1903) (rail line has no duty to remove train from body of trespasser whom it innocently ran over); Union Pac. R. Co. v. Cappier, 66 Kan. 649, 72 P. 281 (1903) (rail line has no duty to help trespasser whom it innocently ran over and who is bleeding to death). Restatement (Third) of Torts: Liability for Physical and Emotional Harm §39 frames the issue this way:

> When an actor's prior conduct, even though not tortious, creates a continuing risk of physical harm of a type characteristic of the conduct, the actor has a duty to exercise reasonable care to prevent or minimize the harm.

If a person negligently injures another, a duty then arises to come to the aid of the injured person. See Parrish v. Atlantic Coast Line R. Co., 221 N.C. 292, 20 S.E.2d 299 (1942). Hit-and-run statutes requiring drivers who injure another, whether negligently or innocently, to stop and give aid may also create a duty the violation of which would be negligence per se or give rise to a presumption or inference of negligence. *See* Brumfield v. Wofford, 143 W. Va. 332, 102 S.E.2d 103 (1958); *see also* Brock v. Watts Realty Co., 582 So.2d 438 (Ala. 1991) (ordinance creates landlord duty to protect tenants from intruders). Would a duty also require a person to act to minimize an unreasonable hazard that the person innocently created? *See* Pacht v. Morris, 107 Ariz. 392, 489 P.2d 29 (1971) (driver whose vehicle accidentally hit horse had duty to remove or warn of horse carcass in order to reasonably protect other drivers).

Reliance. The plaintiff's reliance on the defendant to give aid may in some cases be closely related to an undertaking by the defendant or the defendant's control of an instrumentality threatening the plaintiff, but as Restatement (Second) of Torts §§323-324 suggest, reliance can also be an independent ground on which to find a duty. *See* Wakulich v. Mraz, 322 Ill. App.3d 768, 751 N.E.2d 1, 255 Ill. Dec. 907 (2001) (homeowner's voluntary undertaking to care for drunken minor in home, while preventing others from doing so, creates duty to do so non-negligently); Crowley v. Spivey, 285 S.C. 397, 329 S.E.2d 774 (1985) (grandparent's assurance that they would supervise grandchildren in presence of their mentally disabled mother establishes duty supporting a tort claim after mother killed the grandchildren); *see also* Long v. Broadlawns Med. Ctr., 656 N.W.2d 71 (Iowa 2002) (social worker promising to warn wife when psychotic husband was released owed duty of care with respect to her subsequent murder by husband when no warning was given); Mixon v. Dobbs Houses, Inc., 254 S.E.2d 864 (Ga. App. 1979) (employer's breach of promise to notify employee husband of wife's labor at home was actionable); Morgan v. Yuba County, 230 Cal. App.2d 938, 41 Cal. Rptr. 508 (1964) (sheriff's promise to warn witness when prisoner was released establishes duty supporting claim of witness's estate when prisoner was released without warning and murdered witness); Dudley v. Victor Lynn Lines, Inc., 48 N.J. Super. 457, 138 A.2d 53 (1958), revd. on other grounds, 32 N.J. 479, 161 A.2d 479 (1960) (foreman's promise to call doctor to aid ill trucker establishes duty supporting claim of trucker's estate when foreman failed to do so and trucker died of heart attack).

c. Economic Loss

OBJECTIVE: Given economic loss caused by the negligence of a potential defendant, apply the principles developed in this section of the text to determine whether the potential defendant owed a duty of care the violation of which would give rise to a claim for the economic loss.

Case Study: A delivery truck broke down due to its driver's negligent maintenance. A part to repair a die-casting machine was stuck on the delivery truck for 24 hours while the driver repaired the truck. The 24-hour delay in delivery of the part caused the machine's owner to lose production of 600 parts at a profit of $10 per part. ***Explain whether the machine's owner has a negligence claim against the driver for the $6,000 loss.***

Why, in a section addressing the contours of the duty owed in a negligence action, would we be concerned about economic loss? Get a clear sense of why the economic-loss doctrine is, fundamentally, a duty issue. Otherwise, the economic-loss doctrine can be one of those subjects too difficult to readily grasp, no less recall and apply. The economic-loss doctrine limits the cases in which the actor owes a duty, to those cases in which the event causes a direct injury to person or property. Those cases will be the vast majority of all torts cases, so that lawyers usually need not even consider the economic-loss doctrine. Only the exceptional case involves an economic loss without some direct injury to person or property. The economic loss may be quite substantial. The tort that caused it may be compelling. Yet if the economic-loss doctrine applies, no duty exists, and no recovery is available.

What does the law mean, though, by *direct injury*—that which is necessary before a plaintiff may claim economic loss? A clear sense of the economic-loss doctrine depends on example. In the usual tort case like, say, a fire negligently caused by the installer of an electrical service, the claimant has an obvious direct injury—in that case, the destruction of a building or injury or death of a person by fire. Given that direct injury (the building destruction or personal injury or death), any economic loss that the party who suffered the direct injury can also claim, the party recovers in that action. Thus, the building's owner may sue not only for the diminution in the building's value by fire but also for the lost profits from interruption of the business that the owner would have conducted in the building but for the fire. Or, if the loss was a personal injury, the plaintiff may sue not only for the pain, suffering, and loss of enjoyment of life occasioned by the fire injury but also for the lost wages incurred on account of the personal injury. If, on the other hand, a plaintiff who had suffered no direct injury were to step forward claiming economic loss but was unable to show a direct injury, then the economic-loss doctrine would bar that plaintiff's claim. Consider the example of a neighboring property owner whose building the defendant's fire did not damage and who suffered no personal injury but who suffered economic loss because the fire interrupted the neighbor's business (perhaps by a power outage or fire trucks or gawkers blocking the site). The economic-loss doctrine would bar that owner's claim. The law imposes no duty to prevent economic loss independent of a direct injury.

Getting a clear picture of what the law means by *economic loss* in this context can also be difficult. The classic economic loss is lost profits from a business that a tort affects indirectly, by damaging someone else's person, property, or interest. Economic loss does not mean anything measured by money. Direct injuries we readily measure in economic terms. Building or equipment damage, and medical expense are examples. Tort law even measures pain and suffering in economic terms, albeit uncertainly. *Economic loss* for purposes of the economic-loss doctrine means losses that flow from an interruption in the economy in which a person or entity participates, rather than by a direct injury to the person or entity or their property. Indeed, from that definition one can see the need for the economic-loss doctrine's limitation on duty. Many torts produce ripple effects in local economies that go well beyond the interests of those whose person or property suffered direct injury or damage. When a negligent driver injures a plant manager on the way home from work, certainly the driver should pay the manager's lost wages, medical expense, and pain and suffering. Yet should the driver also pay the plant owner for the business interruption loss the plant owner suffers because of the manager's injury? The economic-loss doctrine limits liability to reasonable bounds. Consider the following illustrative case.

State of Louisiana ex rel. Guste v. M/V Testbank
United States Court of Appeals, Fifth Circuit
752 F.2d 1019 (5th Cir. 1985), cert. denied, 477 U.S. 903 (1986)

HIGGINBOTHAM, J. We are asked to abandon physical damage to a proprietary interest as a prerequisite to recovery for economic loss in cases of unintentional maritime tort. We decline the invitation.[fn]

I. In the early evening of July 22, 1980, the M/V SEA DANIEL, an inbound bulk carrier, and the M/V TESTBANK, an outbound container ship, collided at approximately mile forty-one of the Mississippi River Gulf outlet. At impact, a white haze enveloped the ships until carried away by prevailing winds, and containers aboard TESTBANK were damaged and lost overboard. The white haze proved to be hydrobromic acid and the contents of the containers which went overboard proved to be approximately twelve tons of pentachlorophenol, PCP, assertedly the largest such spill in United States history. The United States Coast Guard closed the outlet to navigation until August 10, 1980 and all fishing, shrimping, and related activity was temporarily suspended in the outlet and four hundred square miles of surrounding marsh and waterways.

Forty-one lawsuits were filed and consolidated before the same judge in the Eastern District of Louisiana. These suits presented claims of shipping interests, marina and boat rental operators, wholesale and retail seafood enterprises not actually engaged in fishing, seafood restaurants, tackle and bait shops, and recreational fishermen. ...

Defendants moved for summary judgment as to all claims for economic loss unaccompanied by physical damage to property. The district court granted the requested summary judgment as to all such claims except those asserted by commercial oystermen, shrimpers, crabbers and fishermen who had been making a commercial use of the embargoed waters. ...

On appeal a panel of this court affirmed, concluding that claims for economic loss unaccompanied by physical damage to a proprietary interest were not recoverable in maritime tort. [C] ... We then took the case en banc... [W]e are unpersuaded that we ought to drop physical damage to a proprietary interest as a prerequisite to recovery for economic loss. To the contrary, our reexamination of the history and central purpose of this pragmatic restriction on the doctrine of foreseeability heightens our commitment to it. Ultimately we conclude that without this limitation foreseeability loses much of its ability to function as a rule of law. ...

IV. Plaintiffs urge that the requirement of physical injury to a proprietary interest is arbitrary, unfair, and illogical, as it denies recovery for foreseeable injury caused by negligent acts. At its bottom the argument is that questions of remoteness ought to be left to the trier of fact. Ultimately the question becomes who ought to decide-judge or jury-and whether there will be a rule beyond the jacket of a given case. The plaintiffs contend that the "problem" need not be separately addressed, but instead should be handled by "traditional" principles of tort law. Putting the problem of which doctrine is the traditional one aside, their rhetorical questions are flawed in several respects.

Those who would delete the requirement of physical damage have no rule or principle to substitute. Their approach fails to recognize limits upon the adjudicating ability of courts. We do not mean just the ability to supply a judgment; prerequisite to this adjudicatory function are preexisting rules, whether the creature of courts or legislatures. Courts can decide cases without preexisting normative guidance but the result becomes less judicial and more the product of a managerial, legislative or negotiated function.[fn]

Review of the foreseeable consequences of the collision of the SEA DANIEL and TESTBANK demonstrates the wave upon wave of successive economic consequences and the managerial role plaintiffs would have us assume. The vessel delayed in St. Louis may be unable to fulfill its obligation to haul from Memphis, to the injury of the shipper, to the injury of the buyers, to the injury of their customers. Plaintiffs concede, as do all who attack the requirement of physical damage, that a line would need to be drawn-somewhere on the other side, each plaintiff would say in turn, of its recovery. Plaintiffs advocate not only that the lines be drawn elsewhere but also that they be drawn on an ad hoc and discrete basis. The result would be that no determinable measure of the limit of foreseeability would precede the decision on liability. We are told that when the claim is too remote, or too tenuous, recovery will be denied. Presumably then, as among all plaintiffs suffering foreseeable economic loss, recovery will turn on a judge or jury's decision. There will be no rationale for the differing results save the "judgment" of the trier of fact. Concededly, it can "decide" all the claims presented, and with comparative if not absolute ease. The point is not that such a process cannot be administered but rather that its judgments would be much less the products of a determinable rule of law. In this important sense, the resulting decisions would be judicial products only in their draw upon judicial resources.

The bright line rule of damage to a proprietary interest, as most, has the virtue of predictability with the vice of creating results in cases at its edge that are said to be "unjust" or "unfair." Plaintiffs point to seemingly perverse results, where claims the rule allows and those it disallows are juxtaposed-such as vessels striking a dock, causing minor but recoverable damage, then lurching athwart a channel causing great but unrecoverable economic loss. The answer is that when lines are drawn sufficiently sharp in their definitional edges to be reasonable and predictable, such differing results are the inevitable result-indeed, decisions are the desired product. But there is more. The line drawing sought by plaintiffs is no less arbitrary because the line drawing appears only in the outcome—as one claimant is found too remote and another is allowed to recover. The true difference is that plaintiffs' approach would mask the results. The present rule would be more candid, and in addition, by making results more predictable, serves a normative function. It operates as a rule of law and allows a court to adjudicate rather than manage.[fn]

V. That the rule is identifiable and will predict outcomes in advance of the ultimate decision about recovery enables it to play additional roles. Here we agree with plaintiffs that economic analysis, even at the rudimentary level of jurists, is helpful both in the identification of such roles and the essaying of how the roles play. Thus it is suggested that placing all the consequence of its error on the maritime industry will enhance its incentive for safety. While correct, as far as such analysis goes, such in terrorem benefits have an optimal level. Presumably, when the cost of an unsafe condition exceeds its utility there is an incentive to change. As the costs of an accident become increasing multiples of its utility, however, there is a point at which greater accident costs lose meaning, and the incentive curve flattens. When the accident costs are added in large but unknowable amounts the value of the exercise is diminished.

With a disaster inflicting large and reverberating injuries through the economy, as here, we believe the more important economic inquiry is that of relative cost of administration, and in maritime matters administration quickly involves insurance. Those economic losses not recoverable under the present rule for lack of physical damage to a proprietary interest are the subject of first party or loss insurance. The rule change would work a shift to the more costly liability system of third party insurance. For the same reasons that courts have imposed limits on the concept of foreseeability, liability insurance might not be readily obtainable for the types of losses asserted here. ... By contrast, first party insurance is feasible for many of the economic losses claimed here. Each businessman who might be affected by a disruption of river traffic or by a halt in fishing activities can protect against that eventuality at a relatively low cost since his own potential losses are finite and readily discernible. Thus, to the extent that economic analysis informs our decision here, we think that it favors retention of the present rule. ...

In conclusion, having reexamined the history and central purpose of the [economic-loss] doctrine ... , we remain committed to its teaching. Denying recovery for pure economic losses is a pragmatic limitation on the doctrine of foreseeability, a limitation we find to be both workable and useful. ...

Accordingly, the decision of the district court granting summary judgment to defendants on all claims for economic losses unaccompanied by physical damage to property is AFFIRMED.

[Concurring opinions omitted.]

WISDOM, Circuit Judge, with whom ALVIN B. RUBIN, POLITZ, TATE, and JOHNSON, Circuit Judges, join, dissenting. ...

The commercial fishing industry in the area sustained serious losses, primarily from the depressed market in that industry in southern Louisiana. Other businesses suffered losses. Numerous parties filed suit against the vessels and their owners, seeking compensation for their expenses and their lost profits caused by the collision, pollution, and bans to navigation and fishing. The claimants may be classified as follows: (1) commercial fishermen, crabbers, oystermen, and shrimpers who routinely operated in and around the closed area; (2) fishermen, crabbers, oystermen, and shrimpers who engaged in these practices only for recreation; (3) operators of marinas and boat rentals, and marine suppliers; (4) tackle and bait shops; (5) wholesale and retail seafood enterprises not actually engaged in fishing, shrimping, crabbing, or oystering in the closed area; (6) seafood restaurants; (7) cargo terminal operators; (8) an operator of railroad freight cars seeking demurrage; (9) vessel operators seeking expenses (demurrage, crew costs, tug hire) and losses of revenues caused by the closure of the outlet. ...

One cannot deny that [the] policy of limiting the set of plaintiffs who can recover for a person's negligence and damage to physical property provides a "bright line" for demarcating the boundary between recovery and nonrecovery. Physical harm suggests a proximate relation between the act and the interference. At bottom, however, the requirement of a tangible injury is artificial because it does not comport with accepted principles of tort law. Mrs. Palsgraf, although physically injured, could not recover. Many other plaintiffs, although physically uninjured, can recover.[fn]

With deference to the majority, I suggest, notwithstanding their well reasoned opinion, that the utility derived from having a "bright line" boundary does not outweigh the disutility caused by the limitation on recovery imposed by the physical-damage requirement. Robins [Dry Dock v. Flint, 275 U.S. 303 (1927) (recognizing the economic-loss doctrine),] and its progeny represent a wide departure from the usual tort doctrines of foreseeability and proximate cause. Those doctrines, as refined in the law of public nuisance, provide a rule of recovery that compensates innocent plaintiffs and holds the defendants liable for much of the harm proximately caused by their negligence.

... Rather than limiting recovery under an automatic application of a physical damage requirement, I would analyze the plaintiffs' claims under the conventional tort principles of negligence, foreseeability, and proximate causation.[fn] ... The majority's primary criticism of this approach to a determination of liability is that it is potentially open ended. Yet, there are well-established tort principles to limit liability for a widely-suffered harm. ... The limitation imposed by "particular" damages, together with refined notions of proximate cause and forseeability, provides a workable scheme of liability that is in step with the rest of tort law, compensates innocent plaintiffs, and imposes the costs of harm on those who caused it.[fn] ...

The advantages of this alternate rule of recovery are that it compensates damaged plaintiffs, imposes the cost of damages upon those who have caused the harm, is consistent with economic principles of modern tort law, and frees courts from the necessity of creating a piecemeal quilt of exceptions to avoid the harsh effects of the Robins rule. ...

If tort law fails to compensate plaintiffs or to impose the cost of damages on those who caused the harm, it should be under a warrant clear of necessity. When a rule of law, once extended, leads to inequitable results and creates principles of recovery that are at odds with the great weight of tort jurisprudence, then that rule of law merits scrutiny. A strict application of the extension denies recovery to many plaintiffs who should be awarded damages.[fn] Conventional tort principles of foreseeability, proximate causation, and "particular" damages would avoid such unfairness.

It is true that application of foreseeability and proximate causation would necessitate case-by-case adjudication. But I have a more optimistic assessment of courts' ability to undertake such adjudication than the majority.[fn] Certainly such an inquiry would be no different from our daily task of weighing such claims in other tort cases.

The majority opinion also states that the Robins rule, being free from the vagaries of factual findings in a case-by-case determination, serves an important normative function because it is more predictable and more "candid." Normative values would also be served, however, by eliminating a broad categorical rule that is insensitive to equitable and social policy concerns that would support allowing the plaintiffs' claims in many individual cases. In assessing "normative concerns," the courts' compass should be a sense of fairness and equity, both of which are better served by allowing plaintiffs to present their claims under usual tort standards. It is not clear, moreover, that a jury's finding of negligence in a case-by-case determination is "less the product of a determinable rule of law" when the finder of fact is guided in its determination by rules of law. The jury's finding of liability in this case would be no more "lawless" than a finding of proximate cause, foreseeability, and particular damages in a physical damage case. ...

The economic arguments regarding allocation of loss that purportedly favor the Robins rule of nonliability are not as clear to me as they appear to be to the majority. It is true that denial of recovery may effectively spread the loss over the victims. It is not certain, however, that victims are generally better insurors against the risk of loss caused by tortious acts having widespread consequences. Although the victims do possess greater knowledge of their circumstances and their potential damages, we do not know whether insurance against these types of losses is readily available to the businesses that may be affected. We do know that insurance against this kind of loss is already available for shippers. Imposition of liability upon the shippers helps ensure that the potential tortfeasor faces incentives to take the proper care. The majority's point is well taken that the incentives to avoid accidents do not increase once potential losses pass a certain measure of enormity. But in truth we have no idea what this measure is: Absent hard data, I would rather err on the side of receiving little additional benefit from imposing additional quanta of liability than err by adhering to Robins' inequitable rule and bar victims' recovery on the mistaken belief that a "marginal incentive curve" was flat, or nearly so. If a loss must be borne, it is no worse if a "merely" negligent defendant bears the loss than an innocent plaintiff absorb the damages. ...

RUBIN, J., with whom WISDOM, POLITZ and TATE, J.J., join, dissenting. ...
Robins should not be extended beyond its actual holding and should not be applied in cases like this, for the result is a denial of recompense to innocent persons who have suffered a real injury as a result of someone else's fault. We should not flinch from redressing injury because Congress has been indifferent to the problem.

INQUIRY

Scope. The *M/V Testbank* decision represents the majority rule following the economic-loss doctrine championed by Justice Holmes' opinion in *Robins Dry Dock & Repair Co. v. Flint* cited in the *M/V Testbank* opinion. *See* 522 Madison Avenue Gourmet Foods, Inc. v. Finlandia Ctr., 750 N.E.2d 1098 (N.Y. 2001) (no liability for pure economic loss from business interruption following nearby building wall's collapse). It is, however, only a majority position. Some jurisdictions decline to apply the economic-loss doctrine limitation. *See* People Express Airlines, Inc. v. Consolidated Rail Corp., 100 N.J. 246, 495 A.2d 107 (1985) (economic-loss liability for evacuation required by tank car accident). Other jurisdictions allow pure-economic-loss recovery depending on the foreseeability and certainty of that loss, moral blame, and other factors. *See* J'Aire Corp. v. Gregory, 598 P.2d 60, 64 (Cal. 1979) (construction contractor liable for business loss attendant on construction delays). The availability of a contract remedy may also affect whether tort relief is available. *See* Just's, Inc. v. Arrington Constr. Co., 583 P.2d 997 (Idaho 1978) (no tort remedy for losses due to construction delays, but contract theory available). Other jurisdictions offer legislative relief, especially in toxic-tort situations. *See* In re Ballard Shipping Co. v Beach Shellfish, 32 F.3d 623 (1st Cir. 1994) (finding Rhode Island statute providing liability for economic loss from pollution not preempted by *Robins Dry Dock*). What if the defendant's negligence causes damage only to the defendant's own product covered by warranty for repair or replacement but the product's damage interrupts the plaintiff's business? The chapter on products liability discusses more cases, but cases have held the economic-loss doctrine to prohibit economic-loss damages in that situation. *See* East River Steamship Corp. v. Transamerica Delaval, Inc., 476 U.S. 858 (1986) (charterer of supertanker not entitled to economic losses from maker of defective turbine that had to be replaced, disabling supertanker).

> **Practice**
> The lawyers knew that their client had suffered serious injury while working for one half of minimum wage, through a yearlong, residential, drug-rehabilitation program. They knew, in other words, that the client had a substance-abuse problem—the relevance and admissibility of which the court would determine on their motion in limine in the client's products-liability case arising out of the workplace injury. The lawyers did not know until later the details of the client's substance-abuse problem. The lawyers did have the strong sense that their client had an intense commitment to stay away from drugs, and they felt that their client deserved that chance.

d. Emotional Distress

OBJECTIVE: Given an event in which a person suffers emotional distress without physical impact, from the negligence of another, recall and apply the rules stated in this section to determine whether the negligent actor owes the person a duty.

Case Study: Felice watched from the kitchen window as her seven-year old son Grant jumped from the day-camp van. Suddenly, she noticed Grant struggling with his coat that appeared to catch when the van door closed. The van started to drag Grant who fell and flipped over repeatedly as the van pulled away from the curb. The negligent van driver brought the van to a sudden halt when he noticed Felice running screaming from the house. Grant survived, but Felice suffered post-traumatic stress disorder including severe gastric distress and weight loss, and sleep disorder. ***Explain whether the van driver owed Felice a duty of care and whether she would have a negligence claim for her emotional distress as a bystander to the incident.***

Another duty issue involves the extent to which one person has a duty to prevent another's emotional distress. What this question addresses is not the right of a person who suffers a physical injury due to the negligence of another to recover for the accompanying emotional distress. That right to recover for mental and emotional distress that accompanies physical harm is clear, although often a causation or damages question rather than a duty question. The duty not to negligently cause physical harm to another, with all that attends the physical harm including mental distress, is not the issue. Instead, this section addresses the right of a person *who has suffered no physical injury* to recover for solely psychical (mental and emotional) effects from another person's negligence. This duty issue is significant. People get upset about many things. Should tort law recognize a cause of action every time, or most of the time, or not at all, when the negligence of one person causes another person only some level of mental or emotional distress? The question suggests the main concern—limitless liability burdening our mutual capacity to compensate. The answer from state to state and from case to case is that duty depends on the circumstance. The courts tend to decide the duty on three criteria—(1) the circumstances of the occurrence, (2) the relationships involved, and (3) the proof and extent of the harm. Consider each of these criteria in a common category in which claims for solely emotional distress can arise.

Bystanders. A good first example involves the right of one who witnesses another's serious injury to make a tort recovery from the person or entity negligently causing that other person's serious injury. The duty toward the one who directly suffers the physical impact and negligent injury is clear enough. What of the emotional distress that the bystander suffers from having to witness it? The tests that the courts have developed and followed include direct-impact, direct-victim, zone-of-danger, and foreseeability tests, each discussed below. First consider the three criteria—circumstance, relationship, and harm—mentioned above, for a sense of how the courts resolve bystander cases:

(1) *Circumstance.* Whether a bystander claim exists may depend on the circumstances of the bystander's witness including whether the bystander was at the scene and how serious was the direct physical harm that the bystander witnessed. To take the clearest example, witnessing first-hand a person's traumatic death through negligence of another would be extremely upsetting to almost anyone. Indeed, the courts have tended to require for bystander claims that the bystander have been a contemporaneous witness to a serious injury. Present at the scene immediately afterward is ordinarily not enough. The witnessed event must also be of a sufficiently violent type and the witnessed injury sufficiently serious, as to produce mental or emotional distress as a result.

(2) *Relationship.* An array of persons may witness another's serious physical harm—say, at a sporting match. Should all 10,000 spectators who witness a horrible injury or wrongful death of a spectator due to the negligence of participants and organizers of a motor-racing event have bystander emotional-distress claims? *See* Frost v. Chief Constable, [1997] 1 All E.R. 504 (App. Ct.) (Hillsborough Football Stadium disaster). The courts have tended to require that bystander plaintiffs show that they were immediate family members of the person who was directly injured or killed by the other person's negligent act. Note that courts consider the relationship between the direct-impact victim and the bystander, not the tortfeasor and victim or bystander.

(3) *Harm.* Finally, in some instances, the bystander's emotional distress will seem too trite to compare to the other person's direct physical injury—or will be difficult to disprove. Bystander claims present both scope and proof problems. Any bystander could claim some mental or emotional distress from another's negligent injury. Rather than allow suits for any psychical harm, the courts have tended to require *severe* mental and emotional distress. Then, almost any bystander could claim that they were severely distressed. To ensure the reliability of psychical proofs, some courts require the bystander plaintiff to show *physical manifestation* of the distress. Now consider the following illustrative bystander case.

Carey v. Lovett
New Jersey Supreme Court
132 N.J. 44, 622 A.2d 1279 (1993)

POLLOCK, J. Once again we are summoned to respond to a family tort arising from an alleged act of medical malpractice. The case arises in the inflammatory setting of the tragic loss of a baby due to physician neglect. The issue is whether parents can recover for their emotional distress caused by medical malpractice in the birth and death of their daughter. ...

... The jury awarded $1,000,000 to the mother and $500,000 to the father, as well as $550,000 to their daughter's estate for her pain and suffering and $450,000 for her wrongful death.

In an unreported opinion, the Appellate Division reversed. ... We hold that a jury could find for Mr. and Mrs. Carey on their claims for emotional distress. ...

On October 9, 1983, in the twenty-sixth week of her third pregnancy, Mrs. Carey awoke feeling tired and short of breath. ...

On the morning of October 11, someone from West Jersey Hospital called Mrs. Carey and told her to report to the hospital in the early afternoon. Mrs. Carey was admitted at 1:00 p.m. Her admission records indicate a diagnosis of "uncontrolled diabetes, six months pregnant." At 2:30 p.m., Dr. Robert Gerard, an internist who was covering for Dr. Osler, examined Mrs. Carey. Dr. Gerard diagnosed Mrs. Carey as suffering from an attack of ketoacidosis, which, in a diabetic woman, frequently causes intrauterine death. ...

At 3:00 p.m., the hospital called Dr. Lovett to inform him that Dr. Gerard had examined Mrs. Carey, had found her to be experiencing diabetic ketoacidosis, and had not detected any fetal heart tones. Based on that telephone call, Dr. Lovett made a tentative diagnosis of fetal demise. ...

Between 4:30 and 5:00 p.m., nurses ... attempted to find a fetal heart sound. ... All attempts were unsuccessful. ... Dr. Lovett advised the nurses to allow Mrs. Carey to deliver the expected stillborn child. ...

At approximately 5:30 p.m., Gregory Carey arrived at the hospital and went to the labor room. Nurse Collins informed the Careys that there were no audible fetal heart tones and that the fetus was dead. Mrs. Carey insisted that the fetus was alive and that she could feel it moving. At Mr. Carey's request, nurse Collins again tested for a fetal heart tone, using both the transducer and the doppler. She also allowed Mr. and Mrs. Carey to listen to the negative results. Mrs. Carey again refused to accept that the fetus was dead. The nurses did not use other available and more accurate methods of determining fetal viability, such as ultrasound or x-rays.

A nurse then escorted Mr. Carey from the labor room and asked him to convince Mrs. Carey that the fetus was dead. The nurse explained that Mrs. Carey's denial of the baby's death was natural, but that he should try to calm his wife by telling her to listen to the nurses. Mr. Carey complied with the nurse's request. Mrs. Carey tearfully maintained that her baby was alive. The nurses did not perform any other test to confirm the diagnosis that the baby was dead.

Dr. Lovett, whom hospital personnel had called periodically, had not come to the hospital during Mrs. Carey's labor. ...

At 9:06 p.m., eight hours after being admitted to the hospital, Mrs. Carey delivered a baby in a breech position. Neither nurse Collins nor nurse Levins, the only hospital personnel present at the birth, assisted in the delivery. The baby dropped unsupported onto the labor bed. Nurse Collins cut the umbilical cord and announced that the baby was a girl. Nurse Levins asked Mrs. Carey if she wished to hold the baby. On his wife's behalf, Mr. Carey declined. Like the nurses and the doctors, he believed that the baby was dead.

The baby was alive [but died ten days later from, as the jury found, malpractice by Drs. Lovett and Osler.] ...

This case poses the question whether parents, without attempting to prove any physical injury to themselves, may recover for their emotional distress caused by medical malpractice resulting in the premature birth and death of their baby. They rely on those cases in which we have recognized a direct duty extending to parents that permits them to maintain a claim for emotional distress. ...

A separate line of cases permits "bystanders" to recover for their emotional distress resulting from injury to another. The progression in this line of cases has been from denying recovery for "indirect" injuries in all circumstances, [cc], to finding "a sufficient guarantee of genuineness, even in the absence of physical injury, if the plaintiff perceives an injury to another at the scene of the accident, the plaintiff and the victim are members of the same family, and the emotional distress is severe," Buckley v. Trenton Saving Fund Soc'y, 111 N.J. 355, 365, 544 A.2d 857 (1988) ([c]). [Cc].

Of particular relevance, we have held that under limited circumstances the medical misdiagnosis of one member of a family may entitle another member to recover for his or her own emotional distress. [C] Recognizing that the death or serious injury of a family member may often produce emotional distress, sometimes quite severe, in another member, we limited recovery to the "observation of shocking events that do not occur in the daily lives of most people." [C] ... Our endeavor has been to balance recognition of psychic injury with concerns for "speculative results or punitive liability," [c], and for the genuineness of the claim, [c].

The characterization of a claim as "indirect" and of the claimant as a "bystander" restricts the class of claimants who may recover for emotional distress. Originally, no claims for emotional distress were compensable unless accompanied by physical impact. [Cc] Later cases allowed recovery for emotional distress in the absence of physical impact, if the distress resulted in physical injury. [C] ...

The characterization of a claim as "direct" or "indirect," although useful for distinguishing claims in which the source of the emotional distress is an injury to the claimant from those in which the injury is to another, should not predetermine the rights of the parties. More important than the characterizations are the principles underlying them.

In the law of negligence, including that pertaining to family torts, the scope of a duty depends generally on the foreseeability of the consequences of a negligent act, as limited by policy considerations and concerns for fairness. [Cc] Concerns about the genuineness of indirect claims for emotional distress have led to limitations on the right to recover to situations in which the distress is severe or is accompanied by physical injury. Additional concerns about speculative results or punitive liability have led us to limit such claims to the observation of shocking events. With medical-malpractice claims, we have required that claimants observe contemporaneously the act of malpractice and the resultant injury. ...

In sum, to prove a claim for emotional distress arising out of the injury or death of a fetus, the mother must prove that she suffered emotional distress so severe that it resulted in physical manifestations or that it destroyed her basic emotional security. The father's emotional distress must be equally severe. The worry and stress that attend the birth of every child will not suffice. Nor will the upset that every parent feels when something goes wrong in the delivery room. In addition, the father must contemporaneously observe the malpractice and its effects on the victim. He must also be shocked by the results. ...

[The court reversed the damages awards as excessive.]

We ... reverse the judgment dismissing the parents' claim for emotional distress, and remand the matter to the Law Division for a trial on both liability and damages.

INQUIRY

Contemporaneous Presence. The above *Carey v. Lovett* case is a compelling example of a mental-and-emotional distress claim in which the bystanders were present at—and intimately involved in—the unfortunate and tortious demise of an immediate family member. How should the courts treat the situation in which family members are not present but at the scene of their close relative's serious injury or death immediately after it? *See* Thing v. La Chusa, 48 Cal.3d 644, 771 P.2d 814, 257 Cal. Rptr. 865 (1989) (no distress recovery for mother who was not present when son was struck by vehicle but saw him lying in roadway immediately after); *see also* Gabaldon v. Jay-Bi Prop. Mgt., Inc., 122 N.M. 393, 925 P.2d 510 (1996) (mother called to scene of son's near drowning not owed a duty with respect to her mental distress). Observation of the sudden event of negligence, and not its aftermath, is the critical factor. *See* Bird v. Saenx, 28 Cal.4th 910, 123 Cal. Rptr.2d 465, 51 P.3d 324 (2002) (no distress recovery where plaintiff was in hospital hallway hearing emergency calls, being told of mother's demise, and seeing mother's body rushed for critical care because plaintiff was not present when mother's artery was negligently transsected); Fernandez v. Walgreen Hastings Co., 126 N.M. 263, 968 P.2d 774 (1998) (witnessing results of misfiled prescription not sufficient). Some cases find a little room to stretch the definition of contemporaneous observation. *See* In re Air Crash Disaster, 967 F.2d 1421 (9th Cir. 1992) (plaintiff whose husband and two children died inside home from plane crash held owed a duty as to her mental distress upon returning home in time to see it ablaze); Wilks v. Hom, 2 Cal. App. 4th 1264, 3 Cal. Rptr.2d 803 (1992) (mother blown out of home by explosion held contemporaneously aware of daughter's serious injury even though not directly observed); Krouse v. Graham, 19 Cal.3d 59, 137 Cal. Rptr. 863, 562 P.2d 1022 (Cal. 1977) (husband in back yard hearing vehicle colliding with and killing wife in front yard held contemporaneously aware and allowed mental distress recovery). A few find even more room. *See* Ferriter v. Daniel O'Connel's Sons, Inc., 381 Mass 507, 413 N.E.2d 690 (1980) (spouse and children seeing seriously injured victim in the hospital "closely on the heels of the accident" permitted recovery). What if a person witnesses an event causing the death of a family member but only learns later that the event involved the family member's death? *See* Cortez v. Macias, 110 Cal. App.3d 640, 167 Cal. Rptr. 905 (Cal. Ct. App. 1980) (no mental distress recovery for parent who watched child die but thought child was falling asleep and was only told about it later).

Acosta v. Castle Construction, Inc.
New Mexico Court of Appeals
868 P.2d 673 (1994)

ALARID, J. ... The sole issue raised on appeal is whether the trial court erred in granting Defendants' motion for summary judgment because Acosta did not establish the element of "contemporary sensory perception of the accident" which is necessary for a claim of negligent infliction of emotional distress. We answer in the affirmative and reverse the grant of summary judgment. ...

FACTS

On April 16, 1988, Acosta was the general project foreman for the renovation of the Loretto Towne Mall, owned by Defendant Loretto Partners. One of the subcontractors on the job, Sid's Plumbing and Heating, Inc., employed Acosta's younger brother, Zacqueo Martinez-Acosta.

On the afternoon of April 16, 1988, Acosta was at his business, which is also located in the Loretto Towne Mall, when he heard a series of screams. Upon hearing the screams, Acosta immediately began to run toward the direction from where he heard the screams. As he ran to the accident scene, a construction worker shouted at Acosta that a worker had been seriously injured. The physical distance between Acosta's office and the accident scene was 322 linear feet. It took Acosta no more than eighteen seconds to arrive at the accident scene after he heard the initial scream.

As Acosta arrived at the Southwest Title Company's office space, he saw Johnny Flores administering cardiopulmonary resuscitation to a body lying on the floor. As Acosta approached, he realized the body was that of his younger brother, Zacqueo Martinez-Acosta. According to Acosta, his brother's mouth and nostrils were still smoking as a result of his brother's electrocution. Acosta did not see the actual electrocution of his brother, but did hear the screams and see the results eighteen seconds later.

Acosta immediately took over for Flores and administered cardiopulmonary resuscitation to keep his brother alive until the ambulance arrived. Acosta's C.P.R. efforts were successful, as his brother was still breathing and had a pulse up until the time the emergency medical technicians arrived on the scene.

Acosta accompanied his brother to Memorial Medical Center and continued his C.P.R. efforts while en route to his hospital. Zacqueo Martinez-Acosta died while being transported by ambulance to Memorial Medical Center in Las Cruces, New Mexico. ...

DISCUSSION

It is clear that all parties recognize Folz v. State, 110 N.M. 457, 797 P.2d 246 (1990), as the case which establishes the elements that must be proven for Acosta to succeed in his claim of negligent infliction of emotional distress. Under *Folz* three elements must be alleged and proven by Acosta to establish a prima facie case[:] "... that (1) the plaintiff and the victim enjoyed a marital or intimate family relationship, (2) the plaintiff suffered severe shock from the contemporaneous sensory perception of the accident, and (3) the accident caused physical injury or death to the victim." [110 N.M. at 471, 797 P.2d at 260.] In the case before us the only element at issue is whether Acosta experienced a contemporary sensory perception of his brother's death.

In this case, Defendants seem to argue that unless the plaintiff is actually present and sees the event in question, there is no contemporary sensory perception. Defendants' position in our view, goes beyond the holding of our Supreme Court in *Folz* and adds elements to the cause of action which the Court could have but did not bring within its holding. If the Court wanted to require presence and sight as elements, it could have easily done so, but it did not. Instead, the Court chose a phrase that has a broader meaning than Defendants urge upon us.

Although no New Mexico appellate court authority directly addresses the narrow question of what specifically is required for establishing "contemporaneous sensory perception," the cases in which this phrase appear do not suggest that the meaning of the phrase is limited solely to visual observance. *See* Solon v. WEK Drilling Co., 113 N.M. 566, 570, 829 P.2d 645, 649 (1992); *Folz*, 110 N.M. at 468-71, 797 P.2d at 257-

60; Ramirez v. Armstrong, 100 N.M. 538, 541-42, 673 P.2d 822, 825-26 (1983); [cc]. In *Solon* and *Ramirez* the Supreme Court noted that the requirement of "contemporary sensory perception" is not satisfied by learning of an accident by "other means" or "after its occurrence." *Solon,* 113 N.M. at 570, 829 P.2d at 649; *see also Ramirez,* 100 N.M. at 541-42d, 673 P.2d at 825-26.

Other jurisdictions have considered, in a variety of factual situations, what is meant by "contemporary sensory perception." [Cc]

In considering whether there has been a "contemporaneous sensory perception," we conclude that visual observance of the accident is merely one of the ways in which the required "sensory perception" may occur. [Cc] We do not believe that the "sensory and contemporaneous observance" requirement should be strictly limited to a visual observance of the accident. [C] Instead, we think even though a party may not actually see the accident, he or she may perceive the event by other than visual means. [Cc]

In sum, we conclude that the facts as alleged by Acosta were sufficient to give rise to a material disputed factual issue as to whether he satisfied the "contemporaneous sensory perception" requirement. [C]

CONCLUSION

In this case, Acosta has made a prima facie case and, by applying the incorrect legal standard, the trial court erroneously granted Defendants' motion for summary judgment. The grant of summary judgment is set aside and the case remanded to the trial court with instructions to reinstate Acosta's claim.

IT IS SO ORDERED.

DONNELLY and BLACK, JJ., concur.

INQUIRY

Elements. Courts take diverse views regarding the elements of bystander claims for emotional distress from the negligent injury of another. The appellate court in *Thing v. La Chusa, supra*, stated the common elements as follows: "We conclude, therefore, that a plaintiff may recover damages for emotional distress caused by observing the negligently inflicted injury of a third person if, but only if, said plaintiff: (1) is closely related to the injury victim; (2) is present as the scene of the injury-producing event at the time it occurs and is then aware that it is causing injury to the victim; and (3) as a result suffers serious emotional distress—a reaction beyond that which would be anticipated in a disinterested witness and which is not an abnormal response to the circumstances." As *Carey v. Lovett* and *Acosta v. Castle Construction, supra,* show, some courts interpret the *closely related* requirement to mean an immediate family member of the victim. *See* Clohessy v. Bachelor, 237 Conn. 31, 675 A.2d 852 (1996). In those states, would a cohabiting relationship suffice? *See* Elden v. Sheldon, 46 Cal.3d 267, 250 Cal. Rptr. 254, 758 P.2d 582 (1988) (no); *see also* Grotts v. Zahner, 115 Nev. 339, 989 P.2d 415 (1999) (no distress recovery for fiancé witnessing spouse-to-be's fatal injury); *but see* Graces v. Estabrook, 149 N.H. 202, 818 A.2d 1255 (2003) (fiancé cohabitant allowed distress recovery). In two sections, the Restatement recognizes the negligent-infliction-of-emotional-distress tort and adopts the *closely related* requirement. The Restatement (Third) of Torts: Liability for

Physical and Emotional Harm §46 (Tentative Draft No. 5, 2007) provides as follows regarding direct claims for negligent infliction of emotional distress:

> An actor whose negligent conduct causes serious emotional disturbance to another is subject to liability to the other if the conduct:
> (a) places the other in immediate danger of bodily harm and the emotional disturbance results from the danger; or
> (b) occurs in the course of specified categories of activities, undertakings, or relationships in which negligent conduct is especially likely to cause serious emotional disturbance.

Restatement (Third) of Torts: Liability for Physical and Emotional Harm §47 (Tentative Draft No. 5, 2007) addresses bystander claims:

> An actor who negligently causes serious bodily injury to a third person is subject to liability for serious emotional disturbance thereby caused to a person who:
> (a) perceives the event contemporaneously, and
> (b) is a close family member of the person suffering the bodily injury.

Skills

The initial client interview is an important moment in an attorney-client relationship in part because of the information that the attorney must gain from the client but also because it establishes a pattern for the relationship. Does the client trust the attorney? Is the attorney a good listener? Does the attorney exhibit a genuine concern for the client? These and other questions are the subtext for the express communications between lawyer and client in an initial interview. Lawyers do well to be sensitive to cultural preferences and have strong communication skills. For instance, a client may choose to speak in five language registers—frozen, formal, consultative, casual, and intimate. Lawyers tend to communicate only in the consultative register, when clients may use or prefer other registers out of habit, emotion, cultural influence, or preference.

Rationales. In defining these limits of the duty to prevent mental distress, the courts divide and vacillate between modern-foreseeability and traditional-categorical approaches. *See* Ramsey v. Beavers, 931 S.W.2d 527 (Tenn. 1996) (foreseeability based on factors); Carey v. Lovett, supra (foreseeability in context); Clohessy v. Bachelor, supra (foreseeability plus elements); Thing v. La Chusa (rejecting foreseeability for elements approach). Rodrigues v. State, 52 Haw. 156, 472 P.2d 509 (1970), in which a homeowner was allowed mental-distress recovery for witnessing the negligent flooding of his house, is a good example of the greater reach of the pure-foreseeability approach because the court did not even require anyone's physical injury or risk of injury. Yet, another Hawaii case applying the foreseeability approach, Kelly v. Kokua Sales & Supply, Ltd., 56 Haw. 204, 532 P.2d 673 (1975), subsequently rejected a man's claim for mental distress at hearing that his daughter and granddaughter had been killed in a motor-vehicle accident because the accident had occurred too far away—perhaps showing the uncertainty of the foreseeability approach. Does it make sense to you to allow recovery for witnessing the flooding of a home but not for hearing of the traumatic death of one's child and grandchild simply because one was physically nearer the first event? *Cf.* Roman v. Carroll, 127 Ariz. 398, 621 P.2s 307 (Ct. App. 1980) (no mental-distress recovery allowed for plaintiff's witnessing a St. Bernard kill plaintiff's poodle). Is it foreseeable that the first event would, and the second event would not, produce mental distress? Which approach—foreseeability or categorical—do you prefer, and why? Here, as elsewhere, the productive tension between categorical and functional approaches, judicial management and judgment, and analogical or analytical forms, define the tort-law rules the courts will apply. Or are the courts simply making rules to fit each new compelling circumstance? *See* Groves v. Taylor, 729 N.E.2d 569 (Ind. 2000) (modifying state's direct-impact rule to allow distress recovery for girl who heard vehicle strike her six-year-old brother and turned in time to see his dead body roll from highway). Should we prefer a rule allowing all mental-distress claims if the distress was severe? *See* Sacco v. High County Indep. Press, Inc., 271 Mont. 209, 896 P.2d 411 (1995) (distress claim allowed so long as foreseeable and severe).

Zone of Danger. An alternative approach followed in many states is simply to permit recovery only for those bystanders who are in the zone of danger—who, in some respect, had their own reason to fear injury. *See* Bovsun v. Sanperi, 61 N.Y.2d 219, 461 N.E.2d 843, 473 N.Y.S.2d 357 (1984); Stadler v. Cross, 295 N.W.2d 552 (Minn. 1980). An example is Waube v. Warrington, 258 N.W. 497 (Wis. 1935), in which the plaintiff's decedent died from the shock of seeing the defendant's vehicle strike and kill her child. The court did not allow recovery because the mother had witnessed the event through a window while in the house, well outside the zone of danger. The text below discusses near-impact cases, akin to the zone-of-danger test. In this age of politicized tort law with frequent statutory reforms, which do you think is the trend—foreseeability tests permitting arguments for broad liability, or zone-of-danger and other categorical approaches tending to restrict liability? The Supreme Court follows the zone-of-danger rule for mental-distress claims brought under the Federal Employer's Liability Act, covering railroad employees. *See* Consolidated Rail Corp. v. Gottshall, 512 U.S. 532 (1994); *see also* Norfolk & Western Ry. v. Ayers, 538 U.S. 135 (2003) (allowing fear-of-asbestosis claims under FELA for exposed workers).

Exceptions. Exceptions to these formulations exist where, although the plaintiff does not fit the jurisdiction's categorical approach, the courts may yet allow the claim for pure mental distress. One traditional exception allows mental distress damages for the negligent handling of corpses. *See* Guth v. Freeland, 96 Ha. 147, 28 P.3d 982 (2001) (morgue defendant); Christensen v. Superior Ct., 54 Cal.3d 868, 820 P.2d 181, 2 Cal. Rtpr.2d 79 (1991) (mortuary and crematorium defendants); Mokry v. University of Texas Health Science Ctr., 529 S.W.2d 802 (Tex. Civ. App. 1975) (research center mishandling body part). A few states limit mishandled-corpse claims to next-of-kin who contemporaneously observe the mishandling. *See* Massaro v. Charles J. O'Shea Funeral Home, Inc., 738 N.Y.S.2d 384 (N.Y. App. Div. 2002); Jaynes v. Strong-Thorne Mortuary, 954 P.2d 45 (N.M. 1997). Should the law allow a mental-distress claim when the mishandled corpse is that of a beloved pet rather than a family member? *See* Campbell v. Animal Quarantine Station, 63 Haw. 557, 632 P.2d 1066 (1981) ($1,000 award for distress over dog's death); Corso v. Crawford Dog and Cat. Hosp., 97 Misc.2d 530, 415 N.Y.S.2d 182 (1979) ($700 award for swap of beloved dog's corpse for cat corpse). Another traditional exception still followed in a minority of states is for the negligent transmission of death notices, again allowing recovery for mental and emotional distress without the usual limitations. *See* Camper v. Minor, 915 S.W.2d 437 (Tenn. 1996) (requiring severe distress and medical proof of it); Oswald v. LeGrand, 453 N.W.2d 634 (Iowa 1990); Johnson v. State, 37 N.Y.2d 378, 334 N.E.2d 590, 372 N.Y.S.2d 638 (1975). Should liability exist for the negligent handling of genetic material? *See* Perry-Rogers v. Obasaju, 723 N.Y.S.2d 28 (N.Y. App. Div. 2001) (fertility-clinic medical providers liable for couple's emotional distress when their embryo was negligently implanted in another woman who gave birth to, and retained custody of, the couple's biological child).

Direct Victims. Another way that mental-distress plaintiffs occasionally avoid the inflexibility of categorical approaches is the *direct-victim* case. Although the plaintiff may not have been present to observe the negligent injury, a special relationship may have existed between plaintiff and defendant such that defendant owed plaintiff a direct duty. Marlene F. v. Affiliated Psychiatric Med. Clinic, Inc., 48 Cal.3d 583, 770 P.2d 278 (1989), is an example permitting the plaintiff mother a cause of action against a therapist for the mother's distress over the therapist's molestation of the mother's child, where the mother was in family therapy with the child. *See also* Larsen v. Banner Health System, 81 P.3d 196 (Wyo. 2003) (distress recovery for twins negligently separated at birth); Burgess v. Superior Ct., 2 Cal.4th 1064, 9 Cal. Rptr.2d 615, 831 P.2d 1197 (1992) (mother's distress recovery against obstetrician delivering negligently brain-damaged child); Molien v. Kaiser Fdn. Hosps., 27 Cal.3d 916, 167 Cal. Rptr. 831, 616 P.2d 813 (1980) (physician owes duty to spouse of patient regarding accurate diagnosis of patient's sexual disease); Johnson v. State, 334 N.E.2d (N.Y. 1975) (daughter has distress claim against hospital for hospital's negligently notifying daughter of mother's death in hospital, when daughter did not discover that mother had not died until the daughter viewed another person's body at the mother's putative wake); *cf.* Schwarz v. Regents of Univ. of California, 226 Cal. App.3d 149, 276 Cal. Rptr. 470 (1990) (father has no mental distress claim for psychiatrist's mistreatment of child, where father had no patient relationship with psychiatrist). Where the direct-impact rule still exists, a court has held it not to bar a mother's distress in witnessing the death of her child in a motor-vehicle accident, where the mother was in the accident vehicle with the child and suffered her own physical injury—an extension, perhaps, of the direct-victim rule. *See* Lee v. State Farm Mut. Ins. Co., 272 Ga. 583, 533 S.E.2d 82 (2000).

Fear of Injury. Bystanders (those who witness another's harm) are not the only ones who can suffer emotional distress from catastrophic events caused by negligence. Those exposed to dangerous events may suffer emotional distress even when exposure injures no one but could have injured. Should tort law recognize mental distress claims where negligence nearly, but not quite, caused serious injury? Some courts have recognized a negligence claim where the plaintiff can prove foreseeable mental or emotional distress from a very-near serious injury as, for instance, when a negligently driven motor vehicle nearly strikes the plaintiff. *See* Niederman v. Brodsky, 436 Pa. 401, 261 A.2d 84 (1970); Falzone v. Busch, 45 N.J. 559, 214 A.2d 12 (1965). A few states continue to restrict pure-mental-distress claims (those not involving someone else's direct physical injury) to those in which there has been a direct, physical impact to the claimant. *See* Lee v. State Farm Mut. Ins. Co., 272 Ga. 583, 533 S.E.2d 82 (2000); R.J. v. Humana of Florida, 652 So.2d 360 (Fla. 1995); *see also* Bosley v.

Andrews, 393 Pa. 161, 142 A.2d 263 (1958) (cardiac insufficiency after near-miss from charging bull), overruled by Falzone, *supra*. Other states add the requirement, seen above in the bystander cases, that the claimant must show a physical manifestation of the mental distress. Consider the following illustrative case.

Daley v. LaCroix
Michigan Supreme Court
384 Mich. 4, 179 N.W.2d 390 (1970)

KAVANAGH, J. This appeal presents as a threshold question ... whether the "impact" rule in emotional distress has any continued vitality in the Michigan civil jurisprudence.

On July 16, 1963, about 10:00 p.m., defendant was traveling west on 15 Mile Road near plaintiffs' farm in Macomb county. Defendant's vehicle left the highway, traveled 63 feet in the air and 209 feet beyond the edge of the road and, in the process, sheared off a utility pole. A number of high voltage lines snapped, striking the electrical lines leading into plaintiffs' house and caused a great electrical explosion resulting in considerable property damage.

Plaintiffs claimed, in addition to property damage, that Estelle Daley suffered traumatic neurosis, emotional disturbance and nervous upset, and that Timothy Daley suffered emotional disturbance and nervousness as a result of the explosion and the attendant circumstances. ...

The case was tried to a jury... . At the conclusion of plaintiffs' proofs, on motion of defendant, the trial judge directed a verdict against Timothy Daley in that no proper evidence of a personal injury to him had been presented, and against Estelle Daley in that she had failed to prove a causal relationship between the accident and her claimed personal injury. ...

The Court of Appeals ([c]) affirmed the trial court's grant of a directed verdict upon the ground that Michigan law denies recovery for negligently caused emotional disturbance absent a showing of physical impact, [cc]. ...

Recovery for mental disturbance caused by defendant's negligence, but without accompanying physical injury or physical consequences or any independent basis for tort liability, has been generally denied with the notable exception of the Sui generis cases involving telegraphic companies and negligent mishandling of corpses. [Cc] ...

Where, however, a mental disturbance results immediately in physical injury, the authorities divide.[fn] ... The final bastion against allowing recovery is the requirement of some impact upon the person of the plaintiff. ...

In the landmark decision of Victorian Railways Commissioners v. Coultas (1888), 13 A.C. 222, recovery for a much disputed damage to plaintiff's nervous system caused by defendant's oncoming train was denied upon the ground that: "... in every case where an accident caused by negligence had given a person a serious nervous shock, there might be a claim for damages on account of mental injury. The difficulty which now often exists in case of alleged physical injuries of determining whether they were caused by the negligent act would be greatly increased, and a wide field opened for imaginary claims." ...

The life of the law, however, has not been logic but experience.[fn] Bowing to the onslaught of exceptions[fn] and the growing irreconcilability between legal fact and

and decretal fiction,[fn] a rapidly increasing majority of courts have repudiated the "requirement of impact" and have regarded the physical consequences themselves or the circumstances of the accident as sufficient guarantee.[fn]

Based upon close scrutiny of our precedential cases and the authority upon which they rested and cognizant of the changed circumstances relating to the factual and scientific information available,[fn] we conclude that the "impact" requirement of the common law should not have a continuing effect in Michigan... .

We hold that where a definite and objective physical injury is produced as a result of emotional distress proximately caused by defendant's negligent conduct, the plaintiff in a properly pleaded and proved action may recover in damages for such physical consequences to himself notwithstanding the absence of any physical impact upon plaintiff at the time of the mental shock.[fn]

The rule we adopt today is, of course, subject to familiar limitations.

Generally, defendant's standard of conduct is measured by reactions to be expected of normal persons. Absent specific knowledge of plaintiff's unusual sensitivity, there should be no recovery for hypersensitive mental disturbance where a normal individual would not be affected under the circumstances. [Cc]

Further, plaintiff has the burden of proof that the physical harm or illness[fn] is the natural result of the fright proximately caused by defendant's conduct. ...

From an examination of the evidence presented on behalf of Timothy Daley, we believe that, even though the question is a close one, on favorable view, he presented facts from which under our new rule, as announced in this case, a jury could reasonably find or infer a causal relation between defendant's alleged negligence and the injuries alleged. We conclude that Timothy Daley should be given an opportunity to prove his alleged cause of action, if he can do so, at a new trial.

Plaintiff Estelle Daley's claim that she suffered physical consequences naturally arising from the fright proximately caused by defendant's conduct is amply supported by the record. Her sudden loss of weight, her inability to perform ordinary household duties, her extreme nervousness and irritability, repeatedly testified to by plaintiffs, are facts from which a jury could find or infer a compensable physical injury.

The plaintiffs' testimony is also supported by the medical expert witness, who diagnosed plaintiff Estelle Daley as "a chronic psychoneurotic * * * in partial remission," and who attributed this state or condition to the explosion directly caused by defendant's acts. ...

The order of the trial court granting directed verdicts against plaintiffs Estelle Daley and Timothy Daley and the Court of Appeals' affirmance thereof are reversed and the causes remanded for new trials. ...

INQUIRY

Manifestation. Some physical manifestations of mental distress, like a heart attack, are obvious. Yet as the facts and outcome of the above *Daley v. LaCroix* case suggest, where the plaintiff must show a physical manifestation of the mental distress, the physical-manifestation requirement tends not to require a literal physical injury. *See* Olson v. Connerly, 151 Wis.2d 663, 445 N.W.2d 706 (Ct. App. 1989) (severe stomach pain is physical manifestation for mental-distress recovery). Weight gain or loss, hair loss, diarrhea, and emesis induced by mental distress may each be physical manifestations. *See* Sullivan v. Boston Gas. Co., 414 Mass. 129, 605 N.E.2d 805 (1993) (need only "objective corroboration" of the distress). An appropriate delimiter may be that the manifestation must be capable of objective determination. Others must be able to observe it in a manner outside the control of the one claiming the distress. *See* Petition of the United States, 418 F.2d 264 (1969) ("susceptible of objective determination"); Robbins v. Kass, 163 Ill. App.3d 927, 114 Ill. Dec. 868, 516 N.E.2d 1023 (Ct. App. 1987) (crying, insomnia, and headaches not physical manifestations); *cf.* Womack v. Eldridge, 215 Va. 338, 210 S.E.2d 145 (1974) (causation as to mental distress must be shown by clear-and-convincing evidence). Yet, some courts require only medical diagnosis of an emotional disorder, perhaps resulting in sleep disturbance, depression, anxiety, or phobias, but not requiring other observable manifestation. *See* Hegel v. McMahon, 136 Wash.2d 122, 960 P.2d 424 (1998); Johnson v. Ruark Obstetrics & Gynecology Assoc., 327 N.C. 283, 395 S.E.2d 85 (1990); *cf.* Hamilton v. Nestor, 265 Neb. 757, 659 N.W.2d 321 (2003) (diagnosis of disorder is sufficient, but it must be severe). Not all states require physical manifestation of the mental distress. *See* Doe v. State, 100 Haw. 34, 58 P.3d 545 (2002) (distress recovery for parents relating to teacher's molestation of child); Hedlund v. Superior Ct., 34 Cal.3d 695, 194 Cal. Rptr. 805, 669 P.2d 41 (1983) (plaintiff's son allowed recovery for witnessing shooting of mother, on pleading only of emotional injury and psychological trauma). Law may not impose a physical-manifestation requirement for claims of intentional infliction of emotional distress. Why not?

Fear of Illness. Fear of injury, like in the *Daley v. LaCroix* case, differs from fear of illness. Should the law allow a claim when the defendant's negligence causes the plaintiff to fear that the plaintiff will become sick or diseased—even when the plaintiff does not? The cases divide, but we can deduce some patterns. First, the courts generally hold that the plaintiff's fear must be severe and reasonable. *See* Norfolk & Western Ry. v. Ayers, 538 U.S. 135 (2003) (fear of contracting lung disease from asbestos product must be severe and genuine); Barrett v. Danbury Hosp., 232 Conn. 242, 654 A.2d 748 (1995) (denying distress recovery for unreasonable fear); Hagerty v. L & L Marine Services, Inc., 788 F.2d 315 (5th Cir. 1986) (recovery allowed for severe mental distress from fear of contracting cancer from soaking by toxic chemicals). Second, the courts often require genuine exposure, not just fear of exposure, to the frightening risk. *See* Roes v. FHP, Inc., 91 Haw. 470, 985 P.2d 661 (1999) (allowing recover for AIDS fear after blood product leaked onto baggage handlers); Majca v. Beekil, 183 Ill.2d 407, 701 N.E.2d 1084 (1998) (allowing recovery for AIDS fear from cut from scalpel negligently discarded in wastebasket); Madrid v. Lincoln County Med. Ctr., 122 N.M. 269, 923 P.2d 1154 (1996) (allowing distress recovery for AIDS exposure while transporting body fluids with paper cuts on hands); *but see* Williamson v. Waldman, 150 N.J. 232, 696 A.2d 14 (1997) (requiring only reasonable fear, not actual exposure). If instead plaintiff had no capability for defendant's negligence to have caused the plaintiff an illness, then the courts are more likely to deny the claim even if the plaintiff's fear of sickness or disease was reasonable. *See* Montalbano v. Tri-Mac Enterps. of Port Jefferson, Inc., 236 A.D.2d 374, 652 N.Y.S.2d 780 (Sup. Ct. App. Div. 1997) (no distress recovery for fear of AIDS from eating blood-covered french fries because there was no plausible route of transmission); Heiner v. Moretuzzo, 73 Ohio St.3d 80, 652 N.E.2d 664 (1995) (no distress recovery after defendant misdiagnosed plaintiff as AIDS-positive because plaintiff was never at risk); *but see* Baker v. Dorfman, 239 F.3d 415 (2d Cir. 2000) (distress recovery allowed for misdiagnosis claim); Chizmar v. Mackie, 896 P.2d 196 (Alaska 1995) (same). One court restricts fear-of-disease claims to those in which the plaintiff shows that more probable than not that the plaintiff will contract the disease—not very sensitive to the plaintiff's plight, when the increased risk is cancer. *See* Potter v. Firestone Tire and Rubber Co., 6 Cal.4th 965, 25 Cal. Rptr.2d 550, 863 P.2d 795 (1993); *see also* Dobran v. Franciscan Med. Ctr., 102 Ohio St.3d 54, 806 N.E.2d 537 (2004) (distress recovery denied where, although defendant lost an irreplaceable tissue sample for a test to determine whether plaintiff's cancer had metastasized, plaintiff's cancer had not spread). Consider a related case.

Keim v. Potter
Indiana Supreme Court
783 N.E.2d 731 (2003)

NAJAM, J. ... David L. Keim appeals the trial court's entry of partial summary judgment in favor of Robert S. Potter, M.D. on Keim's medical malpractice claim. Keim presents two issues for our review, which we consolidate and restate as: whether the trial court erred when it found that the modified impact rule bars Keim's emotional damages claim.

We reverse and remand.

FACTS AND PROCEDURAL HISTORY

In the summer of 1993, Keim donated blood at a Red Cross center. On August 20, 1993, the Central Indiana Regional Blood Center sent Keim a letter informing him that his blood tested positive for hepatitis C and advising him to contact a physician. Accordingly, Keim consulted his family physician, Dr. Potter, who conducted two tests to confirm whether Keim had hepatitis C. The first test was a simple antibody screen, like the one the blood bank had performed, and the results were positive for hepatitis C. The second test was a recombinant immuno-blot assay ("RIBA") test, and the results were indeterminate. Dr. Potter told Keim that the first test, the antibody screen, often results in false positives, so he advised Keim to return in December 1993 to undergo another RIBA test.

On December 27, 1993, Keim returned to Dr. Potter's office for a second RIBA test. But Dr. Potter erroneously ordered another antibody screen instead of the RIBA test. The result of the antibody screen was positive for hepatitis C. In early January 1994, Dr. Potter telephoned Keim to report that the test, which Dr. Potter believed was the RIBA test, indicated that he definitely had hepatitis C. Keim sought clarification from Dr. Potter that the result was not indeterminate again, and Dr. Potter assured Keim that the test result was positive for hepatitis C.

At that time, Keim was thirty-three years old and married, with two young children. Dr. Potter explained that the disease would cause symptoms including fatigue, pain, and jaundice, and that the quality of his life would be substantially diminished. Dr. Potter told Keim that he could develop serious liver damage, including cirrhosis and cancer. Finally, Dr. Potter explained that Keim's hepatitis C would kill him in fifteen to twenty years' time.

Because hepatitis C is transmitted through bodily fluids, Keim was forced to take extreme measures to protect his wife and children from becoming infected through contact with him. Keim and his wife had to begin using condoms every time they had intercourse; he had to keep his toothbrush and razor out of his children's reach; and the children were prohibited from eating or drinking Keim's food and drink. In addition, Dr. Potter instructed Keim to avoid alcoholic beverages, eat healthful foods, exercise regularly, and avoid over-the-counter medications and vitamins. This advice led Keim to become compulsive about what he ate and how much he exercised. Keim's behavior and changed lifestyle had a negative impact on his relationships with his wife and children. Keim and his wife separated in 1995 and later divorced.

When he first diagnosed Keim with hepatitis C, Dr. Potter explained that he should undergo tests every six months to monitor his liver function. Over the ensuing two and one half years, none of those tests indicated any impairment of Keim's liver function. On May 13, 1996, Dr. Potter reviewed Keim's medical file and realized that a second RIBA test was never conducted. Dr. Potter admitted the mistake and told Keim that he might not have hepatitis C after all. In June 1996, Dr. Potter ordered another RIBA test, and the results were indeterminate. When pressed, Dr. Potter acknowledged that another type of test was available to determine, definitively, whether Keim had hepatitis C. The results of that final test indicated that Keim did not have hepatitis C.

Keim filed his proposed complaint with the Department of Insurance, alleging that Dr. Potter was negligent in diagnosing him with hepatitis C.[fn] A medical review panel unanimously concluded that there existed a material issue of fact, not requiring expert opinion, regarding Dr. Potter's liability. Keim filed his complaint with the trial court on November 27, 2000. Dr. Potter subsequently filed a motion for summary judgment or, in the alternative, partial summary judgment, alleging, in relevant part, that Keim's emotional damages claim is barred by the modified impact rule. Following a hearing, the trial court entered partial summary judgment in favor of Dr. Potter on the issue of Keim's alleged emotional damages, and the court specified that there was no just reason for delay in the entry of final judgment on that issue. Keim brings this interlocutory appeal.

DISCUSSION AND DECISION

Keim maintains that the trial court erred when it found that his claim for emotional damages is barred under the modified impact rule. We must agree. ...

In order to maintain a cause of action for negligent infliction of emotional distress under Indiana law, a plaintiff must satisfy the "impact rule." Alexander v. Scheid, 726 N.E.2d 272, 283 (Ind. 2000). This rule originally consisted of three elements: (1) an impact on the plaintiff; (2) that causes physical injury to the plaintiff; (3) that in turn causes the emotional distress. Id. This rule precluded recovery for the case in which a plaintiff experienced real mental stress in the absence of physical injury. Id. But our supreme court later modified the impact rule and held: "When ... a plaintiff sustains a direct impact by the negligence of another and, by virtue of that direct involvement sustains an emotional trauma which is serious in nature and of a kind and extent normally expected to occur in a reasonable person, ... such a plaintiff is entitled to maintain an action to recover for that emotional trauma without regard to whether the emotional trauma arises out of or accompanies any physical injury to the plaintiff." Shuamber v. Henderson, 579 N.E.2d 452, 456 (Ind. 1991).

In Conder v. Wood, 716 N.E.2d 432 (Ind. 1999), our supreme court applied the modified impact rule for the first time since *Shuamber*. The plaintiff in *Conder* witnessed a truck hit her friend as the pair were walking across the street. In an effort to prevent the driver from running the truck's tires over her friend, the plaintiff pounded on the side of the truck to get the driver's attention. The plaintiff later sued the truck driver, claiming emotional damages as a result of witnessing her friend's death. The court held that the plaintiff sustained an "impact" when she pounded on the truck, sufficient to satisfy the direct impact element of the modified impact rule. *Id.* at 435.

Then, in Groves v. Taylor, 729 N.E.2d 569 (Ind. 2000), where an eight-year-old girl witnessed the immediate aftermath of her little brother being struck and killed by a passing police vehicle, our supreme court held that a bystander in such a circumstance need not have sustained any physical impact at all to satisfy the rule. Quoting *Conder*, the court "'recognized the diminished significance of contemporaneous physical injuries in identifying legitimate claims of emotional trauma from the mere spurious. Rather, 'direct impact' is properly understood as the requisite measure of 'direct involvement' in the incident giving rise to the emotional trauma.'" *Id.* at 572. The court explained further:

> In the present case, it is undisputed that the plaintiff did not suffer the kind of direct impact required by *Shuamber* to recover as a bystander for emotional distress. However, as the foregoing passage from *Conder* makes clear, the reason for requiring direct involvement is to be able to distinguish legitimate claims of emotional trauma from the mere spurious. The value of requiring "direct impact" is that it provides clear and unambiguous evidence that the plaintiff was so directly involved in the incident giving rise to the emotional trauma that it is unlikely that the claim is merely spurious.
>
> Given that the prevention of merely spurious claims is the rationale for the *Shuamber* rule, logic dictates that there may well be circumstances where, *while the plaintiff does not sustain a direct impact, the plaintiff is sufficiently directly involved in the incident* giving rise to the emotional trauma that we are able to distinguish legitimate claims from the mere spurious. ...
>
> ... [W]here the direct impact test is not met, a bystander may nevertheless establish "direct involvement" by proving that the plaintiff actually witnessed or came on the scene soon after the death or severe injury of a loved one with a relationship to the plaintiff analogous to a spouse, parent, child, grandparent, grandchild, or sibling caused by the defendant's negligent or otherwise tortious conduct. [*Id.* at 572-573.]

In this case, Keim, Dr. Potter's patient, was mistakenly diagnosed with hepatitis C, a life-altering and deadly disease. As such, he was "directly involved" in the result of Dr. Potter's alleged negligence. [C] Keim was thirty-three years old when he was given the diagnosis; he was forced to modify his lifestyle significantly, to his detriment; and he was given only fifteen to twenty years to live. Keim's claimed emotional injuries are serious in nature and of a kind and extent normally expected to occur in a reasonable person faced with the same circumstances.[fn] [C]

Dr. Potter contends that the holding in *Groves*, requiring direct involvement in an incident giving rise to emotional trauma, applies only to claims brought by *bystanders*. As such, Dr. Potter maintains that Keim did not sustain an "impact" sufficient to meet the requirements of the modified impact rule set out in *Shuamber*. But we do not see the logic in allowing a witness to claim emotional damages while precluding an actual victim of negligence from claiming such damages, where both plaintiffs have suffered a direct involvement reasonably expected to result in emotional injury.

We hold that where, as here, a patient claims emotional damages as a result of alleged medical malpractice, he is sufficiently "directly involved" to satisfy the modified impact rule.[fn] Keim is entitled to present his emotional damages claim to a trier of fact. The trial court erred when it granted Dr. Potter's motion for partial summary judgment. We reverse that order and remand for further proceedings.

Reversed and remanded.

DARDEN and VAIDIK, JJ., concur.

INQUIRY

Food. If the fear for which the plaintiff seeks recovery derives from having consumed a defective food product, even if not quite in the manner the plaintiff reasonably feared, then the courts may well allow recovery. *See* Coca-Cola Bottling Co. v. Hagan, 813 So.2d 167 (Fla. App. 2002) (recovery for distress from condom-like mold in soft-drink product consumed by plaintiff); Ellington v. Coca-Cola Bottling Co., 717 P.2d 109 (Okl. 1986) (recovery for distress from worm-like piece of candy in soft-drink product consumed by plaintiff); Wallace v. Coca-Cola Bottling Co., 269 A.2d 117 (Me. 1970) (recovery for distress from prophylactic in soft-drink product consumed by plaintiff); *but see* Caputzal v. Lindsay Co., 48 N.J. 69, 222 A.2d 513 (1966) (no recovery for alleged heart attack as a result of fear over having drunken water discolored by defendant's water softener).

Participants. One final category in which some courts have treated mental-distress claims differently is where the one claiming distress was in some manner an active participant in the event. For instance, a rescuer may do more than simply witness the serious injury or death of another—the rescuer may be in the process of a life-saving attempt, whether in release of the victim from peril or in the victim's resuscitation. Courts have nevertheless denied mental-distress-only claims for rescuers even under compelling circumstances. *See* Hislop v. Salt River Project Agric. Improvement and Power Dist., 197 Ariz. 553, 5 P.3d 267 (App. 2000) (victim burned alive despite rescuer's actions); Michaud v. Great Northern Nekoosa Corp., 715 A.2d 955 (Me. 1998) (trapped diver torn in half in front of rescuer). On the other hand, a court has allowed recovery for a bystander whose innocent actions caused the victim's horrifying death. *See* Kately v. Barton R. Wilkinson, 148 Cal. App.3d 576, 195 Cal. Rptr. 902 (1983) (bystander triggered defective trash-compactor that crushed co-worker); *but see* Kallstrom v. United States, 43 P.3d 162 (Alaska 2002) (denying active-participant recovery).

e. Prenatal Harm

Prenatal harm is one final area in which difficult tort-law duty issues can arise. Does a tortfeasor owe a duty to the unborn child—to the child not yet conceived, to the child already conceived but still in its mother's womb, and to the child's parents? If so, who owes the duty, what does it entail, and what is the nature of the loss when breached? A common example might be the motor-vehicle driver who negligently injures a pregnant woman who then miscarries or bears a living child so early that it either dies or suffers developmental injuries. Continuing advances in medical technology for examining, genetically testing, diagnosing, and treating children in the womb, and for keeping them alive at earlier stages on premature birth, complicate these duty issues. So do individual commitments, societal norms, political movements, and Supreme Court rulings regarding ending or protecting nascent human life. How does tort law treat duties to prevent prenatal harm in this volatile context in which mothers have constitutional rights to end their children's uterine life in many circumstances? *See* Roe v. Wade, 410 U.S. 113 (1973). The traditional rule, popularized by Justice Oliver Wendell Holmes in Deitrich v. Northhampton, 138 Mass. 14 (1884), before his elevation to the Supreme Court bench and when eugenics still had growing popularity in America, was that the unborn child had no claim for injury in the womb. *See* Endresz v. Friedberg, 24 N.Y.2d 478, 248 N.W.2d 901, 301 N.Y.S.2d 65 (Ct. App. 1969) (twins stillborn due to motor-vehicle accident had no wrongful-death claims against negligent drivers responsible for the accident).

The traditional rule has changed to the point that a substantial majority of courts today allow claims for prenatal harm if the child is born alive. *See* Kalafut v. Gruver, 239 Va. 278, 389 S.E.2d 681 (1990); Torigian v. Watertown News Co., 352 Mass. 446, 225 N.E.2d 926 (1967). That is, when the child injured in utero is born alive with evidence of the uterine injury, the law allows the child's claim. Indeed, most courts would today extend the born-alive rule to a viable-at-time-of-injury rule under which a wrongful-death claim would exist on the part of the estate of a child viable in utero at the time of the injury but not born alive. *See* Parvin v. Dean, 7 S.W.3d 264 (Tex. Ct. App. 1999) (it is a denial of constitutional equal protection not to recognize a viable child's claim, though stillborn); Shaw v. Jendzejek, 717 A.2d 367 (Me. 1998); Cavazos v. Franklin, 867 P.2d 674 (Wash. 1994); *see also* Thibert v. Milka, 419 Mass. 693, 646 N.E.2d 1025 (1995) (child born at 16-week gestational age not viable and not entitled to recover); *but see* Shaw v. Jendzejec, 717 A.2d 367 (Me. 1998) (no claim unless child is born alive). Most courts reject claims on behalf of a child who was never viable and not born alive. *See* Santana v. Zilog, Inc., 95 F.3d 780 (9th Cir. 1996); Crosby v. Glasscock Trucking Co., 340 S.C. 626, 532 S.E.2d 856 (2000); *but see* Wiersma v. Maple Leaf Farms, 543 N.W.2d 787 (S.D. 1996) (wrongful-death-statute claim for child not born alive and never viable); Farley v. Sartin, 195 W. Va. 671, 466 S.E.2d 522 (1995). Other permutations include the recognition of claims on behalf of a non-viable child who was yet born alive (had an instant of life outside the womb), *see* Nealis v. Baird, 996 P.2d 438 (Okla. 1999), and a non-viable child that had quickened (moved) within the womb, *see* Fed. Credit Union v. Tucker, 853 So.2d 104 (Miss. 2003). As you read the following case adopting the born-alive requirement, also adopted in the Restatement (Second) of Torts §869, consider whether you agree with the rule.

Kalafut v. Gruver
Virginia Supreme Court
239 Va. 278, 389 S.E.2d 681 (1990)

COMPTON, J. In this case of first impression in Virginia, involving prenatal harm, we decide whether an action for a child's wrongful death may be maintained against a tortfeasor whose negligence occurred when the decedent was in the mother's womb.

On August 26, 1985 in Roanoke County, a motor vehicle operated by Debra E. Kalafut was struck from the rear by another vehicle driven by appellee John Defrees Gruver, Jr. Kalafut was approximately twenty-one weeks pregnant and suffered personal injuries in the accident.

On September 10, 1985, Kalafut began to experience vaginal bleeding and cramping. She was hospitalized on September 11. On September 14, she went into premature labor and gave birth to a son, Hunter Brandon Kalafut, who was born alive at 7:49 p.m. The child died the same evening at 9:09 p.m. The premature delivery and death were proximately caused by the accident and Gruver's negligence.

In August 1987, appellant Michael Jerome Kalafut, administrator of the estate of Hunter Brandon Kalafut, deceased, filed the present negligence action under the Virginia Death By Wrongful Act statute against Gruver seeking recovery in damages for the infant's death. ...

... We awarded the plaintiff an appeal from the December 1988 final order dismissing the action.

... [W]e are persuaded by the pertinent law elsewhere that maintenance of actions like this should be allowed in Virginia. ...

The law of prenatal injuries has changed considerably in recent years. Formerly, most courts denied recovery for such injuries resulting from a defendant's negligence and denied recovery for the death of such an infant, whether the death occurred before or after birth. The reasons usually assigned for such rulings were that defendant owed no duty to one not in existence at the time of the wrongful act and that fictitious claims would be prevalent due to the great difficulty of proving any causal connection between the negligence and damage. [Cc]

The first American decision on the subject apparently was *Dietrich v. Northampton,* 138 Mass. 14, 52 Am.Rep. 242 (1884). In a wrongful death action resulting from the premature birth of a nonviable fetus, the court, in an opinion by Justice Oliver Wendell Holmes, established the rule of nonliability for prenatal injuries. This decision was widely followed by the courts but was criticized by the commentators. [C] This criticism, together with developments in medical science, especially in the field of embryology, prompted reconsideration of the precedent.

In 1946, a federal court decided that prenatal injuries to a viable unborn child are compensable in a tort action brought on behalf of the child after its live birth. *Bonbrest v. Kotz,* 65 F.Supp. 138 (D.D.C.1946). This decision receives credit for generating a change in the rule. Our research has disclosed no court of last resort, nor have we been referred to any, which presently adheres to the rule of nonliability for prenatal injuries when the child is born alive. [Cc]

Consequently, we adopt the following principle in this case, paraphrasing the Restatement rule: A tortfeasor who causes harm to an unborn child is subject to liability to the child, or to the child's estate, for the harm to the child, if the child is born alive. *See* Restatement (Second) of Torts § 869(1). We do not limit the application of this rule to unborn children who are viable at the time of the tortious act. Thus, an action may be maintained for recovery of damages for any injury occurring after conception, provided the tortious conduct and the proximate cause of the harm can be established. Given the present state of medical technology, however, the proof of causation obviously becomes increasingly more difficult as the focus moves to the beginning of pregnancy. Restatement (Second) of Torts § 869 comment d. But the difficulty of proving the facts should not cause the denial of a right to bring the action. With the complex litigation of today, trial courts are accustomed to applying evidentiary rules and to adjudicating difficult sufficiency of the evidence questions dealing with causation. ...

... In the present case, we have drawn the line between nonliability and liability for prenatal injury at the moment of live birth of the child. At least 12 other jurisdictions adhere to this conditional liability rule, allowing an action for wrongful death only if the child is born alive. [C] At least 21 jurisdictions allow recovery for the wrongful death of a viable stillborn child. [C]

From the standpoint of practicality and fairness, this is the appropriate place to draw the line. For one reason, the beneficiaries' claim for pecuniary compensation for the death of a child who never lives is considerably more speculative and tenuous than is the claim for compensation of a child "who lives to bear the seal of defendant's negligence with all the conscious suffering and economic loss it may entail." [C]

For another reason, the mother is entitled to recover in her action for personal injuries, connected with a stillbirth, damages for her "physical injury and mental suffering associated with [the] stillbirth," [c]. ...

While a fetus is not a "person," it is not a nonentity. For example, an unborn child is protected by the criminal law on abortion. [C] The unborn child is afforded property rights under the statute of descents, [c], and under the statutes on wills, [c]. Such a child is afforded dependency status under the workers' compensation law, [c]. Therefore, in the context of this case, there is no requirement that the plaintiff be in existence at the time of the negligence, only that it be born alive and suffer from the effects of the injury. Indeed, such a concept has been routinely recognized in medical malpractice litigation in Virginia where recovery is permitted for prenatal injuries resulting in permanent disabilities to the child who is born alive and lives for a prolonged period of time. [Cc][fn]

For these reasons, the judgment of dismissal will be reversed, and the action will be remanded for further proceedings on the motion for judgment.

Reversed and remanded.

INQUIRY

Preconception Duties. Should a child born with developmental disabilities have a claim against the one whose negligence caused the mother's reproductive-system defects before the child's conception? *Contrast* Walker v. Rinck, 604 N.E.2d 591 (Ind. 1992) (yes—previous negligent transfusion produces in-utero injury to child years later); Renslow v. Mennonite Hosp., 67 Ill.2d 348, 10 Ill. Dec. 484, 367 N.E.2d 1250 (1977) (yes—injury to unknown child not yet conceived was foreseeable), *with* Albala v. City of New York, 54 N.Y.2d 269, 445 N.Y.S.2d 108, 429 N.E.2d 786 (1981) (no—although injury was foreseeable, there must be an identifiable being within the zone of danger). The *Renslow* decision allowing claims for injury from preconception negligence may reflect the favored rule. *See* Lynch v. Scheiniger, 162 N.J. 209, 744 A.2d 113 (2000) (in accord with Renslow, supra).

Mother's Duty. Mothers certainly owe their children maternal duties. Yet should tort law grant a cause of action in favor of the child whose mother's negligence injures the in-utero child? Courts generally refuse to permit such an action. *See* Remy v. MacDonald, 440 Mass. 675, 801 N.E.2d 260 (2004) (no claim for plaintiff premature infant born alive but injured due to defendant mother's negligent driving); Stallman v. Youngquist, 125 Ill.2d 267, 531 N.E.2d 355, 126 Ill. Dec. 60 (1988) (same); *see also* Chenault v. Huie, 989 S.W.2d 474 (Tex. App. 1999) (no claim against defendant mother for injuries due to cocaine use while plaintiff infant was in utero); *but see* Bonte v. Bonte, 136 N.H. 286, 616 A.2d 464 (1992) (allowing child's claim against mother for negligent prenatal conduct when hit while crossing street); Grodin v. Grodin, 102 Mich. App. 396, 301 N.W.2d 869 (1980) (allowing claim by child against mother for discolored teeth from medication mother took during pregnancy). Can you articulate practical, structural, and philosophical reasons why the law should or should not allow a child's action against its mother for in-utero injuries?

Ethics

Tort trials can occasionally attract public attention and involve issues of public concern. Journalists commonly contact the lawyers involved in a tort case, asking for comment. Rule 3.5 of the ABA Model Rules of Professional Conduct prohibits a lawyer participating in the litigation from making public comments that have a substantial likelihood of prejudicing the litigation's trial. Also, while statements lawyers make within the judicial proceeding (in the courtroom or in filed court papers) are privileged against claims of defamation, the privilege does not extend to statements made to news reporters. In most instances, the tort lawyer's response to a journalist's inquiry will be not to offer any comment. After trial, it may be a different matter. Plenty of tort lawyers have become authors, drawing from their law-practice experience for rich stories of human tragedy and triumph over adversity. Rule 1.8(d) of the ABA Model Rules of Professional Conduct prohibits a lawyer from negotiating an agreement with the client for the literary or media rights to the client's story, before the representation concludes. Any ideas why? Hint: Rule 1.8 is titled "Conflict of Interest: Current Clients: Specific Rules."

Wrongful Conception. To this point, this section has considered tort claims for injuries to or death of a child, from prenatal or preconception negligence. Now consider a fundamentally different question: should tort law recognize claims against those who negligently allow a healthy child's conception and birth? Parties increasingly make, and some courts allow, *wrongful-conception* claims. Those claims may be even more prevalent in the future as prenatal testing and pre-implantation genetic typing increase in use and sophistication. As suggested in the introduction to this section, the constitutional right to abortion stated in *Roe v. Wade* complicates duty issues regarding prenatal life. So does the exercise of the precursor right that the Supreme Court recognized in Griswold v. Connecticut, 381 U.S. 479 (1965), to prevent a child's conception. A substantial opportunity now exists for medical malpractice and other mischief among the half-a-hundred-million U.S. abortions since *Roe v. Wade,* not to mention an equally vast number of contraceptive products and services. How should tort law treat medical-malpractice and genetic-testing claims in which the parents sue for depriving them of the right to avoid conceiving a healthy child? Most courts permit only the costs of pregnancy and delivery of the healthy infant but refuse to allow recovery of the costs of rearing the child. *See* Schork v.

Huber, 648 S.W.2d 861 (Ky. 1983). A few courts permit recovery of child-rearing expenses offset by the benefit of the child—supported by the Restatement (Second) of Torts §920 (1977) regarding offsetting benefits against damages. A very few courts allow the parents to recover the entire cost of child rearing without offset. *See* Zehr v. Haugen, 318 Or. 647, 871 P.2d 1006 (1994); Marciniak v. Lundborg, 153 Wis.2d 59, 450 N.W.2d 243 (1990). In one state, the parents may recover child-rearing expenses only if they prove that their reason for not wanting a child was financial. *See* Burke v. Rivo, 406 Mass. 764, 551 N.E.2d 1 (1990). Consider an illustrative case taking the majority view that refuses to recognize the claim.

Chaffee v. Seslar
Indiana Court of Appeals
751 N.E.2d 773 (Ind. Ct. App. 2001)

DICKSON, J. In this interlocutory appeal, the defendant, Dr. Kenneth Chaffee ("Dr. Chaffee"), challenges the trial court's order permitting the plaintiff, Heather Seslar ("Seslar"), to seek damages including the expenses of raising and educating her child born following an unsuccessful sterilization procedure. We ... hold that damages for an allegedly negligent sterilization procedure may not include the costs of raising a subsequently conceived normal, healthy child.

The facts in this case are relatively uncomplicated. On March 26, 1998, Dr. Chaffee performed a partial salpingectomy on Seslar. [C] The purpose of the procedure was to sterilize Seslar, who had already borne four children, so that she could not become pregnant again. After undergoing the surgery, however, Seslar conceived, and on August 5, 1999, she delivered a healthy baby.

On March 15, 2000, pursuant to Indiana's medical malpractice statutes, Seslar filed a proposed complaint with the Indiana Department of Insurance alleging that Dr. Chaffee's performance of the procedure had been negligent and seeking damages for the future expenses of raising the child through college, including all medical and educational expenses. Dr. Chaffee filed a motion for preliminary determination, requesting an order limiting the amount of recoverable damages and a determination that the costs of raising a healthy child born after a sterilization procedure are not recoverable as a matter of law. The trial court denied Dr. Chaffee's motion but certified its order for interlocutory appeal.

In this appeal from the trial court ruling, the parties identify and disagree regarding two issues: (1) whether the cost of rearing a normal, healthy child born after an unsuccessful sterilization procedure are cognizable, and (2) whether our recent decision in *Bader v. Johnson,* 732 N.E.2d 1212 (Ind.2000) compels the recognition of such damages.

In *Bader,* the plaintiffs alleged that, because of the prior birth of a child with congenital defects, they had consulted the defendants, healthcare providers offering genetic counseling services, during a subsequent pregnancy. The plaintiffs contended that the defendants' failure to communicate adverse test results deprived them of the opportunity to terminate the pregnancy and resulted in the birth of a child whose multiple birth defects led to her death four months after birth. The plaintiffs' claim was not that the defendant caused the resulting abnormalities in their child, but that the defendant's negligence "caused them to lose the ability to terminate the pregnancy and thereby avoid the costs associated with carrying and giving birth to a child with severe defects." [C] The plaintiffs in *Bader* sought various damages including medical costs attributable to the birth defects during the child's minority, [c], but they did not seek the general costs of rearing the child. We permitted the plaintiffs to seek the damages they sought, noting that their claims "should be treated no differently than any other medical malpractice case." [C] We were not confronted with, nor did we address, a challenge to the anticipated ordinary costs of rearing and raising the child. ...

This issue has been receiving considerable attention in other jurisdictions. There are three principal lines of authority regarding resolution of actions for medical negligence resulting in an unwanted pregnancy. In the first, followed by a small group of jurisdictions, the parents of a child born after a negligently performed sterilization procedure are entitled to recover all costs incurred in rearing the child without any offset for the benefits conferred by the presence of the child. ... Generally, these courts find that damages are recoverable using the standard analysis in negligence cases, and refuse to alter that analysis because of public policy considerations or to permit reduction for the benefits conferred by a child.

Under the second approach, the plaintiff may recover all damages that flow from the wrongful act, but the calculation of damages includes a consideration of the offset of the benefits conferred on the parents by the child's birth. This is consistent with the Restatement (Second) of Torts § 920 (1977), which requires that in situations where the defendant's conduct has harmed the plaintiff or the plaintiff's property but "in so doing has conferred a special benefit to the interest of the plaintiff that was harmed, the value of the benefit conferred is considered in mitigation of damages, to the extent that this is equitable." *Id.* The trier of fact is permitted to determine and award all past and future expenses and damages incurred by the parent, including the cost of rearing the child, but is also instructed that it should make a deduction for the benefits, including, for example, the services, love, joy, and affection that the parents will receive by virtue of having and raising the child. [Cc] As between the first and second approaches, we find the latter preferable.

A third view holds that parents of healthy children born after an unsuccessful sterilization procedure involving medical negligence are entitled to pregnancy and childbearing expenses, but not child-rearing expenses. This is the view of the vast majority of jurisdictions,[fn] ... Courts that follow this approach have identified a variety of policy reasons in support of their decisions, including the speculative nature of the damages, the disproportionate nature of the injury to the defendant's culpability, and a refusal to consider the birth of a child to be a compensable "damage." [Cc]

Although raising an unplanned child, or any child for that matter, is costly, we nevertheless believe that all human life is presumptively invaluable. This Court has held that "life ... cannot be an injury in the legal sense." [C] A child, regardless of the circumstances of birth, does not constitute a "harm" to the parents so as to permit recovery for the costs associated with raising and educating the child. We reach the same outcome as the majority of jurisdictions, and hold that the value of a child's life to the parents outweighs the associated pecuniary burdens as a matter of law. Recoverable damages may include pregnancy and childbearing expenses, but not the ordinary costs of raising and educating a normal, healthy child conceived following an allegedly negligent sterilization procedure. ...

We hold that the costs involved in raising and educating a normal, healthy child conceived subsequent to an allegedly negligent sterilization procedure are not cognizable as damages in an action for medical negligence. The order of the trial court denying the defendant's motion for preliminary determination is reversed, and this cause is remanded for further proceedings consistent with this opinion.

INQUIRY

Designer Babies. The above *Chaffee* case involved a parent's claim for the unintended conception of a healthy child. Advances in medical technology now enable some parents to choose the sex and eye color of their children through a combination of genetic typing and fertilization techniques—typically after in-vitro conception before implantation. The costs of these procedures are coming down and their success-rate and availability going up. The demographic and generational implications are in themselves large. What are the implications for tort law? Should the law permit the parents a malpractice claim when the service provider designs the wrong child? In a slightly different case, Harnicher v. University of Utah Med. Ctr., 962 P.2d 67 (Utah 1998), the appellate court refused to recognize a claim when triplets looking unlike the marital father were born, allegedly as a result of the medical provider's negligent failure to mix in the semen of the right donor (chosen by the parents based on blood type and physical appearance) at the time of in-vitro fertilization. The court used the traditional physical-impact rule required for emotional-distress claims. *See also* Stiver v. Parker, 975 F.2d 261 (6th Cir. 1992) (broker owes client a duty to protect against defect-producing semen for artificial insemination of surrogate mother). Do you think that some court somewhere will soon recognize the claim?

Wrongful Birth. The question becomes a little different when the parents' claim has to do with the conception, carriage, and delivery to term of a child who in some respect—typically tied to the cost of child-rearing—does not meet its parents' expectations. (Note that this description avoids some commonly used but value-laden terms like *disability* and *defect* that advocates for the interests of differently abled populations eschew.) For instance, parents abort about ninety percent of Downs Syndrome children. These claims, commonly labeled as *wrongful birth*, typically arise on the negligent failure of a physician, clinic, or laboratory to properly communicate the results of genetic testing on which the parents would have lawfully terminated the pregnancy and not borne the child and its associated costs. Several courts recognize the claims. *See* Thornhill v. Midwest Physician Ctr., 337 Ill. App.3d 1034, 272 Ill. Dec. 432, 787 N.E.2d 247 (2003); Emerson v. Magendantz, 689 A.2d 409 (R.I. 1997) (recovery of all child-rearing costs if defendant knew of possibility of extraordinary costs); Viccaro v. Mulunsky, 406 Mass. 777, 551 N.E.2d 8 (1990) (recovery of extraordinary costs and emotional distress without offset for benefits); Lininger v. Eisenbeaum, 764 P.2d 1202 (Colo. 1988). Other courts have rejected the claims. *See* Grubbs v. Barbourville Family Health Ctr., 120 S.W.3d 682 (Ky. 2003) (but recognizing breach of contract claim); Etkind v. Suarex, 271 Ga. 352, 519 S.E.2d 210 (1999); Wilson v. Kuenzi, 751 S.W.2d 741 (Mo. 1988); Smith v. Cote, 128 N.H. 231, 513 A.2d 341 (1986) (recovery of extraordinary costs only). Several states prohibit the actions by statute. *See* Vernon's Ann. Mo. Stat. §188.130. One court, while allowing a wrongful-birth claim only for the birth of "disabled" children, denied the claim where the disabilities were asthma, fallen arches, and weak ankles. *See* Rice v. Veleanu, 227 A.D.2d 607, 643 N.Y.S.2d 213 (App. Div. 1996). What criteria are the courts using and judgments are they making when they decide which children are such burdens that someone should pay for their existence? The cases obviously implicate profound questions about what it means to be a parent and, indeed, to be human.

Wrongful Life. Wrongful-birth claims are on behalf of the parents for the costs of the child. What about the possibility of a *wrongful-life* claim on behalf of the child for the child having to bear its own life? Troubling enough are the wrongful-birth claims recognizing the possibility that, to his or her parent, a child's life could have negative value. Wrongful-life claims are even more logically problematic because of the question whether life can have negative value to the one living it. Indeed, law gives no clear support for a child's claim to wrongful life. The benefit of being alive must outweigh the pain or other costs of existence. Yet, a few cases do recognize wrongful-life damages for the child, for the extraordinary costs incurred above the usual costs of child rearing. *See* Procanik v. Cillo, 97 N.J. 339, 478 A.2d 755 (1984); Turpin v. Sortini, 31 Cal.3d 220, 182 Cal. Rptr. 337, 643 P.2d 954 (1982). Do the *Procanik* and *Turpin* cases mean that the defendant physician pays for a condition that the physician did not cause and could not have prevented? *See* Canesi v. Wilson, 1588 N.J. 490, 730 A.2d 805 (1999) (medical causation is unnecessary in wrongful-birth claim—causation question is whether parents would have terminated pregnancy).

Wrongful Parenting. Will the courts reach the point of insisting that parents abort certain children—rather than merely granting them compensation when others negligently prevent that option? Curlender v. Bio-Science Labs., 106 Cal. App.3d 811, 165 Cal. Rptr. 477 (1980), was another wrongful-life case against a laboratory for negligently performing blood testing that would have revealed the plaintiff in-utero infant's Tay-Sachs disease. Because the parents would have aborted the child, the appellate court permitted the child to recover pain-and-suffering damages while also suggesting that parents may be liable if they choose to bear a "seriously impaired" and "genetically defective" child. Why do you think that the state legislature reacted promptly to the *Curlender* decision, barring any such claim against the parents for bearing a child? *See* Cal. Civ. Code §43.6 (1981). How should shared understandings regarding the nature of our democratic republic inform courts in this area?

B. Breach

We now turn to the second of the four elements of negligence claims—breach of duty, also called negligence or fault. The Restatement (Third) of Torts: Liability for Physical and Emotional Harm §17 defines a breach of duty, or negligence, as follows: "A person acts with negligence if the person does not exercise reasonable care under all the circumstances. Primary factors to consider in ascertaining whether the person's conduct lacks reasonable care are the foreseeable likelihood that it will result in harm, the foreseeable severity of the harm that may ensue, and the burden that would be borne by the person and others if the person takes precautions that eliminate or reduce the probability of harm." The Restatement's negligence definition reflects the Hand balancing test. Model jury instructions tend, on the other hand, to employ the reasonably prudent-person standard.

As the above cases suggest, cases usually hold duty to be a question of law for the judge, with the right to jury determination only of any underlying fact issues. Judges decide whether a defendant owes the plaintiff a duty of care. By contrast, the law ordinarily considers *breach* of duty a fact issue for the jury. A jury (if any party demands one) will decide whether the defendant has breached the duty. The Restatement (Third) of Torts: Liability for Physical and Emotional Harm §8 addresses the relative role of judge and jury, stating:

> (a) When, in light of all of the evidence, reasonable minds can differ as to the facts relating to the actor's conduct, it is the function of the jury to determine those facts.
> (b) When, in light of all the facts relating to the actor's conduct, reasonable minds can differ as to whether the conduct lacks reasonable care, it is the function of the jury to make that determination.

Proof of breach is therefore a paramount issue. How do tort practitioners show juries that the defendant has or has not breached the duty? This section on breach begins with a glimpse at what evidence torts practitioners gather and present, and how they present it, to help juries decide the breach issue. This sectionthen covers the unusual circumstance where no evidence of breach exists, but the circumstances alone warrant at least an inference that breach occurred—a subject lawyers recognize as the doctrine of res ipsa loquitur. The section concludes with the violation of statute as proof of breach. Consider now what the tort practitioner regards as the core of negligence law and thus of tort practice—how lawyers go about proving and disproving breach of duty.

1. Proof of Fault

OBJECTIVE: Given the opportunity for fact investigation involving negligence claims, identify the direct and circumstantial evidence you would seek on each claim of negligence, and describe the effect of that evidence, consistent with your study of this section of the text.

Case Study: An angler borrowed a motorboat to go fishing. The motorboat's balky engine quit. The angler had a heart attack from the stress of trying to paddle the motorboat with a seat cushion. Others later found the angler dead in the motorboat the next day. ***Identify the direct and circumstantial evidence you would seek to support the estate's claim of negligence against the motorboat's owner.***

The evidentiary proof of fault may be either by direct evidence such as eyewitness testimony or by circumstantial evidence such as by reconstruction of an accident from conditions at the scene. We sometimes assume that direct evidence such as eyewitness testimony is preferable to circumstantial evidence. Yet eyewitness testimony can be notoriously unreliable for several reasons including limitations of time, distance, and vantage point for the observations made; interfering conditions for the observations made; defects in the witness's own ability to observe and recall; and the witness's bias or interest in testifying. Tort cases often present contradictory testimony on how the injury occurred. Juries often resolve liability based on circumstantial evidence presented through the testimony of a disinterested investigator such as a police officer or OSHA investigator. *See* Fairbanks v. J.B. McLoughlin Co., 131 Wash.2d 96, 929 P.2d 433 (1997) (partiers testify that employee was not drunk, but officers investigating employee's motor-vehicle accident minutes later testify that employee was obviously intoxicated—slurring speech, smelling of alcohol, stumbling, and staggering). Circumstantial evidence can thus be more important and persuasive than direct evidence. Consider a case involving circumstantial evidence on a common question encountered by tort practitioners—how long an unreasonably dangerous condition existed before the incident took place.

Ritter v. Meijer, Inc.
Michigan Court of Appeals
128 Mich. App. 783, 341 N.W.2d 220 (1983)

PER CURIAM. On August 22, 1980, Viktoria Ritter, hereinafter plaintiff, was a customer at the defendant's store located in Royal Oak. After finishing her shopping, she paid for her groceries at the store's cashier counter. On her way out of the store, about five or six feet from the checkout counter, she stepped on a grape and fell, sustaining serious injuries. Plaintiff testified that it felt as if the grape had previously been stepped on. Defendant's cashier wiped up the area with a paper towel and then discarded the towel and the grape.

At the close of plaintiffs' evidence, defendant moved for a directed verdict on the ground that there had not been any evidence to establish that the grape had been on the floor a sufficient length of time to give actual or constructive notice to defendant. The trial court denied defendant's motion, noting that there had been evidence that the grape had been previously stepped on, indicating that it had been there for some time. The jury returned a verdict for plaintiff and defendant now brings this appeal. ...

On appeal, defendant's sole argument is that plaintiffs had failed to make out a prima facie case by failing to produce any evidence indicating that the grape had been on the floor for a sufficient length of time to give the defendant notice of it. Specifically, defendant contends that the grape was not described as being dry, dirty, bruised, darkened, discolored or withered. Plaintiff had an opportunity to view the grape after stepping on it and described it as flat, white, and juicy. We note that plaintiff made these observations immediately after sustaining a comminuted fracture of her knee, indicating that she may not have been fully able to observe the condition of the grape. Defendant's employee quickly wiped up the area and discarded the grape. When a party deliberately destroys evidence, a presumption arises that if the evidence were produced at trial, it would operate against the party who deliberately destroyed it. [C] The fact that plaintiff described the grape as being white and wet does not preclude the presumption that it was dirty or partially discolored or withered. The trial court's finding can be sustained on the basis of this presumption.

The trial court also correctly reasoned that the evidence that the grape had previously been stepped on had sufficiently established that it had been there long enough to give defendant actual or constructive notice. A case in negligence may be based on legitimate inferences. [C] A plaintiff makes a prima facie case when sufficient evidence is presented to take the inference out of the realm of conjecture. [C] Defendant contends that it was possible for the grape to be dropped on the floor and stepped on immediately prior to plaintiff's fall. This is pure conjecture. The legitimate inference is that since a grape only occupies a very small portion of the floor space, it would take some time before someone would step on it. Even though this amount of time may be somewhat shorter than it would take for the grape to reach advanced stages of fermentation, we feel that it is sufficient to give defendant constructive notice of the existence of the grape. ...

In *Little v. Borman Food Stores, Inc,* 33 Mich.App. 609, 190 N.W.2d 269 (1971), the plaintiff alleged that she slipped on ice while entering defendant's store. After the plaintiff fell, her slacks were muddy. The court found that, "[t]hese two factors indicate that if there was ice it may well have been covered by or mixed with dirt, which in turn indicates that it may have been there for some time. * * * There was no evidence that affirmatively indicated that the ice had been deposited recently." [C] In the instant case, no evidence was brought forth to rebut the inference created by the fact that the grape had previously been stepped on.

Since the trial court had correctly found that plaintiffs had established a prima facie case, defendant's motion for a directed verdict was properly denied.

Affirmed.

INQUIRY

Spoliation of Evidence. How should courts treat missing evidence? *See* Healey v. Firestone Tire & Rubber Co., 640 N.Y.S.2d 860, 87 N.Y.2d 596, 663 N.E.2d 901 (1996) (circumstantial evidence must exist supporting negligence, or case involving missing direct evidence of allegedly defective truck-tire rim will be dismissed). How should courts treat the intentional destruction (or *spoliation*) of evidence? *See* Bachmeier v. Wallwork Truck Ctrs., 544 N.W.2d 122 (N.D. 1996) (summary judgment for defendant manufacturer where plaintiff failed to preserve allegedly defective wheel hub). How should courts treat the unintentional destruction of evidence? *See* Vodusek v. Bayliner Marine Corp., 71 F.3d 148 (4th Cir. 1995) (jury may draw negative inferences against plaintiff from plaintiff's expert's destruction of allegedly defective boat). The destruction, intentional or otherwise, of electronically stored information such as emails has been a huge issue particularly for corporate litigants recently. Civil-procedure courses address that issue.

Conflicting Testimony. Ordinarily, a party has the right to have a jury decide conflicting evidence on a material issue such as the negligence of a party. How should the court treat conflicting testimony when the conflict is within the story of the only witness? Can a witness change his or her mind? One might think that in those cases, a jury should have the opportunity to decide which of the witness's stories is the more credible and reliable. Should the rule be any different when the witness whose story changes is the plaintiff? *See* Schultz v. Auto-Owners Ins. Co., 212 Mich. App. 199, 536 N.W.2d 784 (1995) (plaintiff cannot contradict the plaintiff's own deposition testimony with an affidavit opposing summary judgment).

Figure

The *National Law Journal* named tort-case mediator and arbitrator Kenneth Feinberg its "Lawyer of the Year" in 2004—and with good reason. As Special Master of the September 11th Victim Compensation Fund of 2001, Mr. Feinberg crafted the regulations and administered the billion dollars in funds set aside by the federal government for 9/11 victims and their families. His other high-profile arbitration work has included helping to

> determine a monetary value for the rare film of President Kennedy's assassination and to allocate legal fees relating to the Hollocaust slave-labor cases. Mr. Feinberg has also served on presidential commissions regarding human radiation experiments and catastrophic nuclear accidents, and has served as the chair of the ABA Special Committee on Mass Torts. In between, he has acted as a court-appointed special master, arbitrator, or mediator in thousands of other mass-tort, business-tort, products-liability, insurance-coverage, and other tort-related cases. Formerly a partner in a major law firm, he currently leads his own law firm The Feinberg Group, LLP, founded in 1993.

Constructive Notice. The above *Ritter* case shows a simple example of how a party can establish fault through a combination of direct and circumstantial evidence bearing on the question of the safety of the defendant's practices. The question of negligence often turns on whether the defendant had notice of the unreasonably unsafe condition or, failing notice, from reasonable inspection should have known, given the passage of time. Constructive notice cases are notoriously unpredictable. *Compare* Ritter, *supra*, *with* Joye v. Great Atlantic & Pacific Tea Co., 405 F.2d 464 (4th Cir. 1968) (banana peel's dark-brown, dirty condition is not evidence of grocer's constructive notice as to how long banana had been on floor). Where no evidence of constructive notice of a dangerous condition exists, alternative liability theories may include negligence in design or construction in a manner that created the dangerous condition. *See* Jasko v. F.W. Woolworth Co., 177 Colo. 418, 494 P.2d 839 (1972) (defendant subject to slip-and-fall liability for negligence in the method of selling pizza on waxed paper over terrazzo floor).

The Plaintiff's Burdens. Keep in mind that the plaintiff has three burdens with respect to fault: to plead it (the burden of pleading), to adduce evidence of it to avoid summary judgment or directed verdict (the burden of production), and to convince the jury that the fact is more likely than not (the burden of proof or persuasion). The investigation, preparation, and presentation of direct and circumstantial evidence for the liability portion of a tort case can be sophisticated and complex. The lawyers may learn the nuances of basic sciences such as hydraulics, aerodynamics, and metallurgy, and applied sciences such as civil, mechanical, and production engineering, ergonomics, and, especially, safety engineering. Consider two cases involving allegations of fault in technically complex judgments—the first case finding no fault and the second case finding fault.

Rhode Island Hosp. Trust Natl. Bank v Zapata Corp.
United States Court of Appeals, First Circuit
848 F.2d 291 (1st Cir. 1988)

BREYER, J. The issue that this appeal presents is whether Zapata Corporation has shown that the system used by Rhode Island Hospital Trust National Bank for detecting forged checks—a system used by a majority of American banks—lacks the "ordinary care" that a bank must exercise under the Uniform Commercial Code § 4-406(3) (1977)....

In early 1985, a Zapata employee stole some blank checks from Zapata. She wrote a large number of forged checks, almost all in amounts of $150 to $800 each, on Zapata's accounts at Rhode Island Hospital Trust National Bank. The Bank, from March through July 1985, received and paid them.

... Ordinarily a bank must reimburse an innocent customer for forgeries that it honors, § 6A-3-401(1) (1985), but § 6A-4-406 makes an important exception to the liability rule. The exception ... applies once a customer has had a chance to catch the forgeries by examining his bank statements and notifying the bank but has failed to do so.

...

The statute goes on to specify an important exception to the exception. It says: "(3) The preclusion under subsection (2) does not apply if the customer establishes lack of ordinary care on the part of the bank in paying the item(s)." § 6A-4-406(3). Zapata's specific claim, on this appeal, is that it falls within this "exception to the exception"—that the bank's treatment of the post-April 24 checks lacked "ordinary care." ...

b. The record convinces us that Zapata failed to carry its burden of establishing "lack of ordinary care" on the part of the Bank. First, the Bank described its ordinary practices as follows: The Bank examines all signatures on checks for more than $1,000. It examines signatures on checks between $100 and $1,000 (those at issue here) if it has reason to suspect a problem, *e.g.*, if a customer has warned it of a possible forgery or if the check was drawn on an account with insufficient funds. It examines the signatures of a randomly chosen one percent of all other checks between $100 and $1,000. But, it does not examine the signatures on other checks between $100 and $1,000. Through expert testimony, the Bank also established that most other banks in the nation follow this practice and that banking industry experts recommend it. Indeed, Trust National Bank's practices are conservative in this regard, as most banks set $2500 or more, not $1,000, as the limit beneath which they will not examine each signature.

This testimony made out a *prima facie* case of "ordinary care." [Cc] Of course, Zapata might still try to show that the entire industry's practice is unreasonable, that it reflects lack of "ordinary care." *The T.J. Hooper,* 60 F.2d 737, 740 (2d Cir.), *cert. denied,* 287 U.S. 662, 53 S.Ct. 220, 77 L.Ed. 571 (1932). ...

Second, both bank officials and industry experts pointed out that this industry practice, in general and in the particular case of the Trust National Bank, saved considerable expense, compared with the Bank's pre-1981 practice of examining each check by hand. ...

Third, both a Bank official and an industry expert testified that changing from an "individual signature examination" system to the new "bulk-filing" system led to *no* significant increase in the number of forgeries that went undetected. ...

Zapata points to *no* testimony or other evidence tending to contradict these assertions. An industry-wide practice that saves money without significantly increasing the number of forged checks that the banks erroneously pay is a practice that reflects at least "ordinary care." [C]

Fourth, even if one assumes, contrary to this uncontradicted evidence, that the new system meant *some* increase in the number of undetected forged checks, Zapata still could not prevail, for it presented *no* evidence tending to show any such increased loss unreasonable in light of the costs that the new practice would save. Instead, it relied simply upon the assertion that costs saved the bank are irrelevant. But, that is not so, for what is reasonable or unreasonable insofar as "ordinary care" or "due care" or "negligence" (and the like) are concerned is often a matter of costs of prevention compared with correlative risks of loss. *See* [c]; *United States v. Carroll Towing Co.,* 159 F.2d 169, 173 (2d Cir.1947) (Hand, J.) ("duty" defined by calculating probability of injury times gravity of harm to determine "burden of precaution" that is warranted). One does not, for example, coat the base of the Grand Canyon with soft plastic nets to catch those who might fall in, or build cars like armored tanks to reduce injuries in accidents even though the technology exists. [Cc] In arguing that the Bank provided "no care" in respect to the checks it did not examine, Zapata simply assumed the very conclusion (namely, the unreasonableness of a selective examination *system*) that it sought to prove. Aside from this assumption, its evidentiary cupboard is bare. ...

As Zapata contends, there are several cases that hold or imply that "ordinary care" necessarily implies individualized scrutiny of every check. But, several of those cases are old, decided in different technological circumstances and before the U.C.C. [Cc]

We have found a few, more modern cases that arguably support Zapata's view, but they involve practices more obviously unreasonable than those presented here. *See, e.g., Hanover Insurance Cos. V. Brotherhood State Bank,* 482 F.Supp. 501 (D.Kan.1979) (no ordinary care where *no* examination of *any size* checks, conspicuous forgeries); [cc].

For these reasons, the judgment of the district court is
Affirmed.

Bernier v. Boston Edison Co.
Massachusetts Supreme Court
380 Mass. 372, 403 N.E.2d 391 (1980)

KAPLAN, J. About 2:30 P.M., May 24, 1972, the plaintiffs Arthur Bernier, Jr., and Patricia J. Kasputys, then eighteen and fifteen years old, were let out of school and, after going to Kasputys's house, sauntered to an ice cream parlor on Massachusetts Avenue in Lexington Center, one of the town's major shopping areas. A half hour later, Alice Ramsdell entered her 1968 Buick Skylark automobile parked, pointed east, on the south side of Massachusetts Avenue... [Another vehicle struck Ms. Ramsdell's vehicle.]

What might have been a commonplace collision turned into a complicated accident. On impact, Ramsdell, a woman of sixty-nine, hit her head against her steering wheel and suffered a bloody nose. She testified she "lost complete control of that car." Dazed, she unknowingly let her foot slip from the power brake to the gas pedal. In the result, after veering right around Boireau's car and perhaps slowing slightly, she accelerated across the remaining twenty feet of Muzzey Street, bounced to the south sidewalk, about nine feet wide, of Massachusetts Avenue, and moved about fifty-five feet down the sidewalk. On this passage the car scraped the front of a camera store, hit and levelled a parking meter, struck and damaged extensively the right rear section of a Chevrolet Chevelle automobile (the third parked car beyond Muzzey Street), knocked down an electric light pole owned by the defendant Boston Edison Company (Edison), and struck the plaintiffs who had left the ice cream parlor and were walking side by side west, into the face of the oncoming car. ...

The electric light pole, when hit, fell away from Ramsdell's car toward the east, struck a Volkswagen automobile parked along Massachusetts Avenue (the fourth car from Muzzey Street), and came down across the legs of Bernier. ... Bernier's thighs and left shin bone were broken, the latter break causing a permanently shortened left leg; and he had other related injuries. Kasputys lay within two feet of the pole further in from the curb than Bernier. ... She suffered a skull fracture on the right side of her head where pieces of metal and a length of wire were found imbedded, and developed permanent pain in her left lower leg.

... [Their c]omplaints alleged against Edison that it had negligently designed, selected, constructed, and maintained the pole at Lexington Center. The cases were consolidated for trial.

The principal witnesses called by the plaintiffs were physicians who testified (orally or through deposition) about the agreement of the injuries with the plaintiffs' theories of how they were caused; two engineers and two supervisors from Edison's staff, responsible for various aspects of the design and maintenance of electric light poles, who were examined on issues of the company's alleged negligence; and a structural engineer, testifying largely as an expert in concrete design. Also called was a police investigator.

...

The jury returned verdicts ... holding Ramsdell and Edison liable. Only Edison appealed.... The company contends ... [that t]here was insufficient evidence for a jury to find with reason (1) that the pole was negligently designed, selected, constructed, or maintained, or, (2) even if Edison was negligent in some way, that the negligence "caused" the plaintiffs' injuries. ...

... The plaintiffs did not claim that an otherwise acceptable pole had been rendered dangerous through damage ([c]), or that a well designed pole had been carelessly constructed. Rather the gravamen of the plaintiffs' case, as it appeared at trial, was that Edison had failed through negligence to design a pole that was accommodated reasonably to foreseeable vehicular impacts so as to avoid pedestrian injuries, and that the continued use of the pole created an unreasonable risk of such injuries. ...

... As designer or codesigner of the pole and in control of its maintenance, Edison "must anticipate the environment in which its product will be used, and it must design against the reasonably foreseeable risks attending the product's use in that setting." Back v. Wickes Corp., [c] 378 N.E.2d 964, 969 (1978). Certainly the evidence showed that a risk of automobiles colliding with Edison poles in particular No. 6 poles was not only foreseeable but well known to the company. About 100 to 120 Edison poles a year were knocked down in such collisions in Edison's "Northeast Service Center" which included Lexington, although there was no evidence that any in Lexington Center had previously been felled. A so-called "knock down truck" worked steadily replacing downed poles in the district and installing new ones, and there were estimates by employees that in their years of field work they had replaced "thousands" of Edison poles. One employee said he had been personally involved in replacing at least a hundred poles of the type involved in the accident at bar.

As in the case of vehicles, design should take into account "foreseeable participation in collisions" ([c]).[fn] And for the speeds to be encountered and consequences entailed in collisions, one analyzes the whole "setting." This was a busy shopping area with heavy pedestrian and vehicular traffics. Parked cars often lined the street but this was not a safety factor that could be greatly relied on.

... Edison installed this No. 6 pole on February 3, 1949. It was of reinforced concrete, twenty-six feet nine inches in height, and ran from an eight inch base to a 5 3/8 inch top diameter. Four anchor bolts held it to a base that extended 4 2/3 feet below the surface. The pole was hollow, allowing for feeder wires to come from an underground cable up to the luminaire. Implanted in the concrete shaft were six vertical steel rods, each .375(3/8) inch thick. Total weight of the pole and luminaire structure was 1,200 pounds.

What precautions were taken in the design to guard against the risk of pedestrian injury through collapse of a No. 6 pole upon impact by a vehicle? According to the evidence, the problem was not seriously adverted to, or so a jury could find. Symptomatic was evidence that no head of a relevant engineering department had authorized a test of Edison poles to determine impact resistance, or knew of such a test. No attempt had been made to design against the risk to pedestrians and no specifications took the impact resistance factor into account. Overall, the major considerations in Edison's design of poles (including their materials) seemed to be cost, adaptability to Edison's existing system of power supply and connecting apparatus, and capacity of Edison employees to install the poles safely.[fn]

... Edison's failure to pay serious attention to the risk of pedestrian injury in designing poles is probative of the actual quality of the poles in that respect, but adequate poles might come about by happenstance. It became necessary to examine the design of the poles in relation to possible impacts and, if that yielded unsatisfactory estimates, to consider what alternative designs were available and feasible and at what costs or with what other effects. [C] To begin with, since injuries might be serious (as the present case indeed indicated), the likelihood of accidents need not be high to warrant careful consideration of safety features. [C]

The plaintiffs' major witness concerning design safety was Howard Simpson, who had a doctorate in engineering and practiced as a consulting structural engineer. His qualifications as an expert on the strength of reinforced concrete were unchallenged. In his opinion, the concrete of the thickness specified for No. 6 poles lacked "ductility," the quality which would allow a pole, when struck by a car, to absorb part of the impact and bend without breaking. No. 6 would shatter when hit with sufficient force; indeed, one of the Edison supervisors testified about No. 6 that the concrete "all crumbles at the point of impact." As the exposed steel rods could not then support the weight of the pole, it would fall. As to the force sufficient to break No. 6 in this fashion, Simpson testified that the pole would succumb to a 1968 Buick Skylark with a passenger, spare tire, and full gas tank going as slowly as six m.p.h. A medium-sized truck weighing 10,000 pounds could level No. 6 when traveling at 1.5 m. p. h.

Simpson went on to say that the strength of the pole could have been substantially improved by using steel rods of larger diameter or by placing steel "hoops" or "spirals" perpendicular to those vertical rods. In his opinion the latter device would have enabled the pole to withstand the impact of the Buick at 11 m. p. h. an important advance, as a car going 9 m.p.h. has an energy considerably greater than that at 6 m.p.h. Such hoops and spirals had been in use since the early 1900's in columns for buildings. Simpson calculated the cost per pole of the hoops at $5.75 and the spirals at $17.50.

We should add here that there was evidence from Edison employees of the existence of other pole-types, possibly of greater strength, that would at least have warranted comparison by Edison with the No. 6 pole in respect to safety values. Various metal poles (aluminum and steel) might have deserved such study. Edison's own No. 26, of prestressed concrete, designed in 1968, might have been an improvement.[fn]

... Edison argues that a finding of negligence here left it in the grip of a "polycentric" problem. If it chose to protect pedestrians by using stronger poles, motorists might be more seriously injured when they hit poles which did not break. If it chose to protect motorists, pedestrians would claim recovery when poles fell on them. No designer or owner, Edison added, is required to make or use a product wholly accident-free. [C] There is some disingenuousness in this argument as the evidence shows Edison paid scant attention in the design of the No. 6 pole to the safety either of motorists or pedestrians. But we think there is nothing in the argument to relieve Edison of a duty to take precautions against knockdowns by cars, and it would seem reasonable for Edison to consider pedestrian safety with particular seriousness. Persons in a car are protected by a metal and glass shield sometimes three times as heavy as the pole's entire weight; pedestrians are exposed. Whether drivers are hurt any less by impact at similar speeds with poles that topple than with poles that bend rather than fall is unknown to us and apparently to Edison as well. To be sure, many more cars will hit poles than poles will hit pedestrians, but a six m.p.h. threshold for cars, and less for trucks, seems little protection indeed. ...

... Here the jury could rationally find negligence of design and maintenance. They could find that the vehicular speed at which No. 6 would topple was grievously low, creating an unacceptable risk of grave injury to persons at the scene (who in shopping areas such as Lexington Center might be numerous). The impact resistance of the pole could have been improved by relatively minor alterations available at the time and not inconveniencing Edison or the public, or possibly by the use of another type of pole with greater resistance. ...

Judgments affirmed.

Skills

Choose four other students with whom to work. In ten minutes, working as a team, plan the investigation of the following tort case involving a personal-injury claim. If you represent the plaintiff, in the first five minutes one student list the areas of inquiry for the deposition of the defendant's representative, another list the areas of inquiry for interrogatories to defendant, another plan the record requests to defendant, another plan the records subpoenas to non-parties, and another plan the liability experts to consult. If you represent the defendant, in the first five minutes one student list the areas of inquiry for the plaintiff's deposition, another list the areas of inquiry for interrogatories to plaintiff, another plan the record requests to plaintiff, another plan the records subpoenas to non-parties, and another plan the liability experts to consult. In the second five minutes, spend one minute reviewing and improving each of those five assignments as a team. Be prepared to report your results to the whole class. *Facts.* Your client is a 38-year-old, married machine operator who suffered the loss of her scalp when her ponytailed hair caught in the drill press she was operating. The drill press's designer-installer is the defendant. The allegations include that the designer-installer failed to guard and warn against the hazard. It has been one year since the accident.

INQUIRY

The Cost of Burden-Balancing. How would you apply the burden-balancing test in a case in which a patron choked to death on food in a casino restaurant, and the defense was that training restaurant employees on the Heimlich maneuver would have cost too much? *See* Lee v. GNLV Corp., 117 Nev. 291, 22 P.3d 209 (2001) (affirming dismissal of case because burden was too high for the "low probability" that choking would occur). Do we properly characterize care as a burden or, instead, as the ultimate intrinsic social value? What does it say about the way in which we conceive of our legal system in general and tort law in particular, when we treat common regard for one another as a burden rather than an opportunity or benefit? Must we base the legal system on a philosophy that we should and do live for ourselves, or does the possibility remain that we might base the law at least in part on the grounds that we might live better by regarding others?

2. Res Ipsa Loquitur

OBJECTIVE: Given descriptions of events involving injury from unknown causes within the control of another, recall and apply the definition of and conditions for res ipsa loquitur to determine whether the plaintiff has the claim and evidence on which to proceed.

Case Study: A man let a woman use his woodworking shop one weekend afternoon for the woman's project. The woman started the table saw near a propane space heater along one side of the shop. There was a flash and explosion severely burning the woman. Because of the fire, investigators were unable to determine just what had caused the explosion. ***Recall and apply the elements of res ipsa loquitur to determine whether the woman has a negligence claim against the man.***

When proof of negligence is unavailable to the plaintiff, but the circumstances compel an inference that negligence occurred, the plaintiff may be entitled to an inference of negligence with the support of the res-ipsa-loquitur doctrine—literally, "the thing speaks for itself." The well-known case Byrne v. Boadle, 2 H.& C. 722, 159 Eng. Rep. 299 (Exch. Ct. 1863), popularized the doctrine, when a barrel of flour inexplicably rolled out from defendant's second-story shop window and onto the plaintiff. Defendant's employee must have been moving the barrel. Barrels of flour do not simply roll out of shop windows of their own accord. But the stricken plaintiff had no way of knowing, and no one else was saying. Plaintiff had no evidence of negligence. The Court of Exchequer nonetheless allowed the plaintiff's negligence claim, holding that defendant must disprove it. The usual effect of the doctrine, as most courts apply it, is to permit (though not require) the jury to draw an inference of negligence if the conditions for res ipsa loquitur apply. *See* K-Mart Corp. v. Gipson, 563 N.E.2d 667 (Ind. App. 1990); *but see* De Leon Lopez v. Corporacion Insular de Seguros, 931 F.2d 116 (1st Cir. 1991) ("hen's-teeth rare" directed verdict for plaintiff on res-ipsa-loquitur circumstance of hospital somehow switching infants immediately after delivery).

Caution is wise when considering whether res ipsa loquitur is available—in part because some judges severely disfavor the maxim as in any sense a true legal rule. *See* Potomac Edison Co. v. Johnson, 160 Md. 33, 152 A. 633 (1930) (Bond, C.J., dissenting). What seems clearer than calling the maxim an independent rule or principle is that the courts will as a matter of procedural fairness grant the plaintiff greater latitude in drawing inferences, when the defendant has the only access to the evidence from which the jury would draw inferences. It is less a rule than an accommodation—a relaxation of evidentiary standards, reserved for the special case and circumstance where defendant is likely concealing an explanation that would establish defendant's own liability.

Several conditions must exist for res ipsa loquitur to apply, and the courts are not necessarily generous in finding them so. First, the mere fact that injury occurred is not sufficient. The circumstances of the injury must be such that injury would ordinarily not have occurred without negligence—that, more probably than not, negligence led to the injury's occurrence. Second, the evidence of negligence must be truly beyond the plaintiff's reach—not merely that plaintiff has not discovered any evidence but that plaintiff was and is in no position to obtain it if it exists. Third, the negligence must have been the defendant's negligence. Traditionally, courts state this condition as the defendant must have had exclusive control over the circumstances giving rise to the plaintiff's injury. Some courts have relaxed the exclusive-control requirement in certain instances. *Contrast* Montgomery Elev. Co. v. Gordon, 619 P.2d 66 (Colo. 1980) (res ipsa theory as to elevator manufacturer even in absence of exclusive control), *with* Ebanks v. New York City Trans. Auth., 512 N.E.2d 297 (N.Y. 1987) (no res ipsa theory as to escalator where defect could have been result of vandalism). The Restatement (Third) of Torts: Liability for Physical and Emotional Harm §17 replaces the exclusive-control requirement with a "class of actors/relevant member" requirement: "The factfinder may infer that the defendant has been negligent when the accident causing the plaintiff's harm is a type of accident that ordinarily happens as a result of the negligence of a class of actors of which the defendant is the relevant member." Some courts have imposed an additional requirement that the incident not have depended on the plaintiff's actions, although other courts have allowed comparative negligence to treat the question of the plaintiff's responsibility for the injury. *See* Peplinski v. Forbes Roofing, Inc., 531 N.W.2d 597 (Wis. 1995) (res ipsa loquitur may apply even in case involving comparative negligence); Giles v. New Haven, 228 Conn. 441, 636 A.2d 1335 (1994) (res ipsa loquitur applied coincident with comparative-negligence instruction). Consider some modern cases attempting to deal with its contours.

Krebs v. Corrigan
District of Columbia Court of Appeals
321 A.2d 558 (D.C. Ct. App. 1974)

YEAGLEY, J. This is an appeal from a directed verdict entered in favor of appellees (defendants) at the conclusion of appellant's (plaintiff's) case in chief. The complaint alleged that defendant Bronson negligently caused damage to personal property belonging to plaintiff and that defendant Donald Corrigan was liable for such damage as Bronson's principal.

... Plaintiff is an artist who creates plexiglass sculptures. ... While ... on the phone, plaintiff glanced back toward where Bronson was working and saw him "flying through the air . . . at least three feet off the ground—and he landed in the middle of (a plexiglass sculpture)." Four sculptures in all were destroyed.

Upon the conclusion of plaintiff's case, defendants moved for a directed verdict on the ground that plaintiff had not presented a prima facie case of negligence. After extended argument, mainly involving the doctrine of res ipsa loquitur, the court granted defendants' motion and directed a verdict in their favor. The judge, in explaining his decision to the jury, indicated that a verdict was directed because plaintiff could not show what caused defendant Bronson's body to fall or be thrown onto the sculptures.

This information was not only unknown to plaintiff but was peculiarly within the knowledge of the defendant Bronson. He, of course, never testified as to any explanation he might have had for the accident, since his motion for a directed verdict was granted. We do not believe a plaintiff ought to be held to that burden on these facts which, left unexplained, support, an inference of negligence. Accordingly, we reverse and remand for a new trial.

It is well established, to the extent that a citation of authority is unnecessary, that the mere happening of an accident does not give rise to any inference of negligence. On the other hand, it is established that the circumstances of certain accidents may be such as to justify an inference that negligence was involved. In the District of Columbia an inference that defendant may have been negligent is permitted when the following three conditions exist: first, the cause of the accident is known; second, the accident-producing instrumentality is under the exclusive control of the defendant; and third, the instrumentality is unlikely to do harm without negligence on the part of the person in control. [Cc] The presence of these factors distinguishes such cases from the vast majority that lack those features, concerning which it is said that negligence is not to be inferred from the mere happening of an accident.

In the case before us there is no doubt that the cause of the accident was known, i.e., the sculpture was damaged by Bronson's falling on it. To say that the cause of the accident was not known, because there was no evidence as to what caused Bronson to come into contact with the sculptures, "confuses the cause of the accident with the manner in which it was caused, lack of knowledge of which, in plaintiff, is a reason for the doctrine of res ipsa loquitur... ." Kerlin v. Washington Gas Light Co., 110 F.Supp. 487, 488 (D.D.C1953) aff'd, 94 U.S.App.D.C. 39, 211 F.2d 649 (1954). ...

Nor is there any doubt that the accident-producing instrumentality, Bronson's body, was within his exclusive control. ... [W]e think it to be a fair presumption that a person's body usually is within his exclusive control; such is the sub silentio presumption in most medical malpractice cases. [C] Defendants' contention that the dent-removing tool was the accident-producing instrumentality, and that Bronson did not have exclusive control over that tool, misses the mark. Moreover, the factual assumption, being without proof of this record, is no more than speculation. ...

Lastly, as in other situations permitting the application of res ipsa loquitur, we consider it of no small significance that the accident-producing instrumentality, Bronson's body, is one which is unlikely to do harm in the absence of negligence on the part of the person in control. Such a conclusion does not ignore the possibility of other explanations for the incident, explanations which might not involve negligence; but human bodies do not generally go crashing into breakable personal property. When they do, as here, we think the facts require the court of permit an inference of negligence. The person in control of the body or instrumentality may come forth with an explanation. To have to explain the actions of one's body is certainly not unreasonable and is less burdensome than to have to explain why a barrel of flour fell out of one's warehouse onto a pedestrian, a situation to which res ipsa loquitur was held applicable in Byrne v. Boadle, 159 Eng.Rep. 299 (Ex. 1863).

Appellees also contend that appellant could not rely on the doctrine of res ipsa loquitur because there was an eyewitness to the accident, i.e., defendant Bronson, and that appellant should have called Bronson as a witness before being allowed to invoke res ipsa loquitur.

To our knowledge this court has never held that a plaintiff may not invoke the doctrine of res ipsa loquitur when the defendant is an eyewitness. In fact on many occasions[fn] we have noted that one of the main reasons for the doctrine is the superior, if not exclusive, knowledge which defendants sometimes have as to the cause of accidents. If requiring a plaintiff to call the defendant as an adverse witness was deemed a sufficient method of determining the cause of an accident, there would be no need for the doctrine of res ipsa loquitur. The doctrine exists because of the realization that examination of a defendant as an adverse witness is not a viable way to discover the cause of an accident.[fn]

In deciding whether or not res ipsa loquitur is applicable, courts necessarily are mindful of the different effects which that decision will have on the parties and the trial. If res ipsa loquitur is not employed, plaintiff's case is terminated even though he suffered an injury that was caused by the defendant. If res ipsa loquitur is found applicable, defendant is put to no greater burden than to produce information peculiarly within his knowledge as to how the incident occurred. Even if that explanation is unsatisfactory or indeed even if no explanation is made, the jury is free to decline to draw an inference of negligence, and it is so instructed.

We find that the plaintiff's evidence, considered in the light most favorable to him, as must be done in ruling on the motion for a directed verdict by a defendant, was sufficient to raise an inference of negligence so as to survive the defendants' motion and to put them to their proof.

Reversed for a new trial.

McDougald v. Perry
Florida Supreme Court
716 So.2d 783 (Fla. 1998)

WELLS, J. ... Lawrence McDougald sued Henry Perry and Perry's employer, C & S Chemical, Inc., (collectively referred to as respondents), for personal injuries sustained in an accident which occurred on July 26, 1990, on U.S. Highway 60 West, in Bartow, Florida. On July 26, McDougald was driving behind a tractor-trailer which was driven by Perry. ... As Perry drove over some railroad tracks, the 130-pound spare tire came out of its cradle underneath the trailer and fell to the ground. The trailer's rear tires then ran over the spare, causing the spare to bounce into the air and collide the windshield of McDougald's Jeep Wagoneer.

The spare tire was housed in an angled cradle underneath the trailer and was held in place by its own weight. Additionally, the tire was secured by a four to six-foot long chain with one-inch links, which was wrapped around the tire. Perry testified that he believed the chain to be the original chain that came with the trailer in 1969. Perry also stated that, as originally designed, the chain was secured to the body of the trailer by a latch device. At the time of the accident, however, the chain was attached to the body of the trailer with a nut and bolt.

Perry testified that he performed a pretrip inspection of the trailer on the day of the accident. This included an inspection of the chain, although Perry admitted that he did not check every link in the chain. After the accident, Perry noticed that the chain was dragging under the trailer. Perry opined that one of the links had stretched and slipped from the nut which secured it to the trailer.[fn] The judge instructed the jury on the doctrine of *res ipsa loquitur.* The jury subsequently returned a verdict in McDougald's favor.

On appeal, the district court reversed... . The district court concluded that the trial court erred by ... instructing the jury on *res ipsa loquitur.* ... For the reasons expressed herein, we quash the decision below and approve the Fifth District's application of *res ipsa loquitur* to the circumstances of a wayward automobile wheel accident. ...

... In *Marrero[v. Goldsmith*, 486 So.2d 530 (Fla. 1986)], we stated: "Res ipsa loquitur is a Latin phrase that translates "the thing speaks for itself." [C] It is a rule of evidence that permits, but does not compel, an inference of negligence under certain circumstances. '[T]he doctrine of *res ipsa loquitur* is merely a rule of evidence. Under it an inference may arise in aid of the proof.' *Yarbrough v. Ball U-Drive System*, 48 So.2d 82, 83 (Fla.1950). In *Goodyear[Tire & Rubber Co. v. Hughes Suply, Inc.*, 358 So.2d 530 (Fla. 1982)], a products liability case, we explained the doctrine as follows: 'It provides an injured plaintiff with a common-sense inference of negligence where direct proof of negligence is wanting, provided certain elements consistent with negligent behavior are present. Essentially the injured plaintiff must establish that the instrumentality causing his or her injury was under the exclusive control of the defendant, and that the accident is one that would not, in the ordinary course of events, have occurred without negligence on the part of the one in control.' *Goodyear*, 358 So.2d at 1341-42, (footnotes omitted)." *Marrero*, 486 So.2d at 531.

In concluding that it was reversible error for the trial court to give the *res ipsa loquitur* instruction, the Second District determined that "McDougald failed to prove that this accident would not, in the ordinary course of events, have occurred without negligence by the defendants." [C] The court explained that, "[t]he mere fact that an accident occurs does not support the application of the doctrine." [C] In support of the Second District's conclusion, respondents cite to *Burns v. Otis Elevator Co.*, 550 So.2d 21 (Fla. 3d DCA 1989), in which the Third District stated: "To prevail at trial, plaintiff must still present sufficient evidence, beyond that of the accident itself, from which the jury may infer that the accident would not have occurred but for the defendants' breach of due care." *Id.* at 22. Respondents assert that this language means that *res ipsa loquitur* did not apply in this case... .

The Second and Third Districts misread and interpret too narrowly what we stated in *Goodyear*. We did not say, as those courts conclude, that "the mere fact that an accident occurs does not support the application of the doctrine." Rather, we stated: "An *injury standing alone, of course, ordinarily does not indicate negligence. The doctrine of res ipsa loquitur simply recognizes that in rare instances an injury may permit an inference of negligence if coupled with a sufficient showing of its immediate, precipitating cause.*" *Goodyear*, 358 So.2d at 1342 (emphasis added). *Goodyear* and our other cases permit latitude in the application of this common-sense inference when the facts of an accident in and of themselves establish that but for the failure of reasonable care by the person or entity in control of the injury producing object or instrumentality the accident would not have occurred. On the other hand, our present statement is not to be considered an expansion of the doctrine's applicability. We continue our prior recognition that *res ipsa loquitur* applies only in "rare instances."

The following comments in section 328D of Restatement (Second) of Torts (1965) capture the essence of a proper analysis of this issue: "*c. Type of event*. The first requirement for the application of the rule stated in this Section is a basis of past experience which reasonably permits the conclusion that such events do not ordinarily occur unless someone has been negligent. There are many types of accidents which commonly occur without the fault of anyone. The fact that a tire blows out, or that a man falls down stairs is not, in the absence of anything more, enough to permit the conclusion

that there was negligence in inspecting the tire, or in the construction of the stairs, because it is common human experience that such events all too frequently occur without such negligence. On the other hand there are many events, such as those of objects falling from the defendant's premises, the fall of an elevator, the escape of gas or water from mains or of electricity from wires or appliances, the derailment of trains or the explosion of boilers, where the conclusion is at least permissible that such things do not usually happen unless someone has been negligent. To such events res ipsa loquitur may apply."
... Restatement (Second) of Torts § 328D cmts. c-d (1965).

We conclude that the spare tire escaping from the cradle underneath the truck, resulting in the tire ultimately becoming airborne and crashing into McDougald's vehicle, is the type of accident which, on the basis of common experience and as a matter of general knowledge, would not occur but for the failure to exercise reasonable care by the person who had control of the spare tire. As the Fifth District noted, the doctrine of *res ipsa loquitur* is particularly applicable in wayward wheel cases. [Cc] ... [C]ommon sense dictates an inference that both a spare tire carried on a truck and a wheel on a truck's axle will stay with the truck unless there is a failure of reasonable care by the person or entity in control of the truck. Thus an inference of negligence comes from proof of the circumstances of the accident. ...

Respondents also contend that the *res ipsa* instruction was inapplicable because McDougald failed to prove that direct evidence of negligence was unavailable. ... Here, ... we find that there was insufficient evidence available to McDougald. The likely cause of this accident, the chain and securing device, were in the exclusive possession of respondents and were not preserved. ...

Accordingly, we quash the decision below, and remand this case with directions that the district court reinstate the trial court's judgment as to respondents' liability based upon the jury's verdict and for further proceedings consistent with the district court's decision on issues related to damages.

It is so ordered. ...

ANSTEAD, Justice, concurring. I fully concur in the majority opinion, and write separately to note that this case presents a classic scenario whereby an aged appellate opinion giving rise to a legal doctrine in the distant past still illuminates and informs today's society. The thread of common sense in human experience ties today's decision to an opinion voiced by Baron Pollock in the 1863 decision in *Byrne v. Boadle,* 2 Hurlet & C. 722, 159 Eng. Rep. 299 (Ex. 1863). ... We can hardly improve upon this explanation for our decision today. The common law tradition is alive and well.

> **Ethics**
>
> A plaintiff's lawyer will not be able to please every client, particularly when the client's expectations for a recovery substantially exceed the merits and value of the claim. Plaintiff's lawyers walk a fine line between expressing confidence in themselves, their clients, and their clients' claims, on one hand, and the frank evaluation necessary to the client's informed decision on settlement, on the other hand. See ABA Model Rules of Professional Conduct, Rule 2.1 ("a lawyer shall ... render candid advice"). Clients are free to terminate the representation and may do so when a lawyer or circumstance does not meet their expectations. What becomes then of the lawyer's contingency fee? The terms of the fee agreement will control, if the fee agreement complies with the ethics rules and other law. A common term grants the plaintiff's lawyer a lien on the client's eventual recovery, for that portion of the fee the lawyer had earned before the client terminated

> the representation. Rule 1.8(i) of the ABA Model Rules of Professional Conduct permits such liens if authorized by law.

INQUIRY

More Res Ipsa Loquitur. Should the plaintiff have the benefit of res ipsa loquitur when plaster falls from a hotel-room ceiling injuring plaintiff (a guest) while in bed? *See* Mintzer v. Wilson, 21 Cal. App.2d 85, 68 P.2d 370 (Cal. App. 1937) (yes). In claims against an airline when an airplane crashes destroying evidence of crash causes? *See* Cox v. Northwest Airlines, Inc., 379 F.2d 893 (7th Cir. 1967) (yes). In a claim against the manager of a fertilizer plant that explodes? *See* Collins v. N-Ren Corp., 604 F.2d 659 (10th Cir. 1979) (yes). In a claim against the rancher whose cattle are found outside the fenced pasture and on a highway? *See* Roberts v. Weber & Sons, 248 Neb. 243, 533 N.W.2d 664 (1995) (yes—split among jurisdictions). In a claim against the driver of a motor vehicle that leaves the highway, striking a roadside object? *See* Bagby v. Commonwealth, 424 S.W.2d 119 (Ky. 1998) (yes); Bavis v. Fonte, 241 Md. 123, 215 A.2d 739 (1966) (yes); Badela v. Karpowich, 152 Conn. 360, 206 A.2d 838 (1965) (yes—majority rule). Should the plaintiff have the benefit of res ipsa loquitur in a claim against a warehouse owner for a fire that destroys the warehouse? *See* Valley Props. Ltd. Ptnrshp. V. Steadman's Hdwe., Inc., 251 Mont. 242, 824 P.2d 250 (1992) (no). In a claim against a property owner for an elevator closing against the plaintiff and bouncing back open? *See* Isaacs v. Warren Terrace, Inc., 60 Ohio Op.2d 214, 277 N.E.2d 88 (1971) (no). In a claim against the manufacturer of a television set that burns? *See* Gast v. Sears Roebuck & Co., 39 Ohio St.2d 29, 68 Ohio Op.2d 17, 313 N.E.2d 831 (1974) (no). In a claim gainst the manufacturer of an escalator that stops suddenly? *See* Barretta v. Otis Elevator Co., 242 Conn. 169, 698 A.2d 810 (1997) (no).

Expert Testimony. In *McDougald, supra,* the court held that expert testimony was not necessary to establish that the injury-causing event would not have happened in the absence of negligence. In other cases, expert testimony may be necessary to prove that the event would not have happened without negligence. *See* States v. Lourdes Hosp., 792 N.E.2d 151 (N.Y. 2003) (expert medical testimony permitted to educate jury on what injuries would be due to substandard care); Brannon v. Wood, 251 Or. 349, 444 P.2d 558 (1968) (expert testimony necessary to establish negligence in spinal surgery resulting in paralysis below incision site). Should the law allow expert testimony in res-ipsa-loquitur cases where, in theory, the event itself speaks of negligence? *See* Newell v. Westinghouse Elec. Corp., 36 F.3d 576 (7th Cir. 1994) (yes, relating to elevator failure); Mireles v. Broderick, 117 N.M. 445, 872 P.2d 863 (1994) (yes, for medical-malpractice claim); *but cf.* Scott v. James, 731 A.2d 399 (D.C. App. 1999) (inference of negligence must be within jurors' common knowledge). In using expert testimony, does the plaintiff run some risk that the court will find an explanation available and reject res ipsa loquitur? *See* Dover Elevator Co. v. Swann, 334 Md. 231, 638 A.2d 762 (1994) (expert's testimony precludes application of doctrine); *see also* Bargmann v. Soll Oil Co., 253 Neb. 1018, 574 N.W.2d 478 (Neb. 1998) (allegations of specific acts or omissions constituting negligence precludes res ipsa loquitur); *but cf.* Weaks v. Rupp, 966 S.W.2d 387 (Mo. Ct. App. 1998) (res ipsa loquitur available as an alternative to specific theory of furnace's malfunction causing carbon-monoxide poisoning).

Exclusive Control. Must the plaintiff prove that the defendant had exclusive control over the circumstances producing the injury? *Compare* Harris v. Amtrak, 79 F. Supp.2d 673 (E.D. Tex. 1999) (yes—res ipsa loquitur not available where defendant did not have exclusive control over train-car doors); Holzhauer v. Saks & Co., 346 Md. 328, 697 A.2d 89 (1997) (yes—res ipsa loquitur not available in claim against retailer for sudden escalator stop, where emergency-stop buttons were accessible to patrons); Larson v. St. Francis Hotel, 83 Cal. App.2d 210, 188 P.2d 513 (1948) (yes—res ipsa loquitur not available for claim against hotel for injury due to armchair being thrown from hotel window, where event may have been guest's, not hotel staff's, fault), *with* Errico v. LaMountain, 713 A.2d 791 (R.I. 1998) (no—res ipsa loquitur available for claim against landlord for apartment balcony giving way when leaned against by guest); Robert v. Aircraft Investment Co., 575 N.W.2d 672 (N.D. 1998) (no—res ipsa loquitur available in claim against installer of aircraft engine, even though installation had occurred years earlier after which other mechanics had made minor repairs); Hill v. Thompson, 484 P.2d 513 (Okl. 1971) (no—res ipsa loquitur available in claim against vehicle driver who parked car on hill four hours earlier, and car eventually ran down hill); Restatement (Second) of Torts §328D(1)(b) (rejecting strict "exclusive control" requirement in favor of "other responsible causes" "are sufficiently eliminated" formulation).

Defendant's Knowledge. Courts sometimes address the exclusive-control requirement in terms of defendant's superior knowledge of the circumstances and superior ability to come forward with the evidence. *See* Reese v. Memorial Hosp., 955 P.2d 425 (Wyo. 1998) (res ipsa loquitur not available unless a showing is made that defendant had superior knowledge and means of explaining the occurrence). Scholarship on the subject tends to agree on this rationale for the doctrine. But many cases do not follow that formulation of the rule. Should, for instance, res ipsa loquitur be available where the putative defendant died or disappeared in the accident that caused the injury, such that the putative defendant has no opportunity at all to come forward with an explanation? *See* Johnson v. Foster, 202 So.2d 520 (Miss. 1967) (doctrine available where vehicle driver and passenger both die in single-car accident); Burkett v. Johnston, 39 Tenn. App. 276, 282 S.W.2d 647 (1955) (same).

Multiple Defendants. Another issue related to the exclusive-control requirement is what to do with multiple potential defendants. In Ybarra v. Spangard, 25 Cal.2d 486, 154 P.2d 687 (1944) (reproduced in pertinent part in the section below on professional negligence), the California Supreme Court permitted a plaintiff to proceed on res ipsa loquitur in a claim against an entire surgical team, when the plaintiff awoke from the surgery with a traumatic injury to a part of the body unrelated to the surgery. A few courts have followed *Ybarra* in the medical-malpractice field, especially in hospital cases, *see* Anderson v. Somberg, 338 A.2d 1 (N.J. 1975); Beaudoin v. Watertown Mem. Hosp., 145 N.W.2d 166 (Wis. 1966), while others have rejected it, *see* Talbot v. W.H. Groves Latter-Day Saints Hosp., Inc., 440 P.2d 872 (Utah 1968). Courts have generally not extended it outside the hospital context. *See* Esco Oil & Gas, Inc., v. Sooner Pipe & Supply Corp., 962 S.W.2d 193 (Tex. Ct. App. 1998) (res ipsa loquitur not available in claim against several defendants over order, manufacture, and distribution of leaky pipes); Samson v. Riesing, 62 Wis.2d 698, 215 N.W.2d 662 (1974) (res ipsa loquitur not available in food-poisoned plaintiff's claim against several defendants each of whom had cooked food independently of the others); *but see* Estate of Chin v. St. Barnabas Med. Ctr., 734 A.2d 778 (N.J. 1999) (res ipsa loquitur available as to multiple defendants in products liability); Martinides v. Mayer, 208 Cal. App.3d 1185, 256 Cal. Rptr. 679 (Cal. Ct. App. 1989) (res ipsa loquitur available in claim against two defendants in hit-and-run accident, where plaintiff was unable to show which of two was driving).

Practice

The plaintiff's lawyer had long been waiting to hear the telephone call. "Look," the lawyer on the other end of the line was saying, "If we pay your 22-grand lien for fees out of the one-third contingency fee, then I'm looking at just 8-grand for my own fees. Give me a break." The plaintiff's lawyer gave a broad smile to himself but kept his tone serious. "No, just send me the check. I did my work, and I am sure that it was much to your benefit," the plaintiff's lawyer replied before politely saying goodbye, hanging up the telephone—and only then giving a great big chuckle to himself. The plaintiff's lawyer had worked hard and long, and with substantial expertise, to get the former client a substantial settlement offer—just under $100,000. The other lawyer had then suddenly come out of nowhere to "steal" the client but had barely been able to improve the offer after 18 more months of delay. It was a shame for the client, but it had been the client's choice. It was a greater shame that the other lawyer had misled the client into thinking that the other lawyer could get a substantially greater offer. "No," the plaintiff's lawyer thought to himself, "I earned that fee"—calculated (according to the contingency-fee agreement) based on the hours the lawyer had worked on the case.

Effects of Res Ipsa Loquitur. Finally, what should the effect of res ipsa loquitur be, when the doctrine is available? As the summary above indicates, most cases hold that the doctrine creates an inference of negligence, *see* Sullivan v. Crabtree, 36 Tenn. App. 469, 258 S.W.2d 782 (1953); George Foltis, Inc. v. New York, 287 N.Y. 108, 38 N.E.2d 455 (1941), although a few hold for a rebuttable presumption or even that it shifts the burden of proof, especially with respect to common carriers, *see* Transcontinental Bus System v. Simons, 367 P.2d 160 (Okla. 1961) (res ipsa loquitur shifts proof burden). Should any circumstances, perhaps like *Byrne v. Boadle*, find the inference of negligence so compelling that the court should grant summary judgment or direct a verdict in the plaintiff's favor? *See* Moore v. Atchison, T. & S.F.R. Co., 28 Ill. App.2d 340, 171 N.E.2d 393 (1960) (trains colliding head-on compels finding of negligence as a matter of law). What if the court does not instruct the jury on res ipsa loquitur but the doctrine is necessary to uphold the jury's verdict for plaintiff on appeal? *See* Grajales-Romero v. American Airlines, Inc., 194 F.3d 288 (1st Cir. 1999) (verdict affirmed on basis of res ipsa loquitur even in absence of jury instruction).

3. Violation of Statute

OBJECTIVE: Given negligence claims in which the defendant or potential defendant violated a statute when causing the injury as to which negligence is claimed, assess and describe the effect of that violation on the negligence claims, consistent with your study of this section of the text.

Case Study: A 17-year old girl piled four other girls in her convertible and headed for the cruising strip. State law prohibited any driver the 17-year-old's age from having more than one other person her age or younger in the vehicle if no adults were also present in the vehicle. The girl's vehicle collided with a tree that had fallen across the road resulting in the injury of one of the other girls when force threw her from her perch atop the backseat of the vehicle. *Assess and describe the effect of the girl's violation of the state law on a negligence claim against her by the injured girl.*

Another way in which parties establish the standard of care is through evidence that the party violated a safety statute. Statutes that require or prohibit conduct are legislative and representative judgments that persons ought to follow a standard of conduct in the situation the statute addresses. Depending on the statute's purpose, those standards may establish standards of care for tort actions, even though the statutes do not expressly so provide. Provisions of a state traffic code are examples. The codes are often criminal, quasi-criminal, civil-infraction, or administrative codes or a combination, making no explicit reference to tort claims. Yet tort practitioners plead and prove their violation to establish the standard of care and its breach in motor-vehicle-negligence cases. Authorities may not have cited the defendant with a statutory violation. Indeed, except in motor-vehicle accident cases (where traffic tickets are frequently issued in connection with a crash), practitioner generally plead and prove statute violations as evidence of breach without benefit of any citation or charge. Even in the case of traffic tickets, the fact of the citation itself may be inadmissible. The plaintiff may have to call the charging officer as a witness to the underlying violation of the statute. Yet even with this constraint, the violation of statute can compel a finding of duty breached.

Distinguish statutes indirectly establishing a tort-law standard of care (those this section addresses) from statutes that expressly create a tort-type cause of action, like consumer-protection and civil-rights statutes. *See* Hickle v. Whitney Farms, Inc., 148 Wash.2d 911, 64 P.3d 1244 (2003) (hazardous-waste disposal statute creates express cause of action). For instance, the federal Consumer Product Safety Act expressly creates a tort-style remedy for knowing violations of safety standards or rules of the Consumer Product Safety Commission. *See* 15 U.S.C. §§2072 (private remedy provision). Other federal statutes do *not* expressly create a statutory right of action but may indirectly establish standards of care. They include the National Traffic and Motor Vehicle Safety Act, 15 U.S.C. §§1381 et seq., the Occupational Safety and Health Act, 29 U.S.C. §§651 et seq., the Flammable Fabrics Act, 15 U.S.C. §§1191 et seq., and the Federal Hazardous Substances Act, 15 U.S.C. §§1261 et seq. Distinguish statutes establishing a standard of care from statutes, like wrongful-death acts, that extend tort remedies to additional classes of beneficiaries. Also, distinguish standard-of-care statutes from statutes like worker's compensation exclusive-remedy provisions and no-fault acts that bar tort actions, and statutes like damages caps that limit and shape tort remedies.

Practice

The family was ecstatic over their new home and, their lawyer felt, much more in control. Theirs had been a desperate situation. Mother and father both worked to support their three daughters—especially their profoundly mentally disabled daughter who required round-the-clock care. The teenage child could not feed herself or communicate. She was growing strong and was able to walk but spent most of her time in a wheelchair, and still wore diapers. The family's sacrifice to keep her at home (mom and dad working staggered shifts) was amazing. The problem had been that the school to which she went each day was refusing to pick her up in front of her home, as the law required. For months her mother struggled to carry her through slush and snow that the wheelchair could not negotiate, to a bus stop well down the street—and sometimes back home when the bus did not appear—while rude school officials continued to refuse the parents' increasingly

> urgent requests. It did not help tensions that this incredibly hard-working and resilient family was minority while the insensitive school officials were not. The last straw was when the mother hurt her back carrying the child to the bus stop and had to take critical time off work. The parents retained the lawyer who sued under the statute that created a private right of action. The school finally relented and complied. The modest monetary settlement turned out to be just enough for the family to make a down payment on a small home—with, for the first time ever, a fenced yard and appropriately furnished room for their profoundly disabled daughter. The burden of the child, literally borne on the back of her mother, had become a gift of a new home.

Using or attempting to use a statutory violation to establish a standard of care in a tort case can raise several issues. A first substantive issue is whether the statute creates a tort-law standard. *See* Charbourne v. Kappaz, 779 A.2d 293 (D.C. 2001) (statute providing that "[n]o owner of an animal shall allow the animal to go at large" was too vague to establish liability for injury by an escaping dog). As the cases below show, the answer ordinarily depends on whether the tort was within the risks the legislature meant the statute to discourage and the tort victim was within the class of persons the legislature meant the statute to protect. This two-prong class-and-risk analysis makes sense, considering tort law's twin policies to deter risk-producing behavior and compensate victims for its harm. The Restatement (Third) of Torts: Liability for Physical and Emotional Harm §14 captures the two prongs, stating, "An actor is negligent if, without excuse, the actor violates a statute that is designed to protect against the type of accident the actor's conduct causes, and if the accident victim is within the class of persons the statute is designed to protect."

A second issue is what the effect should be on the tort case when a statutory violation exists. The violator does not simply lose the tort case, and the violator's victim win. Rather, states split three ways on the effect on a tort claim of a statutory violation. Some states label the violation *negligence per se* and require the violating defendant to prove an excuse—shifting the burden of proof to the defendant. Others hold that a violation gives rise to a *presumption* of negligence that the violating defendant must rebut—leaving the ultimate burden of proof on the plaintiff but shifting the burden of production to the defendant. Others simply hold that the violation permits an *inference* of negligence—shifting no burdens but adding to the overall evidence. A final issue is what constitutes a statute for purposes of these rules—should it include administrative regulations promulgated pursuant to statute and local ordinances? Consider the following case as an introduction.

Dalal v. City of New York
New York Supreme Court, Appellate Division
692 N.Y.S.2d 468 (App. Div. 1999)

MEMORANDUM BY THE COURT. In an action to recover damages for personal injuries, the plaintiff appeals from a judgment of the Supreme Court, Queens County (Price, J.), dated May 28, 1998, which, upon a jury verdict finding, *inter alia,* that the defendant Alicia Ramdhani-Mack was not negligent, is in favor of that defendant and against him, dismissing the complaint.

ORDERED that the judgment is reversed, on the law, and a new trial is granted, with costs to abide the event.

The instant action arises out of an automobile accident that occurred at the intersection of Booth Street and 66th Avenue in Queens. The action against the defendant City of New York was discontinued prior to trial. At trial, the plaintiff testified that he stopped at the stop sign controlling traffic on 66th Avenue, and looked both ways for a distance of about one block, without seeing anything, before he proceeded into the intersection. When he was about halfway through the intersection, his vehicle was struck on the driver's side by a vehicle operated by Alicia Ramdhani-Mack (hereinafter the defendant). The plaintiff further testified that he never saw the defendant's car until impact. The defendant testified that she was about 10 to 15 feet away from the intersection when she noticed the plaintiff's vehicle, which was about 14 feet behind the stop sign but moving, and that about 5 to 7 seconds elapsed from the time that she observed the plaintiff's vehicle until the collision. She stated that she attempted to swerve out of the way, but could not avoid the collision. The defendant further testified that although she was nearsighted and required prescription glasses, she was not wearing her glasses at the time of the accident. She claimed she was still able to see while driving. There was no evidence that either driver was speeding. The jury returned a verdict finding that only the plaintiff was negligent, and that his negligence was the sole proximate cause of the accident.

The plaintiff contends that the trial court erred in refusing to charge that the defendant's violation of Vehicle and Traffic Law § 509(3) was negligence per se, and erred in refusing to allow him to cross-examine the defendant on that issue. Vehicle and Traffic Law § 509(3) provides that "no person shall operate any motor vehicle in violation of any restriction contained on his license." The defendant testified at her examination before trial that her New York State driver's license contained a restriction requiring her to wear corrective lenses while driving.

It is well established that an unexcused violation of a statutory standard of care, if unexplained, constitutes negligence per se ([cc]). The defendant's reliance upon the principle that operating a motor vehicle without a license is not negligence per se ([cc]) is misplaced. The absence or possession of a driver's license relates only to the authority for operating the vehicle and not to the manner thereof ([cc]). However, a restriction placed upon the license requiring the wearing of glasses when driving relates directly to the actual operation of the vehicle. Vehicle and Traffic Law § 509(3) provides that no one shall operate a vehicle in violation of any restriction contained on his or her license, and also relates to the manner in which the vehicle is being operated. Thus, the statute sets up a standard of care, the unexcused violation of which is negligence per se. The trial court erred, therefore, in refusing the plaintiff's request to charge. ...

In view of the verdict, we cannot conclude that these errors were harmless. The plaintiff is therefore entitled to a new trial.

INQUIRY

Applicability of Statute. In many cases like *Dalal* above, the statute clearly establishes a standard of care because it obviously relates to safety. Does the *Dalal* opinion adequately explain why the statute established a standard in that case? Can you articulate a general rule for these cases from it? As the *Dalal* case suggests, parties may not ordinarily use licensing statutes to establish standards of care—although aspects of them (like specific safety-related restrictions on licenses) might establish standards. *See* Kronzer v. First Natl. Bank, 235 N.W.2d 187 (Minn. 1975) (practicing law without a license not a basis for malpractice liability); Fielding v. Driggers, 190 S.E.2d 601 (Ga. Ct. App. 1972) (failure to obtain driver's license is not a basis for negligence liability for motor vehicle accident); Riddell v. Little, 488 S.W.2d 34 (Ark. 1972) (unlicensed operation of aircraft not a basis for negligence liability); Hertz Driv-Ur-Self System v. Hendrickson, 109 Colo. 1, 121 P.2d 483 (1942) (19-year-old unlicensed driver not subject to negligence-per-se treatment); *see also* Fuller v. Sirois, 97 N.H. 100, 82 A.2d 82 (1951) (driving on a suspended license is not a statutory violation from which one can construe evidence of negligence in the vehicle's operation); Brown v. Shyne, 151 N.E. 197 (N.Y. 1926) (fact that defendant physician in medical-malpractice case was unlicensed has no bearing on case). Can you think of other situations in which statutes should not establish a tort-law standard of care—where their violation is unrelated to the safety issue at hand? *See* Chevron U.S.A., Inc. v. Forbes, 783 So.2d 1215 (Fla. App. 2001) (gas station's violation of fire-safety statute to clean up gas spills quickly not negligence per se in customer's claim for slipping and falling in gasoline); Victor v. Hedges, 91 Cal. Rptr.2d 466 (Ct. App. 1999) (when plaintiff was struck on sidewalk by a third person's van while defendant showed plaintiff defendant's vehicle which was parked on sidewalk, fact that defendant had violated statute prohibiting vehicles from being parked on sidewalks was not related to van's striking plaintiff and did not establish negligence per se); Thoma v. Kettler Bros., Inc., 632 A.2d 725 (D.C. 1993) (potential purchaser of townhouse injured while viewing premises was not entitled to negligence-per-se treatment of seller's violation of OSHA workplace regulation).

Criminal Statutes. Justice Traynor authored a well-known opinion on statutes as standards of care, in Clinkscales v. Carver, 22 Cal.2d 72, 136 P.2d 777 (1943). The opinion noted that criminal statutes do not create civil liabilities. At most, they formulate standards of conduct to determine civil liability "only because the court accepts it." "When a legislative body has generalized a standard from the experience of the community and prohibits conduct that is likely to cause harm, the court accepts the formulated standards and applies them." The reasons that a court would do so could include that rights (even ones defined by criminal law) should have remedies (even ones provided by tort law), the legislature may have intended a civil action even though it did not say so, and the criminal statute (with which most people would comply) gives notice of the expected conduct. On these grounds, should a court construe a criminal statute to establish the standard of care in a jurisdiction where it did not apply? *See* Gaines-Tabb v. ICI Explosives USA, Inc., 160 F.3d 613 (10th Cir. 1998) (Kansas fertilizer-labeling statute does not establish standard of care for Oklahoma City federal building-bombing, negligence-per-se claims); *cf.* Sanchez v. Galey, 112 Idaho 609, 733 P.2d 1234 (1986) (federal regulation establishes standard of care as a matter of state law). Consider the following two cases where there were genuine disputes over that very issue, forcing the courts to articulate in greater clarity and detail the standard the courts must apply.

Wawanesa Mut. Ins. Co. v. Matlock
California Supreme Court
60 Cal. App.4th 583, 70 Cal. Rptr.2d 512 (1997)

SILLS, J. ... Timothy Matlock, age 17, bought two packs of cigarettes from a gas station one day in April 1993. Tim gave one of the packs to his friend, Eric Erdley, age 15. Smoking as they walked, the two trespassed onto a private storage facility in Huntington Beach, where a couple of hundred telephone poles were stacked up high upon the ground, held in place by two vertical poles sticking out of the ground. The two had climbed on the logs many times before.

Timothy and Eric were joined by two younger boys, about ten or eleven years old, who walked with them on the logs. Eric was smoking a cigarette held in his left hand. Timothy began to tease the younger boys, telling them the logs were going to fall. The boys started to run, though perhaps more out of laughter than of fear. One of the younger boys ran right into Eric's left arm. Eric dropped his cigarette down between the logs, where it landed on a bed of sand. For about 20 seconds Eric tried to retrieve the cigarette, but he couldn't reach it. He stood up and tried to extinguish it by spitting on it, and again was unsuccessful.

Then Eric caught up with Timothy who was about ten feet ahead. They went into some bunkers about 50 feet away; when they came out again after about twenty minutes, they saw flames at the base of the logs. They were seen running from the location.

The Woodman Pole Company suffered considerable property damage because of the fire. Eric was insured under a $100,000 policy with plaintiff Wawanesa Mutual Insurance Company. Wawanesa paid $89,000 to Woodman, $10,000 to the Orange County Fire Department, and $1,000 to the Huntington Beach Fire Department. Wawanesa, now subrogated to Eric's rights, filed this suit against Timothy and his father Paul Matlock for contribution.

After a bench trial, the court awarded the insurer $44,500 against Timothy and Paul, which included $25,000 against Paul based on a statute which fixes liability on a custodial parent for the willful misconduct of a minor. (See Civ.Code, § 1714.1, subd. (a).) ... The judge stated that the statute which makes it unlawful to give cigarettes to minors, Penal Code section 308, had to have been enacted in 1891 with "more than health concerns" in mind, "since the health issues on tobacco are of considerably more recent concern."[fn]

Timothy and his father Paul now appeal, arguing that there is no basis on which to hold Timothy liable for the damage caused when Eric dropped the cigarette.

We agree. There is no valid basis on which to hold Timothy liable. ...

Just because a statute has been violated does not mean that the violator is necessarily liable for any damage that might be ultimately traced back to the violation. As the court stated in *Olsen v. McGillicuddy* (1971) 15 Cal.App.3d 897, 902-903, 93 Cal.Rptr. 530: "The doctrine of negligence per se does not apply even though a statute has been violated if the plaintiff was not in the class of persons designed to be protected or the type of harm which occurred was not one which the statute was designed to prevent." Mere "but for" causation, as is urged in Wawanesa's brief, is simply not enough. The statute must be designed to protect against the *kind of harm* which occurred.

The statute that makes it illegal to furnish tobacco to minors, Penal Code section 308, has nothing to do with fire suppression. As it *now* stands, it is intended to prevent early *addiction* to tobacco. It may be true, as the trial court opined, that when the first version of the statute was enacted in 1891 (see Stats. 1891, ch. 70, p. 64, § 1) it was not directed primarily at protecting minors' health.[fn] But it is most certainly a health statute as it exists *today*. As our Supreme Court recently noted in *Mangini v. R.J.*

Reynolds Tobacco Co. (1994) 7 Cal.4th 1057, 1060, 31 Cal.Rptr.2d 358, 875 P.2d 73 (quoting from an affirmed decision of the Court of Appeal), section 308 "reflects a statutory policy of protecting minors from addiction to cigarettes." The connection of section 308 with health is emphasized by the court's specifically analogizing section 308 to former Health and Safety Code section 25967, which states that preventing children from "beginning to use tobacco products" is "among the highest priorities in *disease* prevention for the State of California." (See *Mangini, supra*, 7 Cal.4th at pp. 1061-1062, 31 Cal.Rptr.2d 358, 875 P.2d 73, emphasis added [quoting from appellate opinion quoting statute].)

Assuming, for sake of argument, that the Legislature did not have minors' health at heart when it prohibited giving tobacco to them in 1891, the placement of section 308 in chapter 7 of title 9 of the Penal Code, dealing with crimes against religion, conscience and "good morals," furnishes another answer. While we do not have the legislative history from 1891, it appears the statute was most probably enacted to protect minors from the general licentiousness associated with the consumption of cigarettes in the 1890's. (These days—though we recognize that there is altogether too much teenage tobacco smoking—cigarettes tend to be associated more with the World War II generation than with cheesy dens of iniquity.) However, we have found nothing, and certainly Wawanesa has cited us to nothing, which would show that Penal Code section 308 was ever enacted out of some concern that minors with cigarettes would pose a fire hazard.

Nothing suggests that section 308 is part of any scheme to prevent fires. Its placement in the general morals section of the Penal Code belies such an intent. ...

... Because there is no basis on which to hold Timothy liable we need not address the liability of his father. The judgment is reversed with directions to enter a new judgment in favor of Timothy and Paul Matlock. The Matlocks are to recover their costs on appeal.

Stachniewicz v. Mar-Cam Corp.
Oregon Supreme Court
259 Or. 583, 488 P.2d 436 (1971)

HOLMAN, J. The patron of a drinking establishment seeks to recover against the operator for personal injuries allegedly inflicted by other customers during a barroom brawl. The jury returned a verdict for defendant. Plaintiff appealed.

From the evidence introduced, the jury could find as follows:

A fight erupted in a bar between a group of persons of American Indian ancestry, who were sitting in a booth, and other customers who were at an adjacent table with plaintiff. One of plaintiff's friends had refused to allow a patron from the booth to dance with the friend's wife because the stranger was intoxicated. Thereafter, such threats as, "Hey, Whitey, how big are you?" were shouted from the booth at plaintiff and his companions. One of the persons at the table, after complaining to the bartender, was warned by him, "Don't start trouble with those guys." Soon thereafter, those individuals who had been sitting in the booth approached the table and one of them knocked down a person who was talking to a member of plaintiff's party. With that, the brawl commenced.

After a short melee, someone shouted "Fuzz!" and those persons who had been sitting in the booth ran out a door and into the parking lot, with one of plaintiff's friends in hot pursuit. Upon reaching the door, the friend discovered plaintiff lying just outside with his feet wedging the door open[and severe head injuries]. ...

The customers in the booth had been drinking in defendant's place of business for approximately two and one-half hours before the affray commenced.

The principal issue is whether, as plaintiff contends, violations of ORS 471.410(3) and of Oregon Liquor Control Regulation No. 10-065(2) constitute negligence as a matter of law. The portion of the statute relied on by plaintiff reads as follows: "(3) No person shall give or otherwise make available any alcoholic liquor to a person visibly intoxicated * * *."

The portion of the regulation to which plaintiff points provides: "(2) No licensee shall permit or suffer any loud, noisy, disorderly or boisterous conduct, or any profane or abusive language, in or upon his licensed premises, or permit any visibly intoxicated person to enter or remain upon his licensed premises."

The trial court held that a violation of either the statute or the regulation did not constitute negligence per se. It refused requested instructions and withdrew allegations of negligence which were based on their violation.

A violation of a statute or regulation constitutes negligence as a matter of law when the violation results in injury to a member of the class of persons intended to be protected by the legislation and when the harm is of the kind which the statute or regulation was enacted to prevent. [Cc] The reason behind the rule is that when a legislative body has generalized a standard from the experience of the community and prohibits conduct that is likely to cause harm, the court accepts the formulation. [C]

... The statute in question prevents making available alcohol to a person who is already visibly intoxicated. This makes the standard particularly inappropriate for the awarding of civil damages because of the extreme difficulty, if not impossibility, of determining whether a third party's injuries would have been caused, in any event, by the already inebriated person. Unless we are prepared to say that an alcoholic drink given after visible intoxication is the cause of a third party's injuries as a matter of law, a concept not advanced by anyone, the standard would be one almost impossible of application by a factfinder in most circumstances. ...

The regulation promulgated by the commission is an altogether different matter. The regulation requires certain conduct of licensees in the operation of bars. ...

ORS 471.030, entitled "Purpose of Liquor Control Act," provides, in part, as follows: "(1) The Liquor Control Act shall be liberally construed so as: (a) To prevent the recurrence of abuses associated with saloons or resorts for the consumption of alcoholic beverages. ..."

An examination of the regulation discloses that it concerns matters having a direct relation to the creation of physical disturbances in bars which would, in turn, create a likelihood of injury to customers. A common feature of our western past, now preserved in story and reproduced on the screen hundreds of times, was the carnage of the barroom brawl. No citation of authority is needed to establish that the "abuses associated with saloons," which the Liquor Control Act seeks to prevent, included permitting on the premises profane, abusive conduct and drunken clientele (now prohibited by the regulation) which results in serious personal injuries to customers in breach of the bar owner's duty to protect his patrons from harm. We find it reasonable to assume that the commission, in promulgating the regulation, intended to prevent these abuses, and that they had in mind the safety of patrons of bars as well as the general peace and quietude of the community. In view of the quoted purpose of the Act and of the history of injury to innocent patrons of saloons, we cannot assume otherwise.

In addition, we see no reason why the standard is not an appropriate one for use in the awarding of civil damages. Because plaintiff was within the class of persons intended to be protected by the regulation and the harm caused to him was the kind the statute was intended to prevent, we hold that the trial court erred in not treating the alleged violations of the regulation as negligence as a matter of law.[fn]

... We believe it would be fair for the jury to infer, in the circumstances set forth in the statement of the facts, that plaintiff was injured by one of the persons in the booth who had created the disturbance and that the injuries would not have occurred except for defendant's violation of the commission's regulation, as alleged.

The judgment of the trial court is reversed and the case is remanded for a new trial.

INQUIRY

Ordinances and Regulations. Courts typically give local ordinances similar effect as statutes when defining standards of care for tort law. *But see* Elliott v. City of New York, 95 N.Y.2d 730, 747 N.E.2d 760, 724 N.Y.S.2d 397 (2001) (ordinance violation is merely evidence of negligence, not negligence per se). The *Stachniewicz* case shows a court using a regulation, rather than a statute or ordinance, to define a standard of care. As the *Stachniewicz* case shows, administrative regulations enacted under statutory authority may be somewhat broader or significantly more detailed than the enabling legislation. Should regulations establish standards in all cases where an identical statute would have done so? *See* Walton v. Potlach Corp., 781 P.2d 229 (Idaho 1989) (violation of OSHA regulation treated as negligence per se in claim by independent contractor's employee) ; Bayne v. Todd Shipyards Corp., 568 P.2d 771 (Wash. 1977) (regulation's violation is negligence per se, recognizing that courts divide on the issue); *but see* Chambers v. St. Mary's School, 82 Ohio St.3d 563, 697 N.E.2d 198 (1998) (administrative regulation's violation does not warrant finding of negligence per se, but an inference may be drawn from it); Hansen v. Abrasive Engineering & Mfg., Inc., 317 Or. 378, 856 P.2d 625 (1993) (OSHA workplace regulation treated as equivalent to industry custom for purposes of equipment manufacturer's standard of care). Courts do not treat industry standards, promulgated by industry trade associations rather than by governmental agencies, like statutes, ordinances, and regulations. With a proper foundation laid by expert testimony, courts often treat industry standards as admissible evidence on the standard of care. *See* Lemery v. O'Shea Dennis, Inc., 112 N.H. 199, 291 A.2d 616 (1972).

Figure
Gerry Spence is among the best known and most successful of tort lawyers in the nation. His career path was much like many other tort lawyers, beginning as an assistant prosecutor where he gained substantial trial experience, and moving on to insurance defense work, before (as he put it) "seeing the light" and deciding to represent individual victims of wrong. Spence represented the estate of whistleblower Karen Silkwood, winning

> a $10.5 million-dollar verdict against her employer for radiation exposure, spawning a book and film about her life. He has won a $52 million-dollar verdict against McDonald's on behalf of a family-owned competitor, a $33 million-dollar verdict for a quadriplegic client against an insurance company, and other multi-million-dollar verdicts in medical-malpractice, nursing-care, and other torts cases. He also successfully defended Ruby Ridge-resident Randy Weaver on murder charges and Imelda Marcos on conspiracy charges. He has not lost a tort-case jury trial in 40 years. Spence, the author of 16 books and founder of several non-profits, conducts trial-lawyer training at his Wyoming ranch.

Class and Risk. What if the plaintiff was clearly in the class the statute meant to protect but did not need the protection? *See* Thomas v. Baltimore & O.R. Co., 19 Md. App. 217, 310 A.2d 186 (1973) (regulation requiring that defendant warn public of railway crossing does not establish standard of care as to plaintiff who already knew); *see also* Rains v. Bend of the River, 124 S.W.3d 580 (Tenn. App. 2003) (although illegal gun sale to minor was negligence per se, statutory violation was not the proximate cause of minor's suicide). Is there a specificity requirement—that the statute be more than a general guideline for good conduct? *See* Ridge v. Cessna Aircraft Co., 117 F.3d 126 (4th Cir. 1997) (FAA regulations too general to establish pilot's standard of care). Is a statute that prohibits an operator from leaving the key in the ignition of an unattended vehicle meant to stop only vehicle theft or also tort injuries caused by vehicle thiefs? May a statute have more than one purpose? *See* Kozkicki v. Dragon, 255 Neb. 248, 583 N.W.2d 336 (1998) (both—thief had wrecked four to five stolen vehicles); Vining v. Avis Rent-A-Car Systems, 354 So.2d 54 (Fla. 1977) (both); Ney v. Yellow Cab. Co., 2 Ill.2d 74, 117 N.E. 2d 74 (1954) (both); *see also* Hines v. Foreman, 243 S.W. 479 (Tex. Com. App. 1922) (statute prohibiting modification of vehicle exhaust pipes had dual purpose of abating noise and enabling vehicle operators to hear approaching hazards); *but see* DeCastro v. Boylan, 367 So.2d 83 (La. App. 1979) (unattended-vehicle statute meant only to protect against theft).

Other Factors. We have seen that the primary criteria for determining whether a statute establishes a tort-law standard of care are whether the plaintiff is within the class the statute protects and the plaintiff's harm within the hazard or risk. The Restatement (Second) of Torts §§287-288 states that statutes that protect the state, secure only public (not private or individual) rights, require service only to the public, protect a different class, protect a different interest, or protect against other harm or hazards, do not establish a standard of care. Courts also use other criteria based in public policy, to determine whether a statute establishes the tort-law standard of care. Another consideration may be whether the statute merely confirms or reinforces an existing common-law duty. Courts are reluctant to allow statutes to create duties not usually recognized by the common law, such as a duty to rescue. *See* Lacey v. United States, 98 F. Supp. 219 (D. Miss. 1951) (no duty to rescue); Cuffy v. City of New York, 505 N.E.2d 937 (N.Y. 1987) (same); *but see* Minn. Stat. Ann. §604A.01(1) (2001) (criminal statute requiring assistance to strangers if possible without danger or peril); Ky. Rev. Stat. §189.580(1) (2001) (those involved in a motor-vehicle accident have a duty to render or seek aid to others injured in the accident). Courts may not apply negligence-per-se rules to the conduct of children. *See* Bauman v. Crawford, 104 Wash.3d 241, 704 P.2d 1181 (1985). Fault remains an important consideration. Statutes that would, if taken as the tort-law standard, impose strict liability, less likely establish the standard.

Liability should also remain proportionate to the defendant's culpability and be an insurable risk. Consider the following illustrative case.

Perry v. S.N.,
Texas Supreme Court
973 S.W.2d 301 (Tex. 1998)

PHILLIPS, C.J. ... This is a suit for injuries arising out of the abuse of children at a day care center. Plaintiffs filed suit individually and as next friends of their two children, alleging that defendants witnessed the abuse and failed to report it to the police or child welfare officials. The sole issue before us is whether plaintiffs may maintain a cause of action for negligence per se based on the Family Code, which requires any person having cause to believe a child is being abused to report the abuse to state authorities and makes the knowing failure to do so a misdemeanor. ... We reverse the judgment of the court of appeals and render judgment that plaintiffs take nothing. ...

B.N. and K.N. attended a day care center operated by Francis Keller and her husband Daniel Keller from March 25, 1991, to August 28, 1991. Their parents, S.N. and S.N., allege that during that period, Daniel Keller regularly abused B.N. and K.N. and other children at the center both physically and sexually. Mr. and Mrs. N. brought suit against the Kellers and three of the Kellers' friends, Douglas Perry, Janise White, and Raul Quintero. Plaintiffs claim that Francis Keller confided in White at an unspecified time that Daniel Keller had "abusive habits toward children." They further allege that on one occasion in August 1991, while visiting the Kellers, defendants Perry, White, and Quintero all saw Daniel Keller bring a number of children out of the day care center into the Kellers' adjoining home and sexually abuse them. ... According to plaintiffs, Perry, White, and Quintero did not attempt to stop Daniel Keller from abusing the children or report his crimes to the police or child welfare authorities. ...

... Mr. and Mrs. N. alleged only that Perry, White, and Quintero were negligent per se because they violated a statute requiring any person who "has cause to believe that a child's physical or mental health or welfare has been or may be adversely affected by abuse" to file a report with the police or the Department of Protective and Regulatory Services. Tex. Fam.Code § 261.109(a). ... They claimed that Perry, White, and Quintero's failure to report the abuse proximately caused them harm by permitting the day care center to remain open, thus enabling Daniel Keller to continue abusing the children at the center. ...

The threshold questions in every negligence per se case are whether the plaintiff belongs to the class that the statute was intended to protect and whether the plaintiff's injury is of a type that the statute was designed to prevent. ... [T]he current Family Code provision governing the investigation of reports of child abuse states that "[t]he primary purpose of the investigation shall be the protection of the child." Tex. Fam.Code § 261.301(d).

B.N. and K.N. are within the class of persons whom the child abuse reporting statute was meant to protect, and they suffered the kind of injury that the Legislature intended the statute to prevent.[fn] But this does not end our inquiry. [C] The Court must still determine whether it is appropriate to impose tort liability for violations of the statute. [C] This determination is informed by a number of factors.... .

We first consider the fact that, absent a change in the common law, a negligence per se cause of action against these defendants would derive the element of duty solely from the Family Code. At common law there is generally no duty to protect another from the criminal acts of a third party or to come to the aid of another in distress. [Cc] ...

In contrast, the defendant in most negligence per se cases already owes the plaintiff a pre-existing common law duty to act as a reasonably prudent person, so that the statute's role is merely to define more precisely what conduct breaches that duty. ...

When a statute criminalizes conduct that is also governed by a common law duty, as in the case of a traffic regulation, applying negligence per se causes no great change in the law because violating the statutory standard of conduct would usually also be negligence under a common law reasonableness standard. [Cc] But recognizing a new, purely statutory duty "can have an extreme effect upon the common law of negligence" when it allows a cause of action where the common law would not. [C] In such a situation, applying negligence per se "bring[s] into existence a new type of tort liability." Burnette v. Wahl, 284 Or. 705, 588 P.2d 1105, 1109 (1978). The change tends to be especially great when, as here, the statute criminalizes inaction rather than action. [Cc] ...

The court of appeals in this case listed several factors to consider in deciding whether to apply negligence per se. [Cc] According to the court of appeals, the principal factors favoring negligence per se are that the Legislature has determined that compliance with criminal statutes is practicable and desirable and that criminal statutes give citizens notice of what conduct is required of them. [C] ...

On the question of notice, this Court has held that one consideration bearing on whether to apply negligence per se is whether the statute clearly defines the prohibited or required conduct. [Cc] The Family Code's reporting requirement is triggered when a person "has cause to believe that a child's physical or mental health or welfare has been or may be adversely affected by abuse or neglect." Tex. Fam.Code § 261.109(a). In this case, defendants allegedly were eyewitnesses to sexual abuse. Under these facts, there is no question that they had cause to believe abuse was occurring, and thus that the statute required them to make a report. In many other cases, however, a person may become aware of a possible case of child abuse only through second-hand reports or ambiguous physical symptoms, and it is unclear whether these circumstances are "cause to believe" that such conduct "may be" taking place.[fn] [C] A statute that conditions the requirement to report on these difficult judgment calls does not clearly define what conduct is required in many conceivable situations.[fn]

The next factor the court of appeals considered was whether applying negligence per se to the reporting statute would create liability without fault. [C] We agree with the court of appeals that it would not, because the statute criminalizes only the "knowing[ ]" failure to report.[fn] [Cc] This characteristic of the statute weighs in favor of imposing civil liability.

Our next consideration is whether negligence per se would impose ruinous liability disproportionate to the seriousness of the defendant's conduct. In analyzing this factor, the court of appeals treated child abuse as the relevant conduct. [C] The conduct criminalized by section 261.109, however, is not child abuse but the failure to report child abuse. Through its penal laws, the Legislature has expressed a judgment that abuse and nonreporting deserve very different legal consequences. ... This evidence of legislative intent to penalize nonreporters far less severely than abusers weighs against holding a person who fails to report suspected abuse civilly liable for the enormous damages that the abuser subsequently inflicts. The specter of disproportionate liability is particularly troubling when, as in the case of the reporting statute, it is combined with the likelihood of "broad and wide-ranging liability" by collateral wrongdoers... .

We conclude by noting that for a variety of reasons, including many of those we have discussed, most other states with mandatory reporting statutes similar to Texas's have concluded that the failure to report child abuse is not negligence per se. [Cc]

In summary, we have considered the following factors regarding the application of negligence per se to the Family Code's child abuse reporting provision: (1) whether the statute is the sole source of any tort duty from the defendant to the plaintiff or merely supplies a standard of conduct for an existing common law duty; (2) whether the statute puts the public on notice by clearly defining the required conduct; (3) whether the statute would impose liability without fault; (4) whether negligence per se would result in ruinous damages disproportionate to the seriousness of the statutory violation, particularly if the liability would fall on a broad and wide range of collateral wrongdoers; and (5) whether the plaintiff's injury is a direct or indirect result of the violation of the statute. Because a decision to impose negligence per se could not be limited to cases charging serious misconduct like the one at bar, but rather would impose immense potential liability under an ill-defined standard on a broad class of individuals whose relationship to the abuse was extremely indirect, we hold that it is not appropriate to adopt Family Code section 261.109(a) as establishing a duty and standard of conduct in tort. Therefore, Mr. and Mrs. N. and their children may not maintain a claim for negligence per se or gross negligence based on defendants' violation of the child abuse reporting statute. ...

For the foregoing reasons, we reverse the judgment of the court of appeals and render judgment that plaintiffs take nothing.

INQUIRY

Negligence Per Se. Finally, we come to the question of the effect of a violation of a statute that establishes a standard of care. Judge Cardozo authored another one of the more well-known opinions in this area, Martin v. Herzog, 126 N.E. 814 (N.Y. App. Ct. 1920). In *Martin*, the plaintiff violated a statute that required vehicle-headlight use after sunset. The trial court instructed the jury that it could treat the violation as evidence of contributory negligence. Judge Cardozo wrote, "We think the unexcused omission of the statutory signals is more than some evidence of negligence. It *is* negligence in itself. ... Jurors have no dispensing power by which they may relax the duty that one traveler on the highway owes under the statute to another. It is error to tell them that they have." The above cases that construe a statutory violation as negligence per se represent the rule advocated by Judge Cardozo and adopted by the great majority of courts. In those jurisdictions, the court will direct a verdict for the plaintiff if the defendant does not come forward with an excuse for the violation. In effect, the negligence-per-se rule requires the defendant to prove that circumstance compelled the violation, altering the conditions under which the court would apply the statute.

Presumptions and Inferences. Some courts have shaped other rules regarding the effect of a statutory violation on a tort claim. Can you sense from the above cases why courts might show some pause in treating statutory violations with such force? The middle ground, illustrated by the following case, construes the violation as giving rise to a presumption of negligence. The defendant must come forward with some evidence that the defendant was not negligent, or the court will direct a verdict for the plaintiff. Yet the defendant does not assume the burden in presumption states. Only the burden of producing evidence shifts. Once the defendant comes forward with evidence that the defendant was not negligent, the case will go to the jury with the plaintiff retaining the proof burden. A few remaining states treat the statutory violation as giving rise only to an inference of negligence, shifting no burdens—a significantly weaker effect. *See* Rev. Code Wash. §5.40.050; Kalata v. Anheuser-Busch Cos., 144 Ill.2d 425, 581 N.E.2d 656, 163 Ill. Dec. 502 (1991). As you read the following case, consider how the three different rules would affect your handling of the defense of a tort case in which your client violated a safety statute. What would be an acceptable excuse?

Zeni v. Anderson
Michigan Supreme Court
397 Mich 117, 243 N.W.2d 270 (1976)

WILLIAMS, J. Two issues confront us in this negligence case. The first is the effect of an alleged violation of statute by plaintiff. ... We hold that violation of a statute by plaintiff or defendant creates a prima facie case from which a jury may draw an inference of negligence. The jury may also consider whether a legally sufficient excuse has been presented to refute this inference. ...

The accident which precipitated this action occurred one snowy morning, March 7, 1969, when the temperature was 11 F, the sky was clear and the average snow depth was 21 inches. Plaintiff Eleanor Zeni, then a 56-year-old registered nurse, was walking to her work at the Northern Michigan University Health Center in Marquette. Instead of using the snow-covered sidewalk, which in any event would have required her to walk across the street twice to get to her job, she traveled along a well-used pedestrian snowpath, with her back to oncoming traffic.

Defendant Karen Anderson, a college student, was driving within the speed limit in a steady stream of traffic on the same street. Ms. Anderson testified that she had turned on the defroster in the car and her passenger said she had scraped the windshield. An eyewitness whose deposition was read at trial, however, testified that defendant's windshield was clouded and he doubted that the occupants could see out. He also testified that the car was traveling too close to the curb and that he could tell plaintiff was going to be hit.

Defendant's car struck the plaintiff on the driver's right side. ...

Ms. Zeni's injuries were serious and included an intra-cerebral subdural hematoma which required neurosurgery. She has retrograde amnesia and therefore, because she does not remember anything from the time she began walking that morning until sometime after the impact, there is no way to determine whether she knew defendant was behind her. ...

Testimony at trial indicated that it was common for nurses to use the roadway to reach the Health Center, and a security officer testified that in the wintertime it was safer to walk there than on the one sidewalk. Apparently, several days before the accident, Ms. Zeni had indeed fallen on the sidewalk. ...

Defendant, however, maintained that plaintiff's failure to use that sidewalk constituted contributory negligence because, she said, it violated M.C.L.A. s 257.655;

M.S.A. s 9.2355, which requires: "Where sidewalks are provided, it shall be unlawful for pedestrians to walk upon the main traveled portion of the highway. Where sidewalks are not provided, pedestrians shall, when practicable, walk on the left side of the highway facing traffic which passes nearest." ...

The jury found defendant "guilty of subsequent negligence" and awarded plaintiff damages of $30,000. ...

A. Violation of Statute as Rebuttable Presumption. In a growing number of states, the rule concerning the proper role of a penal statute in a civil action for damages is that violation of the statute which has been found to apply to a particular set of facts establishes only a prima facie case of negligence, a presumption which may be rebutted[fn] by a showing on the part of the party violating the statute of an adequate excuse[fn] under the facts and circumstances of the case. ...

This is the approach we follow today. ...

The approach is logical. Liability without fault is not truly negligence, and in the absence of a clear legislative mandate to so extend liability, the courts should be hesitant to do so on their own. ... The rule of rebuttable presumption has arisen in part in response to this concern, and in part because of the reluctance to go to the other extreme and in effect, discard or disregard the legislative standard.[fn] ...

B. Violation of Statute as Negligence Per Se. ... [T]he judge-made rule of negligence per se has still proved to be too inflexible and mechanical to satisfy thoughtful commentators and judges. It is forcefully argued that no matter how a court may attempt to confine the negligence per se doctrine, if defendant is liable despite the exercise of due care and the availability of a reasonable excuse, this is really strict liability, and not negligence. ... It is troublesome, too, that "potentially ruinous civil liability" may follow from a "minor infraction of petty criminal regulations," 49 Col.L.Rev. 21, 23, or may, in a jurisdiction burdened by contributory negligence, serve to deprive an otherwise deserving plaintiff of a much-needed recovery.

C. Violation of Statute as Evidence of Negligence. Just as the rebuttable presumption approach to statutory violations in a negligence context apparently arose, at least in part, from dissatisfaction with the result of a mechanical application of the per se rule, a parallel development in our state with respect to infractions of ordinances and of administrative regulations, has been that violations of these amount to only evidence of negligence. [Cc]

We have not, however, chosen to join that small minority[fn] which has decreed that violation of a statute is only evidence of negligence. In view of the fairness and ease with which the rebuttable presumption standard has been and can be administered, we believe the litigants are thereby well served and the Legislature is given appropriate respect.

... [W]e find the jury was adequately instructed as to the effect of the violation of this particular statute on plaintiff's case. ...

The Court of Appeals is reversed and the trial court is affirmed. Costs to the plaintiff.

INQUIRY

Excusing the Violation. Consider the following two cases. For each, determine if you would excuse the statute's violation: (1) Busby v. Quail Creek Golf & Country

Club, 885 P.2d 1326 (Okla. 1994) (defendant club may be excused from violating statute prohibiting sale of alcohol to a minor if it shows that minor used realistic false identification and it had no other means of knowing); and (2) Tedla v. Ellman, 19 N.E.2d 987 (1939) (plaintiff who violated statute requiring pedestrians to walk along a road facing the traffic, held to have an excuse to walk with her back to the traffic to minimize the traffic's effects). What do we decide when we ask whether law should excuse a violation? If the reasonableness of the violating actor's conduct determines excuse, are we back to basic tort principles—and not really considering the statute's effect? What may be going on here is that the statute changes who decides whether conduct is reasonable. The Restatement (Second) of Torts §288A, Comment J, gives the court the role of determining whether an excuse for a statutory violation exists (presumably, whether the violation was reasonable or not) but the jury the role of determining any fact issues as to the underlying conditions necessary to establish the excuse. Ordinarily, the jury would decide both the facts and the reasonableness of the conduct established by the facts. The Restatement (Third) of Torts: Liability for Physical and Emotional Harm §15 summarizes the conditions for excusing a violation of statute as follows:

> An actor's violation of a statute is excused and not negligence if:
> (a) the violation is reasonable in light of the actor's childhood, physical disability, or physical incapacitation;
> (b) the actor exercises reasonable care in attempting to comply with the statute;
> (c) the actor neither knows nor should know of the factual circumstances that render the statute applicable;
> (d) the actor's violation of the statute is due to the confusing way in which the requirements of the statute are presented to the public; or
> (e) the actor's compliance with the statute would involve a greater risk of physical harm to the actor or to others than noncompliance.

Reasonableness. On the question of the reasonableness of an actor's excuse, should a court permit evidence that others customarily violate the statute? *See* Robinson v. District of Columbia, 580 A.2d 1255 (D.C. App. 1990) (rejecting evidence that jaywalking in violation of crosswalk statute was the customary practice at the accident's location). Of what significance should it be, on the other hand, that an actor has complied with all safety statutes? Compliance with safety statutes may be relevant—though ordinarily, not conclusive—evidence that a party was not negligent. *See* Huntwork v. Voss, 525 N.W.2d 632 (Neb. 1995) (relevant evidence); *see also* Duncan v. Corbetta, 178 A.D.2d 459, 577 N.Y.S.2d 129 (1991) (actor might still be negligent even if complying with all safety statutes); *cf.* Deshotels v. Southern Farm Bureau Cas. Ins. Co., 164 So.2d 688 (La. Ct. App. 1964) (compliance with specific statute setting more than minimum standard for specific conduct may establish non-negligence as a matter of law).

Knowledge

When applying elements of tort claims to the facts, deductive reasoning has limited value in justifying legal conclusions. Another analytic skill is to state interests. Interests are the broader public motives for bringing about the client's more specific objective. Judges sometimes decide cases by weighing the interests they implicate. For example, individual and corporate clients may have interests in discouraging distracting litigation, avoiding adverse publicity, preserving reputation, preventing future claims or injuries, or educating the public or a specific community about significant dangers. Courts have interests in managing dockets, maintaining services, preserving integrity, and promoting public trust. Agencies have interests in protecting the public, preserving public order, protecting the environment, providing for orderly commerce, preserving public revenues, and promoting the economy.

Chapter VI

Causation

We live in a crucible of cause and effect, perhaps meaning to do good to others and perhaps not, but constantly challenged by the consequences of our actions. That sense of the untoward is no more acute than in tort law's treatment of causation. Causation is the third of the four elements of a negligence claim—duty, breach, causation, and damages. Causation has broader application, as an element of other torts in addition to negligence. Treating causation as an element of intentional torts makes less sense because the law presumes damages for most intentional-tort causes of action (assault, battery, false imprisonment, and trespass to land). When the evidence supports it, intentional-tort claimants may still argue that the defendant's actions caused the claimant damages, especially when those damages are greater than the nominal damages that a jury might award when presuming damages in intentional-tort actions. Yet negligence cases, which represent the bulk of tort practice, present the causation element most clearly. Negligence cases often involve disputes over causation.

Causation means a connection between the defendant's wrong and the harm for which the plaintiff demands that the defendant compensate. Causation is the tie that connects negligence to damages, binding the defendant to pay those damages. The plaintiff might suffer in several ways—destitute, homeless, missing a limb, in pain, humiliated, and embarrassed. Yet the defendant must compensate the plaintiff for only that suffering the defendant's tortious actions caused. If the defendant acted negligently, but the defendant's negligence caused plaintiff no harm, then the plaintiff will have no claim—even if the defendant's other, non-negligent actions did cause plaintiff harm. Lyons v. Midnight Sun Trans. Services, Inc., 928 P.2d 1202 (Alaska 1996), is an example. Plaintiff's decedent died in a collision when she drove her vehicle out from a stop sign into the path of defendant's speeding vehicle. The jury found the defendant negligent but also found that the defendant's negligence was not a cause of decedent's death—that, in effect, she would have died anyway, even if defendant had not been negligently speeding. The appellate court affirmed the defense verdict.

In its broadest sense, causation has not only logical and scientific but also equitable dimensions. Causation implies a scientific cause-and-effect relationship—especially obvious in a case such as one for the negligent marketing of a defective drug. Scientific evidence must establish that the drug produced compensable harms. If it had no such effect, then negligence in marketing had no effect. The plaintiff might suffer from other causes, but the cause-in-fact connection would be absent. Cause in fact is the first of two major studies within causation. Yet in a social context, causation also has equitable dimensions. Every life has many connections. Many acts arguably involve negligence. Logical or scientific cause-in-fact relationships may exist in so many ways that law must use some formulation other than scientific cause to limit the reach of tort liability. An example is the worker who negligently awakes ten minutes later than planned one morning and then is an innocent (non-negligent) participant in an accident on the way to work that would not have occurred but for the worker's being ten minutes behind the usual schedule. To the sensible mind, the late moment of the worker's awakening would have been pure fortuity in the accident's occurrence. Yet one harmed in the accident could argue that but-for the worker's negligent late awakening, the accident would not have happened—a causal connection. Thus, causation includes a second aspect known as *proximate* or *legal* cause, representing a policy judgment as to liability's extent. Proximate or legal cause is the second of two major studies within causation. Courts are not always so careful in their use of terms in this area, sometimes calling proximate cause what is instead clearly cause in fact. Consider first the topic of cause in fact.

A. Cause in Fact

OBJECTIVE: Given various negligence claims involving unusual injuries, apply cause-in-fact principles to determine whether that element is satisfied as to each claim, consistent with this text.

Case Study: A secretary negligently left the key in the door when leaving for the evening. The tenant of the next office noticed the key and decided to see if the secretary was in the office. While groping for the light switch inside the door, the tenant's hand touched a plug plugged into an outlet that an electrician had negligently installed against code immediately above the light switch. A cleaning-service employee had negligently loosened the plug while vacuuming. The tenant received a severe burn from the plug. **Determine and explain whether causation in fact exists as to the negligence of the secretary, cleaning-service employee, and electrician for the tenant's injury.**

As the above introduction states, cause in fact (also known as actual cause) is the scientific or *but-for* connection the plaintiff must make between the defendant's tortious conduct and the plaintiff's harm, for the plaintiff to satisfy this first aspect of the causation element of a negligence claim. The plaintiff must ordinarily show that but for the defendant's negligence, the plaintiff's harm or loss would not have occurred. The defendant's negligence (not merely the occurrence or accident) must bring about the plaintiff's harm or loss. But-for cause only begins to suggest the subtleties that causation proofs can generate. Indeed, causation has a lexicon all its own. The plaintiff's lawyer will shudder to hear the judge or opposing counsel describe the causation proofs as "guess," "conjecture," "speculation," or "mere possibility," because dismissal for lack of causation evidence is next. Causation must instead be a matter of probability, not possibility—indeed, under the traditional burden of proof, *more probable than not*. Watch closely for these and other similar verbal formulations as you consider the following two introductory cause-in-fact cases.

Jordan v. Jordan
Virginia Supreme Court
220 Va. 160, 257 S.E.2d 761 (1979)

PER CURIAM. Plaintiff, John Will Jordan, obtained a jury verdict of $6,000 for personal injuries suffered as a result of being struck by an automobile operated by his wife, Lena Jordan, the defendant. Judgment was entered on the verdict. …

The evidence shows that in the early afternoon of September 14, 1976, the Jordans drove to the home of a friend to pay a social visit. ...

Defendant, called as an adverse witness, testified that she left the friend's home by the front door approximately forty-five to fifty minutes after she had told her husband that she was not ready to leave. When she left the house, she looked for her husband but did not see him. She assumed that he had become angry and walked home through the woods, since such a walk took only five minutes. After she unlocked the door on the passenger's side of the car, she entered the automobile, closed the door, and slid across the seat to the driver's side. She started the motor and backed up in order to avoid a hole in the driveway and a truck that had been parked nearby. The car struck her husband after she had backed up one and one-half to two feet. She testified that she did not look behind her or use the rearview mirror before backing her car, and that she could not have seen her husband if she had looked immediately before backing because of his "squatting position" behind the car.

The plaintiff testified that he squatted down approximately three to four feet behind the left back side of the car about twenty to thirty minutes before his wife came out of the house and entered her automobile. ... The plaintiff said that he did not hear his wife leave the home and bid her friend good-bye, nor did he pay attention to the sound of the car door closing. The plaintiff attempted to move only after hearing the car engine start. When he stood up, the car knocked him down and ran over him. He sustained a broken leg, a fractured hip, and minor injuries.

To constitute actionable negligence, there must be a legal duty, a breach thereof, and a consequent injury which could have been reasonably foreseen by the exercise of reasonable care and prudence. [Cc] Negligence cannot be presumed from the mere happening of an accident, and the burden is on the plaintiff who alleges negligence to present evidence of preponderant weight from which a jury can find that the defendant's negligence was a proximate cause of the accident. [Cc] ...

The failure of the defendant to look in the rearview mirror at the very moment she started the engine and moved her car backward does not constitute actionable negligence under the evidence here. There is no evidence that the defendant could have seen the plaintiff if she had looked in the rearview mirror. Indeed, the uncontradicted testimony of the plaintiff indicates that her looking in the rearview mirror would not have detected his presence. Since there is no evidence to suggest that the plaintiff could have seen the defendant, we conclude that the defendant's failure to look in the rearview mirror did not cause the plaintiff's injuries and, therefore, does not constitute actionable negligence.

For the reasons stated, the judgment of the court below will be set aside and final judgment entered here for the defendant.

Reversed and final judgment.

Ethics

Plaintiff's lawyers often represent individuals who have physical, mental, and emotional injuries from torts that the clients retain the lawyers to address. Rule 1.14(a) of the ABA Model Rules of Professional Conduct requires a lawyer representing a client who has a diminished capacity to keep the professional relationship as normal as reasonably possible. That effort means that the lawyer will continue to meet and communicate with the client, and otherwise keep the client informed, even when it requires accommodations like home, hospital, and nursing home visits, wheelchair accommodation, and services for the sight or hearing impaired. Only when the client is

> unable to adequately act in the client's own interest may the lawyer consult about the client's matter with other individuals who have the ability to protect the client—and only then to the extent necessary to protect the client's interests, as Rule 1.14(b) and (c) provide.

Perkins v. Texas & New Orleans Ry. Co.
Lousiana Supreme Court
243 La. 829, 147 So.2d 646 (1962)

SANDERS, J. This is a tort action. Plaintiff, the 67-year-old widow of Tanner Perkins, seeks damages for the death of her husband in the collision of an automobile, in which he was riding, with a train of the defendant railroad. The district court awarded damages. The Court of Appeal affirmed.[fn] We granted certiorari to review the judgment of the Court of Appeal.

The tragic accident which gave rise to this litigation occurred at the intersection of Eddy Street and The Texas and New Orleans Railroad Company track in the town of Vinton, Louisiana, at approximately 6:02 a.m., after daylight, on September 28, 1959. At this crossing Eddy Street runs north and south, and the railroad track, east and west. Involved was a 113-car freight train pulled by four diesel engines traveling east and a Dodge automobile driven by Joe Foreman in a southerly direction on Eddy Street. Tanner Perkins, a guest passenger, was riding in the front seat of the automobile with the driver.

Located in the northwest quadrant of the intersection of the railroad track and Eddy Street was a warehouse five hundred feet long. ... This warehouse obstructed the view to the west of an automobile driver approaching the railroad crossing from the north on Eddy Street. It likewise obstructed the view to the north of trainmen approaching the crossing from the west. Having previously served on this route, the engineer and brakeman were aware of this obstruction.

To warn the public of the approach of trains, the defendant railroad had installed at the crossing an automatic signal device consisting of a swinging red light and a bell. At the time of the accident, this signal was operating. A standard Louisiana railroad stop sign and an intersection stop sign were also located at the crossing.

Proceeding east, the train approached the intersection with its headlight burning, its bell ringing, and its whistle blowing.

The engineer, brakeman, and fireman were stationed in the forward engine of the train. The engineer was seated on the right or south side, where he was unable to observe an automobile approaching from the left of the engine. The brakeman and fireman, who were seated on the left or north side of the engine, were looking forward as the train approached the intersection. These two crewmen saw the automobile emerge from behind the warehouse. At that time the front wheels of the automobile were on or across the north rail of the house track. The fireman estimated that the train was approximately 60 feet from the crossing when the automobile emerged from behind the warehouse. The brakeman, however, estimated that the train was 30 to 40 feet from the crossing at the time the automobile came into view. Both crewmen immediately shouted a warning to the engineer, who applied the emergency brakes. The train struck the right side of the automobile and carried it approximately 1250 feet. The two occupants were inside the automobile when it came to rest. Both were killed.

The speed of the automobile in which Tanner Perkins was riding was variously estimated from 3-4 miles per hour to 20-25 miles per hour.

The plaintiff and defendant railroad concede in their pleadings that Joe Foreman, the driver of the automobile, was negligent in driving upon the track in front of the train and that his negligence was a proximate cause of the death of Tanner Perkins.[fn]

It is conceded that the railroad's safety regulations imposed a speed limit of 25 miles per hour on trains in the town of Vinton. The plaintiff has conceded in this Court that this self-imposed speed limit was a safe speed at the crossing. The train was in fact traveling at a speed of 37 miles per hour.

Applicable here is the rule that the violation by trainmen of the railroad's own speed regulations adopted in the interest of safety is evidence of negligence.[fn] The rule has special force in the instant case because of the unusually hazardous nature of the crossing. We find, as did the Court of Appeal, that the trainmen were negligent in operating the train 12 miles per hour in excess of the speed limit.

As one of several defenses, the defendant railroad strenuously contends that the excessive speed of the train was not a proximate cause of the collision for the reason that the accident would not have been averted even had the train been traveling at the prescribed speed of 25 miles per hour. Contrariwise, the plaintiff contends that the speed of the train constituted a "proximate, direct and contributing cause" of the accident.

Thus presented, the prime issue in this case is whether the excessive speed of the train was a cause in fact[fn] of the fatal collision.

It is fundamental that negligence is not actionable unless it is a cause in fact of the harm for which recovery is sought.[fn] It need not, of course, be the sole cause. Negligence is a cause in fact of the harm to another if it was a substantial factor in bringing about that harm. Under the circumstances of the instant case, the excessive speed was undoubtedly a substantial factor in bringing about the collision if the collision would not have occurred without it. On the other hand, if the collision would have occurred irrespective of such negligence, then it was not a substantial factor.[fn]

The burden of proving this causal link is upon the plaintiff.[fn] Recognizing that the fact of causation is not susceptible of proof to a mathematical certainty, the law requires only that the evidence show that it is more probable than not that the harm was caused by the tortious conduct of the defendant.[fn] Stated differently, it must appear that it is more likely than not that the harm would have been averted but for the negligence of the defendant.

In the instant case the train engineer testified that at a speed of 25 miles per hour he would have been unable to stop the train in time to avoid the accident. Other facts of record support his testimony in this regard. With efficient brakes, the mile-long train required 1250 feet to stop at a speed of 37 miles per hour. It is clear, then, that even at the concededly safe speed of 25 miles per hour, the momentum of the train would have, under the circumstances, carried it well beyond the crossing. This finding, of course, does not fully determine whether the collision would have been averted at the slower speed. The automobile was also in motion during the crucial period. This necessitates the further inquiry of whether the automobile would have cleared the track and evaded the impact had the train been moving at a proper speed at the time the trainmen observed the automobile emerge from behind the warehouse.[fn] Basic to this inquiry are the speed of the automobile and the driving distance between it and a position of safety.

The testimony of the witnesses is in hopeless conflict as to the speed of the automobile at the time of the collision. ...

Although the record discloses that the train struck the automobile broadside, it does not reflect the driving distance required to propel the vehicle from the danger zone. ...

... [T]he plaintiff argues that had the train been traveling at a proper speed the driver of the automobile would "conceivably" have had some additional time to take measures to avert disaster and the deceased would have had some additional time to extricate himself from danger. Hence, the plaintiff reasons, the collision and loss of life "might not" have occurred.

... The record contains no probative facts from which the Court can draw a reasonable inference of causation under this theory. In essence, the argument is pure conjecture.

Based upon the evidence of record, it appears almost certain that the fatal accident would have occurred irrespective of the excessive speed of the train. It follows that this speed was not a substantial factor in bringing about the accident.

We conclude that the plaintiff has failed to discharge the burden of proving that the negligence of the defendant was a cause in fact of the tragic death. The judgment in favor of plaintiff is manifestly erroneous.

For the reasons assigned, the judgment of the Court of Appeal is reversed, and the plaintiff's suit is dismissed at her cost.

INQUIRY

Causation Scenarios. What must one do to determine whether a defendant's negligence caused harm or loss? Cause-in-fact issues require the practitioner to imagine how the scenario would have unfolded in the *absence* of negligence. One must assume that the defendant did *not* act negligently and then reconstruct whether the plaintiff would have suffered injury given that absence of the defendant's negligence. *See* Viner v. Sweet, 30 Cal.4th 1232, 70 P.3d 1046, 135 Cal. Rptr.2d 629 (2003) (causation requires comparing historical events to hypothetical scenarios). Has the plaintiff shown cause in fact if a defendant landowner negligently constructs a dam and an unprecedented storm sweeps away the defendant's dam and several others, causing the destruction of the plaintiff's property? *See* Restatement (Second) of Torts §432 (a), Comment *b*, Illus. 2 (no). Has the plaintiff shown cause in fact if the defendant railroad's engineer fails to continue to sound the train whistle while an eighty-seven-car train crosses a road, as required by statute, and a vehicle driver runs into the sixty-eighth car in the train? *See* Sullivan v. Boone, 205 Minn. 437, 286 N.W. 350 (Minn. 1939) (no because the driver would no longer have heard the whistle).

Proof of Causation. Determining what happened given the negligence to what would have happened in the absence of negligence can lead not only to conjecture but also proof problems. One of those problems may have to do with just what happened to cause the injury, when the parties know the fact of negligence and injury but not the connection between the two. Circumstantial evidence is certainly appropriate on causation issues, just as on other issues. Cause-in-fact evidence need not be direct evidence. A plaintiff can establish cause in fact by reasonable inferences drawn from proven circumstances. Yet the plaintiff must establish cause in fact beyond a mere possibility. The plaintiff must prove that the asserted cause was more probably than not the cause in fact. The following two cases illustrate causation-proof problems. In the first case, the one witness who would have known and been able to testify to the cause was unavailable because he had died allegedly because of the negligence. In the second case, the one witness who could have made the causal connection between the negligence and the harm was unable or unwilling to do so. As you read these cases, consider how you might have proven causation.

Skinner v. Square D Co.
Michigan Supreme Court
445 Mich 153, 516 N.W.2d 475 (1994)

CAVANAGH, C.J. Plaintiffs, representatives for the decedent Chester W. Skinner, appeal from the Court of Appeals decision affirming the trial court's grant of the defendant's motion for summary disposition....

We find that the plaintiffs failed to offer evidence from which reasonable minds could infer that the alleged defect caused the decedent's death. ...

I

[The opinion borrowed the Court of Appeals summary of the facts:] Plaintiffs brought this products liability action against defendant, Square D Company, following the death of plaintiffs' decedent, Chester W. Skinner. Mr. Skinner was electrocuted by his own homemade tumbling machine on which he had installed a switch manufactured by defendant. ...

[Mr. Skinner] was in the business of cleaning and finishing metal parts. To this end, [he] routinely used a homemade tumbling machine that he had designed and built himself. ..

Because of the way Mr. Skinner had designed the machine, reversing the direction of the drum's rotation was a dangerous task. The motor that turned the drum was controlled by a switch manufactured by defendant. Mr. Skinner had connected the Square D switch to the motor by using three wires with insulated "alligator clips" on the ends. In order to reverse the direction of the machine, the operator was required to disconnect two of the alligator clips from the motor by hand and reverse them. For obvious reasons, it was important for the operator to make sure that the Square D switch was in the "off" position before disconnecting the wires from the motor.

On February 21, 1986, Mr. Skinner was in his shop, working in the room with the tumbling machines. Mrs. Skinner and two other women, Beulah McBride and Violet Whiting, were in another room, racking parts. Suddenly, the women heard Mr. Skinner cry out. They ran into the room where Mr. Skinner was, and found him standing with his hands above his head, each hand grasping an alligator clip. Electric current was passing through Mr. Skinner's body. Aware of what was happening, Mr. Skinner cried out to the women, "don't touch me!" He then freed his left hand from the alligator clip and reached for the Square D switch. Mr. Skinner threw the switch into the "off" position, twisted, and fell over dead. ...

Plaintiffs claim that the Square D switch was defectively designed because it had a large "phantom zone" that sometimes made the switch appear to be "off" when it was actually "on." Plaintiffs assert that this defect proximately caused Mr. Skinner's death.

The defendant responds that, even assuming the switch is defective, the plaintiffs' evidence does not show that Mr. Skinner was misled by the switch when he was fatally electrocuted.[fn] ...

II

It is well settled under Michigan law that a prima facie case for products liability requires proof of a causal connection between an established defect and injury. [C] While the plaintiff bears the burden of proof, the plaintiff is not required to produce evidence that positively eliminates every other potential cause. Rather, the plaintiff's evidence is sufficient if it "establishes a logical sequence of cause and effect, notwithstanding the existence of other plausible theories, although other plausible theories may also have evidentiary support." ...

IV

So as to avoid any possible confusion, we make plain that the specific causation issue before the Court in this case is one of cause in fact, and not legal cause or "proximate cause." ...

The cause in fact element generally requires showing that "but for" the defendant's actions, the plaintiff's injury would not have occurred. [C] On the other hand, legal cause or "proximate cause" normally involves examining the foreseeability of consequences, and whether a defendant should be held legally responsible for such consequences. [Cc]

Because no one was present in the shop with the decedent immediately before the accident, the plaintiffs had to rely on circumstantial evidence to establish that the alleged defective switch was the cause in fact of the decedent's death. This Court has repeatedly recognized that plaintiffs may utilize circumstantial proof to show the requisite causal link between a defect and an injury in products liability cases. [Cc]

While plaintiffs may show causation circumstantially, the mere happening of an unwitnessed mishap neither eliminates nor reduces a plaintiff's duty to effectively demonstrate causation: "That there was no eyewitness to the accident does not always prevent the making of a possible issue of fact for the jury. But the burden of establishing proximate cause ... always rests with the complaining party, and no presumption of it is created by the mere fact of an accident." [C]

To be adequate, a plaintiff's circumstantial proof must facilitate reasonable inferences of causation, not mere speculation. In Kaminski v. Grand Trunk W.R. Co., 347 Mich. 417, 422, 79 N.W.2d 899 (1956), this Court highlighted the basic legal distinction between a reasonable inference and impermissible conjecture with regard to causal proof: "As a theory of causation, a conjecture is simply an explanation consistent with known facts or conditions, but not deducible from them as a reasonable inference. There may be 2 or more plausible explanations as to how an event happened or what produced it; yet, if the evidence is without selective application to any 1 of them, they remain conjectures only. On the other hand, if there is evidence which points to any 1 theory of causation, indicating a logical sequence of cause and effect, then there is a juridical basis for such a determination, notwithstanding the existence of other plausible theories with or without support in the evidence."

We want to make clear what it means to provide circumstantial evidence that permits a reasonable inference of causation. As Kaminski explains, at a minimum, a causation theory must have some basis in established fact. However, a basis in only slight evidence is not enough. Nor is it sufficient to submit a causation theory that, while factually supported, is, at best, just as possible as another theory. Rather, the plaintiff must present substantial evidence from which a jury may conclude that more likely than not, but for the defendant's conduct, the plaintiff's injuries would not have occurred.[fn] ...

... [T]he plaintiffs' circumstantial evidence here did not afford a reliable basis from which reasonable minds could infer that more probably than not, but for the defect in the Square D switch, Mr. Skinner would not have been electrocuted.

Plaintiffs' causation theory is that the faulty switch caused the decedent to be confused about whether the machine was on or off; that this confusion induced him to touch the live wires; and that this contact resulted in his electrocution. To support this theory, the plaintiffs offered testimony from co-workers who stated that, in the past, the decedent was always a careful worker, and always turned the power off before he manually reversed the alligator clips. On the basis of this testimony, the plaintiffs urge that the switch must have confused the decedent regarding whether the machine was on or off on the day that he touched the wires and that this confusion led to his electrocution. The lower courts explicitly exposed the critical problem with this theory.

If the machine had been operating, the decedent could not have been confused by the switch in the way that the plaintiffs contend. The plaintiffs do not dispute that when the tumbler is running, it makes a considerable amount of noise, and that the drum moves in a circular motion. The decedent could not have been confused regarding the power's status because either the noise or the visual appearance of movement would have affirmatively cued him regarding whether the power was on or off-regardless of what the switch may have indicated.

... The plaintiffs proposed an hypothesis under which Mr. Skinner thought that the machine was off because of a faulty indication from the switch, the power was actually on, but the machine was not running because the wires were not attached to the alligator clips. Under this hypothetical situation, the following antecedent events would necessarily had to have transpired: the machine had to have been turned off, the wires then unhooked, and, the machine thereafter turned back on. This scenario is fatally flawed in two respects.

First, the plaintiffs failed to produce any evidence from which a jury could reasonably conclude that the wires were unhooked when Mr. Skinner began using the machine just before the accident. In fact, the only record evidence pertaining to how the wires and clips were maintained indicated that they would probably have been connected. Second, the plaintiffs did not offer any proof from which it rationally could be inferred how the machine would have been turned back on after the wires had been unhooked.[fn]

Of course, the plaintiffs' offered scenario is a possibility. However, so are countless others. ...

Plaintiffs' expert testimony did not sufficiently establish causation. Plaintiffs' experts maintained that the switch was defective, and that the defect was the proximate cause of the decedent's death. The experts' causation theories were deficient, however, because each lacked a basis in established fact. Specifically, each expert either assumed, or was asked to assume, that (somehow) the wires were unhooked, and that the power was on when Mr. Skinner began working on the machine. Because the experts' conclusions regarding causation are premised on mere suppositions, they did not establish an authentic issue of causation. ...

Accordingly, we affirm the judgment of the Court of Appeals.

Gentry v. Douglas Hereford Ranch, Inc.
Montana Supreme Court
290 Mont. 126, 962 P.2d 1205 (1998)

TRIEWEILER, J. The plaintiff, John L. Gentry, brought this action in the District Court for the Seventh Judicial District in Wibaux County to recover damages from the defendants, Douglas Hereford Ranch, Inc., and Pard Cattle Company, for the wrongful death of Barbara Gentry, and for damages she sustained prior to her death. The District Court awarded summary judgment to both defendants. Gentry appeals from the District Court's order and judgment. We affirm the judgment of the District Court. ...

Defendant Douglas Hereford Ranch, Inc., is the owner of ranch land located in Wibaux County, Montana. ... Defendant Pard Cattle Company was the lessee of the ranch land.

... [O]n the morning of November 5, Brent Bacon drove from Wibaux, where the couple lived, to the ranch with the intention of first starting the furnace and then hunting for deer on the ranch property. He took with him a Marlin lever action 30-30 rifle and headed to the ranch in his personal vehicle.

On his way to the ranch, Brent observed a fox, loaded six or seven rounds of ammunition into the rifle magazine, "cocked in a shell," and fired one shot at the fox. He apparently missed and "cocked in a second shell," but was too late to fire a second shot. According to his statement to investigators, he then pulled the trigger and released the hammer so that the hammer was resting on a live round of ammunition. He then proceeded to the ranch...

Adjoining the house was a wooden deck accessed by two wooden steps. As Brent approached the deck, he was holding his rifle on his shoulder with his right hand. He had three of his fingers on the lever and one of them on the trigger. His thumb was on the hammer. At about the time he reached the deck, Barbara exited the house to retrieve a radio from the ranch pickup. She headed in the same direction that Brent was going and did not see him. As he reached the deck and was watching her, he stumbled and fell. Sometime after he stumbled, but before he landed on the deck, his rifle discharged; the bullet struck Barbara in the head; and, after surviving for a period of sixty-nine days, she died from the head injuries she sustained when she was shot.

In a taped interview given by Brent Bacon later in the day on November 5, he was asked the following question and gave the following answer:

> Q: You don't know how you slipped or ... ?
> A: I don't know how I slipped....

A negligence action requires proof of four elements: (1) existence of a duty; (2) breach of the duty; (3) causation; and (4) damages. If the plaintiff fails to offer proof of one of these elements, the action in negligence fails and summary judgment in favor of the defendant is proper. [C] The causation element requires proof of both cause in fact and proximate cause. [Cc] ...

Gentry alleged that the ranch company and the cattle company were negligent by failing to maintain the stairs to the deck adjoining the "new house" in a reasonably safe condition. He contended that the bottom stair was unstable and that the area leading to it was cluttered by debris, including a drain pipe, electric wires, and rocks. However, the defendants' motions for summary judgment were based on Bacon's testimony that he was unable to attribute his fall to any of those conditions. When he was deposed on May 2, 1997, he gave the following testimony in response to the following questions:

> Q: Do you remember stumbling as you started up the steps?
> A: I don't remember hardly anything. ...
> Q: And you don't remember exactly where you were when you began to stumble; is that right?
> A: That's correct.
> Q: And you don't know whether it was-whether there was even some object that caused you to slip or stumble; is that right?
> A: I don't remember anything. ...
> Q: You don't remember where you were?
> A: No.
> Q: And from the time after the rifle discharged, you don't know exactly where you were when you fell or what caused you to fall; is that right?
> A: Correct. ...
> Q: And you don't recall if you had even reached the steps at the time that you fell; is that right?
> A. That's correct. ...
> Q: Did you want to add something?
> A: Yes. I've stated umpteen numerous times that I don't remember if I tripped or if I was just clumsy or if I missed the step or hit it or whatever. I've stated that and stated that, and I don't recall.

Bacon also testified that while he had stumbled climbing those same steps prior to the incident in question, he had done so as the result of his own clumsiness, and not because of the condition of the steps.

In response to Bacon's deposition testimony, which was cited to the District Court in support of the defendants' motions for summary judgment, Gentry cited the District Court, and now cites this Court, to the following statement made by Bacon during an interview with investigators on November 16, 1995.

> TW: Okay. So, you remember stumbling, and you don't remember on what?
> BB: No, I don't remember if I went to step up on the step or if ... there's a rock there also underneath the step to keep it level. I don't think it was that, I think it was the step.

Gentry contends that based on this isolated statement a reasonable finder of fact could infer that it was the step which caused Bacon's fall. However, earlier in the same interview, he was asked the following question and gave the following answer:

> TW: Do you remember what you stumbled on?
> BB: No I don't.

... [T]he isolated statement relied on by Gentry does not support the contention that it was the condition of the step or the area surrounding the step which caused Bacon to stumble and fall. The most that could be inferred was that he was about to ascend the stairs when he did stumble and fall. Why he stumbled and fell would still require speculation. In the context of summary judgment proceedings, we have previously held that neither a suspicion nor speculation is sufficient to defeat a motion for summary judgment. ...

Gentry has offered no substantial evidence that any condition on the property owned by the ranch company and leased by the cattle company caused Bacon to stumble and fall immediately before his rifle discharged and struck the decedent, Barbara Gentry. Therefore, we conclude that cause in fact cannot be proven as a matter of law, and the District Court did not err when it held that the defendants, Douglas Hereford Ranch, Inc., and Pard Cattle Company were not negligent in a manner that contributed to the injuries and death of Barbara Gentry. ...

We affirm the judgment of the District Court.

> *Practice*
> The meeting was one of the most painful that the lawyer had ever conducted. Oh, the elderly couple was exceedingly polite toward and appreciative of the lawyer. Yet they were also despondent. Their adult daughter had been murdered by the father of her young son after a long-running and bitter custody dispute. The father had planted drugs in their daughter's car, accused her of sexually abusing her son, and, when that did not succeed in gaining him custody, tried to hire a hit man and then finally choked her to death himself in front of their son. The elderly couple now had custody of their grandson, whose murderer-father was in prison for life. The lawyer soberly explained to the elderly couple that, of course, he would open a probate estate and maintain a civil action against the murderer-father for their daughter's death. The elderly couple assured the lawyer that they wanted any recovery that resulted to go to the grandson. But the lawyer knew that with the murderer-father spending his life-savings on his criminal defense and secreting anything that remained, all of the lawyer's work for the elderly couple and their grandson would result in nothing more than an uncollectible judgment—and a deeply abiding sharing of the elderly couple's unmitigated pain.

INQUIRY

Presumptions. How does one prove or disprove causation when the one person who would be able to testify to it is unavailable—perhaps because the tort killed them? Cases such as Tarasoff v. Regents of the Univ. of California, 551 P.2d 334 (Cal. 1976), involving the necessity and efficacy of a warning, are good examples. *Tarasoff* involved a psychologist's failure to warn a third person that the psychologist's patient had threatened to kill her. In *Tarasoff*, the causation question was what effect the defendant psychologist's warning, if given, would have had on the decedent. If the psychologist had warned the decedent, would she have listened to the warning and changed her behavior? The courts have given some latitude to family members and others who knew the decedent to testify to the decedent's responsible character, allowing jurors to draw an inference that the decedent would have heeded the warning. *See* Affiliated Ute Citizens v. United States, 406 U.S. 128 (1972) (court may presume that persons to whom information should have been given would have conformed their conduct to take prudent account of the information); *cf.* Reisner v. Regents of the Univ. of California, 31 Cal. App.4th 1195 (1995) (plaintiff retains burden to show that plaintiff would have heeded defendant's warning that defendant's patient had HIV). See the section on the read-and-heed presumption for product warnings.

Coincidences. From the above *Gentry* case, is coincidence between the negligence and the harm enough to draw an inference of causation? The coincidence-establishing-cause question often arises in trip-and-fall or slip-and-fall cases. *See* Fedorczyk v. Caribbean Cruise Lines, Ltd., 82 F.3d 69 (3d Cir. 1996) (plaintiff slipping in bathtub without knowing why is not entitled to inference that her feet were between the negligently placed non-slip strips). But the coincidence question goes beyond falls. *See* Kramer Service, Inc. v. Wilkins, 184 Miss. 483, 186 So. 625 (1939) (1-out-of-100 possibility that skin cancer developed at site of cut caused by defendant's negligence not sufficient to take causation question to jury). The logical danger that the courts wish to avoid is reasoning by *post hoc ergo propter hoc*—because it happened after, it must have happened because. The best-known statement and illustration of the rule, Smith v. Rapid Transit, Inc., 58 N.E.2d 754, 755 (Mass. 1945), involved an unidentified bus that ran plaintiff's vehicle off the road. The plaintiff tried using transit schedules to identify the bus, but the court ruled that the probability of the defendant's bus having been the cause of the harm must be "more likely or probable in the sense that actual belief in its truth, derived from the evidence, exists in the mind or minds of the tribunal... ." Why is tort law so concerned with the causal connection when the plaintiff has already established both negligence and harm? Do you think that in some cases the reprehensibility of the tortious wrong influences the outcome of the causation issue? *See* Zuchowicz v. United States, 140 F.3d 381 (2d Cir. 1998) (causation established that negligent over-prescription of dangerous drug caused woman's fatal lung disease, despite no evidence that drug had caused disease in any other patient—no other women having been given such a dangerously high dose).

Expert Testimony. Parties often need to retain experts to resolve the causation issue. The next chapter on professional negligence addresses the peculiar expert-testimony issues for causation in medical, legal, and other malpractice cases. Yet in many other kinds of negligence cases, causation will involve sufficiently technical and scientific judgments that the jury must rely on experts. The validity of expert opinions on causation has been a large area of concern in tort law. The concern exists that juries have based at least some tort verdicts on "junk science." In two tort-law cases, Daubert v. Merrell Dow Pharmaceuticals, Inc., 509 U.S. 579 (1993), and Kumho Tire Co. v. Carmichael, 526 U.S. 137 (1999), the Supreme Court established standards for the admissibility of expert testimony in all federal cases. Evidence courses address this standard in depth. Suffice here to say that *Daubert* abandoned the former *Frye*-"general acceptance" test, under which expert testimony was admissible if the relevant scientific community generally accepted the opinions expressed. *Daubert* replaced the general-acceptance test with the requirement that the trial court act as a "gatekeeper" to ensure that expert evidence meets a methods-reliability standard based on factors including peer review and publication, testability, and error rate. *Kumho Tire* then extended that standard to all expert testimony—not just scientific testimony. Many (although not all) state courts and some legislatures have adopted the *Daubert* and *Kumho Tire* standards or similar standards. *See* Farm Bureau Mut. Ins. Co. v. Foote, 14 S.W.3d 512 (Ark. 2000) (adopting *Daubert* to exclude expert testimony on dog capabilities); *but see* Goeb v. Theraldson, 615 N.W.2d 800 (Minn. 2000) (rejecting *Daubert* in favor of preserving former general-acceptance principle). Consider now how the federal appellate court applied the *Daubert* standard, on remand of *Daubert*, to the causation issue in a tort case.

Daubert v. Merrell Dow Pharmaceuticals, Inc.
United States Court of Appeals, Ninth Circuit
43 F.3d 1311 (9th Cir. 1995)

KOZINSKI, C.J. On remand from the United States Supreme Court, we undertake "the task of ensuring that an expert's testimony both rests on a reliable foundation and is relevant to the task at hand." *Daubert v. Merrell Dow Pharmaceuticals, Inc.,* 509 U.S. 579... (1993). ...

Two minors brought suit against Merrell Dow Pharmaceuticals, claiming they suffered limb reduction birth defects[fn] because their mothers had taken Bendectin, a drug prescribed for morning sickness to about 17.5 million pregnant women in the United States between 1957 and 1982. [C] This appeal deals with an evidentiary question: whether certain expert scientific testimony is admissible to prove that Bendectin caused the plaintiffs' birth defects.

For the most part, we don't know how birth defects come about. We do know they occur in 2-3% of births, whether or not the expectant mother has taken Bendectin. [C] Limb defects are even rarer, occurring in fewer than one birth out of every 1000. [C] But scientists simply do not know how teratogens (chemicals known to cause limb reduction defects) do their damage: They cannot reconstruct the biological chain of events that leads from an expectant mother's ingestion of a teratogenic substance to the stunted development of a baby's limbs. Nor do they know what it is about teratogens that causes them to have this effect. No doubt, someday we will have this knowledge, and then we will be able to tell precisely whether and how Bendectin (or any other suspected teratogen) interferes with limb development; in the current state of scientific knowledge, however, we are ignorant.

Not knowing the mechanism whereby a particular agent causes a particular effect is not always fatal to a plaintiff's claim. Causation can be proved even when we don't know precisely *how* the damage occurred, if there is sufficiently compelling proof that the agent must have caused the damage *somehow*. One method of proving causation in these circumstances is to use statistical evidence. If 50 people who eat at a restaurant one evening come down with food poisoning during the night, we can infer that the restaurant's food probably contained something unwholesome, even if none of the dishes is available for analysis. This inference is based on the fact that, in our health-conscious society, it is highly unlikely that 50 people who have nothing in common except that they ate at the same restaurant would get food poisoning from independent sources.

It is by such means that plaintiffs here seek to establish that Bendectin is responsible for their injuries. They rely on the testimony of three groups of scientific experts. One group proposes to testify that there is a statistical link between the ingestion of Bendectin during pregnancy and limb reduction defects. These experts have not themselves conducted epidemiological (human statistical) studies on the effects of Bendectin; rather, they have reanalyzed studies published by other scientists, none of whom reported a statistical association between Bendectin and birth defects. Other experts proffered by plaintiffs propose to testify that Bendectin causes limb reduction defects in humans because it causes such defects in laboratory animals. A third group of experts sees a link between Bendectin and birth defects because Bendectin has a chemical structure that is similar to other drugs suspected of causing birth defects.

It is by such means that plaintiffs here seek to establish that Bendectin is responsible for their injuries. ...

Federal judges ruling on the admissibility of expert scientific testimony face a far more complex and daunting task in a post-*Daubert* world than before. ... Under *Daubert*, we must engage in a difficult, two-part analysis. First, we must determine nothing less than whether the experts' testimony reflects "scientific knowledge," whether their findings are "derived by the scientific method," and whether their work product amounts to "good science." [C] Second, we must ensure that the proposed expert testimony is "relevant to the task at hand," [c], i.e., that it logically advances a material aspect of the proposing party's case. ...

The first prong of *Daubert* puts federal judges in an uncomfortable position. The question of admissibility only arises if it is first established that the individuals whose testimony is being proffered are experts in a particular scientific field... . Yet something doesn't become "scientific knowledge" just because it's uttered by a scientist; nor can an expert's self-serving assertion that his conclusions were "derived by the scientific method" be deemed conclusive... . As we read the Supreme Court's teaching in *Daubert,* therefore, though we are largely untrained in science and certainly no match for any of the witnesses whose testimony we are reviewing, it is our responsibility to determine whether those experts' proposed testimony amounts to "scientific knowledge," constitutes "good science," and was "derived by the scientific method." ...

Our responsibility, then, unless we badly misread the Supreme Court's opinion, is to resolve disputes among respected, well-credentialed scientists about matters squarely within their expertise, in areas where there is no scientific consensus as to what is and what is not "good science," and occasionally to reject such expert testimony because it was not "derived by the scientific method." Mindful of our position in the hierarchy of the federal judiciary, we take a deep breath and proceed with this heady task. ...

... [T]he Court said, "in order to qualify as 'scientific knowledge,' an inference or assertion must be derived by the scientific method." [C] Our task, then, is to analyze not what the experts say, but what basis they have for saying it.

Which raises the question: How do we figure out whether scientists have derived their findings through the scientific method or whether their testimony is based on scientifically valid principles? Each expert proffered by the plaintiffs assures us that he has "utiliz[ed] the type of data that is generally and reasonably relied upon by scientists" in the relevant field, [c], and that he has "utilized the methods and methodology that would generally and reasonably be accepted" by people who deal in these matters, [c]. The Court held, however, that federal judges perform a "gatekeeping role," [c]; to do so they must satisfy themselves that scientific evidence meets a certain standard of reliability before it is admitted. ...

While declining to set forth a "definitive checklist or test," [c], the Court did list several factors federal judges can consider in determining whether to admit expert scientific testimony under Fed.R.Evid. 702: whether the theory or technique employed by the expert is generally accepted in the scientific community; whether it's been subjected to peer review and publication; whether it can be and has been tested; and whether the known or potential rate of error is acceptable. [C][fn] ...

That an expert testifies based on research he has conducted independent of the litigation provides important, objective proof that the research comports with the dictates of good science. *See* Peter W. Huber, Galileo's Revenge: Junk Science in the Courtroom

206-09 (1991) (describing how the prevalent practice of expert-shopping leads to bad science). ...

We have examined carefully the affidavits proffered by plaintiffs' experts, as well as the testimony from prior trials that plaintiffs have introduced in support of that testimony, and find that none of the experts based his testimony on preexisting or independent research. While plaintiffs' scientists are all experts in their respective fields, none claims to have studied the effect of Bendectin on limb reduction defects before being hired to testify in this or related cases.

If the proffered expert testimony is not based on independent research, the party proffering it must come forward with other objective, verifiable evidence that the testimony is based on "scientifically valid principles." One means of showing this is by proof that the research and analysis supporting the proffered conclusions have been subjected to normal scientific scrutiny through peer review and publication. [C]

Peer review and publication do not, of course, guarantee that the conclusions reached are correct; much published scientific research is greeted with intense skepticism and is not borne out by further research. But the test under *Daubert* is not the correctness of the expert's conclusions but the soundness of his methodology. [C]

Bendectin litigation has been pending in the courts for over a decade, yet the only review the plaintiffs' experts' work has received has been by judges and juries, and the only place their theories and studies have been published is in the pages of federal and state reporters. None of the plaintiffs' experts has published his work on Bendectin in a scientific journal or solicited formal review by his colleagues. Despite the many years the controversy has been brewing, no one in the scientific community—except defendant's experts—has deemed these studies worthy of verification, refutation or even comment. It's as if there were a tacit understanding within the scientific community that what's going on here is not science at all, but litigation.[fn]

Establishing that an expert's proffered testimony grows out of pre-litigation research or that the expert's research has been subjected to peer review are the two principal ways the proponent of expert testimony can show that the evidence satisfies the first prong of Rule 702.[fn] Where such evidence is unavailable, the proponent of expert scientific testimony may attempt to satisfy its burden through the testimony of its own experts. For such a showing to be sufficient, the experts must explain precisely how they went about reaching their conclusions and point to some objective source—a learned treatise, the policy statement of a professional association, a published article in a reputable scientific journal or the like—to show that they have followed the scientific method, as it is practiced by (at least) a recognized minority of scientists in their field. [C][fn]

Plaintiffs have made no such showing. As noted above, plaintiffs rely entirely on the experts' unadorned assertions that the methodology they employed comports with standard scientific procedures. In support of these assertions, plaintiffs offer only the trial and deposition testimony of these experts in other cases. While these materials indicate that plaintiffs' experts have relied on animal studies, chemical structure analyses and epidemiological data, they neither explain the methodology the experts followed to reach their conclusions nor point to any external source to validate that methodology. We've been presented with only the experts' qualifications, their conclusions and their assurances of reliability. Under *Daubert*, that's not enough. ...

In elucidating the second requirement of Rule 702, *Daubert* stressed the importance of the "fit" between the testimony and an issue in the case ... . Here, the pertinent inquiry is causation. In assessing whether the proffered expert testimony "will assist the trier of fact" in resolving this issue, we must look to the governing substantive standard, which in this case is supplied by California tort law.

Plaintiffs do not attempt to show causation directly; instead, they rely on experts who present circumstantial proof of causation. Plaintiffs' experts testify that Bendectin is a teratogen because it causes birth defects when it is tested on animals, because it is similar in chemical structure to other suspected teratogens, and because statistical studies show that Bendectin use increases the risk of birth defects. Modern tort law permits such proof, but plaintiffs must nevertheless carry their traditional burden; they must prove that their injuries were the result of the accused cause and not some independent factor. In the case of birth defects, carrying this burden is made more difficult because we know that some defects—including limb reduction defects—occur even when expectant mothers do not take Bendectin, and that most birth defects occur for no known reason.

California tort law requires plaintiffs to show not merely that Bendectin increased the likelihood of injury, but that it more likely than not caused *their* injuries. [C] In terms of statistical proof, this means that plaintiffs must establish not just that their mothers' ingestion of Bendectin increased somewhat the likelihood of birth defects, but that it more than doubled it—only then can it be said that Bendectin is more likely than not the source of their injury. Because the background rate of limb reduction defects is one per thousand births, plaintiffs must show that among children of mothers who took Bendectin the incidence of such defects was more than two per thousand.[fn]

None of plaintiffs' epidemiological experts claims that ingestion of Bendectin during pregnancy more than doubles the risk of birth defects.[fn] ... While plaintiffs' epidemiologists make vague assertions that there is a statistically significant relationship between Bendectin and birth defects, none states that the relative risk is greater than two. These studies thus would not be helpful, and indeed would only serve to confuse the jury, if offered to prove rather than refute causation. A relative risk of less than two may suggest teratogenicity, but it actually tends to *dis*prove legal causation, as it shows that Bendectin does not double the likelihood of birth defects.[fn] ...

As the district court properly found below, "the strongest inference to be drawn for plaintiffs based on the epidemiological evidence is that Bendectin could *possibly* have caused plaintiffs' injuries." [C] ... Plaintiffs do not quantify this possibility, or otherwise indicate how their conclusions about causation should be weighted, even though the substantive legal standard has always required proof of causation by a preponderance of the evidence.[fn] ...

The district court's grant of summary judgment is AFFIRMED.

INQUIRY

Reasonable Probability. In tort law generally, the plaintiff must prove causation to a more-probable-than-not (also known as "preponderance-of-the-evidence") standard. Would the reprehensibility of the misconduct in, say, toxic-tort cases be a reason to adopt a more relaxed causation standard? *See* Rubanick v. Witco Chem. Corp., 125 N.J. 421, 593 A.2d 733 (1991) (scientific-causation testimony for toxic torts warrants a broadened admissibility standard). Similarly, would the broad compensatory nature of worker's compensation and other no-fault schemes also warrant a more relaxed causation standard? *See* McAllister v. Workmen's Comp. Appeals Bd., 69 Cal.2d 408, 445 P.2d 313, 71 Cal. Rptr. 697 (1968) (causation testimony admissible in worker's compensation case if to a "reasonable probability"). In an especially noteworthy case, the appellate court in Gardner v. National Bulk Carriers, Inc., 310 F.2d 284 (4th Cir. 1962), held that the plaintiff proves causation when a ship's master refuses to return to search for a person who could have fallen overboard hours earlier (and thus had no chance of rescue) because the master has destroyed "the reasonable possibility of rescue." Do not expect courts to apply this broadened causation standard in the usual case.

Acting in Concert. Causation is satisfied as to all defendants who act in concert with respect to the harm. Thus, when one person encourages another to commit an assault, causation is present as to both persons when the assault occurs. *See* Loeb v. Kimmerle, 215 Cal. 143, 9 P.2d 199 (Cal. 1932). Or when one drag racer participates in a street race with another racer, and that other injures a third person, both racers have caused the other's injuries. *See* Agovino v. Kunze, 181 Cal. App.2d 591, 5 Cal. Rptr. 534 (1960).

Ethics

Defense lawyers constantly evaluate their clients' tort-liability risk, to plan litigation and settlement. Yet occasionally, a client will ask a defense lawyer to evaluate the client's tort liability for the benefit of a third party—perhaps for a bank so that the client may extend a line of credit, or for a prospective purchaser of a business to which the tort-liability attaches. The ABA Model Rules of Professional Conduct admonish in Rule 2.3(a) that a lawyer evaluating a client's matter for a third party may do so only if the lawyer "reasonably believes that making the evaluation is compatible with other aspects of the lawyer's relationship with the client." If the evaluation is likely to affect the client's matter, then Rule 2.3(b) requires that the lawyer not make the evaluation unless the client gives informed consent. Can a lawyer who is vigorously defending a client in tort litigation, on one hand, at the same time write a candid evaluation of the litigation for a third party, on the other hand? Would the opinion be discoverable by the opposition in the tort case? What if the opinion was dire—that the client was likely to lose in a manner that would seriously affect its finances? Defense lawyers hesitate to act as both an advocate and a neutral evaluator, and are more likely to advise the client to retain, or have the third party retain, other counsel to make the evaluation.

Multiple Causes. The law can sometimes use cause in fact to sort the relative liability of multiple tortfeasors for separate injuries occurring close in time or coincidentally, when the tortfeasors do not act in concert. If a nurse anesthetist negligently infects a patient by impermissibly re-using an anesthetic line and pump, at the same time that the surgeon severs the patient's nerves in the surgical site after failing to identify and retract them as the standard of care required, then the nurse may be liable for the infection injury and the physician for the nerve injury. Cause in fact is more complex when the actions of two or more defendants combine to cause the same harm. If primary and attending surgeons proceed in concert with a surgery without identifying and retracting the nerves as the standard of care required, with the result that they sever the nerves, then both will have caused the patient's nerve injury. The malpractice of each will have been a combining cause of the patient's injury. *See* LeJeune v. Allstate Ins. Co., 365 So.2d 471 (La. 1978) (common duty of deputy to clear intersection and driver to observe it were both but-for causes of injury); *see also* Nisbet v. Bucher, 949 S.W.2d 111 (Mo. Ct. App. 1997) (common responsibility of defendants for decedent's hazing death). Likewise, two negligent drivers who each drive their vehicles into an intersection without the appropriate care to observe and yield, and as a result collide causing injury to a passenger in one of the vehicles, will have combined to cause that passenger's injury. Neither alone would have been a cause, but both together are causes, and both are accordingly liable.

Preempted Causes. In the rare case, tortious action may have caused harm but for the fact that some other event first caused the harm. A motorist strikes and kills a pedestrian. A second motorist then negligently runs over the deceased pedestrian. The second motorist, though negligent, has not caused the deceased pedestrian's death. A different situation occurs when the defendant has negligently caused harm, but a subsequent event removes the injurious effect of the harm. Baker v. Willoughby, 2 W.L.R. 50 (H.L. 1970), is such a case in which the defendant injured the plaintiff's leg which surgeons subsequently amputated due to other causes. Although in *Baker* the House of Lords granted the plaintiff leg-injury damages for the rest of the plaintiff's expected life (notwithstanding the absence of the injured leg), and some American courts have followed *Baker*, *see* Spose v. Ragu Foods, Inc., 537 N.Y.S.2d 739 (Sup. Ct. 1989) (subsequent total disability from other cause does not bar partial disability claim from first cause), question the logic and soundness of holding a defendant liable beyond that period for which the plaintiff would have suffered damages. *See* Dillon v. Twin State Gas & Elec. Co., 163 A. 111 (N.H. 1932) (defendant subject to liability only for difference between crippling of boy from fall and death of boy from grabbing defendant's uninsulated power lines in an attempt to prevent fall); *see also* Candia v. Estepan, 734 N.Y.S.2d 37 (App. Div. 2001) (patient's estate has no cause of action for defendant physician's misdiagnosis of patient's disease where disease would have resulted in patient's death even if promptly diagnosed).

Substantial Factor. Cause in fact grows significantly more complex when coincident causes are not each but-for causes. In some cases, two or more negligent actors will have acted coincidentally to cause the same harm, under circumstances where the same harm would have occurred if only one of them acted. In these cases of multiple sufficient causes, but-for causation does not exist as to either actor's negligence. Each actor can say correctly that the harm would have occurred even without their own negligence. Yet it would obviously be inequitable to allow both negligent actors to escape liability and the plaintiff to bear the burden of the uncompensated harm. In those cases, the courts apply a *substantial-factor test* finding causation as to both actors even though the injury would have occurred without one of the actors. *See* Kingston v. Chicago & N.W. Ry., 211 N.W. 913 (Wis. 1927); Anderson v. Minneapolis, St. P. & S. St. M. R.R. Co., 146 Minn. 430, 179 N.W. 45 (1920). But-for causation applies unless producing obviously inequitable results, in the case of multiple sufficient causes, where the substantial-factor test instead applies. *See* Busta v. Columbus Hosp. Corp., 276 Mont. 342, 916 P.2d 122 (1996); Restatement (Second) of Torts §431 (1965). Concurrent independent causes arise where destructive agents (fire, water, toxic chemicals), unleashed by independent actors, reach the plaintiff or plaintiff's land coincidentally to cause the harm. *See* Rutherford v. Owens-Illinois, Inc., 16 Cal.4th 953, 941 P.2d 1203 (1997) (adopting substantial-factor test for plaintiff's injury from exposure to asbestos); *see also* Northington v. Marin, 102 F.3d 1564 (1996) (defendant deputy's labeling plaintiff a jailhouse snitch was a substantial factor, along with other deputies' doing the same act, in bringing about plaintiff's harm).

Trivial Causes. An insignificant contribution to harm is ordinarily not enough to establish causation. The one who flips a lit match into an already-blazing conflagration has not contributed to the blaze's harm. This concern—that we not hold persons liable for actions the causative effects of which are no more than trivial—gave rise to the *substantial-factor* label used in the multiple-sufficient-cause cases. The idea was that each cause of multiple causes must alone be substantial. Yet the two rules—(1) that liability for trivial causes is not recognized but (2) that liability for multiple sufficient causes is recognized—are actually independent rules. The Restatement (Third) of Torts: Liability for Physical Harm §27 (Tentative Draft Mar. 25, 2002) wisely abandons the "substantial factor" label for multiple sufficient causes. It states simply that, "When an actor's tortious conduct is not a factual cause of physical harm ... only because another causal set exists that is also sufficient to cause the physical harm at the same time, the actor's tortious conduct is a factual cause of the harm." As you read the following case illustrative of the substantial-factor test, followed by a second case involving a somewhat different causation issue, see if you can articulate the difference between the two cases and the principles they represent.

Horton v. Harwick Chem. Corp.
Ohio Supreme Court
73 Ohio St.3d 679, 653 N.E.2d 1196 (1995)

PFEIFER, J. We are asked in this case to set forth the appropriate summary judgment standard for causation in asbestos cases.... .

In *Pang v. Minch* (1990), 53 Ohio St.3d 186, 559 N.E.2d 1313, paragraph five of the syllabus, this court held that "[w]here a plaintiff suffers a single injury as a result of the tortious acts of multiple defendants, the burden of proof is on the plaintiff to demonstrate that the conduct of each defendant was a substantial factor in producing the harm." In the asbestos cases, the plaintiff also has the burden of proving exposure to asbestos-containing products. [C] ...

Medical science suggests that very limited exposure to asbestos can cause mesothelioma, perhaps the worst of asbestos-related diseases. [Cc]

Dr. Cohen described in his affidavit the process of "re-entrainment," by which the physical action of air movement, vibration, or physical trauma causes aerodynamically active asbestos fibers and particles to "take flight" and sail into the air. He stated that it was "more likely than not that some of the fibers and particles released in one corner of the [DTR] plant would travel on drafts and air currents throughout the plant, including to its furthest opposite point." Dr. Cohen stated that the theory that a worker would only be exposed to asbestos released in the immediate vicinity of his workplace is a "scientific impossibility," due to the aerodynamic quality of the fibers and the plant's inevitable air turbulence. Dr. Cohen stated that the plaintiffs "were more likely than not substantially exposed to asbestos and talc fibers and particles from all manufacturers whose asbestos and talc containing products were used in the [DTR] facility during the periods they worked there."

It is not the province of the judge to immediately foreclose the validity of testimony such as Dr. Cohen's. ...

The true worth of testimony like Dr. Cohen's is determined in the jury room when weighed against competing testimony. We are unwilling to close the door on the legitimacy of the "fiber drift" theory in every case in Ohio courts. ...

For each defendant in a multidefendant asbestos case, the plaintiff has the burden of proving exposure to the defendant's product and that the product was a substantial factor in causing the plaintiff's injury. A plaintiff need not prove that he was exposed to a specific product on a regular basis over some extended period of time in close proximity to where the plaintiff actually worked in order to prove that the product was a substantial factor in causing his injury.

Instead, we adopt the definition of "substantial factor" contained in Restatement of the Law 2d, Torts (1965), Section 431, Comment *a*: "The word 'substantial' is used to denote the fact that the defendant's conduct has such an effect in producing the harm as to lead reasonable men to regard it as a cause, using that word in a popular sense, in which there always lurks the idea of responsibility, rather than the so-called 'philosophical sense,' which includes every one of the great number of events without which any happening would not have occurred." ...

Judgments reversed and causes remanded.

Practice

Cross-examination is a powerful tool. The plaintiff motorcyclist had nearly lost his leg when a woman pulled her mini-van from a stop sign out in front of the motorcyclist—seemingly a clear-cut case of liability. Yet the motorcyclist was not a particularly sympathetic plaintiff—notwithstanding his very serious injury. He was single, had been out of work, and was living at home with his parents while tinkering with his motorcycle. And the trial judge had admitted testimony from a farmer who had been out behind his barn when he heard the motorcycle go by "winding it out," from which defense counsel argued that the accident was due to the motorcyclist's speeding—even if he did have the right-of-way. The bailiff and court reporter, both old friends of defense counsel, agreed with defense counsel's crowing that the jury would only be out five minutes before returning a no-cause verdict. Then the defense counsel made the mistake of calling his client as a defense witness. She did fine on direct examination—on the way home with her two daughters from soccer practice, looked both ways, never saw the motorcyclist, she testified. Yet on cross-examination, plaintiff's counsel patiently and ever so politely asked her each detail leading up to the accident, until she suddenly broke down in tears of apology for so seriously injuring the young man so negligently. As plaintiff's counsel handed her a tissue and said "no further questions, Your Honor," he looked at defense counsel whose head hung down staring at his legal pad. The verdict took just 25 minutes—for the plaintiff.

Summers v. Tice
California Supreme Court
33 Cal.3d 80, 199 P.2d 1 (1948)

CARTER, J. Each of the two defendants appeals from a judgment against them in an action for personal injuries. ...

Plaintiff's action was against both defendants for an injury to his right eye and face as the result of being struck by bird shot discharged from a shotgun. ... [P]laintiff and the two defendants were hunting quail on the open range. Each of the defendants was armed with a 12 gauge shotgun loaded with shells containing 7 1/2 size shot. Prior to going hunting plaintiff discussed the hunting procedure with defendants, indicating that they were to exercise care when shooting and to "keep in line." In the course of hunting plaintiff proceeded up a hill, thus placing the hunters at the points of a triangle. The view of defendants with reference to plaintiff was unobstructed and they knew his location. Defendant Tice flushed a quail which rose in flight to a ten foot elevation and flew between plaintiff and defendants. Both defendants shot at the quail, shooting in plaintiff's direction. At that time defendants were 75 yards from plaintiff. One shot struck plaintiff in his eye and another in his upper lip. Finally it was found by the court that as the direct result of the shooting by defendants the shots struck plaintiff as above mentioned and that defendants were negligent in so shooting and plaintiff was not contributorily negligent. ...

The problem presented in this case is whether the judgment against both defendants may stand. It is argued by defendants that ... there is not sufficient evidence to show which defendant was guilty of the negligence which caused the injuries the shooting by Tice or that by Simonson. ...

... [The trial court] determined that the negligence of both defendants was the legal cause of the injury or that both were responsible. Implicit in such finding is the assumption that the court was unable to ascertain whether the shots were from the gun of one defendant or the other or one shot from each of them. The one shot that entered plaintiff's eye was the major factor in assessing damages and that shot could not have come from the gun of both defendants. It was from one or the other only.

It has been held that where a group of persons are on a hunting party, or otherwise engaged in the use of firearms, and two of them are negligent in firing in the direction of a third person who is injured thereby, both of those so firing are liable for the injury suffered by the third person, although the negligence of only one of them could have caused the injury. ... When we consider the relative position of the parties and the results that would flow if plaintiff was required to pin the injury on one of the defendants only, a requirement that the burden of proof on that subject be shifted to defendants becomes manifest. They are both wrongdoers both negligent toward plaintiff. They brought about a situation where the negligence of one of them injured the plaintiff, hence it should rest with them each to absolve himself if he can. The injured party has been placed by defendants in the unfair position of pointing to which defendant caused the harm. If one can escape the other may also and plaintiff is remediless. Ordinarily defendants are in a far better position to offer evidence to determine which one caused the injury. This reasoning has recently found favor in this Court. In a quite analogous situation this Court held that a patient injured while unconscious on an operating table in a hospital could hold all or any of the persons who had any connection with the operation even though he could not select the particular acts by the particular person which led to his disability. Ybarra v. Spangard, 25 Cal.2d 486, 154 P.2d 687, 162 A.L.R. 1258. ...

In addition to that, however, it should be pointed out that the same reasons of policy and justice shift the burden to each of defendants to absolve himself if he can relieving the wronged person of the duty of apportioning the injury to a particular defendant, apply here where we are concerned with whether plaintiff is required to supply evidence for the apportionment of damages. If defendants are independent tort feasors and thus each liable for the damage caused by him alone, and, at least, where the matter of apportionment is incapable of proof, the innocent wronged party should not be deprived of his right to redress. The wrongdoers should be left to work out between themselves any apportionment. [C] …

The judgment is affirmed.

INQUIRY

Burden Shifting. *Summers v. Tice*, a well-known case, holds that the burden of proof on causation shifts to the defendants (that they must each disprove causation) when all were negligent, plaintiff cannot show whose negligence caused the harm, and the negligence of one or more unquestionably caused the harm. Can you think of other circumstances beyond hunting incidents where the burden-shifting rule of *Summers v. Tice* should apply? *See* Michie v. Great Lakes Steel Div., 495 F.2d 213 (6th Cir. 1974) (burden shifts to polluting defendants to disprove that their actions caused the harm); Huston v. Konieczny, 556 N.E.2d 505 (Ohio 1990) (plaintiff entitled to proceed on alternative-causation theory against any of several defendants who could have been the one to serve the intoxicated minor); Hood v. Hagler, 606 P.2d 548 (Okla. 1979) (burden shifts to defendant dog owners to disprove that their dog was the one who bit the plaintiff from behind); Haft v. Lone Palm Hotel, 3 Cal.3d 756, 91 Cal. Rptr. 745, 478 P.2d 465 (Cal. 1970) (burden of proof on causation shifts in drowning death of two in pool, where drownings were not witnessed and claim was for failure to provide a lifeguard); Cummings v. Kendall, 41 Cal. App.2d 549, 107 P.2d 282 (1940) (burden of proof on causation shifts to defendants in successive vehicle collisions, one of which killed plaintiff's decedent); *see also* James v. Bessemer Processing Co., 155 N.J. 279, 714 A.2d 898 (1998) (causation issue goes to jury where plaintiff adduced expert testimony that one of several chemicals manufactured by defendants caused his cancer). Consider one special circumstance that has challenged the traditional causation rules.

Sindell v. Abbott Laboratories
California Supreme Court
26 Cal.3d 588, 607 P.2d 924, 163 Cal. Rptr. 132,
cert. denied, 449 U.S. 912 (1980)

MOSK, J. This case involves a complex problem both timely and significant: may a plaintiff, injured as the result of a drug administered to her mother during pregnancy, who knows the type of drug involved but cannot identify the manufacturer of the precise product, hold liable for her injuries a maker of a drug produced from an identical formula?

Plaintiff Judith Sindell brought an action against eleven drug companies…. The complaint alleges [that b]etween 1941 and 1971, defendants were engaged in the business of manufacturing, promoting, and marketing diethylstilbesterol (DES), a drug which is a synthetic compound of the female hormone estrogen. The drug was administered to plaintiff's mother and the mothers of the class she represents,[fn] for the purpose of preventing miscarriage. … DES may cause cancerous vaginal and cervical growths in the daughters exposed to it before birth, because their mothers took the drug during pregnancy. The form of cancer from which these daughters suffer is known as adenocarcinoma, and it manifests itself after a minimum latent period of 10 or 12 years.

It is a fast-spreading and deadly disease, and radical surgery is required to prevent it from spreading. ... In 1971, the Food and Drug Administration ordered defendants to cease marketing and promoting DES for the purpose of preventing miscarriages, and to warn physicians and the public that the drug should not be used by pregnant women because of the danger to their unborn children. ...

We begin with the proposition that, as a general rule, the imposition of liability depends upon a showing by the plaintiff that his or her injuries were caused by the act of the defendant or by an instrumentality under the defendant's control. ...

There are, however, exceptions to this rule. Plaintiff's complaint suggests several bases upon which defendants may be held liable for her injuries even though she cannot demonstrate the name of the manufacturer which produced the DES actually taken by her mother. The first of these theories, classically illustrated by Summers v. Tice (1948) 33 Cal.2d 80, 199 P.2d 1, places the burden of proof of causation upon tortious defendants in certain circumstances. The second basis of liability emerging from the complaint is that defendants acted in concert to cause injury to plaintiff. There is a third and novel approach to the problem, sometimes called the theory of "enterprise liability," but which we prefer to designate by the more accurate term of "industry-wide" liability,[fn] which might obviate the necessity for identifying the manufacturer of the injury-causing drug. We shall conclude that these doctrines, as previously interpreted, may not be applied to hold defendants liable under the allegations of this complaint. However, we shall propose and adopt a fourth basis for permitting the action to be tried, grounded upon an extension of the Summers doctrine. ...

A third theory upon which plaintiff relies is the concept of industry-wide liability, or according to the terminology of the parties, "enterprise liability." This theory was suggested in Hall v. E. I. Du Pont de Nemours & Co., Inc. (E.D.N.Y.1972) 345 F.Supp. 353. In that case, plaintiffs were 13 children injured by the explosion of blasting caps in 12 separate incidents which occurred in 10 different states between 1955 and 1959. The defendants were six blasting cap manufacturers, comprising virtually the entire blasting cap industry in the United States, and their trade association. There were, however, a number of Canadian blasting cap manufacturers which could have supplied the caps. The gravamen of the complaint was that the practice of the industry of omitting a warning on individual blasting caps and of failing to take other safety measures created an unreasonable risk of harm, resulting in the plaintiffs' injuries. The complaint did not identify a particular manufacturer of a cap which caused a particular injury.[fn]

The court reasoned as follows: there was evidence that defendants, acting independently, had adhered to an industry-wide standard with regard to the safety features of blasting caps, that they had in effect delegated some functions of safety investigation and design, such as labelling, to their trade association, and that there was industry-wide cooperation in the manufacture and design of blasting caps. In these circumstances, the evidence supported a conclusion that all the defendants jointly controlled the risk. Thus, if plaintiffs could establish by a preponderance of the evidence that the caps were manufactured by one of the defendants, the burden of proof as to causation would shift to all the defendants. The court noted that this theory of liability applied to industries composed of a small number of units, and that what would be fair and reasonable with regard to an industry of five or ten producers might be manifestly unreasonable if applied to a decentralized industry composed of countless small producers.[fn] ...

We decline to apply this theory in the present case. At least 200 manufacturers produced DES; Hall, which involved 6 manufacturers representing the entire blasting cap industry in the United States, cautioned against application of the doctrine espoused therein to a large number of producers. [C] Moreover, in Hall, the conclusion that the defendants jointly controlled the risk was based upon allegations that they had delegated some functions relating to safety to a trade association. There are no such allegations here... .

... There are, however, forceful arguments in favor of holding that plaintiff has a cause of action.

In our contemporary complex industrialized society, advances in science and technology create fungible goods which may harm consumers and which cannot be traced to any specific producer. The response of the courts can be either to adhere rigidly to prior doctrine, denying recovery to those injured by such products, or to fashion remedies to meet these changing needs. ...

The most persuasive reason for finding plaintiff states a cause of action is that advanced in Summers: as between an innocent plaintiff and negligent defendants, the latter should bear the cost of the injury. Here, as in Summers, plaintiff is not at fault in failing to provide evidence of causation, and although the absence of such evidence is not attributable to the defendants either, their conduct in marketing a drug the effects of which are delayed for many years played a significant role in creating the unavailability of proof.

From a broader policy standpoint, defendants are better able to bear the cost of injury resulting from the manufacture of a defective product. ... The manufacturer is in the best position to discover and guard against defects in its products and to warn of harmful effects; thus, holding it liable for defects and failure to warn of harmful effects will provide an incentive to product safety. [Cc] These considerations are particularly significant where medication is involved, for the consumer is virtually helpless to protect himself from serious, sometimes permanent, sometimes fatal, injuries caused by deleterious drugs.

Where, as here, all defendants produced a drug from an identical formula and the manufacturer of the DES which caused plaintiff's injuries cannot be identified through no fault of plaintiff, a modification of the rule of Summers is warranted. As we have seen, an undiluted Summers rationale is inappropriate to shift the burden of proof of causation to defendants because if we measure the chance that any particular manufacturer supplied the injury-causing product by the number of producers of DES, there is a possibility that none of the five defendants in this case produced the offending substance and that the responsible manufacturer, not named in the action, will escape liability.

But we approach the issue of causation from a different perspective: we hold it to be reasonable in the present context to measure the likelihood that any of the defendants supplied the product which allegedly injured plaintiff by the percentage which the DES sold by each of them for the purpose of preventing miscarriage bears to the entire production of the drug sold by all for that purpose. Plaintiff asserts in her briefs that Eli Lilly and Company and 5 or 6 other companies produced 90 percent of the DES marketed. If at trial this is established to be the fact, then there is a corresponding likelihood that this comparative handful of producers manufactured the DES which caused plaintiff's injuries, and only a 10 percent likelihood that the offending producer would escape liability.[fn]

If plaintiff joins in the action the manufacturers of a substantial share of the DES which her mother might have taken, the injustice of shifting the burden of proof to defendants to demonstrate that they could not have made the substance which injured plaintiff is significantly diminished. ...

The presence in the action of a substantial share of the appropriate market also provides a ready means to apportion damages among the defendants. Each defendant will be held liable for the proportion of the judgment represented by its share of that market unless it demonstrates that it could not have made the product which caused plaintiff's injuries. In the present case, as we have see, one DES manufacturer was dismissed from the action upon filing a declaration that it had not manufactured DES until after plaintiff was born. ...

Under this approach, each manufacturer's liability would approximate its responsibility for the injuries caused by its own products. Some minor discrepancy in the correlation between market share and liability is inevitable.... . But just as a jury cannot be expected to determine the precise relationship between fault and liability in applying the doctrine of comparative fault ([cc]) or partial indemnity ([c]), the difficulty of apportioning damages among the defendant producers in exact relation to their market share does not seriously militate against the rule we adopt. As we said in Summers with regard to the liability of independent tortfeasors, where a correct division of liability cannot be made "the trier of fact may make it the best it can." (33 Cal.2d at p. 88, 199 P.2d at p. 5.) ...

The judgments are reversed.

INQUIRY

Alternative Liability. The market-share alternative-liability rule crafted in *Sindell* is novel. Five state supreme courts (Illinois, Iowa, Missouri, Ohio, and Rhode Island) reject the theory even for DES cases and instead require that plaintiff prove causation in the traditional manner—that the defendant manufacturer made the ingested drug. Of the few states following California's lead in *Sindell* and fashioning an alternative-liability theory for DES cases, each state has adopted slightly different forms than *Sindell*, which requires the plaintiff to name a "substantial share" of the manufacturers and permits manufacturers to exculpate themselves. For instance, Wisconsin uses the degree of risk each manufacturer contributed rather than market share as the measure on which to allocate liability. *See* Collins v. Eli Lilly Co., 116 Wis.2d 166, 342 N.W.2d 37 (1984). New York does not allow defendant manufacturers to prove that they did not make the drug ingested by the plaintiff's mother. *See* Hymowitz v. Eli Lilly and Co., 73 N.Y.2d 487, 539 N.E.2d 1069, 541 N.Y.S.2d 941 (1989). Washington and Florida permit a plaintiff to sue just one of the culpable DES manufacturers, permit that manufacturer to implead others, and presumptively assign equal (rather than market) shares unless the defendant can prove otherwise. *See* Conley v. Boyle Drug Co., 570 So.2d 275 (Fla. 1990); Martin v. Abbott Labs., 102 Wash.2d 581, 689 P.2d 368 (1984).

Other Applications. Courts generally do not extend *Sindell*'s market-share alternative liability beyond DES cases. Courts have rejected it for vaccines, asbestos, breast implants, gasoline, grocery carts, guns, and lead paint, *see* Marshall v. Celotex Corp., 691 F. Supp. 1045 (E.D. Mich. 1988) (asbestos); Hamilton v. Beretta U.S.A.

Corp., 750 N.E.2d 1055 (N.Y. 2001) (guns); Santiago v. Sherwin Williams Co., 3 F.3d 546 (1st Cir. 1993) (lead paint), and permitted it only for blood-clotting proteins, *see* Smith v. Cutter Biological, Inc., 72 Haw. 416, 823 P.2d 717 (1991).

Knowledge

Lawyers make policy arguments. A policy argument begins by identifying an interest of a party, person, entity, agency, industry, or community. It then proposes a measure (a law, rule, or ruling) that promotes the articulated interest. Policy arguments are instrumental. The lawyer must show the cause and effect between the proposed measure and an outcome desired because it supports a legitimate interest. A policy argument thus requires three cognitive performances: (1) identifying a legitimate interest; (2) articulating the proposed ruling or measure; and (3) convincingly demonstrating that the ruling or measure promotes the interest.

B. Proximate or Legal Cause

OBJECTIVE: **Given various negligence claims involving unusual injuries, apply proximate-cause principles to determine whether proximate cause is satisfied, consistent with this text.**

Case Study: A man loaned his fishing boat to a homeowner one evening, negligently forgetting to tell the homeowner that its gas tank was nearly empty. No sooner had the homeowner gotten the boat out on the lake, than its engine died with the gas tank empty. As a result, the homeowner was unable to get home in time to take his dinner out of the oven. Fire personnel responded to thick smoke from the burned dinner while the homeowner floated helplessly on the lake. Repairs from smoke and fire-personnel damage cost the homeowner several thousand dollars. ***Evaluate whether proximate cause is satisfied on the homeowner's negligence claim against the boat owner for those damages.***

As the introduction at the beginning of your studies on causation made clear, causation has a second aspect (after cause in fact) that falls under the unfortunate rubric of *proximate cause*. To be *proximate* means to be next in line, close to, or near. In that sense, the phrase *proximate cause* is somewhat appropriate as a description for this aspect of causation requiring a judgment whether defendant's negligence is sufficiently near to plaintiff's harm to make defendant's liability appropriate—given that plaintiff has already established cause in fact. On the other hand, the word *proximate* is easy to confuse, especially in lay jurors' minds but also in the minds of lawyers and judges, with other words like *approximate* and with concepts like cause in fact. That confusion is why some writers have adopted the phrase *legal cause* to describe this aspect of causation representing a societal judgment whether, given the existence of weak cause in fact, liability is nonetheless just and fair. *See* Restatement (Second) of Torts §431 (1965) ("legal cause" substituted for "proximate cause"). Yet the proximate-cause label seems to have stuck.

As you will see from the cases, statutes, and principles below, there is little or no certainty about the analytical approach to proximate cause. The best that a torts practitioner can do may be to: (1) recognize the basic direct-sequence and foreseeability tests for proximate cause; (2) employ a proximate-cause vocabulary including words like natural, remote, extraordinary, predictable, direct, dependent, continuous, improbable, and foreseeable; (3) assemble facts into accurate accounts and coherent patterns suggesting a proximate-cause outcome; and (4) develop an intuitive feel for the element and how courts will treat it in its factual context within the relevant jurisdiction. As you explore the complex subject of proximate cause, consider how the visceral responses of lawyers, judges, and jurors to the proximate-cause issue, and the occasionally trite phrases the law seems to employ to decide it, reflect fundamental understandings of the nature of human action, volition, responsibility, and existence. Although proximate cause is not an issue in the great majority of cases, consider a case illustrating the struggle that proximate cause can present in any one instance.

Union Pump Co. v. Allbritton
Texas Supreme Court
898 S.W.2d 773 (Tex. 1995)

OWEN, J. The issue in this case is whether the condition, act, or omission of which a personal injury plaintiff complains was, as a matter of law, too remote to constitute legal causation. ... Because we conclude that there was no legal causation as a matter of law, we reverse the judgment of the court of appeals and render judgment that plaintiff take nothing.

On the night of September 4, 1989, a fire occurred at Texaco Chemical Company's facility in Port Arthur, Texas. A pump manufactured by Union Pump Company caught fire and ignited the surrounding area. ... Sue Allbritton, a trainee employee of Texaco Chemical, had just finished her shift and was about to leave the plant when the fire erupted. She and her supervisor Felipe Subia, Jr., were directed to and did assist in abating the fire.

Approximately two hours later, the fire was extinguished. However, there appeared to be a problem with a nitrogen purge valve, and Subia was instructed to block in the valve. Viewing the facts in a light most favorable to Allbritton, there was some evidence that an emergency situation existed at that point in time. Allbritton asked if she could accompany Subia and was allowed to do so. To get to the nitrogen purge valve, Allbritton followed Subia over an aboveground pipe rack, which was approximately two and one-half feet high, rather than going around it. It is undisputed that this was not the safer route, but it was the shorter one. Upon reaching the valve, Subia and Allbritton were notified that it was not necessary to block it off. Instead of returning by the route around the pipe rack, Subia chose to walk across it, and Allbritton followed. Allbritton was injured when she hopped or slipped off the pipe rack. There is evidence that the pipe rack was wet because of the fire and that Allbritton and Subia were still wearing fireman's hip boots and other firefighting gear when the injury occurred. Subia admitted that he chose to walk over the pipe rack rather than taking a safer alternative route because he had a "bad habit" of doing so.

Allbritton sued Union Pump... . But for the pump fire, she asserts, she would never have walked over the pipe rack, which was wet with water or firefighting foam.

... The question before this Court is whether Union Pump established as a matter of law that neither its conduct nor its product was a legal cause of Allbritton's injuries. ...

Negligence requires a showing of proximate cause... .

At some point in the causal chain, the defendant's conduct or product may be too remotely connected with the plaintiff's injury to constitute legal causation. As this Court noted in City of Gladewater v. Pike, 727 S.W.2d 514, 518 (Tex.1987), defining the limits of legal causation "eventually mandates weighing of policy considerations." See also Springall v. Fredericksburg Hospital and Clinic, 225 S.W.2d 232, 235 (Tex.Civ.App.-San Antonio 1949, no writ), in which the court of appeals observed: "[T]he law does not hold one legally responsible for the remote results of his wrongful acts and therefore a line must be drawn between immediate and remote causes. The doctrine of 'proximate cause' is employed to determine and fix this line and 'is the result of an effort by the courts to avoid, as far as possible the metaphysical and philosophical niceties in the age-old discussion of causation, and to lay down a rule of general application which will, as nearly as may be done by a general rule, apply a practical test, the test of common experience, to human conduct when determining legal rights and legal liability.'" Id. at 235 (quoting City of Dallas v. Maxwell, 248 S.W. 667, 670 (Tex.Comm'nApp.1923, holding approved)).

Drawing the line between where legal causation may exist and where, as a matter of law, it cannot, has generated a considerable body of law.[fn] ... [T]he Restatement (Second) of Torts, section 431, [is] instructive on the issue of legal causation: "In order to be a legal cause of another's harm, it is not enough that the harm would not have occurred had the actor not been negligent.... The negligence must also be a substantial factor in bringing about the plaintiff's harm. The word 'substantial' is used to denote the fact that the defendant's conduct has such an effect in producing the harm as to lead reasonable men to regard it as a cause, using that word in the popular sense, in which there always lurks the idea of responsibility, rather than in the so-called 'philosophic sense,' which includes every one of the great number of events without which any happening would not have occurred." Lear Siegler, [Inc. v. Perez,] 819 S.W.2d [470,] 472 [(Tex. 1991)] (quoting Restatement (Second) of Torts § 431 cmt. a (1965)).

... [T]he connection between the defendant and the plaintiff's injuries simply may be too attenuated to constitute legal cause. [C] Legal cause is not established if the defendant's conduct or product does no more than furnish the condition that makes the plaintiff's injury possible. [C] This principle applies with equal force to proximate cause and producing cause. [C] ...

... The principles underlying the various legal theories of causation overlap in many respects, but they are not coextensive. While in Bell [v. Campbell, 434 S.W.2d 117, 122 (Tex. 1968)], this Court held "the injuries involved in this suit were not proximately caused by any negligence of [defendants] but by an independent and intervening agency," id., we also held "[a]ll forces involved in or generated by the first collision had come to rest, and no one was in any real or apparent danger therefrom[,]" id. at 120, and accordingly, that the "[defendants'] negligence was not a concurring cause of [the plaintiffs'] injuries." Id. at 122. This reasoning applies with equal force to Allbritton's claims.

Even if the pump fire were in some sense a "philosophic" or "but for" cause of Allbritton's injuries, the forces generated by the fire had come to rest when she fell off the pipe rack. The fire had been extinguished, and Allbritton was walking away from the scene. Viewing the evidence in the light most favorable to Allbritton, the pump fire did no more than create the condition that made Allbritton's injuries possible. We conclude that the circumstances surrounding her injuries are too remotely connected with Union Pump's conduct or pump to constitute a legal cause of her injuries. [C]

Accordingly, we reverse the judgment of the court of appeals and render judgment that plaintiff take nothing. ...

CORNYN, J., concurring. I concur in the Court's judgment, but for different reasons than those given in its opinion. I would hold that although the defective pump was a cause-in-fact of Sue Allbritton's injury, neither Union Pump's negligence nor the defective pump was a legal cause of her injury. Because the Court's opinion conflates foreseeability and other policy issues with its cause-in-fact analysis, I do not join its opinion. ...

This case does not present a question of cause-in-fact. The pump defect clearly was a "but for" cause of Allbritton's injuries: assuming the truth of Allbritton's allegations, as we must in this summary judgment case, if the pump had not been defective, there would have been no fire, and Allbritton would have gone home uninjured at the end of her shift. Assuming the substantial factor test from Section 432(2) of the Restatement (Second) applies, the pump defect was also a substantial factor in her injury. The pump was the undisputed cause of the fire, which created a crisis at the plant.[fn] Because the pump defect was clearly a but-for cause and a substantial factor, the pump defect was a cause-in-fact of Allbritton's injury.

But determining that the defect was the cause-in-fact of Allbritton's injuries does not end the inquiry. [C] We must decide whether the pump defect meets the second prong of both proximate cause and producing cause. In proximate cause, this other element is foreseeability, but it also incorporates policy driven decisions such as when subsequent events will be treated as intervening causes. [C] In this case, the injury to Allbritton was not foreseeable. Allbritton's injuries were the result of a needlessly dangerous shortcut taken after the crisis had subsided.[fn] Holding Union Pump liable for Allbritton's failure to use proper care in exiting the area of the fire after the crisis has ended is akin to holding it liable for an auto accident she suffered on the way home, even though the accident probably would not have occurred had she left after her normal shift. Foreseeability allows us to cut off Union Pump's liability at some point; I would do so at the point the crisis had abated or at the point that Allbritton and Subia departed from their usual, safe path. ...

SPECTOR, J., dissenting. The summary judgment evidence in this case does not negate causation as a matter of law.

The record reflects that at the time Sue Allbritton's injury occurred, the forces generated by the fire in question had not come to rest. Rather, the emergency situation was continuing. The whole area of the fire was covered in water and foam; in at least some places, the water was almost knee-deep. Allbritton was still wearing hip boots and other gear, as required to fight the fire. Viewing all the evidence in the light most favorable to Allbritton, I agree with Justice Cornyn that the pump defect was both a "but-for" cause and a substantial factor in bringing about Allbritton's injury, and was therefore a cause in fact.

This case is markedly different from the two main cases on which the majority relies... . In each of those cases, a defendant's negligence simply created a condition that attracted an individual to the scene, where a negligent third party inflicted an injury. Here, in contrast, there was no negligent third party. To whatever extent Allbritton's own negligence may have contributed to her injury, a jury should be allowed to allocate comparative responsibility.

Because Union Pump has failed to establish its right to summary judgment as a matter of law, I dissent.

Figure

Torts practitioner Lori Cohen, a partner and co-chair of the litigation group at the law firm Greenberg Traurig in Atlanta, has defended, tried, and won dozens of medical-device, pharmaceutical, and other products-liability and medical-malpractice cases. She has been appointed and served as National Counsel for major companies like Johnson & Johnson, Medtronic, GlaxoSmithKline, and Novartis, in mass-tort cases involving drugs, medical devices, and other products, and represented many hospitals and physicians. Her extensive writing and lecturing has focused on using technology in the courtroom to present complex scientific and medical evidence, *Daubert* challenges to expert testimony, and the conduct and strategy of mass-tort litigation. Ms. Cohen also edits three national legal publications relating to medical and products liability.

---

1. Direct Sequence

How should the law best resolve difficult proximate-cause cases like the above one? A simpler form of test with which to begin our studies of proximate cause is the direct-sequence test. The direct-sequence test concerns itself less with whether the harm that resulted from the defendant's negligence was predictable (probable or foreseeable) and more with whether, in hindsight, the case shows such a direct, immediate, and unbroken sequence of events between the negligence and the harm that liability should exist. *See* Lynch v. Scheininger, 162 N.J. 209, 744 A.2d 113 (2000) (proximate cause can be satisfied for unforeseeable harms); *see also* Depew v. Crocodile Enterps, Inc., 63 Cal. App.4th 480, 73 Cal. Rptr.2d 673 (Cal. Ct. App. 1998) (employer not liable under direct-sequence test for over-worked employee falling asleep at the wheel on the way home from work and killing a third person); Snowbarger v. Tri-County Elec. Coop., 793 S.W.2d 348 (Mo. 1990) (employer liable under foreseeability test in same circumstances). The direct-sequence test looks back from the reconstructed evidence to trace how immediate and direct—how *proximate*—the harmful result was. Many jurisdictions favor verbal formulations that combine some aspect of the direct-sequence test ("direct," "natural," "proximate") with different considerations of probability or foreseeability. When used in jury instructions, these verbal formulations must be relatively clear and concise for the lay person to understand. Thus, for instance, under Michigan's model jury instruction SJI2d 15.01 on proximate cause, the trial judge simply tells the jury, "When I use the words 'proximate cause' I mean first, that the negligent conduct must have been a cause of plaintiff's injury, and second, that the plaintiff's injury must have been a *natural and probable result* of the negligent conduct" (emphasis added). *See also* Ark. Model Jury Instr. 501 (2004) ("a natural and continuous sequence"). You are about to read a few thousand words on what jury instructions reduce to two: "natural" and "probable." Consider first the relative simplicity with which the courts in the following cases disposed of the proximate-cause issue, under various formulations ("direct," "natural and proximate," "unbroken sequence," "directly traceable") of the direct-sequence test, without considering probability or foreseeability.

Chistianson v. Chicago, St. P., M. & O. Ry. Co.
Minnesota Supreme Court
67 Minn. 94, 69 N.W. 640 (1896)

MITCHELL, J. This action... was brought to recover for personal injuries caused by the alleged negligence of defendant's servants. ... The plaintiff was in defendant's employ as a section hand. On the day in question, he and two other sectionmen started easterly on a hand car, to meet their section foreman. In the meantime, another section crew, with plaintiff's section foreman, had started westerly from another point, on another hand car. When the two cars came within a short distance of each other, those on the west-bound signaled those on the east-bound car to go back. Thereupon those on the latter car turned back, and both cars proceeded westerly, the car on which plaintiff was going ahead, and the other car following. It appears from the evidence that those on the rear car had, before starting out that morning, imbibed several drinks of whisky; and that, while both cars were going westerly, some of them once or twice signaled to those on the forward car as if wanting them to go faster. ... The cars were running down [a] grade at a rate of speed variously estimated at from 10 to 20 miles an hour. The front car, on which plaintiff was, was of old style, not capable of as great a rate of speed as the rear car; and, owing to the nature of its gearing, the handles attached to the lever moved very rapidly; so much so that it was difficult for one standing on the car to hold on to them. Plaintiff was standing on the rear end of the car, with nothing to hold on to except these handles. ... The usual distance at which hand cars kept apart, according to the rules of the company, was "three telegraph poles," which would be 540 feet. At the rate of speed at which it was going, the rear car could not have been brought to a stop by the application of the brake in less than 100 feet. The cars had traveled in this way about a mile and a quarter, the rear car gaining on the forward one, until it got within 60 feet of it. The plaintiff testified that at this point he looked back, and, seeing the other car so near, and going so fast, became dizzy, lost his balance, and fell off. It is perhaps unimportant whether his fall was the result of fright caused by seeing the other rapidly moving car so near, or whether he accidentally lost his hold on the handle of the lever, and lost his balance. The fact is undisputed that he did fall off. We think the evidence shows that, after the men on the rear car saw him fall, they did all they could to stop their car; but going, as they were, at so great a rate of speed, and being within 60 feet of the front car, it was impossible for them to avoid colliding with the plaintiff. The result was that the car ran upon him while lying on the track, and inflicted very severe injuries. ...

3. The main contention... of defendant's counsel, is that, conceding that those on the rear car were negligent, yet plaintiff's injuries were not the proximate result of such negligence; or, perhaps to state their position more accurately, that it is not enough to entitle plaintiff to recover that his injuries were the natural consequence of this negligence, but that it must also appear that, under all the circumstances, it might have been reasonably anticipated that such injury would result. With this legal premise assumed, counsel argues that those on the rear car could not have reasonably anticipated that plaintiff would fall from the car. It is laid down in many cases and by some text writers that, in order to warrant a finding that negligence (not wanton) is the proximate cause of an injury, it must appear that the injury was the natural and probable consequence of the negligent act, and that it (the injury) was such as might or ought, in the light of attending circumstances, to have been anticipated. ... What a man may reasonably anticipate is important, and may be decisive, in determining whether an act is

negligent, but is not at all decisive in determining whether that act is the proximate cause of an injury which ensues. If a person had no reasonable ground to anticipate that a particular act would or might result in any injury to anybody, then, of course, the act would not be negligent at all; but, if the act itself is negligent, then the person guilty of it is equally liable for all its natural and proximate consequences, whether he could have foreseen them or not. Otherwise expressed, the law is that if the act is one which the party ought, in the exercise of ordinary care, to have anticipated was liable to result in injury to others, then he is liable for any injury proximately resulting from it, although he could not have anticipated the particular injury which did happen. Consequences which follow in unbroken sequence, without an intervening efficient cause, from the original negligent act, are natural and proximate; and for such consequences the original wrongdoer is responsible, even though he could not have foreseen the particular results which did follow. [Cc] ... Tested by this rule, we think that it is clear that the negligence of those on the rear car was the proximate cause of plaintiff's injuries; at least, that the evidence justified the jury in so finding. Counsel admitted on the argument that if, by derailment or other accident, the front car had been suddenly stopped, and a collision and consequent injuries to plaintiff had resulted, the negligence of those on the rear car would have been the proximate cause. But we can see no difference in principle between the case supposed and the present case. The causal connection between the negligent act and the resulting injury would be the same in both cases. The only possible difference is that it might be anticipated that the sudden stoppage of the car was more likely to happen than the falling of one of its occupants upon the track. ...

Order affirmed.

In re Arbitration Between Polemis and Furness, Withy & Co., Ltd.
King's Bench, Court of Appeals
3 K.B. 560 (Court of Appeal 1921)

BANKES, J. By a time charter party dated February 21, 1917, the respondents chartered their vessel to the appellants. ... The vessel was employed by the charterers to carry a cargo to Casablanca in Morocco. The cargo included a quantity of benzine or petrol in cases. While discharging at Casablanca a heavy plank fell into the hold in which the petrol was stowed, and caused an explosion, which set fire to the vessel and completely destroyed her. The owners claimed the value of the vessel from the charterers, alleging that the loss of the vessel was due to the negligence of the charterers' servants. The charterers contended that ... the damages claimed were too remote. The claim was referred to arbitration, and the arbitrators stated a special case for the opinion of the Court. Their findings of fact are as follows[: That the ship was lost by fire. That the fire arose from a spark igniting petrol vapour in the hold. That the spark was caused by the falling board coming into contact with some substance in the hold. That the fall of the board was caused by the negligence of [those] engaged in the work of discharging. That the causing of the spark could not reasonably have been anticipated from the falling of the board, though some damage to the ship might reasonably have been anticipated.] Then they state the damages, 196,165l. 1s. 11d. ...

... In Smith v. London and South Western Ry. Co.[fn] Channell B. said: "... [W]hen it has been once determined that there is evidence of negligence, the person guilty of it is equally liable for its consequences, whether he could have foreseen them or not." ... [A]nd again, to use the words of an eminent English jurist (Sir F. Pollock[fn]), "In whatever form we state the rule of 'natural and probable consequences,' we must remember that it is not a logical definition, but only a guide to the exercise of common sense. The Lawyer cannot afford to adventure himself with philosophers in the logical and metaphysical controversies that beset the idea of cause." In the latter case Lord Sumner said[fn]: "What are 'natural, probable and necessary' consequences? Everything that happens, happens in the order of nature and is therefore 'natural.' ... To speak of 'probable' consequence is to throw everything upon the jury. ..."

In the present case the arbitrators have found as a fact that the falling of the plank was due to the negligence of the defendants' servants. The fire appears to me to have been directly caused by the falling of the plank. Under these circumstances I consider that it is immaterial that the causing of the spark by the falling of the plank could not have been reasonably anticipated. The appellants' junior counsel sought to draw a distinction between the anticipation of the extent of damage resulting from a negligent act, and the anticipation of the type of damage resulting from such an act. He admitted that it could not lie in the mouth of a person whose negligent act had caused damage to say that he could not reasonably have foreseen the extent of the damage, but he contended that the negligent person was entitled to rely upon the fact that he could not reasonably have anticipated the type of damage which resulted from his negligent act. I do not think that the distinction can be admitted. Given the breach of duty which constitutes the negligence, and given the damage as a direct result of that negligence, the anticipations of the person whose negligent act has produced the damage appear to me to be irrelevant. I consider that the damages claimed are not too remote. ...

WARRINGTON, J. ... The accident happened in the port of Casablanca, in Morocco, to which the ship had been directed by the charterers with a cargo which included cases of benzine and/or petrol stored in No. 1 hold. These cases had leaked on the voyage and there was a considerable quantity of petrol vapour in the hold. Arab stevedores employed by the charterers were engaged in shifting certain cargo in the hold, and for the purpose of their work had placed some heavy planks across the forward end of the hatchway. In the course of the work one of the planks came in contact with the sling or the rope by which the sling was worked, was thereby dislodged, and fell into the hold. The fall was instantly followed by a rush of flames, and the result was the total destruction of the ship. ...

... [It is contended that "a person guilty of negligence is not responsible in respect of mischief which could by no possibility have been foreseen and which no reasonable person would have anticipated."[fn]

The result may be summarised as follows: The presence or absence of reasonable anticipation of damage determines the legal quality of the act as negligent or innocent. If it be thus determined to be negligent, then the question whether particular damages are recoverable depends only on the answer to the question whether they are the direct consequence of the act. ... In the present case it is clear that the act causing the plank to fall was in law a negligent act, because some damage to the ship might reasonably be anticipated. If this is so then the appellants are liable for the actual loss, that being on the findings of the arbitrators the direct result of the falling board... .

SCRUTTON, J. ... Experienced arbitrators, by whose findings of fact we are bound, have decided that the fire was caused by a spark igniting petrol vapour in the hold, the vapour coming from leaks from cargo shipped by the charterers, and that the spark was caused by the Arab workmen employed by the charterers negligently knocking a plank out of a temporary staging erected in the hold, so that the plank fell into the hold, and in its fall by striking something made the spark which ignited the petrol vapour. ...

The second defence is that the damage is too remote from the negligence, as it could not be reasonably foreseen as a consequence. ... I cannot think it useful to say the damage must be the natural and probable result. This suggests that there are results which are natural but not probable, and other results which are probable but not natural. I am not sure what either adjective means in this connection; if they mean the same thing, two need not be used; if they mean different things, the difference between them should be defined. And as to many cases of fact in which the distinction has been drawn, it is difficult to see why one case should be decided one way and one another. ... In this case, however, the problem is simpler. To determine whether an act is negligent, it is relevant to determine whether any reasonable person would foresee that the act would cause damage; if he would not, the act is not negligent. But if the act would or might probably cause damage, the fact that the damage it in fact causes is not the exact kind of damage one would expect is immaterial, so long as the damage is in fact directly traceable to the negligent act, and not due to the operation of independent causes having no connection with the negligent act, except that they could not avoid its results. Once the act is negligent, the fact that its exact operation was not foreseen is immaterial. ... In the present case it was negligent in discharging cargo to knock down the planks of the temporary staging, for they might easily cause some damage either to workmen, or cargo, or the ship. The fact that they did directly produce an unexpected result, a spark in an atmosphere of petrol vapour which caused a fire, does not relieve the person who was negligent from the damage which his negligent act directly caused. ...

Appeal dismissed.

INQUIRY

Limits. The blessing of the direct-sequence test is its simplicity. Its shortfall is that it has no natural limit. *See* Colonial Inn Motor Lodge, Inc. v. Gay, 288 Ill. App.3d 32, 680 N.E.2d 407 (1997) (holding driver liable for building that exploded when he backed truck into a gas line on its air conditioning unit, allowing natural gas to escape and accumulate up until the point of explosion); Bunting v. Hogsett, 139 Pa. 363, 21 A. 31 (1891) (defendant rail line held liable for damage occurring when the collision of its engine with a train on a crossing caused the engine controls to jar loose, sending the engine in reverse at a high rate of speed, eventually causing a second collision in which the plaintiff was injured). Two cases arising out of the same occurrence wonderfully illustrate the scope or limit of the direct-sequence test for proximate cause. In Petition of Kinsman Transit Co., 338 F.2d 708 (2d Cir. 1964), known as "Kinsman No. 1," the defendants negligently moored a ship, the *Shivas*, at a dock during the winter season when the river was filled with rapidly flowing ice and debris. The ice and debris built up against the *Shiras*, breaking it free, from whence it crashed downstream into another ship, the *Tewksbury*, causing the two ships to crash further downstream into a bridge, the collapse of which caused flooding well up the river. Applying a direct-sequence test like that above, the trial court held the defendants liable to property owners flooded upstream, notwithstanding that these consequences were unforeseeable. When years later the owner of a ship that had been downstream of the bridge and was blocked from its unloading destination upriver sued in "Kinsman No. 2," Petition of Kinsman Transit Co., 388 F.2d 821 (2d Cir. 1968), the same trial court rejected the claim as too remote and indirect—the holding upheld on the cited appeal.

> **Ethics**
> A tort-lawyer favorite is to act as a neutral mediator or case evaluator in a tort case prepared and defended by other lawyers. Tort lawyers—both plaintiff's lawyers and defense counsel—will often select and retain neutral lawyer-mediators and -evaluators for court-imposed or voluntary settlement procedures. A neutral lawyer's review and evaluation of other lawyers' tort cases can help the lawyer stay current with the law, theories, claims, and professional contacts and resources necessary to a strong tort-law practice. The ABA Model Rules of Professional Conduct permit, in Rule 2.4, a lawyer to serve as a third-party neutral mediator or evaluator but caution the lawyer to ensure that unrepresented parties understand the lawyer's neutral role.

Rationale. What is the direct-sequence test's justification or rationale? The above cases show that once a court determines negligence (separately, without reference to the foreseeability of the particular harm that resulted), the reprehensible quality of negligence as an act of carelessness toward one's fellow person in itself justifies that the defendant compensate for any harm (peculiar or not) that follows from the reprehensible act. Wrongdoers, it seems, should not complain about the peculiar nature of the harm flowing from their wrong, when they should expect harm of some kind from their tortious acts. On that theory, should the law extend proximate cause to an even larger scope for mor-reprehensible intentional torts? *See* DeRosier v. New England Tel. & Tel. Co., 81 N.H. 451, 130 A.145 (1925) ("For an intended injury the law is astute to discover even very remote causation.").

Judge or Jury. In theory, the procedural treatment of proximate-cause issues is like that of the other elements of a negligence claim—if reasonable minds can differ, proximate cause goes to the jury. On the other hand, trial judges and appellate courts have a definite tendency to treat the realm of juror-reasonableness as narrower for proximate cause than for the breach, cause-in-fact, and damages issues. Put simply, courts are more likely to grant summary judgment on proximate cause than they are on those other elements. *See* Metts v. Griglak, 264 A.2d 684 (Pa. 1970) (affirming judgment notwithstanding the verdict, that defendant's bus's speeding was not the proximate cause of plaintiff's injury riding on another bus that collided with a car crowded from the road by defendant's speeding bus). In that respect, courts treat proximate cause more like a policy or duty issue than an issue of fact—even though courts will repeat the same procedural litany that the proximate-cause issue is for the jury where reasonable minds could differ.

2. Foreseeability

As an alternative to direct-sequence tests, proximate cause often resolves around the concept of foreseeability. To decide whether holding defendant liable for having negligently caused an unusual harm is appropriate, one asks whether the reasonable person would have foreseen that harm at the time of acting, before the harm occurred. Think of the foreseeability test as the conceptual mirror of the direct-sequence test. The direct-sequence test looks back from the occurrence, tracing how direct the line is from the negligence to the harm. The foreseeability test looks forward from the negligence, estimating how probable it would have seemed that harm would occur. Each test has its advantages. The direct-sequence test involves no conjecture over defendant's state of mind before the harm occurred, as to the foreseeability of the harm. It focuses instead on the real, physical, and objective occurrences accumulating to cause the harm. By contrast, the foreseeability test concerns itself less with the (occasionally quite odd) occurrences that lead to the harm and instead focuses on the broader spectrum of probability that harm would somehow occur. In that sense, each test balances the other, working better where the other test works less well.

Applying the foreseeability test for proximate cause shows again that the elements of negligence overlap. Analyzing one element tends to affect how you analyze another element. The more reprehensible the conduct, the more likely proximate cause exists; the more foreseeable the harm, the more likely negligence exists; the greater risk action will cause harm, the greater likelihood duty exists—and so on. Do not grow frustrated over the nebulous nature of the proximate-cause issue. Rather, embrace its ambiguity as reassurance of the comprehensive and integrated nature of life, of how we discern, choose, and act. Separating negligence elements gives us artificial means of analyzing what are essentially unified circumstances. Accept proximate cause and its direct-sequence and foreseeability signposts as clues to what justice requires of us under holistic circumstance. As to the foreseeability test for proximate cause, consider first a simple, illustrative case, then followed by the grandfather of all proximate-causes cases—possibly the best known of any tort case.

Ventricelli v. Kinney System Rent a Car, Inc.
New York Court of Appeals
45 N.Y.2d 950, 411 N.Y.S.2d 555, 383 N.E.2d 1149, as modified,
46 N.Y.2d 770, 413 N.Y.S.2d 655, 386 N.E.2d 263 (1978)

[The defendant rental-car service leased to plaintiff Ventricelli a vehicle that had a defective trunk lid that would not close properly. As Ventricelli and his passenger were trying to slam the lid of the vehicle, which was parked on the side of the street, another vehicle ran into Ventricelli, who subsequently received a $550,000 jury verdict in his negligence action against the defendant rental-car service. The Appellate Division opinion below reversed and ordered dismissal as to the defendant rental-car service.]

MEMORANDUM[by BREITEL, C.J.] Order of the Appellate Division affirmed, with costs. Proximate cause and foreseeability are relative terms, "nothing more than a convenient formula for disposing of the case" (Prosser, Law of Torts (4th ed.), s 43, p. 267). In writing of the "orbit of the duty," Chief Judge Cardozo said "(t)he range of reasonable apprehension is at times a question for the court, and at times, if varying inferences are possible, a question for the jury" (Palsgraf v. Long Is. R. R. Co., 248 N.Y. 339, 345, 162 N.E. 99, 101). So it is with proximate cause and foreseeability ([cc]).

Although the negligence of the automobile renter, defendant Kinney, is manifest, and was, of course, a "cause" of the accident, it was not the proximate cause. "What we do mean by the word 'proximate' is, that because of convenience, of public policy, of a rough sense of justice, the law arbitrarily declines to trace a series of events beyond a certain point" (Palsgraf v. Long Is. R. R. Co., 248 N.Y. 339, 352, 162 N.E. 99, 103, Supra (Andrews, J., dissenting)). The immediately effective cause of plaintiff's injuries was the negligence of Maldonado, the driver of the second car, in striking plaintiff while he was standing behind his parked automobile. That Kinney's negligence in providing an automobile with a defective trunk lid would result in plaintiff's repeated attempts to close the lid was reasonably foreseeable. Not "foreseeable," however, was the collision between vehicles both parked a brief interval before the accident. Plaintiff was standing in a relatively "safe" place, a parking space, not in an actively traveled lane. He might well have been there independent of any negligence of Kinney, as, for example, if he were loading or unloading the trunk. Under these circumstances, to hold the accident a foreseeable consequence of Kinney's negligence is to stretch the concept of foreseeability beyond acceptable limits ([cc]).

FUCHSBERG, J. (dissenting). When Dean Prosser suggested that proximate cause may at times seem to be "nothing more than a convenient formula for disposing of the case," he also observed that the existence of proximate cause must "'be determined on the facts of each case upon mixed considerations of logic, common sense, justice, policy and precedent'" (Prosser, Law of Torts (4th ed.), s 42, pp. 267, 249).

The generality of both these statements recognizes that torts is a branch of the law in which the decisional process is usually so dependent on the vagaries of particular facts in individual cases that it calls for a high degree of flexibility in judgment ([c]). Thus, disputes as to whether conduct is negligent, contributorily negligent or the proximate cause of an injury are usually best left to the fact finder. Since the record here convinces me that this case fails well within the range of these cautions, I believe the Trial Judge did not err as a matter of law in leaving the issue of proximate cause to the jury.

Ample was the proof that, to the knowledge of the rental company, the trunk door on the automobile it furnished to the plaintiff had a penchant for flying open so as to obstruct the operator's view while the vehicle was moving. Given those facts, it was not only foreseeable, but a most reasonable rather than a remote expectation, that a driver confronted by such an emergency would alight and promptly proceed to the rear of the car to attempt to secure the lid manually so that he might continue on his way without further danger to others and himself. The seemingly ineluctable consequence was to expose the driver to the danger of being struck by another vehicle while he was positioned behind the trunk. On these facts, it could readily be found, as the jury apparently did here, that the choice between the alternatives the danger from the obstruction of the driver's view from the vehicle and the danger of being struck while engaged in the act of removing the danger was thrust on the plaintiff by Kinney's negligence. …

Moreover, I perceive no sufficient reason to depart from these principles because the plaintiff, before exiting from the car to make the trunk adjustment, thought it preferable to park the car at an available spot in the curb lane instead of the middle lane of the block of New York City's busy and narrow Pell Street, where he found himself when the trunk suddenly sprung open. In either case, he was where he could be expected to be in the roadway with his attention diverted by the trunk on which he was working. Those who drive along a curb lane or pull in or out of one for the purpose of parking are not necessarily more careful or more observant than those to be found in an inner lane. In any event, being at most but a quantitative factor which did not detract from the qualitative risk, it was peculiarly one for consideration by the jury under all the circumstances and not a basis for determination as a matter of law.

All this is not to say that the jury had to find that there was a reasonable likelihood of danger resulting from the act of which plaintiff complains. It could have found that there was not. But, by its verdict it did in effect find that the accident that caused the plaintiff to lose his leg was at least in part the "ordinary and natural result" of the defendant's negligent act. And that it also had a right to do. [C]

I therefore would vote to reverse the order of the Appellate Division and remit the case to it for the determination of any remaining questions.

Palsgraf v. Long Island R. Co.
New York Court of Appeals
248 N.Y. 339, 162 N.E. 99 (1928)

CARDOZO, C.J. Plaintiff was standing on a platform of defendant's railroad after buying a ticket to go to Rockaway Beach. A train stopped at the station, bound for another place. Two men ran forward to catch it. One of the men reached the platform of the car without mishap, though the train was already moving. The other man, carrying a package, jumped aboard the car, but seemed unsteady as if about to fall. A guard on the car, who had held the door open, reached forward to help him in, and another guard on the platform pushed him from behind. In this act, the package was dislodged, and fell upon the rails. It was a package of small size, about fifteen inches long, and was covered by a newspaper. In fact it contained fireworks, but there was nothing in its appearance to give notice of its contents. The fireworks when they fell exploded. The shock of the explosion threw down some scales at the other end of the platform many feet away. The scales struck the plaintiff, causing injuries for which she sues.

The conduct of the defendant's guard, if a wrong in its relation to the holder of the package, was not a wrong in its relation to the plaintiff, standing far away. Relatively to her it was not negligence at all. Nothing in the situation gave notice that the falling package had in it the potency of peril to persons thus removed. Negligence is not actionable unless it involves the invasion of a legally protected interest, the violation of a right. "Proof of negligence in the air, so to speak, will not do." Pollock, Torts (11th Ed.) p. 455; [cc]. "Negligence is the absence of care, according to the circumstances." Willes, J., in Vaughan v. Taff Vale Ry. Co., 5 H. & N. 679, 688; [cc]. The plaintiff, as she stood upon the platform of the station, might claim to be protected against intentional invasion of her bodily security. Such invasion is not charged. She might claim to be protected against unintentional invasion by conduct involving in the thought of reasonable men an unreasonable hazard that such invasion would ensue. These, from the point of view of the law, were the bounds of her immunity, with perhaps some rare exceptions, survivals for the most part of ancient forms of liability, where conduct is held to be at the peril of the actor. [C] If no hazard was apparent to the eye of ordinary vigilance, an act innocent and harmless, at least to outward seeming, with reference to her, did not take to itself the quality of a tort because it happened to be a wrong, though apparently not one involving the risk of bodily insecurity, with reference to some one else. "In every instance, before negligence can be predicated of a given act, back of the act must be sought and found a duty to the individual complaining, the observance of which would have averted or avoided the injury." McSherry, C. J., in West Virginia Central & P. R. Co. v. State, 96 Md. 652, 666, 54 A. 669, 671 (61 L. R. A. 574). [Cc] "The ideas of negligence and duty are strictly correlative.' Bowen, L. J., in Thomas v. Quartermaine, 18 Q. B. D. 685, 694. The plaintiff sues in her own right for a wrong personal to her, and not as the vicarious beneficiary of a breach of duty to another. …

The argument for the plaintiff is built upon the shifting meanings of such words as 'wrong' and 'wrongful,' and shares their instability. What the plaintiff must show is 'a wrong' to herself; i. e., a violation of her own right, and not merely a wrong to some one else, nor conduct 'wrongful' because unsocial, but not 'a wrong' to any one. We are told that one who drives at reckless speed through a crowded city street is guilty of a negligent act and therefore of a wrongful one, irrespective of the consequences. Negligent the act is, and wrongful in the sense that it is unsocial, but wrongful and unsocial in relation to other travelers, only because the eye of vigilance perceives the risk of damage. If the same act were to be committed on a speedway or a race course, it would lose its wrongful quality. The risk reasonably to be perceived defines the duty to be obeyed, and risk imports relation; it is risk to another or to others within the range of apprehension. [Cc] This does not mean, of course, that one who launches a destructive force is always relieved of liability, if the force, though known to be destructive, pursues an unexpected path. "It was not necessary that the defendant should have had notice of the particular method in which an accident would occur, if the possibility of an accident was clear to the ordinarily prudent eye." Munsey v. Webb, 231 U. S. 150, 156, 34 S. Ct. 44, 45 (58 L. Ed. 162); [cc]. Some acts, such as shooting are so imminently dangerous to any one who may come within reach of the missile however unexpectedly, as to impose a duty of prevision not far from that of an insurer. Even to-day, and much oftener in earlier stages of the law, one acts sometimes at one's peril. [Cc] Under this head, it may be, fall certain cases of what is known as transferred intent, an act willfully dangerous to A resulting by misadventure in injury to B. [C] These cases aside, wrong is defined in terms of the natural or probable, at least when unintentional. [Cc] The range of reasonable apprehension is at times a question for the court, and at times, if varying inferences are possible, a question for the jury. Here, by concession, there was nothing in the situation to suggest to the most cautious mind that the parcel wrapped in newspaper would spread wreckage through the station. If the guard had thrown it down knowingly and willfully, he would not have threatened the plaintiff's safety, so far as appearances could warn him. His conduct would not have involved, even then, an unreasonable probability of invasion of her bodily security. Liability can be no greater where the act is inadvertent.

Negligence, like risk, is thus a term of relation. Negligence in the abstract, apart from things related, is surely not a tort, if indeed it is understandable at all. [C] Negligence is not a tort unless it results in the commission of a wrong, and the commission of a wrong imports the violation of a right, in this case, we are told, the right to be protected against interference with one's bodily security. But bodily security is protected, not against all forms of interference or aggression, but only against some. One who seeks redress at law does not make out a cause of action by showing without more that there has been damage to his person. If the harm was not willful, he must show that the act as to him had possibilities of danger so many and apparent as to entitle him to be protected against the doing of it though the harm was unintended. Affront to personality is still the keynote of the wrong. Confirmation of this view will be found in the history and development of the action on the case. Negligence as a basis of civil liability was unknown to mediaeval law. [Cc] For damage to the person, the sole remedy was trespass, and trespass did not lie in the absence of aggression, and that direct and personal. [Cc] Liability for other damage, as where a servant without orders from the master does or omits something to the damage of another, is a plant of later growth. [Cc] When it emerged out of the legal soil, it was thought of as a variant of trespass, an offshoot of the parent stock. This appears in the form of action, which was known as trespass on the case. [Cc] The victim does not sue derivatively, or by right of subrogation, to vindicate an interest invaded in the person of another. Thus to view his cause of action is to ignore the fundamental difference between tort and crime. [C] He sues for breach of a duty owing to himself.

The law of causation, remote or proximate, is thus foreign to the case before us. The question of liability is always anterior to the question of the measure of the consequences that go with liability. If there is no tort to be redressed, there is no occasion to consider what damage might be recovered if there were a finding of a tort. We may assume, without deciding, that negligence, not at large or in the abstract, but in relation to the plaintiff, would entail liability for any and all consequences, however novel or extraordinary. [Cc] There is room for argument that a distinction is to be drawn according to the diversity of interests invaded by the act, as where conduct negligent in that it threatens an insignificant invasion of an interest in property results in an unforeseeable invasion of an interest of another order, as, e. g., one of bodily security. Perhaps other distinctions may be necessary. We do not go into the question now. The consequences to be followed must first be rooted in a wrong.

The judgment of the Appellate Division and that of the Trial Term should be reversed, and the complaint dismissed, with costs in all courts.

ANDREWS, J. (dissenting). Assisting a passenger to board a train, the defendant's servant negligently knocked a package from his arms. It fell between the platform and the cars. Of its contents the servant knew and could know nothing. A violent explosion followed. The concussion broke some scales standing a considerable distance away. In falling, they injured the plaintiff, an intending passenger.

Upon these facts, may she recover the damages she has suffered in an action brought against the master? The result we shall reach depends upon our theory as to the nature of negligence. Is it a relative concept—the breach of some duty owing to a particular person or to particular persons? Or, where there is an act which unreasonably threatens the safety of others, is the doer liable for all its proximate consequences, even where they result in injury to one who would generally be thought to be outside the radius of danger? This is not a mere dispute as to words. We might not believe that to the average mind the dropping of the bundle would seem to involve the probability of harm to the plaintiff standing many feet away whatever might be the case as to the owner or to one so near as to be likely to be struck by its fall. If, however, we adopt the second hypothesis, we have to inquire only as to the relation between cause and effect. We deal in terms of proximate cause, not of negligence.

Negligence may be defined roughly as an act or omission which unreasonably does or may affect the rights of others, or which unreasonably fails to protect one's self from the dangers resulting from such acts. Here I confine myself to the first branch of the definition. Nor do I comment on the word "unreasonable." For present purposes it sufficiently describes that average of conduct that society requires of its members.

There must be both the act or the omission, and the right. It is the act itself, not the intent of the actor, that is important. [Cc] In criminal law both the intent and the result are to be considered. Intent again is material in tort actions, where punitive damages are sought, dependent on actual malice-not one merely reckless conduct. But here neither insanity nor infancy lessens responsibility. [C]

As has been said, except in cases of contributory negligence, there must be rights which are or may be affected. Often though injury has occurred, no rights of him who suffers have been touched. A licensee or trespasser upon my land has no claim to affirmative care on my part that the land be made safe. [C] Where a railroad is required to fence its tracks against cattle, no man's rights are injured should he wander upon the road because such fence is absent. [C] An unborn child may not demand immunity from personal harm. [C] …

The proposition is this: Every one owes to the world at large the duty of refraining from those acts that may unreasonably threaten the safety of others. Such an act occurs. Not only is he wronged to whom harm, might reasonably be expected to result, but he also who is in fact injured, even if he be outside what would generally be thought the danger zone. There needs be duty due the one complaining, but this is not a duty to a particular individual because as to him harm might be expected. Harm to some one being the natural result of the act, not only that one alone, but all those in fact injured may complain. We have never, I think, held otherwise. Indeed in the Di Caprio Case we said that a breach of a general ordinance defining the degree of care to be exercised in one's calling is evidence of negligence as to every one. We did not limit this statement to those who might be expected to be exposed to danger. Unreasonable risk being taken, its consequences are not confined to those who might probably be hurt. …

The right to recover damages rests on additional considerations. The plaintiff's rights must be injured, and this injury must be caused by the negligence. We build a dam, but are negligent as to its foundations. Breaking, it injures property down stream. We are not liable if all this happened because of some reason other than the insecure foundation. But, when injuries do result from our unlawful act, we are liable for the consequences. It does not matter that they are unusual, unexpected, unforeseen, and unforeseeable. But there is one limitation. The damages must be so connected with the negligence that the latter may be said to be the proximate cause of the former.

These two words have never been given an inclusive definition. What is a cause in a legal sense, still more what is a proximate cause, depend in each case upon many considerations, as does the existence of negligence itself. Any philosophical doctrine of causation does not help us. A boy throws a stone into a pond. The ripples spread. The water level rises. The history of that pond is altered to all eternity. It will be altered by other causes also. Yet it will be forever the resultant of all causes combined. Each one will have an influence. How great only omniscience can say. You may speak of a chain, or, if you please, a net. An analogy is of little aid. Each cause brings about future events.

Without each the future would not be the same. Each is proximate in the sense it is essential. But that is not what we mean by the word. Nor on the other hand do we mean sole cause. There is no such thing.

Should analogy be though helpful, however, I prefer that of a stream. The spring, starting on its journey, is joined by tributary after tributary. The river, reaching the ocean, comes from a hundred sources. No man may say whence any drop of water is derived. Yet for a time distinction may be possible. Into the clear creek, brown swamp water flows from the left. Later, from the right comes water stained by its clay bed. The three may remain for a space, sharply divided. But at last inevitably no trace of separation remains. They are so commingled that all distinction is lost.

As we have said, we cannot trace the effect of an act to the end, if end there is. Again, however, we may trace it part of the way. A murder at Serajevo may be the necessary antecedent to an assassination in London twenty years hence. An overturned lantern may burn all Chicago. We may follow the fire from the shed to the last building. We rightly say the fire started by the lantern caused its destruction.

A cause, but not the proximate cause. What we do mean by the word 'proximate' is that, because of convenience, of public policy, of a rough sense of justice, the law arbitrarily declines to trace a series of events beyond a certain point. This is not logic. It is practical politics. Take our rule as to fires. Sparks from my burning haystack set on fire my house and my neighbor's. I may recover from a negligent railroad. He may not. Yet the wrongful act as directly harmed the one as the other. We may regret that the line was drawn just where it was, but drawn somewhere it had to be. We said the act of the railroad was not the proximate cause of our neighbor's fire. Cause it surely was. The words we used were simply indicative of our notions of public policy. Other courts think differently. But somewhere they reach the point where they cannot say the stream comes from any one source. …

There are some hints that may help us. The proximate cause, involved as it may be with many other causes, must be, at the least, something without which the event would not happen. The court must ask itself whether there was a natural and continuous sequence between cause and effect. Was the one a substantial factor in producing the other? Was there a direct connection between them, without too many intervening causes? Is the effect of cause on result not too attentuated? Is the cause likely, in the usual judgment of mankind, to produce the result? Or, by the exercise of prudent foresight, could the result be foreseen? Is the result too remote from the cause, and here we consider remoteness in time and space. [C] … Clearly we must so consider, for the greater the distance either in time or space, the more surely do other causes intervene to affect the result. When a lantern is overturned, the firing of a shed is a fairly direct consequence. Many things contribute to the spread of the conflagration—the force of the wind, the direction and width of streets, the character of intervening structures, other factors. We draw an uncertain and wavering line, but draw it we must as best we can.

Once again, it is all a question of fair judgment, always keeping in mind the fact that we endeavor to make a rule in each case that will be practical and in keeping with the general understanding of mankind. …

… In fairness he should make good every injury flowing from his negligence. Not because of tenderness toward him we say he need not answer for all that follows his wrong. We look back to the catastrophe, the fire kindled by the spark, or the explosion.

We trace the consequences, not indefinitely, but to a certain point. And to aid us in fixing that point we ask what might ordinarily be expected to follow the fire or the explosion.

This last suggestion is the factor which must determine the case before us. The act upon which defendant's liability rests is knocking an apparently harmless package onto the platform. The act was negligent. For its proximate consequences the defendant is liable. If its contents were broken, to the owner; if it fell upon and crushed a passenger's foot, then to him; if it exploded and injured one in the immediate vicinity, to him also... . Mrs. Palsgraf was standing some distance away. How far cannot be told from the record—apparently 25 or 30 feet, perhaps less. Except for the explosion, she would not have been injured. We are told by the appellant in his brief, "It cannot be denied that the explosion was the direct cause of the plaintiff's injuries." So it was a substantial factor in producing the result—there was here a natural and continuous sequence—direct connection. The only intervening cause was that, instead of blowing her to the ground, the concussion smashed the weighing machine which in turn fell upon her. There was no remoteness in time, little in space. And surely, given such an explosion as here, it needed no great foresight to predict that the natural result would be to injure one on the platform at no greater distance from its scene than was the plaintiff. Just how no one might be able to predict. Whether by flying fragments, by broken glass, by wreckage of machines or structures no one could say. But injury in some form was most probable.

Under these circumstances I cannot say as a matter of law that the plaintiff's injuries were not the proximate result of the negligence. That is all we have before us. The court refused to so charge. No request was made to submit the matter to the jury as a question of fact, even would that have been proper upon the record before us.

The judgment appealed from should be affirmed, with costs.

POUND, LEHMAN, and KELLOGG, JJ., concur with CARDOZO, C. J.

ANDREWS, J., dissents in opinion in which CRANE and O'BRIEN, JJ., concur.

INQUIRY

Relevance. The challenge that the 4-3 decision in *Palsgraf* presents is not only understanding the difference between Judge Cardozo's majority opinion conflating negligence elements and linking proximate cause to foreseeability, and Judge Andrews' dissent keeping the elements distinct and determining proximate cause under a list of factors like a direct-sequence test. How is *Palsgraf* relevant to tort practice? Do that many cases involve unforeseeable plaintiffs suffering direct but unforeseeable harms? A few cases do. *See* Edwards v. Honeywell, Inc., 50 F.3d 484 (7th Cir. 1995) (Indiana law does not require alarm company to foresee harm to firefighter's widow from delay in alarm); Mellon Mortgage Co. v. Holder, 5 S.W.2d 654, 42 Tex. Sup. J. 1159 (Tex. 1999) (victim of sexual assault occurring in defendant's garage not a foreseeable plaintiff because plaintiff had no relationship to defendant); Whiteford v. Yamaha Motor Corp., 582 N.W.2d 916 (Minn. 1998) (manufacturer need not have foreseen that child would toboggan into the underside of snowmobile); *see also* In re September 11 Litigation, 280 F. Supp.2d 279 (S.D. N.Y. 2003) (airport security interests should foresee possibility of harm not only to those in the airplanes but to those on the ground). But *Palsgraf* has a different value in exposing, through the conflicting views of two eminent jurists, the fluidly representational nature of tort law generally and negligence law specifically. We can only imprint or superimpose our verbal formulations, whatever they are, over actions and relationships, the actions and relationships being much more vital and genuine than the formulations we choose to represent them. As much as lawyers and judges try to treat tort law within a coldly analytical framework, the humanity tort law governs repeatedly forces its way through that framework. Our law language merely creates forums in which to discern truths of a justice that reaches much deeper than language. Tort law will always remain a study of the conflict between human corruption and its awful effects, on the one hand, and on the other hand our agreement that we must address that corruption and those effects through a responsible and merciful justice system—accountable while still forgiving.

Knowledge

Trends and tendencies are two useful analytical tools. Law cannot be definitive without losing sensitivity. If law is too clear, then it will be insensitive—a scoundrel's blunderbuss rather than an artist's brush or surgeon's scalpel. Static law loses its ability to adapt to new technological and social circumstances. One way in which tort law keeps it basic rules and principles sensitive is to permit and even encourage those who apply it—judges, jurors, and practitioners—to adopt certain tendencies. The rule may be for one outcome, but the trend or tendency may be to broaden or loosen the rule in certain settings or circumstances. The usefulness of tort advice, and a practitioner's economic survival, can depend on the practitioner's knowledge of trends and tendencies. The law may appear to say one thing, but the practitioner needs to know if the trend or tendency in a specific circumstance would say something else.

Foreseeability. Two cases involving the same occurrence wonderfully illustrate the foreseeability test for proximate cause. In Overseas Tankship (U.K.) Ltd. v. Morts Dock & Eng. Co., Ltd., [1961] A.C. 388 (Privy Council 1961), a case commonly known as "Wagon Mound No. 1," the owner of a wharf that was destroyed by fire sued the owners of a ship that had discharged furnace oil into the harbor. The furnace oil had drifted across the harbor's surface until it reached the dock, where molten metal from welding on the wharf fell onto cotton waste floating in the oil, igniting the oil and destroying the dock. The trial court found that the defendant ship-owners "did not know and could not reasonably be expected to have known" that the oil floating on the water's surface could catch fire but, in the direct-sequence sense of *Polemis* (above), nonetheless found for the plaintiff wharf-owner. The Privy Council reversed, rejecting the direct-sequence test and instead applying the foreseeability test. One of the Wagon Mound No. 1 opinions held that "it does not seem consonant with current ideas of justice or morality that for an act of negligence, however slight or venial, which results in some trivial foreseeable damage, the actor should be liable for all consequences however unforeseeable and however grave, so long as they can be said to be 'direct.'" Rather, proximate cause "is judged by the standard of the reasonable man, that he ought to have foreseen" those consequences—that they were "reasonably foreseeable" or "natural or necessary or probable."

Proof. How does one prove or disprove foreseeability? Overseas Tankship (U.K.) Ltd. v. Miller Steamship Co., [1967] 1 A.C. 617 (Privy Council 1966), known as "Wagon Mound No. 2," involved the same defendant ship-owners as Wagon Mound No. 1. The Wagon Mound No. 2 plaintiffs were the owners of two ships docked at the wharf whose owner sued and lost in Wagon Mound No. 1. One would think that the plaintiff ship-owners in Wagon Mound No. 2 would lose just as did the plaintiff wharf-owner in

Wagon Mound No. 1. The proximate-cause arguments were identical, the law had not changed, and their appeal after the (presumably expected) dismissal in the trial court was to the same Privy Council that had decided Wagon Mound No. 1. Yet the Privy Council reversed the trial court, finding proximate cause. What was the difference? The astute trial lawyers in Wagon Mound No. 2 had the benefit of hindsight as to the outcome of Wagon Mound No. 1. The Privy Council held that defendants' ship's engineer should have foreseen the risk of a fire on the water from the discharge of the ship's furnace oil because "the ship's engineer probably ought to have known that this had in fact happened before." The Wagon Mound decisions illustrate that proximate cause (like duty, breach, cause in fact, and damages) depends on the competence of counsel and quality of proofs.

Manner of Harm. Foreseeability, as a conceptual standard, seems clear enough, even if the outcome from its application in any one case may be uncertain. One looks to the reasonable probability of the harm occurring to determine whether defendant should have predicted it. Yet are we predicting the harm or the manner in which it occurs? It seems reasonably clear that the culpable actor need not have predicted the manner in which the harm occurs, if harm is reasonably probable. The facts of United Novelty Co. v. Daniels, 42 So.2d 395 (Miss. 1949), present the classic example. A rat happened by the defendant's lighted flame, catching its tail on fire. It scurried past a nearby gas outlet, causing an explosion that injured a worker. The appellate court held that the facts satisfied proximate cause because even though the odd manner of harm was not foreseeable, an explosion from maintaining a lighted flame adjacent to a gas outlet was foreseeable. Thus, even within the foreseeability cases, we find liability under less-predictable events.

Spreading-Fire Cases. As in other areas of tort law, proximate cause can depend on the peculiar kind or category of case. Cases involving spreading fire must determine for how much of the harm the defendant who negligently set the fire must pay. The cases differ along a spectrum from near to remote. Some cases have held defendant liable only for the loss of the first building to which the fire spreads. *See* Ryan v. New York C. R.R. Co., 35 N.Y. 210, 91 Am. Dec. 49 (1866). Others have held that the defendant should pay for the loss of the first adjoining landowner. *See* Webb v. Rome, W. & O.R. Co., 49 N.Y. 420, 10 Am. Rep. 389 (1872). Others have held that the defendant should pay for the loss on the first property set afire, without regard to whether it is adjoining. *See* Homac Corp. v. Sun Oil Co., 258 N.Y. 462, 180 N.E. 172 (1932). Most accept that liability should extend at least some distance beyond the first building, first adjacent land, or first property set afire. *See* Willner v. Wallinder Sash & Door Co., 28 N.W.2d 682 (Minn. 1947); Hoyt v. Jeffers, 30 Mich. 181 (1874). One plains-state court has held the defendant liable for damage to uninsured croplands four miles away. *See* Atchison, T. & S.F. R. Co. v. Stanford, 12 Kan. 354, 15 Am. Rep. 362 (1874). The majority of courts probably would follow a foreseeability test rather than attempting to craft bright-line rules. *See* Silver Falls Timber Co., v. Eastern & W. Lumber Co., 40 P.2d 703 (Or. 1935); Hardy v. Hines Bros. Lumber Co, 75 S.E. 855 (N.C. 1912). Should the ability to insure against fire loss influence decisions on proximate cause? *See* Ryan, *supra* (the ability to insure against fire loss justifies in part more limited fire-loss liability).

Predictability. Certain events and outcomes are inherently unpredictable. What about harms from negligence but that require some contribution from the (inherently unpredictable) weather? Under the foreseeability test, whether proximate cause exists when the harm depended on the weather depends on how predictable the weather. *See*

Johnson v. Kosmos Portland Cement Co., 64 F.2d 193 (6th Cir. 1933) (defendant liable for lightning-sparked explosion of gas collecting in the bottom of defendant's barge, where the season required foresight of bad weather); Kimble v. Mackintosh Hemphill Co., 359 Pa. 461, 59 A.2d 68 (1948) (defendant liable for roof collapse despite very high winds, where roof defect was one that made it subject to collapse from wind loads). The intervening-cause section below further addresses this issue. How to treat the unpredictability of human conception and characteristic? *See* Simmerer v. Dabbas, 89 Ohio St. 3d 586, 733 N.E.2d 1169 (2000) (holding defendant physician who negligently failed to sterilize the patient liable for costs of pregnancy but not for costs associated with child's birth defects).

Eggshell-Skull Rule. Do not confuse the foreseeability test for proximate cause with the question of the extent of the harm once some foreseeable harm has ensued. The general rule is that when some foreseeable harm results from the defendant's negligence, the defendant must pay for all harm whether its full extent is foreseeable or not. This rule, also treated briefly above in the battery studies, is the eggshell-skull or thin-skull rule, attributed in its original to Dulieu v. White, 2 K.B. 669 (King's Bench 1901), in which the court conjectured a claim for serious injury based on an unknown weakness of the victim's skull. By contrast, the foreseeability test for proximate cause asks whether *any* damage was foreseeable. For example, in Wagon Mound No. 1, evidence showed that the defendants' furnace oil had soiled the piers of the wharf before the fire destroyed it. The fact that the oil's sullying of the piers was foreseeable (which it much more likely was than the occurrence of the fire) could have satisfied proximate cause as to *some* damage. Would the eggshell-skull rule then have extended the plaintiff wharf-owner's claim to encompass the fire loss? The distinction may lie in that the fire loss still required the welders to drop molten metal into the water, making the sequence leading to the fire loss distinct enough from the oil-on-the-piers problem for the defendants to avoid the application of the eggshell-skull rule. In any case, consider now one of the best-known American cases illustrating the eggshell-skull rule.

McCahill v. New York Transp. Co.
New York Court of Appeals
201 N.Y. 221, 94 N.E. 616 (1911)

HISCOCK, J. One of the appellant's taxicabs struck respondent's intestate on Broadway, in the city of New York, in the nighttime under circumstances which, as detailed by the most favorable evidence, permitted the jury to find that the former was guilty of negligence and the latter free from contributory negligence. As a result of the accident the intestate was thrown about 20 feet, his thigh broken and his knee injured. He immediately became unconscious, and was shortly removed to a hospital, where he died on the second day thereafter of delirium tremens. A physician testified that the patient when brought to the hospital "was unconscious or irrational rather than unconscious. ... He rapidly developed delirium tremens. ... I should say with reasonable certainty the injury precipitated his attack of delirium tremens, and understand I mean precipitated, not induced." And, again, that in his opinion "the injury to the leg and the knee hurried up the delirium tremens." He also stated: "He might have had it (delirium tremens) anyway. Nobody can tell that." Of course, it is undisputed that the injuries could not have led to delirium tremens except for the pre-existing alcoholic condition of the intestate, and under these circumstances the debatable question in the case has been whether appellant's negligence was, legally speaking, the proximate cause of intestate's death. It seems to me that it was, and that the judgment should be affirmed.

In determining this question, it will be unnecessary to quote definitions of proximate cause which might be useful in testing an obscure, involved, or apparently distant relationship between an act and its alleged results, for the relationship here is perfectly simple and obvious. The appellant's automobile struck and injured the traveler. The injuries precipitated, hastened, and developed delirium tremens, and these caused death. There can be no doubt that the negligent act directly set in motion the sequence of events which caused death at the time it occurred. Closer analysis shows that the real proposition urged by the appellant is that it should not be held liable for the results which followed its negligence, either, first, because those results would not have occurred if intestate had been in a normal condition; or, secondly, because his alcoholism might have caused delirium tremens and death at a later date even though appellant had not injured him. This proposition cannot be maintained in either of its branches which are somewhat akin.

This principle has become familiar in many phases that a negligent person is responsible for the direct effects of his acts, even if more serious, in cases of the sick and infirm as well as in those of healthy and robust people, and its application to the present case is not made less certain because the facts are somewhat unusual and the intestate's prior disorder of a discreditable character. [Cc] ...

I think the judgment should be affirmed, with costs.

INQUIRY

Relevance. What is the significance of the eggshell-skull rule today—or is it merely an old-English curiosity needlessly injected into tort law by a creative quip in the *Dulieu* case? Although *Dulieu* and *McCahill* are old cases, and the idea of an eggshell skull seems obscure, the rule remains significant today. *See* Fuller v. Merten, 173 Or. App. 592, 22 P.3d 1221 (2001) (osteoporitic neck fracture due to relatively minor collision); Bartolone v. Jeckovich, 481 N.Y.S.2d 545 (App. Div. 1984) (liability for acute psychotic breakdown from minor physical injuries). The tort practitioner quickly learns that clients present a wide variety of physical and mental capacities to withstand traumatic injuries and to recover from them. A substantial percentage of cases dispute the nature and extent of the plaintiff's injury due to defendant's negligence. Courts instruct juries on the eggshell-skull rule in the form that "the defendant takes the plaintiff as he finds her" (with appropriate adaptations for the pronoun gender). *See* Aflague v. Luger, 8 Neb. App. 150, 589 N.W.2d 177 (Neb. Ct. App. 1999) (negligent defendant-driver liable for plaintiff's mental disability from minor accident, due to plaintiff's prior brain injury); Thompson v. Lupone, 135 Conn. 236, 62 A.2d 861 (1948) (defendant liable for obese plaintiff's eight-month-long recovery notwithstanding that a non-obese person would have recovered in two weeks).

Limits. Should we distinguish between the plaintiff's unusual physical susceptibilities and unusual mental susceptibilities? A few courts do so. *See* Ragin v. Harry Macklowe Real Est. Co., 6 F.3d 898 (2d Cir. 1993) (mental and emotional susceptibility due to past discrimination not protected under housing discrimination law);

Munn v. Algee, 924 F.2d 568 (5th Cir. 1991) (mental susceptibility due to religious beliefs not protected under Mississippi law). Most courts do not. *See* Steinhauser v. Hertz Corp., 421 F.2d 1169 (2d Cir. 1970) (New York law affords damages for schizophrenia from car accident). In most cases, like *McCahill*, the defendant will pay for harm due to the plaintiff's mental instability, if the case involves a physical impact. Do not confuse rules for unusual harms due to unusual susceptibilities with duty-of-care questions. As we saw in a prior section of this text, the defendant ordinarily does not have to anticipate unusual mental susceptibilities when shaping the conduct in which the defendant will engage. But as to the proximate-cause issue, once the defendant acts negligently in causing some physical harm, then the defendant pays for additional harm due to unusual mental susceptibilities.

Risk Rule. Where does proximate cause stand today? Some have argued more recently for a reformulation of the direct-sequence and foreseeability tests for proximate cause, around the concept of risk. Under that formulation, recognized in part by the Restatement (Third) of Torts: Liability for Physical Harm (Basic Principles) §29 (Tentative Draft No. 3, Apr. 7, 2003), proximate cause exists when the harm is within the risk that made the defendant's act negligent in the first place. This formulation fits neatly with cases like the one involving the rat's tail catching fire in the flame (United Novelty Co. v. Daniels, supra). If the defendant creates the risk of the harm that actually occurred (in United Novelty, an explosion), we are less concerned with the specific manner of its occurrence and more willing to accept that proximate cause exists. Marshall v. Nugent, 222 F.2d 604 (1st Cir. 1955), may be another such case, in which the defendant truck driver negligently forced a car from the road. Another car struck and injured an occupant of the car who was trying to get into position to direct traffic away from the first accident. The *Marshall* opinion held that proximate cause existed because the risks created by the defendant truck driver "were in the bosom of time, as yet unrevealed"—in other words, because the harm was within the class of risks that the defendant truck driver had created. *Cf.* Charles v. Lavergne, 412 So.2d 726 (La. App. 1982) (risk of vehicle tires bouncing cable up from pavement, wrapping cable around vehicle axle, pulling cable taut, snapping cable pole, and injuring worker on pole, was not within risk addressed by duty to slow down to avoid striking workers). Time may tell the extent to which the risk rule finds favor, although if history is any guide, even if it does, *Palsgraf* will survive to challenge and bedevil future law students.

Practice

"What do you mean by 'failure analysis'?" the expert witness asked. The plaintiff's lawyer groaned inwardly at the expert witness's response. The discovery deposition of an expert witness can be simple, or it can be a challenge—depending in large part on whether the expert witness thinks that he or she can avoid straight answers and on how much the expert witness wants to play games and fight. This deposition was going to be a challenge. "Have you heard that phrase before?" the lawyer responded. "Well, of course," said the expert. "And where have you heard that phrase used?" asked the lawyer. "In my education, at conferences—it's in the literature," the expert answered, cringing at that last admission. "Do you have any indication from your review of the records in this case that the defendant manufacturer was at all familiar with that phrase 'failure analysis'?" the lawyer asked. The expert cringed again, sensing now no point in playing games. "I think that they knew what a failure analysis was," the expert sheepishly

> answered. "Then when I ask you this next series of questions about the defendant's failure analyses, just give the phrase its ordinary meaning in your field," the lawyer instructed.

3. Intervening Causes

OBJECTIVE: Given various negligence claims in which other causes intervene between the negligence and the injury, apply the principles in this section of the text to determine whether proximate cause is satisfied as to each claim notwithstanding the intervening cause.

Case Study: An apartment management company hired a maintenance person. The maintenance person had a criminal history of thefts that the company negligently failed to discover. The maintenance person used a master key to enter an apartment one night, thinking mistakenly that the tenant was away. When the maintenance person entered the bedroom, the tenant awoke and screamed. The maintenance person ran out. The tenant grew so upset by the incident that she suffered a miscarriage. *Evaluate and discuss whether these events satisfy proximate cause in the tenant's claim against the company for harm related to her miscarriage.*

To this point, we have treated proximate cause as involving the connection between the defendant's conduct and plaintiff's harm. Law also evaluates proximate cause from a different standpoint, by looking at what intervened after the defendant's negligence in order to bring about plaintiff's harm. Bringing about a harm ordinarily involves a host of combining factors, some natural and others artificial (of human agency), and some intentional and others negligent or with due care. Law can examine the quality and predictability of the intervening acts and events that were necessary (in combination with the defendant's wrong) to bring about the harm. Courts have recognized that these two ways of looking at proximate cause—either the connection between the conduct and the harm or the quality of the intervening events—are alike, so that the latter intervening-cause approach may be superfluous. *See* Barry v. Quality Steel Prods., Inc., 263 Conn. 424, 820 A.2d 258 (2003). Indeed, with the advent of comparative-fault systems allocating fault among plaintiffs, defendants, and even non-parties, some courts have abandoned intervening-cause analyses. *See* Barry, *supra*; Control Techniques, Inc., v. Johnson, 762 N.E.2d 104 (Ind. 2002); Torres v. El Paso Elec. Co., 127 N.M. 729, 987 P.2d 386 (1999). But the majority of states retain intervening-cause analysis as an important supplement to the traditional hindsight and foresight tests of proximate cause. *See* Exxon Co. v. Sofec, Inc., 517 U.S. 830 (1996) (rejecting argument in admiralty cases that superseding cause has been replaced by risk allocation).

The basic intervening-cause rule is that when the intervening acts or events necessary to bring about the harm are extraordinary and therefore unforeseeable, those intervening acts supersede and cut off the causation set in motion by defendant's negligence. Proximate cause remains for harm that follows *intervening* acts or events but not for *superseding* causes, *see* Restatement (Second) of Torts §477 (1965)—although not all courts are conscientious in distinguishing those terms—*see* Control Techniques, Inc. v. Johnson, 762 N.E.2d 104 (Ind. 2002) (terms used interchangeably). The defendant will not be liable for harm resulting from the defendant's negligence combined with extraordinary acts or events that the defendant did not foresee and need not have foreseen. As you read the following cases involving unusual intervening causes, identify, classify, and evaluate the intervening act until you are able to state whether law should treat those intervening causes as superseding and cutting off causation as to prior negligence.

Bigbee v. Pacific Tel. and Tel. Co.
California Supreme Court
34 Cal.3d 49, 192 Cal. Rptr. 857, 665 P.2d 947 (1983)

BIRD, C.J. This appeal questions the correctness of a summary judgment entered in favor of four defendants in this personal injury action. The determinative issue is whether, under the evidence presented on the motion, foreseeability remains a question of fact for the jury. [C] ...

On November 2, 1974, plaintiff, Charles Bigbee, was severely injured when an automobile driven by Leona North Roberts struck the telephone booth in which he was standing. ... [P]laintiff sued the companies allegedly responsible for the design, location, installation, and maintenance of the telephone booth.... .

Plaintiff sought recovery against the latter defendants on theories of negligence and strict liability in tort. A second amended complaint (hereafter, the complaint), filed in 1978, alleged in substance that on the night of the accident, at approximately 12:20 a.m., plaintiff was standing in a public telephone booth located in the parking lot of a liquor store on Century Boulevard in Inglewood, California. Roberts, who was intoxicated, was driving east along Century Boulevard. She lost control of her car and veered off the street into the parking lot, crashing into the booth in which plaintiff was standing.

Plaintiff saw Roberts' car coming toward him and realized that it would hit the telephone booth. He attempted to flee but was unable to do so. According to the allegations of the complaint, the telephone booth was so defective in design and/or manufacture, or so negligently installed or maintained that the door to the booth "jammed and stuck, trapping" plaintiff inside. Had the door operated freely, he averred, he would have been able to escape and would not have suffered injury.

Additionally, plaintiff alleged that the telephone booth was negligently located in that it was placed too close to Century Boulevard.... .

Defendants contend that their duty to use due care in the location, installation, and maintenance of telephone booths does not extend to the risk encountered by plaintiff[fn] and that neither their alleged negligence in carrying out these activities nor any defect in the booth was a proximate cause of plaintiff's injuries. These contentions present the same issue in different guises. Each involves this question—was the risk that a car might crash into the phone booth and injure plaintiff reasonably foreseeable in this case? [Cc] Ordinarily, foreseeability is a question of fact for the jury. [C] It may be decided as a question of law only if, "under the undisputed facts there is no room for a reasonable difference of opinion." [Cc] ...

Turning to the merits of this case, the question presented is a relatively simple one. Is there room for a reasonable difference of opinion as to whether the risk that a car might crash into the phone booth and injure an individual inside was reasonably foreseeable under the circumstances set forth above?

In pursuing this inquiry, it is well to remember that "foreseeability is not to be measured by what is more probable than not, but includes whatever is likely enough in the setting of modern life that a reasonably thoughtful [person] would take account of it in guiding practical conduct." (2 Harper & James, Law of Torts, *supra*, § 18.2, at p. 1020.) One may be held accountable for creating even "'the risk of a slight possibility of injury if a reasonably prudent [person] would not do so.'" (*Ewart v. Southern Cal. Gas Co.* (1965) 237 Cal.App.2d 163, 172, 46 Cal.Rptr. 631, quoting from *Vasquez v. Alameda* (1958) 49 Cal.2d 674, 684, 321 P.2d 1 (dis. opn. of Traynor, J.); [cc].) Moreover, it is settled that what is required to be foreseeable is the general character of the event or harm—e.g., being struck by a car while standing in a phone booth—not its precise nature or manner of occurrence. [Cc]

Here, defendants placed a telephone booth, which was difficult to exit, in a parking lot 15 feet from the side of a major thoroughfare and near a driveway. Under these circumstances, this court cannot conclude as a matter of law that it was unforeseeable that the booth might be struck by a car and cause serious injury to a person trapped within. A jury could reasonably conclude that this risk was foreseeable. [Cc] This is particularly true where, as here, there is evidence that a booth at this same location had previously been struck. [Cc]

Indeed, in light of the circumstances of modern life, it seems evident that a jury could reasonably find that defendants should have foreseen the possibility of the very accident which actually occurred here. Swift traffic on a major thoroughfare late at night is to be expected. Regrettably, so too are intoxicated drivers. [C] Moreover, it is not uncommon for speeding and/or intoxicated drivers to lose control of their cars and crash into poles, buildings or whatever else may be standing alongside the road they travel—no matter how straight and level that road may be.

Where a telephone booth, which is difficult to exit, is placed 15 feet from such a thoroughfare, the risk that it might be struck by a car veering off the street, thereby causing injury to a person trapped within, cannot be said to be unforeseeable as a matter of law.

It is of no consequence that the harm to plaintiff came about through the negligent or reckless acts of Roberts.[fn] "If the likelihood that a third person may act in a particular manner is the hazard or one of the hazards which makes the actor negligent, such an act whether innocent, negligent, intentionally tortious, or criminal does not prevent the actor from being liable for harm caused thereby." (Rest.2d Torts, § 449; [cc]) Here, the risk that a car might hit the telephone booth could be found to constitute one of the hazards to which plaintiff was exposed.

Other courts considering cases presenting factual situations similar to this one have reached precisely the same conclusions. [Cc] …

Considering the case law and the circumstances of this case, this court cannot conclude as a matter of law that injury to plaintiff, inflicted by negligent or reckless third party drivers, was unforeseeable. "[J]ust as we may not rely upon our private judgment on this issue, so the trial court may not impose its private judgment upon a situation, such as this, in which reasonable minds may differ." (*Schwartz v. Helms Bakery Limited, supra*, 67 Cal.2d 232, 244, 60 Cal.Rptr. 510, 430 P.2d 68.)

This is not to say, of course, that defendants are liable for plaintiff's injury. This court decides only that this question is one that should be reserved for a jury.

Since the foreseeability of harm to plaintiff remains a triable issue of fact, the judgment is reversed and the case is remanded to the trial court for further proceedings consistent with the views expressed in this opinion.

Derdiarian v. Felix Contracting Corp.
New York Court of Appeals
51 N.Y.2d 308, 414 N.E.2d 666, 434 N.Y.S.2d 166 (1980)

COOKE, C.J. The operator of a motor vehicle, who failed timely to ingest a dosage of medication, suffered an epileptic seizure and his vehicle careened into an excavation site where a gas main was being installed beneath the street surface. The automobile crashed through a single wooden horse-type barricade put in place by the contractor and struck an employee of a subcontractor, who was propelled into the air. Upon landing the employee was splattered by boiling liquid enamel from a kettle also struck by the vehicle. Principally at issue on this appeal is whether plaintiffs, the employee and his wife, failed to establish as a matter of law that the contractor's inadequate safety precautions on the work site were the proximate cause of the accident. [Although plaintiff's body ignited into a fire ball, he miraculously survived the incident.] …

The order of the Appellate Division, [c], should be affirmed. As a general rule, the question of proximate cause is to be decided by the finder of fact, aided by appropriate instructions. There is no basis on this record for concluding, as a matter of law, that a superseding cause or other factor intervened to break the nexus between defendant's negligence and plaintiff's injury. …

At trial, plaintiff's theory was that defendant Felix had negligently failed to take adequate measures to insure the safety of workers on the excavation site. …

To support his claim of an unsafe work site, plaintiff called as a witness Lawrence Lawton, an expert in traffic safety. According to Lawton, the usual and accepted method of safeguarding the workers is to erect a barrier around the excavation. Such a barrier, consisting of a truck, a piece of heavy equipment or a pile of dirt, would keep a car out of the excavation and protect workers from oncoming traffic. The expert testified that the barrier should cover the entire width of the excavation. He also stated that there should have been two flagmen present, rather than one, and that warning signs should have been posted advising motorists that there was only one lane of traffic and that there was a flagman ahead.

… Defendant Felix now argues that plaintiff was injured in a freakish accident, brought about solely by defendant Dickens' negligence, and therefore there was no causal link, as a matter of law, between Felix' breach of duty and plaintiff's injuries.[fn] …

Where the acts of a third person intervene between the defendant's conduct and the plaintiff's injury, the causal connection is not automatically severed. In such a case, liability turns upon whether the intervening act is a normal or foreseeable consequence of the situation created by the defendant's negligence ([cc]). If the intervening act is extraordinary under the circumstances, not foreseeable in the normal course of events, or independent of or far removed from the defendant's conduct, it may well be a superseding act which breaks the causal nexus ([cc]). Because questions concerning what is foreseeable and what is normal may be the subject of varying inferences, as is the question of negligence itself, these issues generally are for the fact finder to resolve.

There are certain instances, to be sure, where only one conclusion may be drawn from the established facts and where the question of legal cause may be decided as a matter of law. Those cases generally involve independent intervening acts which operate upon but do not flow from the original negligence. Thus, for instance, we have held that where an automobile lessor negligently supplies a car with a defective trunk lid, it is not liable to the lessee who, while stopped to repair the trunk, was injured by the negligent driving of a third party (Ventricelli v. Kinney System Rent A Car, supra). Although the renter's negligence undoubtedly served to place the injured party at the site of the accident, the intervening act was divorced from and not the foreseeable risk associated with the original negligence. And the injuries were different in kind than those which would have normally been expected from a defective trunk. In short, the negligence of the renter merely furnished the occasion for an unrelated act to cause injuries not ordinarily anticipated ([c]).

By contrast, in the present case, we cannot say as a matter of law that defendant Dickens' negligence was a superseding cause which interrupted the link between Felix' negligence and plaintiff's injuries. From the evidence in the record, the jury could have found that Felix negligently failed to safeguard the excavation site. A prime hazard associated with such dereliction is the possibility that a driver will negligently enter the work site and cause injury to a worker. That the driver was negligent, or even reckless, does not insulate Felix from liability ([cc]). Nor is it decisive that the driver lost control of the vehicle through a negligent failure to take medication, rather than a driving mistake ([c]). The precise manner of the event need not be anticipated. The finder of fact could have concluded that the foreseeable, normal and natural result of the risk created by Felix was the injury of a worker by a car entering the improperly protected work area. An intervening act may not serve as a superseding cause, and relieve an actor of responsibility, where the risk of the intervening act occurring is the very same risk which renders the actor negligent.

In a similar vein, plaintiff's act of placing the kettle on the west side of the excavation does not, as a matter of law, absolve defendant Felix of responsibility.[fn] Serious injury, or even death, was a foreseeable consequence of a vehicle crashing through the work area. The injury could have occurred in numerous ways, ranging from a worker being directly struck by the car to the car hitting an object that injures the worker. Placement of the kettle, or any object in the work area, could affect how the accident occurs and the extent of injuries. That defendant could not anticipate the precise manner of the accident or the exact extent of injuries, however, does not preclude liability as a matter of law where the general risk and character of injuries are foreseeable. ...

For the foregoing reasons, the order of the Appellate Division should be affirmed, with costs. The certified question is answered in the affirmative.

INQUIRY

Negligence of Others. The *Bigbee* and *Derdiarian* cases involve intervening acts that were presumably negligent—leaving the highway and crashing into a telephone booth in the first case and crashing through a construction barrier in the second case. Must we, when predicting the effects of our own negligence, anticipate the negligence of others? *Contrast* Hairston v. Alexander Tank and Equip. Co., 310 N.C. 227, 311 S.E.2d 559 (1984) (defendant liable on basis of negligence in vehicle maintenance requiring that vehicle be stopped on the side of the road, even though the harm occurred through the "inexcusable" negligence of another driver in leaving the road and striking the vehicle's driver), *with* Quirke v. City of Harvey, 266 Ill. App.3d 664, 639 N.E.2d 1355 (1994) (city and power company defendants not liable for turning off power to prevent a suicide, when power shut-off resulted in negligent driver causing injury at unlit intersection); Falk v. Finkelman, 268 Mass. 524, 168 N.E. 89 (1929) (no proximate cause as to claim against defendant for negligently parking car on street where fire truck ran into it resulting in injury to pedestrian). Restatement (Second) of Torts §477 (1965) suggests that intervening acts of third persons that are extraordinarily negligent will be superseding causes cutting off causation as to the prior negligent of the defendant. *See* Georgia Pipe Co. v. Lawler, 584 S.E.2d 634 (Ga. Ct. App. 2003) (jury question whether trucker who saw that bands had broken on load was superseding cause of load falling from truck); Roberts v. Benoit, 605 So.2d 1032 (La. 1991) (deputy's foolishly playing with gun supersedes defendant's negligent training of deputy). Restatement (Second) of Torts §442 (1965) lists factors to consider including how extraordinary is the act, whether it was independent of the defendant's negligence, whether another person is liable for the harm, and how culpable was that other person's misconduct. Courts are more likely to regard negligent acts as intervening rather than superseding.

> **Ethics**
>
> Of all the ethics rules tort lawyers know, probably the most often encountered and fundamental is the rule to pursue only meritorious claims and defenses. The ABA Model Rules of Professional Conduct admonish in Rule 3.1 that "[a] lawyer shall not bring or defend a proceeding, or assert or controvert an issue therein, unless there is a basis in law and fact for doing so that is not frivolous, which includes a good faith argument for an extension, modification, or reversal of existing law." Note the latitude lawyers have to file certain cases that would require an extension or even reversal of law—but only with a good-faith argument (perhaps a trend, authority in another jurisdiction, or a compelling equity). Any impression that plaintiff's lawyers routinely file meritless claims is simply wrong. A lawyer who does so could lose the license to practice law, suffer court sanction, and face civil actions. One's professional reputation and practice, not to mention peace of mind and well-being of soul, depend on making well-informed, good-faith judgments about the merits of claims and defenses.

Intentional Acts. Are intentional acts more likely superseding than unintentional acts? *See* Wiener v. Southcoast Childcare Ctrs., Inc., 32 Cal.4th 1138, 12 Cal. Rptr.3d 615, 88 P.3d 517 (2004) (motorist's intentionally driving his vehicle through defendant's inadequate fence killing children was superseding cause); Kozicki v. Dragon, 255 Neb. 248, 583 N.W.2d 336 (Neb. 1998) (defendant liable for injury from collision caused by car thief after defendant left his car running in a high crime area because defendant should have foreseen that thieves are more negligent drivers); *see also* Herrera v. Quality Pontiac, 134 N.M. 43, 73 P.3d 181 (2003) (proximate-cause issue to jury on liability of negligent vehicle-driver who left keys in ignition, for thief's collision). Is a trespass a foreseeable intervening act or an unpredictable superseding act? *See* Aetna Ins. Co. v. 3 Oaks Wrecking and Lumber Co., 65 Ill. App.3d 618, 382 N.E.2d 283, 21 Ill. Dec. 919 (1978) (defendant liable for negligently maintaining condemned house in which trespassing vagrants started a fire that burned down an adjacent building insured by plaintiff). Should the law find proximate cause when the defendant repossession agent sets off a car alarm in the middle of the night, and a third person shoots a neighbor in the ensuing confusion? *See* Griffith v. Calley of Sun Recovery & Adj. Bureau, Inc., 126 Ariz. 227, 613 P.2d 1283 (1988) (proximate-cause issue to jury). When the defendant negligently enables a stranger to impersonate an elevator boy who insidiously ushers the plaintiff into an open elevator shaft? Cole v. German Savings & Loan Society, 124 Fed. 113 (8th Cir. 1903) (no proximate cause). At least in some cases, the knowledge of the intervening person (whether they knew that injury was substantially certain) will make a difference in whether proximate cause exists as to the negligent defendant. *See* Lockhart v. Loosen, 943 P.2d 1074 (Okla. 1997) (if husband knew that he had sexually transmitted disease from affair, when he infected plaintiff wife, then his infection of wife was superseding cause as to negligence of husband's girlfriend for not warning wife).

Criminal Acts. Should the fact that an intentional act is also criminal make a difference in determining whether it is a superseding cause? To put it another way, should a defendant be held to foresee that someone might go so far as to commit a crime that combines with the defendant's negligence in a way that causes harm for which the defendant would then be held liable? One well-known old case on a criminal act as superseding cause is Watson v. Kentucky & Indiana Bridge & R.R. Co., 137 Ky. 619, 126 S.W. 146 (1910). The defendant railroad's negligence resulted in a gasoline spill into the street. When a man struck a match "to light a cigar" (as he testified), the ensuing explosion injured the plaintiff bystander. Others testified that the man had said, "Let's go set the damn thing on fire," and had thus caused the explosion deliberately. The appellate court held that the jury should resolve the superseding-cause issue by deciding which of the two stories was true. If the man had caused the explosion intentionally, then no proximate cause existed as to the railroad's negligence because "if the intervening agency is something so unexpected or extraordinary as that he could not or ought not to have anticipated it, he will not be liable, and certainly he is not bound to anticipate the criminal acts of others… ." The general rule, though, is not so clear. Criminal acts do not automatically end proximate cause as to harm flowing from prior negligent acts that combine with them. Consider the following case and summary of more recent law, from the same jurisdiction that produced the *Watson* opinion.

Britton v. Wooten
Kentucky Supreme Court
817 S.W.2d 443 (Ky. 1991)

LEIBSON, J. On May 8, 1983, Wooten's Pic Pac Grocery in Louisa, Kentucky, was destroyed by fire. A portion of the grocery store premises consisted of a building owned by the movant, Genoa Britton (the lessor), and leased to L. Wayne Wooten d/b/a Wooten's Pic Pac and Wooten's Grocery Company, Inc. (collectively, the lessee). The movant filed suit against her lessee alleging negligence in the operation of the grocery store. Allegedly, the store employees stacked trash that was flammable, combustible material next to the building all the way up to the eaves, in violation of the fire marshal's regulations and the fire code of the State of Kentucky. Consequently, a fire originating in the trash progressed up the exterior wall to the combustible roof, causing the building to burn to the ground.

The only evidence of record specifically identifying how the fire started was the testimony of Andrew Reed, an arson investigator from the Kentucky State Police, who had investigated the cause of the fire at length. He stated that in his opinion "someone set fire to the paper boxes in or near the dempsey dumpsters." ...

In seeking Summary Judgment, the lessee had ... relied upon "several general principles of law pertaining to proximate causation" and, more specifically, "that the act of the arsonist in setting the fire was a superseding cause as a matter of law, thereby breaking the chain of causation." [The trial court granted summary judgment on that and another basis. The Court of Appeals affirmed on the other grounds, not reaching the superseding cause issue.] ...

The Complaint alleges, and the record suggests, that the manner in which the lessee's employees permitted trash and refuse to accumulate and pile up next to the grocery building was in violation of a safety code, [c]. Such violations of administrative regulations, like statutory violations, constitute negligence, per se, and the basis for liability if found to be a substantial factor in causing the result. [Cc] ...

Even if there were no safety code, stacking rubbish and boxes close to a building and too high in the dumpsters, to such extent that if a fire started it would climb the masonry wall to the inflammable material in the roof of the building constitutes acts which might well be viewed as actionable negligence. ...

If the boxes and trash were piled high against the masonry wall in such a manner as to permit a fire started in the refuse access up the masonry wall to the inflammable roof of the building, undoubtedly this was a proximate cause, or a substantial factor, in the destruction of the building regardless of how the fire started. The proximate cause issue lacks substance, and the respondent really has only one argument, that "the act of the arsonist in setting the fire was a superseding cause as a matter of law."

... [W]e reject any all-inclusive general rule that, as respondent contends, "criminal acts of third parties ... relieve the original negligent party from liability."

This archaic doctrine has been rejected everywhere. The only Kentucky case movant cites in support of it *Watson v. Kentucky & Indiana Bridge and R. Co.,* 137 Ky. 619, 126 S.W. 146 (1910), a case over 80 years old. In it the court draws a distinction in the railroad company's liability for a fire ignited following a train derailment and gas spillage on the basis of a fact question presented as to whether the man who ignited the gasoline did so maliciously or inadvertently. That case indeed holds that the railroad company is "not bound to anticipate the criminal act of others by which damage is inflicted and hence is not liable therefor." *Id.* at 151.... . The question is whether that case is still viable.

Respondent cites *Restatement (Second) of Torts,* § 448 in support of the continued viability of criminal acts, per se, as sufficient to cut the chain of causation. That section postulates that "an intentional tort or crime is a superseding cause" where the defendant's "negligent conduct" only creates "a situation which afforded an opportunity" for another to commit an intentional tort or crime, but it adds an all important caveat: "... unless the actor [the defendant] at the time of his negligent conduct realized or should have realized the likelihood that such a situation might be created, and that a third person might avail himself of the opportunity to commit such a tort or crime."

Restatement (Second) of Torts, § 449, expands on the meaning of § 448. Section 449 postulates: "If the likelihood that a third person may act in a particular manner is the hazard or one of the hazards which makes the actor [the defendant] negligent, such an act [by another person] whether innocent, negligent, intentionally tortious, or criminal, does not prevent the actor [the defendant] from being liable for harm caused thereby." And these two sections, 448 and 449, also must be read in conjunction with *Restatement*

(Second) of Torts, § 302B, "Risk of Intentional or Criminal Conduct," which states: "An act or an omission may be negligent if the actor realizes or should realize that it involves an unreasonable risk of harm to another through the conduct of the other or a third person which is intended to cause harm, even though such conduct is criminal."

The fact is that the appendices to the *Restatement (Second) of Torts,* §§ 448 and 449, are replete with numerous cases, perhaps one hundred in number, from throughout these United States, acknowledging the *Restatement (Second) of Torts* §§ 448 and 449 as authority and deciding the negligence of a defendant is actionable as a contributing cause, wherein the immediate cause is a subsequent criminal act. ...

In the present case whether the spark ignited in the trash accumulated next to the building was ignited negligently, intentionally, or even criminally, or if it was truly accidental, is not the critical issue. The issue is whether the movant can prove that the respondent caused or permitted trash to accumulate next to its building in a negligent manner which caused or contributed to the spread of the fire and the destruction of the lessor's building. If so, the source of the spark that ignited the fire is not a superseding cause under any reasonable application of modern tort law.

The Summary Judgment in the trial court is vacated, and the decision in the Court of Appeals affirming it is reversed. The within case is remanded to the trial court for further proceedings consistent with this Opinion.

INQUIRY

Other Crimes. Do not misread *Britton* and the many cases it cites, holding negligent defendants to foreseeing how criminal conduct might combine with their negligence, to suggest that landowners, businesses, and other concerns have a general duty to protect against criminal conduct. *See* Medcalf v. Washington Heights Condominium Assn., 747 A.2d 532 (Conn. App. 2000) (defendant's malfunctioning intercom system not a proximate cause of violent assault by building intruder); State v. Dierker, 961 S.W.2d 58 (Mo. 1998) (unforeseeable to highway department that teenager would throw chunk of concrete from freeway overpass onto windshield of car); Thomas v. United States Soccer Fed., 236 A.D.2d 600, 653 N.Y.S.2d 958 (N.Y. App. Div. 1997) (federation's negligent failure to train referee and provide a safe sporting environment not a proximate cause of player's injury when unruly fans held the player down for opposing player to bite off his ear); Nola M. v. University of Southern California, 20 Cal. Rptr.2d 97 (Cal. Ct. App. 1993) (no basis to hold that better campus security would not have prevented plaintiff's injury); Morales v. City of New York, 521 N.E.2d 425 (N.Y. 1988) (sale of gasoline in milk jugs rather than approved containers was not a proximate cause of damage from arson accomplished by use of gasoline from jugs); Toone v. Adams, 262 N.C. 403, 137 S.E.2d 132 (1964) (criminal assault on baseball umpire was unforeseeable); Bence v. Crawford Savings & Loan Assn., 400 N.E.2d 39 (Ill. App. 1980) (bank not liable for death of patron shot by robber who panicked when bank personnel refused to open automated door to allow robber to escape); Beneneson v. National Surety Co., 260 N.Y. 299, 183 N.E. 505 (1932) (check forgery was unforeseeable). To the contrary, duty and proximate cause exist in such cases only when other special circumstances are present.

Special Relationships. A special relationship between the plaintiff and defendant may support proximate cause and liability when the defendant breaches a duty and a foreseeable crime occurs, harming the plaintiff. *See* Bell v. Board of Educ., 90 N.Y.2d 944, 687 N.E.2d 1325, 665 N.Y.S.2d 42 (1997) (proximate-cause issue is for jury where teacher left field-trip site without waiting for missing student, who was then raped on walk home alone); Stevens v. Des Moines Indep. Commun. Sch. Dist., 528 N.W.2d 117 (Iowa 1995) (proximate-cause issue to jury on allegation that school failed to adequately supervise hallways to prevent student beating). The defendant may have negligently defeated security designed to frustrate the crime. *See* Garceau v. Engel, 169 Minn. 62, 210 N.W. 608 (1926) (defendant liable for plaintiff's loss after defendant left keys to plaintiff's store in the store's front door). The defendant may have negligently placed the criminal in a position to accomplish the crime. *See* Easley v. Apollo Det. Agency, 69 Ill. App.3d 920, 26 Ill. Dec. 313, 387 N.E.2d 1241 (1979) (defendant security firm negligently hired violent employee, given access to plaintiff's apartment where assault occurred). Or the defendant may have negligently performed a duty specifically with respect to the criminal who committed the intervening crime. *See* Christensen v. Epley, 36 Or. App. 535, 585 P.2d 416 (1978) (youth center director held liable for death of person shot by youths escaping from detention center); *but see* Shepard v. South Carolina Dept. of Corrections, 299 S.C. 370, 385 S.E.2d 35 (Ct. App. 1989) (highway department not liable for rape and murder committed by convict escapee from cleanup crew); Dunn v. State, 29 N.Y.2d 313, 277 N.E.2d 647, 327 N.Y.S.2d 622 (1971) (no proximate cause where psychotic ward escaped from defendant's center, stole car, and negligently collided with plaintiff's vehicle).

Products. Superseding cause can also be a proximate-cause issue relating to the manufacture and sale of defective products. *See* Morguson v. 3M Co., 857 So.2d 796 (Ala. 2003) (perfusionist hooking up heart-lung machine backward, causing patient's death, was superseding cause as to heart-lung machine manufacturer's design defect enabling machine to be hooked up backward); Stahlecker v. Ford Motor Co., 266 Neb. 601, 667 N.W.2d 244 (2003) (manufacturer of defective tire not liable for unforeseeable rape and murder of motorist stranded when tire failed); Briscoe v. Amazing Prods., Inc., 23 S.W.2d 228 (Ky. App. 2000) (manufacturer of drain cleaner not liable for extraordinary criminal assault by purchaser who threw cleaner in another's face); Tabb v. ICI Explosives, USA, Inc., 160 F.3d 613 (10th Cir. 1998) (fertilizer manufacturer not liable for federal-building bombing enabled by negligent mislabeling of explosive-grade fertilizer). Some circumstances exist, though, under which the manufacturer should have anticipated the criminal misuse of the manufacturer's product. For instance, the defendant may have marketed a dangerous product in a manner that its criminal misuse was foreseeable. *See* Ileto v. Glock Inc., 349 F.3d 1191 (9th Cir. 2003) (foreseeable that over-marketing guns would create secondary market for criminal users); *see also* Pavlides v. Niles Gun Show, Inc., 93 Ohio App.3d 46, 637 N.E.2d 404 (1994) (jury issue whether gun show promoters were liable for shooting that occurred after youth stole gun from show).

Effect of Statute. In the *Britton* case above, the defendant had failed to comply with a statute arguably intended to protect against the kind and manner of harm that occurred. Should the law extend proximate cause to include the harmful effects of the violation of statute, even if the intervening cause that the statute anticipates is criminal and extraordinary? *See* Liberty Natl. Life Ins. Co., v. Weldon, 267 Ala. 171, 100 So.2d 696 (1957) (aunt's murder of child was foreseeable to defendant life-insurance company, the negligence of which enabled the aunt to purchase a policy on the child in the company's violation of an insurable-interest statute). The presence or absence of a statute against leaving keys in a car's ignition appears to make a difference in some of the stolen-car cases. *Compare* Ney v. Yellow Cab Co., 2 Ill.2d 74, 117 N.E.2d 74 (1954) (liability—statute), *with* Hergenrether v. East, 61 Cal.2d 440, 393 P.2d 164, 39 Cal. Rptr. 4 (1964) (no liability—no statute). Car-lot owners are apparently less likely to be liable for harms caused by vehicle-thieves whose thefts the car-lot owner negligently enabled. *See* Kim v. Budget Rent A Car, 143 Wash.2d 190, 15 P.3d 1283 (2001) (no lot-owner liability).

The Rescue Doctrine. Negligence can create the need for help or rescue, exposing the helpers or rescuers to perils of their own. Under the *rescue doctrine*, a defendant whose negligence creates a need for rescue may be liable to a rescuer who suffers injury. Think of the amateur adventurer whose foolishness requires others to go to great lengths and considerable peril to rescue the amateur from the adventure. *See* Sears v. Morrison, 90 Cal. Rptr.2d 528, 76 Cal. App.4th 577 (1999) (proximate cause extends to rescuer's claim against person needing rescue); In re Est. of Keck v. Blair, 71 Wash. App. 105, 856 P.2d 740 (1993) (same). Or think of the innocent traveler who requires rescue because of the negligent acts of the person or entity whose negligence caused the traveler's need for rescue. *See* McCoy v. American Suzuki Motor Corp., 136 Wash.2d 350, 961 P.2d 952 (1998) (proximate cause extends to rescuer's claim against manufacturer whose defective vehicle rolled over, causing need for rescue). Or think of the manufacturer whose product failed, endangering its user to the point of rescue, and resulting in injury to the rescuer. *See* Dillard v. Pittway Corp., 719 So.2d 188 (Ala. 1998) (proximate cause extends to manufacturer of defective smoke detector, in claim by rescuer of homeowners threatened by fire). What makes the question appropriate for intervening-cause treatment is that the acts of the person who requires rescue, or the acts of the rescuer, may each be so extraordinary that holding liable the defendant whose negligence set the need for rescue in motion is injust. *See* Atchison, T. & S.F.R. Co. v. Calhoun, 213 U.S. 1 (1909) (no proximate cause for claim against defendant railroad over rescuer's foolish attempt to return child to alighting passenger, that resulted in injury to child); *see also* Lambert v. Parrish, 492 N.E.2d 289 (Ind. 1986) (proximate cause does not extend to injury of non-rescuer husband who rushed to scene of wife's accident). Consider an illustrative case.

Lowrey v. Horvath
Missouri Supreme Court
689 S.W.2d 625 (Mo. 1985)

DONNELLY, J. Sherry Lowrey and her three minor children, Roxanna Lowrey, Dallas Lowrey and Robert Lowrey, instituted this action against Carolyn Horvath and the estate of Charles Horvath to recover damages for the wrongful death of their husband and father, Bobby Lowrey, and to recover damages for personal injuries sustained by Sherry Lowrey. …

… The averments in Count I of plaintiffs' petition include the following facts: … that Bobby Lowrey, at the request of Carolyn Horvath, entered a well located on property owned jointly by Carolyn and Charles Horvath in order to render assistance to Charles Horvath who had previously entered the well for the purpose of cleaning and repairing it; that Carolyn Horvath requested Bobby Lowrey's help in the belief that her husband may have been injured or ill; that Bobby Lowrey, after receiving Carolyn Horvath's request for help, attempted to render assistance to Charles Horvath inside of the well and thereafter collapsed and died as a result of asphyxiation; that Carolyn and Charles Horvath were negligent in the manner in which they undertook to clean and repair the well in that Carolyn and/or Charles Horvath placed a gasoline powered pump in or immediately above the well and Carolyn and Charles Horvath knew or in the exercise of ordinary care should have known that locating the pump in such a position created a grave risk of death or serious physical injury to those entering the well; and that as a direct and proximate result of the negligence of Carolyn and Charles Horvath and the death of Bobby Lowrey, plaintiffs have sustained damages.

... Plaintiffs... contend that under the "rescue doctrine" the petition sufficiently charges defendant-decedent Charles Horvath with negligence in placing himself in a perilous situation that was likely to invite a rescue attempt by others.

... Under the rule which has developed, a person who is injured in the course of undertaking a rescue may recover from the person whose negligence created the peril necessitating the rescue so long as the rescuer's conduct is not rash or reckless. [Cc] The rescue doctrine offers ... important benefits to the person who is attempting to recover for injuries incurred during a rescue attempt. ... [T]he plaintiff may invoke the rescue doctrine to establish "that the defendant's negligence in creating the peril which induced the injured person to attempt to rescue another who was imperiled was the proximate cause of the injury for which recovery is sought * * *." 57 Am.Jur.2d *Negligence* § 418 (1971). [C] ...

Recovery under the rescue doctrine is based upon the theory that danger invites rescue and therefore "the negligence or wrong that imperils life is not only a wrong to the imperiled victim but is also a wrong (negligence) to his rescuer." *Dulley[v. Berkly]*, 304 S.W.2d [878,] 883[(Mo. 1957)]. For this reason, persons who have negligently forced some "third party" into a situation inviting the plaintiff's rescue have been held liable for the plaintiff's injury even though they might not have contemplated that someone would attempt to extricate the third party from danger. In the oft repeated words of Judge Cardozo, although the wrongdoer "may not have foreseen the coming of a deliverer [h]e is accountable as if he had." *Wagner v. International Ry. Co.*, 232 N.Y. 176, 180, 133 N.E. 437, 438 (1921).

There is no logical basis for distinguishing between the situation in which recovery is sought against a defendant whose negligence imperiled some third party, and the situation in which recovery is sought against a defendant who negligently imperiled himself. A person with reasonable foresight who negligently imperils another or who negligently imperils himself will normally contemplate the probability of an attempted rescue, in the course of which the rescuer may sustain injury. ...

We conclude that given the natural reactions and conduct to be expected of ordinary people in a life-threatening situation, there is a probability of injury sufficiently serious that a reasonable person will take precautions to avoid placing himself in a position of peril that is likely to invite rescue. [Cc] ...

... The judgment dismissing Count I of plaintiffs' petition is reversed and the case is remanded for a trial upon the merits.

All concur.

INQUIRY

Firefighter Rule. In the *Wagner* opinion cited in the above case, Justice Cardozo added the famously Delphic statement, "Danger invites rescue," to justify a passenger's claim against a rail line, when the passenger's cousin fell from the train while it passed over a high trestle, and the passenger was hurt climbing down the trestle in an attempt to locate the cousin. Should professional rescuers have claims against those whom they rescue? A majority of jurisdictions bar rescue-doctrine claims by professional rescuers including firefighters and police, if their injury is of the kind that their profession anticipates. *See* Smith v. Tully, 665 A.2d 1333 (R.I. 2002) (police officer's claim for injury responding to bar-fight call barred by rule); Farmer v. B & G Enterprises, Inc., 818 So.2d 1154 (Miss. 2002); Pinter v. American Family Mut. Ins. Co., 613 N.W.2d 110 (Wis. 2000); Flowers v. Rock Creek Terrace Ltd. Partnership, 520 A.2d 361 (Md. 1987) (rule applies even to volunteer firefighters). The firefighter rule's rationales include the rescuer's voluntary assumption of job-related risks and that the job itself will provide adequate compensation either in hazard pay or in disability-benefits systems. The firefighter's rule is, nonetheless, a disfavored doctrine that some states have abolished recently, *see* Fla. Stat. ch. 112.182 (1990); Mich. Comp. L. §600.2965; N.J. Stat. Ann. 2A:62A-21 (1994); Christensen v. Murphy, 296 Or. 610, 678 P.2d 1210 (1984), or if not abolished, then limited, *see* Cole v. Hubanks, 272 Wis.2d 539, 681 N.W.2d 147 (2004); Neighbarger v. Irwin Indus., Inc., 882 P.2d 347 (Cal. 1994) (rule does not apply to privately employed rescuer); Mahoney v. Carus Chem. Co., 102 N.J. 564, 510 A.2d 4 (1986) (rule does not apply if defendant intended to create firefighter's risk). Even where the rule survives, if the professional's injury is unrelated to the usual professional risks of rescue, then the professional's rescue-doctrine claim exists. *See* Tucker v. Shoemake, 354 Md. 413, 731 A.2d 884 (1999) (rule does not bar police officer's claim for injury due to negligence unrelated to professional call); Melton v. Crane Rental Co., 742 A.2d 875 (D.C. 1999) (rule does not bar claim by EMT injured by crane collapse while taking patient to hospital in ambulance); Solgaard v. Guy F. Atkinson Co., 6 Cal.3d 361, 491 P.2d 821, 99 Cal. Rptr. 29 (1971) (construction-site physician entitled to bring claim for injury while trying to rescue worker from landslide).

Medical Care. Should a defendant whose negligence injures another in a manner that requires medical treatment have to pay for additional harm caused by medical malpractice in the course of that treatment? *See* Weber v. Charity Hosp., 475 So.2d 1047 (La. 1985) (proximate cause satisfied as to claim against defendant whose negligence caused injuries requiring transfusion, when transfusion led to plaintiff's hepatitis). Courts accept that medical malpractice occurs at a sufficient incidence for the negligent defendant to foresee and compensate for it. Liability for another's malpractice may seem academic because the plaintiff would have claims against the defendant who caused the original injury and the medical-care provider who committed the malpractice. Yet the cost and uncertainty of the malpractice claim may make the liability claim against the first defendant more palatable. The plaintiff's additional injury may also not have been from malpractice but merely from the need for treatment. *See* Anaya v. Superior Ct., 78 Cal. App.4th 971, 93 Cal. Rptr. 228 (2000) (proximate cause satisfied as to negligence claim against defendant driver, for death of person whom defendant injured in car crash, when emergency helicopter crashed on way to the hospital). On the other hand, the courts may find that a medical-care provider who commits an egregious form of malpractice has superseded proximate cause as to the defendant whose negligence caused the harm that required the treatment. *See* Purchase v. Seelye, 231 Mass. 434, 121 N.E. 413 (1918) (operating on the wrong side of the patient). Should a defendant whose negligence harms the plaintiff in a way that subjects the plaintiff to other injury or disease, have to pay for the harm of that other injury or disease? *See* Hammerstein v. Jean Developm. West, 111 Nev. 1471, 902 P.2d 975 (1995) (landlord subject to liability for diabetic's gangrene caused by blister following ankle twist from walking down stairs due to negligently maintained fire alarm); Mitchell v. Legarsky, 95 N.H. 214, 60 A.2d 136 (1948) (defendant liable for second breaking of plaintiff's limb weakened by original injury); Wallace v. Ludwig, 292 Mass. 251, 198 N.E. 159 (1935) (defendant liable for infection from plaintiff's weakened condition). The cases just cited are examples of a principle that the Restatement (Second) of Torts §441, Comment *c* (1965), recognizes, that a defendant will more likely be held liable for harm flowing from intervening causes that are dependent on the defendant's original negligence. They are also examples of a second principle that once the defendant must pay for some harm (sufficiently direct and foreseeable in nature), then the defendant is more likely to be liable for additional harm that is indirect and not foreseeable.

Plaintiff's Conduct. To this point, we have examined cases in which the intervening causes were outside of the plaintiff's control. One would think that when the plaintiff's own extraordinary acts combine with the defendant's negligence to bring about the harm, that liability would depend on comparative negligence, assumption of risk, the open-and-obvious defense, product misuse, and other defenses that focus on the plaintiff's conduct. Yet in the truly extraordinary case in which the defendant could not have foreseen the plaintiff's actions, law may instead evaluate the plaintiff's conduct within the intervening-cause framework, treating the plaintiff's own actions as having superseded the chain of causation set in motion by the defendant's negligence. *Cf.* Mesick v. State of New York, 118 A.D.2d 214, 504 N.Y.S.2d 279 (1986) (plaintiff's falling from rope into shallow water-hole with jagged rocks not a superseding cause, where defendant knew of rope's use). As you read the following case, consider why the plaintiff's decedent acted as he did, and decide whether you think his actions were sufficiently extraordinary to cut off the chain of proximate cause set in motion by the defendant's negligence. Note that a higher appellate court reversed the opinion you are about to read. If you had represented the losing appellant in the opinion below, would you have advised and undertaken the further appeal that resulted in reversal?

Yun v. Ford Motor Co.
New Jersey Superior Court
276 N.J. Super. 142, 647 A.2d 841, reversed,
143 N.J. 162, 669 A.2d 1378 (1994)

VILLANUEVA, J. Plaintiffs Gloria Yun (as administrator *ad prosequendum* of the estate of Chang Hak Yun)[fn] and Nam Yi Yun, the decedent's widow,[fn] appeal from a summary judgment dismissing their claims against defendants Ford Motor Company (Ford), Castle Ford (Castle), Universal Motor Coach (Universal), Kim's Mobile Service Center, Inc. (Kim) and Miller Manufacturing Corporation (Miller).

Chang Hak Yun (Chang) was struck by an automobile on the Garden State Parkway while retrieving a spare tire that had fallen off of a Ford van in which he was a passenger. Approximately seven months later, he died of the injuries sustained.

Plaintiffs brought suit against the defendants, claiming that the apparatus connecting the spare tire to the rear of the van was defective. ...

On November 27, 1988, between 11:10 p.m. and 11:40 p.m., Chang was a passenger in a 1987 Ford van owned and driven by his daughter, Yun Cho Shim (Yun), northbound in the local lanes of the Garden State Parkway (Parkway). While driving on the Parkway returning from Atlantic City, Yun heard a "rattling type" noise coming from the rear of the van. According to the plaintiffs, at approximately mile post 50.8 the plastic cover and spare tire and part of the support bracket which was screwed to the rear of the van, landed directly behind Yun's van and then rolled across both lanes of traffic or were pushed there by another vehicle, ultimately coming to a rest against the wooden guard rail separating the Parkway lanes.

Yun safely drove the van onto the right berm of the highway and stopped. Chang, a rear seat passenger who was sixty-five years old at the time, exited the vehicle, then ran across two lanes of the dark, rain-slicked Parkway and retrieved the spare tire and some of the other parts. During the course of returning back to the Ford van across the Parkway, Chang was struck by the vehicle operated by defendant Precious Linderman. Precious Linderman had been driving northbound in the right lane when she saw and struck Chang as he was crossing the Parkway. ...

On October 27, 1988, approximately one month prior to the subject accident, defendant Kim had serviced the Ford van. According to Kim, Yun and Chang had brought the van to Kim for an oil change and a tune up. Kim changed the oil but advised Chang and his daughter that a tune-up was not necessary. However, Kim also advised them that the front driver's side tire was extremely bald and should not be driven in that condition. Consequently, Chang and his daughter requested Kim to change the tire with the spare located in the bracket on the outside rear of the van. Kim removed the spare tire from the bracket and used it to replace the worn left front tire. Kim thereafter placed the worn tire in the bracket and secured it.

Additionally, Chang and Yun advised Kim that the bracket holding the spare tire was damaged, "bent down," apparently as a result of a motor vehicle accident that occurred several months earlier. Chang and Yun told Kim not to repair same, because they knew where to get the parts and that it was going to be repaired by the dealer and handled through the insurance company of the other driver who was involved in that motor vehicle accident. ...

Shortly after the accident, on behalf of plaintiffs, Seymour S. Bodner, a consulting engineer, examined the van and the remains of the spare tire assembly. He opined that the bracket frame remained secured to the van's left rear door at its three attachment areas but a portion of the mounting bracket had sheared off from the assembly. Bodner concluded that an aluminum strap, which secured the attached spare tire, was defectively welded to the bracket frame. ... The resulting "fatigue failure" of the strap then caused it to fracture... .

... [P]laintiffs must prove that the alleged defect in the spare tire bracket assembly proximately caused the injuries sustained by Chang. [C] Proximate cause is "'any cause which in the natural and continuous sequence, unbroken by an efficient intervening cause, produces the result complained of and without which the result would not have occurred.'" *Daniel v. State, Dep't of Transp.*, 239 *N.J.Super.* 563, 595, 571 *A.*2d 1329 (App.Div.) (quoting *Polyard v. Terry*, 160 *N.J.Super.* 497, 511, 390 *A.*2d 653 (App.Div.1978), *aff'd o.b.*, 79 *N.J.* 547, 401 *A.*2d 532 (1979)).

Proximate cause has been described as a standard for limiting liability for the consequences of an act based "'upon mixed considerations of logic, common sense, justice, policy and precedent.'" *Scafidi v. Seiler*, 119 *N.J.* 93, 101, 574 *A.*2d 398 (1990) (quoting *Caputzal v. The Lindsay Co.*, 48 *N.J.* 69, 77-78, 222 *A.*2d 513 (1966)). Proximate cause "'must be limited to those causes which are so closely connected with the result and of such significance that the law is justified in imposing liability.'" *Caputzal, supra,* 48 *N.J.* at 78, 222 *A.*2d 513 (quotations omitted). ... Thus, our focus must be on whether Chang's conduct was reasonably foreseeable versus "highly extraordinary," thereby breaking the chain of causation. [C]

The present case presents extraordinary circumstances. ... Assuming plaintiffs' allegations are true, an alleged defect in the spare tire assembly caused the spare tire and other parts to fall off the van and roll across the Parkway. Because the van in which Chang was travelling came safely to rest at the side of the Parkway, his actions were "highly extraordinary." Chang's attempt to retrieve the parts involved crossing the Parkway in both directions—an activity which cannot be described as anything short of extraordinarily dangerous, if not suicidal, as the action proved. In the process of returning from the middle of the Parkway, Chang was struck by Mrs. Linderman and fatally injured. ...

Logic and fairness dictate that liability should not extend to injuries received as a result of Chang's senseless decision to cross the Parkway under such dangerous conditions. Common sense should have persuaded Chang, who was only a passenger, to wait for assistance or abandon the bald tire and damaged assembly. The van could have been driven safely home. ...

... [T]he alleged defect in the spare tire assembly did not injure Chang. The driver of the van was able to pull the vehicle to the side of the road safely and without incident. ...

... Assuming, arguendo, that the spare tire assembly was a substantial factor in causing Chang's injuries, Chang's highly extraordinary and dangerous actions in crossing the Parkway twice with complete disregard for his own personal safety clearly constitute a superseding and intervening cause of his own injuries. ...

... The allegedly defective product (the spare tire carrier) did not cause Chang's injuries. Chang's and Yun's joint decision, thirty days before this accident, not to repair the allegedly defective assembly and Chang's flagrant disregard for his personal safety by crossing the Parkway late at night and the injuries he received when struck by Linderman's vehicle constitute intervening superseding causes. Logic, common sense, justice and fairness dictate that the alleged product defect was not a proximate cause of Chang's injury.

Usually, the issue of proximate cause is reserved for the jury's determination. [Cc] In certain cases, however, the issue of proximate cause has been held so intertwined with issues of policy as to be treated as a matter of law for the court to determine. [C] ... This position is consistent with that of the *Restatement (Second) Torts* § 435(2) (1965): "The actor's conduct may be held not to be a legal cause of harm to another where after the event and looking back from the harm to the actor's negligent conduct, it appears to the court highly extraordinary that it should have brought about the harm." ...

... It was not reasonably foreseeable to defendants that if the spare wheel assembly was defective, and the driver-owner of the car and Chang refused to have it repaired and later while they were driving on the Parkway at night, it fell off but they safely brought the car to a stop on a berm, that Chang would then violate the law by twice crossing the Parkway to go to the median to retrieve the parts and be killed by a passing car. Furthermore, reasonable people could not differ that the continued driving for thirty days with knowledge of the defect and the senseless, and illegal crossing of the Parkway were intervening superseding causes of the accident which broke the chain of causation.

Affirmed.

Ethics

Tort practice often involves filing briefs and making motion arguments in court about certain facts and law on various issues. Obligations to the court temper such client advocacy. The ABA Model Rules of Professional Conduct admonish in Rule 3.3(a) that a lawyer must not misrepresent the law or facts to the court, must correct a false statement of fact or law, must disclose adverse controlling law not disclosed by opposing counsel, and must not offer false evidence. The careers and reputations of tort lawyers are made and broken over their willingness and ability to comply with Rule 3.3.

INQUIRY

Suicide. Cases hold that a negligent defendant is not liable for the suicide of another—that suicide is so extraordinary of a deliberate act that the fact of the suicide cuts off the chain of causation that began with the defendant's negligence. *See* Doe v. Doe, 409 Ill.Dec. 308, 67 N.E.3d 520 (Ill. Ct. App. 2016) (suicide allegedly due to social-media interaction); Cleveland v. Rotman, 297 F.3d 569 (7th Cir. 2002) (Illinois law) (summary judgment for defendant where suicide was by a competent adult); Daniels v. New York, N.H. & H.R. Co., 183 Mass. 393, 67 N.E. 424 (1903). Some of those cases hold that suicide ends the causal chain even when the decedent's suicidal condition began with the defendant's intentional and highly reprehensible (not merely negligent) act. *See* Lancaster v. Montesi, 216 Tenn. 50, 390 S.W.2d 217 (1965) (torture). Another line of cases disagrees and allows an estate's wrongful-death recovery for the decedent's suicide if defendant's intentional (rather than negligent) act induced it. *See* R.D. v. W.H., 875 P.2d 26 (Wyo. 1994); State v. Edgeworth, 214 So.2d 579 (Miss. 1968). Another line of cases, taking a middle ground, finds proximate cause and allows recovery only when the suicide is an "irresistible impulse." *See* Clift v. Narragansett Television, 688 A.2d 805 (R.I. 1996); Padula v. State, 48 N.Y.2d 366, 398 N.E.2d 548, 422 N.Y.S.2d 943 (1979); Wallace v. Bounds, 369 S.W.2d 138 (Mo. 1963). The decedent's planning tends to be taken as evidence against, and impulsiveness as evidence of, an "irresistible impulse," but the standard can be problematic. *See* Brown v. American Steel and Wire Co., 43 Ind. App. 560, 88 N.E. 80 (1909) (careful manner in which decedent cut his throat is evidence suicide was not irresistible impulse). Consider the following case.

Fuller v. Preis
New York Court of Appeals
35 N.Y.2d 425, 322 N.E.2d 263, 363 N.Y.S.2d 568 (1974)

BREITEL, C.J. Plaintiff executor, in a wrongful death action, recovered a jury verdict for $200,000. The Appellate Division set aside the verdict and judgment in favor of plaintiff executor and dismissed the complaint. ... Plaintiff executor appeals.

Decedent, Dr. Lewis, committed suicide some seven months after an automobile accident from which he had walked away believing he was uninjured. In fact he had suffered head injuries with consequences to be detailed later. The theory of the case was that defendants, owner and operator of the vehicle which struck decedent's automobile, were responsible in tort for the suicide as a matter of proximate cause and effect. The issue is whether plaintiff's evidence of cause of the suicide was sufficient to withstand dismissal of the complaint. ...

On December 2, 1966, decedent Dr. Lewis, a 43-year-old surgeon, was involved in an intersection collision. Upon impact, the left side of his head struck the frame and window of his automobile. Suffering no evident injuries, he declined aid and drove himself home. Early the next day he experienced an episode of vomiting. An examination later that day at his hospital was inconclusive.

Two days after the accident, Dr. Lewis had a seizure followed by others. After a four- or five-day stay in the hospital as a patient he was diagnosed as having had a subdural contusion and cerebral concussion. Medication was prescribed.

He sustained recurring seizures, was hospitalized again, was further tested, and after five days, was discharged with diagnosis of "post traumatic focal seizures." Then ensued a period of deterioration and gradual contraction of his professional and private activities. Meanwhile, his wife, partially paralyzed as a result of an old poliomyelitis, suffered 'nervous exhaustion' and his mother became ill with cancer.

On July 7, 1967, the day he learned of his mother's illness, decedent executed his will. On July 9, after experiencing three seizures that day, he went to the bathroom of his home, closed the door and shot himself in the head. He died the following day. Just before the gunshot, his wife heard him say to himself, "I must do it, I must do it," or words to that effect.

Two suicide notes, both dated July 9, 1967, were found next to the body. One, addressed to his wife, professed his love. The other, addressed to the family, contained information about a bank account and the location of his will and requested discreet disposition of certain personal property. He warned that the note "must never be seen by anyone except the three of you as it would alter the outcome of the 'case'—i.e., it's worth a million dollars to you all." And he went on to say that "I am perfectly sane in mind" and "I know exactly what I am doing." Alluding to the accident, the loss of his office and practice, his mother's and his wife's illnesses, the imposition caused thereby to his children, and his mounting responsibilities, he professed inability to continue.

Precedent of long standing establishes that public policy permits negligent tort-feasors to be held liable for the suicide of persons who, as the result of their negligence, suffer mental disturbance destroying the will to survive ([cc]). ...

In any event, this case was tried for all purposes in accordance with the prevailing law. Indeed, the jury was instructed, primarily, upon the theory of liability for a suicide by an accident victim suffering from ensuing mental disease, who was unable to control the "irresistible impulse" to destroy himself. ...

Dr. Lewis was physically and mentally healthy immediately prior to the automobile accident in which he struck his head against the interior of his own vehicle. After the accident he suffered several epileptic seizures, often with unconsciousness. Before the accident he had never suffered a seizure. For seven months between the accident and his death, Dr. Lewis experienced no fewer than 38 separate seizures. ...

The only authentic issue is whether the suicide was an "irresistible impulse" caused by traumatic organic brain damage. ...

The brain damage and the seizures compelled Dr. Lewis to give up his surgical practice and many other activities. The seizures were acceleratedly and progressively severe and uncontrolled by drugs. ... He was constantly depressed, unsteady on his feet, irritable, complained of headaches, and walked askew.

On the day of the suicide, only seven months after the accident, when Dr. Lewis had had three seizures, his daughter tried to speak with him but he did not respond. After the third seizure he seemed unable to recognize his wife, had a strange look, and locked himself in the bathroom. Twenty minutes later, his wife heard him mutter, "I must do it, I must do it," and then a gunshot rang out. Dr. Lewis had shot himself in the head and died the following day. ...

That Dr. Lewis believed himself sane should, of course, not control. Most insane people are certain of their sanity. Sanity is never established by a self-serving certification. He was not mentally retarded and his belief that his death might secure a large amount of money is hardly surprising.

In tort law, as contrasted with criminal law, there is recognition that one may retain the power to intend, to know, and yet to have an irresistible impulse to act and therefore be incapable of voluntary conduct. ... The issue in this case was, precisely, whether Dr. Lewis, who obviously knew what he was doing and intended to do what he did, nevertheless, was, because of mental derangement, incapable of resisting the impulse to destroy himself. Precedents and modern knowledge say that that could have been. The jury found that it was so. ...

Accordingly, the order of the Appellate Division should be reversed, with costs, and a new trial directed.

INQUIRY

Caretakers. A separate line of intervening-cause cases considers the liability not of the person who caused the injury that led to the suicide but of persons or entities that had an affirmative duty to prevent it. In most of these cases, proximate cause exists notwithstanding the intervening suicide. *See* White v. Lawrence, 975 S.W.2d 525 (Tenn. 1998) (jury question whether physician who negligently prescribed secret dose of Antabuse for alcoholic patient was liable for patient's resulting suicide); Jacoves v. United Merchandising Corp., 9 Cal. App.4th 88, 11 Cal. Rptr.2d 468 (1992) (hospital liability); McNamara v. Honeyman, 406 Mass. 43, 546 N.E.2d 139 (1989) (psychiatrist liability). On what rationale do courts base these cases? Should proximate cause exist as to the defendant who negligently supplies the decedent with the means of suicide? *See* Scoggins v. Wal-Mart Stores, Inc., 560 N.W.2d 564 (Iowa 1997) (no—ammunition sale to minor); Runyon v. Reid, 510 P.2d 943 (Okla. 1973) (no—prescription drug refill with authorization).

Utility. The courts in some of these intervening-cause cases may not be looking solely at the nature and quality of the intervening acts and events. They may also be considering the nature and quality of the defendant's acts. One well-known intervening-cause case is Weirum v. RKO Gen., Inc., 15 Cal.3d 40, 539 P.2d 36, 123 Cal. Rptr. 468 (1975). The defendant radio station conducted a contest encouraging its teenage listeners to pursue a disc jockey around the city, rewarding the first listener to reach the disc jockey with a prize. One of those listeners, driving recklessly at speeds up to eighty miles per hour, forced a vehicle from the highway, killing its driver. The appellate court affirmed a jury verdict for the plaintiff, rejecting the claim that the listener's reckless acts were a superseding cause. In another case involving conduct of questionable utility, Kolar v. Bergo, 280 Mont. 262, 929 P.2d 867 (1996), the defendant played an April Fool's Day prank telling an acquaintance that his young daughter was at home alone and frightened. The acquaintance seriously injured another motorist in his rush to get home to care for his child. The appellate court reversed the trial court's summary judgment for the defendant who had arranged the prank, remanding the case for trial. Courts may be more willing to find that an intervening negligent or reckless act has not superseded the cause set in motion by a defendant whose negligent act had no utility.

Media. A related area where the utility of the conduct is very much in question, but counter-balancing First Amendment principles are at work, involves media negligence facilitating individual acts of violence. Cases involving hit-man advertisements are instructive. In Eimann v. Soldier of Fortune Magazine, 880 F.2d 830 (5th Cir. 1989), cert. denied, 493 U.S. 1024 (1990), the federal appeals court applied Texas law to find unforeseeable to the defendant magazine that a person would suffer harm by the hiring of a gunman who had advertised his hit-man services in the magazine. Then in Braun v. Soldier of Fortune Magazine, 968 F.2d 1110 (11th Cir. 1992), cert. denied, 506 U.S. 1071 (1993), another federal appeals court, applying Georgia law, reached the opposite result. And in Rice v. Paladin Enterps., Inc., 128 F.3d 233 (4th Cir. 1997), the federal appeals court applied Maryland law to allow a cause of action for a triple murder planned using the defendant publisher's hit-man technical manual. *See also* Wilson v. Paladin Enterps., 186 F. Supp.2d 1140 (D. Ore. 2001) (same). A state appeals court has also allowed a claim to proceed against a film company and producer for harm caused by individuals allegedly encouraged to emulate the film's killers. *See* Byers v. Edmondson, 712 So.2d 681 (La. App. 1998); *but see* James v. Meow Media, Inc., 300 F.3d 683 (6th Cir. 2002) (Kentucky law does not recognize claim against Internet companies whose violent depictions allegedly desensitized killer); Sanders v. Acclaim Ent., Inc., 188 F. Supp.2d 1264 (D. Colo. 2002) (estate of teacher killed in Columbine High School incident has no claim against makers of violent media killers allegedly imitated).

Intoxication. Should a defendant who legally makes alcohol available have to anticipate that a person would over-imbibe, causing another harm? With but a very few exceptions, the courts have been unwilling to find proximate cause to extend liability to the defendant who lawfully serves alcohol to another. *See* Ferreira v. Strack, 652 A.2d 965 (R.I. 1995) (refusing to create a common-law cause of action for social-host liability); Klein v. Raysinger, 504 Pa. 141, 470 A.2d 507 (1983) (no social-host liability for injury caused by drunken adult); *cf.* Hickingbotham v. Burke, 140 N.H. 28, 662 A.2d 297 (1995) (social-host liability only if serving of alcohol is reckless). The traditional view is that the intoxicated person's voluntarily imbibing is the sole proximate cause of the attendant injury. *See* Cruse v. Aden, 127 Ill. 231, 20 N.E. 73 (1889). On the other hand, courts more commonly recognize proximate cause and liability for harm resulting from serving alcohol to a minor. *See* Hansen v. Friend, 118 Wash.2d 476, 824 P.2d 483 (1992) (adults liable for drowning death of minor intoxicated by alcohol they provided); Sutter v. Hutchings, 254 Ga. 194, 327 S.E.2d 716 (1985) (adult who purchased beer keg for minors liable to estate of person killed by drunken minor driver leaving party); *but* *see* Smith v. Merritt, 940 S.W.2d 602 (Tex. 1997) (no liability for intoxicating minor). These negligent-intoxication cases should be distinguished from the negligent-entrustment cases holding defendants liable when they negligently equip a person they knew to be drunk with the means of causing harm. *See* Kitchen v. K-Mart Corp., 697 So.2d 1200 (Fla. 1997) (sold a gun to a visibly intoxicated person); Deck v. Sherlock, 162 Neb. 86, 75 N.W.2d 99 (1956) (loaned a car to a visibly intoxicated person).

Dram-Shop Acts. Some states provide for the tort liability of a commercial dispenser of alcohol through what we know as *dram-shop acts*, typically creating liability for harm caused by sales to minors and visibly intoxicated persons. States without a dram-shop act that creates a civil cause of action for harm from sales to minors and intoxicated persons, will still have alcohol-control laws making such sales illegal. Where a commercial dispenser of alcohol violates alcohol-control laws that prohibit serving a minor or a visibly intoxicated adult, some courts recognize a negligence-per-se claim against the alcohol server for harm the intoxicated person does to a third person, notwithstanding no-proximate-cause arguments. *See* Stachniewicz v. Mar-Cam Corp., 259 Or. 583, 488 P.2d 436 (1971); *see also* Ontiveros v. Borak, 136 Ariz. 500, 667 P.2d 200 (1983); *but see* Ling v. Jan's Liquors, 237 Kan. 629, 703 P.2d 731 (1985). Courts differ on whether proximate cause exists in claims against employers for harm caused by intoxicated employees leaving work or work-related parties. *See* Slade v. Smith's Mgt. Corp., 119 Idaho 482, 808 P.2d 401 (1991) (employer liability); Otis Eng. Corp., v. Clark, 668 S.W.2d 307 (Tex. 1983) (employer liability); *but see* Overbaugh v. McCutcheon, 183 W.Va. 386, 396 S.E.2d 153 (1990) (no employer liability); Johnson v. KFC Ntl. Mgt. Co., 71 Haw. 229, 788 P.2d 159 (1990) (no employer liability). Consider a representative dram-shop act:

MICH. COMP. L. §456.1801 Licensees' bonds; dram shop act
(1) Except as otherwise provided in this act, before the approval and granting, or renewal, of a license, the following licensees or applicants for that license shall make, execute, and deliver to the commission a bond... .
(2) A retail licensee shall not directly, individually, or by a clerk, agent, or servant sell, furnish, or give alcoholic liquor to a minor except as otherwise provided in this act. A retail licensee shall not directly or indirectly, individually or by a clerk, agent, or servant sell, furnish, or give alcoholic liquor to a person who is visibly intoxicated.
(3) Except as otherwise provided in this section, an individual who suffers damage or who is personally injured by a minor or visibly intoxicated person by reason of the unlawful selling, giving, or furnishing of alcoholic liquor to the minor or visibly intoxicated person, if the unlawful sale is proven to be a proximate cause of the damage, injury, or death, or the spouse, child, parent, or guardian of that individual, shall have a right of action in his or her name against the person who by selling, giving, or furnishing the alcoholic liquor has caused or contributed to the intoxication of the person or who has caused or contributed to the damage, injury, or death. ...
(4) An action under this section shall be instituted within 2 years after the injury or death. A plaintiff seeking damages under this section shall give written notice to all defendants within 120 days after entering an attorney-client relationship for the purpose of pursuing a claim under this section. ...
(5) An action under this section against a retail licensee shall not be commenced unless the minor or the alleged intoxicated person is a named defendant in the action and is retained in the action until the litigation is concluded by trial or settlement.
(6) Any licensee subject to the provisions of subsection (3) regarding the unlawful selling, furnishing, or giving of alcoholic liquor to a visibly intoxicated person shall have

the right to full indemnification from the alleged visibly intoxicated person for all damages awarded against the licensee.

(7) All defenses of the alleged visibly intoxicated person or the minor shall be available to the licensee. In an action alleging the unlawful sale of alcoholic liquor to a minor, proof that the defendant retail licensee or the defendant's agent or employee demanded and was shown a Michigan driver license or official state personal identification card, appearing to be genuine and showing that the minor was at least 21 years of age, shall be a defense to the action.

(8) There shall be a rebuttable presumption that a retail licensee, other than the retail licensee who last sold, gave, or furnished alcoholic liquor to the minor or the visibly intoxicated person, has not committed any act giving rise to a cause of action under subsection (3).

(9) The alleged visibly intoxicated person shall not have a cause of action pursuant to this section... .

(10) This section provides the exclusive remedy for money damages against a licensee arising out of the selling, giving, or furnishing of alcoholic liquor. ...

INQUIRY

Limitations. Notice the several significant limitations that the Michigan legislature places on dram-shop actions, including that the plaintiff must name and retain the intoxicated person in the suit, the intoxicated person has no cause of action, and the plaintiff must give notice within 120 days. Are these limitations tacit recognition that proximate cause is problematic where the intoxicated person directly causing the harm has voluntarily imbibed? Do the legislatures have the correct (political) sense of dram-shop liability? New Jersey's experience is instructive. Its supreme court recognized social-host liability for harm caused by a person whom the social host had continued to serve after the person was visibly intoxicated. *See* Kelly v. Gwinnell, 96 N.J. 538, 476 A.2d 1219 (1984). The legislature subsequently limited the cause of action to third persons injured by a visibly intoxicated person whose blood alcohol exceeded .10%—with an additional rebuttable presumption that the person was not visibly intoxicated if the blood alcohol was under .15%—and abolished the social host's joint and several liability, further limiting the recovery. N.J. Stat. Ann. 2A:15-5.7. The *Ferreira* opinion, cited above, gives a detailed history of social-host liability.

Non-Human Causes. To this point, we have been considering primarily the effect of acts by other persons, on the chain of causation set in motion by the negligent defendant. How should proximate-cause law treat intervening natural events? Restatement (Second) of Torts §§450 and 451 define forces of nature and suggest when they should supersede prior negligence, cutting off proximate cause. The root distinction is, obviously, between foreseeable versus unforeseeable natural forces. Thus, courts have held sufficiently foreseeable for proximate cause, a heavy snow, *see* Bowman v. Columbia Tel. Co., 406 Pa. 455, 179 A.2d 197 (1962), a deep cold spell, *see* Fox v. Boston & Maine R. Co., 148 Mass. 220, 19 N.E. 222 (1889), and a late frost, *see* Benedict Pineapple Co. v. Atlantic Coast Line R. Co., 55 Fla. 514, 46 So. 732 (1908). Would a volcanic eruption be an unpredictable and therefore superseding cause? *See* Doss v. Big Stone Gap, 145 Va. 520, 134 S.E. 563 (1926) (yes).

Chapter VII

Malpractice

OBJECTIVE: Given injury or loss due to the actions of a professional using a specialized body of knowledge and expertise, articulate how the standard of care for a professional-malpractice claim will differ from the standard for an ordinary negligence claim, and how proof of that standard will also differ, consistent with your study of this section of the text.

Case Study: A pediatrician treated a child patient's fractured wrist resulting in the fracture's disunion after eight weeks in a soft splint. The patient's parents retained a lawyer to pursue a malpractice claim, but the lawyer did not file the case within the statutory limitations period. The lawyer's accountant did not file the lawyer's tax return by the deadline. The accountant's plumber left a drain line uncapped resulting in the flooding of the accountant's basement. *Articulate probable standards of care for each professional, also describing how to prove that standard for each professional.*

Professional negligence, or malpractice, is a negligence claim against a professional for harm in the course of professional service. In providing service, a professional typically draws on specialized knowledge, skill, and experience that a judge, juror, or other layperson does not possess. This circumstance requires several adaptations to basic negligence principles, requiring treatment of professional negligence (malpractice) separately from claims of ordinary negligence. Malpractice claims still require proof of all elements of an ordinary negligence claim—duty, breach, causation, and damages. Merely because a doctor mistreats a patient, or a lawyer mishandles a client's matter, does not mean that a malpractice claim exists. The person claiming the loss must show that the professional owed a duty and that the mistreatment or mishandling caused a loss or injury that the professional should pay. The negligence principles covered in the chapters above will already have given you good sense of how the law treats these issues. Consider below some special issues, unique to professional-malpractice claims.

A. Duty

Duty is not ordinarily a significant issue in malpractice claims—at least those in which a physician has allegedly caused an injury to a patient in the course of treatment, or a lawyer or other professional has failed to serve a client, causing the patient or client making the malpractice claim some provable injury or loss. The professional and person whom the professional serves are usually not strangers. The parties will ordinarily have been in a physician-patient, lawyer-client, or other professional relationship, of which duties of professional care are an obvious part. Yet peculiar duty questions may still exist. Consider two of them.

Emergency Aid or Rescue. One question has to do with the need for emergency assistance from a professional—typically, a doctor or other medical professional who just happens to be present when the need suddenly arises. Tort law does not impose a duty on a physician to render emergency aid, unless before the emergency arises the physician already stands in a role or relationship that would compel the duty. *See* Hurley v. Eddington, 156 Ind. 416, 59 N.E. 1058 (1901); *cf.* AMA Principles of Medical Ethics, No. 5 (physician should render emergency medical services when possible). The obvious exception where a duty would exist is if the physician is on duty in an emergency room awaiting the next medical emergency. Can you think of any other examples, other than where the physician has a hospital role, where the physician might owe a duty to a person who is not, in the usual sense, the physician's patient? *See* Coffee v. McDonnell-Douglas Corp., 8 Cal.3d 551, 503 P.2d 1366, 105 Cal. Rptr. 358 (1972) (duty to disclose disease discovered in physical examination for job). Physicians and other medical-care providers who voluntarily come to the aid of a stranger have the benefit in every state of some form of protective statute. *See* McCain v. Batson, 233 Mont. 288, 760 P.2d 725 (1988) (vacationing physician immune for suturing a hiker's wounds). California's statute grants broad immunity, stating simply that "[n]o licensee, who in good faith renders emergency care at the scene of an emergency, shall be liable for any civil damages as a result of any acts or omissions by such person in rendering emergency care." West's Ann. Cal. Bus. & Prof. Code §2395. The statute also protects physicians pressed into service in hospital emergency rooms during medical disasters. *See* Burciaga v. St. John's Hosp., 187 Cal. App.3d 710 (Cal. App. 1986). Contrast California's broad immunity with the following statute.

MICH. COMP. L. §691.1502. Hospital or other medical care facility personnel
(1) If an individual's actual hospital duty does not require a response to the emergency situation, a physician, physician's assistant, dentist, podiatrist, intern, resident, registered nurse, licensed practical nurse, registered physical therapist, clinical laboratory technologist, inhalation therapist, certified registered nurse anesthetist, x-ray technician, or paramedic, who in good faith responds to a life threatening emergency or responds to a request for emergency assistance in a life threatening emergency within a hospital or other licensed medical care facility, is not liable for civil damages as a result of an act or omission in the rendering of emergency care, except an act or omission amounting to gross negligence or willful and wanton misconduct.

(2) The exemption from liability under subsection (1) does not apply to a physician if a physician-patient relationship, to a physician's assistant if a physician's assistant-patient relationship, or to a licensed nurse if a nurse-patient relationship existed before the emergency.

(3) The exemption from liability under subsection (1) does not apply to a physician's assistant unless the response by the physician's assistant is within the scope of the license held by the physician's assistant or within the expertise or training of the physician's assistant.

(4) This act does not diminish a hospital's responsibility to reasonably and adequately staff hospital emergency facilities if the hospital maintains or holds out to the general public that it maintains emergency room facilities.

INQUIRY

Emergency Facilities. Some cases have held that statutes governing emergency facilities create a duty to provide emergency services. *See* Thompson v. Sun City Commun. Hosp., Inc., 141 Ariz. 597, 688 P.2d 605 (1984). The practice of private hospitals dumping uninsured, Medicare, and Medicaid patients to public hospitals to avoid the cost, but delaying critical treatment in the process, was of sufficient concern that Congress outlawed the practice with the Emergency Medical Treatment and Active Labor Act, 42 U.S.C. §1395dd. Other courts have held that a common-law duty to treat exists independent of any authorizing statute. *See* Wilmington Gen. Hosp. v. Manlove, 54 Del. (4 Storey) 15, 174 A.2d 135 (1961). The federal courts have interpreted the federal anti-dumping statute's civil remedy so narrowly that state-law duties may be the more significant ones.

Ethics

Litigating professional-negligence (malpractice) cases can, like litigating other tort cases, involve substantial discovery including exhaustive (some would say "exhausting") interrogatories and extensive depositions. The ABA Model Rules of Professional Conduct admonish in Rule 3.4 that a lawyer must be fair to opposing parties and counsel in all pretrial and trial matters. Fairness includes not obstructing access to evidence or concealing documents, not counseling witnesses to refrain from giving information or to testify falsely, not offering false evidence, and not alluding in trial to irrelevant matters. Fairness also includes not serving frivolous discovery requests or failing to make a diligent effort to comply with proper discovery requests. The manner in which a lawyer conducts and responds to discovery reveals the lawyer's professional character and establishes the lawyer's reputation, as much as any other professional activity.

Third Persons. Duty can also be an issue in malpractice cases when the professional service was meant for someone other than or in addition to the person contracting with the professional for the service. Some unfortunate examples include the physician who failed to tell a treated hepatitis patient that the disease will be sexually communicable for an additional six months, *see* DiMarco v. Lynch Homes, 525 Pa. 558, 583 A.2d 422 (1990) (physician liable to person contracting the disease from patient), and the physician who failed to tell the father of a polio-vaccinated child regarding the risk of contracting the disease from the child, *see* Tenuto v. Lederle Labs., 90 H.Y.2d 606, 687 N.E.2d 1300, 665 N.Y.S.2d 17 (1997) (physician subject to liability to father). The general rule is that a professional owes a duty only to the person with whom the professional contracts for service, with relatively rare exceptions where the patient or treatment involves known specific material risks to identifiable others. *See* McKenzie v. Hawai'I Permanente Medical Group, Inc., 98 Haw. 296, 47 P.3d 1209 (2002) (physician subject to liability to accident victim after failing to warn patient that medication could impair driving); Joy v. Eastern Maine Med. Ctr., 529 A.2d 1364 (Me. 1987) (physician owes duty to third person injured by driving patient whom physician had negligently failed to warn of drug's drowsiness side effect); *but see* Praesel v. Johnson, 967 S.W.2d 391 (Tex. 1998) (physician has no duty to those injured by epileptic seizure of patient whom physician failed to advise not to drive); Kirk v. Michael Reese Hosp. & Med. Ctr., 117 Ill.2d 507, 513 N.E.2d 387, 111 Ill. Dec. 944 (1987) (no duty of care to third person injured by physician's negligent failure to warn driving patient of drug's drowsiness side effect). Consider the following well-known case.

Tarasoff v. Regents of the Univ. of California
California Supreme Court
17 Cal.3d 425, 551 P.2d 334, 131 Cal. Rptr. 14 (1976)

TOBRINER, J.   On October 27, 1969, Prosenjit Poddar killed Tatiana Tarasoff.[fn] Plaintiffs, Tatiana's parents, allege that two months earlier Poddar confided his intention to kill Tatiana to Dr. Lawrence Moore, a psychologist employed by the Cowell Memorial Hospital at the University of California at Berkeley. They allege that on Moore's request, the campus police briefly detained Poddar, but released him when he appeared rational. They further claim that Dr. Harvey Powelson, Moore's superior, then directed that no further action be taken to detain Poddar. No one warned plaintiffs of Tatiana's peril.

Concluding that these facts set forth causes of action against neither therapists and policemen involved, nor against the Regents of the University of California as their employer, the superior court sustained defendants' demurrers to plaintiffs' second amended complaints without leave to amend.[fn] This appeal ensued.

Plaintiffs' complaints predicate liability on ... defendants' failure to warn plaintiffs of the impending danger... . Defendants, in turn, assert that they owed no duty of reasonable care to Tatiana... .

We shall explain that defendant therapists cannot escape liability merely because Tatiana herself was not their patient. When a therapist determines, or pursuant to the standards of his profession should determine, that his patient presents a serious danger of violence to another, he incurs an obligation to use reasonable care to protect the intended victim against such danger. The discharge of this duty may require the therapist to take one or more of various steps, depending upon the nature of the case. Thus it may call for him to warn the intended victim or others likely to apprise the victim of the danger, to notify the police, or to take whatever other steps are reasonably necessary under the circumstances. ...

Although, as we have stated above, under the common law, as a general rule, one person owed no duty to control the conduct of another[fn] ([cc]), nor to warn those endangered by such conduct ([cc]), the courts have carved out an exception to this rule in cases in which the defendant stands in some special relationship to either the person whose conduct needs to be controlled or in a relationship to the foreseeable victim of that conduct ([c]). Applying this exception to the present case, we note that a relationship of defendant therapists to either Tatiana or Poddar will suffice to establish a duty of care... .

Although plaintiffs' pleadings assert no special relation between Tatiana and defendant therapists, they establish as between Poddar and defendant therapists the special relation that arises between a patient and his doctor or psychotherapist.[fn] Such a relationship may support affirmative duties for the benefit of third persons. Thus, for example, a hospital must exercise reasonable care to control the behavior of a patient which may endanger other persons.[fn] A doctor must also warn a patient if the patient's condition or medication renders certain conduct, such as driving a car, dangerous to others.[fn]

Although the California decisions that recognize this duty have involved cases in which the defendant stood in a special relationship both to the victim and to the person whose conduct created the danger,[fn] we do not think that the duty should logically be constricted to such situations. Decisions of other jurisdictions hold that the single relationship of a doctor to his patient is sufficient to support the duty to exercise reasonable care to rotect others against dangers emanating from the patient's illness. The courts hold that a doctor is liable to persons infected by his patient if he negligently fails to diagnose a contagious disease ([c]) or, having diagnosed the illness, fails to warn members of the patient's family ([cc]). ...

Defendants contend, however, that imposition of a duty to exercise reasonable care to protect third persons is unworkable because therapists cannot accurately predict whether or not a patient will resort to violence. In support of this argument amicus representing the American Psychiatric Association and other professional societies cites numerous articles which indicate that therapists, in the present state of the art, are unable reliably to predict violent acts; their forecasts, amicus claims, tend consistently to overpredict violence, and indeed are more often wrong than right.[fn] Since predictions of violence are often erroneous, amicus concludes, the courts should not render rulings that predicate the liability of therapists upon the validity of such predictions. ...

We recognize the difficulty that a therapist encounters in attempting to forecast whether a patient presents a serious danger of violence. ...

In the instant case, however, the pleadings do not raise any question as to failure of defendant therapists to predict that Poddar presented a serious danger of violence. On the contrary, the present complaints allege that defendant therapists did in fact predict that Poddar would kill, but were negligent in failing to warn. ...

The risk that unnecessary warnings may be given is a reasonable price to pay for the lives of possible victims that may be saved. We would hesitate to hold that the therapist who is aware that his patient expects to attempt to assassinate the President of the United States would not be obligated to warn the authorities because the therapist cannot predict with accuracy that his patient will commit the crime.

Defendants further argue that free and open communication is essential to psychotherapy ([c]); that "unless a patient . . . is assured that . . . information (revealed by him) can and will be held in utmost confidence, he will be reluctant to make the full disclosure upon which diagnosis and treatment . . . depends." (Sen.Com. on Judiciary, comment on Evid.Code, s 1014.) The giving of a warning, defendants contend, constitutes a breach of trust which entails the revelation of confidential communications.[fn]

We recognize the public interest in supporting effective treatment of mental illness and in protecting the rights of patients to privacy ([c]) and the consequent public importance of safeguarding the confidential character of psychotherapeutic communication. Against this interest, however, we must weigh the public interest in safety from violent assault. The Legislature has undertaken the difficult task of balancing the countervailing concerns. In evidence Code section 1014, it established a broad rule of privilege to protect confidential communications between patient and psychotherapist. In Evidence Code section 1024, the Legislature created a specific and limited exception to the psychotherapist-patient privilege: "There is no privilege . . . if the psychotherapist has reasonable cause to believe that the patient is in such mental or emotional condition as to be dangerous to himself or to the person or property of another and that disclosure of the communication is necessary to prevent the threatened danger."[fn]

Our current crowded and computerized society compels the interdependence of its members. In this risk-infested society we can hardly tolerate the further exposure to danger that would result from a concealed knowledge of the therapist that his patient was lethal. … The containment of such risks lies in the public interest. For the foregoing reasons, we find that plaintiffs' complaints can be amended to state a cause of action against defendants Moore, Powelson, Gold, and Yandell and against the Regents as their employer, for breach of a duty to exercise reasonable care to protect Tatiana.[fn] …

The judgment of the superior court in favor of defendants Atkinson, Beall, Brownrigg, Hallernan, and Teel is affirmed. The judgment of the superior court in favor of defendants Gold, Moore, Powelson, Yandell, and the Regents of the University of California is reversed, and the cause remanded for further proceedings consistent with the views expressed herein.

INQUIRY

Conditions. Do not read the *Tarasoff* case too broadly. The risk that the patient presents to the third person must be particularized (specific), imminent, and as to an identifiable person. *See* Brady v. Hopper, 751 F.2d 329 (10th Cir. 1984) (would-be presidential assassin John Hinckley's psychiatrist had no duty to warn where Hinckley made no specific threat); Thompson v. County of Alameda, 27 Cal.3d 741, 614 P.2d 728, 167 Cal. Rptr. 70 (1980) (releasee's threat to take the life of some young child not sufficiently specific to establish duty to warn). Statutes enacted in response to professional concern over *Tarasoff*-like liability tend to reinforce and strengthen these requirements. *See* Cal. Civil Code §43.92 (requiring "serious threat of physical violence against a reasonably identifiable victim"); Minn. Stat. §148.975(2) ("specific, serious threat of physical violence against a specific, clearly identified or identifiable potential victim").

Taking Charge. Some jurisdictions facing the same circumstance—a medical-care provider's knowledge that a patient presents a risk to a third person—follow the Restatement (Second) of Torts §319's requirement that the provider must also have "taken charge" of the patient. *See* Estate of Morgan v. Fairfield Family Counseling Ctr., 77 Ohio St.3d 284, 673 N.E.2d 1311 (1997) (psychotherapist's outpatient treatment of patient who subsequently killed his parents could have been sufficiently controlling as to create duty to warn); Nasser v. Parker, 249 Va. 172, 455 S.E.2d 502 (1995) (no duty where no control of the kind anticipated by §319). Section 319 states, "One who takes charge of a third person whom he knows or should know to be likely to cause bodily harm to others if not controlled is under a duty to exercise reasonable care to control the third person to prevent him from doing such harm." Does the taken-charge requirement solve the problem? Or does it create too limited a duty to protect third persons whom the law should protect?

Suicide. Beyond the concern that a medical-care provider's patient might harm someone else lies the concern that patients might harm themselves. Certainly, a medical-care provider has a duty to take reasonable precautions to prevent the suicide of one under the provider's control. But does that duty extend to create a duty to warn others that a patient might commit suicide? *See* Nally v. Grace Commun. Church, 47 Cal.3d 278, 763 P.2d 948, 253 Cal. Rptr. 97 (1988) (church counselor had no duty to refer suicidal counselee for mental health review); Bellah v. Greenson, 81 Cal. App.3d 614, 146 Cal. Rptr. 535 (1978) (psychiatrist has no duty to warn patient's parents of patient's suicidal condition); *but see* Eisel v. Board of Educ., 324 Md. 376, 597 A.2d 447 (1991) (school counselor has duty to warn parents of 13-year-old suicidal student, where danger of suicide was acute). Why would, except in the school situation, the duty be less for suicide than for harm to a third person?

Conflicts of Interest. Replete throughout these cases of professional duties to third persons is the concern that any such duty will compromise the professional's service or negatively affect the professional relationship. Physicians, lawyers, accountants, and others depend on their client's trust and loyalty in order to provide fully effective service. Confidentiality is not, as the public sometimes thinks, a matter of enabling a client's or patient's misconduct. Rather, it ensures that the client shares with the attorney, or the patient shares with the medical-care provider, the most worrisome of concerns—so that the professional can address it in the most-effective manner. That the duty flows only to the patient or client and not to third persons (except in extraordinary circumstances) ensures the integrity of the professional's service. Consider the following case also involving a potential conflict of interest, but from outside the medical context.

Clagett v. Dacy
Maryland Court of Appeals
47 Md. App. 23, 420 A.2d 1285 (1980)

WILNER, J. Appellants were the high bidders at a foreclosure sale, but because the attorneys conducting the sale failed to follow the proper procedures, the sale was set aside. This occurred twice. Ultimately, the debtor discharged the loan, thus "redeeming" his land, and appellants lost the opportunity to acquire the property and make a profit on its resale. They sued the attorneys in the Circuit Court for Prince George's County to recover their loss, alleging that the attorneys in question owed them, as bidders, a duty to use care and diligence and to conduct the sale "properly and carefully." By sustaining the attorneys' demurrer without leave to amend, the court concluded that no such duty existed—at least not one from which an action for damages will arise....

... [A]ppellants claimed that appellees had "an obligation ... running to the plaintiffs, as prospective bidders, to see that the sale was properly and carefully conducted ..." and that appellants, as bidders had a right to rely on appellees "having exercised due care and diligence" in following the requisite procedures and conducting the sale properly. ...

The traditional rule, in Maryland and elsewhere, is that an attorney's duty of diligence and care flows only to his direct client/employer, and that, whether in an action of contract or tort, only that client/employer can recover against him for a breach of that duty. ...

The only departure from the direct privity requirement on the part of the Court of Appeals came in Prescott v. Coppage, 266 Md. 562, 296 A.2d 150 (1972), a unique case. ...

Although the case has a most unusual factual setting, it does seem to suggest a modest relaxation of the strict privity requirement to the extent of allowing a true third party beneficiary to sue an attorney as he could sue any other defaulting or tortious party to a contract made for his benefit. This extension is not unique to Maryland. ...

It is, however, a limited one with a special utility. It is most often seen and applied in actions based on drafting errors in wills and other such documents or on erroneous title reports—errors that, by their very nature, will likely have a long or delayed effect and will most probably impact upon persons other than the attorney's immediate employer ([cc]), although it has been applied in other contexts as well. See Donald v. Garry, 19 Cal.App.3d 769, 97 Cal.Rptr. 191 (1971) (creditor who assigned claim to collection agency for collection allowed to sue agency's attorney for negligence in prosecuting his claim). ...

It will, moreover, take more than general conclusory allegations to satisfy that requirement. Attorneys are not quite the free agents as some others are in the world of commerce. There are well-recognized limitations, judicially imposed and enforced, upon how they may conduct themselves, and who they may, and may not, represent in certain situations. Except in very limited circumstances, they may not represent or act for conflicting interests in a transaction; their manifest duty of loyalty to their employer/client forbids it. ...

These limitations, predominant but not necessarily exclusive with attorneys, must, of necessity, be taken into account when dealing with actions founded upon an implied duty owed by an attorney to a person who is not his direct employer/client, or upon an employment relationship alleged to arise by implication rather than by express agreement. Thus, the duties or obligations inherent in an attorney-client relationship will not be presumed to flow to a third party and will not be presumed to arise by implication when the effect of such a presumption would be tantamount to a prohibited or improbable employment, absent the clearest exposition of facts from which such an employment may be fairly and rationally inferred.

When judged against these principles, it becomes clear that the Declaration at issue here has failed to state a cause of action. It does not sufficiently allege a proper standing on the part of appellants to sue the appellee attorneys; nor, from what is alleged, could it do so. Appellees were engaged to represent the mortgagee (deed of trust beneficiary), not the bidders, whose interest would likely be in conflict with that of the mortgagee. The mortgagee's economic interest, and legal obligation, is to secure the highest possible price for the property, whereas the bidders' goal is to pay as little as possible. It is evident, in that circumstance, that an attorney could not lawfully represent both the mortgagee and the bidder in the transaction; and it will not be lightly presumed or inferred that appellees did so.

Nor may the prohibited employment be inferred from an allegation that appellees' fees would ultimately be paid from the proceeds of sale. The mere fact that those fees, along with the other costs of the proceeding, may be taken from the purchase price paid by the successful bidder does not mean that the purchaser is actually paying the fees. Quite the contrary. The debtor/mortgagor ultimately pays the fees and all other costs, for he gets only the net surplus (if any) available after all such fees and costs are discharged. The bidder pays only for the property, not the cost of selling it; and he is not, therefore, the client (express or implied) of the attorney engaged to sell the property.

JUDGMENT AFFIRMED; APPELLANTS TO PAY THE COSTS.

INQUIRY

Legal Malpractice. Ordinarily, lawyers have malpractice liability only to their clients. A common (though not uniform) exception is when a lawyer drafts a will for a client to benefit a third party. The lawyer is subject to the third party for loss caused by the lawyer's failure to practice within the applicable professional standard. *See* Heyer v. Flaig, 70 Cal.2d 223, 449 P.2d 161, 74 Cal. Rptr. 225 (1969) (lawyer held liable to intended-beneficiary daughters for failure to advise client mother regarding effect of marriage on her will). Another exception is when a lawyer prepares an opinion letter for a client to benefit a third party. *See* Vereins-Und Westbank v. Carter, 691 F. Supp. 704 (S.D. N.Y. 1988) (lawyer liable to third party for whom lawyer drafted client's opinion letter); Prudential Ins. Co. v. Dewey, Ballantine, Bushby, Palmer & Wood, 80 N.Y.2d 377, 590 N.Y.S.2d 831, 605 N.E.2d 318 (1992) (law firm liable to third party); *but see* Bily v. Arthur Young & Co., 3 Cal.4th 370, 11 Cal. Rptr.2d 51, 834 P.2d 745 (1992) (accounting firm not liable to third party). The party suffering the loss in these opinion-letter cases may attempt to skirt the duty issue by alleging fraudulent, negligent, or innocent misrepresentation. In these cases, though, courts do not hold the attorney liable to a third person whose interests are adverse to the client—as the above *Clagett* case shows. *See* One Ntl. Bank v. Antonelis, 80 F.3d 606 (1st Cir. 1996) (under Massachusetts law, attorneys owe no duty to non-client relying on title, where the non-client had an interest conflicting with the client); Weaver v. Superior Ct., 95 Cal. App.3d 166, 156 Cal. Rptr. 745 (1979) (attorneys owe no duty to physician against whom attorneys brought malpractice action); *see also* Hawkins v. King County, 24 Wash. App. 338, 602 P.2d 361 (1979) (attorney owes no duty to warn a third person of client's violent tendencies, where third person was already aware).

Practice

The partner and associate drove together to the insurance-company seminar. Their law firm was on the insurance company's approved counsel list, and over the years they had defended dozens of cases the insurer's adjusters assigned to them. They knew that several of this insurer's adjusters expressed bad attitude about claimants—more so than other insurance companies' adjusters. Until this day, the lawyers had attributed the adjusters' cynicism to personality. Years of working for only one side might do that to a person, they thought. Then began the seminar, held at the company's sparking new regional headquarters to bring the adjusters and approved counsel together around the corporate mission. The first speaker began with a joke about malingering claimants before moving on to the insurer's fraud-detection measures, interspersing his talk with stories of cheating claimants—to the assembled crowd's delight. The next speaker shared more of the same, until a break for the defense lawyers and adjusters to share their own such stories over fine coffee and pastries. Getting the drift, the partner and associate slipped out the back and headed for their car. Neither said much on the way

> back to the office. Within a year, they no longer accepted the insurer's assignments. Although they continued to take assignments from other insurers, they also began representing more claimants.

B. Standard of Care

OBJECTIVE: Given professional malpractice claims arising in a variety of professions, fields, and other circumstances, identify the applicable standard of care for each, consistent with your study of this section of the text, and describe the evidence supporting or contradicting the claim.

Case Study: A pediatrician treated a child patient's fractured wrist resulting in the fracture's disunion after eight weeks in a soft splint. The patient's parents retained a lawyer to pursue a malpractice claim, but the lawyer did not file one within the statutory limitations period. The lawyer's accountant did not file the lawyer's tax return by the deadline. The accountant's plumber left a drain line uncapped resulting in the flooding of the accountant's basement. ***Identify the applicable standard of care for each professional.***

The prior section shows that whether a professional duty exists is straightforward. A much harder challenge is to establish what that professional duty requires. Fundamentally, what distinguishes professional malpractice from ordinary negligence is that the standard differs. Malpractice is the negligence form of action when defendant applies specialized knowledge, skills, and experience acquired through professional training. The standard of care for professionals is therefore not what would have been *reasonably prudent* but, instead, what professionals in the same field *customarily* do. Restatement (Second) of Torts §299A (1965), states the professional's standard of care as follows: "Unless [a professional] represents that [the professional] has greater or less skill or knowledge, one who undertakes to render services in the practice of a profession or trade is required to exercise the skill and knowledge normally possessed by members of that profession or trade in good standing in similar communities." Because the professional's standard of care encompasses specialized knowledge and skills, its proof requires special considerations. Consider the following case illustrating the difference between a prudent-person standard and the professional's standard—but reinforcing that the professional's standard remains an objective one.

Heath v. Swift Wings, Inc.
North Carolina Court of Appeals
40 N.C. App. 158, 252 S.E.2d 526 (1979)

On 3 August 1975 a Piper 180 Arrow airplane crashed immediately after takeoff from the Boone-Blowing Rock Airport. Killed in the crash was the pilot, Fred Heath; his wife, Jonna; their son, Karl; and a family friend, Vance Smathers. …

The plaintiff's complaint alleged several grounds of negligence: (1) operation of the aircraft in an overloaded condition beyond its performance capabilities, (2) failure to follow the operating manual with regard to takeoff distance for short and soft field takeoffs, (3) failure to take into account specific runway and weather conditions, (4) failure to take appropriate emergency steps including aborting takeoff, (5) flying below safe speed, (6) improper control after takeoff, and (7) violation of federal aircraft safety regulations. ...

... Mary Payne Smathers Curry, widow of Vance Smathers, observed the takeoff of the Piper aircraft shortly after 5:00 o'clock on 3 August 1975. She observed Fred Heath load and reload the passengers and luggage, apparently in an effort to improve the balance of the aircraft. He also "walked around (the airplane) and looked at everything... She remembers seeing him and thinking that he's doublechecking it to be sure no one has slashed the tires." The airplane engine started promptly and the plane was taxied to the end of the runway where it paused for approximately five minutes before takeoff. The airplane came very close to the end of the runway before takeoff. However "(t)he engine sounded good the entire time, and she did not recall hearing the engine miss or pop or backfire." After takeoff, the airplane "gained altitude but it didn't go up very high" and then "leveled off pretty low." ...

William B. Gough, Jr., a free-lance mechanical engineering consultant and pilot, testified concerning the operation and flight performance of the Piper 180 Arrow. He testified concerning the many factors affecting the takeoff capabilities of the Piper and the calculations to be made by the pilot before takeoff, utilizing flight performance charts. He testified that in his opinion, according to his calculations, the pilot should have used flaps to aid in the takeoff. Furthermore, he stated that in his opinion the reasonably prudent pilot should have made a controlled landing in the corn field shortly after takeoff if he were experiencing difficulty attaining flight speed, and that if he had done so Jonna Heath and Karl Heath would have survived. ...

The jury returned a verdict answering the following issue as indicated: "1. Was Fred Heath, Jr., negligent in the operation of PA-28R 'Arrow' airplane on August 3, 1975 as alleged in the complaint?" Answer: "No." ... [Plaintiffs appealed on the basis in part of the jury instructions on negligence.]

MORRIS, C.J. ... Assignment of error No. 4 is directed to the trial court's charge concerning the definition of negligence and the applicable standard of care: "Negligence, ladies and gentlemen of the jury, is the failure of someone to act as a reasonably and careful and prudent person would under the same or similar circumstances. Obviously, this could be the doing of something or the failure to do something, depending on the circumstances. With respect to aviation negligence could be more specifically defined as the failure to exercise that degree of ordinary care and caution, which an ordinary prudent pilot having the same training and experience as Fred Heath, would have used in the same or similar circumstances."

It is a familiar rule of law that the standard of care required of an individual, unless altered by statute, is the conduct of the reasonably prudent man under the same or similar circumstances. [Cc] While the standard of care of the reasonably prudent man remains constant, the quantity or degree of care required varies significantly with the attendant circumstances. [Cc]

The trial court improperly introduced a subjective standard of care into the definition of negligence by referring to the "ordinary care and caution, which an ordinary prudent pilot *having the same training and experience as Fred Heath*, would have used in the same or similar circumstances." (Emphasis added.) We are aware of the authorities which support the application of a greater standard of care than that of the ordinary prudent man for persons shown to possess special skill in a particular endeavor. [C] Indeed, our courts have long recognized that one who engages in a business, occupation, or profession must exercise the requisite degree of learning, skill, and ability of that calling with reasonable and ordinary care. [Cc] Furthermore, the specialist within a profession may be held to a standard of care greater than that required of the general practitioner. [C] Nevertheless, the professional standard remains an objective standard. For example, the recognized standard for a physician is established as "the standard of professional competence and care customary in similar communities among physicians engaged in his field of practice." Dickens v. Everhart, 284 N.C. at 101, 199 S.E.2d at 443.

Such objective standards avoid the evil of imposing a different standard of care upon each individual. The instructions in this case concerning the pilot's standard of care are misleading at best, and a misapplication of the law. They permit the jury to consider Fred Heath's own particular experience and training, whether outstanding or inferior, in determining the requisite standard of conduct, rather than applying a minimum standard generally applicable to all pilots. The plaintiff is entitled to an instruction holding Fred Heath to the objective minimum standard of care applicable to all pilots. ...

... [F]or prejudicial errors in the charge, there must be a
New trial.

INQUIRY

The Standard. If the professional's standard of care is to exercise the knowledge, skill, and training of a competent professional within the same field, does that mean an "average" member of the profession? *See* Nowatske v. Osterloh, 198 Wis.2d 419, 543 N.W.2d 265 (1996) (jury instructions should not define the professional standard as the "average"). Does it mean a highly skilled member of the profession? *See* Corbitt v. Tatagari, 804 A.2d 1057 (Del. 2002) (the professional standard is neither the highly skilled nor the average because a professional of less than average skill could still be competent). Should law hold professionals providing pro-bono service to a lower standard? *See* Becker v. Janinski, 15 N.Y.S. 675, 677 (1891) (no). Should law hold a lawyer appointed to represent an indigent to a lower standard? *See* Ferri v. Ackerman, 444 U.S. 193 (1979) (appointed counsel is not entitled to immunity from malpractice suit).

Professions. Do teachers practice to a sufficiently defined and specialized set of standards that they could be liable for professional malpractice? *See* Brantley v. District of Columbia, 640 A.2d 181 (D.C. App. 1994) (stating that there is overwhelming authority against recognizing failure-to-educate claims); *see also* Ross v. Creighton Univ., 957 F.2d 410 (7th Cir. 1992); *cf.* Sain v. Cedar Rapids Commun. Sch. Dist., 626 N.W.2d 115 (Iowa 2001) (rejecting educational malpractice but recognizing negligent-misrepresentation claim against guidance counselor who misled student athlete on NCAA regulations); Christensen v. Southern Normal Sch., 790 So2d 252 (Ala. 2001) (rejecting educational malpractice but recognizing breach of contract and misrepresentation claims). Do clergy? *See* Lightman v. Flaum, 736 N.Y.S.2d 300, 97 N.Y.2d 128, 761 N.E.2d 1027 (2001) (rejecting malpractice or breach of fiduciary duty claim for disclosure in court dispute of confidential information shared in rabbinical counseling); F.G. v. MacDonell, 150 N.J. 550, 696 A.2d 697 (1997) (rejecting malpractice claim for clergy-parishioner intimate relationship during marital counseling); Bladen v. First Presbyterian Church, 857 P.2d 789 (Okla. 1993) (same); *but see* Doe v. Evans, 814 So.2d 370 (Fla. 2002) (permitting breach of fiduciary duty claim for misusing marital counseling).

Breach of Contract. Why not simply sue a negligent professional for breach of contract? By and large, professionals promise to perform, not to guarantee a result. *See* McComas v. Bocci, 166 Or. App. 150, 996 P.2d 506 (2000) (attorney allegedly promising to "kick ass" on appeal held not to have promised results); Sciacca v. Polizzi, 403 So.2d 728 (La. 1981) (claim for injuries from defendant's implantation of defective intra-uterine device sound in tort because defendant made no specific guarantees with respect to the procedure); *but see* Sullivan v. O'Connor, 363 Mass. 579, 296 N.E.2d 183 (1973) (affirming breach of contract judgment for plaintiff where there was clear proof that defendant plastic surgeon guaranteed a specific-shape nose). Although most cases find the cause of action to be in tort—a malpractice action—rather than contract, a few decisions permit both. *See* Collins v. Reynard, 154 Ill.2d 48, 607 N.E.2d 1185, 180 Ill. Dec. 62 (1992). Why might a plaintiff want to plead a contract rather than malpractice claim? *See* Sciacca, *supra* (malpractice claim barred by statute of limitations). The limitations periods for malpractice claims tend to be shorter, and sometimes much shorter, than for contract claims.

Reasonableness of Customs. What if professionals in the field adopt a custom that may be expedient but creates unreasonable risks? Should the professional be protected by an unreasonably lax professional standard? Consider the following case.

Hodges v. Carter
North Carolina Supreme Court
239 N.C. 517, 80 S.E.2d 144 (1954)

Civil action to recover compensation for losses resulting from the alleged negligence of defendant D. D. Topping and H. C. Carter, now deceased, in prosecuting, on behalf of plaintiff, certain actions on fire insurance policies.

On 4 June 1948 plaintiff's drug store building located in Belhaven, N. C., together with his lunch counter, fixtures, stock of drugs and sundries therein contained, was destroyed by fire. At the time plaintiff was insured under four policies of fire insurance against loss of, or damage to, said mercantile building and its contents. He filed proof of loss with each of the four insurance companies which issued said policies. The insurance companies severally rejected the proofs of loss, denied liability, and declined to pay any part of the plaintiff's losses resulting from said fire.
...
On 7 April 1949 plaintiff entered into a written contract of employment with defendants to prosecute an action against each of the insurers on the policy issued by it. The compensation to be paid was fixed on a contingent basis and defendants bound themselves "to do whatever may be necessary in order to bring the matters to a successful conclusion, to the best of their knowledge and ability."

On 3 May 1949 defendants, in behalf of plaintiff, instituted in the Superior Court of Beaufort County four separate actions—one against each of the four insurers. Complaints were filed and summonses were issued, directed to the sheriff of Beaufort County. In each case the summons and complaint, together with copies thereof, were mailed to the Commissioner of Insurance of the State of North Carolina. The Commissioner accepted service of summons and complaint in each case and forwarded a copy thereof by registered mail to the insurance company named defendant therein.

[The insurance company defendants successfully challenged the attorney defendants' choice to serve process by mail rather than in person as the statute on service required.]

On 4 March 1952 plaintiff instituted this action in which he alleges that the defendants were negligent in prosecuting his said actions in that they failed to (1) have process properly served, and (2) sue out alias summonses at the time the insurers filed their motions to dismiss the actions for want of proper service of summons, although they then had approximately sixty days within which to procure the issuance thereof.

Defendants, answering, deny negligence and plead good faith and the exercise of their best judgment.

At the hearing in the court below the judge, at the conclusion of plaintiff's evidence in chief, entered judgment of involuntary nonsuit. Plaintiff excepted and appealed. ...

BARNHILL, C.J. This seems to be a case of first impression in this jurisdiction. ...

Ordinarily when an attorney engages in the practice of the law and contracts to prosecute an action in behalf of his client, he impliedly represents that (1) he possesses the requisite degree of learning, skill, and ability necessary to the practice of his profession and which others similarly situated ordinarily possess; (2) he will exert his best judgment in the prosecution of the litigation entrusted to him; and (3) he will exercise reasonable and ordinary care and diligence in the use of his skill and in the application of his knowledge to his client's cause. [Cc]

An attorney who acts in good faith and in an honest belief that his advice and acts are well founded and in the best interest of his client is not answerable for a mere error of judgment or for a mistake in a point of law which has not been settled by the court of last resort in his State and on which reasonable doubt may be entertained by well-informed lawyers. [Cc]

Conversely, he is answerable in damages for any loss to his client which proximately results from a want of that degree of knowledge and skill ordinarily possessed by others of his profession similarly situated, or from the omission to use reasonable care and diligence, or from the failure to exercise in good faith his best judgment in attending to the litigation committed to his care. [Cc]

When the facts appearing in this record are considered in the light of these controlling principles of law, it immediately becomes manifest that plaintiff has failed to produce a scintilla of evidence tending to show that defendants breached any duty the law imposed upon them when they accepted employment to prosecute plaintiff's actions against his insurers or that they did not possess the requisite learning and skill required of an attorney or that they acted otherwise than in the utmost good faith.

The Commissioner of Insurance is the statutory process agent of foreign insurance companies doing business in this State, G.S. s 58-153, Hodges v. New Hampshire

Insurance Co., 232 N.C. 475, 61 S.E.2d 372, and when defendants mailed the process to the Commissioner of Insurance for his acceptance of service thereof, they were following a custom which had prevailed in this State for two decades or more. Foreign insurance companies had theretofore uniformly ratified such service, appeared in response thereto, filed their answers, and made their defense. The right of the Commissioner to accept service of process in behalf of foreign insurance companies doing business in this State had not been tested in the courts. Attorneys generally, throughout the State, took it for granted that under the terms of G.S. s 58-153 such acceptance of service was adequate. And, in addition, the defendants had obtained the judicial declaration of a judge of our Superior Courts that the acceptance of service by the Commissioner subjected the defendants to the jurisdiction of the court. Why then stop in the midst of the stream and pursue some other course?

Doubtless this litigation was inspired by a comment which appears in our opinion on the second appeal, Hodges v. Home Insurance Co., 233 N.C. 289, 63 S.E.2d 819. However, what was there said was pure dictum, injected—perhaps ill advisedly—in explanation of the reason we could afford plaintiff no relief on that appeal. We did not hold, or intend to intimate, that defendants had been in any wise neglectful of their duties as counsel for plaintiff.

The judgment entered in the court below is
Affirmed.

INQUIRY

Aspects of the Standard. As the *Hodges* case intimates, the professional's standard has procedural, subjective, and objective aspects. The procedural aspect requires the professional to possess *or acquire* the knowledge and skill to handle the matter. And so, a lawyer unfamiliar with a case must research the law, investigate the facts, and engage in such other professional study to act competently with respect to the matter. *See* Smith v. Lewis, 13 Cal.3d 349, 530 P.2d 589, 118 Cal. Rptr. 621 (1975) (affirming judgment for plaintiff for attorney's failure to know or research the law of community property); *but see* Lucas v. Hamm, 56 Cal.2d 583, 364 P.2d 685, 15 Cal. Rptr. 821 (1961) (attorney not liable for drafting will that violated rules against perpetuities and on restraint against alienation because these areas are fraught with confusion). The subjective aspect permits the professional to exercise judgment within the standard of care—even if the judgment is ultimately in error. *See* Crosby v. Jones, 705 So.2d 1356 (Fla. 1998) (attorney exercising best judgment is not liable for errors in tactics); Thomas v. Bethea, 351 Md. 513, 718 A.2d 1187 (1998) (attorney recommending settlement not liable for judgment error); Cosgrove v. Grimes, 774 S.W.2d 662 (Tex. 1989) ("If an attorney makes a decision which a reasonably prudent attorney *could* make in the same or similar circumstance, it is not an act of negligence even if the result is undesirable."); Blankenship v. Baptist Mem. Hosp., 26 Tenn. App. 131, 168 S.W.2d 491 (1942) (physician making diagnosis is allowed error in exercising best judgment); *but see* Pleasants v. Alliance Corp., 209 W.Va. 39, 543 S.W.2d 320 (2000) (rejecting "mistake of judgment" instruction because it incorrectly suggests that standard of care is subjective); Wood v. McGrath, North, Mullin & Kratz, 256 Neb. 109, 589 N.W.2d 103 (1999) (failure to disclose material information in recommending settlement is not exercise of best judgment). The objective aspect requires that the professional perform within the customs of the field. *See* Watkins v. Sheppard, 278 So.2d 890 (La. App. 1973) (lawyer's standard requires that suit be timely filed within the limitations period).

Medical Malpractice. After the two introductory cases above from other fields (piloting and law), the professional-negligence cases studied below are all medical-malpractice cases. Our concentration on medical malpractice does not mean that the demonstrated principles apply only in that context. Medicine is so highly specialized, and when performed outside the standard of care so readily leads to injury, that it offers the most highly developed case law. But professional malpractice cases sharing the same conceptual features as medical malpractice against physicians, nurses, psychologists, dentists, and other medical-care providers, claimants also pursue against lawyers, accountants, architects, engineers, veterinarians, pharmacists, and other professionals. The line between an ordinary-negligence claim and a malpractice claim can be hard to draw, especially considering that a professional may commit both ordinary negligence and professional malpractice—as when a physician negligently bumps over a patient whose illness the physician has misdiagnosed, resulting in a fractured hip from the fall and a worsened illness from the wrong treatment.

Practice

The leading practice field for malpractice claims against lawyers is personal injury. The second-leading field is real-estate transactions. The reasons that these two areas lead in malpractice claims differ. Real-estate work can be highly technical, especially in reviewing title-insurance commitments, drafting or confirming property descriptions, and ensuring to discover, disclose, and address easements and other rights and interests. Real property can have substantial value, and when something goes wrong, the attorneys who mismanaged the transaction are natural targets. Personal-injury lawyers face fewer technical challenges. Their problems tend to be (1) filing in time to satisfy limitations periods and (2) managing their clients' expectations. The lawyer who exaggerates claims in order to impress potential clients ends up with unhappy clients only too happy to sue. No matter what the professional field—lawyer, doctor, or other—poor professional relationships increase malpractice claims.

Expert-Testimony Requirement. Another peculiarity of malpractice claims is that expert testimony must ordinarily prove them. Lay judges and jurors, without an expert's education, training, and experience, do not know the technical standards to which a competent professional would perform. Law requires expert testimony for claims against attorneys, *see* Wong v. Ekberg, 148 N.H. 369, 807 A.2d 1266 (2002) (standard for pretrial preparation of criminal defense), architects, *see* Aetna Ins. Co. v. Hellmuth, Obata & Kassabaum, Inc., 392 F.2d 472 (8th Cir. 1968) (Missouri law), and other professionals—including, especially, physicians. Consider the following case.

Smith v. Knowles
Minnesota Supreme Court
281 N.W.2d 653 (Minn. 1979)

SCOTT, J. This is an appeal by plaintiff, Clinton E. Smith, as trustee for the heirs of Diane Smith (his wife) and Baby Girl Smith (his stillborn child), from an order of the district court in Blue Earth County dismissing plaintiff's wrongful death actions against defendant, Dr. William David Knowles. The dismissals were granted, upon motion of defendant at the close of plaintiff's case, on the ground that the plaintiff failed to offer sufficient expert evidence for the jury to consider his claims of negligence and causation. We affirm.

The actions giving rise to this appeal arose from the deaths of Diane Smith and her unborn child. Both mother and child died as a result of toxemia of pregnancy, or "eclampsia." These actions were commenced against Diane's attending physician, Dr. Knowles. Essentially, plaintiff claims that Dr. Knowles was negligent in failing to make a timely diagnosis of Diane's pre-eclampsia and that he was further negligent in his treatment of that condition once it was diagnosed. …

… Diane Smith consulted [Dr. Knowles] on September 18, 1973, at which time he diagnosed her second pregnancy. From September until her death in February, 1974, she saw Dr. Knowles at one-month intervals.

Clinton Smith testified at trial that his wife's pregnancy differed markedly from her first one. He indicated that beginning in November she experienced headaches, heartburn, blurred vision, swelling in her legs and ankles and some vomiting. He related that these symptoms continued into December and that Diane took aspirin and antacid tablets throughout this period to alleviate these symptoms. Plaintiff further testified that his wife continued to suffer from nausea, blurred vision, headaches, chest pains and swelling through January and that these symptoms intensified in early February. …

Diane was admitted to the hospital at approximately 11:45 a. m. [on February 13, 1974, under Dr. Knowles' care. She suffered convulsions and lost consciousness.] …

… Late that evening, after the doctors could no longer hear fetal heart tones, Dr. Howard performed a Caesarean section and delivered a stillborn baby girl. Diane's condition continued to deteriorate following the operation. On February 19, the doctors administered an encephalogram and determined that Diane's brain had ceased functioning. Mr. Smith gave his permission for the doctors to discontinue artificial means of life support, and Diane expired.

At trial, plaintiff sought to show that Dr. Knowles was negligent in both his diagnosis and treatment of Diane's condition. The trial court concluded that plaintiff failed to present sufficient competent medical testimony to allow the case to go to the jury, and thus granted defendant's motion to dismiss. …

Clearly, expert testimony is crucial to plaintiff's claims. To establish a prima facie case in an action such as this, the plaintiff here must introduce expert testimony as to both the standard of care and the defendant doctor's departure from that standard. [Cc] Moreover, plaintiff's claims required expert testimony to show that Dr. Knowles' action or inaction was a direct cause of the decedents' deaths. [C]

Here, plaintiff called no independent medical witnesses. Instead, he chose to prove his case through his cross-examination of Dr. Knowles[fn] and the introduction of excerpts from several recognized medical treatises.[fn] The trial court carefully reviewed this evidence and concluded that it was legally insufficient. We agree.

At trial, plaintiff called Dr. Knowles for cross-examination and asked him a series of hypothetical questions. Dr. Knowles was most forthright and candid in his answers.

… His testimony was corroborated, to a large extent, by excerpts from several learned treatises.[fn] Giving this general evidence the benefit of all legitimate inferences, we conclude that it was, at best, minimally sufficient to establish the requisite standard of care. Never was any specific expert testimony presented which tended to show that Dr. Knowles departed from this standard.

Even more troubling, however, is the lack of expert testimony on the causation elements of plaintiff's claims. Here, as in Silver v. Redleaf, supra, plaintiff had the burden to prove, by expert testimony, that, "* * * it was more probable that death resulted from some negligence for which defendant was responsible than from something for which he was not responsible." 292 Minn. 465, 194 N.W.2d 273. (Citations omitted.) Such proof is absent from this case. Instead, the record would have compelled the jury to speculate as to whether earlier diagnosis or different treatment would have resulted in a cure. The trial court could not permit this, and thus had no alternative but to grant defendant's motion for a dismissal. In light of our disposition of this case, we need not reach the other issues raised by the briefs.

Affirmed.

INQUIRY

Treatises. Could an ingenious plaintiff establish the standard of care using medical treatises? In the above case, *Smith v. Knowles*, the plaintiff succeeded in introducing medical treatises as substantive evidence on the medical standard of care. Federal Rule of Evidence 803(18), which Minnesota and other states have adopted in the same form, provides that learned treatises are admissible once established as reliable authority. But as *Smith v. Knowles* shows, the admission into evidence of a treatise will ordinarily not, alone, establish the standard of care. Other jurisdictions reject FRE 803(18), prohibiting a learned treatise as substantive evidence. *See* Aldridge v. Edmunds, 561 Pa. 323, 750 A.2d 292 (2000) (textbook evidence is inadmissible to establish a standard of care but may be used to impeach on cross-examination); *see also* Hilgendorf v. St. John Hosp. & Med. Ctr. Corp., 245 Mich. App. 670, 630 N.W.2d 356 (2001) (learned treatises may only first be used for cross-examination but then may be used to rehabilitate the challenged expert).

> **Ethics**
> Tort lawyers must often gather, record, and preserve evidence for inspection, disclosure, evaluation, and trial. The temptation may exist for the lawyer to take the accident-scene photographs, make inspections and measurements, record witness statements, and do other important investigation, rather than hire a private investigator, accident reconstructionist, or other expert investigator. A lawyer can gain much from seeing things first-hand, while saving time and expense. But a lawyer can also lose much if the lawyer becomes a witness in the litigation. Rule 3.7 of the ABA Model Rules of Professional Conduct prohibits a lawyer from acting as an advocate and witness at trial—from assuming two conflicting roles—except in special cases. The advocate lawyer who inadvertently becomes a witness can lose the opportunity to earn a fee and places the client's case in jeopardy. Tort lawyers, and especially plaintiff's lawyers, do well to have a reliable, credible, and skilled private investigator available to gather evidence. Retired police officers can make excellent tort-claim investigators when

> already trained and having already had substantial experience in accident-investigation, interviewing witnesses, and recording statements. They can also make highly credible witnesses as to any evidence they gathered that parties later dispute. Some investigators also have the qualifications to serve as expert witnesses in accident reconstruction and related fields.

Obviousness of Standard. Must an expert witness testify to the standard of care in absolutely every malpractice case, or do some instances exist when even a lay person would know that the defendant's conduct fell below the standard of care? *Compare* Dickerson v. Fatehi, 253 Va. 324, 484 S.W.2d 880 (1997) (expert testimony unnecessary for claim based on surgeon's leaving hypodermic needle and attachment in surgical site); Coleman v. Rice, 706 So.2d 696 (Miss. 1997) (expert testimony unnecessary when sponge left in laparotomy-surgery site); Welte v. Bello, 482 N.W.2d 437 (Iowa 1992) (expert testimony unnecessary when defendant caused third-degree burns to arm from misdirected anesthetic, during surgery on nose); Timbrell v. Suburban Hosp., 4 Cal.2d 68, 47 P.2d 737 (1935) (expert testimony unnecessary regarding hot-water bottle-shaped burns on stomach after surgery and recovery), *with* Hightower-Warren v. Silk, 548 Pa. 459, 698 A.2d 52 (1997) (expert testimony necessary for paralyzed vocal chords after thyroid surgery); Mireles v. Broderick, 117 N.M. 445, 872 P.2d 863 (1994) (expert testimony necessary for arm numbness after mastectomy); Connors v. University Assocs., 4 F.3d 123 (2d Cir. 1993) (expert testimony necessary for loss of leg function after abdominal surgery). Consider one well-known case in which the court did not require expert testimony but instead permitted the plaintiff to rely on res ipsa loquitur.

Ybarra v. Spangard
California Supreme Court
25 Cal.2d 486, 154 P.2d 687 (1944)

GIBSON, C.J. This is an action for damages for personal injuries alleged to have been inflicted on plaintiff by defendants during the course of a surgical operation. The trial court entered judgments of nonsuit as to all defendants and plaintiff appealed.

On October 28, 1939, plaintiff consulted defendant Dr. Tilley, who diagnosed his ailment as appendicitis, and made arrangements for an appendectomy to be performed by defendant Dr. Spangard at a hospital owned and managed by defendant Dr. Swift. Plaintiff entered the hospital, was given a hypodermic injection, slept, and later was awakened by Drs. Tilley and Spangard and wheeled into the operating room by a nurse whom he believed to be defendant Gisler, an employee of Dr. Swift. Defendant Dr. Reser, the anesthetist, also an employee of Dr. Swift, adjusted plaintiff for the operation, pulling his body to the head of the operating table and, according to plaintiff's testimony, laying him back against two hard objects at the top of his shoulders, about an inch below his neck. Dr. Reser then administered the anesthetic and plaintiff lost consciousness. When he awoke early the following morning he was in his hospital room attended by defendant Thompson, the special nurse, and another nurse who was not made a defendant.

Plaintiff testified that prior to the operation he had never had any pain in, or injury to, his right arm or shoulder, but that when he awakened he felt a sharp pain about half way between the neck and the point of the right shoulder. He complained to the nurse, and then to Dr. Tilley, who gave him diathermy treatments while he remained in the hospital. The pain did not cease but spread down to the lower part of his arm, and after his release from the hospital the condition grew worse. He was unable to rotate or lift his arm, and developed paralysis and atrophy of the muscles around the shoulder. ...

... In the opinion of Dr. Clark, plaintiff's condition was due to trauma or injury by pressure or strain applied between his right shoulder and neck.

Plaintiff was also examined by Dr. Fernando Garduno, who expressed the opinion that plaintiff's injury was a paralysis of traumatic origin, not arising from pathological causes, and not systemic....

Plaintiff's theory is that the foregoing evidence presents a proper case for the application of the doctrine of res ipsa loquitur, and that the inference of negligence arising therefrom makes the granting of as nonsuit improper. Defendants take the position that, assuming that plaintiff's condition was in fact the result of an injury, there is no showing that the act of any particular defendant, nor any particular instrumentality, was the cause thereof. They attack plaintiff's action as an attempt to fix liability "en masse" on various defendants, some of whom were not responsible for the acts of others; and they further point to the failure to show which defendants had control of the instrumentalities that may have been involved. ... We are satisfied, however, that these objections are not well taken in the circumstances of this case. ...

The present case is of a type which comes within the reason and spirit of the doctrine more fully perhaps than any other. The passenger sitting awake in a railroad car at the time of a collision, the pedestrian walking along the street and struck by a falling object or the debris of an explosion, are surely not more entitled to an explanation than the unconscious patient on the operating table. Viewed from this aspect, it is difficult to see how the doctrine can, with any justification, be so restricted in its statement as to become inapplicable to a patient who submits himself to the care and custody of doctors and nurses, is rendered unconscious, and receives some injury from instrumentalities used in his treatment. Without the aid of the doctrine a patient who received permanent injuries of a serious character, obviously the result of some one's negligence, would be entirely unable to recover unless the doctors and nurses in attendance voluntarily chose to disclose the identity of the negligent person and the facts establishing liability. [C] ...

The argument of defendants is simply that plaintiff has not shown an injury caused by an instrumentality under a defendant's control, because he has not shown which of the several instrumentalities that he came in contact with while in the hospital caused the injury; and he has not shown that any one defendant or his servants had exclusive control over any particular instrumentality. Defendants assert that some of them were not the employees of other defendants, that some did not stand in any permanent relationship from which liability in tort would follow, and that in view of the nature of the injury, the number of defendants and the different functions performed by each, they could not all be liable for the wrong, if any.

We have no doubt that in a modern hospital a patient is quite likely to come under the care of a number of persons in different types of contractual and other relationships with each other. ... But we do not believe that either the number or relationship of the defendants alone determines whether the doctrine of res ipsa loquitur applies. Every defendant in whose custody the plaintiff was placed for any period was bound to exercise ordinary care to see that no unnecessary harm came to him and each would be liable for failure in this regard. Any defendant who negligently injured him, and any defendant charged with his care who so neglected him as to allow injury to occur, would be liable. The defendant employers would be liable for the neglect of their employees; and the doctor in charge of the operation would be liable for the negligence of those who became his temporary servants for the purpose of assisting in the operation. ...

It may appear at the trial that, consistent with the principles outlined above, one or more defendants will be found liable and others absolved, but this should not preclude the application of the rule of res ipsa loquitur. The control at one time or another, of one or more of the various agencies or instrumentalities which might have harmed the plaintiff was in the hands of every defendant or of his employees or temporary servants. This, we think, places upon them the burden of initial explanation. Plaintiff was rendered unconscious for the purpose of undergoing surgical treatment by the defendants; it is manifestly unreasonable for them to insist that he identify any one of them as the person who did the alleged negligent act. ...

... [T]here can be no justification for the rejection of the doctrine in the instant case. As pointed out above, if we accept the contention of defendants herein, there will rarely be any compensation for patients injured while unconscious. A hospital today conducts a highly integrated system of activities, with many persons contributing their efforts. There may be, e.g., preparation for surgery by nurses and internes who are employees of the hospital; administering of an anesthetic by a doctor who may be an employee of the hospital, an employee of the operating surgeon, or an independent contractor; performance of an operation by a surgeon and assistants who may be his employees, employees of the hospital, or independent contractors; and post surgical care by the surgeon, a hospital physician, and nurses. The number of those in whose care the patient is placed is not a good reason for denying him all reasonable opportunity to recover for negligent harm. It is rather a good reason for re-examination of the statement of legal theories which supposedly compel such a shocking result.

We do not at this time undertake to state the extent to which the reasoning of this case may be applied to other situations in which the doctrine of res ipsa loquitur is invoked. We merely hold that where a plaintiff receives unusual injuries while unconscious and in the course of medical treatment, all those defendants who had any control over his body or the instrumentalities which might have caused the injuries may properly be called upon to meet the inference of negligence by giving an explanation of their conduct.

The judgment is reversed.

INQUIRY

Multiple Defendants. When a case involves only one defendant, res ipsa loquitur is available for medical-malpractice claims just as for negligence claims. *See* Kambat v. St. Francis Hosp., 678 N.E.2d 456 (N.Y. 1997) (doctrine applied to case in which defendant surgeon left 18-by-18-inch pad in surgical site after hysterectomy). The *Ybarra* case involves the unusual instance of applying res ipsa loquitur to multiple defendants. It represents only a small minority position. *Compare* Estate of Chin v.

St. Barnabas Med. Ctr., 312 N.J. Super 81, 711 A.2d 352 (N.J. Super. Ct. App. Div. 1998) (followed); Beaudoin v. Watertown Mem. Hosp., 32 Wis.2d 132, 145 N.W.2d 166 (1966) (followed); *with* Golden v. Kishwaukee Commun. Health Services Ctr., 269 Ill. App.3d 37, 206 Ill. Dec. 314, 645 N.E.2d 319 (Ill. App. Ct. 1994) (rejected); King v. Searle Parmaceuticals, Inc., 832 P.2d 858 (Utah 1992) (rejected); Talbot v. Dr. W.H. Groves' Latter-Day Saints Hosp., 21 Utah 2d 73, 440 P.2d 872 (1968) (rejected). Take care to distinguish the *Ybarra* case, where plaintiff joined all potentially liable defendants, from cases in which the plaintiff fails to name as defendants one or more medical-care providers who may well have breached the standard of care causing the plaintiff's injury. Res ipsa loquitur will not apply in those instances. *See* Darrah v. Bryan Mem. Hosp., 253 Neb. 710, 571 N.W.2d 783 (1998) (res-ipsa-loquitur theory against hospital dismissed for plaintiff's failure to join medical treaters). Also, some state legislatures have limited the reach of res ipsa loquitur in medical-malpractice cases. *See* 18 Del. Code Ann. 18 §6853 (1992).

Vicarious Liability. When a case involves multiple potential defendants, vicarious-liability theories may be available based on respondeat-superior (employer liability), agency-by-estoppel, and ostensible- or apparent-agency theories. *See* Dias v. Brigham Med. Assocs., Inc., 438 Mass. 317, 780 N.E.2d 447 (2002) (medical group employer vicariously liable in respondeat superior for malpractice of employed physician); Clark v. Southview Hosp. & Family Health Ctr., 68 Ohio St.3d 435, 628 N.W.2d 46 (1994) (hospital vicariously liable on agency theory for malpractice of physician if patient looks to the hospital for service); Jackson v. Power, 743 P.2d 1376 (Alaska 1987) (hospital subject to ostensible agency or agency-by-estoppel vicarious liability for malpractice of emergency-room physician); *see also* Petrovich v. Share Health Plan of Illinois, Inc., 188 Ill.2d 17, 241 Ill. Dec. 627, 719 N.E.2d 756 (1999) (HMO vicarious liability on apparent-agency theory, for professional negligence of participating physician); *but see* Fla. Stat. Ann. §641.51 (barring HMO apparent-agency vicarious liability); W. Va. Code §55-7B-9 (medical-care providers not vicariously liable on agency theory unless agent's liability insurance was under $1 million); Fletcher v. South Peninsula Hosp., 71 P.3d 833 (Alaska 2003) (hospital not vicariously liable for malpractice of physician to whom patient was referred outside of the hospital before hospital admission for physician's treatment); Baptist Mem. Hosp. System v. Sampson, 969 S.W.2d 945 (Tex. 1998) (hospital not vicariously liable for emergency-room physician's malpractice where patient signed consent form acknowledging that physician was independent contractor). In the ostensible-agency formulation, the patient looks to the hospital to provide the physician, while in the agency-by-estoppel formulation the hospital holds itself out as providing services through the physician. Emergency-room services are the classic agency situation—as to which a hospital may also have vicarious liability under a non-delegable-duty theory. Hospital vicarious liability by agency is not generally available where the patient has an office-based relationship with the physician independent of that which arises when the patient seeks care at the hospital.

Direct Corporate Claims. When a physician commits medical malpractice, there may also be direct claims of corporate negligence against hospitals, clinics, or even health-maintenance organizations (HMOs) and other managed-care organizations, for negligently providing the physician with staff privileges or assignments of patients. *See* Jones v. Chicago HMO Ltd., 191 Ill.2d 278, 730 N.E.2d 1119, 246 Ill. Dec. 654

(2000) (HMO alleged to have assigned overload of patients to physician); Insinga v. LaBella, 543 So.2d 209 (Fla. 1989) (hospital); Darling v. Charleston Commun. Mem. Hosp., 33 Ill.2d 326, 211 N.E.2d 253 (1965) (hospital).

> **Ethics**
>
> Medical-malpractice litigation can be complex, requiring a lawyer to possess specialized knowledge, exercise special skills, and have special resources. Rule 1.1 of the ABA Model Rules of Professional Conduct requires that lawyers "provide competent representation to a client," defining that representation to require "the legal knowledge, skill, thoroughness and preparation reasonably necessary for the representation." Lawyers who are unfamiliar with a legal field will often refer cases to lawyers who have the necessary expertise, although Comment 2 to Rule 1.1 acknowledges that competent representation "in a wholly novel field can also be provided through necessary study." An alternative is to associate as co-counsel with a lawyer experienced and competent in the field, to gain the requisite experience for the next case.

The Reasonable Physician. Opinions have raised concerns that custom standard-of-care requirements are an elitist manner of protecting professionals from juries, especially in those states that do not extend custom standards to protect the trades, and that they retard improved practices. A very few states reject an explicit, custom standard and let juries decide malpractice cases on ordinary-negligence principles as to what the reasonable professional would have done under the same circumstances. *See* Helling v. Carey, 83 Wash.2d 514, 519 P.2d 981 (Wash. 1974); *see also* Nowatske v. Osterloh, 198 Wis.2d 419, 543 N.W.2d 265, 272 (1996) ("customary conduct is not dispositive and cannot overcome the requirement that physicians exercise ordinary care"); Philp G. Peters, Jr., *The Role of the Jury in Modern Malpractice Law*, 87 Iowa L.Rev. 909 (2002). The Washington legislature responded to *Helling v. Carey* by statutorily requiring that the plaintiff prove "that the defendant ... failed to exercise that degree of skill, care and learning possessed by other persons in the same profession...," *see* Wash. Rev. Code §4.24.290, but the Washington Supreme Court subsequently held that the statute did not change *Helling v. Carey's* reasonableness standard, *see* Gates v. Jensen, 595 P.2d 919 (Wash. 1979). Other courts will on rare occasions permit a special instruction that law does not shield an unreasonable but customary practice if the physician has not used best judgment. *See* Burton v. Brooklyn Doctors Hosp., 88 A.D.2d 217, 452 N.Y.S.2d 875 (1982). Assuming (as is usually the case) that the plaintiff must call an expert witness to testify to the standard of care, what kind of expert may the plaintiff call? Consider the following case, on the need for qualified testimony in the same field.

Melville v. Southward
Colorado Supreme Court
791 P.2d 383 (Colo. 1990)

QUINN, C.J. The question in this case is whether a plaintiff in a medical malpractice action against a podiatrist, who performed foot surgery and rendered postoperative care and treatment to the plaintiff, may elicit expert opinion testimony from a practitioner of another school of medicine, namely orthopedic surgery, on the standard of care applicable to podiatric surgery and post-operative care and treatment. The trial court permitted the plaintiff, over the defendant's objection, to elicit an expert opinion from an orthopedic surgeon that the podiatric surgery performed on the plaintiff's foot and the post-operative treatment rendered to the plaintiff fell below the standard of care applicable to the surgery in question and also fell below the standard of care applicable to the post-operative care and treatment of the patient. The court of appeals, in an unpublished opinion, reversed the judgment entered on the jury verdict for the plaintiff and ordered the dismissal of the plaintiff's complaint with prejudice, reasoning that the testimony of the orthopedic surgeon was insufficient as a matter of law to establish a *prima facie* case of negligence against the podiatrist. [C] We agree with the court of appeals that the lack of any foundation for the orthopedic surgeon's familiarity with the podiatric standard of care for the surgery in question and the post-operative care and treatment of the patient rendered the orthopedic surgeon's opinion testimony inadmissible. However, contrary to the court of appeals' decision, we believe that the proper disposition of this matter is to return the case to the trial court for a new trial.

I.

The plaintiff-petitioner, Lulu Melville (plaintiff), filed a negligence action in the district court of Fremont County against the defendant-respondent, Dr. Stanton C. Southward (defendant), a licensed podiatrist. The complaint, as pertinent here, alleged that on or about August 14, 1980, the defendant performed a surgical procedure in his office on the plaintiff's right foot, that the surgical procedure fell below the standard of reasonably careful podiatric surgery, that defendant failed to provide adequate post-operative care and treatment, and that the plaintiff sustained a serious infection and developed osteomyelitis as a result of defendant's negligence. ...

... The evidence at trial established the following sequence of events. The plaintiff first consulted the defendant in July 1980 for an ingrown toenail. The defendant removed the ingrown toenail and subsequently, on August 14, 1980, recommended that plaintiff undergo a surgical procedure known as a metatarsal osteotomy in order to relieve the discomfort that the plaintiff had been experiencing. The recommended surgery consisted of the cutting and shortening of the metatarsal shaft of the second toe in the right foot.

The plaintiff agreed to the surgery, and it was performed on August 14 in the defendant's office. ...

On August 26, 1980, the plaintiff telephoned the defendant and complained that her foot was swollen, red, and quite painful. The defendant advised her to increase the amount of vinegar in the prescribed solution and to soak the foot more frequently, and stated that he would check the foot again in two days at the plaintiff's scheduled office appointment. The defendant, at the scheduled office visit, told the plaintiff that her foot was healing, and he rewrapped the foot with clean bandages. The next day, August 29, the plaintiff noticed a sore spot near the surgical site and a fluid exuding from that area when it was touched. The plaintiff telephoned her family physician, Joseph R. McGarry, for an appointment.

[Dr. McGarry examined, treated, and hospitalized the plaintiff, before referring her to orthopedic surgeon Dr. Barnard.]

Doctor Barnard first saw the plaintiff on October 17, 1980, and noted that the plaintiff's foot was swollen and slightly red. X-rays revealed an erosion of the bone in the area of the second metatarsal. Such bone erosion, according to Barnard, was consistent with osteomyelitis which, in his view, had been caused by the osteotomy performed by the defendant.

Plaintiff's counsel asked Doctor Barnard whether he had an opinion to a reasonable medical probability on whether the osteotomy was performed below the standard of care for such a surgical procedure. ... Barnard testified that the osteotomy performed by the defendant was below the standard of care for two reasons: first, the surgery was unnecessary because none of the pre-surgical X-rays indicated a deformity in the metatarsal; and second, even assuming the surgery was necessary, the osteotomy was performed in an unsterile office environment and thereby subjected the bone to a high risk of infection. Barnard acknowledged in his testimony that he was unfamiliar with the standards applicable to podiatric foot surgery, was not familiar with podiatric literature, had never received any instruction on podiatry, and had never performed the surgical procedure involved in this case.

Doctor Barnard also testified, again over the defendant's objection, that the defendant's post-operative treatment of the plaintiff fell below the proper standard of care for treating an osteotomy. ...

... It was Barnard's opinion that the plaintiff had sustained a permanent disability as a result of the defendant's surgery and would have difficulty walking and balancing herself.

At the close of the plaintiff's case, the defendant moved for a directed verdict, claiming that the plaintiff had failed to establish a *prima facie* case of negligence due to the lack of any expert testimony on the applicable standard of care for podiatric surgery and post-operative care and treatment. The trial court denied the motion, ruling that an orthopedic surgeon has more training and expertise than a podiatrist and thus is competent to provide an opinion on the standard of care applicable to the podiatric surgery performed by the defendant. ...

The jury found that the plaintiff had sustained damage in the amount of $56,000 as a result of the defendant's negligence. ...

II.

... To establish a *prima facie* case, the plaintiff must establish that the defendant failed to conform to the standard of care ordinarily possessed and exercised by members of the same school of medicine practiced by the defendant. [Cc] The standard of care in a medical malpractice action is measured by whether a reasonably careful physician of the same school of medicine as the defendant would have acted in the same manner as did the defendant in treating and caring for the plaintiff. [C]

Unless the subject matter of a medical malpractice action lies within the ambit of common knowledge or experience of ordinary persons, the plaintiff must establish the controlling standard of care, as well as the defendant's failure to adhere to that standard, by expert opinion testimony. [Cc] The reason for the requirement of expert opinion testimony in most medical malpractice cases is obvious: matters relating to medical diagnosis and treatment ordinarily involve a level of technical knowledge and skill beyond the realm of lay knowledge and experience. Without expert opinion testimony in such cases, the trier of fact would be left with no standard at all against which to evaluate the defendant's conduct. [Cc] ...

... [T]he dispositive consideration in ruling on the admissibility of expert opinion testimony by a medical witness regarding whether the defendant, who practices in another school of medicine, has adhered to or deviated from the requisite standard of care in diagnosing or treating the plaintiff should be the following: (1) whether the testifying expert, although practicing a specialty different from that of the defendant, nonetheless is, by reason of knowledge, skill, experience, training, or education, so substantially familiar with the standard of care applicable to the defendant's specialty as to render the witness' opinion testimony as well-informed as would be the opinion of an expert witness practicing the same specialty as the defendant; or (2) whether the standard of care for the condition in question is substantially identical for both specialties.[fn] If a proper foundation establishes either of these evidentiary predicates for admissibility, the witness should be permitted to offer an expert opinion on the standard of care applicable to the defendant's specialty and on whether the defendant breached that standard of care. On the other hand, absent the proper foundation evidence, the expert witness practicing a specialty different from that of the defendant should not be permitted to offer an expert opinion on those matters.

III.

The practice of podiatry is defined by statute as "the diagnosis and the medical, surgical, mechanical, manipulative, and electrical treatment of disorders of the human toe and foot, including the ankle and tendons that insert into the foot." § 12-32-101(3), 5 C.R.S. (1985).[fn] The practice of medicine, in contrast, includes the diagnosis, treatment, or prevention of "any human disease, ailment, pain, injury, deformity, or physical or mental condition, whether by the use of drugs, surgery, manipulation, electricity, or any physical, mechanical, or other means whatsoever." Section 12-36-106(1)(a), 5 C.R.S. (1985). Orthopedic surgery is a medical subspecialty that involves the utilization of medical, surgical, and physical methods in treating the extremities, spine, and associated structures, and, as such, includes not only foot surgery encompassed by the practice of podiatry but also other treatments and medical practices not within podiatric practices. [C] …

The plaintiff failed to establish an evidentiary foundation that Doctor Barnard, by reason of his knowledge, skill, experience, training, or education, was so substantially familiar with the standard of care for podiatric surgery as to render his opinion testimony as well-informed as that of a podiatrist. On the contrary, Barnard expressly acknowledged that he was not familiar either with podiatric foot care or with the standard of care applicable to a podiatrist. … Nor did the plaintiff establish by way of an evidentiary predicate that the standard of care for a metatarsal osteotomy was substantially identical for both the practice of orthopedic surgery and podiatry. …

We accordingly affirm that part of the court of appeals' judgment which holds that the trial court improperly permitted an orthopedic surgeon to offer opinion testimony on the standard of care applicable to a podiatrist. We, however, reverse that part of the judgment which orders the dismissal of the plaintiff's complaint with prejudice, and we remand the case to the court of appeals with directions to return it to the trial court for a new trial consistent with the views herein expressed.

INQUIRY

Matching Expertise. If a similarly qualified physician must testify to the standard of care as to a defendant physician, then why do some courts allow physicians to testify to the standard of care for nurses? *See* Hall v. Sacred Heart Med. Cntr., 100

Wash. App. 53, 995 P.2d 621 (2000). What if the defendant professional lacked the qualifications to provide service in the field but told the plaintiff that the professional had the qualifications? Does the law hold the professional to the standard of the professional's own field or the field in which the professional falsely claimed expertise? *See* Duffey Law Office v. Tank Transport, Inc., 194 Wis.2d 674, 535 N.W.2d 91 (App. 1995) (attorney claiming expertise in labor law held to the standard of a specialist in that field); Aves v. Shah, 997 F.2d 762 (10th Cir. 1993) (physician claiming obstetrical specialty held, under Kansas law, to that higher standard).

Emergencies. Does the standard of care change in an emergency? Medical-care providers who already owe a patient the duty to provide medical care—including emergency care—are held to the usual standard of care for medical emergencies. But some states provide statutory protection for medical-care providers who act as a Good Samaritan when they have no pre-existing duty. *See* HIRPA v. IHC Hosps., Inc., 948 P.2d 785 (Utah 1997) (hospital physician protected by emergency-immunity statute when responding to "Code Blue" call to save another physician's patient within hospital); *cf.* N.C. Gen. Stat. §20-166(d) (liability remains for gross negligence); *but see* Velazquez v. Jiminez, 172 N.J. 240, 798 A.2d 51 (2002) (emergency-immunity statute does not apply to hospital physician).

Figure

In his day, trial lawyer Melvin Belli, whose career spanned the 1940s into the 1990s, had the reputation of the "King of Torts." Some of his cases, such as *Escola v. Coca-Cola Bottling Co.*, 150 P.2d 436 (Cal. 1944), in which Justice Traynor's concurrence laid the groundwork for strict products liability, and some of his trial practices such as the liberal use of demonstrative evidence and expert witnesses, helped to establish what tort lawyers today regard as commonplace. In his first torts-trial win shortly after graduating from law school, he used as trial exhibits the mechanical parts involved in his client's injury and a model of the intersection—an uncommon practice until then. He wrote many books including *Ready for the Plaintiff* and a six-volume work *Modern Trials* on demonstrative evidence. But he was better known for representing famous figures like Muhammad Ali, Jim and Tammy Bakker, Sirhan Sirhan, and Mae West, and for his flamboyant style—like shooting a cannon from the roof of his office building to announce another case win and to call celebrants to another one of his extravagant parties. His law firm went bankrupt in 1995 when he won a class-action breast-implant lawsuit only to have the defendant declare bankruptcy, leaving Belli without a way to pay the $5 million dollars in expenses his firm advanced on the case. Always an entertainer, Belli appeared in the Star Trek television series and several other films and television shows.

Objective Standard. When the plaintiff identifies, retains, and calls an appropriately qualified expert witness, exactly to what must the expert testify to establish a standard of care? Expert testimony must establish both (1) the professional's standard of care and (2) causation. The causation issue, discussed below, can be more troublesome than it initially seems. But even as to the standard-of-care issue, the testifying expert faces challenges. An expert testifying to the standard of care cannot simply state what the expert would have done because standards may permit more than one permissible professional judgment. The expert's testimony must be in terms of what the standard of care required. *See* Johnson v. Riverdale Anesthesia

Assocs., 275 Ga. 240, 563 S.W.2d 431 (2002) (expert's testimony that he personally would have treated the plaintiff does not establish a standard of care to do so); Boyce v. Brown, 51 Ariz. 416, 77 P.2d 455 (1938) (expert's testimony that he personally would have ordered a radiograph does not establish a standard of care to do so). As you read the following case, consider why the expert witness might have testified as he did and what responsibility, if any, the plaintiff's lawyer had for it.

Walski v. Tiesenga
Illinois Supreme Court
72 Ill.2d 249, 21 Ill. Dec. 201, 381 N.E.2d 279 (1978)

KLUCZYNSKI, J. This appeal involves an action in malpractice against two doctors, Marvin Tiesenga and James Walsh, for personal injuries arising from the alleged negligence of the doctors during an operation on plaintiff's thyroid gland in which her left recurrent laryngeal nerve was cut. ... The trial court directed a verdict in favor of the defendants. The appellate court affirmed on the ground that plaintiff had failed to establish the requisite professional standard of care against which the defendants' conduct was to be judged. [C] ... [W]e agree that the trial court did not err in directing a verdict for defendants.

... During an office visit on July 19, 1971, Dr. Walsh detected that plaintiff's thyroid gland was enlarged and was pressing on her trachea. The enlarged thyroid interfered with plaintiff's breathing. Dr. Walsh arranged for Dr. Tiesenga, a general surgeon, to perform a subtotal thyroidectomy on November 30, 1971. Dr. Walsh assisted in the surgery. After surgery, plaintiff experienced problems in breathing and speaking.

Plaintiff called Dr. Tiesenga as an adverse witness.... He indicated that a recurrent laryngeal nerve lies on either side of the thyroid gland. If that nerve is severed, cut or crushed, paralysis of the vocal chords would be expected. ... Dr. Tiesenga identified the right recurrent laryngeal nerve. He stated he made no attempt to identify the nerve on the left but, in removing tissue from the left side of the gland, made a wide cut so as to avoid the area where the nerve might possibly be.

Dr. David M. Berger testified as an expert witness on plaintiff's behalf. He examined plaintiff in January of 1976 and found vocal-chord paralysis. His direct testimony concerning acceptable procedures for thyroid surgery was that "in my feeling the standards by which I feel are acceptable practice, one must identify and preserve the recurrent laryngeal nerves on all occasions." On cross-examination Dr. Berger testified that there are always options available in surgery but that in his own mind it was not a proper option to skirt the left recurrent laryngeal nerve. He stated he could not testify generally but only "on the basis of my own opinion as to what I consider a proper option." When asked on cross-examination if there existed a contemporary school of surgeons that will skirt the nerve when they encounter a host of adhesions, Dr. Berger responded that "in the institutions in which I trained that is not the teaching. And I can't speak for other institutions or other areas of training. I can only speak for my own." Defense counsel read a quotation to Dr. Berger from a medical textbook which indicated that there existed a certain amount of controversy in the medical community concerning deliberate exposure of the laryngeal nerve. The quotation concluded with the remark that the situation remained one in which each surgeon will find the approach which suits him best. Dr. Berger indicated that he did not fully agree with that statement, but indicated the decision whether or not to expose the nerve depends on the surgeon and the technique and care he uses. Dr. Berger stated that "(e)verbody who is a certified surgeon doesn't use the same methods, obviously." ...

The malpractice alleged here was Dr. Tiesenga's failure to identify the left recurrent laryngeal nerve during what the defendants testified was extremely difficult thyroid surgery involving a thyroid gland which was surrounded by scar tissue as a result of prior surgery and treatment. This is not the type of situation in which the common sense of laymen could provide the standard of care. ...

Plaintiff here had the burden of establishing that the defendant doctors were guilty of malpractice. She failed, however, to introduce evidence of the standard of care to which the defendants were bound to adhere. Plaintiff's expert, Dr. Berger, testified only concerning his own personal preference for isolating the laryngeal nerve under the facts presented to him in the hypothetical question. He at no time testified that there was a generally accepted medical standard of care, or skill which required the identification of the laryngeal nerve under the circumstances. Plaintiff's witness Dr. Kowal testified that the decision whether to isolate the nerve varied from case to case.

The appellate courts have held that the testimony of the defendant doctor may be sufficient to establish the standard of care ([cc]), but it is apparent that the defendants' testimony here did not indicate a standard at variance with their actual conduct. Dr. Tiesenga testified that because of prior surgery on and treatment of plaintiff's thyroid, it would have been unwise to attempt to isolate her laryngeal nerve. The better practice, according to Dr. Tiesenga's testimony, was to skirt the area where the nerve might possibly be. Dr. Walsh concurred. When confronted with a statement from a recognized treatise that the first step in performing a thyroidectomy is to expose and identify the recurrent laryngeal nerve, Dr. Tiesenga agreed with the statement only as a general proposition. He testified that where there has been prior surgery and treatment, it is not always good practice to follow the procedure indicated in the treatise. ...

It is insufficient for plaintiff to establish a Prima facie case merely to present testimony of another physician that he would have acted differently from the defendant, since medicine is not an exact science. It is rather a profession which involves the exercise of individual judgment within the framework of established procedures. Differences in opinion are consistent with the exercise of due care. [Cc] ...

The testimony of other physicians that they would have followed a different course of treatment than that followed by the defendant, or a disagreement of doctors of equal skill and learning as to what the treatment should have been, does not establish negligence. ...

For the above reasons the judgment of the appellate court is affirmed.

INQUIRY

The Locale. In medical-malpractice cases, for counsel to retain and call an expert witness qualified in the same general or specialty field as the defendant medical care provider may not be sufficient to establish the standard of care. Substantial authority exists for the proposition that medical standards of care vary depending on the region and facility in which the defendant provides the care—that the country doctor performing only occasional surgery in a small, county hospital with relatively antiquated facilities and equipment does not have the same standard of care as the physician who practices in a large, metropolitan hospital having the best equipment available. The facilities, supplies, equipment, support personnel, information resources, and currency of the medical-care provider's training can all depend on the locale. The legal rules vary, but experts testifying to the standard of care may have to show that they are familiar with the local practice standard (a "strict-locality rule") or familiar with practice standards in similar locales. *See* Robinson v. LeCorps, 83 S.W.3d 718 (Tenn. 2002) (statutory strict-locality rule). Other states representing a trend hold that in an age when information is readily available in electronic form to even the most remote medical practitioners, and medical training has taken on so clearly a national character, that a unified, national standard of care exists—at least in specialties requiring national-board certification. *See* Morrison v. McNamara, 407 A.2d 555 (D.C. App. Ct. 1979) (standard of care for board certified medical-care providers is a national standard). Consider the following case and statute imposing further requirements on the qualifications necessary for a health professional to testify to the standard of care in a medical-malpractice action.

Vergara v. Doan
Indiana Supreme Court
593 N.E.2d 185 (Ind. 1992)

SHEPARD, C.J. Javier Vergara was born on May 31, 1979, at the Adams Memorial Hospital in Decatur, Indiana. His parents, Jose and Concepcion, claimed that negligence on the part of Dr. John Doan during Javier's delivery caused him severe and permanent injuries. A jury returned a verdict for Dr. Doan and the plaintiffs appealed. The Court of Appeals affirmed. [C] Plaintiffs seek transfer, asking us to abandon Indiana's modified locality rule. We grant transfer to examine the standard of care appropriate for medical malpractice cases.

In most negligence cases, the defendant's conduct is tested against the hypothetical reasonable and prudent person acting under the same or similar circumstances. [C] In medical malpractice cases, however, Indiana has applied a more specific articulation of this standard. It has become known as the modified locality rule: "The standard of care ... is that degree of care, skill, and proficiency which is commonly exercised by ordinarily careful, skillful, and prudent [physicians], at the time of the operation and *in similar localities.*" Burke v. Capello (1988), Ind., 520 N.E.2d 439, 441 (emphasis added). Appellants have urged us to abandon this standard, arguing that the reasons for the modified locality rule are no longer applicable in today's society. We agree.

The modified locality rule is a less stringent version of the strict locality rule, which measured the defendant's conduct against that of other doctors in the same community. When the strict locality rule originated in the late 19th century, there was great disparity between the medical opportunities, equipment, facilities, and training in rural and urban communities. Travel and communication between rural and urban communities were difficult. The locality rule was intended to prevent the inequity that would result from holding rural doctors to the same standards as doctors in large cities. [Cc]

With advances in communication, travel, and medical education, the disparity between rural and urban health care diminished and justification for the locality rule waned. The strict locality rule also had two major drawbacks, especially as applied to smaller communities. First, there was a scarcity of local doctors to serve as expert witnesses against other local doctors. Second, there was the possibility that practices among a small group of doctors would establish a local standard of care below that which the law required. [C] In response to these changes and criticisms, many courts adopted a modified locality rule, expanding the area of comparison to similar localities. This is the standard applied in Indiana. [C] ...

Use of a modified locality rule has not quelled the criticism. [Cc] Many of the common criticisms seem valid. The modified locality rule still permits a lower standard of care to be exercised in smaller communities because other similar communities are likely to have the same care. [C] We also spend time and money on the difficulty of defining what is a similar community. [C] The rule also seems inconsistent with the reality of modern medical practice. The disparity between small town and urban medicine continues to lessen with advances in communication, transportation, and education. In addition, widespread insurance coverage has provided patients with more choice of doctors and hospitals by reducing the financial constraints on the consumer in selecting caregivers. These reasons and others have led our Court of Appeals to observe that the modified locality rule has fallen into disfavor. [C] Many states describe the care a physician owes without emphasizing the locality of practice.[fn] Today we join these states and adopt the following: a physician must exercise that degree of care, skill, and proficiency exercised by reasonably careful, skillful, and prudent practitioners in the same class to which he belongs, acting under the same or similar circumstances. Rather than focusing on different standards for different communities, this standard uses locality as but one of the factors to be considered in determining whether the doctor acted reasonably. Other relevant considerations would include advances in the profession, availability of facilities, and whether the doctor is a specialist or general practitioner. [C]

... Plaintiff was permitted to present his expert witness, Dr. Harlan Giles, even though he was from Pittsburgh, Pennsylvania (not Decatur or a similar locality). Dr. Giles testified regarding his experience and knowledge of the standard of care in communities similar to Decatur and in hospitals similar in size to Adams County Memorial Hospital. He testified that in his opinion, considering all the factors incident to the pregnancy and birth of Javier Vergara, the standard of care required Dr. Doan to have delivered the baby by cesarean section. He stated that this opinion was based on the standard of care as it existed in 1979 in Decatur or similar communities. He also testified that the failure to have either an anesthesiologist or a qualified nurse anesthetist present at the delivery was a breach of the national standard of care for hospitals the size of Adams County Memorial and smaller. Evidently the jury disagreed with Dr. Giles and found Dr. Doan's conduct reasonable under the circumstances.

We regard our new formulation of a doctor's duty as a relatively modest alteration of existing law. It is unlikely to have changed the way this case was tried. We are satisfied that an instruction without the locality language would not lead a new jury to a different conclusion.

Therefore, we hold that giving instruction 23 was harmless and does not require reversal. In a different factual situation, however, an erroneous instruction with the locality language present might well constitute reversible error.[fn] The standard that we set out today, without the locality language, should be used from today forward.

MICH. COMP. L. §600.2169. Medical malpractice action; expert witnesses; criteria and qualifications; contingency fee

(1) In an action alleging medical malpractice, a person shall not give expert testimony on the appropriate standard of practice or care unless the person is licensed as a health professional in this state or another state and meets the following criteria:

(a) If the party against whom or on whose behalf the testimony is offered is a specialist, specializes at the time of the occurrence that is the basis for the action in the same specialty as the party against whom or on whose behalf the testimony is offered. However, if the party against whom or on whose behalf the testimony is offered is a specialist who is board certified, the expert witness must be a specialist who is board certified in that specialty.

(b) Subject to subdivision (c), during the year immediately preceding the date of the occurrence that is the basis for the claim or action, devoted a majority of his or her professional time to either or both of the following:

(*i*) The active clinical practice of the same health profession in which the party against whom or on whose behalf the testimony is offered is licensed and, if that party is a specialist, the active clinical practice of that specialty.

(*ii*) The instruction of students in an accredited health professional school or accredited residency or clinical research program in the same health profession in which the party against whom or on whose behalf the testimony is offered is licensed and, if that party is a specialist, an accredited health professional school or accredited residency or clinical research program in the same specialty.

(c) If the party against whom or on whose behalf the testimony is offered is a general practitioner, the expert witness, during the year immediately preceding the date of the occurrence that is the basis for the claim or action, devoted a majority of his or her professional time to either or both of the following:

(*i*) Active clinical practice as a general practitioner.

(*ii*) Instruction of students in an accredited health professional school or accredited residency or clinical research program in the same health profession in which the party against whom or on whose behalf the testimony is offered is licensed. …

INQUIRY

Similar Community. The majority of jurisdictions follow a similar-community rule for medical standards of care. What makes a community similar? What information does a lawyer need to determine the similarity of communities? How can a lawyer identify experts who are familiar with standards of care in similar communities? How can a lawyer help familiarize an expert with the similar-community standard? Lawyers face these questions when selecting and preparing experts to testify to medical standards of care in most states. Number of beds is one standard measure for hospital size. The population of the city or region in which the defendant practiced is another common measure for determining the similarity of communities. Experts who trained or have practiced in hospitals having an equivalent number of beds, in cities of the same size, may qualify. Medical-staff size may be another equivalency consideration.

National standards. National standards of care are common for medical specialties. *See* Sheeley v. Memorial Hosp., 710 A.2d 161 (R.I. 1998); Wall v. Stout, 310 N.C. 184, 311 S.E.2d 571 (1984); Shilkret v. Annapolis Emerg. Hosp. Assn., 276 Md. 187, 349 A.2d 245 (1975). Who is a specialist? *See* Jordan v. Bogner, 844 P.2d 664 (Colo. 1993) ("family practice" held a specialist owing national standard of care). National-board certifications for specialists in internal medicine, emergency medicine, neurology, orthopedics, orthopedic surgery, pediatrics, anesthesiology, ophthalmology, and other medical fields, suggest national standards for these specialties. Will a neurosurgeon who supervises a surgery by a non-specialist surgeon face the higher neurosurgery standard? *See* Baker v. Story, 621 S.W.2d 639 (Tex. Civ. App. 1981) (yes). Would a blended standard—national in some respects but local in others—make more sense? *See* Hall v. Hilbun, 466 So.2d 856 (Miss. 1985) (national standard for skill and care but local standard for resources). What region or locale should determine the lawyer's standard of care? *See* Russo v. Griffin, 147 Vt. 20, 510 A.2d 436 (1986) (attorney's standard of care is statewide standard); Wright v. Williams, 121 Cal. Rptr. 194, 47 Cal. App.3d 810 (1975) (attorneys held to standard "in the same or similar locality").

Practice

Statutes complicate medical-malpractice litigation today in nearly every state, the statutes enacted in response to a perceived crisis in that litigation. The statutes have no uniformity. Some, like the statute reproduced above, impose expert-witness requirements. Some alter the standard of care, while others alter informed consent. Others require pre-suit notice of claim and exchange of medical records, and redefine when claims accrue and the period within which the claimant must file them. Others require that the parties file affidavits of merit with the complaint. Others require case evaluation before a panel that includes medical-care providers. Some cap damages—some overall, others addressing only non-economic damages, and still others providing for broad or narrow exceptions. Policymakers debate the crisis's reality, depth, and cause. Increases in the number of medical-malpractice suits occurred, but they tended to be in certain regions and specialties. Rises in malpractice-insurance premiums also occurred, but the greatest increases tended to be in high-risk specialties, and some attribute much of the overall rise not to increased litigation but to decreased investment earnings of insurance companies. One specialty—anesthesiology—attacked the problem instead of the messenger, leading to significant medical (rather than legal) reforms and, with them, substantially decreased mortality and morbidity rates and lower insurance premiums. Medical malpractice remains. The Harvard Medical Practice Study of about 10,000 patients reported that 4% of hospitalizations result in iatrogenic (physician-caused) injury, 28% of those injuries are due to negligence, 14% of iatrogenic injuries result in death, and 51% of the deaths are due to negligence. Estimates are that 44,000 Americans die from medical error every year—more than in motor-vehicle accidents or from breast cancer or AIDS.

C. Causation

Patients and clients often have such a high degree of confidence in professionals that when harm occurs under a professional's care, the assumption is that their failure to comply with the standard of care was the cause of the harm. Those who suffer injury or loss at the hands of a professional often overlook the cause-in-fact element. Malpractice cases involve proof not only of the duty, its breach, and damages, but also the connection between the breach and damages. Proving or disproving causation can involve peculiar challenges in malpractice cases. In medical-malpractice cases, the question of what difference the defendant medical-care provider's breach of the standard of care made to the plaintiff's health can be a highly technical (biological and medical) question. Medical-malpractice cases are often fought on causation, rather than the standard-of-care issue. Even in legal-malpractice cases, causation can be a substantial question, especially when the claim has to do with the lawyer's alleged failure to pursue or defend a case. In that instance, the malpractice plaintiff must prove the *case-within-a-case* in order to establish that the lawyer's substandard performance made a difference in the outcome. A lawyer does not commit malpractice by providing substandard service in a case that the client would have lost anyway. That claim does not satisfy the causation element. *See* Togstad v. Vesely, Otto, Miller & Keefe, 291 N.W.2d 686 (Minn. 1980). As an introduction to the malpractice-case causation problem, consider the following case in which the defendant lawyer failed to pursue the promised appeal. In that case, what must the plaintiff prove, and how would the plaintiff prove it?

Charles Reinhart Co. v. Winiemko
Michigan Supreme Court
444 Mich. 579, 513 N.W.2d 773 (1994)

RILEY, J. At issue in the instant case is whether proximate cause in a legal malpractice action alleging negligence during an appeal is an issue of law reserved for the court or an issue of fact reserved for the jury. More specifically, we are presented with the question whether a court or a jury should determine whether the underlying appeal would have been successful. We hold that the issue is reserved to the court because whether an appeal would have been successful intrinsically involves issues of law within the exclusive province of the judiciary. ...

I

Dr. and Mrs. William Kauffman brought suit against plaintiff The Charles Reinhart Company,[fn] a real estate firm... . The Kauffmans alleged that plaintiff had improperly altered an instrument conveying real estate that they had purchased by reserving a previously undisclosed utility easement. In July 1983, the jury found that plaintiff defrauded the Kauffmans and awarded $70,000 in damages. The jury also found that plaintiff negligently conveyed the property and awarded an additional $30,000 in damages.[fn]

Plaintiff's corporate counsel, deciding to proceed with another attorney on appeal, retained Ronald C. Winiemko as counsel. In September 1983, they discussed the case and determined that the appeal would focus on the claim that the jury awards for both fraud and negligence were cumulative. Although Winiemko timely filed an appeal, he failed to timely file his brief and formally answer his adversary's motion for dismissal.[fn] Accordingly, the Court of Appeals dismissed the appeal. ...

Thus, in September 1987, plaintiff filed the instant action against Winiemko ... averring that Winiemko had committed professional malpractice by, inter alia, irretrievably losing plaintiff's right to appeal. Plaintiff alleged that but for Winiemko's negligence, plaintiff would have succeeded in its appeal of the underlying litigation.
...

... Winiemko argued that the underlying appeal, as a matter of law, could not have succeeded.[fn] ... Finding the question a jury issue, the trial court denied Winiemko's motions and permitted plaintiff's legal experts to testify that the appeal would have succeeded. The jury found Winiemko guilty of professional malpractice and breach of contract, and awarded damages.

The Court of Appeals affirmed.[fn] It ruled that proximate cause in a legal malpractice suit is a question of fact,[fn] and found that even in an appellate malpractice action "issues that were questions of law in the underlying case ... become questions of fact" in the malpractice action.[fn] Thus, the Court held that "[i]n a case charging appellate malpractice, the question for the trier of fact is whether a reasonable appellate court would, more likely than not, have granted the appellant in the underlying case some relief."[fn] ...

II

... [A] plaintiff "must show that but for the attorney's alleged malpractice, he would have been successful in the underlying suit." Id. (emphasis added).[fn] In other words, ""'the client seeking recovery from his attorney is faced with the difficult task of proving two cases within a single proceeding.'"" Id. at 64 [internal citation omitted] ...

As at least one court has noted, "[t]he apparent irony, however, is that the attorney now attempts to show that his previous client's appeal would have failed even though he may have accepted the duty of pursuing it. ..." Jablonski v. Higgins, 6 Ohio Misc.2d 8, 11, 6 OBR 548, 453 N.E.2d 1296 (1983). ...

In a legal malpractice action alleging negligence in an appeal a plaintiff must prove two aspects of causation in fact: whether the attorney's negligence caused the loss or unfavorable result of the appeal, and whether the loss or unfavorable result of the appeal in turn caused a loss or unfavorable result in the underlying litigation. [C] Whether the court as a matter of law or the jury as an issue of fact determines these aspects of proximate cause is the issue in the instant case.[fn]

... "Since the basic premise of trying the underlying action is to prove what the result should have been, the guiding principle in identifying issues of law and fact is to utilize the same classifications as should have been applied in the underlying case." 2 Mallen & Smith, supra, § 27.10, p. 652.[fn] Thus, whether an appeal lost because of an attorney's negligence would have succeeded if properly pursued is an issue for the court because the resolution of the underlying appeal originally would have rested on a decision of law. [Cc] ...

The Michigan Constitution exclusively vests the "judicial power" of the state in one court of justice composed of the Supreme Court, the Court of Appeals, and the courts of original jurisdiction. [C]

Thus, in the instant case, because the issue whether the underlying appeal would have succeeded is resolved by legal principle, the issue is one for the court, not the jury. Simply because issues of law are presented in a unique procedural posture does not eviscerate this basic governing principle of Michigan jurisprudence.[fn] ...

... Issues of law are resolved by a reasoned application of neutral principles to a particular factual situation.[fn] That the resolution of a particular case may not appear obvious at the outset of litigation or an appeal does not belie the notion that a neutral and principled application of legal authority will result in one principled result.[fn] While ambiguities within the law exist, they are resolved not by the predilections of individual judges, but by a reasoned application of legal principles. That dissents and conflicting opinions exist within the same legal system reveal only that some members of the judiciary disagree over the application or interpretation of guiding principles, not that a correct result is not achievable, or has not been achieved.[fn]

... As Thomas Paine declared, "in America The Law is King. For as in absolute governments the King is law, so in free countries the law ought to be King; and there ought to be no other."[fn] We are a nation, and a Court, ruled by law. Any suggestion that this Court or others might deviate from a pure application of the law and its guiding principles is unwarranted and contrary to the fundamental principles of adjudication. Furthermore, this hypothesis must be rejected wholeheartedly for it strikes at the very core of the law's legitimacy. The rulings of this Court are legitimate only as long as they rely primarily on the application of neutral principles originating from the constitution, statutes, regulations, or the common law. ... Although the rule of law may be said to be an ideal, we do violence to this fundamental principle by encouraging its disregard.

Justice Scalia explained the importance of rule of law: "Rudimentary justice requires that those subject to the law must have the means of knowing what it prescribes.... As laws have become more numerous, and as people have become increasingly ready to punish their adversaries in the courts, we can less and less afford protracted uncertainty regarding what the law may mean." Scalia, *The Rule of Law as a Law of Rules*, 56 U Chi L R 1175, 1179 (1989). ...

Nor is this holding elitist. Juries traditionally do not decide the law or the outcome of legal conflicts. Juries are not appellate courts. To maintain the traditional role of the jury, the jury must remain the factfinder; a jury may determine what happened, how, and when, but it may not resolve the law itself. The determination of questions of law by the courts is not a new elitist prerogative—to the contrary, it is a vindication of the existence of the judiciary. Indeed, it is the very purpose of the judiciary.[fn] ...

Thus, we hold that the issue of proximate cause in the instant case is reserved to the court because whether an appeal would have been successful intrinsically involves issues of law within the exclusive province of the courts, and remand the legal issue presented in the underlying litigation for resolution by the trial court. ...

[A]t no time has the right to a jury trial in any fashion been understood to displace the authority and duty of the judiciary to determine legal issues. For as long as the right to a jury has been recognized, the exclusive province of the court to rule on matters of law has been acknowledged. [C] As Justice Cooley summarized, over a century and a half of jurisprudence has recognized that a judge's duty is to inform the jury "what ... the law is," while the jury "should be left free and unbiased by [the judge's] opinion to determine for themselves whether the facts in evidence," under the instructions of the judge, show a guilty verdict. Cooley, supra at 678. ...

In summary, we hold that the question whether a court or a jury should determine whether the underlying appeal would have been successful is reserved to the court because whether an appeal would have been successful intrinsically involves issues of law within the exclusive province of the judiciary. ...

INQUIRY

Suit Within a Suit. The suit-within-a-suit requirement imposed in the case above makes this type of legal-malpractice case significantly more uncertain in its outcome than the usual negligence case. The requirement is, however, both the logical and traditional causation rule for such cases. Indeed, as to an underlying civil-damages case, the plaintiff has more to show on causation than simply that the plaintiff would have won but-for the attorney's negligence. The legal-malpractice plaintiff must also show the amount of damages *and* that the plaintiff could have collected those damages. *See* Kituskie v. Corbman, 552 Pa. 275, 714 A.2d 1027 (1998). Is there any other causation theory you can discern in those cases where prevailing in the underlying case was unlikely? The *Winiemko* plaintiff also argued that the attorney's failure to perfect and pursue the appeal lost the plaintiff the opportunity to settle the underlying case on advantageous terms. *See also* Vahila v. Hall, 77 Ohio St.3d 421, 674 N.E.2d 1164 (1997) (damages of a less favorable result). To prove causation on the could-have-settled theory, must the plaintiff have testimony of the other party in the underlying case that they would have settled the case for less than the judgment? *See* Viner v. Sweet, 30 Cal.4th 1232, 70 P.3d 1046, 135 Cal. Rptr.2d 629 (2003) (legal-malpractice plaintiff may establish more-favorable terms by circumstantial evidence, not merely by adversary's admission). Legal malpractice in defense of criminal charges involves its own challenges. *See* Coscia v. McKenna & Cuneo, 25 Cal.4th 1194, 25 P.3d 670, 108 Cal. Rptr.2d 471 (2001) (legal-malpractice plaintiff alleging that defendant attorney's negligence resulted in wrongful conviction must first obtain post-conviction reversal).

Probabilities. Another causation problem that can arise in malpractice cases (especially medical malpractice) has to do with causation probabilities that are less than the plaintiff's traditional more-probable-than-not burden of proof. Is causation satisfied when the defendant's negligence made it 10%, 20%, or 40% more likely that the plaintiff would suffer or the decedent die? The problem is that those causation proofs might mean that there was a 90%, 80%, or 60% probability that something *other* than the defendant's negligence was the cause of the plaintiff's suffering or decedent's death. The plaintiff may not have proven—in fact, may have disproven—that the defendant's causation was more probable than not (greater than 50%). And yet, the defendant's action *could* (to a substantial probability) have been a cause and one that law should therefore deter. Sound bases exist for both liability and no-liability so that, not surprisingly, states divide on whether less-than-half evidence makes a causation issue for the jury. Some states allow less-than-half evidence if defendant's negligence was a substantial factor. *See* Gardner v. Pawliw, 696 A.2d 599 (N.J. 1997) (allowing causation proofs at less than 50%, so long as "sufficiently significant" in relation to the harm); McKellips v. St. Francis Hosp., 741 P.2d 467 (Okla. 1987) (allowing causation proofs at less than 50%, so long as a "substantial factor"); Herskovits v. Group Health Coop., 99 Wash.2d 609, 664 P.2d 474 (1983); Kallenberg

v. Beth Israel Hosp., 357 N.Y.S.2d 508 (N.Y. App. Div. 1974) (expert testimony that patient had a 20 to 40% chance of survival if properly treated sufficient to allow jury to find causation under preponderance burden). Others require that the evidence reflect a probability of greater than half. *See* Murray v. United States, 215 F.3d 460 (4th Cir. 2000) (Virginia law); Smith v. Parrott, 833 A.2d 843 (Vt. 2003). Other states find a middle ground under a value-of-the-chance approach, allowing less-than-half causation but permitting the plaintiff to recover only that proportion of the loss. *See* McMackin v. Johnson Cty. Healthcare Ctr., 88 P.3d 491 (Wyo. 2004); Scafdi v. Seiler, 119 N.J. 93, 574 A.2d 398 (N.J. 1990) (value of the lost chance of survival); *see also* Smith v. State, 676 So.2d 543 (La. 1996) (jury may value the lost chance); Delaney v. Cade, 255 Kan. 199, 873 P.2d 175 (Kan. 1994) (lost chance cases limited to those in which the lost chance is substantial). The following trial court opinion illustrates the issue and summarizes how the states have divided on its treatment.

Beswick v. City of Philadelphia
United States District Court
185 F. Supp.2d 418 (E.D. Pa. 2001)

GILES, C.J. ...

Ralph Raymond Beswick, Jr. and Rose Wiegand, Co-Administrators of the Estate of Ralph Richard Beswick, Sr., bring ... state law negligence claims against Julie Rodriguez, and Father and Son Transport Leasing Inc., d/b/a CareStat Ambulance and Invalid Coach Transportation, Inc. ("CareStat"), a private ambulance service, its record owner, Slawomir Cieloszcyk, a purported owner and manager, Gregory Sverdlev, and two CareStat employees, Ruslan Ilehuk and Ivan Tkach (collectively "CareStat defendants"). ...

For the reasons that follow, ... the CareStat defendants' motions [for summary judgment] are denied, and the motions of Sverdlev, Tkach, and Ilehuk are denied. ...

Plaintiffs' claims all arise from the death of Ralph Richard Beswick, Sr. on February 11, 2000. ...

On the evening of February 11, 2000, Ralph Richard Beswick, Sr. collapsed on the dining room floor of the South Kensington home that he and Wiegand had shared for 23 years. [C] From the living room where she had been watching television, Wiegand heard the "thump" of Beswick falling and went to him.[fn] Upon entering the kitchen and finding Beswick lying prone on the floor, Wiegand immediately dialed the City's medical emergency response number, 911, and told the answering call-taker, Julie Rodriguez, that Beswick had fallen and needed urgent assistance, and requested an ambulance. Rodriguez asked if Beswick was breathing. Wiegand responded that he was. Without obtaining any further information, Rodriguez told Wiegand that "somebody" was "on the way."

Fire Department regulations require 911 operators to refer all emergency medical calls to the Fire Department, which then dispatches Fire Rescue Units appropriately equipped and staffed to respond to medical emergencies. ...

Instead of following established procedure, which would have continued the process to trigger the Rescue Unit's response, Rodriguez abandoned protocol and used a telephone located next to her console to call a private ambulance company, CareStat, to see if it could respond to the Wiegand call. Rodriguez, without the knowledge of the

City, had recently begun working for CareStat as a dispatcher in her off hours, and had a secret deal with CareStat to refer to it all calls received in her City 911 capacity that she believed CareStat could handle. ...

Immediately after speaking with Wiegand, Rodriguez telephoned Slawomir Cieloszcyk (also known as "Slavik"), the owner and dispatcher of CareStat. Upon telling Cieloszcyk that Ralph Beswick, Sr. was age 65 and unconscious from a fall, Rodriguez asked how long it would take CareStat to get to the Beswick home. [C] ... Cieloszcyk estimated a response time of fifteen minutes. He ended the conversation by saying, "We're on the way."

... All 911 calls are assumed to be medical emergencies unless and until actual response and evaluation by the City Fire Department might determine otherwise. CareStat had no permission from the City to use 911 call-taker Rodriguez to refer calls to it and knew that the 911 call was being diverted from the City's established response system. ...

Ten minutes after the first 911 call had been made, because there was yet no emergency vehicle at the Beswick home, Wiegand's sister placed another 911 call at 8:02 p.m. to make sure that the City's rescue services had already been dispatched. This call also happened to have been received and handled by Rodriguez. Despite this second urgent call, Rodriguez did not punch it over to the City's emergency dispatch system. She called CareStat again, seeking assurance that its ambulance dispatched would arrive soon. Cieloszcyk assured Rodriguez that the CareStat ambulance was on the way as he had promised her.

Because an emergency equipped unit still had not arrived, Wiegand called 911 a third time. The third call came to a call-taker other than Rodriguez. He followed all Fire Department procedures and within a very short time period a City Fire Department Rescue Unit arrived at the Beswick home. ... By the time that the CareStat ambulance arrived, the Fire Rescue Unit had already removed Beswick from the home. ...

The first emergency telephone call concerning Beswick was received by Rodriguez at the Fire Command Center ("FCC") at 19:53:41. The second call, placed by Wiegand's sister, was received by Rodriguez at 20:02:54. The third Wiegand call was received at the FCC by dispatcher Jose Zayes at 20:04:57, and the City Fire Department response was immediately dispatched.

... Based upon this information, the total delay in getting a Medic Unit to respond to Beswick has been estimated by Battalion Chief Schweizer to be 16 minutes and 16 seconds. [C][fn: It is undisputed that Beswick died of a heart attack upon his arrival at the hospital. He was cremated two days later without an autopsy, so the exact magnitude of his heart attack can never be known.]

Plaintiffs have introduced evidence that this 16 minute, 16 second delay caused or contributed to the cause of Beswick's death, through the deposition testimony of Kale Etchberger and Joanne Przeworski, the two Fire Department paramedics who arrived on the scene as part of Medic Unit 31. ... Plaintiffs' expert, Dr. Norman Makous, a cardiologist, would opine to a reasonable degree of medical certainty that based on established medical literature regarding observed cardiac arrests due to ventricular fibrillation, and assuming that Beswick was still breathing at the time of the first 911 call, that had Medic Unit No. 2 arrived after the first call, Beswick's chance of survival would have equaled, if not exceeded, thirty-four (34) percent. ...

CareStat defendants argue that on its face, a statistical survival rate of 34 percent, which plaintiffs' medical expert concludes is the chance for survival Beswick would have had if a City ambulance had been appropriately dispatched, is insufficient as a matter of law to establish proximate cause. ...

Pennsylvania tort law follows the Restatement Second of Torts, § 323, which provides: "§323. Negligent Performance of Undertaking to Render Services One who undertakes, gratuitously or for consideration, to render services to another which he should recognize as necessary for the protection of the other's person or things, is subject to liability to the other for physical harm resulting from his failure to exercise reasonable care to perform his undertaking, if (a) his failure to exercise such care increases the risk of such harm, or (b) the harm is suffered because of the other's reliance upon the undertaking." (emphasis added). ... See Hamil v. Bashline, 481 Pa. 256, 392 A.2d 1280, 1286 (1978). In Hamil, ... the court adopted the following standard: "Once a plaintiff has introduced evidence that a defendant's negligent act or omission increased the risk of harm to a person in plaintiff's position, and that the harm was in fact sustained, it becomes a question for the jury as to whether or not that increased risk was a substantial factor in producing the harm. Such a conclusion follows from an analysis of the function of Section 323(a)." [Cc] ...

... Accordingly, this court will permit Dr. Makous' testimony regarding the increased risk of harm to Beswick of 34 percent, and will allow the jury to determine, by a preponderance of the evidence, whether this increased risk brought about Beswick's death. ...

The doctrine of loss of chance has two versions. Under one, the plaintiff can recover only for the value of the lost chance. [Cc] Under this theory, the burden of proof for causation is not changed; rather, the injury is defined as the loss of a chance in itself, as opposed to the resultant harm to the plaintiff. With the injury thus defined, a plaintiff is able to prove causation for that injury under the traditional preponderance test. Recovery is generally the percentage of the damages defendant was found to have caused.

Under the other version of the lost chance doctrine, the nature of plaintiff's injury remains unchanged; rather, the court permits a lower burden of proof, allowing plaintiff to prove that the defendant caused the injury, even though plaintiff cannot prove more likely than not, but for the defendant's negligence, the injury would not have occurred. [Cc]

Pennsylvania law has not adopted either of these approaches. ...

For the foregoing reasons, the City's Motion for Summary Judgment is granted, the CareStat defendants' Motions are denied, and Sverdlev, Tkach, and Ilehuk's Motion is denied.

INQUIRY

Less-than-Half Probabilities. In the age of continuing statutory reform of tort laws, some legislatures require that the plaintiff establish causation by evidence that the defendant's negligence caused a greater than one-half lost opportunity to survive. *See* Mich. Comp. L. §600.2912a; *see also* Weymers v. Khera, 454 Mich. 639, 563 N.W.2d 647 (1997) (acknowledging that MCL §600.2912a was a response to prior case law permitting less-than-half loss-of-a-chance causation). Courts have also been unwilling to extend the less-than-half rule outside of the medical context. *See* Lowmack v. Century Prods. Co., 139 F.3d 890 (4th Cir. 1998) (special less-than-half rules would not extend to products-liability claim under Virginia law); Hardy v. Southwestern Bell Tel. Co., 910 P.2d 1024 (Okla. 1996) (special rule does not apply to design-flaw claim involving 911 system). If the plaintiff may not offer causation evidence when it has to do with less-than-half probabilities, then should law also prohibit the defendant from offering less-than-half probabilities that the injury had some *other* cause? *See* Wilder v. Eberhart, 977 F.2d 673 (1st Cir. 1992) (yes). What would justify the rules being different for the plaintiff and the defendant? If the plaintiff's burden is to prove causation by evidence that it was more probable than not, then perhaps the defendant should be permitted to "chip away" at the plaintiff's evidence by proving an accumulation of small probabilities that it was not a cause.

D. Informed Consent

OBJECTIVE: Given evidence regarding communication between the plaintiff patient and defendant physician in a malpractice claim involving a result the plaintiff claims to be a compensable injury, recall and apply the principles described in this section of the text to determine whether the plaintiff has a claim for failure to obtain informed consent.

Case Study: An orthopedist recorded in medical records that she consulted with a patient about the risks and benefits of soft splinting of the patient's fractured wrist. The patient will testify that the orthopedist said only that soft splinting was the recommended treatment and that there were no other viable alternatives. *Apply the principles of informed consent to determine whether, or under what circumstances, the patient would have a malpractice claim for failure to obtain informed consent.*

Consider now some issues having less to do with the procedures and proof of malpractice cases and having more to do with their substance. The usual malpractice claim is one in which the professional fails to conform the professional's conduct to the standard of care, causing the patient (or client) a loss or injury. A second common form of malpractice claim is one for lack of informed consent. In those cases, the service that the professional provides may conform to the standard of care in every operational respect (or it may not), but the professional fails to advise the patient of information material to the patient's decision to proceed with the professional's service. Lack-of-informed-consent claims often accompany claims based on a breach of the standard of care in the professional service itself. Lack-of-informed-consent claims involve a breach of the standard of care to supply appropriate information. The standard of care defines not only the professional's technical performance but also the material information that the professional must disclose. A malpractice claim for lack of informed consent approaches an intentional tort claim for battery. Indeed, the shift from intentional-tort claims for battery to malpractice claims for lack of informed consent was a trend that did not culminate until the year 2000 when Georgia became the last state to adopt lack-of-informed-consent claims as a part of medical-malpractice law. *See* Ketchup v. Howard, 543 S.E.2d 371 (Ga. Ct. App. 2000).

> **Practice**
> One challenge that plaintiff's lawyers face in preparing medical-malpractice cases is the understandable reluctance of medical-care providers to testify against local colleagues. Medical-care providers, like other professionals, can depend on referrals from other providers. They may also maintain professional relationships through local professional organizations and activities. Testifying against a colleague could burden those relationships and lose referrals, creating a litigation-expert phenomenon known (in its conspiratorial characterization) as "the code of silence." *See* Mulder v. Parke Deavis & Co., 288 Minn. 332, 181 N.W.2d 882 (1970). Thus, plaintiff's lawyers ordinarily must locate experts from outside the region—not necessarily an easy task, and one that can add substantial travel expense to the litigation. Defendants and their counsel do not face the same challenge because professionals are more willing to come to the aid of an accused colleague. See McGulpin v. Bessmer, 241 Ia. 1119, 43 N.W.2d 121 (1950) (criticizing strict-locality rule). How would you respond if, in closing argument, defense counsel pointed out to the jury that the plaintiff "had to go all the way across the country to find a doctor willing to testify against my client"?

Lack-of-informed-consent claims in medical-malpractice cases usually involve the professional's failure to advise of a risk of the treatment. When the patient realizes the risk—even without any breach of the standard of care—the patient may justly complain that the patient would have refused the treatment or procedure if the defendant care provider had disclosed the risk. This question of whether the patient would have had the treatment anyway if the physician had disclosed the risk, is a causation issue. *See* Scott v. Bradford, 606 P.2d 554 (1979) (adopting a subjective test for causation in lack-of-informed-consent cases, based on what the patient would have done). A majority of states adopt an objective, rather than subjective, test for causation in these cases, asking what the reasonable patient would have done. Others ask what the plaintiff patient would have done. All such claims still require expert testimony on what the standard of care required the physician to advise. *See* Carr v. Strode, 79 Haw. 475, 904 P.2d 489 (1995) (expert testimony required as to inherent risks, probability of success, frequency with which risks are realized, and alternative treatment); Roberts v. Young, 369 Mich. 133, 119 N.W.2d 627 (1963) (physician's duty to warn of risks depends on "the general practice customarily followed by the medical profession"). In addressing that standard-of-care question as to what the physician should have advised (rather than the causation question as to what the patient would have done if advised), a minority of courts impose a standard of what the reasonable patient would have needed to know to make an informed decision. *See* Cobbs v. Grant, 8 Cal.3d 229, 104 Cal. Rptr. 505, 502 P.2d 1 (1972).

Keep in mind that a physician's failure to obtain any consent at all (not merely informed consent) may result in a battery claim—where expert testimony on a standard of care would not be required at all. *See* Walls v. Shreck, 265 Neb. 683, 658 N.W.2d 686 (2003) (battery claim established without expert testimony, where surgeon operated on wrong eye); Blanchard v. Kellum, 975 S.W.2d 522 (Tenn. 1998); Morgan v. Rose, 550 Pa. 202, 704 A.2d 617 (1997). Now consider an unusual but compelling case involving lack of informed consent.

Moore v. Regents of the Univ. of California
California Supreme Court
51 Cal.3d 120, 793 P.2d 479, 271 Cal. Rptr. 146 (1990)

PANELLI, J. We granted review in this case to determine whether plaintiff has stated a cause of action against his physician and other defendants for using his cells in potentially lucrative medical research without his permission. Plaintiff alleges that his physician failed to disclose preexisting research and economic interests in the cells before obtaining consent to the medical procedures by which they were extracted. ... We hold that the complaint states a cause of action for breach of the physician's disclosure obligations, but not for conversion. ...

[Plaintiff John Moore was treated at UCLA Medical Center in 1976 for leukemia. During the course of Moore's treatment, his physician Dr. Golde and other defendants discovered from tissue that they removed from Moore that they had a special use for Moore's cells in their genetic research. Dr. Golde told Moore that Moore's disease would be slowed by the removal of Moore's spleen. They then patented a line from Moore's cells and licensed the line for commercial production in return for financial interests. They had Moore repeatedly return to the Medical Center for further "treatment" of Moore's condition, even though Moore had moved to the Seattle area and was unaware of defendants' independent research and financial interests in the tissue that they had been removing from him. When he learned of their interests, he sued for conversion, failure to obtain his informed consent, breach of fiduciary duty, and other claims. The trial court dismissed all counts. The Court of Appeals reversed on conversion and remanded, occasioning this appeal to the California Supreme Court. Only a small portion of the lengthy opinion is reproduced, on the malpractice-related allegations.]

A. Breach of Fiduciary Duty and Lack of Informed Consent

Moore repeatedly alleges that Golde failed to disclose the extent of his research and economic interests in Moore's cells[fn] before obtaining consent to the medical procedures by which the cells were extracted. These allegations, in our view, state a cause of action against Golde for invading a legally protected interest of his patient. This cause of action can properly be characterized either as the breach of a fiduciary duty to disclose facts material to the patient's consent or, alternatively, as the performance of medical procedures without first having obtained the patient's informed consent.

Our analysis begins with three well-established principles. First, "a person of adult years and in sound mind has the right, in the exercise of control over his own body, to determine whether or not to submit to lawful medical treatment." (*Cobbs v. Grant* (1972) 8 Cal.3d 229, 242 [104 Cal.Rptr. 505, 502 P.2d 1]; [c].) Second, "the patient's consent to treatment, to be effective, must be an informed consent." (*Cobbs v. Grant*, supra, 8 Cal.3d at p. 242, 104 Cal.Rptr. 505, 502 P.2d 1.) Third, in soliciting the patient's consent, a physician has a fiduciary duty to disclose all information material to the patient's decision. [Cc]

These principles lead to the following conclusions: (1) a physician must disclose personal interests unrelated to the patient's health, whether research or economic, that may affect the physician's professional judgment; and (2) a physician's failure to disclose such interests may give rise to a cause of action for performing medical procedures without informed consent or breach of fiduciary duty.

To be sure, questions about the validity of a patient's consent to a procedure typically arise when the patient alleges that the physician failed to disclose medical risks, as in malpractice cases, and not when the patient alleges that the physician had a personal interest, as in this case. The concept of informed consent, however, is broad enough to encompass the latter. "The scope of the physician's communication to the patient ... must be measured by the patient's need, and that need is whatever information is material to the decision." (*Cobbs v. Grant*, supra, 8 Cal.3d at p. 245, 104 Cal.Rptr. 505, 502 P.2d 1.)

Indeed, the law already recognizes that a reasonable patient would want to know whether a physician has an economic interest that might affect the physician's professional judgment. ... As the Court of Appeal has said, "[c]ertainly a sick patient deserves to be free of any reasonable suspicion that his doctor's judgment is influenced by a profit motive." (*Magan Medical Clinic v. Cal. State Bd. Of Medical Examiners* (1967) 249 Cal.App.2d 124, 132, 57 Cal.Rptr. 256.) ...

It is important to note that no law prohibits a physician from conducting research in the same area in which he practices. Progress in medicine often depends upon physicians, such as those practicing at the university hospital where Moore received treatment, who conduct research while caring for their patients.

Yet a physician who treats a patient in whom he also has a research interest has potentially conflicting loyalties. This is because medical treatment decisions are made on the basis of proportionality—weighing the benefits *to the patient* against the risks *to the patient*. ... A physician who adds his own research interests to this balance may be tempted to order a scientifically useful procedure or test that offers marginal, or no, benefits to the patient. The possibility that an interest extraneous to the patient's health has affected the physician's judgment is something that a reasonable patient would want to know in deciding whether to consent to a proposed course of treatment. It is material to the patient's decision and, thus, a prerequisite to informed consent. [C] ...

We acknowledge that there is a competing consideration. To require disclosure of research and economic interests may corrupt the patient's own judgment by distracting him from the requirements of his health. But California law does not grant physicians unlimited discretion to decide what to disclose. Instead, "it is the prerogative of the patient, not the physician, to determine for himself the direction in which he believes his interests lie." (*Cobbs v. Grant,* supra, 8 Cal.3d at p. 242, 104 Cal.Rptr. 505, 502 P.2d 1.) "Unlimited discretion in the physician is irreconcilable with the basic right of the patient to make the ultimate informed decision...." (Id., at p. 243, 104 Cal.Rptr. 505, 502 P.2d 1.) ...

Accordingly, we hold that a physician who is seeking a patient's consent for a medical procedure must, in order to satisfy his fiduciary duty[fn] and to obtain the patient's informed consent, disclose personal interests unrelated to the patient's health, whether research or economic, that may affect his medical judgment. ...

The decision of the Court of Appeal is affirmed in part and reversed in part. ...

INQUIRY

Tangential Risks. If a sensible rule is that medical-care providers should disclose conflicts of interest if they are of the type likely to affect medical judgment, then what about disclosing circumstances (other than conflicts) that may also implicate medical judgment—like the provider's alcoholism? *See* Hidding v. Williams, 578 So.2d 1192 (La. App. 1991) (must disclose); *but see* Albany Urology Clinic v. Cleveland, 272 Ga. 296, 528 S.W.2d 777 (2000) (no duty to disclose cocaine use). Or like comparative morbidity rates? *See* Howard v. University of Medicine & Dentistry, 172 N.J. 537, 800 A.2d 73 (2002) (to require disclosure, there must be substantial difference in physician's actual and represented rates likely to affect reasonable patient); *but see* Johnson v. Kokemoor, 199 Wis.2d 615, 545 N.W.2d 495 (1996) (inexperienced surgeon must disclose comparative success rates of experienced surgeons). Do you think that the *Johnson v. Kokemoor* case may represent a new trend toward requiring hospitals and other care providers to disclose success and failure rates? *Cf.* Duttry v. Patterson, 771 A.2d 101 (Pa. 2001) (physician's misrepresentation of frequency in which and number of times he had performed plaintiff's surgical procedure cannot form basis for lack-of-informed-consent claim). Can you see how tort law might influence disclosures by managed-care organizations?

Size of Risk. Recognizing that most lack-of-informed-consent cases involve the failure to advise of material risks associated with the proposed treatment, one still has to ask how big of a risk is a material risk. Can it include, for instance, one that presents nothing more than a one-percent risk of an adverse event? *See* Canterbury v. Spence, 464 F.2d 772 (D.C. Cir. 1972) (materiality of small risk depends on severity of complication); Martin v. Richards, 192 Wis.2d 156, 531 N.W.2d 70 (1995) (risk of death is not too remote for disclosure at one to three percent). Can the claustrophobia (a psychological effect) from an MRI be a material risk of a diagnostic test? *See* Curtis v. MRI Imaging Services II, 327 Or. 9, 956 P.2d 960 (1998) (yes). Can not telling a patient of the availability of a CAT scan as an alternative test be failure of informed consent? *See* Martin v. Richards, 192 Wis.2d 156, 531 N.W.2d 70 (1995) (yes—physician liable). Can not telling a patient of the risks of refusing a pap-smear test be failure of informed consent? *See* Truman v. Thomas, 27 Cal.3d 285, 611 P.2d 902, 165 Cal. Rptr. 308 (1980) (yes—physician liable). To obtain informed consent, must a physician inform a patient that one of the treatment options is no treatment, if no-treatment is within the standard of care? *See* Wecker v. Amend, 22 Kan. App.2d 498, 918 P.2d 658 (1996) (yes).

Causation. Lack-of-informed-consent cases can present special causation questions. One concern is that patients will, in hindsight, falsely claim (out of shock, injury, and need) that they would not have had the medical treatment if they had been advised of the realized risk. *See* Sard v. Hardy, 281 Md. 432, 379 A.2d 1014 (1977). In many medical procedures, the risks include substantial injury or death. Patients generally accept the risk of serious harm in small percentages. How, other than by the usual methods of oaths and cross-examination, might courts reduce the risk of a verdict based on self-serving, after-the-fact testimony? Although the logical way to address cause in fact would be to simply ask whether the plaintiff, subjectively, would have chosen not to have the treatment had the defendant informed plaintiff of the risk, some courts have instead applied an objective test and required evidence that the reasonable patient would not have had the treatment. *See* Aronson v. Harriman, 321 Ark. 359,

901 S.W.2d 832 (1995) (adopting objective test); *cf.* Schreiber v. Physicians Ins. Co., 223 Wis.2d 417, 588 N.W.2d 26 (1999) (adopting objective test unless plaintiff subjectively withdrew consent during treatment). The objective, reasonable-patient test presents its own proof problems including who is to testify as to what the reasonable patient would have done—physicians? *See* Hartke v. McKelway, 707 F.2d 1544 (D.C. Cir. 1983).

Career

Portfolios can make a difference in finding employment and succeeding in tort practice. Professionals benefit by reflecting on their competence and demonstrating it to others. Portfolios promote your ability to reflect on your developing skill. They also make it easier to assemble evidence of your skill and distribute it. You can make an electronic portfolio simply by using an operating system's folders, stored on hard drive, flash drive, or in the cloud, and accessible to you through the Internet. An electronic portfolio allows you to collect, organize, study, maintain, and distribute files, photographs, video, and other indications of your skill. The key is to start a portfolio now and to use it consistently, storing your schoolwork and evidence of your law-related co-curricular and extra-curricular activities. Consider organizing it into three main folders marked Knowledge, Skill, and Ethics, and then sorting your course-work and other files into those three dimensions of legal education. That act alone will encourage you to balance and improve your legal education, while preparing to demonstrate to others its quality.

Chapter VIII

Premises Liability

A. Generally

OBJECTIVE: Given a person's injury occurring on or about a premises, classify the injured person within the traditional premises-liability framework, and recall and apply the applicable standard of care, consistent with this chapter.

Case Study: A local pizzeria paid a boy to tuck pizza-delivery advertisements in the doors of units at an apartment complex, where a sign at the entrance to the complex said "no advertising or soliciting." The boy tripped and fell on a loose piece of carpet the apartments had installed and maintained on one of its stairways. The following week after the boy's injury, an apartment tenant was injured tripping and falling on the same piece of loose carpet. The following week, an apartment guest was injured tripping and falling on the same piece of loose carpet. ***Classify the boy, tenant, and guest for purposes of their premises-liability claims against the apartment, applying the standard of care for each to determine whether they would prevail, consistent with this chapter.***

Negligence claims take on a somewhat different form when they involve the duties of a landowner, or if not the landowner then the tenant or other one occupying and controlling the land, to prevent injuries from occurring to others because of conditions on the land. The factual context for the claims differs. The cases typically involve not so much the defendant's actions (the usual source for negligence claims) but rather conditions of the land or its vegetation and structures. The law framework, while still an action for *negligence*, differs, so much that lawyers frequently style the claims as for *premises liability* rather than ordinary negligence, although again, premises liability is still a negligence claim. Indeed, while conventions differ, a plaintiff's lawyer representing a client injured on another's premises may title the complaint's first count "Negligence," alleging acts and omissions of the defendant, and the second count "Premises Liability," alleging unreasonably dangerous conditions of the premises—even though a premises-liability action is still, at its root, a negligence action. Attitudes of judges, jurors, and others toward premises-liability claims can differ from that toward negligence claims because of the freedom we grant one another to act as we please within our own domains. Must we really keep our own property in the condition others demand?

Courts in the great majority of states follow a traditional, English common-law, premises-liability framework. That framework begins by classifying the plaintiff as an *invitee*, *licensee*, or *trespasser*, and then assigns to the defendant a higher or lower level of duty depending on the plaintiff's classification. The next section of this chapter defines, illustrates, and explores those classifications. A significant minority of courts rejects the traditional framework and instead applies the usual elements of a negligence claim to all claimants, even where the traditional framework would treat claimants quite differently. *See* Hopkins v. Fox & Lazo Realtors, 132 N.J. 426, 625 A.2d 1110 (1993). England also changed its traditional framework in 1957 to adopt, under the Occupiers' Liability Act, a unified duty of care. *See* Tomlinson v Congleton Borough Council, [2004] 1 A.C. 46; British Rys. Bd. v. Herrington, [1972] A.C. 877 (House of Lords). The courts in that minority of American states taking the new, non-traditional approach hold that the defendant who controls the land owes a duty of reasonable care to the plaintiff injured on it. *See* Nelson v. Freeland, 507 S.E.2d 882 (N.C. 1998); Smith v. Arbaugh's Restaurant, 469 F.2d 97 (D.C. Cir. 1972); Pickard v. City & County of Honolulu, 452 P.2d 445 (Haw. 1969). What constitutes reasonable care may depend in part on the status of the plaintiff—whether invited or expected to be there, and whether a trespasser—but the landowner still owes a duty of reasonable care. *See* Scurti v. City of New York, 354 N.E.2d 794 (N.Y. 1976) (duty of reasonable care owed to child trespassing into railroad yard and onto top of freight car, where child was electrocuted by overhead wires powering locomotive) ("The fact that plaintiff entered without permission is also a relevant circumstance... .").

In that minority of states applying the unified reasonable-care standard, trespassers presumably more-frequently maintain claims than they would in states with the traditional standard, even though some trespasser claims can be unusual. *See* Mark v. Pacific Gas & Elec. Co., 7 Cal.3d 170, 496 P.2d 1276, 101 Cal. Rptr. 908 (1972) (trespasser college student electrocuted while unscrewing a street lamp owed a reasonable-care duty). One accommodation that several courts have made is to eliminate the distinction between the invitee and licensee statuses, affording both classes the duty of reasonable care, but to preserve the trespasser status and its no-duty rule. *See* Alexander v. The Medical Assocs. Clinic, P.C., 646 N.W.2d 74 (Iowa 2002); Tantimonico v Allendale Mut. Ins. Co., 637 A.2d 1056 (R.I. 1994); Hudson v. Gaitan, 675 S.W.2d 699 (Tenn. 1984); Mounsey v. Ellard, 297 N.E.2d 43 (Mass. 1973). Another action that most legislatures have taken is to pass recreational-use statutes granting landowners limited immunity against claims brought by persons making recreational use of private lands. *See* Cal. Civ. Code §846 (a landowner "owes no duty of care to keep the premises safe for entry or use by others for any recreational purpose"); Mich. Comp. L. §324.73301 (1995); N.Y. Gen. Oblig. Law §9-103. In those states, the hiker, deer hunter, or cross-country skier injured on another's land, whether present with or without permission, should not expect warnings or other protection against hazards on the land. Many other states have simply reaffirmed the traditional classifications. *See* Pinnell v. Bates, 838 So.2d 198 (Miss. 2002); Sims v. Giles, 343 S.C. 708, 541 S.E.2d 857 (2001); Franconia Assocs. v. Clark, 250 Va. 444, 463 S.E.2d 670 (1995).

The California Supreme Court rejected the traditional premises-liability framework in the following case and imposed a duty of reasonable care without respect to the plaintiff's classification. Media reports followed of settlements and awards in favor of two trespassers, one of whom had fallen through a skylight while trying to burglarize a school and the other of whom was thrown from the motorcycle he had stolen, while riding across the defendant farmer's land. The state legislature then enacted legislation to protect landowners against certain claims by trespassers. *See* Cal. Civil Code §1714.7 (moving-train exception); Cal. Civil Code §847 (felony exception); Calvillo-Silva v. Home Grocery, 968 P.2d 65 (Cal. 1998) (recognizing felony exception); Perez

v. Southern Pacific Transp. Co., 267 Cal. Rptr. 100 (Cal. App. 1990) (recognizing moving-train exception). As you read the following case and the legislative response rejecting it, decide with which law you agree, the traditional standard or uniform duty.

Rowland v. Christian
California Supreme Court
69 Cal.2d 108, 70 Cal. Rptr. 97, 443 P.2d 561 (1968)

PETERS, J. Plaintiff appeals from a summary judgment for defendant Nancy Christian in this personal injury action.

In his complaint plaintiff alleged that about November 1, 1963, Miss Christian told the lessors of her apartment that the knob of the cold water faucet on the bathroom basin was cracked and should be replaced; that on November 30, 1963, plaintiff entered the apartment at the invitation of Miss Christian; that he was injured while using the bathroom fixtures, suffering severed tendons and nerves of his right hand; and that he has incurred medical and hospital expenses. He further alleged that the bathroom fixtures were dangerous, that Miss Christian was aware of the dangerous condition, and that his injuries were proximately caused by the negligence of Miss Christian. …

… Although it is true that some exceptions have been made to the general principle that a person is liable for injuries caused by his failure to exercise reasonable care in the circumstances, it is clear that in the absence of statutory provision declaring an exception to the fundamental principle… , no such exception should be made unless clearly supported by public policy. [Cc]

A departure from this fundamental principle involves the balancing of a number of considerations; the major ones are the foreseeability of harm to the plaintiff, the degree of certainty that the plaintiff suffered injury, the closeness of the connection between the defendant's conduct and the injury suffered, the moral blame attached to the defendant's conduct, the policy of preventing future harm, the extent of the burden to the defendant and consequences to the community of imposing a duty to exercise care with resulting liability for breach, and the availability, cost, and prevalence of insurance for the risk involved. [Cc]

One of the areas where this court and other courts have departed from the fundamental concept that a man is liable for injuries caused by his carelessness is with regard to the liability of a possessor of land for injuries to persons who have entered upon that land. It has been suggested that the special rules regarding liability of the possessor of land are due to historical considerations stemming from the high place which land has traditionally held in English and American thought, the dominance and prestige of the landowning class in England during the formative period of the rules governing the possessor's liability, and the heritage of feudalism. [C]

The departure from the fundamental rule of liability for negligence has been accomplished by classifying the plaintiff either as a trespasser, licensee, or invitee and then adopting special rules as to the duty owed by the possessor to each of the classifications. Generally speaking a trespasser is a person who enters or remains upon land of another without a privilege to do so; a licensee is a person like a social guest who is not an invitee and who is privileged to enter or remain upon land by virtue of the possessor's consent, and an invitee is a business visitor who is invited or permitted to enter or remain on the land for a purpose directly or indirectly connected with business dealings between them. [C] ...

Although the invitor owes the invitee a duty to exercise ordinary care to avoid injuring him ([cc]), the general rule is that a trespasser and licensee or social guest are obliged to take the premises as they find them insofar as any alleged defective condition thereon may exist, and that the possessor of the land owes them only the duty of refraining from wanton or willful injury. ([cc]) The ordinary justification for the general rule severely restricting the occupier's liability to social guests is based on the theory that the guest should not expect special precautions to be made on his account and that if the host does not inspect and maintain his property the guest should not expect this to be done on his account. [C]

An increasing regard for human safety has led to a retreat from this position.... .

In refusing to adopt the rules relating to the liability of a possessor of land for the law of admiralty, the United States Supreme Court stated: "The distinctions which the common law draws between licensee and invitee were inherited from a culture deeply rooted to the land, a culture which traced many of its standards to a heritage of feudalism. In an effort to do justice in an industrialized urban society, with its complex economic and individual relationships, modern common-law courts have found it necessary to formulate increasingly subtle verbal refinements, to create subclassifications among traditional common-law categories, and to delineate fine gradations in the standards of care which the landowner owes to each. Yet even within a single jurisdiction, the classifications and subclassifications bred by the common law have produced confusion and conflict. As new distinctions have been spawned, older ones have become obscured. Through this semantic morass the common law has moved, unevenly and with hesitation, towards 'imposing on owners and occupiers a single duty of reasonable care in all circumstances.'" (Footnotes omitted.) (Kermarec v. Compagnie Generale, 358 U.S. 625, 630-631[(1959)]; [cc]. ...

There is another fundamental objection to the approach to the question of the possessor's liability on the basis of the common law distinctions based upon the status of the injured party as a trespasser, licensee, or invitee. Complexity can be borne and confusion remedied where the underlying principles governing liability are based upon proper considerations. Whatever may have been the historical justifications for the common law distinctions, it is clear that those distinctions are not justified in the light of our modern society and that the complexity and confusion which has arisen is not due to difficulty in applying the original common law rules—they are all too easy to apply in their original formulation—but is due to the attempts to apply just rules in our modern society within the ancient terminology.

Without attempting to labor all of the rules relating to the possessor's liability, it is apparent that the classifications of trespasser, licensee, and invitee, the immunities from liability predicated upon those classifications, and the exceptions to those immunities, often do not reflect the major factors which should determine whether immunity should be conferred upon the possessor of land. Some of those factors, including the closeness of the connection between the injury and the defendant's conduct, the moral blame attached to the defendant's conduct, the policy of preventing future harm, and the prevalence and availability of insurance, bear little, if any, relationship to the classifications of trespasser, licensee and invitee and the existing rules conferring immunity. ...

Although in general there may be a relationship between the remaining factors and the classifications of trespasser, licensee, and invitee, there are many cases in which no such relationship may exist. Thus, although the foreseeability of harm to an invitee would ordinarily seem greater than the foreseeability of harm to a trespasser, in a particular case the opposite may be true. The same may be said of the issue of certainty of injury. The burden to the defendant and consequences to the community of imposing a duty to exercise care with resulting liability for breach may often be greater with respect to trespassers than with respect to invitees, but it by no means follows that this is true in every case. In many situations, the burden will be the same, i.e., the conduct necessary upon the defendant's part to meet the burden of exercising due care as to invitees will also meet his burden with respect to licensees and trespassers. The last of the major factors, the cost of insurance, will, of course, vary depending upon the rules of liability adopted, but there is no persuasive evidence that applying ordinary principles of negligence law to the land occupier's liability will materially reduce the prevalence of insurance due to increased cost or even substantially increase the cost.

Considerations such as these have led some courts in particular situations to reject the rigid common law classifications and to approach the issue of the duty of the occupier on the basis of ordinary principles of negligence. ([Cc]) And the common law distinctions after thorough study have been repudiated by the jurisdiction of their birth. (Occupiers' Liability Act, 1957, 5 and 6 Eliz. 2, ch. 31.)

A man's life or limb does not become less worthy of protection by the law nor a loss less worthy of compensation under the law because he has come upon the land of another without permission or with permission but without a business purpose. Reasonable people do not ordinarily vary their conduct depending upon such matters, and to focus upon the status of the injured party as a trespasser, licensee, or invitee in order to determine the question whether the landowner has a duty of care, is contrary to our modern social mores and humanitarian values. The common law rules obscure rather than illuminate the proper considerations which should govern determination of the question of duty. …

Once the ancient concepts as to the liability of the occupier of land are stripped away, the status of the plaintiff relegated to its proper place in determining such liability, and ordinary principles of negligence applied, the result in the instant case presents no substantial difficulties. As we have seen, when we view the matters presented on the motion for summary judgment as we must, we must assume defendant Miss Christian was aware that the faucet handle was defective and dangerous, that the defect was not obvious, and that plaintiff was about to come in contact with the defective condition, and under the undisputed facts she neither remedied the condition nor warned plaintiff of it. Where the occupier of land is aware of a concealed condition involving in the absence of precautions an unreasonable risk of harm to those coming in contact with it and is aware that a person on the premises is about to come in contact with it, the trier of fact can reasonably conclude that a failure to warn or to repair the condition constitutes negligence. Whether or not a guest has a right to expect that his host will remedy dangerous conditions on his account, he should reasonably be entitled to rely upon a warning of the dangerous condition so that he, like the host, will be in a position to take special precautions when he comes in contact with it. …

The judgment is reversed.

CAL. CIV. CODE §847. Immunity from liability; injuries or death occurring on property during or after the commission of certain felonies

(a) An owner, including, but not limited to, a public entity, as defined in Section 811.2 of the Government Code, of any estate or any other interest in real property, whether possessory or nonpossessory, shall not be liable to any person for any injury or death that occurs upon that property during the course of or after the commission of any of the felonies set forth in subdivision (b) by the injured or deceased person.

(b) The felonies to which the provisions of this section apply are the following: (1) Murder or voluntary manslaughter; (2) mayhem; (3) rape; (4) sodomy by force, violence, duress, menace, or threat of great bodily harm; (5) oral copulation by force, violence, duress, menace, or threat of great bodily harm; (6) lewd acts on a child under the age of 14 years; (7) any felony punishable by death or imprisonment in the state prison for life; (8) any other felony in which the defendant inflicts great bodily injury on any person, other than an accomplice, or any felony in which the defendant uses a firearm; (9) attempted murder; (10) assault with intent to commit rape or robbery; (11) assault with a deadly weapon or instrument on a peace officer; (12) assault by a life prisoner on a noninmate; (13) assault with a deadly weapon by an inmate; (14) arson; (15) exploding a destructive device or any explosive with intent to injure; (16) exploding a destructive device or any explosive causing great bodily injury; (17) exploding a destructive device or any explosive with intent to murder; (18) burglary; (19) robbery; (20) kidnapping; (21) taking of a hostage by an inmate of a state prison; (22) any felony in which the defendant personally used a dangerous or deadly weapon; (23) selling, furnishing, administering, or providing heroin, cocaine, or phencyclidine (PCP) to a minor; (24) grand theft as defined in Sections 487 and 487a of the Penal Code; and (25) any attempt to commit a crime listed in this subdivision other than an assault.

(c) The limitation on liability conferred by this section arises at the moment the injured or deceased person commences the felony or attempted felony and extends to the moment the injured or deceased person is no longer upon the property. ...

(g) The limitation on liability provided by this section shall be in addition to any other available defense.

INQUIRY

Cycles. The above case and legislative response represent a typical pattern in tort law—case rulings and results linked to publicity leading to tort-law reform by legislative action or other court rulings. Query whether premises-liability plaintiffs in California actually have less rather than more (as the supreme court intended) protection after the cycle shown above. *See* Calvillo-Silva v. Home Grocery, 19 Cal.4th 714, 968 P.2d 65, 80 Cal. Rptr.2d 506 (1998) (trespasser statute protects landowner against claim for actively inflicted harm). Query also whether the modern trend to abandon the plaintiff-classification framework for a broad duty of reasonable care to anyone entering the land has ended—and, where states adopted it, whether it increases personal integrity and protection or simply leaves jurors more free than ever to do as they wish in protecting invited guests but not trespassers. While tort law remains an important part of our system of governance as a democratic republic, the sensible and responsible compassion lying in the hearts and souls of individual well-informed jurors should shape and inform tort law, just as much as the views and visions of justices, legislators, regulators, and academics. The Restatement (Third) of Torts: Liability for Physical and Emotional Harm §§51 and 52 (Tentative Draft No. 6, 2009), take a middle ground between the traditional framework and a modern reasonable-care standard. Do you prefer the Restatement framework? Does it just introduce new categories around which the courts must draw new lines?

REST. (THIRD) OF TORTS: LIABILITY FOR PHYSICAL AND EMOTIONAL HARM §51 (Tentative Draft No. 6, 2009)
Subject to §52, a land possessor owes a duty of reasonable care to entrants on the land with regard to:
(a) conduct by the land possessor that creates risks to entrants on the land;
(b) artificial conditions on the land that pose risks to entrants on the land;
(c) natural conditions on the land that pose risks to entrants on the land; and
(d) other risks to entrants on the land when any of the affirmative duties provided in Chapter 7 is applicable.

REST. (THIRD) OF TORTS: LIABILITY FOR PHYSICAL AND EMOTIONAL HARM §52 (Tentative Draft No. 6, 2009)
(a) The only duty a land possessor owes to flagrant trespassers is the duty not to act in an intentional, willful, or wanton manner to cause physical harm.
(b) Notwithstanding Subsection (a), a land possessor has a duty to exercise reasonable care for flagrant trespassers who reasonably appear to be imperiled and
(1) helpless; or
(2) unable to protect themselves.

Practice
The two plaintiff's lawyers had not seen one another for years—somewhat typical of personal-injury practice, that the interaction is greater between opposing counsel than among counsel of the same side of the bar. "Hey, so how's the practice?" one asked the other. "Not bad, you know," the other replied, "Sure, 'tort reform' has hit a lot of the smaller claims in medical malpractice, products liability, premises liability, and motor-vehicle no-fault. It's tough for a lot of people. But the bigger cases are still there. The practice just changed from volume to quality, and you still try to help where you can."

Defendants. A common question in premises-liability cases—whether the courts apply the majority plaintiff-classification framework explored below or use the minority approach shown above—is who are the appropriate defendants. The question takes special significance when one party leases to another the real property on which the injury occurs, in an agreement that divides responsibilities for the property's maintenance. The traditional rule is that the tenant, not the property owner, owes the duties (if any) to third persons. Yet both commercial and residential leases will often assign to the property owner the responsibility of maintaining the exterior and any interior common spaces like hallways, stairways, and vestibules, while assigning to the tenant the responsibility for the interior of the leased premises. Even inside the leased premises the property owner may retain the right—and with it, the responsibility—to maintain mechanical and electrical systems and appliances. Courts generally recognize these and other exceptions to the traditional no-landlord-duty rule, although a few courts go farther and simply recognize that the property owner continues to owe a general duty of care. *See* Young v. Garwacki, 380 Mass. 162, 402 N.E.2d 1045 (1980) (landlord liable for injury to guest of tenant who leaned against balcony railing in need of landlord's repair); Pagelsdorf v. Safeco Ins. Co., 91 Wis.2d 734, 284 N.W.2d 55 (1979) (same). When a plaintiff suffers injury, parties must often look to lease terms, notice to property owner and tenant of the dangerous condition causing the injury, and the course of dealing between property owner and tenant with respect to that dangerous condition. *See also* Restatement (Second) of Torts §328E (1965) (duty may arise with right to occupy, whether or not exercised). Consider the following case setting out as a basic rule that the landlord is not liable after leasing the premises but then listing the many exceptions—so many, that they may have swallowed the rule.

Borders v. Roseberry
Kansas Supreme Court
216 Kan. 486, 532 P.2d 1366 (1975)

PRAGER, J. This case involves the liability of a landlord for personal injuries suffered by the social guest of the tenant as the result of a slip and fall on the leased premises. ... The defendant-appellee, Agnes Roseberry, is the owner of a single-family, one-story residence... . Several months prior to January 9, 1971, the defendant leased the property on a month to month basis to a tenant, Rienecker. Just prior to the time the tenant took occupancy of the house the defendant landlord had work performed on the house. The remodeling of the house included a new roof. In repairing the house the repairmen removed the roof guttering from the front of the house but failed to reinstall it. The landlord knew the guttering had been removed by the workmen, intended to have it reinstalled, and knew that it had not been reinstalled. The roof line on the house was such that without the guttering the rain drained off the entire north side of the house onto the front porch steps. In freezing weather water from the roof would accumulate and freeze on the steps. The landlord as well as the tenant knew that the guttering had not been reinstalled and knew that without the guttering, water from the roof would drain onto the front porch steps and in freezing weather would accumulate and freeze. The tenant had complained to the landlord about the absence of guttering and the resulting icy steps.

On January 9, 1971, there was ice and snow on the street and ice on the front steps. During the afternoon the tenant worked on the front steps, removing the ice accumulation with hammer. The plaintiff-appellant, Gary D. Borders, arrived on the premises at approximately 4:00 p. m. in response to an invitation of the tenant for dinner. It is agreed that plaintiff's status was that of a social guest of the tenant. There was ice on the street and snow on the front steps when plaintiff arrived. At 9:00 p. m. as plaintiff Borders was leaving the house he slipped and fell on an accumulation of ice on the steps and received personal injuries. ... Following submission of the case the trial court entered judgment for the defendant... . The trial court based its judgment upon a conclusion of law which stated that a landlord of a single-family house is under no obligation or duty to a social guest, a licensee of his tenant to repair or remedy a known condition... .

... The issue raised involves the liability of a lessor who has leased his property to a tenant for a period of time. ...

Traditionally the law in this country has placed upon the lessee as the person in possession of the land the burden of maintaining the premises in a reasonably safe condition to protect persons who come upon the land. It is the tenant as possessor who, at least initially, has the burden of maintaining the premises in good repair. [Cc] ... There is therefore, as a general rule, no liability upon the landlord, either to the tenant or to others entering the land, for defective conditions existing at the time of the lease.

The general rule of non-liability has been modified, however, by a number of exceptions which have been created as a matter of social policy. Modern case law on the subject today usually limits the liability of a landlord for injuries arising from a defective condition existing at the time of the lease to six recognized exceptions. These exceptions are as follows:

1. Undisclosed dangerous conditions known to lessor and unknown to the lessee.

This exception is stated in Restatement, Second, Torts §358 as follows:

"§358. Undisclosed Dangerous Conditions Known to Lessor.
"(1) A lessor of land who conceals or fails to disclose to his lessee any condition, whether natural or artificial, which involves unreasonable risk of physical harm to persons on the land, is subject to liability to the lessee and others upon the land with the consent of the lessee or his sublessee for physical harm caused by the condition after the lessee has taken possession, if (a) the lessee does not know or have reason to know of the condition or the risk involved, and (b) the lessor knows or has reason to know of the condition, and realizes or should realize the risk involved, and has reason to expect that the lessee will not discover the condition or realize the risk. ..."

2. Conditions dangerous to persons outside of the premises.
This exception is stated in Restatement, Second, Torts §379 as follows:

"§379. Dangerous Conditions Existing When Lessor Transfers Possession. A lessor of land who transfers its possession in a condition which he realizes or should realize will involve unreasonable risk of physical harm to others outside of the land, is subject to the same liability for physical harm subsequently caused to them by the condition as though he had remained in possession." ...

3. Premises leased for admission of the public.

The third exception arises where land is leased for a purpose involving the admission of the public. The cases usually agree that in that situation the lessor is under an affirmative duty to exercise reasonable care to inspect and repair the premises before possession is transferred, to prevent any unreasonable risk or harm to the public who may enter. This exception is stated in §359 of Restatement, Second, Torts.... .

4. Parts of land retained in lessor's control which lessee is entitled to use.

When different parts of a building, such as an office building or an apartment house, are leased to several tenants, the approaches and common passageways normally do not pass to the tenant, but remain in the possession and control of the landlord. Hence the lessor is under an affirmative obligation to exercise reasonable care to inspect and repair those parts of the premises for the protection of the lessee, members of his family, his employees, invitees, guests, and others on the land in the right of the tenant. This exception is covered in Restatement, Second, Torts ss 360 and 361....

5. Where lessor contracts to repair.

... This exception is found in Restatement, Second, Torts s 357 which states as follows:

> "§357. Where Lessor Contracts to Repair. A lessor of land is subject to liability for physical harm caused to his lessee and others upon the land with the consent of the lessee or his sublessee by a condition of disrepair existing before or arising after the lessee has taken possession if (a) the lessor, as such, has contracted by a covenant in the lease or otherwise to keep the land in repair, and (b) the disrepair creates an unreasonable risk to persons upon the land which the performance of the lessor's agreement would have prevented, and (c) the lessor fails to exercise reasonable care to perform his contract." ...

6. Negligence by lessor in making repairs.

When the lessor does in fact attempt to make repairs, whether he is bound by a covenant to do so or not, and fails to exercise reasonable care, he is held liable for injuries to the tenant or others on the premises in his right, if the tenant neither knows nor should know that the repairs have been negligently made. This exception is stated in Restatement, Second, Torts s 362....

With the general rule and its exceptions in mind we shall now examine the undisputed facts in this case to determine whether or not the landlord can be held liable to the plaintiff here. It is clear that the exceptions pertaining to undisclosed dangerous conditions known to the lessor (exception 1), conditions dangerous to persons outside of the premises (exception 2), premises leased for admission of the public (exception 3), and parts of land retained in the lessor's control (exception 4) have no application in this case. Nor do we believe that exception 5, which comes into play when the lessor has contracted to repair, has been established by the court's findings of fact. It does not appear that the plaintiff takes the position that the lessor contracted to keep the premises in repair; nor has any consideration for such an agreement been shown. As to exception 6, although it is obvious that the repairs to the roof were not completed by installation of the guttering and although the landlord expressed his intention to replace the guttering, we do not believe that the factual circumstances bring the plaintiff within the application of exception 6 where the lessor has been negligent in making repairs. As pointed out above, that exception comes into play only when the lessee lacks knowledge that the purported repairs have not been made or have been negligently made. Here it is undisputed that the tenant had full knowledge of the icy condition on the steps created by the absence of guttering. It seems to us that the landlord could reasonably assume that the tenant would inform his guest about the icy condition on the front steps. We have concluded that the factual circumstances do not establish liability on the landlord on the basis of negligent repairs made by him. ...

The judgment of the district court is affirmed.

INQUIRY

Lessors. A majority of courts still follow a no-liability rule for lessors, with many exceptions. *See* Johson County Sheriff's Posse, Inc. v. Endsley, 926 S.W.2d 284 (Tex. 1996); Ortega v. Flaim, 902 P.2d 199 (Wyo. 1995); Chandler v. Furrer, 823 S.W.2d 27 (Md. Ct. App. 1991). Courts in a substantial minority of jurisdictions have abolished the lessor non-liability rule to impose the usual duty of reasonable care. *See* Favreau v. Miller, 591 A.2d 68 (Vt. 1991); Stevens v. Stearns, 678 P.2d 41 (Idaho 1984); Mansur v. Ewbanks, 401 So.2d 1328 (Fla. 1981); Sargent v. Ross, 308 A.2d 528 (N.H. 1973). In states where the non-liability rule persists, landlord/tenant statutes often impose varying duties on residential property owners. Although those statutes are to ensure adequate living conditions for apartment tenants, when their violation leads to personal injury, the injured may invoke them for a presumption or inference of negligence, or as negligence per se. *See* Peterson v. Superior Court, 899 P.2d 905 (Cal. 1995). In a regime that is no less complicated than that suggested by the above case, and probably more so, the Restatement (Third) of Torts: Liability for Physical and Emotional Harm §53 (Tentative Draft No. 6, 2009), summarizes the duties that a lessor retains as follows:

> Except as provided in §52, a lessor owes to the lessee and all other entrants on the leased premises the following duties:
> (a) A duty of reasonable care under §51 for those portions of the leased premises over which the lessor retains control;
> (b) A duty of reasonable care under §7 for any risks that are created by the lessor in the condition of the leased premises;
> (c) A duty to disclose to the lessee any dangerous condition that satisfies all of the following:
> (1) it poses a risk to entrants on the leased premises;
> (2) it exists on the leased premises when the lessee takes possession;
> (3) it is latent and unknown to the lessee; and
> (4) it is known or should be known to the lessor;
> (d) A duty of reasonable care for any dangerous condition on the leased premises at the time the lessee takes possession if:
> (1) the lease is for a purpose that includes admission of the public; and
> (2) the lessor has reason to believe that the lessee will admit persons onto the leased premises without rectifying the dangerous condition;
> (e) A duty of reasonable care:
> (1) for any contractual undertaking; or
> (2) for any voluntary undertaking, under §§42–43, with regard to the condition of the leased premises;
> (f) A duty based on an applicable statute imposing obligations on lessors with regard to the condition of leased premises, unless the court finds that recognition of a tort duty is inconsistent with the statute;
> (g) A duty of reasonable care to comply with an applicable implied warranty of habitability; and
> (h) A duty of reasonable care to lessees under §40, Comment *m*, as well as any other affirmative duties that may apply. See Chapter 7.

B. Classifying the Plaintiff

Although it rejected them in favor of a minority reasonable-care rule, the *Rowland v. Christian* decision above has already introduced the reader to the traditional, majority-rule classifications for premises liability. First, keep in mind that law classifies the plaintiff, not the defendant. Then, the classifications themselves are reasonably straightforward as follows. *Invitees*, whom courts sometimes call *business invitees* or *business visitors*, are on the defendant's land for pecuniary (monetary) purposes. The classic examples are shoppers at a retail store. Property owners owe invitees a duty of reasonable care. Warning an invitee of dangers on the premises is not sufficient if the dangers are unreasonable. *See* Wilk v. Georges, 514 P.2d 877 (Ore. 1973) (Christmas-tree nursery liable for customer's slip and fall despite warning); Restatement (Second) of Torts §343A (obviousness of risk does not defeat invitee's claim). *Licensees*, by contrast, are on the defendant's premises with the defendant's permission (even by invitation, although do not confuse it with an "invitee") for other than pecuniary purposes—like social guests at a residence. Property owners owe licensees a duty to warn of hidden dangers about which the landowner knew. Trespassers are on the premises without the defendant's permission—like vandals entering an abandoned building. Property owners generally owe trespassers no duty, except as to active operations when the owner knows of their presence and hazard. *But see* Gladon v. Greater Cleveland Reg. Trans. Auth., 75 Ohio St. 3d 312, 662 N.E.2d 287 (1996). A person accompanying another onto land will often adopt the status of that other person whom the first person accompanies. *See* Ellis v. Luxury Hotels, Inc., 716 N.E.2d 951 (2000) (guest of hotel-guest invitee is also invitee). Defining the classifications and standards of care is not the difficult part. The difficulty is applying the classifications and standards to bring out their subtlety and accomplish their purpose. Consider each classification in turn.

1. Invitees

Property owners owe invitees a duty of reasonable care because of the economic benefit the landowner expects from their visit. *See* Restatement (Second) of Torts §332. If the classic invitee—on the premises for the owner's business purpose—is the retail shopper considering a purchase, then what are the boundary issues? They begin with whether the plaintiff can change statuses as the plaintiff's and defendant's intentions change as to the plaintiff's presence on the land. A shopper (an invitee) can with the passage of time or a change in intentions become a looker (still an invitee), the seeker of a recreation or gratuity (a licensee), or an unwelcome intruder (a trespasser). With a change in the nature or scope of the plaintiff's activities on the premises, a social guest (a licensee) can become a shopper (an invitee) or an unwelcome intruder (a trespasser). How should the law patrol the borders of the invitee classification? The answer may not be clear, but consider the following case.

Campbell v. Weathers
Kansas Supreme Court
153 Kan. 316, 111 P.2d 72 (1941)

WEDELL, J. ...

The defendants were the lessee of a building, who operated a cigar and lunch business, the owner of the building and the owner's manager of the building.

... Plaintiff had been a customer of the defendant lessee for a number of years. On Sunday morning, June 4, 1939, between 8:30 and nine o'clock, plaintiff entered the place of business operated by the defendant lessee, as a cigar and lunch business. He spent probably fifteen or twenty minutes in the front part of the building and then started for the toilet. He stepped into the open trap door in the floor of the hallway, broke his right arm and sustained some other injuries. ...

The first issue to be determined is the relationship between plaintiff and the lessee. Was plaintiff a trespasser, a lessee or an invitee? ... It is conceded lessee operated a business which was open to the public. Lessee's business was that of selling cigars and lunches to the public. ... Plaintiff had been a customer of the lessee for a number of years. ... He was a switchman for one of the railroads. He stopped at the lessee's place of business whenever he was in town. He had used the hallway and toilet on numerous occasions, whenever he was in town, and had never been advised the toilet was not intended for public use. ...

The evidence of lessee's own employee was that the toilet was not regarded as a private toilet. The evidence is that it was not used only by the lessor, the lessee, or by lessee's employees. Did the evidence disclose that in addition to the lessor, the lessee and his employees, it was to be used only by customers of the lessee? It did not. The positive and unqualified testimony was: "It was used by everybody, used by the public." ... In a densely populated business district such a privilege may have constituted a distinct inducement to bring not only old customers like appellant, but prospective customers into lessee's place of business. ...

The writer cannot subscribe to the theory that a regular customer of long standing is not an invitee to use toilet facilities required by law to be provided by the operator of a restaurant, simply because the customer had not actually made a purchase on the particular occasion of his injury, prior to his injury. It would seem doubtful whether such a doctrine could be applied justly to regular customers of a business which the law does not specifically require to be supplied with toilet facilities, but which does so for the convenience or accommodation of its guests. Women do a great deal of shopping. They sometimes shop all day in their favorite stores and sometimes fail to make a single purchase. Shall courts say, as a matter of law, they were not invitees of the business simply because on a particular occasion they had not yet made a purchase? No business concern would contend they were not invitees unless perchance an injury had occurred. Men frequently, during spare moments, step into a place of business, which they patronize regularly, where drinks, cigars and lunches are sold. They may not have intended definitely to presently make a purchase. They may, nevertheless, become interested, for example, in a new brand of cigars on display which they may purchase then or on some future occasion. Would the owner or operator of the business contend they were not invitees? We do not think so. Then why should courts arbitrarily say so, as a matter of law? It is common knowledge that business concerns invest huge sums of money in newspaper, radio and other mediums of advertising in order to induce regular and prospective customers to frequent their place of business and to examine their stocks of merchandise. They do not contemplate a sale to every invitee. ... In the case of Kinsman v. Barton & Company, 141 Wash. 311, 251 P. 563, that court had occasion to determine what constituted an invitee and said: "An invitee is one who is either expressly or impliedly invited onto the premises of another in connection with the business carried on by that other. If one goes into a store with the view of then, or at some other time, doing some business with the store, he is an invitee." [C] ...

Of course, if it appears a person had no intention of presently or in the future becoming a customer he could not be held to be an invitee as there would be no basis for any thought of mutual benefit. [C]

It is true, in the instant case, there was no direct evidence of appellant's intention to make a purchase on this particular occasion. We cannot, however, well ignore the pertinent fact that this appellant had been a customer of lessee of long standing. He had patronized lessee's business for a number of years and had done so whenever he was in town. In view of this record, we think it unreasonable to say, as a matter of law, appellant lost his status as an invitee, simply because he had not actually made a purchase prior to his injury on this single occasion, or because the record did not affirmatively disclose he actually intended to make a specific purchase presently or in the future. There is nothing in the record which remotely indicates appellant had abandoned his practice to continue patronizing the lessee and his presence there on this occasion is some evidence he had not abandoned such previous custom. …

Did the lessee violate any duty to appellant, an invitee? …

The trap door in the hallway was opened on the day before the accident. It was opened in order to obtain ventilation underneath the floor and in order to get relief from dampness and the muddy ground preparatory to re-enforcing the floor. It was left open on Sunday, the day of the accident, at the suggestion of the lessee. … On the morning of the accident the hallway was dark or dimly lighted. There was an electric light suspended from the ceiling but it was not lighted at the time of the injury. … Appellant did not know the trap door was open. He saw no signs to warn him it was open and no one in person advised him concerning it. The lessee previously had been expressly warned by one of his own employees that he had almost fallen into the hole and that it should be closed or someone would be injured and sue him. …

The order sustaining the demurrers of the landlord and the manager of the building is affirmed. The order sustaining the demurrer of the lessee is reversed.

INQUIRY

Retailers. The above case suggests that owners of retail premises will have a hard time showing that persons on the premises are present for other than some present or potential business purpose—even when making a foreseeable personal use of the facilities. *See* Martin v. B.P. Exploration & Oil, 769 So.2d 261 (Miss. Ct. App. 2000) (plaintiff using a gas-station restroom without buying gas remains an invitee); Knapp v. Connecticut Theatrical Corp., 122 Conn. 413, 190 A. 291 (1937) (theater patron opening wrong door while attempting to find restroom remains an invitee); *but see* Liveright v. Max Lifsitz Furniture Co., 117 N.J.L. 243, 187 A. 583 (1936) (licensee while using restroom not intended for public). Yet a clear change away from a business purpose might turn an invitee into a licensee. *See* Whelan v. Van Natta, 382 S.W.2d 205 (1964) (grocery-store shopper is a licensee when searching back room for a free box for son). So might using a prohibited shortcut through the premises. *See* Nicoletti v. Westcor, Inc., 131 Ariz. 140, 639 P.2d 330 (1982). How should premises-liability law classify those who have no intention of shopping but are accompanying others who do, such as a child for whom the shopper expects to make a purchase? *See* Anderson v. Cooper, 214 Ga. 164, 104 S.E.2d 90 (1958) (invitee). What if the person accompanying the shopper is only an adult friend for whom the shopper plans no purchase? *See* Goldsmith v. Cody, 351 Mich. 380, 88 N.W.2d 268 (1958) (invitee). What if the injured visitor is simply on a tour of the landowner's plant? *See* Gilliland v. Bondurant, 51 S.W.2d 559 (Mo. App. 1932), affd., 332 Mo. 881, 59 S.W.2d 679 (1933) (invitee). Or attracted by a free give-away? Edwards v. Gulf Oil Corp., 69 Ga. App. 140, 24 S.E.2d 843 (1943) (free comics at gas station—invitee); Ward v. Avery, 113 Conn. 394, 155 A. 502 (1931) (free telephone service—invitee).

Ethics

Witnesses can be reluctant to share their information, especially when they believe that disclosure may mean that they will have to testify at a trial—and when the case is a tort case. They may not know that insurance is available and may instead believe that their information will cost an individual—perhaps a family member or friend—their savings or even their home. Lawyers must not misrepresent their role or purpose in speaking with witnesses. Rule 4.1 of the ABA Model Rules of Professional Conduct prohibits lawyers from making false statements to third persons. Rule 4.3 provides that a lawyer who deals on behalf of a client with an unrepresented person must not misrepresent the lawyer's interest in the matter. If a witness will not voluntarily share information with a lawyer, then the lawyer usually has other lawful means, such as a subpoena for a discovery deposition, to gain the witness's information. Indeed, better to have a reluctant witness's testimony preserved in a deposition than to have the witness disappear or change the story.

Business Interests. More than just retail-store owners have business interests sufficient to turn a visitor into an invitee. Any business interest may justify classification as an invitee. *See* Suarez v. Trans World Airlines, Inc., 498 F.2d 612 (7th Cir. 1974) (airline passenger preparing to purchase ticket is invitee); First Natl. Bank of Birmingham v. Lower, 263 Ala. 36, 81 So.2d 284 (1955) (getting change at a bank—invitee); Restatement (Second) of Torts §343 (pecuniary-business transactions would make the visitor an invitee); *see also* McCann v. Anchor Line, 79 F.2d 338 (2d Cir. 1935) (accompanying travelers at train station classifies as invitee). Homeowners conduct significant business from the home—not only in the form of in-home meetings for employment and commercial purposes, but also contracting for household cleaning, garbage pick-up, improvement and repair services, and utility services (necessitating meter-readers). What classification should we give the social guest at a home "Tupperware" (kitchen-storage-product) party? *See* Beebe v. Moses, 113 Wash. App. 464, 54 P.3d 188 (Wash. Ct. App. 2002) (question of licensee or invitee status was for jury). What is the status of the visitor who attends a social-organization meeting? Older cases have found invitee status, although doing so goes beyond the modern pecuniary-interest rule. *See* Geiger v. Simpson M.E. Church, 174 Minn. 389, 219 N.W. 463 (1928) (invitee—social meeting at church); Howe v. Ohmart, 7 Ind. App. 32, 33 N.E. 466 (1893) (invitee—literary society meeting); *but see* Barmore v. Elmore, 83 Ill. App.3d 1056, 38 Ill. Dec. 751, 403 N.E.2d 1355 (Ill. App. Ct. 1980) (licensee—Masonic lodge business in home). The cases also treat as invitees, spectators at public events and users of public facilities and parks. *See* Adams v. United States, 239 F. Supp. 503 (E.D. Okl. 1965) (national park); Mesa v. Spokane World Expos., 18 Wash. App. 609, 570 P.2d 157 (1977) (public amusement); Lowe v. Gastonia, 211 N.C. 564, 191 S.E. 7 (1937) (golf course).

Reasonable Care. What constitutes reasonable care toward an invitee? The landowner's duties to an invitee certainly include making reasonable inspections for, and warning about, unreasonable dangers. Yet the invitee duty also includes making reasonably necessary repairs and maintenance to prevent unreasonable dangers from arising or continuing on the premises. Warning, in other words, may not be enough from the legal standpoint. *See* Wilk v. Georges, 267 Or. 19, 514 P.2d 877 (1973). On the other hand, landowners owe no absolute duty to prevent an invitee's injury. Law requires only reasonable care, not perfect safety. *See* Kay v. Kay, 306 Ark. 322, 812 S.W.2d 685 (Ark. 1991) (homeowners do not owe invitee maid a duty to prevent her from being bitten by brown recluse spider). Some courts find no duty as to natural accumulations of snow and ice. *See* Luebeck v. Safeway Stores, Inc., 152 Mont. 88, 446 P.2d 921 (1968). Many courts find no duty to warn or protect against open-and-obvious hazards. *See* O'Sullivan v. Shaw, 431 Mass. 201, 726 N.E.2d 951 (2000) (affirming dismissal of claim for injury from diving into shallow pool on basis that no duty was owed); General Motors Corp. v. Hill, 752 So.2d 1186 (Ala. 1999) (no duty as to obvious conditions); *cf.* Shaw v. Petersen, 169 Ariz. 559, 821 P.2d 220 (Ct. App. 1991) (no negligence regarding obvious conditions because injury event not foreseeable).

Acts of Others. Some authority holds landowners liable for the unruly actions of others on or about the premises, if those actions are foreseeable and related to the defendant's business. *See* Silva v. Showcase Cinemas Concessions of Dedham, Inc., 736 F.2d 810 (1st Cir. 1984), cert. denied, 469 U.S. 883 (1984) (theater has a duty to reasonably address foreseeable violence in theater and parking lot); McFarlin v. Hall, 127 Ariz. 220, 619 P.2d 729 (1980) (duty of reasonable care with respect to intoxicated patron). Criminal-injury hazards relating to structures or equipment used on the premises may contribute to the finding of a duty. *See* Kelly v. Kroger Co., 484 F.2d 1362 (10th Cir. 1973) (silent alarm endangered customer hostage when police arrive); Erickson v. Curtis Investment Co., 447 N.W.2d 165 (Minn. 1989) (duty owed to take reasonable care to prevent rape in parking ramp). Although some authority extends the duty to prevent intentional criminal acts against another without respect to the landowner's contributing business, structures, or equipment, *see* Taco Bell, Inc.v. Lannon, 744 P.2d 43 (Colo. 1987), courts are often not so inclined. *See* Boyd v. Racine Currency Exchange, Inc., 56 Ill.2d 95, 306 N.E.2d 39 (1973). Consider the following illustrative case.

Williams v. Cunningham Drug Stores, Inc.
Michigan Supreme Court
429 Mich. 495, 418 N.W.2d 381 (1988)

CAVANAGH, J. In this case of first impression we are asked to determine whether a store owner must provide armed, visible security guards to protect customers from the criminal acts of third parties.

I

On May 4, 1979, plaintiff Willie Williams was shopping in a Cunningham drug store located in a high crime area of the City of Detroit. A plainclothes security guard was employed by the store, but on the day in question he was sick. Store personnel called the main office to request a substitute, but one was not sent.[fn]

While plaintiff was shopping, an armed robbery occurred. During the resulting confusion and panic, plaintiff ran out of the store, directly behind the fleeing robber. As the two men were outside, the robber turned and shot plaintiff.[fn]

In May of 1980, plaintiff filed a complaint against defendant Cunningham Drug Stores, alleging that defendant had breached its duty to exercise reasonable care for the safety of its patrons. Specifically, plaintiff alleged that defendant had failed to provide armed, visible security guards and had failed to intercede after having noticed that an armed robbery was in progress. ...

Upon the close of plaintiffs' proofs at trial, defendant moved for a directed verdict ... on the basis that defendant did not have a duty to protect plaintiff from the unforeseeable acts of a third party. The trial court granted defendant's motion as a matter of law and directed a verdict of no cause of action.

Plaintiff appealed by right in the Court of Appeals, which affirmed, holding that as a matter of law defendant's duty of reasonable care did not extend to providing the degree of protection plaintiffs claimed was due. [C]

We granted plaintiffs' application for leave to appeal, [c], and now affirm.

II

... [A]s a general rule, there is no duty that obligates one person to aid or protect another.[fn]

Social policy, however, has led the courts to recognize an exception to this general rule where a special relationship exists between a plaintiff and a defendant.[fn] Thus, a common carrier may be obligated to protect its passengers, an innkeeper his guests, and an employer his employees.[fn] The rationale behind imposing a duty to protect in these special relationships is based on control. In each situation one person entrusts himself to the control and protection of another, with a consequent loss of control to protect himself.[fn] The duty to protect is imposed upon the person in control because he is best able to provide a place of safety.

Owners and occupiers of land are in a special relationship with their invitees and comprise the largest group upon whom an affirmative duty to protect is imposed. The possessor of land has a duty to exercise reasonable care to protect invitees from an unreasonable risk of harm caused by a dangerous condition of the land.[fn] Consequently, a landlord may be held liable for an unreasonable risk of harm caused by a dangerous condition in the areas of common use retained in his control such as lobbies, hallways, stairways and elevators.[fn] Likewise, a business invitor or merchant may be held liable for injuries resulting from negligent maintenance of the premises or defects in the physical structure of the building.[fn]

The duty a possessor of land owes his invitees is not absolute, however. It does not extend to conditions from which an unreasonable risk cannot be anticipated or to dangers so obvious and apparent that an invitee may be expected to discover them himself.[fn] Furthermore, "the occupier is not an insurer of the safety of invitees, and his duty is only to exercise reasonable care for their protection."[fn]

III

The question before us in this case is whether a merchant's duty to exercise reasonable care includes providing armed, visible security guards to protect invitees from the criminal acts of third parties. Plaintiffs contend that it does and that the trial court erred in granting defendant's motion for a directed verdict rather than allowing the jury to determine whether defendant's conduct met the standard of reasonable care.

In deciding this question, we note that the court and jury perform different functions in a negligence case. Among other things, the court decides the questions of duty and the general standard of care, and the jury determines what constitutes reasonable care under the circumstances. However, in cases in which overriding public policy concerns arise, the court determines what constitutes reasonable care. [C] Such public policy concerns exist in the present case, and therefore the question whether defendant's conduct constituted reasonable care is one the court should determine as a matter of law.

We agree with the Court of Appeals that a merchant's duty of reasonable care does not include providing armed, visible security guards to deter criminal acts of third parties.[fn] We decline to extend defendant's duty that far in light of the degree of control in a merchant's relationship with invitees, the nature of the harm involved, and the public interest in imposing such a duty.[fn] ...

The duty advanced by plaintiffs is essentially a duty to provide police protection. That duty, however, is vested in the government by constitution and statute.[fn] We agree with the Court of Appeals in this case that neither the Legislature nor the constitution has established a policy requiring that the responsibility to provide police protection be extended to commercial businesses.

Furthermore, although defendant can control the condition of his premises by correcting physical defects that may result in injuries to his invitees, he cannot control the incidence of crime in the community. Today a crime may be committed anywhere and at any time. To require defendant to provide armed, visible security guards to protect invitees from criminal acts in a place of business open to the general public would require defendant to provide a safer environment on his premises than his invitees would encounter in the community at large. Defendant simply does not have that degree of control and is not an insurer of the safety of his invitees.[fn]

In addition, any duty we might impose on defendant to protect his invitees from the criminal acts of third parties would be inevitably vague, given the nature of the harm involved. Fairness requires that if a merchant could be held liable for the failure to provide security guards, he should be able to ascertain in advance the extent of his duty and whether he has fulfilled it.[fn] ... Even if a merchant were not required to prevent all crime, defining a reasonable standard of care short of that goal might well be impossible.

Finally, we note that imposing the duty advanced by plaintiffs is against the public interest. The inability of government and law enforcement officials to prevent criminal attacks does not justify transferring the responsibility to a business owner such as defendant. To shift the duty of police protection from the government to the private sector would amount to advocating that members of the public resort to self-help. Such a proposition contravenes public policy.[fn]

IV

We conclude as a matter of law that the duty of reasonable care a merchant owes his invitees does not extend to providing armed, visible security guards to protect customers from the criminal acts of third parties. The merchant is not an insurer of the safety of his invitees, and for reasons of public policy he does not have the responsibility for providing police protection on his premises. Accordingly, the decision of the Court of Appeals is affirmed.

INQUIRY

Apartments. The *Williams* case mentions that a special relationship may form the basis for a landowner's duty with respect to security. It also mentions the factor of control—that a duty may arise where the landowner has the sole or primary control. One place where both a special relationship and landlord control are often present is in residential-apartment leases. The traditional rule would relieve a landlord of any duty with respect to criminal attacks by third parties. *See* Goldberg v. Housing Auth. of Newark, 38 N.J. 578, 186 A.2d 291 (1962). Some courts have held that a landowner owes a duty to a tenant to prevent foreseeable criminal attacks in hallways and other common areas, especially with repeated prior attacks, landowner exclusive control, and tenant reliance on landowner. *See* Jardel Co. v. Hughes, 523 A.2d 518 (Del. 1987); Lay v. Dworman, 732 P.2d 455 (Okl. 1986); Kline v. 1500 Massachusetts Ave. Apt. Corp., 141 U.S. App. D.C. 370, 439 F.2d 477 (D.C. Cir. 1970). The decisions may require a high degree of foreseeability. *See* McClung v. Delta Square Ltd. Partnership, 937 S.W.2d 891 (Tenn. 1996). Other courts find a duty only where the landowner assumes one. *See* Feld v. Merriam, 506 Pa. 383, 485 A.2d 742 (1984). Where a duty exists, claimants must show how the landowner could reasonably have satisfied it. *See* Sherman v. Concourse Realty Corp., 47 A.D.2d 134, 365 N.Y.S.2d 239 (1975) (tenant's claim against landlord for third-party assault submitted to jury on theory of failure to provide working lock); Johnston v. Harris, 387 Mich. 569, 198 N.W.2d 409 (1972) (breach of landlord's duty a jury question on theory that landlord should have provided lights and locks).

2. Licensees

The licensee status raises both classification and duty issues. The classic licensee is the social guest in the landowner's home—not present for a business interest but nonetheless on the land with the owner's permission. Thompson v. Katzer, 86 Wash. App. 280, 936 P.2d 421 (Ct. App. 1997) (incidental service to host does not transform licensee guest into invitee); Zuther v. Schild, 224 Kan. 528, 581 P.2d 385 (1978); Stevens v. Dovre, 248 Md. 15, 234 A.2d 596 (1967); *but see* Burrell v. Meads, 569 N.E.2d 637 (Ind. 1991) (expanding invitee class to include social guests). The boundary issues for licensees arise in much the same manner that they do for invitees—through the passage of time, changes in the intentions of the licensee and landowner, and changes in the nature and scope of the licensee's activities. Although older authority provides that a licensee's only duty is to avoid willful and wanton injury, *see* Duff v. United States, 171 F.2d 846 (4th Cir. 1949) (Maryland law), the licensee duty today is clearly broader in most states, including a duty to warn of known hidden dangerous conditions. *See* Barry v. Cantrell, 150 Ga. App. 439, 258 S.E.2d 61 (1979) (duty to warn of dead tree supporting hammock); Laube v. Stevenson, 137 Conn. 469, 78 A.2d 693 (1951) (duty to warn of absence of handrail and other defects in unlit stairway); *see also* Restatement (Second) of Torts §342 (also warn where there is reason to know). Consider the following case illustrative of how the classification as a licensee rather than invitee can dispose of the case. As you read the case, also note the duty of care owed a licensee.

Younce v. Ferguson
Washington Supreme Court
106 Wash.2d 658, 724 P.2d 991 (1986)

GOODLOE, J. In this case, we determine whether the common law classifications of entrants as invitees, licensees, or trespassers should continue to be determinative of the standard of care owed by an owner or occupier of land and whether the status of the entrant in this case was correctly determined. We answer both questions affirmatively and affirm the trial court.

Appellant Lisa Younce appeals the dismissal of respondents Charles, Thelma, and Dean Strunk from the suit. Lisa was injured when a car driven by Tamera Ferguson ran into her on a parcel of Strunk property, where a high school graduation "kegger" party was being held.

Dean Strunk, the son of Charles and Thelma Strunk, was a member of the 1977 Evergreen High School graduating class. Class members planned a graduation party to follow commencement exercises on June 7, 1977. Tickets to the party were sold for $4.00 to purchase beer, food, and music. Dean made arrangements to and did buy 15 kegs of beer from a local tavern for the party with ticket proceeds. The party was originally scheduled to be held on another class member's property, but during the commencement exercises it was generally agreed that the party would be moved to the Strunk property on 109th Avenue. ...

When Dean arrived at the 109th Avenue property around 11 p.m. with the kegs, 100-400 minors were present, including graduating seniors, school mates, students from other schools, and other minors not attending school. Brad was collecting tickets, directing cars to parking areas, and advising cars' occupants of the kegs' location.

Tamera Ferguson, a minor, paid for attendance when she arrived. Lisa Younce, a minor, arrived around 11:30 p.m. with Judy Bock, who had previously bought two tickets for their admission. Lisa and Judy had had one mixed drink before arriving. They mixed another after arriving but Lisa did not drink it.

When the accident occurred, at approximately 12:15 a.m., drinking had been going on at the site for at least an hour, but the party attendees were well behaved. There had been no excessive drinking except for Dean and Tamera, who both admitted they were intoxicated from alcohol consumed at the party site. No automobile had been driven through the area where party attendees were standing. Lisa was standing in a dimly lit grassy and gravel area near the main barn and approximately 150 feet away from the kegs. Lisa was hit from behind by a Volkswagen driven by Tamera. The car hit her in the right knee and knocked her to the ground. Lisa was not under the influence of or affected by alcohol at the time she was hit. ...

Lisa ... sued the Strunks. ... Lisa's ... theory which is the basis of the entire appeal relates to the common law classifications between invitee, licensee, and trespasser and the duty of care owed by the owner or occupier of land.

The trial court found that liability on the part of the Strunks depended upon Lisa's status on the property. The court found Lisa was a social guest, and therefore only a licensee. Applying the duty of care applicable to licensees and articulated in

Restatement (Second) of Torts § 332 (1965), the trial court found the duty had not been breached. The Strunks were dismissed with prejudice. The court explained in its memorandum opinion, however, that if Lisa had been an invitee and the duty of care therefore had been one of reasonable care under all the circumstances, the court would have concluded that the Strunks had breached their duty to Lisa. ...

Lisa argues ... that ... she was incorrectly characterized as a licensee at trial. Lisa argues that she should have been characterized as an invitee under the facts of this case. Lisa's status on the property determines the standard of care owed her by the Strunks. ...

In *McKinnon v. Washington Fed. Sav. & Loan Ass'n*, 68 Wash.2d 644, 650, 414 P.2d 773 (1966), this court adopted the Restatement (Second) of Torts § 332 (1965) definition of invitee. An invitee is owed a duty of ordinary care.

Section 332 defines an invitee as follows:

> (1) An invitee is either a public invitee or a business visitor.
> (2) A public invitee is a person who is invited to enter or remain on land as a member of the public for a purpose for which the land is held open to the public.
> (3) A business visitor is a person who is invited to enter or remain on land for a purpose directly or indirectly connected with business dealings with the possessor of the land.

A licensee is defined as "a person who is privileged to enter or remain on land only by virtue of the possessor's consent." Restatement, § 330. A licensee includes a social guest, that is, a person who has been invited but does not meet the legal definition of invitee. In *Memel v. Reimer*, 85 Wash.2d 685, 689, 538 P.2d 517 (1975), this court replaced the willful and wanton misconduct standard of care toward licensees with a duty to exercise reasonable care toward licensees where there is a known dangerous condition on the property which the possessor can reasonably anticipate the licensee will not discover or will fail to realize the risks involved. *Memel* specifically adopted the standard of care for licensees outlined in Restatement, § 342:

> A possessor of land is subject to liability for physical harm caused to *licensees* by a condition on the land *if, but only if,*
> (a) the possessor knows or has reason to know of the condition and should realize that it involves an *unreasonable risk of harm* to such licensees, *and* should expect that they will not discover or realize the danger, *and*
> (b) he fails to exercise reasonable care to make the condition safe, or to warn the licensees of the condition and the risk involved, *and*
> (c) *the licensees do not know or have reason to know of the condition and the risk involved.*

(Italics ours.) *Memel*, at 689, 691, 538 P.2d 517. The possessor fulfills his duty by making the condition safe or warning of its existence.

Lisa contends that she was a member of the public on the land for a purpose for which the land is held open and therefore is an invitee. We disagree. The facts of this case do not parallel the facts of other cases where the plaintiff was found to be a public invitee. In *McKinnon*, a federal savings and loan association posted a sign saying it had meeting rooms available for public use. The plaintiff in *McKinnon* was part of a Girl Scout group using the room for Scout meetings. In *Fosbre v. State*, 70 Wash.2d

578, 424 P.2d 901 (1967), the plaintiff was injured at a recreational area on a National Guard fort. The area had been improved and maintained for use by National Guard families of which plaintiff was a member. In these "invitee" cases, "the occupier, *by his arrangement of the premises or other conduct,* has led the entrant to believe that the premises were intended to be used by visitors, as members of the public, for the purpose which the entrant was pursuing, and *that reasonable care was taken to make the place safe for those who enter for that purpose.*" (Italics ours.) *McKinnon,* 68 Wash.2d at 649, 414 P.2d 773. [Cc]

This implied assurance helps to distinguish between invitees and social guests, who are considered licensees. As explained in comment *h*(3) to Restatement, § 330: "The explanation usually given by the courts for the classification of social guests as licensees is that there is a common understanding that the guest is expected to take the premises as the possessor himself uses them, and does not expect and is not entitled to expect that they will be prepared for his reception, or that precautions will be taken for his safety, in any manner in which the possessor does not prepare or take precautions for his own safety, or that of the members of his family."

Under the facts of this case, it is hard to imagine how the Strunks could have prepared or could have been expected to prepare a dairy farm for a kegger.

We are not persuaded by Lisa's argument that payment of a $4.00 admission price made her an invitee. Analysis in cases where an admission was paid and the plaintiff was characterized as an invitee did not focus on the money as indicative of the plaintiff's status as an invitee. [Cc]

The trial court correctly identified Lisa as a licensee. She was privileged to enter or remain on the land only by virtue of the owner's consent. We question whether Charles and Thelma did consent to her presence on the property, but recognize that Dean did consent. In any event, we find the duty owed licensees was not breached because no known dangerous condition existed of which Lisa was not aware or of which she did not realize the risks involved. Lisa had knowledge of the risks involved by staying on the property. We affirm the trial court.

INQUIRY

Duty to Warn. As the above *Younce v. Ferguson* case shows, the landowner's duty toward a licensee is principally that to warn. The landowner need not exercise reasonable care to correct an unreasonably dangerous condition if the landowner instead prefers to warn. This limitation on the duty owed a licensee is what distinguishes it from the duty owed an invitee. While the landowner who expects invitees on the premises must make the premises reasonably safe for them, by contrast the landowner need only warn licensees if the land is not reasonably safe. Also, the landowner need only warn about *unreasonable* dangers—not every danger. *See* Barmore v. Elmore, 83 Ill. App.3d 1056, 38 Ill. Dec. 751, 403 N.E.2d 1355 (Ill. App. Ct. 1980) (homeowner had no duty to warn of mentally ill, adult child in the home, who stabbed licensee in the chest, where there was no apparent risk). Must the landowner inspect for conditions about which to warn? Restatement (Second) of Torts §342, set forth in the above case, states that the landowner must correct or warn as to unreasonably dangerous conditions about which the landowner "knows or has reason to know"—not requiring inspection, *see* Singleton v. Jackson, 85 Wash. App. 835, 935 P.2d 644 (Wash. Ct. App. 1997) (no duty to warn licensee home-solicitor of unknown slippery condition of outside deck), but leaving some room for constructive-notice evidence ("reason to know"). Note also that the duty to warn extends to both artificial and natural conditions but not to conditions about which the licensee knows or has reason to know. *See* Carter v. Kinney, 896 S.W.2d 926 (Mo. 1995) (no duty to warn social guest of obviously icy driveway); King v. Jackson, 302 Ark. 540, 790 S.W.2d 904 (Ark. 1990) (no duty to warn social guest not to trip over shoes left in plain sight on porch).

Skills

Although typically, torts practitioners may jury-try only a couple or few cases each year (most cases settling), tort-law practice still centers on the courts and litigation. Jury trials may be few, but frequent court hearings occur on various motions—to amend pleadings, to add parties, for discovery, to add witnesses, to schedule or adjourn matters. Find out from your professor or the local court the day and time for one of the judge's general-civil motion dockets. Then attend and observe, while considering the following practical questions: What are the attorneys wearing? What are the attorneys carrying their files in? When do the attorneys arrive? What do the attorneys do to be sure that they are on the docket? How do the attorneys get their cases in line on the docket? Have the attorneys brought their clients? Why or why not? How do the attorneys address the judge? How do the attorneys address their opposing counsel? What attitude do the attorneys exhibit toward the authority (rulings) of the judge? What attitude do the attorneys exhibit toward the argument of their opposing counsel? Where do the attorneys sit (plaintiff's counsel and defense counsel)? What are the attorneys doing while waiting for their turn on the docket? How many motions will the judge hear and decide on this docket? How does the court record those decisions? How does the judge arrive at decisions? Has the judge read the motions and briefs? How much reading was the judge required to do for this motion docket? What (if anything) did the judge refer to or read during the arguments? What was the best argument you heard? The worst? How could the advocate have improved? What was the best ruling you saw? Any with which you disagreed? What surprised you the most about the proceedings? How did the judge keep the docket moving? Did anyone waste time? At what cost? Who helped the judge in the courtroom? How? What role, if any, did humor play in any proceeding? How many of the matters were tort cases?

Public-Safety Officers. Courts have held police and firefighters to be licensees. *See* Rogers v. Cato Oil & Grease Co., 396 P.2d 1000 (Okl. 1964); James v. Cities Serv. Oil Co., 66 Ohio App. 87, 31 N.E.2d 872 (1939), affd., 140 Ohio St. 314, 23 Ohio Ops. 571, 43 N.E.2d 276 (1942). Other courts have refused to classify public-safety officers as either licensees or invitees and have instead afforded them a reasonable-care standard. Armstrong v. Mailand, 284 N.W.2d 343 (Minn. 1989); Mounsey v. Ellard, 297 N.E.2d 43 (Mass. 1973). The question is academic in states applying the firefighters rule, barring actions by professional emergency personnel for injuries in the line of duty, *see* Pinter v. American Family Mut Ins. Co., 613 N.W.2d 110 (Wis. 2000), although as indicated in a prior chapter, case law or statutes have abrogated the rule in some states. *See* Kreski v. Modern Wholesale Elec. Supply Co., 151 Mich. App. 376, 390 N.W.2d 244 (1986); Christensen v. Murphy, 296 Or. 610, 678 P.2d 1210 (1984).

3. Trespassers

The fighting issues regarding trespassers can be either their classification (if evidence shows that the landowner knew of their presence and may have impliedly consented to it) or whether an exception should apply to the no-duty rule. The circumstances are often reasonably clear whether the plaintiff had permission to be on the land, or if not clear, then at least the parties know that permission—express or implied—will be the fact issue. Trespasser of course include those entering the land as a burglar or vandal or to commit other harm. Yet trespassers may also simply walk onto the land for recreational purposes, be mistaken as to a right to enter, or even enter for the landowner's benefit but without permission. In the modern reasonable-care approach, the trespasser's motive could make a difference in whether the landowner would owe a duty—and could certainly influence jurors to treat the trespasser better or more poorly. In the categorical approach, the trespasser's reason for entry should not affect the outcome. Consider the following illustrative case.

Buzzell v. Jones
Vermont Supreme Court
151 Vt. 4, 556 A.2d 106 (1989)

ALLEN, C.J. The defendant appeals from a judgment in favor of plaintiff George Buzzell for injuries he received on defendant's land while fleeing from her dogs.

The defendant lives on a mostly wooded 100 acre parcel of land that is uninhabited except for her home. She owned two dogs, a malamute and a border collie. The former had shown no dangerous tendencies, but the latter had bitten visitors on several occasions.

The plaintiff was a county forester and went to the defendant's property at her request to inspect her woodlot in connection with a federal cost-sharing program. He accompanied defendant through a twenty-acre stand of trees and marked ones that in his opinion should be cut. He recommended that she hire a private forester to do the required work. It was understood that she would inform the plaintiff when the work was completed so that he could inspect the woodlot to certify if it qualified for the cost-sharing program.

The defendant informed the plaintiff's secretary that the work had been completed, and the plaintiff later arrived unannounced at defendant's home to inspect the work. When he was unable to find the defendant, he went alone to the woodlot. Defendant and the two dogs were in another section of the property. When the dogs discovered the plaintiff they barked and ran after him. The border collie bit his left leg and the plaintiff injured his kneecap while attempting to flee the attack. ...

Defendant's first claim is that the trial court erred in refusing to grant her requested instructions that one who exceeds the scope of a limited invitation becomes a trespasser and that a landowner owes no duty to a trespasser other than to refrain from wilfully or wantonly injuring him. The trial court instead charged that the defendant owed a duty of reasonable care to restrain her dogs and that recovery could be had for negligence defined as the want or lack of ordinary care.

Under our well-established caselaw, a landowner generally owes no duty of care to a trespasser to protect him from injury caused by unsafe and dangerous conditions on the premises. [C] The question presented for our review is whether under the evidence the plaintiff could have been considered a trespasser. One who enters the land of another by invitation is a business invitee if the purpose is one that is of interest or advantage to the occupant. [C] Limitations of place, purpose and time may be tied to the invitation, however, which, if exceeded, would prevent business invitee status or deprive the invitee of that status. [C] Thus, the owner's duty of reasonable care to an invitee extends only to those portions of the premises to which he has been invited and to which the purpose of his visit may reasonably be expected to take him. [C] Or, if he "effects an entry for purposes other than ... for which the permission was granted, or, after entering, engages in activities beyond the scope of his permission, whatever duty may be owed to him comes to an end." *Hillier[v. Noble]*, 142 Vt. [552,] 556, 458 A.2d [1101,] 1103[(1983)].

More importantly to this case, limitations of time may be imposed upon the invitation and if they are not complied with or are exceeded, one may not attain the status of an invitee. [Cc]

Plaintiff argues that his status as a business visitor should be implied from the permission originally given, particularly in light of defendant's knowledge that plaintiff would be returning to inspect the work. While one may attain the status of a business visitor without an express invitation, [c], where the invitation is express and is conditioned or limited, the conditions or limitations must be complied with before one can become a business visitor. ...

Here, the defendant's evidence was sufficient to permit the jury to find that the defendant had limited the invitation by requiring notice to her about when the plaintiff would be inspecting and that such notice was not given. There was a conflict as to the extent of the invitation given, and the court erred in instructing the jury only as to the duty of care owed to the business invitee. Because the instructions were incomplete on a critical issue material to a correct decision, we reverse and remand for a new trial. ...

INQUIRY

Exceptions. The classification of trespassers is not especially difficult. Neither is the no-duty rule for trespassers. Yet the traditional rule has exceptions in many states:

1. One exception is for *active operations*—that the landowner must exercise reasonable care in activities (such as the use of heavy machinery) that present a risk of serious harm to known trespassers. *See* Sheehan v. St. Paul & Duluth Ry. Co., 76 F. 201 (7th Cir. 1896) (no railway liability to trespasser stuck on track because peril not discovered until too late); Maldonado v. Jack M. Berry Grove Corp., 351 So.2d 967 (Fla. 1977) (landowner subject to liability for injury of trespassing child while operating hydraulic-lift machine); Restatement (Second) of Torts §§334, 336.

2. Another exception, or a corollary of the active-operations rule, is a *discovered-peril* rule—where landowners owe a duty of reasonable care once they discover a trespasser's peril. *See* Pridgen v. Boston Hous. Auth., 364 Mass. 696, 308 N.E.2d 467 (1974) (reasonable care owed to trespassing boy trapped in elevator shaft); Frederick v. Philadelphia Rapid Trans. Co., 337 Pa. 136, 10 A.2d 576 (1940) (subway liable for

failing to exercise reasonable care after plaintiff fell onto track, tripping shutoff); Restatement (Second) of Torts §§342, 343.

3. Another exception some states recognize is for known *artificial conditions* that present a *concealed risk* of harm to the trespasser—that the landowner need not exercise reasonable care to inspect for or correct those conditions but must give reasonable warning of them when known. *See* Martin v. Jones, 122 Utah 597, 253 P.2d 359 (1953); Restatement (Second) of Torts §§335, 337.

4. Another exception a court might recognize involves *tolerated intruders*, particularly where the landowner is aware that trespassers are frequently using a particular path. *See* Imre v. Riegel Paper Corp., 24 N.J. 438, 132 A.2d 505 (1957). In effect, the tolerated intruder becomes a licensee.

Can you articulate why the difference between active operations and artificial conditions? The law affords landowners much liberty to leave their lands as they please and even to do on their lands as they please—drawing the lines at active risks to known trespassers and known concealed risks. Are these the two most compelling situations warranting care toward the trespasser? Do care and warning satisfy whatever hidden concern compels these limited duties? Consider the following case.

Salaman v. City of Waterbury
Connecticut Supreme Court
717 A.2d 161 (Conn. 1998)

McDONALD, J. The named defendant,[fn] the city of Waterbury (city), appeals from the Appellate Court's decision reversing the trial court's judgment granting the city's motion for judgment notwithstanding the verdict. [C] ... We reverse the judgment of the Appellate Court.

The plaintiff, Julio Salaman, administrator of the estate of his decedent, Jaime C. Salaman, brought an action against the city in three counts: nuisance, custodial negligence[fn] and premises liability negligence. The jury reasonably could have found the following facts. The plaintiff's decedent drowned while attempting to swim across the East Mountain Reservoir (reservoir) in Waterbury on September 2, 1991. Approximately halfway across the reservoir, he experienced difficulty swimming and called for help. Two people tried to rescue the decedent, but were unsuccessful.

At the time of his death, the decedent was part of a group of people from the defendant New Opportunities for Waterbury, Inc. (NOW), a residential counseling program. Following a picnic and a basketball game, the group, supervised by the defendant Michael Trotman, a residential supervisor employed by NOW, had traveled by van to the reservoir to swim. The reservoir, which was owned by the city, was not surrounded by a fence. There was an area to the side of the access road that was used for parking, and a trail that led to the water. The reservoir had not been used as a public water supply for more than thirty years, and the city allowed fishing with a permit. On occasion, some people may have used the reservoir for swimming. The city, however, did not permit swimming in the reservoir. There were no lifeguards or lifesaving equipment at the reservoir. There were several old signs posted on the reservoir property which read: "City of Waterbury, No Trespassing, Public Water Supply." There were no such signs in the parking area, on any of the trails or at the beach area. The decedent, a twenty-two year old former high school athlete, was an excellent swimmer who had been swimming since childhood. [C] ...

In its charge to the jury, the trial court, after explaining the status of a trespasser on a landowner's property, stated: "Therefore, if you find that the plaintiff's decedent, Jaime Salaman, was a trespasser upon the reservoir property, then you must further find the defendant city of Waterbury owed no duty to [him]. If you find no duty, then you must return a verdict in favor of the defendant city...." ...

The jury returned a verdict in favor of the plaintiff, allocating comparative negligence as follows: the city, 28 percent; NOW and Trotman, 57 percent; and the plaintiff's decedent, 15 percent. The jury awarded total damages of $1,226,264.60, and the city's allocation amounted to $343,354.08. [C]

Thereafter, the trial court granted the city's motions to set aside the verdict and for judgment notwithstanding the verdict, concluding that the evidence was insufficient to impose liability on the city. ...

The Appellate Court reversed the trial court's judgment, concluding that the jury could have found that the decedent was a licensee because the jury reasonably could have inferred that the city had constructive knowledge of the general public's use of the reservoir for swimming. The Appellate Court concluded that this constructive knowledge gave rise to the duty "to exercise reasonable care to warn ... of conditions posing an unreasonable risk of harm." [C] On the basis of that conclusion, the Appellate Court further concluded that the verdict should not have been set aside. [C] ...

The status of an entrant on another's land, be it trespasser, licensee or invitee, determines the duty that is owed to the entrant while he or she is on a landowner's property. [C] In this case, the jury was properly instructed as to the city's duty to the decedent if he was either a trespasser or a licensee. If the decedent was a trespasser, the city's only duty was to refrain from causing him injury "intentionally, or by willful, wanton or reckless conduct." [C] It is undisputed that the city did not intentionally or recklessly injure the decedent and the trial court was correct in its instructions. Therefore, as the Appellate Court observed, the jury must have concluded that the decedent was a licensee or it could not have imposed liability on the city. [C] ...

We now turn to the issue of whether the trial court could have granted the city's motion for judgment notwithstanding the verdict. We conclude that the trial court's action was proper. ...

... The plaintiff had introduced some evidence that people were swimming in the reservoir, which was relevant to both licensee and trespasser status. [Cc] The motion for directed verdict, based on the decedent's status as a trespasser, therefore, addressed the issue of sufficiency of the evidence to support a verdict based on licensee status. We conclude, therefore, that the trial court and the plaintiff were given adequate notice of the city's claim that there was insufficient evidence that the decedent was other than a trespasser and thereby could be considered a licensee. We conclude that the trial court properly could have granted the motion upon the ground on which it relied. ...

The judgment of the Appellate Court is reversed and the case is remanded to that court with direction to affirm the judgment of the trial court.

> **Figure**
> Robin Conrad is the executive vice president of the National Chamber Litigation Center in Washington, D.C.—the public policy arm of the three-million-member business federation the U.S. Chamber of Commerce. The Supreme Court and eleven of the nation's federal appellate courts have admitted her to practice. Ms. Conrad has filed amicus briefs in every Supreme Court punitive-damages case since 1989, many mass-tort class-action cases, and other major tort cases relating to business all over the nation. She has also represented the Chamber as lead petitioner in two Supreme Court cases involving air-quality standards and corporate speech. Her responsibilities include developing and implementing strategies to shape the law in ways favorable to United States businesses, through Supreme Court decisions on punitive damages, class actions, federal preemption, and securities litigation. Ms. Conrad and her husband and son live on a horse farm in Maryland.

4. Children

Premises-liability law sometimes affords children special protection that it does not afford to adults. Law does so under two alternative formulations. The traditional formulation is that landowners owe children of *tender years* (those unable to appreciate safety risks) a duty of reasonable care with respect to an *attractive nuisance* (an unreasonably dangerous condition that would attract children) on the land. *See* Sioux City & Pac. R. Co. v. Stout, 84 U.S. (17 Wall.) 657 (1873). The modern formulation of the rule, resting on foreseeability and risk/burden considerations, rejects the attractive-nuisance and tender-years labels to consider instead the landowner's knowledge of the likelihood of harm to trespassing children who would not recognize the risk of serious injury from a condition having too little utility. *See* Restatement (Second) of Torts §339. The difference may be that the modern formulation would permit recovery by a child whom a dangerous condition did not attract but one that injured the child. *Contrast* McGettigan v. Natl. Bank of Washington, 320 F.2d 703 (D.C. Cir. 1963) (recovery by trespassing boy injured by flare found on defendant's land), *with* Carroll v. Jagoe Homes, 677 N.E.2d 612 (Ind. Ct. App. 1997) (no recovery by trespassing boy injured on construction site that had not allured boy—rejecting *Restatement* view). In either case, the plaintiff must show that the landowner should have anticipated that children would come onto the premises where they would experience an unreasonable danger of serious harm. *See* Goll v. Muscara, 211 Pa. Super. 93, 235 A.2d 443 (1967).

When neither common-law formulation supplies a duty, legislative enactment may do so. *See* Johnson v. Harris, 530 P2d 1136 (Ariz. Ct. App. 1975) (pool-fence ordinance establishes duty and violation its breach); *but see* Osterman v. Peters, 272 A.2d 21 (Md. 1971) (pool-fence ordinance does not establish duty to trespassers). The common-law duty arises only when the child is so young as not to appreciate the hazard. *See* Racine v. Moon's Towing, 817 So.2d 21 (La. 2002) (attractive-nuisance doctrine not available to 14- and 15-year-olds); Texas Utils. Elec. Co. v. Timmons, 947 S.W.2d 191 (Tex. 1997) (teenager too old not to appreciate risk of electric lines); Hollis v. Norfolk Southern Rwy. Co., 667 So.2d 727 (Ala. 1995) (teenager too old not to appreciate risk of falling from cliff). Although the tender-years doctrine has been around for quite a while, it does not garner uniform approval. *See* United Zinc & Chem. Co. v. Britt, 258 U.S. 268 (1922) (Holmes, J.) (reversing verdict for estate of two trespassing children who were poisoned in defendant's industrial-land waters). A trend may exist moving from traditional toward modern rules. Yet the traditional attractive-nuisance rule has continuing vitality. Consider the following extraordinary recent case adopting the attractive-nuisance formulation.

Bennett v. Stanley
Ohio Supreme Court
92 Ohio St.3d 35, 748 N.E.2d 41 (2001)

PFEIFER, J. In this case we are called upon to determine what level of duty a property owner owes to a child trespasser. We resolve the question by adopting the attractive nuisance doctrine set forth in Restatement of the Law 2d, Torts (1965), Section 339. ...

When Rickey G. Bennett, plaintiff-appellant, arrived home in the late afternoon of March 20, 1997, he found his two young daughters crying. The three-year-old, Kyleigh, told him that "Mommy" and Chance, her five-year-old half-brother, were "drowning in the water." Bennett ran next door to his neighbors' house to find mother and son unconscious in the swimming pool. Both died.

The Bennetts had moved next door to defendants-appellees, Jeffrey and Stacey Stanley, in the fall of 1996. The Stanleys had purchased their home the previous June. At the time of their purchase, the Stanleys' property included a swimming pool that had gone unused for three years. At that time, the pool was enclosed with fencing and a brick wall. After moving in, the Stanleys drained the pool once but thereafter they allowed rainwater to accumulate in the pool to a depth of over six feet. They removed a tarp that had been on the pool and also removed the fencing that had been around two sides of the pool. The pool became pond-like: it contained tadpoles and frogs, and Mr. Stanley had seen a snake swimming on the surface. The pool contained no ladders, and its sides were slimy with algae.

... The Bennetts rented the house next to the Stanleys. The houses were about one hundred feet apart. There was some fencing with an eight-foot gap between the two properties.

The Stanleys were aware that the Bennetts had moved next door and that they had young children. They had seen the children outside unsupervised. Stacey Stanley had once called Chance onto her property to retrieve a dog. The Stanleys testified, however, that they never had any concern about the children getting into the pool. ...
Kyleigh told her father that she and Chance had been playing at the pool on the afternoon of the tragedy. The sheriff's department concluded that Chance had gone to the pool to look at the frogs and somehow fell into the pool. His mother apparently drowned trying to save him. ...

Appellees filed a motion for summary judgment, which the trial court granted on September 4, 1998. The trial court found that Chance and Cher were trespassers on appellees' property and that appellees therefore owed them only a duty to refrain from wanton and willful misconduct. ...

Ohio has long recognized a range of duties for property owners vis-à-vis persons entering their property. ... Today, we face the issue of whether child trespassers should become another class of users who are owed a different duty of care.

This court has consistently held that children have a special status in tort law and that duties of care owed to children are different from duties owed to adults: "[T]he amount of care required to discharge a duty owed to a child of tender years is necessarily greater than that required to discharge a duty owed to an adult under the same circumstances. This is the approach long followed by this court and we see no reason to abandon it. 'Children of tender years, and youthful persons generally, are entitled to a degree of care proportioned to their inability to foresee and avoid the perils that they may encounter. * * * The same discernment and foresight in discovering defects and dangers cannot be reasonably expected of them, that older and experienced persons habitually employ; and therefore the greater precaution should be taken, where children are exposed to them.'" *Di Gildo v. Caponi* (1969), 18 Ohio St.2d 125, 127, 47 O.O.2d 282, 283, 247 N.E.2d 732, 734, [c]. ...

Despite the fact that in premises liability cases a landowner's duty is defined by the status of the plaintiff, and that children, even child trespassers, are accorded special protection in Ohio tort law, this court has never adopted the attractive nuisance doctrine. The doctrine as adopted by numerous states is set forth in Restatement of the Law 2d, Torts (1965), Section 339:

"A possessor of land is subject to liability for physical harm to children trespassing thereon caused by an artificial condition upon land if:

"(a) the place where the condition exists is one upon which the possessor knows or has reason to know that children are likely to trespass, and

"(b) the condition is one of which the possessor knows or has reason to know and which he realizes or should realize will involve an unreasonable risk of death or serious bodily harm to such children, and

"(c) the children because of their youth do not discover the condition or realize the risk involved in intermeddling with it or in coming within the area made dangerous by it, and

"(d) the utility to the possessor of maintaining the condition and the burden of eliminating the danger are slight as compared with the risk to children involved, and

"(e) the possessor fails to exercise reasonable care to eliminate the danger or otherwise to protect the children." ...

Adopting the attractive nuisance doctrine would be merely an incremental change in Ohio law, not out of line with the law that has developed over time. It is an appropriate evolution of the common law. ...

We therefore use this case to adopt the attractive nuisance doctrine contained in Restatement of the Law 2d, Torts (1965), Section 339. In doing so, we do not abandon the differences in duty a landowner owes to the different classes of users. In this case we simply further recognize that children are entitled to a greater level of protection than adults are. ...

The Restatement's version of the attractive nuisance doctrine balances society's interest in protecting children with the rights of landowners to enjoy their property. Even when a landowner is found to have an attractive nuisance on his or her land, the landowner is left merely with the burden of acting with ordinary care. A landowner does not automatically become liable for any injury a child trespasser may suffer on that land. ...

The requirement of foreseeability is built into the doctrine. The landowner must know or have reason to know that children are likely to trespass upon the part of the property that contains the dangerous condition. See Section 339(a). Moreover, the landowner's duty "does not extend to those conditions the existence of which is obvious even to children and the risk of which should be fully realized by them." *Id.* at Comment *i*. Also, if the condition of the property that poses the risk is essential to the landowner, the doctrine would not apply: "The public interest in the possessor's free use of his land for his own purposes is of great significance. A particular condition is, therefore, regarded as not involving unreasonable risk to trespassing children unless it involves a grave risk to them which could be obviated without any serious interference with the possessor's legitimate use of his land." *Id.* at Comment *n*.

We are satisfied that the Restatement view effectively harmonizes the competing societal interests of protecting children and preserving property rights. In adopting the attractive nuisance doctrine, we acknowledge that the way we live now is different from the way we lived in 1907, when *Harvey* was decided. We are not a rural society any longer, our neighbors live closer, and our use of our own property affects others more than it once did.

Despite our societal changes, children are still children. They still learn through their curiosity. They still have developing senses of judgment. They still do not always appreciate danger. They still need protection by adults. Protecting children in a changing world requires the common law to adapt. Today, we make that change. …

Judgment reversed and cause remanded.

Skills

How can lawyers dispel negative attitudes about the tort system? Tort lawyers face that question when selecting jurors, a process called *jury voir dire*. The trial judge typically allows the lawyers to ask questions of the jury panel and individual jurors. The judge then asks whether the lawyers have challenges for cause. Cause challenges have to do with personal knowledge or biases that would interfere with a juror's ability to decide fairly. The judge then allows the lawyers to exercise peremptory challenges to remove up to three jurors (in civil cases) without cause. Jury voir dire is not simply about picking jurors. It is also about educating them—reminding them of rights and duties that are important to justice. Jury voir dire is also the jurors' only substantial opportunity to speak in the courtroom (other than through their verdict), making especially important that lawyers listen and follow up on juror answers. Some judges require lawyers to submit written questions in advance. Below is an example. How helpful do you think the questions are to help the jurors understand the tort system?

[case caption]

PLAINTIFF'S PROPOSED JURY VOIR DIRE

Plaintiff Robert Roe proposes the following jury voir dire:

1. My purpose in speaking with you is to get at the truth about how you feel about lawsuits in general and certain things which may come up in this lawsuit in particular. I want to be sure that you will be fair to my client Mr. Roe. If you were in Mr. Roe's place, looking to strangers to bring him justice, would you want to have a fair jury?

2. Will you be sure to tell me especially those views you hold, which you think I would not want to hear? In other words, do not just tell me what you think I want to hear.

3. Mr. Roe asked me to file this lawsuit. Does that create a bad taste in your mouth? Do you think, "Well, I don't like people who file lawsuits"? Or do you feel that lawsuits are

sometimes necessary to right a wrong? Can you think of an example when a lawsuit put right a wrong? Do you think that lawsuits sometimes make things right?

4. Mr. Roe had me file this lawsuit against the retailer EZ-Mart, where he was injured. Do you shop at EZ-Mart? Do you own any stock in EZ-Mart? So if you awarded what Mr. Roe asked in this case, which may be as much as $100,000, do you think that it would affect you in any way?

5. Do you believe that a retailer like EZ-Mart is capable of doing something wrong? Can you think of an example of a retailer engaging in an illegal or dangerous practice? If a retailer caused you harm that cost you hundreds or even thousands of dollars, would you hesitate to file a lawsuit if it refused to pay what the law said it is supposed to pay?

6. Have you ever made a claim? Even for health benefits? If a company refuses to pay an honest claim that it should have paid, costing you hundreds or thousands of dollars, would you hesitate to file a lawsuit?

7. How important do you think juries are to keeping businesses safe and honest? Can you think of an example when a company was doing something illegal or unsafe but a jury held them accountable for it? Would you want a jury of your peers to decide your case, if a serious wrong was done to you that needed to be addressed?

8. How important do you think the military and the police are to keeping our country free and orderly? How important do you think this civil justice system is, where people can bring their claims against companies they believe are doing something harmful? Do you think that this civil justice system, like the military and law enforcement, helps preserve our liberty and order? Can you think of a better way to resolve civil disputes?

9. If you had a day in court to prove something very important to you, like a company's responsibility to pay for your injury because of their unsafe practices or violation of the law, what kind of juror would you want? Can you be that kind of juror?

10. Although I do not advertise on television, as a lawyer I do help individuals who need help. Do you have something against lawyers like me, who help those who are financially in need or who are wronged or oppressed by companies? Do you think you would need to hire a lawyer like me if you had to come to court for civil justice?

11. We have a tort law that a shopkeeper like EZ-Mart must reasonably inspect and maintain its premises to keep them reasonably safe. Will you under any circumstances follow the law as Judge Ricks instructs you to follow it?

[signature block]

C. Off the Premises

Landowners face one other potential responsibility, to those who are merely passing by the land but may be injured by some condition on it. The case below illustrates one of the more common examples, that of something on the land obstructing the vision of passerby vehicle drivers. Trees falling from the land, and golf balls and baseballs flying from the land, may also injure passers-by. *See* Akins v. Glens Falls City Sch. Dist., 53 N.Y.2d 325, 441 N.Y.S.2d 644, 424 N.E.2d 531 (1981) (reasonable care requires ballpark proprietor only to screen behind home plate); Salevan v. Wilmington Park, Inc., 45 Del. (6 Terry) 290, 72 A.2d 239 (Sup. Ct. 1950) (liability for injury from one of 16 to 18 foul balls hit out of park onto abutting street each game). Conditions on the land may also affect the flow or accumulation of water, *see* Middlesex County v. McCue, 149 Mass. 103, 21 N.E. 230 (1889), snow and ice, *see* Norville v. Hub Furniture Co., 59 App. D.C. 29, 32 F.2d 420 (1929), or blowing sand, *see* Ettl v. Land & Loan Co., 122 N.J.L. 401, 5 A.2d 689 (1939), on adjacent roadways and premises. One rule in these cases is that the landowner owes no duties to passers-by for natural conditions on the land but must exercise reasonable care with respect to artificial conditions. *See* Adlington v. Viroqua, 155 Wis. 472, 144 N.W. 1130 (1914) (landowner liable for slip-and-fall injury from discharge of freezing water onto abutting sidewalk). Other courts have extended a duty of reasonable care to all conditions, whether natural or artificial. *See* Sprecher v. Adamson Cos., 30 Cal.3d 358, 178 Cal. Rptr. 783, 636 P.2d 1121 (Cal. 1981) (uphill landowner owes duty to protect downhill landowners from mudslides). The Restatement (Third) of Torts: Liability for Physical and Emotional Harm §54 (Tentative Draft No. 6, 2009) takes a mixed approach that recognizes but modifies the natural-artificial distinction:

(a) For artificial conditions or conduct on land that pose a risk of physical harm to persons or property not on the land, the possessor of the land has a duty of reasonable care.
(b) For natural conditions on land that pose a risk of physical harm to persons or property not on the land, the possessor of the land
(1) has a duty of reasonable care if the land is commercial; and
(2) otherwise has a duty of reasonable care only if the possessor knows of the risk or if the risk is obvious.
(c) Unless Subsection (b) applies, a possessor of land adjacent to a public walkway has no duty under this Chapter with regard to a risk posed by the condition of the walkway to pedestrians or others if the land possessor did not create the risk.

As you read the following case, consider how workable the natural-artificial distinction is and whether it succeeds in distinguishing between acts and omissions.

Spears v. Blackwell
Indiana Court of Appeals
666 N.E.2d 974 (Ind. Ct. App. 1996)

BARTEAU, J. Tim W. Spears and Kim Spears ("Spearses") appeal the trial court's granting of Gale Blackwell and Toni Blackwell's ("Blackwells") Motion for Summary Judgment, raising several issues on appeal. ...

We reverse and remand. ...

In the afternoon of June 14, 1991, Tim Spears was driving his car in a southerly direction on Ladoga Road in Montgomery County, Indiana. The Blackwells owned six acres of real estate ("Property") abutting the west side of Ladoga Road, including a house located approximately 500 feet from Ladoga Road. The Property was in a rural area, with farmers' fields in the immediate area.

... [Stacey] Brier was driving her car in an easterly direction down the Blackwells' driveway to leave the Property. ... At the end of the driveway, Brier stopped her car and looked both ways before proceeding onto Ladoga Road. Due to the height of the vegetation, described as weeds, growing on the area of raised land, Brier was unable to see if any vehicles were approaching, so she had to roll down her window to listen for oncoming vehicles. Neither Brier nor Tim Spears saw each other's car as Brier entered onto Ladoga Road, at which point Tim Spears's car struck the side of Brier's car. Tim Spears sustained various injuries from the accident. ...

The key issue is whether the Blackwells, as owners of the realty in a rural area, owed Tim Spears, as a user of the public thoroughfare of Ladoga Road, a duty of care to maintain the vegetation in a way that protected him from harm that could result from the condition of the vegetation.

The Spearses' claim is a negligence action. To prevail in a negligence action, the plaintiff must prove the elements of a cause of action for negligence, being: (1) defendants' duty to conform their conduct to a standard of care arising from their relationship with the plaintiff; (2) breach of that duty; and (3) injury to the plaintiff resulting from that breach. [C] Here, we are asked to address the issue of whether a duty exists. …

Generally, an owner of realty does not owe a duty to passersby using an adjacent public thoroughfare to protect them from harm that could result from natural conditions of the land. [C] Conversely, such a duty is owed regarding an artificial condition of the land about which the landowner knew or should have known. [Cc]

The trial court granted summary judgment because it determined that the vegetation was a natural condition. The Spearses contend that the trial court erred when it determined that the vegetation was a natural condition, contending that the issue of whether the vegetation was a natural or an artificial condition is a genuine issue of material fact.[fn] We agree.

The Restatement defines natural conditions as land that was not changed by any acts of humans, including the possessor or any predecessors in interest. Restatement (Second) of Torts § 363 cmt. b (1965).[fn] Natural conditions also include the natural growth of vegetation, such as weeds, on land that is not artificially made receptive to them. *Id.* Also, vegetation that humans plant is non-natural despite whether they are inherently harmful or become so only because of subsequent changes due to natural forces. *Id.* Additionally, the Restatement defines "natural condition" of land to be "a condition that is not in any way the result of human activity." Restatement (Second) of Torts § 840 cmt. a (1979). "Natural condition" includes "soil that has not been cultivated, graded or otherwise disturbed." *Id.* Vegetation is not considered a "natural condition" if it "grows on land only because it has been plowed," even if no one planted or cultivated the vegetation. *Id.*

The vegetation on the raised area is described as having been tall weeds at the time of the accident. Before the Blackwells' ownership of the property, the owners of the property had planted juniper shrubs and a rock garden in the area where the vegetation was growing. Evidence of this rock and juniper garden was still present in August of 1993 when a large amount of rock and dirt was removed from the area where the vegetation was growing.[fn] Also, a corn field existed in the vicinity of the raised area when the Blackwells first acquired the property. And, on at least one occasion before the accident, the Blackwells mowed the area of the vegetation.[fn]

The Spearses presented evidence from which a reasonable trier of fact could determine that the vegetation was not a natural condition. This created a genuine issue of material fact precluding summary judgment. [Cc] We reverse the entry of summary judgment and remand this case to the trial court.

Reversed.

INQUIRY

Trees. Trees are natural conditions (when not cultivated, *cf.* Coates v. Chinn, 51 Cal.2d 304, 332 P.2d 289 (1958)) that can carry with them some considerable and foreseeable risks to travelers. Should the law treat trees differently than other natural conditions? *See* Meyers v. Delaney, 529 N.W.2d 288 (Iowa 1995) (no duty to discover natural rot in tree branch that fell on neighbor's property). Many courts have followed an urban/rural distinction, requiring owners of urban land, on which trees are less—and passers-by more—common, to reasonably inspect for rot and other weakness and to take reasonable precautions to prevent trees and limbs from falling, striking passers-by, and presenting obstacles to passing vehicles. *See* O'Brien v. United States, 275 F.2d 696 (9th Cir. 1960); Staples v. Duell, 494 S.E.2d 639 (S.C. Ct. App. 1997) (rural landowner has no duty to inspect trees); Valinet v. Eskew, 574 N.E.2d 283 (Ind. Ct. App. 1991) (urban landowner has duty to inspect trees for decay threatening passing motorists). Others reject any categorical distinction in favor of a straightforward duty of reasonable care. *See* Taylor v. Olsen, 282 Or. 348, 578 P.2d 779 (1978) (affirming dismissal of claim for tree falling across road, in absence of discoverable decay). Others require that the landowner know that the tree is defective before imposing a duty of reasonable care. *See* Lewis v. Krussel, 101 Wash. App. 178, 2 P.3d 486 (2000); Plesko v. Allied inv. Co., 12 Wis.2d 168, 107 N.W.2d 201 (1961). The rare court will extend a tree-inspection duty even to rural, not just urban, lands. *See* Valinet v. Eskew, 557 N.E.2d 702 (Ind. Ct. App. 1990) (rural landowner liable to passing motorist for injury from falling tree). The Restatement (Second) of Torts §363, Comment *e* (1965), suggests a duty should exist only "where traffic is relatively frequent, land is less heavily wooded, and acreage is small." If an adjoining landowner has the property right to cut off tree branches or roots that intrude from the neighboring land, so as to prevent injury or property damage, how should that affect liability? *See* Melnick v. C.S.X. Corp., 68 Md. App. 107, 510 A.2d 592 (1986) (self-help right is only remedy regarding trees without decay).

Ethics

Occasionally, a tort lawyer will meet the opposing party or, if the opposing party is a corporate entity, the opposing party's employees, without opposing counsel being present. It may happen at a social event. It may happen when counsel and witnesses appear for office depositions or court hearings before opposing counsel arrives. An opposing party or employee may attempt to contact the tort lawyer with information that the opposing party or employee feels that the lawyer needs to know. Rule 4.2 of the ABA Model Rules of Professional Conduct prohibits a lawyer from communicating about the matter with a person whom another lawyer represents, unless the other lawyer consents. Significantly, the privilege belongs to the opposing lawyer, not the opposing party. Small talk about sports or the weather may be acceptable. Talk about the case must await opposing counsel's arrival.

Sidewalks. How does premises liability law treat city-sidewalk injuries? City liability depends first on the state's governmental-immunity law (whether case law or statutory). *See* Mich. Comp. L. §§691.1401(e), 691.1402(1) (waiving governmental immunity for sidewalk defects). If a municipality is not immune and is instead subject to liability for negligently maintained sidewalks, then the statutes or courts will typically require that the plaintiff prove notice to the municipality of the defect before the injury. *See* Mich. Comp. L. §691.1402a(1)(a) (municipality liable only if it knew or should have known of defect for 30 days before injury). Case law or statute may also impose substantive conditions regarding the size or nature of the defect. *See* Mich. Comp. L. §691.1402a(2) (imposing minimum two-inch discontinuity-defect rule like that of prior common law). Some municipalities provide by ordinance for the abutting landowner to share or assume the municipality's sidewalk-injury liability. *See* New York City Code §§7-210, 7-211, 7-212. Courts have also occasionally held landowners to have a duty of reasonable care with respect to maintaining municipal sidewalks and signs abutting their property. *See* Monaco v. Hartz Mtn. Corp., 178 N.J. 401, 840 A.2d 822 (2004); Cogliati v. Ecco High Frequency Corp., 92 N.J. 402, 456 A.2d 524 (1983); Moeller v. Fleming, 136 Cal. App.3d 241, 186 Cal. Rptr. 24 (1982) (landowner liable for trip from tree root breaking abutting sidewalk).

Career

Law firms can make a difference to your finding employment and succeeding in tort practice. Each firm has its own culture and practice models. Some firms provide substantial professional-development opportunities for their lawyers, such as conferences, seminars, in-house trainings, and formal mentors. Others do not. Tort-law expertise can take years to fully develop. Professional-development opportunities, such as the chance to attend a national conference on tort law, accelerate that development. Some firms encourage bar and pro-bono service in ways that enhance the careers and career satisfaction of their lawyers. Others do not. Bar and pro-bono service can quickly enhance torts-practice expertise, broadening one's contacts, knowledge, interpersonal skills, and torts-practice areas. Study firms in the geographic area where you want to practice. Look for opportunities that will enhance your career and career satisfaction.

Chapter IX

Negligence—Defenses

The plaintiff's ability to prove the elements of a tort claim does not guarantee a recovery. To accommodate a range of other policies and interests not adequately reflected in the elements of a tort cause of action, tort law allows defendants to plead and prove any number of affirmative defenses. The modifier *affirmative* may seem redundant to the basic concept that the defendant may yet be able to defend a prima-facie claim that the plaintiff establishes. Affirmative connotes the defendant's responsibility to positively plead those defenses in the defendant's answer in the tort action, come forward with evidence that the circumstances supporting the defenses exist, and satisfy the burden of proof on those defenses. Practitioners might commonly plead no duty and no breach (for instance) as a defense to an action. Yet using terms and proof burdens properly, the law would instead provide that the plaintiff has no claim in those instances. When a court rule or case addresses *affirmative defenses*, the matter involves theories on which the defendant has the burdens of pleading, production, and proof. As the following sections show, defenses can involve the plaintiff's conduct before or after the incident, the plaintiff's or defendant's status, the relationship of the parties, or matters of procedure including how much time passed before plaintiff filed the action or notified of the claim.

A. Contributory or Comparative Negligence

Objective: Given a negligence claim, identify the plaintiff's standard of care, evaluate the evidence of the plaintiff's breach of that standard, and compare and contrast how the defendant's liability and plaintiff's recovery would be affected under the doctrines of contributory and comparative negligence, consistent with this section.

Case Study: A hunter stepped outside his cabin with his rifle to walk down a lane for a few minutes in the plain clothes he happened to be wearing. Another hunter on an overlooking ridge, who had just seen two does walk down the lane, was sure that a buck would follow. He fired at and hit what he thought was a good-sized buck but turned out to be the other hunter. ***Evaluate the effect of each hunter's negligence under the doctrines of contributory and comparative negligence.***

Contributory Negligence. A common defense at issue in many negligence cases has to do with the plaintiff's own conduct. If the plaintiff can examine the defendant's conduct to complain of the defendant's negligence in bringing about the harm, then the law should permit the defendant to examine the plaintiff's conduct to see to what extent it may have constituted negligence contributing to the harm. The traditional defense of the plaintiff's *contributory negligence*, retained in only a small minority of four states plus the District of Columbia, is that the plaintiff's negligence bars the plaintiff's claim completely. Under the defense of contributory negligence, if the plaintiff negligently caused the plaintiff's own harm in any part, then the plaintiff would have no recovery from the defendant for any portion of plaintiff's damages. The early English case of Butterfield v. Forrester, 11 East 59, 103 Eng. Rep. 926 (King's Bench 1809), took that approach. Although the defendant was negligent in leaving a pole across the road while repairing his house, the plaintiff was contributorily negligent and his claim barred for riding his horse violently into the pole when it should have been visible from far enough away to avoid it. Policies supporting the defense are penal (in punishment of the plaintiff), equitable (that the plaintiff must come to court with clean hands), and economic (that allowing negligent plaintiffs to recover dilutes incentive to self-care and increases system costs). The defendant has the burden of proof on contributory negligence. *See* Brown v. Piggly-Wiggly Stores, 454 So.2d 1370 (Ala. 1984). Consider the following illustrative case.

Poyner v. Loftus
District of Columbia Court of Appeals
694 A.2d 69 (D.C. 1997)

SCHWELB, J. This action for personal injuries was brought by William J. Poyner, who is legally blind, after he fell from an elevated walkway. The trial judge granted summary judgment in favor of the defendants, concluding that Mr. Poyner was contributorily negligent as a matter of law. On appeal, Mr. Poyner contends that, in light of his handicap, a genuine issue of material fact existed as to whether he exercised reasonable care, and that the entry of summary judgment was therefore erroneous. We affirm. …

… Mr. Poyner suffers from glaucoma and retrobulbar neuritis. He testified that he is able to see approximately six to eight feet in front of him. Notwithstanding his handicap, Mr. Poyner does not use a cane or a seeing eye dog in pursuing his daily activities.

On August 24, 1993, Mr. Poyner was proceeding from his home to Parklane Cleaners, a dry cleaning establishment located on the west side of the 4300 block of Connecticut Avenue, N.W. in Washington, D.C. The entrance to Parklane Cleaners is adjacent to an inclined platform which is located approximately four feet above street level. Mr. Poyner testified that he had walked by the area on three or four previous occasions, and that he was aware of the general layout. He stated that there were bushes along the edge of the platform, and that these bushes provided a natural barrier which would prevent him from falling if he attempted to walk too far. On the day of the accident, however, and unbeknownst to Mr. Poyner, one of the bushes was missing, and there was thus nothing to restrain him from falling off the platform.

Mr. Poyner testified that as he was walking along the elevated area, he heard someone call "Billy!" from Connecticut Avenue. He turned his head to the right, but continued to walk forward to the location at the end of the platform where he thought that a bush would be. There was no bush, however, and Mr. Poyner fell, suffering personal injuries. ...

Ordinarily, questions of negligence and contributory negligence must be decided by the trier of fact. [C] A party asserting the defense of contributory negligence is required to establish, by a preponderance of the evidence, that the plaintiff failed to exercise reasonable care. [C] ... The issue of contributory negligence should not be submitted to the jury, however, where the evidence, taken in the light most favorable to the plaintiff, establishes contributory negligence so clearly that no other inference can reasonably be drawn. [C]

The trial judge concluded that this was one of those rare cases in which contributory negligence—a defense with respect to which the defendants had the burden of proof—had been established as a matter of law. We agree. Indeed, we are satisfied, as was the trial judge, that Mr. Poyner's own testimony established that he did not exercise reasonable care and that his own contributory negligence proximately caused the accident.

It is undisputed that, at the time of the accident, a shrub at the end of the elevated platform was missing. A photograph which is a part of the record demonstrates that this was readily apparent, at least to any sighted person who chose to look. "[A] person must see what is reasonably there to be seen." *Jackson v. Schenick*, 174 A.2d 353, 355 (D.C.1961) (citation omitted). ... In this case, Mr. Poyner acknowledged that his attention was distracted when someone called his name, and that he turned his head to the right, but continued to walk forward. At the critical moment, according to his own testimony, Mr. Poyner, who could see six to eight feet in front of him and was aware of his handicap, did not look where he was going. We agree with the trial judge that this constituted contributory negligence and that no impartial jury could reasonably find otherwise. ...

Mr. Poyner argues, however, that he is not a sighted person, and that "it is reasonable *for a legally blind person* ... as a response to his name being called, [to] turn towards the direction of his caller, reach for the handle and continue his step towards the door." (Emphasis added.) He claims that those actions "do not constitute contributory negligence." He contends, in other words, that on account of his visual impairment, his conduct should be tested against a different standard of care.

... "It seems to be the general rule that a blind or otherwise handicapped person, in using the public ways, must exercise for his own safety due care, or care commensurate with the known or reasonably foreseeable dangers. Due care is such care as an ordinarily prudent person with the same disability would exercise under the same or similar circumstances." *Cook v. City of Winston-Salem*, 241 N.C. 422, 85 S.E.2d 696, 700-01 (1955) (citing, *inter alia, Keith v. Worcester & Blackstone Valley St. Ry. Co.*, 196 Mass. 478, 82 N.E. 680 (1907)). As the court explained in *Keith*, however, "it is also correct to say that in the exercise of common prudence one of defective eyesight must usually as a matter of general knowledge take more care and employ keener watchfulness in walking upon the streets and avoiding obstructions than the same person with good eyesight, in order to reach the standard established by the law for all persons alike, whether they be weak or strong, sound or deficient." *Id.*, 82 N.E. at 681; [c]. ...

... [T]he plaintiff was walking alone, and he did not use a guide dog or a cane. As a result, he fell from the walkway. ... Mr. Poyner, who could see six to eight feet in front of him, acknowledged that, at the moment that he fell, he was not looking where he was going. ...

... Mr. Poyner was alone, and he used neither a cane nor a seeing eye dog. He also looked away at the critical moment. Under these circumstances, he was contributorily negligent as a matter of law, and summary judgment was properly granted.

Affirmed.

INQUIRY

Ameliorating Doctrines. In familiar tort-law pattern, courts have used other rules and doctrines to soften the all-or-nothing harshness of the contributory-negligence defense. One approach has been to allow juries to nullify the harsh workings of contributory negligence even in cases that would seem to require the reasonable juror to find at least some fault on the part of the plaintiff. *See* Paraskevaides v. Four Seasons Washington, 292 F.3d 886 (D.C. Cir. 2002) (plaintiff hotel guest fails to place jewelry worth $1.2 million in hotel's safe deposit box); Baltimore Gas and Elec. Co. v. Flippo, 248 Md. 680, 705 A.2d 1144 (1998) (plaintiff grabs electric wire); Urban v. Wait's Supermarket, Inc., 294 N.W.2d 793 (S.D. 1980) (plaintiff store-customer trips over watermelon); Lazar v. Cleveland Elec. Illuminating Co., 43 Ohio St.2d 131, 331 N.E.2d 424 (1975) (plaintiff grabs uninsulated utility wire). Another approach has been to ensure that the plaintiff's contributory negligence is a substantial factor (not merely a cause in any degree) in bringing about the harm. *See* Hofstrom v. Share, 295 N.J. Super. 186, 684 A.2d 981 (1996) (no evidence that patient's failure to follow defendant physician's instructions contributed to her injury); Bahm v. Pittsburgh & Lake Erie R. Co., 6 Ohio St.2d 192, 217 N.E.2d 217 (1966) (erroneous jury instruction eliminating substantial-factor requirement); *see also* Furukawa v. Uoshio Ogawa, 236 F.2d 272 (9th Cir. 1956) (under California law, limiting scope of proximate cause as to contributory negligence). Yet another approach has been to disallow the plaintiff's contributory negligence to defend intentional or wanton misconduct, *see* Adkisson v. City of Seattle, 42 Wash.2d 676, 258 P.2d 461 (1953), or conduct violating statutes protecting plaintiffs who are unable to protect themselves, *see* Restatement (Second) of Torts §483, such as liquor sales to the intoxicated or firearms sales to minors.

Last Clear Chance. Last clear chance is another ameliorating doctrine for contributory negligence. The doctrine relieves the plaintiff from the bar of contributory negligence when the defendant is aware of the plaintiff's negligence and yet fails to exercise reasonable care to avoid its consequences—a preventable injury. If the defendant has the last *clear* chance to avoid the plaintiff's injury, then the plaintiff's prior contributory negligence will not have mattered. Fuller v. Illinois Cent. R. Co., 100 Miss. 705, 56 So. 783 (1911), is an example where the court held that although the decedent pedestrian's presence crossing the track just ahead of a train was contributory negligence, the engineer's wanton failure to sound the signal to warn the decedent when the engineer was aware of the decedent's negligence compelled application of the last-clear-chance doctrine. Davies v. Mann, 152 Eng. Rep. 588 (Ct. of Exch. Ch. 1842), is a colorful early case in which the plaintiff negligently fettered his donkey to graze alongside a road when the defendant negligently ran his horses and wagon into it, killing it. The Court of Exchequer Chamber affirmed a verdict for the plaintiff, holding that the defendant had the last clear chance to prevent the harm. Must the plaintiff be helpless or only inattentive? *See* Restatement (Second) of Torts §§479, 480 (either will do). In its most generous form, the last-clear-chance doctrine relieves the plaintiff of contributory negligence when the defendant should have known that the plaintiff's carelessness put the plaintiff at risk (known as the doctrine of discovered peril). As clear as the two examples above may seem, courts occasionally limit, disfavor, and eschew the last-clear-chance doctrine. *See* WMATA v. Johnson, 726 A.2d 172 (D.C. Ct. App. 1999) (no last clear chance for train operator to avoid decedent jumping in front of train); Williams v. Harrison, 255 Va. 272, 497 S.E.2d 467 (1998) (no last clear chance for either of colliding cars).

Practice

Why, the personal-injury lawyer wondered, did her friends and family members always ask her the medical questions—why did she seem to know a little bit about so much medicine? Then one day, when she felt a rare need to look back over her 20 years of practice, she decided to make a list of the injuries her clients had suffered. Among them were fractured jaw, skull, eye orbit, cervical spine, lumbar spine, sacrum, hip, clavicle, upper-arm, forearm, wrist, fingers, femur, tibia-fibula, foot, and ankle; lacerated heart, spleen, and appendix; severed facial and wrist nerves and bile duct; amputated hand, foot, and leg; staphylococcus, HIV, and herpes infections; and closed-head injury, post-traumatic stress syndrome, and depression. Then there were the deaths—so many profound moments sharing with loved ones what unexpectedly sudden, premature, and sometimes violent deaths meant. As the lawyer reflected, she realized again that knowledge—indeed truth itself—is not propositional but personal, without meaning until attached to a person and relationship. The question is not so much "what is truth" but "who is truth."

Comparative Negligence. The most-favored means of making a more equitable comparison of the plaintiff's and defendant's fault has been to abolish the defense of contributory negligence and replace it with a comparative-negligence defense that allocate fault on percentage bases between plaintiff and defendant. Only four states—Alabama, Maryland, North Carolina, and Virginia—reject the comparative-negligence approach and retain contributory negligence. Although many states have only recently adopted comparative negligence, the English admiralty courts were applying comparative-negligence rules even before the 1809 *Butterfield* decision recognizing contributory negligence. The defendant has the burden of proof on comparative negligence. *See* Restatement (Third) of Torts: Apportionment of Liability §4 (2000).

McIntyre v. Balentine
Supreme Court of Tennessee
833 S.W.2d 52 (1992)

DROWOTA, J. In this personal injury action, we granted Plaintiff's application for permission to appeal in order to decide whether to adopt a system of comparative fault in Tennessee. ... We now replace the common law defense of contributory negligence with a system of comparative fault. ...

In the early morning darkness of November 2, 1986, Plaintiff Harry Douglas McIntyre and Defendant Clifford Balentine were involved in a motor vehicle accident resulting in severe injuries to Plaintiff. ...

Both men had consumed alcohol the evening of the accident. After the accident, Plaintiff's blood alcohol level was measured at .17 percent by weight. Testimony suggested that Defendant was traveling in excess of the posted speed limit.

... After trial, the jury returned a verdict stating: "We, the jury, find the plaintiff and the defendant equally at fault in this accident; therefore, we rule in favor of the defendant."

After judgment was entered for Defendants, Plaintiff brought an appeal alleging the trial court erred by ... refusing to instruct the jury regarding the doctrine of comparative negligence... . The Court of Appeals affirmed, holding that ... comparative negligence is not the law in Tennessee... .

I.

The common law contributory negligence doctrine has traditionally been traced to Lord Ellenborough's opinion in *Butterfield v. Forrester,* 11 East 60, 103 Eng.Rep. 926 (1809). ... Stating as the rule that "[o]ne person being in fault will not dispense with another's using ordinary care," plaintiff was denied recovery on the basis that he did not use ordinary care to avoid the obstruction. [C]

The contributory negligence bar was soon brought to America as part of the common law, [c], and proceeded to spread throughout the states. [C] ...

In Tennessee, ... we have continued to follow the general rule that a plaintiff's contributory negligence completely bars recovery. [Cc]

Equally entrenched in Tennessee jurisprudence are exceptions to the general all-or-nothing rule: contributory negligence does not absolutely bar recovery where defendant's conduct was intentional, [cc]; where defendant's conduct was "grossly" negligent, [cc]; where defendant had the "last clear chance" with which, through the exercise of ordinary care, to avoid plaintiff's injury, [cc]; *Davies v. Mann,* 152 Eng.Rep. 588 (1842); or where plaintiff's negligence may be classified as "remote." [Cc]

In contrast, comparative fault has long been the federal rule in cases involving injured employees of interstate railroad carriers, [c], and injured seamen. [Cc] ...

Between 1920 and 1969, a few states began utilizing the principles of comparative fault in all tort litigation. [C] Then, between 1969 and 1984, comparative fault replaced contributory negligence in 37 additional states. [C] In 1991, South Carolina became the 45th state to adopt comparative fault, [c], leaving Alabama,[fn] Maryland, North Carolina, Virginia, and Tennessee as the only remaining common law contributory negligence jurisdictions.

Eleven states have judicially adopted comparative fault.[fn] Thirty-four states have legislatively adopted comparative fault.[fn] ...

II.

... After exhaustive deliberation that was facilitated by extensive briefing and argument by the parties, amicus curiae, and Tennessee's scholastic community, we conclude that it is time to abandon the outmoded and unjust common law doctrine of contributory negligence and adopt in its place a system of comparative fault. Justice simply will not permit our continued adherence to a rule that, in the face of a judicial determination that others bear primary responsibility, nevertheless completely denies injured litigants recompense for their damages. ...

III.

Two basic forms of comparative fault are utilized by 45 of our sister jurisdictions, these variants being commonly referred to as either "pure" or "modified." In the "pure" form[fn], a plaintiff's damages are reduced in proportion to the percentage negligence attributed to him; for example, a plaintiff responsible for 90 percent of the negligence that caused his injuries nevertheless may recover 10 percent of his damages. In the "modified" form,[fn] plaintiffs recover as in pure jurisdictions, but only if the plaintiff's negligence either (1) does not exceed ("50 percent" jurisdictions) or (2) is less than ("49 percent" jurisdictions) the defendant's negligence. [C]

Although we conclude that the all-or-nothing rule of contributory negligence must be replaced, we nevertheless decline to abandon totally our fault-based tort system. We do not agree that a party should necessarily be able to recover in tort even though he may be 80, 90, or 95 percent at fault. We therefore reject the pure form of comparative fault.

We recognize that modified comparative fault systems have been criticized as merely shifting the arbitrary contributory negligence bar to a new ground. [C] However, we feel the "49 percent rule" ameliorates the harshness of the common law rule while remaining compatible with a fault-based tort system. [C] We therefore hold that so long as a plaintiff's negligence remains less than the defendant's negligence the plaintiff may recover; in such a case, plaintiff's damages are to be reduced in proportion to the percentage of the total negligence attributable to the plaintiff. ...

V.

We recognize that today's decision affects numerous legal principles surrounding tort litigation. ...

First, and most obviously, the new rule makes the doctrines of remote contributory negligence and last clear chance obsolete. ...

Second, in cases of multiple tortfeasors, plaintiff will be entitled to recover so long as plaintiff's fault is less than the combined fault of all tortfeasors.

Third, today's holding renders the doctrine of joint and several liability obsolete. ...

Further, because a particular defendant will henceforth be liable only for the percentage of a plaintiff's damages occasioned by that defendant's negligence, situations where a defendant has paid more than his "share" of a judgment will no longer arise, and therefore the Uniform Contribution Among Tort-feasors Act, T.C.A. §§ 29-11-101 to 106 (1980), will no longer determine the apportionment of liability between codefendants.

Fourth, fairness and efficiency require that defendants called upon to answer allegations in negligence be permitted to allege, as an affirmative defense, that a nonparty caused or contributed to the injury or damage for which recovery is sought.

In cases where such a defense is raised, the trial court shall instruct the jury to assign this nonparty the percentage of the total negligence for which he is responsible. However, in order for a plaintiff to recover a judgment against such additional person, the plaintiff must have made a timely amendment to his complaint and caused process to be served on such additional person. ...

For the foregoing reasons, the judgment of the Court of Appeals is reversed in part and affirmed in part, and the case is remanded to the trial court for a new trial in accordance with the dictates of this opinion. The costs of this appeal are taxed equally to the parties.

INQUIRY

Forms. As the above case suggests, comparative negligence has different forms—pure and modified. The pure form requires the factfinder to allocate fault to each party along a sliding scale from zero to one-hundred percent—provided that the total fault must always be one-hundred percent—so that the judge can then apportion damages according to the assigned fault. Thus, a plaintiff whom the court finds to have incurred $100,000 in damages but to have been forty percent at fault will receive $60,000 in damages. If one defendant has the remaining sixty-percent fault, then law obligates that defendant to pay the $60,000 in damages. If instead two defendants are at fault, one with twenty-five percent of the fault and the other with thirty-five percent of the fault, then they must pay $25,000 and $35,000 respectively. Although the Restatement (Third) of Torts: Apportionment of Liability §7 (2000), favors comparative negligence's pure form, only about one dozen states follow it. Modified comparative negligence comes in two forms—*less than* and *not greater than*. In the dozen or so less-than jurisdictions, the plaintiff's negligence must be less than the combined negligence of all other defendants—less, in other words, than fifty percent—or the plaintiff has no recovery. In the twenty or so not-greater-than states, the plaintiff's negligence must be not more than the combined negligence of all other defendants—not more, in other words, than fifty percent—or the plaintiff has no recovery. Can you discern why the difference in the two forms of modified comparative negligence may be important? Which interests do you think favor which forms? Some states use pure comparative negligence for some claims and modified comparative negligence for others. *See* Mich. Comp. L. §500.3135(2)(b) ("Damages shall be assessed on the basis of comparative fault, except that damages shall not be assessed in favor of a party who is more than 50% at fault.") (motor-vehicle liability). Some states limit the degree of comparative negligence that the factfinder may assign for certain conduct, like the failure to wear a seatbelt. *See* Iowa Code §321.445(4)(b) (1997) (five percent); Mich. Comp. L. §257.710e(6) (no more than five percent comparative negligence); Wis. Stat. §347.48(7)(g) (1999) (fifteen percent). A small minority of states bar the plaintiff's recovery if the plaintiff's fault is greater than each defendant's fault but less than half the fault—for example, where the plaintiff's fault is forty percent and each of two defendants' fault is thirty percent. *See* Minn. Stat. Ann. §604.01 (West 2000); Idaho Code §6-801 (Michie 1998).

Rationales. Responsibility, accountability, and equity are the primary and obvious rationales supporting comparative negligence. The consequences for both plaintiff and defendant should be proportional to the fitness or unfitness of their actions toward the plaintiff's safety. Yet what are jurors comparing—the reprehensibility of each party's conduct, how much it contributed to the plaintiff's injury (its causal proximity), or a combination of the two? Spier v. Barker, 323 N.E.2d 164 (N.Y. 1974), illustrated the issue when it held, contrary to what other courts would have held, that the plaintiff's failure to wear a seatbelt was not contributory negligence in her ejection from the car. Why not? *See* Eaton v. McLain, 891 S.W.2d 587 (Tenn. 1994) (consider "such factors as: (1) the relative closeness of the causal relationship between the conduct of the defendant and the injury to the plaintiff; (2) the reasonableness of the party's conduct in confronting a risk, such as whether the party knew of the risk, or should have known of it; (3) the extent to which the defendant failed to reasonably utilize an existing opportunity to avoid the injury to the plaintiff; (4) the existence of a sudden emergency requiring a hasty decision; (5) the significance of what the party was attempting to accomplish by the conduct, such as an attempt to save another's life; and (6) the party's particular capacities, such as age, maturity, training, education, and so forth") (footnotes omitted). Do these factors make the evaluation any easier? What fault allocation would you make between the entity that fails to train a snow-blower user and the user who puts her hand in the snow-blowing chute? *See* Hunt v. Ohio Dept. of Rehab. & Correc., 696 N.E.2d 674 (Ohio Ct Cl. 1997) (forty percent to plaintiff, sixty percent to defendant). Between a college-football player who in a psychotic episode scuffles with the defendant police officers, resulting in his getting shot? *See* Baldwin v. City of Omaha, 607 N.W.2d 841 (Neb. 2000) (fifty-five percent to plaintiff, forty-five percent to defendants, and therefore no recovery under modified regime).

Disclosure to Jury. To achieve the purposes of comparative negligence, should the judge tell the jury how their allocation of fault affects the damages recovered by the plaintiff? In the above *McIntyre* case, the court ruled so, and many agree. *See* Russell v. Stricker, 635 N.W.2d 734 (Neb. 2001). Not every court agrees—some adopting the "blindfold rule." *See* McGowan v. Story, 70 Wis.2d 189, 234 N.W.2d 325 (1975). Can you articulate the basis for not disclosing the effects—catching the "blindfold" reference? Disclosure of the effects of allocation could be especially critical in states adopting the less-than form of modified comparative negligence. Can you see why?

Other Modifications. As the above *McIntyre* case states, a change from the traditional contributory-negligence rule to comparative negligence may require several other changes in traditional tort doctrines. Most courts, like *McIntyre*, abolish the last-clear-chance doctrine along with the abolition of contributory negligence. *See* Spahn v. Town of Port Royal, 499 S.E.2d 205 (S.C. 1998); *but see* Fountain v. Thompson, 312 S.E.2d 788 (Ga. 1984) (preserving the last-clear-chance doctrine after adopting comparative negligence); *see also* Restatement (Third) of Torts: Apportionment of Liability §3, Comment *b* (2000). With percentages of fault already assigned, law has no further need for rights of contribution between defendants. Defendants pay only their portion of the recovery. How should law treat the uncollectible defendant? Who bears that loss? Some states let the burden fall on the plaintiff, while other states reallocate uncollectible portions among all parties (plaintiff included) or among defendants. Which rule do you prefer? Should the law abolish joint-and-several liability? Some courts do so. *See* McIntyre, supra; *but see* Fernanders v. Marks Constr. of South Carolina, Inc., 330 S.C. 470, 499 S.E.2d 509 (1998) (retaining joint-and-several liability and listing the choice made by other jurisdictions). A later study on multiple parties further discusses apportionment issues. Courts applying comparative negligence have been more willing to permit the jury to compare the plaintiff's negligence to the defendant's recklessness—that is, to reduce awards for comparative negligence even when the defendant knew that the defendant's conduct created a high probability of harm. *See* White v. Hansen, 837 P.2d 1229 (Colo. 1992) (plaintiff pedestrian's recovery against drunk driver reduced for plaintiff's having walked with his back to traffic); Vining v. City of Detroit, 413 N.W.2d 486 (Mich. Ct. App. 1987) (plaintiff's negligence reduces recovery notwithstanding recklessness of defendant police officer). Some things have not changed under comparative negligence. Courts generally continue to decline to reduce plaintiff recoveries for comparative negligence where the defendant's tortious conduct is intentional. *See* Hampton Tree Farms, Inc. v. Jewett, 974 P.2d 738 (Or. App. Ct. 1999); Winkler v. Rocky Mtn. Conf. of United Methodist Church, 923 P.2d 152 (Colo. Ct. App. 1995); *but see* Wijngaarde v. Parents of Guy, 720 So.2d 6 (La. Ct. App. 1998).

Figure

Consumer lawyer Brian Panish's best-known credit is to have won the largest personal-injury, products-liability verdict in the nation's history—a $4.9 billion verdict against a motor-vehicle manufacturer for six individuals who suffered severe burn injuries resulting from defects in a fuel system. He also claims ten verdicts over $10 million and over 100 verdicts or settlements of greater than $1 million. But Mr. Panish's real credit is drawn from his tireless work on behalf of consumers—work that won him nominations or awards as trial lawyer of the year from the national organization Trial Lawyers for Public Justice and the Consumer Attorneys Association of Los Angeles. He has also served on the plaintiffs' steering committees for Tryptophan and Fen-Phen litigation, and speaks for national and state lawyer organizations, on consumer-tort law and civil procedure.

Uncollectible Defendants. Another question the *McIntyre* decision addressed was the fault of non-parties. Should law allocate fault to them? Of course, that portion of the fault allocated to a non-party goes uncollected. Some states, as in *McIntyre*, provide for non-party fault allocations on the demand of the defendant but ensure that the plaintiff has an opportunity to amend the complaint to add the non-party. Why do you think the plaintiff did not add the non-party in the first place? The question of non-party fault also raises the issue of the immune non-party. For instance, employers are occasionally at fault in part for their employees' injuries, where the employee has the opportunity to pursue a negligence or products-liability claim against a third party who, in turn, would wish to shift some of the fault back to the employer. But worker's compensation disability acts make employers immune from employee negligence actions. On whom—plaintiff or defendant—should the cost of the immunity fall? Many courts do not allocate fault to an immune non-party. *See* Snyder v. LTG Lufttechnische GmbH, 955 S.W.2d 252 (Tenn. 1997); Sears, Roebuck & Co. v.

Huang, 652 A.2d 568 (Del. 1995); *but see* Mack Trucks, Inc. v. Tackett, 841 So.2d 1107 (Miss. 2003) (fault may be allocated to immune employer).

B. Assumption of Risk

OBJECTIVE: Given a negligence claim in which there is evidence that the plaintiff was aware of and deliberately accepted the risk of injury, evaluate the likelihood that the plaintiff's claim will be affected by the assumption of risk doctrine, consistent with this section of the text.

Case Study: An outdoor-recreation enthusiast insisted on renting a canoe despite warnings that the river was running high from snowmelt and spring rains. The rental agreement stated the risks of canoeing. At the first bend in the river, the enthusiast broke an old paddle in the swift current, leaving the enthusiast helpless to prevent the canoe's swamping. Witnesses were unable to save the enthusiast from drowning. ***Discuss and evaluate the effect of the assumption-of-risk defense on the wrongful death claim of the enthusiast's estate against the canoe-rental company.***

Assumption of risk is, like contributory and comparative negligence, an affirmative defense having to do with the plaintiff's conduct. Its most basic formulation is that the plaintiff voluntarily encountered and accepted the hazards of a known risk and so should not complain about the injury that results from the realization of those risks. Bungee jumping and other high-risk recreational pursuits make the best examples. *See* Plant v. Wilbur, 47 S.W.2d 889 (Ark. 2001) (racetrack's exculpatory clause bars claim by pit-crew member); Jones v. Dressel, 623 P.2d 370 (Colo. 1981) (exculpatory clause in sky-diving agreement bars claim for plane crash on takeoff to skydive). Individuals who choose to engage in those pursuits should not complain against others when they realize one of the risks of injury that makes the recreation exciting. Assumption of risk differs from contributory and comparative negligence in that it focuses on the plaintiff's actual knowledge of the conduct's risks, resulting in injury, rather than what the plaintiff should have known. The proofs focus on the subjective rather than objective, showing what the plaintiff knew rather than what the reasonable person would have known.

Assumption of risk takes two forms, express and implied. Although it is a defense to a negligence action, express assumption of risk has a contractual nature. It involves the participant's agreement, often but not always in writing, *see* Boyle v. Revici, 961 F.2d 1060 (2d Cir. 1992), that the participant accepts the risks and consequences of the activity in which the participant is about to engage, in exchange for the activity provider's permission to participate. Obviously, then, the actual terms of the express assumption are critical to whether it bars a tort action in the event that the participant is injured by the provider's negligence or more serious misconduct. A participant might accept certain risks that are a natural part of the central service while rejecting other risks, like the risk of injury due to facility design or maintenance by the service provider. However, because providers are usually the ones drafting the assumption-of-risk agreements—in many instances without the ability of the participant to negotiate other terms—the agreements often require the participant to assume the risk of the provider's negligence. Tort law enforces assumption-of-risk agreements much as contract law would enforce them—according to the express, unambiguous, and bargained terms of the agreement unless they are adhesion (non-negotiable) contracts on essential services. The classic example of an unenforceable assumption-of-risk agreement would be one that required a patient to assume the risk of an emergency physician's malpractice in providing emergency-room service. *See* Cudnik v. William Beaumont Hosp., 207 Mich. App. 378, 525 N.W.2d 891 (1994); *see also* Tunkl v. Regents of Univ. of California, 60 Cal.2d 92, 383 P.2d 441, 32 Cal. Rptr. 33 (1963) (does not matter if medical treatment is free). As you read the following case, consider where it should fall along a spectrum of cases involving essential to non-essential services.

Seigneur v. National Fitness Inst., Inc.
Maryland Court of Special Appeals
132 Md. App. 271, 752 A.2d 631 (Md. Ct. Sp. App. 2000)

SALMON, J. In this case, we are asked to examine the enforceability of an exculpatory clause found in a fitness club's contract.

On September 4, 1998, Gerilynne Seigneur and her husband James filed a complaint in the Circuit Court for Montgomery County against National Fitness Institute, Inc. ("NFI"). The Seigneurs asserted that Ms. Seigneur was injured as a result of NFI's negligence while she was undergoing an initial evaluation at a fitness club owned and operated by NFI. NFI filed a motion to dismiss the complaint based on an exculpatory clause found in its contract with Ms. Seigneur. ... The motion for summary judgment was granted... . Does the exculpatory clause in the agreement entered into by the parties validly release NFI from all liability for injuries to Ms. Seigneur caused by NFI's negligence?[fn] We answer that question in the affirmative.
...

When she signed her membership contract, Ms. Seigneur had a history of serious lower back problems, including a herniated disc. Moreover, her general physical condition was poor. These facts were disclosed to NFI prior to the accident.

As part of the application process, Ms. Seigneur was required to complete and sign a document ... contain[ing] the following clause: "Important Information: I, the undersigned applicant, agree and understand that I must report any and all injuries immediately to NFI, Inc. staff. *It is further agreed that all exercises shall be undertaken by me at my sole risk and that NFI, Inc. shall not be liable to me for any claims, demands, injuries, damages, actions, or courses of action whatsoever, to my person or property arising out of or connecting with the use of the services and facilities of NFI, Inc., by me,* or to the premises of NFI, Inc. Further, I do expressly hereby forever release and discharge NFI, Inc. from all claims, demands, injuries, damages, actions, or courses of action, and from all acts of active or passive negligence on the part of NFI, Inc., its servants, agents or employees." (Emphasis added.)

... Kim Josties, an NFI employee, then performed an initial evaluation of Ms. Seigneur, in which Ms. Seigneur was first directed to perform various flexibility tests. Ms. Josties next directed her to the weight machines for strength testing. ... Ms.

Seigneur next used an upper torso weight machine. Ms. Josties placed a ninety-pound weight on this machine and instructed Ms. Seigneur to lift this weight once with her arms. While attempting to lift this load, Ms. Seigneur felt a tearing or ripping sensation in her right shoulder. ...

Ms. Seigneur claims that since this incident, she has had pain and difficulty using her shoulder. In addition, she has undergone shoulder surgery for a condition that her doctor attributed to the use of NFI's upper torso machine. ...

The Seigneurs' complaint against NFI alleged, *inter alia,* that NFI was vicariously liable because Ms. Josties, as an employee or agent of NFI, was "negligent in instructing, directing, and/or guiding the [appellant] to lift ninety (90) pounds of weight on the upper torso machine in the manner previously described... ." ...

To decide this case, we must first determine whether the exculpatory clause quoted at the beginning of this opinion unambiguously excused NFI's negligence. ...

Not all attempts to limit liability by way of exculpatory clauses are successful. ...

In the foregoing cases where the clause was held to be ambiguous, the common thread was that the clause did not clearly indicate that the injured party was releasing the health clubs from liability for the clubs' own negligence. Without this clear expression of intent, the courts in those cases felt compelled to invalidate the exculpatory clauses in question. Nevertheless, given the judiciary's reluctance to interfere with the right of parties to contract, courts are almost universal in holding that health clubs, in their membership agreements, may limit their liability for future negligence if they do so unambiguously. [C] ...

In the instant case, there is no suggestion that the agreement between NFI and Ms. Seigneur was the product of fraud, mistake, undue influence, overreaching, or the like. The exculpatory clause unambiguously provides that Ms. Seigneur "expressly hereby forever release[s] and discharge[s] NFI, Inc. from all claims, demands, injuries, damages, actions, or courses of action, and from all acts of *active or passive negligence on the part of NFI, Inc., its servants, agents or employees.*" (emphasis added). Under these circumstances, we hold that this contract provision expresses a clear intention by the parties to release NFI from liability for all acts of negligence. ...

Three exceptions have been identified where the public interest will render an exculpatory clause unenforceable. They are: (1) when the party protected by the clause intentionally causes harm or engages in acts of reckless, wanton, or gross negligence; (2) when the bargaining power of one party to the contract is so grossly unequal so as to put that party at the mercy of the other's negligence; and (3) when the transaction involves the public interest. [Cc]

Appellants argue that NFI "possess[es] a decisive advantage in bargaining strength against members of the public who seek to use its services." She also claims that she was presented with a contract of adhesion and that this is additional evidence of NFI's grossly disproportionate "bargaining power."

It is true that the contract presented to Ms. Seigneur was a contract of adhesion.[fn] But that fact alone does not demonstrate that NFI had grossly disparate bargaining power. [C] As discussed *infra,* there were numerous other competitors providing the same non-essential services as NFI. The exculpatory clause was prominently displayed in the Participation Agreement and Ms. Seigneur makes no claim that she was unaware of this provision prior to her injury.

To possess a decisive bargaining advantage over a customer, the service offered must usually be deemed essential in nature. [Cc] ... In *Schlobohm[v. Spa Petite, Inc., 326 N.W.2d 920 (Minn. 1982)]* the Court said: "[I]n the determination of whether the enforcement of an exculpatory clause would be against public policy, the courts consider whether the party seeking exoneration offered services of great importance to the public, which were a practical necessity for some members of the public. ..." ...

... The services offered by the appellee simply cannot be accurately characterized as "essential." ...

The Washington metropolitan area, of which Montgomery County is a part, is home to many exercise and fitness clubs. Ms. Seigneur ... was free to choose among scores of facilities providing essentially the same services. [C] She also had the option of purchasing her own fitness equipment and exercising at home or of exercising without any equipment by doing aerobic or isometric exercises. Ms. Seigneur's bargaining position was not grossly disproportionate to that of NFI. ...

NFI does not provide an essential public service such that an exculpatory clause would be "patently offensive" to the citizens of Maryland. The services offered by a health club are not of great importance or of practical necessity to the public as a whole. [C] Nor is a health club anywhere near as socially important as institutions or businesses such as innkeepers, public utilities, common carriers, or schools. ...

The following is as true today as when it was first uttered: "I, for one, protest ... against arguing too strongly upon public policy; it is a very unruly horse and when once you get astride it you never know where it will carry you. It may lead you from the sound law. It is never argued at all but when other points fail." *Anne Arundel County v. Hartford Acc. and Indem. Co.,* 329 Md. 677, 686, 621 A.2d 427 (1993) (quoting *Richardson v. Mellish,* 2 Bing. 229, 130 Eng.Rep. 303 (1824)). As it relates to exculpatory clauses, unless the clause is patently offensive, Maryland has this unruly horse securely in the stable. Here, the clause passes the not patently offensive test.

We affirm the trial court's ruling that NFI's exculpatory clause is enforceable so as to release NFI from liability for injuries Ms. Seigneur sustained while on its premises. ...

INQUIRY

Essential Services. The above *Seigneur* case holds that a fitness center does not provide an essential service for purposes of the public-policy exception to an express-assumption-of-risk agreement. Medical care, by contrast, would be an essential service in many cases, as would public transportation by common carrier. Is daycare an essential service? *See* Gavin W. v. YMCA of Metropolitan Los Angeles, 131 Cal. Rptr.2d 168, 106 Cal. App.4th 662 (2003) (express-assumption clause void as against public policy). Would a parent's waiver of a child's negligence claim be effective, if not for an essential service like daycare but instead for recreation? *See* Cooper v. Aspen Skiing, 48 P.3d 1229 (Colo. 2002) (parents could not waive 17-year-old skiier's claims); Hawkins v. Peart, 37 P.3d 1062 (Utah 2001) (parent cannot waive child's right); Scott v. Pacific West Mtn. Resort, 119 Wash.2d 484, 834 P.2d 6 (1992) (same);

but see Sharon v. City of Newton, 437 Mass. 99, 769 N.E.2d 738 (2002) (parent can waive child's claim); Zivich v. Mentor Soccer Club, Inc., 82 Ohio St.3d 367, 696 N.E.2d 201 (1998) (same). Does one spouse's express assumption of risk also assume the risk on behalf of the other spouse? *See* Hardy v. St. Claire, 739 A.2d 368 (Maine 1999) (no—signer spouse only); Huber v. Hovey, 501 N.W.2d 53 (Iowa 1993) (same). What if a carrier offers a free ride in exchange for a liability waiver? *See* Gonzales v. Baltimore & Ohio R. Co., 318 F.2d 294 (4th Cir. 1963) (claim held barred).

Public Policy. Public policy does not always depend on the essential nature of the services. It may also consider the public's interest in access to places of public accommodation. *See* Dalury v. S-K-I, Ltd., 670 A.2d 795 (Vt. 1995) (exculpatory clause for negligence in operation of ski resort is void as against public policy). Statutes or regulations may also prohibit service providers from requiring that customers assume risks, *see* N.Y. Gen. Oblig. L. §5-321 (2004) (voiding rental-property release clauses); N.Y. Gen. Oblig. L. §5-326 (2001) (voiding recreational-facility release clauses), or, contrarily, may grant service-providers an assumed-risk defense, *see* N.J. Stat. Ann. §5:13-5 (1979) (skiers assume risks inherent in sport); 12 Vt. Stat. Ann. §1037 (1978) (sports participants assume risks "obvious and necessary" to sport). Courts have also on occasion refused to enforce express assumption-of-risk clauses purporting to waive claims for gross negligence. *See* Gross v. Sweet, 400 N.E.2d 306 (N.Y. 1979).

Ethics

Rule 5.4 of the ABA Model Rules of Professional Conduct provides that a lawyer must not share legal fees with a nonlawyer except in a few special circumstances. Rule 7.2(b) prohibits a lawyer from giving anything of value to a person for recommending the lawyer's services. One of the restrictions that Rules 5.4 and 7.2 impose on tort practice is that plaintiff's lawyers may not pay nonlawyers such as secretaries, legal assistants, investigators, or nonlawyers who refer cases, referral fees or a portion of the contingency fee when earned. Rule 5.4(a)(3) does permit a lawyer to include nonlawyer employees in a compensation plan based on a profit-sharing arrangement, but compensation of nonlawyer employees must not be contingent on case outcomes and paid out of those earned fees. In practice, law firms representing plaintiffs and earning contingent fees will often have a year-end bonus plan based on the law firm's general success for that year—not dividing fees with nonlawyers. What do you think is the basis for Rule 5.4's prohibition? Hint: Rule 5.4 bears the title, "Professional Independence of a Lawyer."

Risk. In order for express assumption of risk to bar the plaintiff's claim, the plaintiff's injury must have been within the risk that the plaintiff expressly assumed. *See* Woodall v. Wayne Steffner Prods., Inc., 201 Cal. App.2d 800, 20 Cal. Rptr. 572 (1962) (plaintiff human kite did not expressly assume risk that driver pulling kite would exceed instructed speed). The issue often arises when the injury is unusual. *Cf.* Grabill v. Adams County Fair and Racing Assn., 666 N.W.2d 592 (Iowa 2003) (injury from fireworks is within risk assumed by participants at racetrack); Karr v. Brant Lake Camp, 261 A.D.2d 342, 691 N.Y.S.2d 427 (N.Y. App. Div. 1999) (plaintiff 11-year-old ballplayer did not assume risk of being hit by ball thrown by older camp counselor); Wright v. Loon Mtn. Rec. Corp., 140 N.H. 166, 663 A.2d 1340 (1995) (jury question whether plaintiff assumed risk that guide's horse would kick her). Is negligence an ordinary risk of an activity, or must it be expressly mentioned in order to be held to have been assumed? *Contrast* Boehm v. Cody Country Chamber of Commerce, 748 P.2d 704 (Wyo. 1987) (releasing "all claims" is sufficient—negligence need not be mentioned), and Restatement (Third) of Torts: Apportionment of Liability §2, Comment *c* (2000) (negligence need not be mentioned if other language is sufficiently clear), *with* Hyson v. White Water Mtn. Resorts, 265 Conn. 636, 829 A.2d 827 (2003) (must mention negligence for it to be expressly assumed).

Implied Assumption of Risk. In other cases, assumption of risk is not by express agreement but law instead implies from circumstances compelling the conclusion that the participant knew and voluntarily encountered the risk. Turcotte v. Fell, 502 N.E.2d 964 (N.Y. 1986), is an example in which the appellate court dismissed the negligence claims of jockey Ron Turcotte (the rider of Triple-Crown winner Secretariat) against a competing jockey who allegedly rode foul causing Turcotte's mount to stumble, the racetrack's allegedly cuppy track contributing to the mount's fall that paralyzed Turcotte. The court held Turcotte to have known and voluntarily encountered both the foul-riding and cuppy-track risks. The distinction between implied assumption of risk and contributory or comparative negligence is in the plaintiff's knowledge. If the plaintiff knew, then assumption of risk applies. *See* Hunn v. Windsor Hotel Co., 119 W. Va. 215, 193 S.E. 57 (1937). If the plaintiff did not know but should have known, then only contributory or comparative negligence applies. *See* Robinson v. BF Goodrich Tire Co., 444 Pa. Super. 640, 664 A.2d 616 (1995); *see also* Wallace v. Rosen, 765 N.E.2d 192 (Ind. Ct. App. 2002). In lay terms, the difference may be one of carelessness versus foolishness. Can you see why contributory or comparative negligence might also apply when the plaintiff knew, not just should have known, the risk? *See* Gonzalez v. Garcia, 75 Cal. App.3d 874, 142 Cal. Rptr. 503 (1977) (both defenses apply to plaintiff who voluntarily rides with intoxicated driver). Another distinction between implied assumption of risk and comparative negligence is that the former is a complete bar and the latter only a partial bar. When the defendant asserts implied assumption of risk, the defendant must show the plaintiff's awareness of the risk and voluntariness of the conduct. Contrast the following two cases, one illustrating a non-essential and the other an essential activity where the risk was apparent and assumed in one but the risk not apparent and not assumed in the other.

Murphy v. Steeplechase Amusement Co.
New York Court of Appeals
250 N.Y. 479, 166 N.E. 173 (1929)

CARDOZO, C.J. The defendant, Steeplechase Amusement Company maintains, an amusement park at Coney Island, N.Y. One of the supposed attractions is known as "the Flopper." It is a moving belt, running upward on an inclined plane, on which passengers sit or stand. Many of them are unable to keep their feet because of the movement of the belt, and are thrown backward or aside. The belt runs in a groove, with padded walls on either side to a height of four feet, and with padded flooring beyond the walls at the same angle as the belt. An electric motor, driven by current furnished by the Brooklyn Edison Company, supplies the needed power.

Plaintiff, a vigorous young man, visited the park with friends. One of them, a young woman, now his wife, stepped upon the moving belt. Plaintiff followed and stepped behind her. As he did so, he felt what he describes as a sudden jerk, and was thrown to the floor. His wife in front and also friends behind him were thrown at the same time. Something more was here, as every one understood, than the slowly moving escalator that is common in shops and public places. A fall was foreseen as one of the risks of the adventure. There would have been no point to the whole thing, no adventure about it, if the risk had not been there. The very name, above the gate, "the Flopper," was warning to the timid. If the name was not enough, there was warning more distinct in the experience of others. We are told by the plaintiff's wife that the members of her party stood looking at the sport before joining in it themselves. Some aboard the belt were able, as she viewed them, to sit down with decorum or even to stand and keep their footing; others jumped or fell. The tumbling bodies and the screams and laughter supplied the merriment and fun. "I took a chance," she said when asked whether she thought that a fall might be expected.

Plaintiff took the chance with her, but, less lucky than his companions, suffered a fracture of a knee cap. He states in his complaint that the belt was dangerous to life and limb, in that it stopped and started violently and suddenly and was not properly equipped to prevent injuries to persons who were using it without knowledge of its dangers, and in a bill of particulars he adds that it was operated at a fast and dangerous rate of speed and was not supplied with a proper railing, guard, or other device to prevent a fall therefrom. No other negligence is charged.

We see no adequate basis for a finding that the belt was out of order. It was already in motion when the plaintiff put his foot on it. He cannot help himself to a verdict in such circumstances by the addition of the facile comment that it threw him with a jerk. ... An aberration so extraordinary, if it is to lay the basis for a verdict, should rest on something firmer than a mere descriptive epithet, a summary of the sensations of a tense and crowded moment. [Cc] But the jerk, if it were established, would add little to the case. Whether the movement of the belt was uniform or irregular, the risk at greatest was a fall. This was the very hazard that was invited and foreseen. [C]

Volenti non fit injuria. One who takes part in such a sport accepts the dangers that inhere in it so far as they are obvious and necessary, just as a fencer accepts the risk of a thrust by his antagonist or a spectator at a ball game the chance of contact with the ball. [Cc] The antics of the clown are not the paces of the cloistered cleric. The rough and boisterous joke, the horseplay of the crowd, evokes its own guffaws, but they are not the pleasures of tranquillity. The plaintiff was not seeking a retreat for meditation. Visitors were tumbling about the belt to the merriment of onlookers when he made his choice to join them. He took the chance of a like fate, with whatever damage to his body might ensue from such a fall. The timorous may stay at home. ...

... Nothing happened to the plaintiff except what common experience tells us may happen at any time as the consequence of a sudden fall. Many a skater or a horseman can rehearse a tale of equal woe. A different case there would also be if the accidents had been so many as to show that the game in its inherent nature was too dangerous to be continued without change. The president of the amusement company says that there had never been such an accident before. A nurse employed at an emergency hospital maintained in connection with the park contradicts him to some extent. She says that on other occasions she had attended patrons of the park who had been injured at the Flopper, how many she could not say. None, however, had been badly injured or had suffered broken bones. Such testimony is not enough to show that the game was a trap for the unwary, too perilous to be endured. According to the defendant's estimate, 250,000 visitors were at the Flopper in a year. Some quota of accidents was to be looked for in so great a mass. One might as well say that a skating rink should be abandoned because skaters sometimes fall. …

The judgment of the Appellate Division and that of the Trial Term should be reversed, and a new trial granted, with costs to abide the event.

Rush v. Commercial Realty Co.
New Jersey Supreme Court
7 N.J. Misc. 337, 145 A. 476 (1929)

PER CURIAM. The case for the plaintiffs was that they were tenants of the defendant, which controlled the house wherein they lived and also the adjoining house, and provided a detached privy for the use of both houses; that Mrs. Rush having occasion to use this privy, went into it and fell through the floor, or through some sort of trap door therein, descended about nine feet into the accumulation at the bottom, and had to be extricated by use of a ladder. The defendant denied that there was any pit at all, and claimed the floor was only about nine inches above solid ground. This, like several other features of the case, presented a disputed question of fact for the jury. The two grounds of appeal are that the trial court erred in refusing a nonsuit, and erred in refusing to direct a verdict for the defendant.

Taking the facts as the jury were entitled to find them, most favorably for the plaintiffs, the situation was that of a building under the control of the landlord for the use of tenants generally, and maintained by the landlord; a consequent duty of care in maintenance; a defective condition in the floor which the jury might say was due to negligent maintenance by the defendant; and an accident resulting therefrom. In such a situation it would seem that the argument for a nonsuit or for a direction must be restricted to the questions of contributory negligence and assumption of risk. In dealing with these, it should be observed that Mrs. Rush had no choice, when impelled by the calls of nature, but to use the facilities placed at her disposal by the landlord, to wit, a privy with a trap door in the floor, poorly maintained. We hardly think this was the assumption of a risk; she was not required to leave the premises and go elsewhere. Whether it was contributory negligence to step on a floor, which she testified was in bad order, was a question for the jury to solve according to its finding of the conditions and her knowledge of them, or what she should have known of them; it does not seem to be a court question.

We conclude that there was no error in denying motions to take the case from the jury, and the judgment will accordingly be affirmed.

INQUIRY

Boundaries. The above two cases show each end of spectrums on the voluntariness of the conduct and awareness and acceptance of the risk. *See also* Wyly v. Burlington Indus., 452 F.2d 807 (5th Cir. 1971) (under Texas law, participant assumes risk of chair collapse when 14 wrinkle-free-slacks contestants sit on his lap); Thurmond v. Prince Wm. Prof. Baseball Club, Inc., 265 Va. 59, 574 S.E.2d 246 (2003) (baseball-game spectator assumes risk of being hit by foul ball); American Golf Corp. v. Becker, 93 Cal. Rptr.2d 683 (Cal. Ct. App. 2000) (golfer assumes risk of ball's richet off yardage marker and injury to golfer's eye); Herrle v. Estate of Marshall, 53 Cal. Rptr.2d 713 (Cal. Ct. App. 1996) (nurse caring for Alzheimer's patient assumes the risk that patient will strike her); Vanderlei v. Heideman, 83 Ill. App.3d 158, 403 N.E.2d 756, 38 Ill. Dec. 525 (1980 (horseshoer assumes risk of being kicked by horse). Other cases present closer calls. *See* Sayed v. Azizullah, 238 Ga. App. 642, 519 S.E.2d 732 (1999) (17-year-old boy assumes risk of swimming in dangerous waters); Telega v. Security Bureau, Inc., 719 A.2d 372 (Pa. Super. 1998) (trampling by unruly spectators is not an assumed risk of attending a football game); McDermott v. Platte County Agric. Society, 245 Neb. 698, 515 N.W.2d 121 (1994) (plaintiff does not assume risk of falling on icy parking lot, when there is only one route to be taken); Ridgway v. Yenny, 223 Ind. 16, 57 N.E.2d 581 (1944) (accepting ride home in bad weather with reckless driver not an assumed risk of accident, when plaintiff was in unfamiliar neighborhood needing to get home). Which defense—implied assumption of risk or contributory/comparative negligence—applies to a plaintiff's negligence claim against a beginning driver whom the plaintiff voluntarily agreed to teach? *See* Le Fleur v. Vergilia, 280 App. Div. 1035, 117 N.Y.S.2d 244 (1952) (assumption of risk). Which applies to a plaintiff's negligence claim against an intoxicated driver with whom the plaintiff voluntarily seeks a ride home at night? *See* Young v. Wheby, 126 W. Va. 741, 30 S.E.2d 6 (1944) (assumption of risk); Sutherland v. Davis, 286 Ky. 743, 151 S.W.2d 1021 (1941) (assumption of risk).

Abolition. Some cases hold that implied assumption of risk does not apply where the defense would defeat the policy behind a protective statute—as, for instance, with child-labor laws. *See* Terry Dairy Co. v. Nalley, 146 Ark. 448, 225 S.W. 887 (1920. With the near-complete acceptance of comparative negligence, and with continuing frustration over the definition and boundaries of implied assumption of the risk, an increasing number of jurisdictions have abolished the implied-assumption-of-risk defense. See Mass. Gen. Laws Ch. 231, §85 (West 2000); Kopischke v. First Continental Corp., 187 Mont. 471, 610 P.2d 668 (1980). The Restatement (Third) of Torts: Apportionment of Liability §3, Comment *c* (2000), favors the comparative-negligence approach over implied assumption of risk. Other jurisdictions have preserved both defenses. *See* Neb. Rev. Stat. §25-21, 185.12 (2004). New York preserved the implied-assumption-of-risk defense but modified it to work like comparative negligence—reducing, but not eliminating, the plaintiff's recovery depending on the "proportion which the culpable conduct attributable to the claimant" represents to the total culpable conduct. N.Y. C.P.L.R. §1411; *see also* Colo. Rev. Stat. §13-21-111.7 (2001); Alaska Stat. §9.17.90 (Michie 2000). The statute just quoted is the state's comparative-fault statute, but New York's courts have interpreted it to apply to the assumption-of-risk defense, *see* McCabe v. Easter, 516 N.Y.S.2d 515 (App. Div. 1987), except where the plaintiff is injured in a recreational activity where the defense's all-or-nothing operation remains, *see* Turcotte v. Fell, 502 N.E.2d 964 (N.Y. 1986). As you read the following case abolishing implied assumption of risk, consider which approach you prefer.

Blackburn v. Dorta
Florida Supreme Court
348 So.2d 287 (Fla. 1977)

SUNDBERG, J. ... Since our decision in Hoffman v. Jones, [280 So.2d 431 (Fla. 1973)], contributory negligence no longer serves as a complete bar to plaintiff's recovery but is to be considered in apportioning damages according to the principles of comparative negligence. We are now asked to determine the effect of the Hoffman decision on the common law doctrine of assumption of risk. If assumption of risk is equivalent to contributory negligence, then Hoffman mandates that it can no longer operate as a complete bar to recovery. However, if it has a distinct purpose apart from contributory negligence, its continued existence remains unaffected by Hoffman. ...

At the outset, we note that assumption of risk is not a favored defense. There is a puissant drift toward abrogating the defense.[fn] The argument is that assumption of risk serves no purpose which is not subsumed by either the doctrine of contributory negligence or the common law concept of duty.[fn] It is said that this redundancy results in confusion and, in some cases, denies recovery unjustly. ... Joining the intensifying assault upon the doctrine, a number of comparative negligence jurisdictions have abrogated assumption of risk.[fn] Those jurisdictions hold that assumption of risk is interchangeable with contributory negligence and should be treated equivalently. Today we are invited to join this trend of dissatisfaction with the doctrine. For the reasons herein expressed, we accept the invitation.

At the commencement of any analysis of the doctrine of assumption of risk, we must recognize that we deal with a potpourri of labels, concepts, definitions, thoughts, and doctrines. The confusion of labels does not end with the indiscriminate and interchangeable use of the terms "contributory negligence" and "assumption of risk." In the case law and among text writers, there have developed categories of assumption of risk. Distinctions exist between express and implied;[fn] between primary and secondary;[fn] and between reasonable and unreasonable or, as sometimes expressed, strict and qualified.[fn] It will be our task to analyze these various labels and to trace the historical basis of the doctrine to unravel what has been in the law an "enigma wrapped in a mystery." ...

The breed of assumption of risk with which we deal here is that which arises by implication or implied assumption of risk. Initially it may be divided into the categories of primary and secondary. The term primary assumption of risk is simply another means of stating that the defendant was not negligent, either because he owed no duty to the plaintiff in the first instance, or because he did not breach the duty owed. Secondary assumption of risk is an affirmative defense to an established breach of a duty owed by the defendant to the plaintiff. ...

It is apparent that no useful purpose is served by retaining terminology which expresses the thought embodied in primary assumption of risk. This branch (or trunk) of the tree of assumption of risk is subsumed in the principle of negligence itself. ...

Having dispensed with express and primary-implied assumption of risk, we recur to secondary-implied assumption of risk which is the affirmative defense variety that has been such a thorn in the judicial side. The affirmative defense brand of assumption of risk can be subdivided into the type of conduct which is reasonable but nonetheless bars recovery (sometimes called pure or strict assumption of risk), and the type of conduct which is unreasonable and bars recovery (sometimes referred to as qualified assumption of risk). [C] ... There is little to commend this doctrine of implied-pure or strict assumption of risk... . [T]here is no reason supported by law or justice in this state to give credence to such a principle of law.

There remains, then, for analysis only the principle of implied-qualified assumption of risk... . The opinion of the United States Supreme Court in Tiller v. Atlantic Coast Line R. R., 318 U.S. 54, 63 S.Ct. 444, 87 L.Ed. 610 (1943), demonstrates that the doctrine has not only been indiscriminately misapplied historically but also represents a morally unacceptable social policy which was calculated to advance the industrial revolution regardless of the cost in human suffering. Mr. Justice Frankfurter, concurring, put it aptly when he stated: "The phrase 'assumption of risk' is an excellent illustration of the extent to which uncritical use of words bedevils the law. A phrase begins life as a literary expression; its felicity leads to its lazy repetition; and repetition soon establishes it as a legal formula, undiscriminatingly used to express different and sometimes contradictory ideas. ...

Plainly enough only mischief could result from using a single phrase to express two such different ideas. Such ambiguity necessarily does harm to the desirability of clarity and coherence in any civilized system of law. But the greater mischief was that in one of its aspects the phrase 'assumption of risk' gave judicial expression to a social policy that entailed much human misery. The notion of 'assumption of risk' as a defense that is, where the employer concededly failed in his duty of care and nevertheless escaped liability because the employee had 'agreed' to 'assume the risk' of the employer's fault rested, in the context of our industrial society, upon a pure fiction. ..." ...

We find no discernible basis analytically or historically to maintain a distinction between the affirmative defense of contributory negligence and assumption of risk. ...

... Therefore, we hold that the affirmative defense of implied assumption of risk is merged into the defense of contributory negligence and the principles of comparative negligence enunciated in Hoffman v. Jones, supra, shall apply in all cases where such defense is asserted. ...

It is so ordered.

Inquiry

Precautions. One other class of cases arises in which implied assumption of risk provides a conceptual framework for evaluating the plaintiff's conduct. Usually the question is whether the plaintiff was aware of the risks of engaging in certain conduct, such as operating a motor vehicle or motorcycle. Yet there are instances when the plaintiff was aware of and assumed the risks of engaging in the activity but did so without taking certain available precautions—like wearing a seatbelt in a motor vehicle or a helmet while operating a motorcycle. Statutes requiring seatbelt or helmet use reinforce the significance of the failure-to-use-available-safety-devices issue. Should a negligent defendant driver who collides with the plaintiff motorcyclist not wearing a helmet, be able to shift the damages for the plaintiff's skull fracture to the plaintiff by arguing assumption of risk? *See* Rogers v. Rush, 257 Md. 233, 262 A.2d 549 (1970) (expert testimony on increased risk of skull fracture without helmet inadmissible where no law required helmet use). As noted above, some jurisdictions treat the issue by statutorily limiting the plaintiff's comparative negligence to a certain amount—in Michigan, for instance, to five percent for failure to wear a seatbelt. How should such a statute affect the defendant's right to claim an implied-assumption-of-risk defense? *See* Klinke v. Mitsubishi Motors Corp., 458 Mich. 582, 581 N.W.2d 272 (1998) (statutory cap on comparative negligence in motor-vehicle-accident claim, for failure to wear seatbelt, does not limit defendant manufacturer's comparative-negligence defense in products-liability claim).

Other Defenses. This study concludes consideration of negligence defenses for the Torts I course. The Torts II course considers several other negligence including statutes of limitation, statutes of repose, notice-of-claim statutes, intra-family immunities, charitable immunity, governmental immunity, worker's compensation exclusive-remedy provisions, and motor-vehicle no-fault immunity. The Torts II course also addresses products-liability defenses like product misuse, open and obvious, sophisticated user, learned intermediary, federal preemption, and government contractor, and damages defenses involving apportionment and failure to mitigate. Look forward to studying those additional defenses in your next torts studies.

CONCLUSION

I hope that you have appreciated your first-term Torts I studies, recognizing that you have more studies to complete in Torts II. Your Torts I studies of negligence gave you the knowledge essential to the core of torts practice. You could, with the requisite skills and ethics, practice much of tort law using what you learned here in Torts I. You are still missing, though, the study of damages, which is a Torts II study essential to maintaining negligence claims. You have also not yet directly studied significant Torts II multiple-party issues like release, satisfaction, joint-and-several liability, vicarious liability, contribution, indemnity, and apportionment of damages. Torts II will also address several new torts or torts fields including products liability, strict liability, misrepresentation, defamation, invasion of privacy, business torts, and torts involving misuse of legal procedures. Torts II also addresses the worker's compensation and motor-vehicle no-fault systems. You thus have significantly more to learn about torts, even while you have a solid grounding in the civil-liability system. Look forward to your Torts II studies, even as you celebrate finishing Torts I.

www.ingramcontent.com/pod-product-compliance
Lightning Source LLC
Chambersburg PA
CBHW051358070526
44584CB00023B/3211